# A History of Economic Thought

Eric Roll has had three careers, the first as a student and teacher of economics for many years, including spells at a number of American universities. He then spent more than twenty years in the Public Service where he was concerned with many aspects of economic problems and policies. He was particularly active in international negotiations relating to such diverse concerns as the organization of the international sugar market and Britain's entry into the European Community. He retired from the Public Service as Permanent Under-secretary of State of the Department of Economic Affairs and entered upon his third career as a director, later Chairman and now President of a leading merchant banking group.

# A History of
# Economic Thought

# ERIC ROLL

### Fifth Edition
REVISED AND ENLARGED

*faber and faber*
LONDON · BOSTON

First published in 1938
by Faber and Faber Limited
3 Queen Square, London, WC1N 3AU
Second impression 1939
Second edition revised and enlarged 1945
Reprinted 1946, 1949 and 1950
Third edition 1954
Reprinted 1956 and 1961
New and revised edition 1973
Reprinted 1978, 1983, 1987 and 1990

Fifth edition revised 1992

Photoset by Parker Typesetting Service, Leicester
Printed in England by Clays Ltd, St Ives Plc
All rights reserved

© Eric Roll, 1938, 1945, 1954, 1973, 1992

Eric Roll is hereby identified as author of this book
in accordance with the Copyright, Designs and Patents Act 1988

A CIP record for this book is available
from the British Library

ISBN 0 571 16553 2

To
the memory of
my father
and
my mother

# Contents

# Foreword to the Fifth Edition

Two reasons seem to justify a revised edition of this book. First, it is seventeen years since the last one was completed, which is long enough to justify an examination of recent changes in any discipline. Second, the book seems to continue to be useful to the general reader as well as to professional students of the subject, although it has been in print for over fifty years.

As on earlier occasions, I have had to make up my mind on four difficult questions. First, is the general structure of the book and the balance of treatment of different ideas and of individual authors still right? Secondly, is the general approach, particularly to the relation between economic ideas and the broad changes, political, economic and cultural, of the societies in which these ideas arise and grow in need of change? Thirdly, have recent researches thrown new light on individual thinkers or particular aspects of theorizing of the past to such an extent that statements made about them in this book would need to be amended? And, finally, how are the most recent developments in economic thought – say the forty years or so since the death of Keynes – to be dealt with?

I have concluded that there would be no point in changing a structure which to a large extent imposes itself and which has for that reason been adopted by most writers on this subject. When writing history it is not easy, even if it were sensible, to do without a substantial measure of chronology. As for the segments into which I had divided the subject matter, apart from the final chapters dealing with the last fifty years, the phasing and, therefore, classification of the different divisions of this history, seem to me also to have proved themselves in wide and long usage. In short, I have not been able to think of one that would better present the historical process which I wished to describe.

I was much more uncertain about balance. Is it, for example, really still useful, either for the general reader or the student, to seek, identify, and analyse the antecedents of the elements of the present body of economics in antiquity (including the shadowland of the Scriptures) or in the musings of medieval thinkers? Even if the speculations of mercantilists and bullionists cannot be omitted (if only for the stubborn persistence of their remnants into the present day), is too much made of them? Here again, I decided against a radical change. Only about forty pages in all – about one-fifteenth of the whole book – are devoted to the period up to the mercantilists.

There are two questions that have to be asked in regard to the approach: how does one define economic thought; and therefore what does one include? Secondly, are there any broad general principles of explanation that can be applied to an individual idea, or to the whole body of ideas of an individual writer? On both these points, the Introduction which follows sets out my views in general terms. I would, however, add the following. It is, I believe, inevitable that one has to accept a distinction between not only the methods (which is fairly obvious) but also the scope and perhaps even the essential purpose of the natural and the social sciences. This means, particularly, that when one studies the history of ideas in the latter realm – perhaps especially the economic – one is faced with a dilemma. In his presidential address to the American Economic Association in 1961, Professor Samuelson, surely the most brilliant representative of modern economics, drew a sharp distinction between the 'mere textbook' of Gide and Rist's *History of Economic Doctrines* and the 'work of scholarship' of Schumpeter's *History of Economic Analysis*, a monumental tome, published just after the 1954 edition of the present work. He based this distinction – and it is not quite clear on the evidence of the rest of Professor Samuelson's lecture how far it was meant to be one denoting merit or merely highlighting a dilemma – on, for example, the relative treatment of Robert Owen and Robert Malthus (Professor Samuelson may well have meant the Malthus of the *Principles* and not of the *Essay*), of Fourier and Saint-Simon on the one side, and Walras and Pareto on the other, and of Arthur Young as against Allyn Young. In short, he made a distinction based on the extent to which 'analytics' is to be the criterion for the selection and treatment of different writers. Is this to be the correct standard? If it is, my own principle of selection does not conform. Yet is this really the right way of looking at it? Admittedly, while I have not dealt with all professional analytical economists, I have also left out a good many non-professionals (as now defined); but I was not then writing, and am not now attempting to write, only about those politico-economic writers whose ideas have gone to form, or at least to influence, the residue of popular beliefs about the economic processes of society. However, neither have I attempted to write – as Schumpeter did – only for the professional student who wishes to trace in meticulous detail the *provenance* of particular theories in economics, and their gradual climb up the ladder of sophistication.

Professor Samuelson himself seems to have come to believe more definitely in a more eclectic approach than perhaps he did in the lecture I have quoted, for in the 1970 edition of the *Readings in Economics*, which accompanies his immensely successful textbook, he explains in his Introduction that 'life is not a Who's Who' and that in choosing authors whose texts might be suitable for illustrating to his students the problems he is dealing with, he has 'not asked for their union cards as professional economists'. It seems, therefore, that one must be free to adopt some blend of the 'analytical' and the more 'popular' types of economics; and I make no excuse for my own limited admixture to the treatment of 'analytics' of certain ingredients taken from less rigorous economic theorizing.

The more difficult question is whether there exists some general principle of explanation which can be applied to the study of ideas in general and to that of economic ones in particular. There are two possible, extreme, positions: one that the appearance of ideas is wholly fortuitous, the other – identified with various types of unitary interpretations of history such as the Marxist – that it is ultimately dependent on some permanently operating factors, in particular, the material. As further explained in the Introduction, I take something of a middle position, believing that neither of these two views can be relied upon by itself to provide consistently an adequate explanation. The Sociology of Knowledge is of all branches of that contentious discipline still the most obscure.

A certain amount of new material has been made available in recent years on the lives and ideas of a number of important economists of the past. To some of these reference was made in the last edition. Further new studies have appeared since on a number of economists. However, I do not think anything has come to light that would make me alter my general assessment of the thinkers concerned.

My major problem has been to decide on the treatment of the most recent developments. I shall have more to say about this aspect below, and at greater length in the final chapters, but the volume of economic literature during this period, which is very much greater (and growing at an accelerated pace) than that of the twenty years that separated the last edition from its predecessor, would alone seem to justify further treatment. I should, however, say at once that I believe the recent additions to the body of economic theory to be neither as significant nor as important as those of the preceding three or four decades. What has, however, been important in the period since the last edition has been the relationship between economic theory and economic policy, provoked largely by the requirements of the latter in the light of changes in economic conditions as well as in social attitudes. It is this increasing 'politization' of economics and a growing partisanship, already discernible in the developments described in the last edition, which in my opinion form the most important current feature of the subject. Accordingly, while I have tried in the final chapters to give a succinct account of some of the new theoretical developments for which much – often too much – is claimed, I have concentrated on the continuation and exacerbation of the fight for ascendancy of different theoretical approaches to the policy of economic management, which must remain, I believe, the practical objective of economic theory.

I have omitted the bibliography that was included in earlier editions. While not many books on the subject in general have appeared in recent years, there has been a flood of books and, particularly, articles on individual topics and writers. Many of these, which I have considered to be particularly helpful in the terms of the general theme of this book, are mentioned in the text and in footnotes.

E. R.
London, November 1991

# INTRODUCTION

# Economics and the History of Ideas

Interest in the development of economic science is less than a hundred and fifty years old. There are a few unimportant works in the eighteenth century and there is a book in the *Wealth of Nations* which surveys earlier systems of political economy. But when Adam Smith wrote, the theories which he considered erroneous had not been completely ousted and his survey had a largely polemical aim. We have to wait until the supremacy of classical economy is being challenged before interest in earlier thought revives. Indeed, the earliest attempts at a systematic treatment of the history of economic doctrine were made by adherents of the historical and socialist schools which developed in Germany after the middle of the nineteenth century. Those, like Roscher, who were anxious to develop the historical approach in competition with the deductive were naturally pre-occupied with the history of ideas. Socialists, on the other hand, hoped to draw inspiration in their attack upon the prevailing liberal-capitalist theory from a critical study of the origins of that theory. This aim is particularly obvious in Marx; but it is present in the writings of many nineteenth-century authors.

With the spread of economic teaching at the end of the nineteenth and beginning of the twentieth centuries, the history of doctrine becomes a more popular subject of study. Sometimes, as in the case of Ashley, it is still an adjunct to economic history and a consequence of methodological preference. But most histories of this modern period become matter-of-fact outlines, often because (as in France, where Gide and Rist produced their widely read history) the teaching of the history of political economy remained for a long time the only form of academic economic instruction. Recently a more directly 'technical' interest has also arisen. As the conceptual 'tools' of the economist have increased in number and complexity, the practitioners have become

I

interested in the evolution of the individual concepts and the methods of application of their technical apparatus. Special studies of neglected aspects of past thought are now more frequent.

It is not the purpose of this book to provide an exhaustive survey on such purely 'technical' lines. It is doubtful whether such a specialized history is the one most urgently needed at the moment. Nor is this volume intended to supplant those encyclopedic compendia to which teachers and professional students must necessarily refer from time to time.

As far as the student is concerned the exigencies of the study of modern economics create two serious dangers. In the first place, the intricacies of modern theoretical refinements may make the student forget the essentially practical nature of his discipline. As the increasing attention given to the theory of economic policy shows, the skilled practitioner is less exposed to this danger, but the student may become excessively 'conceptually' oriented before he has time to see the connection between 'analytics' and policy. The modern student of economics is also apt to lose sight of the contribution which his own subject has made, and is making, to the general stream of human thought. English and American teaching of economics has escaped the undue subservience to the historical approach characteristic until fairly recently of French faculties. But there is not enough evidence that the opposite extreme, that of complete neglect of the history of doctrine, is being avoided. A broad statement of the evolution of economic thought written as an introduction to modern theory may provide the corrective of which many students seem to be in need.

Other readers, if they are interested in the development of thought, may welcome an account of one of the most important of the speculations of the human mind. Economic theories are always, though often tortuously, related to economic practice. A study of the interplay between the conditions of life and the theorizing of man can be a helpful guide through the conflicts of ideas. Many ideas of the past had their roots in institutional arrangements, in the relations between different economic groups, in their conflicting interests. In so far as the same or similar arrangements and relations still exist, the ideas to which they gave birth are not dead. Aristotle's views on the different classes of human labour, the strictures of medieval schoolmen on usury, mercantilist theories of foreign trade and physiocratic notions about agriculture, Ricardo's theory of rent and the practical conclusions drawn from it, and the revolt of the German romantics against economic liberalism are all still with us. They have gone into the stockpot of ideas from which successive generations have drawn their mental food.

In the works of the greatest of modern economists, Keynes, Sismondi and Proudhon come alive again. Not so many years ago Gray, in his popular history of economics, could neglect completely Malthus's *Principles*; pre-war controversies between the protagonists of capital accumulation and the under-consumptionists directed attention again to one of the greatest economic controversies of the past – that between Ricardo and Malthus.

Many writers have stressed the longevity of economic ideas, but they have generally been led to regard with contempt those who still cling to fallacies which the expert has long since discarded. Some, in their enthusiasm for modern developments, have looked upon past theories as imperfections steadily overcome; while others have tried to produce an apologia for earlier ideas by stressing their 'rightness' relative to time and place. The approach which I adopt is based on neither of these extremes. Analogies should not merely be pointed out; an examination and comparison of contemporaneous conditions is necessary before their full significance can be understood. I cannot hope to have done more than provide a first guide for such a treatment of economic ideas, but as such it may have its use both for the student and the general reader.

A history of ideas is by nature selective and interpretative; by virtue of what he leaves out and by his manner of presenting that which he includes, the author allows for his own interests, predilections and prejudices. Too often, however, the principle which underlies the author's treatment remains implied. Where the ideas presented relate to social institutions and policy and have a bearing upon human welfare, implied assumptions can be particularly misleading. An express statement of the writer's assumptions may help the reader to form his own views.

The approach of this book is based on the view that the process by which ideas are formed is susceptible to systematic analysis. In the main, the appearance of a major trend of thought is not fortuitous but is dependent upon causes which can be discovered. Often our knowledge of the circumstances of the lives and times of certain thinkers is not complete enough for an exhaustive demonstration of the causes which have produced certain ideas; but we usually know enough to be able to form a broad opinion of the manner in which economic theories arise.

This book is also based on the conviction that the economic structure of any given epoch and the changes which it undergoes are major influences on economic thinking. Much of this conviction is shared by most writers on this subject, though it is seldom made explicit. Few people would doubt that the economic thought produced in a community in which slave labour predominates is different from that which either a feudal society, or one based on wage-labour, brings forth. Reluctance to accept this proposition arises partly because it is often stated in a way which appears to make the economic system the *sole* determinant; partly because it is difficult to present convincingly any casual relation between economic practice and economic theory in more detailed discussions of their history; partly also, no doubt, because this approach is usually associated with schools of thought which try to turn the resulting analysis to purposes which it cannot and should not be made to serve, namely to provide guidance for desired changes in economic policy, let alone social structure.

It must, therefore, be emphasized that the economic factor is a major factor only in a very general sense which it is not always possible to demonstrate precisely. The causal chain is long and devious. In the history of economic ideas a host of other causal factors have been operative to produce a given theory or attitude at a given time, many of more direct influence than the economic one to which they may be ultimately linked.

Nor is it to be denied that ideas, in their turn, influence the development of economic practice. Indeed, in the short run, as Keynes remarked, the vapourings of some obscure scribbler may have an altogether disproportionate effect on current policy. The history of this century has shown this only too clearly. In the development of economic doctrine itself, the stage of evolution reached by the existing body of economic theory is of outstanding importance. This is particularly so once the advancement of economic science has come to depend upon specialist scholars generally attached to academic institutions. Every thinker must then begin with the technical apparatus which he finds ready at hand, even though the original factors which produced this apparatus are no longer operative.

Political theory and political practice are other factors which have influenced economists at different times. Many economists were sometimes social philosophers as well; this was particularly true of the classical economists. And the works of both old and modern writers show the influence of prevailing philosophical argument and of the

4

general quality of scientific thought of their time. Other writers were either themselves engaged in politics or had a considerable influence upon policy; and many a theory bears the mark of the political climate in which it was conceived.

There is no inevitable order in which these influences appear. However clear the succession of forms of social organization and economic structure may be, it must not be thought that ideas relating to them show an equally clear-cut sequence. Ideas which have arisen in a past social order often influence thought and action within a later institutional framework. Together with the existing combinations of economic factors they shape contemporaneous social change; and, in this process of interaction, it is not always easy to say which is the proximate and which the remote influence.

Keynes, himself, in a celebrated and often quoted passage, espoused a somewhat different theory. The world, he claimed, is ruled by little else than 'the ideas of economists and political philosophers'; practical men, thinking themselves not subject to any intellectual influences being, in fact, 'the slaves of some defunct economist'; and he went even further to assert, apparently in diametrical opposition to economic, materialist, or Marxist interpretations, that 'soon or late it is ideas, not vested interests, which are dangerous for good or evil'. Fortunately, being brought up in the Anglo-Saxon tradition with its strong practical bent, Keynes did not develop these views into the rigid socio-ideological system of a Pareto.

This absence of a neat chronological sequence in the evolution of economic doctrine is most striking when different countries are compared. During the last hundred and fifty years industrial society has grown up in very irregular fashion in different countries. The variation of tempo has created apparent anomalies in the history of economics. Ideas, dead in one country, reappear in another if the economic environment is more suitable. The emergence of pre-liberal economic doctrines, for example, in Germany, in which capitalist industry developed late and at a time when there were already full-grown rivals, could hardly be ascribed exclusively to differences of national temperament and mentality. It is true that these economic ideas will be found to be part of a general system of thought referring especially to such subjects as the nation, foreign trade, and the relation between the state and economic life. But the existence of this general national outlook as anything like a long-term determinant in its own right is none the less doubtful; in the long run it is itself determined by economic and other conditions.

The purpose and guiding principle of this book have determined its plan. In the first place many names which a different type of history would have had to include have been omitted, while some thinkers who have seldom been regarded as important are here dealt with. My choice has been determined by two considerations. First, apart from the most outstanding economists of the past, only those have been included whose contributions to economic thought appear to have significance in relation to present-day theory and controversy in the wider field of political economy, rather than in the narrowly technical branches of economic science. Secondly, stress has been laid both on writers and views which, to my mind, exemplify most clearly different trends of thought. I have also had to be selective in the treatment of the work of individual authors who have been chosen for inclusion, particularly among the more modern ones. Where I have concentrated on certain aspects of these authors' work to the exclusion of others, I have done so in order to illustrate most clearly the evolution of a particular idea or group of ideas. No injustice to the range of an author's work is intended.

Another result of the particular approach here adopted has been that technical developments of economic analysis have not been given uniform attention. Particularly in the earlier sections, the reader will find less emphasis laid upon the more obscure antecedents of individual economic concepts; and it is only in dealing with the developments of the last two hundred years or so that the discussion becomes more detailed. My main concern has been with the wider questions of economic scope and method, of the relations between Economics and politics, and of the place which economic theory has occupied in social change. And many special fields, such as the theories of money and crises, have, as a rule, only been dealt with if they formed an integral part of an author's work or had a special bearing on the evolution of Economics as an essentially practical discipline.

The last thirty years or so have presented a special problem. Already in the inter-war period there were signs that economics was attracting more and more students – professional and amateur alike. This trend has continued and been intensified in the period since the end of the war. With some ups and downs, the numbers studying the subject in academic institutions has gone on increasing. The new categories of economists – 'business economists', 'economic' or 'financial' analysts and commentators in specialist as well as general periodic publications

– have grown enormously. The largest increase has been in the number of those concerned with current economic events and problems of economic policy. There has also been a substantial increase in more theoretical and esoteric enquiry, some explicit, some by a fairly obvious, though not always avowed, route linked with practical problems of policy. It is to sort the wheat from the chaff of the latter, to identify those developments – if any – which significantly affect the position and future development of the discipline that has presented the most difficult problem of all.

As far as the practitioners of the more academic aspects of the discipline are concerned, it might have been thought that the institution of a Nobel Prize in Economic Sciences in 1969 – with thirty laureates to date – would provide, as it were, a ready-made list of the outstanding scholars in this field. However, I decided that this would be a hazardous assumption to make, for while some of the laureates would command universal approval, the claims of others would be highly controversial. Perhaps the one significant fact that emerges from a study of the list is that more than half of them are American, thus continuing a tendency for the science to become increasingly American, which has been noted before.

In this connection it is interesting to note one new development in the Nobel Prize awards. The Prize for 1990 was awarded jointly to three economists (all American, thus increasing their preponderance in the list to date) – Merton Miller, Harry Markowitz and William Sharpe, all of whom had worked in the field of corporate finance and financial economics. Merton Miller has been known for many years for his work with the distinguished MIT economist (and earlier Nobel Prize winner) Franco Modigliani. However, this award, in respect of work in a field not hitherto regarded as really within the ambit of theoretical economics and somehow on the fringes of the 'proper' preoccupations of distinguished economists (leading, incidentally, one of the prize-winners, Merton Miller, to extol the virtues of recent financial innovations such as 'junk bonds' in his acceptance speech), clearly marks some kind of important development. It is not yet clear, however, what exactly that development is and whether it says anything significant about economics or about the Nobel Prize – or both!

One extremely valuable aid, however, has become available recently and must be acknowledged here, *The New Palgrave Dictionary of Economics*, edited by John Eatwell, Murray Milgate and Peter Newman (4 vols., 1987). This is undoubtedly an indispensable reference book for the professional; and general readers may also consult it with advantage because of its high degree of comprehensiveness and the generally exceptional quality of the individual articles. It is not easy to understand why it has been criticized in some quarters of the 'New Right' – possibly on the ground of being too tolerant of views and writers who do not pass the test of acceptability applied by these particular critics!

Whether or not I have succeeded in the way I have tackled the problem of selection must be left to each reader's own judgement. But it will be quite some time before an objective, or at least widely acceptable, judgement can be formed.

# I

# The Beginnings

## *The Old Testament*

There has been much disagreement among economists as to the scope of economics. The quality of this agreement is of some significance for an estimate of the present and future of the science. At this stage it is useful to summarize briefly the points of agreement. Most professional economists today would say that the primary purpose of economics is analytical, that is, to discover what is. In other words, whatever other aims some of them may have in mind, and whatever hypothetical examples they may devise for expository purposes, economists' concern is to establish the principles upon which the present economic system works. It is sometimes argued that economics is capable of becoming as exact and as 'universally valid' as the physical sciences; by implication, the essentially social and historical nature of economics is denied. These views, however, are put forward only on the occasion of methodological discussion and do not seem to affect the scope of the bulk of the work of members of this school of thought: they are still mainly interested in the working of the present-day economy.

It should be said at once that the general public is very rarely aware of this positive and analytical purpose which the professional regards as the paramount, or even as the only legitimate one. The public knows that it can justifiably demand of the economist a statement of how the system works (though its faith in the explanation which is forthcoming is not always great); but it generally wants to know also what is the right thing to *do*. Economists cannot always shirk this question; and when they answer they reveal more far-reaching differences of opinion than any that arise in the analysis upon which they all claim to base their advice. Such disagreement over the diagnosis of an actual economic problem and the prescription of a remedy, more than a desire for scientific neatness, leads economists from time to time to an examination of the limits of their discipline. Thus we return to the differences of definition.

Although this circuitous route has been travelled frequently in the last two hundred years, the main development of economic thought has proceeded without constant methodological discussion. The broad social framework of the present-day economy was taken as given. Private property and enterprise, private exchange, the market economy, in short, capitalist production was the soil in which the principal concepts grew. Capital, labour, value, price, supply, demand, rent, interest, profit – these are the elements of the system and, therefore, of its theoretical analysis.

The earliest systematic development of these concepts is to be found at the end of the seventeenth and beginning of the eighteenth centuries. The particular set of economic conditions to which they refer was not present in developed and comprehensive form at any earlier stage of human history. We shall see that the great minds to whom we owe the foundations of classical political economy claimed that they had discovered more than the laws appropriate to a particular social system. But it is important to stress here that political economy as a science begins at a time when the foundations of industrial capitalism were already well laid. There is a surprising unanimity of opinion among historians of economic doctrine on this point; and many writers have even gone so far as to ignore completely any earlier economic thought, or to refer to it only in very slighting terms.[1] It is perfectly true that the total volume of economic theory, in any modern sense, to be found in the writings of, for example, the Greek philosophers is very small; but we can only expect statements of an economic character in the present-day sense of the term to the extent to which certain of the economic conditions of our society were already present in the society in which the Greek philosophers lived.

1 Gide and Rist begin their history with the physiocrats of the eighteenth century. Cannan, in his *Review of Economic Theory* (1929), p. 2, says that 'we should be disappointed' if we expected to find 'interesting economic speculation in the writings of the Greek philosophers'. Dühring (*Kritische Geschichte der National Ökonomie und des Sozialismus*, 1874) claims that neither ancient nor medieval thought contributed anything 'positive' to economic science. Schumpeter (*Epochen der Dogmen und Methodengeschichte*, 2nd ed., 1925) admits the indirect influence of Greek philosophy but minimizes its detailed contribution. Marx, in a chapter which he wrote for Engels's *Anti-Dühring*, gives Greek economic thought (or, at least, Aristotle), its due, though with his customary tendentiousness.

That society, or that earlier one which is described in the Old Testament, undoubtedly possessed some of the characteristics of modern capitalism. There was private property, division of labour, market exchange, and money. Some writers have gone farther than appears justified in their attempt to find ancient analogies for modern economic phenomena. But there can be no doubt that ancient thinkers, discussing the problems of their society, have made statements which have become the starting-point of all social theory. The fact that these statements are fragmentary and scattered does not detract from their importance. The views of the Hebrew prophets, set in the ethical or metaphysical system of a patriarchal society, may appear extremely primitive to a modern economist; but their power to influence men's minds is not necessarily inferior to that of many a refined and scientific theory; indeed it is often greater. The systems of philosophy, of which such isolated economic statements formed part, continue to live; and whenever critical convulsions occur in the economic system, their influence grows. When belief in established institutions and practices declines, the search for comprehensive philosophies of life and rival policies compete in the name of one or another *Weltanschauung*. No one would deny that most ideas in the body of human thought during more than two thousand years still have their champions.

It is not intended to exaggerate either the volume or the importance of early economic thought. Man cannot begin to theorize about the economic process as long as this is so simple as to require no special explanation. Modern economists make even Robinson Crusoe speculate upon the implications of choice which they regard as the essence of economy; but all that anthropology shows is that the earliest human theorizing was concerned with what contemporary economists would call the technical aspects of the process of want-satisfaction. In so far as we can discover the ideas which primitive man consciously held they appear to be designed to supply some explanation of the changes of season, of the powers of the soil, of the habits of animals, and of the bearing of all these upon the ability to satisfy human wants. Even at comparatively developed stages of tribal society no specifically social economic problems seem to call for explanation. The economic process of a community in which the technique of production is simple, in which property (at any rate, that which is applied to productive uses) is communally owned and in which division of labour exists but has not led to habitual private exchange of products, are unlikely to appear incomprehensible to the members. The connections between individual effort and individual satisfaction is obvious to every one: the process of production and the product are under the individual's control throughout and there is no need for any elaborate social or economic theory.

But technique of production develops and wants become more complex; and there comes a stage when different social arrangements are devised to give the possibilities of the community their full scope. Division of labour develops to the point at which it involves the establishment of private exchange and the extension of private property from consumable to productive goods. Production is then habitually for purposes of private exchange; the easy supervision and control over the social economic process is gone: the process has become impersonal. It is at this stage in man's development that we should expect to find the first gropings after a theory of society and an explanation of the economic process. In spite of increasing anthropological work we know little of the detailed forms which this economic transformation actually took; we know still less of the change in ideas which was part of it. To the collection of records as well as myths of varying evidential worth which we call the Bible anthropologists have, during the last hundred years, added material which may eventually enable us to be reasonably certain of how primitive man thought of his society and its changes. What evidence we have so far of ancient social thought consists entirely of myths concerned with justifying or attacking in supernatural terms an existing social order.

In the Old Testament and the subsequent collections of laws and interpretations which constitute original Hebrew thought, there is mirrored a conflict between the tribal society, with communal property and primitive economic activity, and the impersonal economic process of a more complex, stratified society with classes and castes, based in large measure on private property. The animistic views of early Semitic religion give way to an idealized conception of divinity. But the unearthly majesty of God is tempered not only by two other basic attributes, justice and mercy, but also by the covenant between the Deity and his people. It is possible to see in this union an idealized substitute for older and closer social bonds that had already been loosened. There was no attempt as yet to remove from religious doctrine any concern with physical welfare in the life on earth. The code of conduct enjoined upon members of the community was strict and included a recognition of certain overriding social obligations that were little different from those of the patriarchal family and the tribal community.

Although the scope of private property grew to include land, the individual's rights over property remained severely restricted for a long time. Laws to preserve a family's connection with the ownership of land and the institution of a year of jubilee[1] (even though no record of its enforcement appears to exist) are examples of communal limitation of individual rights. But the disintegration of the primitive community could not be stopped. With the development of private property there came trade, both home and foreign, and with it the possibilities of accumulating wealth. It was in that period that the Hebrew monarchy grew up. The picture of the society of the time which is drawn in Kings, and more emphatically still in the laments, protests, and visions of the prophets, is one of marked division between rich and poor. The luxury of the court was based upon the gradual development of an enslaved class. The expenses of the royal household, wars, and lavish public building were financed by tolls and the profits of the king's foreign trade monopoly, by conscription of labour and heavy taxation.[2] The results were impoverishment of the masses, alienation of land, and the development of an 'underprivileged' class.

This change in the economic climate is reflected in the spiritual revolt of the prophets. By their denunciation of the covetousness of the new society they sought to guide men back to the way of living of the covenant, to revive justice and mercy as the principles of social behaviour. They castigated the excesses of the new commercial classes, of the usurers and the 'land robbers'; and they preached once again limitations upon the rights of private property. In some matters they were successful. The prohibition of the levying of execution upon a debtor's clothes or tools[3] remains a cardinal principle of Jewish law, and it is also one which has influenced the laws of many other nations down to the present day.

But the prophets' major attack was fruitless. They were able to describe clearly the consequences of the existing social order, but they did not understand the forces which were responsible for the appearance of the order itself. They could only sigh for the return of an earlier age, not realizing that its social structure had become

1 e.g. Leviticus, xxv, 10, 11.
2 e.g. 1 Kings, v, 13 sqq.
3 e.g. Exodus, xii, 26–7; Deuteronomy, xxiv, 6.

inappropriate. Some of the prophets appear to have been dimly aware of the Utopian nature of their protest; these have no hope of the future, and they expect to see the wrath of God bringing about the universal destruction which they regard as the only fate their world deserves.[1] Others put their faith in the coming of the Messiah who would deliver mankind from evil and lead it back to the ways of the patriarchal community.[2]

Underlying both the despair of some prophets and the hope which others attached to the coming of the Redeemer is a wholly idealistic view of social change. The evils which the prophets denounced were not realized to be in part the result of the growth of a new economic structure; they were ascribed exclusively to a change of men's hearts. Covetousness and corruption, unrelated to the more favourable soil in which they could now flourish, were alone regarded as the cause of misery. The remedy was equally a wholly idealistic one: a full acceptance of God's law, a life led, once again, according to the religious code. A clear vision of a new social structure of the future was no part of this view. The expansion of production and man's growing mastery over nature demanded the recently established institutions. In so far, therefore, as the prophets were concerned with the social order as well as with man's behaviour they could only express a vain hope for a return to more primitive conditions. The prophetic revolt, significant in its day, was doomed to failure. It reached its zenith with the rise of Christianity; but even this last and strongest outburst of discontent did not succeed in improving the people's conditions in its own time. With progressive idealization it lost its direct relevance to the social problems of its time. But it remained as one of the most powerful influences over men's minds for all time and as the most potent single source of inspiration for individual conduct.

## Greece: Plato and Aristotle

Meanwhile, another ancient civilization which left a mark upon European thought had developed in not altogether dissimilar ways. We know little about the heroic period of Greek history; but from the myths that remain and from such legends as the constitution of

1 e.g. Amos, viii.
2 e.g. Isaiah, xi.

Theseus, it seems that already in that period the decay of tribal organization had gone far. Private property in land, a high degree of division of labour, trade – particularly maritime – and the use of money were already established. The close bonds of the tribe were broken and had been replaced by those of a society rigorously divided into classes and ruled by a landed aristocracy. Certain democratic forms of government which had survived from earlier times, such as the popular assembly, had lost their content in the Greek city state of the eighth century; real power lay in the hands of the owners of the land and of an hereditary ruling class.

Although this kind of state had arisen through the disappearance of the economic foundation of tribal society, it still preserved too many features of a self-sufficient agricultural community to be entirely appropriate to the needs of growing commerce. Not only did the rising trading classes come into conflict with the landed aristocracy; the increasing reliance of agriculture on export markets and the growing power of money led to the same impoverishment and gradual enslavement of free peasants which had roused the prophets of the Old Testament.

The constitution of Solon in the sixth century BC is a symptom of this growing conflict. It attempted by a number of reforms to prevent the worst consequences of new economic practices and to provide for a peaceful adaptation of political institutions. The personal enslavement of the debtor was forbidden and some slaves freed; and although the taking of interest was not prohibited, nor a maximum rate for it fixed, many existing debts were reduced or cancelled. The machinery of government was altered by dividing the free citizens into four classes according to the property they owned. Although all classes of citizens had the right to vote in the popular assembly, thus retaining the ultimate power of checking the government, offices were reserved for those who owned property.

These ingenious reforms, which attempted to blend an aristocratic with a democratic constitution, which buttressed the property qualification for government while at the same time limiting certain property rights, were not lastingly successful. The struggle between the aristocracy and the commercial classes, clamouring for their due share of government and supported by the impoverished peasants, continued. The inner conflicts of the individual Greek states until the collapse of Greek civilization itself are all variants on the same theme: the fight between the old ruling class and the expanding commercial classes, complicated by the existence of a mass of slaves and impoverished peasants and artisans.

With the rule of the tyrants, such as Peisistratus of Athens, and particularly with the democratic constitution of Cleisthenes (509 BC), the aristocratic power, at any rate in Athens, appeared to be broken. The growth of its trade and the threat of the Persians made Athenian democracy become, under Themistocles, the protagonist of a new Hellenic imperialism; it was still based on the economic power of the commercial class, but it had become aggressive, nationalist, and reluctant to return to the confined conditions of the earlier city states. In the ensuing conflict with other Greek states, particularly with aristocratic Sparta, Athenian democracy was unable to survive. Its own internal decay, no less than the threat from outside, brought about its collapse. The development of trade and manufacture on a basis of slavery led to the impoverishment of the bulk of free citizens. A new ruling class developed; but being in a small minority and lacking the cohesion of the old aristocracy, it proved itself inferior to its more aggressive Greek rivals. In the hundred years that followed its defeat at the hands of Sparta Athens did succeed in reviving again; and the ideas of democracy and national confederation for which she had stood at the height of her power received a new lease of life. But this revival only lasted until 338 BC, when the Macedonian conquest of the whole of Greece was completed.

It was during the latter part of this long period of violent transformation that Greek philosophy made its main contribution to social thought. Greek political theory was born of a social conflict similar to that which had called forth the protests of the Hebrew prophets. It, too, was inspired by discontent and was concerned with social reform. But although it lacked the revolutionary fervour of the prophets, it achieved a much more penetrating analysis of its own society than anything to be found in the Bible or for many hundreds of years after Greek civilization. Chronologically, it was Plato who first attempted to offer a systematic exposition of the principles of society and of the origin of the city state, as well as a plan for the ideal social structure. But it was his pupil Aristotle who laid the foundations of much of later economic thought.

Plato's principal work which is significant for our purpose is *The Republic*. In that dialogue and, to a less extent, in some of the books of *Laws*, Plato's main economic ideas are contained. In considering these ideas it is important to remember certain facts. Plato was essentially an aristocrat; but his dislike of Athenian democracy was not consciously based upon an opposition to the economic power of the rising commercial class. Rather was it a spiritual and romantic revolt aroused by the excesses of commercialism. Plato was, however, also a man of the world who, with certain interruptions caused by the inevitable disillusionment suffered by the philosopher in politics, was continually drawn into the political arena. It has been suggested[1] that *The Republic* was written with an eye to an invitation to Syracuse, where Plato later became tutor and adviser to Dionysius II. His blueprint of the ideal society may thus be not only a Utopia; it may bear the marks of an immediate political aim.

On the purely analytical side Plato's main achievement is the account of the division of labour and the origin of the city (then identical with the state) with which he prefaces his outline of the ideal republic. The city, he says,[2] arises because of division of labour, which is itself the result of natural inequalities in human skill and the multiplicity of human wants. Specialization becomes necessary since a given piece of work cannot wait for the worker (which it would have to do when men perform a multitude of tasks) for fear of deterioration. But when men specialize and are no longer self-sufficient, a commercial organization becomes necessary. Plato does not pursue this argument; nor does he consider the specifically social and economic aspects of division of labour. To him it is a natural phenomenon; and he thinks of its effects exclusively in terms of superior quality of products (increased use-value, as modern economists would say). There is as yet no concern with the cheapening of products which specialization brings about. It is not surprising, therefore, that Plato should have had no idea of that connection between the size of the market and the degree of division of labour which Adam Smith was to make famous. Plato's contemporary, Xenophon, however, who gives in his *Cyropaedia* a similar account of the division of labour, seems to have gone a little farther in his appreciation of the nature of private exchange: he distinguishes between the big cities in which division of labour is developed and the small cities in which it hardly exists.

Plato put his theory of the division of labour to an essentially retrograde use. In his hands, it became an idealization of a caste system and a support for the aristocratic tradition which was by then on the

1 R. H. S. Crossman, *Plato To-day* (1937), p. 111
2 Plato, *The Republic*, Book II.

defensive. The Athenian state which had inspired Plato to draw up his programme was a state torn by rivalries. Plato was aware of this conflict and of its terrible consequences in misery, corruption, and general degradation. In the ideal republic, therefore, class antagonism was to be absent. This was not to be achieved by abolishing class divisions altogether. On the contrary, as might be expected from an aristocrat, the distinction between the rulers and the ruled was to be made much more marked. But Plato envisaged his rulers as a caste rather than as a class, freed, he hoped, from any motive of economic exploitation by their acceptance of rigorous standards of conduct. This is the secret of the 'communism' of Plato's republic. The concept of the rulers was, however, a highly idealized one. It ignored the corrupting effects of absolute power; it also ignored the economic aspects of a caste system. In the end it turned out to be admirably suited to become an apologia for an actual oligarchy.

In Plato's ideal state there are two classes: the rulers and the ruled. The former is divided into guardians and auxiliaries; the latter are the artisans. No one in the latter class, devoted as it was to the menial occupations of the production and exchange of wealth, could have the ability necessary for government. The members of the ruling class must be set apart from early childhood, carefully educated not only in philosophy but also in the arts of war, since they will have to protect their state against foreign attack. At the age of thirty they will have to pass an examination which will select the future 'philosopher-kings', as they have been called, while all those who cannot pass the examination remain auxiliaries concerned with general administrative duties. Plato, then, believed in rule by an élite. It was for this élite that he postulated a communistic life of Spartan rigour. Free from the degrading pursuit of wealth, they would be able to devote themselves to governing their community with a rule of reason.

This ideal state was far removed both from Athenian democracy and from the society of its great rival, aristocratic Sparta. In the former, class-conflicts and injustice were rife and the virtues of a more stable social order were fast disappearing. In the latter, government was in the hands of an hereditary class that could not claim to have gone through that careful process of education and selection which Plato postulated for his guardians. It showed little concern for the welfare of its subjects, whom it ruled not by reason and benevolence (nor even by the lying propaganda which Plato had regarded as a justifiable weapon of his ideal governing class), but by brutal tyranny. Moreover, when brought into contact with commercialism and colonization, it developed the same vices of corruption and decadence that were ruining democratic Athens.

Nevertheless, it did not at first appear impossible to carry out some of Plato's ideas in his own day. Some of his pupils, like Dion, occupied influential positions; and there were in existence oligarchies, like Syracuse, which offered the hope of avoiding the evils of both Athens and Sparta. But Plato's idealistic view of social change was twisted out of all recognition in its practical application; it was made to justify not merely lies used by a benevolent despot in the interests of his subjects but the most violent acts of self-seeking politicians. The rule of reason did not conquer in Plato's lifetime; it was the aristocratic counter-revolution that was victorious, until it too had to give way to the foreign invader.

But Plato's ideas survived; again and again, the romantic and the Utopian have gone to him for inspiration. Pareto and Wells revive the idea of the governing élite; the one as the moving force of all past social development; the other as a caste specially fitted for the task of rational, just, and benevolent government of the future. In the writings of the rationalist philosophers the belief in the rule of reason comes to life again. To this day there persists the view, common to Plato and Aristotle, that some occupations are unworthy. And Plato's very small regard for foreign trade is shared by many romantic schools of economics.

The most striking analogies to Plato's blend of reaction and Utopia appear in periods of history during which radical and rapid changes in the economic and social structure are taking place. It is then that there can be found those who are distressed by the decay in established values, but who cannot rise to more than an idealization of the past. They want to re-establish a mythical golden age, since they cannot understand the forces which are transforming their own society. This characteristic is well marked in the German romantics of the nineteenth century; as we shall see, Fichte and Adam Müller urge such a 'going-back' to the 'serenity' and 'peace' of the Middle Ages. And many of the suggestions for social reform that are finding adherents today have the same romantic quality. The degree of sincerity and good intention with which such views are put forward varies, but intention is, perhaps, in the end not of decisive importance. Plato may well have been genuinely troubled about the evils of the new democracy of his day, and his may not have been a selfish opposition concerned with safeguarding the threatened interests of the aristocracy to which he belonged; nor does his *Republic* create the mental fog so characteristic of many later romantics. Yet even he, apparently sincere and clear-headed and writing at a time when philosophical speculation had a great chance of practical influence, was doomed to see his ideas perverted. This fate has been suffered by many later reformers whose sincerity may have been as great. The romantic garb has often also been added to demagogic purposes: to hide the grim purpose which those who develop or exploit certain views really have. Plato and Dion are not the last examples of the gulf which separates intention and performance.

If Plato was the first of a long line of reformers, his pupil, Aristotle, was the first analytical economist; he was not of aristocratic origin, and he appears to have been much more reconciled to the growth of the new society than was his teacher. Throughout his *Politics* and those parts of his *Ethics* which have a relevance to political and economic questions, there is evident a keen understanding of the principles on which his own society was based. It was he who laid the foundations of science and who first posed the economic problems with which all later thinkers have been concerned.

Aristotle also discussed the constitution of the ideal state. He criticized the plans of others, including those of Plato, and gave his own. In Book II of the *Politics* Aristotle strongly opposes the communistic elements of Plato's ideal republic. The arguments which he uses against community of wives and children are of little relevance to our present purpose, although they are interesting in regard to the development of the family unit in the Greek state. Aristotle's attack on the community of property is almost entirely based on the 'incentive' argument; communal property will not be looked after as carefully as private property; in addition, quarrels are bound to develop when men, unequal by nature in skill and industry, are not differentiated by varying opportunities of enjoyment. Not the abolition of private property, but a more enlightened and liberal use of it is required.

Aristotle's own ideal city lacks Plato's imagination but it retains the belief in reason and benevolence. The state is still divided into rulers and ruled. The former are the military class, the statesmen, magistrates, and the priesthood. These functions are not to be divided among different groups; according to age the members of the ruling class will perform these tasks of government; they will be soldiers when they are young and strong, statesmen in the prime of life, and priests in old age. The ruled are the farmers, craftsmen, and labourers. And though he still regarded trade as an unnatural occupation, Aristotle was prepared to admit it to a limited extent into his ideal city. The basis of this city still remained slavery. Aristotle justified it by appealing to the fact that some people were slaves by nature. He did, however, make some breach into the existing institution of slavery by emphasizing that slaves should be recruited from those of non-Hellenic origin.

But his part in the controversy about the ideal state is the least important of Aristotle's contributions to early economic thought. His analytical ideas can be summarized under three headings: (a) the definition of the scope of economics; (b) the analysis of exchange; and (c) the theory of money. To these may be added a number of other incidental remarks which are made in the course of the main discussion. The particular merit of this discussion is that the argument proceeds logically, each step leading to the next. According to Aristotle, economy is divided into two parts: economy proper, which was the science of household management; and the science of supply, which was concerned with the art of acquisition. Nothing need be said about his discussion of the former except that it deals with the development of the city from the household and the village and that it contains Aristotle's famous defence of slavery.

In discussing the science of supply Aristotle is soon led to analyse the art of exchange through which the needs of the household are increasingly met. Here he distinguishes between a natural and an unnatural form of exchange. The former is merely an extension of the economy of the household designed 'for the satisfaction of men's natural wants';[1] it arises from the existence of varying stocks of goods and the enlargement of the association of men beyond the confines of the household. It is from this simple form of exchange that a more complicated and unnatural practice arises.

'Of everything which we possess there are two uses: both belong to the thing as such, but not in the same manner, for one is the proper, and the other the improper or secondary use of it. For example, a shoe is used for wear, and is used for exchange; both are uses of the shoe.'[2] In these words, Aristotle laid the foundation of the distinction between use-value and exchange-value, which has remained a part of economic

1 Aristotle, *Politics* (Jowett's translation), Book I, 9.
2 ibid.

21

thought to the present day. Although his words are obscure, Aristotle seems to say that the secondary value of an article – as a means of exchange – is not necessarily 'unnatural'. Men may exchange without being engaged in the unnatural form of supply, the art of money-making. They would in that case exchange only until they had enough; but barter does not stop there. Men become more and more dependent upon exchange for the supply of their needs and they develop a medium of exchange. They make a convention to use an article useful in itself, such as iron or silver, for the purpose of facilitating exchange.

Thus Aristotle carries a little further Plato's definition of money as a symbol for the sake of exchange. He shows how the inconveniences of barter lead to the development of indirect exchange, how measurement by size and weight is replaced by coinage, and how trade for its own sake, the pursuit of money-making, arises. The natural purpose of exchange, the more abundant satisfaction of wants, is lost sight of; the accumulation of money becomes an end in itself. The worst form of money-making is that which uses money itself as the source of accumulation: usury. Money is intended to be used in exchange, but not to increase at interest; it is by nature barren; through usury it breeds, and this must be the most unnatural of all the ways of making money. In these views Aristotle shows himself to be still anxious to limit the scope of commerce by setting it on an ethical basis and by distinguishing between different forms of it. To this extent he is still in the Platonic tradition; it is not surprising, therefore, that when Christian doctrine of the Middle Ages sought to condemn the baser aspects of trade – the search for gain for its own sake, and particularly usury – it looked to Aristotle for support.

Aristotle's long discussion of the two arts of money-making was not just an attempt to drive home an ethical distinction. It was also a true analysis of two different forms in which money acts in the economic process: as a medium of exchange whose function is completed by the acquisition of the good required for the satisfaction of a want; and in the shape of money capital leading men to the desire for limitless accumulation. For the first time in the history of economic thought the dichotomy of money and real capital (Aristotle already distinguished those goods which are used for further acquisition) is stated; but later economists stripped it of its ethical garb.

In his discussion of the quality of money Aristotle concludes that money has a conventional rather than a natural origin. It was the rendering of the Greek word *nomos* into the Latin *lex* which caused considerable difficulty to later interpreters, particularly to the medieval schoolmen. They were unable to distinguish clearly between legal-tender money and money in a more general sense, as the medium of exchange created by usage. It has been suggested[1] that Aristotle's view on this point anticipated Knapp's state theory of money, which makes money a creature of the law. But it seems clear that Aristotle meant by *nomos* nothing but the convention of the market, a very different thing from the law. He distinguished this from the 'natural' institutions of the economic process only in order to bring out the development which the household economy had undergone and also to differentiate between the medium of exchange and the money-capital aspects of money.

Aristotle's appreciation of the real quality of market exchange is revealed even more by the attention which he gives to the problem of exchange-value and to the function of money in its determination. The relevant passages in Book V of the *Ethics* are somewhat obscure, but they show that Aristotle was able to formulate the problem of the function of money as a 'measure' of value. Again the question of the establishment of exchange-value is made in part an ethical problem. It appears in Aristotle's discussion of justice, and in particular of the corrective justice which should underlie commercial transactions. Aristotle realizes that exchange is based on equivalence. He regards exchange as ultimately based on wants, but he considers at the same time that 'proportionate equality'[2] prior to exchange is essential. He thus appears on the side of those who regard exchange-value as existing apart from price and prior to any particular act of exchange.

He did not, however, develop a theory of the factors determining that exchange-value. He is content to state that although goods which are exchanged are essentially incommensurable, they must somehow be comparable in order to be exchanged. This possibility of general exchange he bases, in the first place, on the existence of mutual demand which unites society, 'for if people had no wants, or their wants were dissimilar, there would be either no exchange or it would not be the same as it is now'. In the second place, he takes money as 'a sort of recognized representative' of demand. 'It measures everything ... e.g. the number of shoes which are equivalent to a house or a meal.' What begins with the promise of being a theory of value ends up

1 A. Gray, *The Development of Economic Doctrine* (1931), p. 27
2 Aristotle, *Ethics* (Welldon's translation), Book V.

with a mere statement of the accounting function of money. But the problem is correctly stated; so also is that of the 'store of value' function of money. Aristotle recognizes that 'money is serviceable with a view to future exchanges', but also that its value, like that of other things, is subject to change. Although Aristotle is thus responsible for the beginning of a real analysis of the problem of exchange-value, it was the ethical form of Aristotle's views which served as the content for medieval theories of exchange: they found their first extension in the doctrine of the 'just price'. It was not until the rise of the classical political economy of the eighteenth century that a positive theory of value was first developed.

In Aristotle we see the first separation and reunion of the positive and the ethical approach to the economic process. His is a view of society similar to Plato's. For example, Aristotle ascribes the evils of property not to that institution itself, but to the vicious manner in which men administer it. But the distinction between the forms which economic activity actually takes and the ethical precepts which should underlie it is clearly brought out. In his analysis of the principles of a society in transition from agricultural self-sufficiency to trade and commerce he remained unsurpassed for centuries. He remains also the chief source of inspiration of all those who wish to effect a worthy compromise between the baser and the higher pursuits of man. There was one institution, a fundamental one of his society, with which he was quite unable to grapple – slavery; and it was this which brought low his civilization. It was not in Greece, however, but in Rome that the conflict between this exploited class of the ancient world and its rulers came to a head.


## The Roman Empire and Christianity

Rome has left a meagre legacy of specifically economic discussion. The great empire, by the side of which the Greek city state looks a negligible unit, was incapable of producing great social thinkers. It is not possible to develop here an analysis of the reasons for this paucity of philosophical speculation in ancient Rome. All one can say in relation to economic thought is that the struggle between the old and the new society in its specifically economic aspects, which was vividly before the eyes of Greek philosophers and which inspired their views, appears not to have been so marked in Rome.

The Roman Empire also had its beginnings in small agricultural communities with very little trade and a rigid division of social classes. But favourable geographical conditions, a wealth of natural resources, an early achievement of something approaching national cohesion, and the conquest of colonies, which for a time solved the problem of impoverished farmers, caused a rapid transition to a larger and more complex social structure. This transition, though smoother, apparently, than in Greece, was not without its conflicts. The wars and conquests which extended the power of Rome were accompanied by serious economic dislocation and an intensified opposition of interests between poor and rich. While they impoverished the small farmer through increasing tax burdens, they added to the wealth of the large landowners, moneylenders, and merchants, and created a new wealthy class of those who were able to profit from the quickened economic activity of war and reconstruction. Soon, however, the establishment of the empire and the consequent consolidation of administration and finance led to a period of prosperity which made it possible to lighten the tax burden and to quieten discontent by bread and circuses.

It is not until the decline of imperial splendour that there is some concern with economic questions. But even then it is little more than a second-hand version of Greek doctrine that holds the field. A desire for a return to the more primitive conditions of the past (again romantically viewed), a high regard for agriculture, a strong condemnation of the newer forms of money-making, an attack upon the *latifundia*, the large domains which had grown up after the Punic wars: these are the recurring elements of Roman social thought. There is little that is original in the writings of the philosophers, though Pliny may be said to have carried a little further the discussion of money by pointing out the qualities which make gold a particularly suitable medium of exchange.

The only important new development is the perceptible change in the view of slavery. There is no longer the constantly repeated justification of slavery that runs through the writings of the Greek philosophers; it even begins to be questioned whether slavery is a natural institution. In the works of writers on agriculture (such as Columella) who were concerned with technical matters, slave labour is generally described as inefficient; and this view was shared by Pliny. It was true that on the large *latifundia*, with their difficulties of supervision, slavery was becoming an uneconomical form of labour. And when after the end of the period of conquests the supply of fresh slaves ceased, the whole economic basis of slavery on the land was destroyed. The expansion of urban industry, too, could not be carried out except through the gradual disappearance of the slave; and while industry and trade (though not money-lending) continued to be looked upon as ungentlemanly pursuits worthy only of slaves, foreigners, or plebeians, this only led to the gradual decline of the old ruling class and to the rise of a class of freedmen who occupied more and more important political positions.

For the problems that developed after the second century AD the Roman Empire could find no solution. A ruling class whose economic power was vanishing was faced by plebeians and freedmen, crushed by the weight of taxation which an overgrown administrative apparatus imposed, and by a mass of despairing slaves. This inner decay and the weakening hold of military rule over distant provinces, brought about the final downfall of the empire. Although it did not produce a body of economic doctrine, it left two important legacies.

During the height of its power when, for a time, the patricians, the new landowners, and the commercial classes lived in comparative peace, there was evolved a body of laws which has had the most profound influence on later legal institutions. In the first place, the intercourse with other peoples which Rome had had from very early times brought into contact different legal systems and created an interest in the problems of their relationship. The *ius gentium* was the body of all those laws which were the same in different nations and were created by the necessities of the same historical development. This concept led later to the idea of the natural law which had a considerable influence on the evolution of economic thought. Of more direct economic importance were the doctrines which Roman jurists evolved for the regulation of economic relations. They upheld the rights of private property almost without limit and guaranteed freedom of contract to an extent which seems to go beyond what was appropriate to the conditions of the day.

These two features of Roman law, basic in so far as economic relations were concerned, show the great extent to which Rome had developed the mechanism of modern commerce. They reflect the strongly individualist quality of the Roman economic structure, in marked contrast to the survival of more rigid group elements in the much less highly developed economy of Greek society. Nothing could be more striking than the difference between Aristotle's view of property and that inherent in Roman law: in the former, a strong ethical element limiting the rights of property, and in the latter, an unrestricted individualism. Thus while Aristotle becomes the philosopher of the Middle Ages and one of the sources of the Canon Law, it is Roman law which serves as an important basis for the legal doctrines and institutions of capitalism.

Although the Roman Empire's law and practice do not appear to have been exercised over the evils of its social order, Rome was the birthplace of the greatest movement of revolt of antiquity. In its origins Christianity is in the tradition of the Hebrew prophets. The Messiah would come, Isaiah had said, 'to preach good tidings to the meek, ... to bind up the broken-hearted, to proclaim liberty to the captives and the opening of the prison to them that are bound'.[1] And Jesus, having read out these words in the synagogue at Nazareth, added, 'Today hath this scripture been fulfilled in your ears'.[2] Whatever view one may take of the Gospels, it is clear that Jesus was conscious that His mission as the Messiah included that of emancipator of the poor and oppressed. Like the prophets, He castigates the exploiters of the weak and those who, regardless of their fellow men, accumulate private riches. Like them, He threatens retribution through the wrath of God.

There are, however, considerable differences between the teachings of Jesus and those of the earlier Hebrew prophets. When the latter were making their protest, the memory of the tribal community with its group obligations was still vivid. They could look back to it and could appeal to its customs and laws in their attack upon the invading force of the new society divided into social classes. With some exceptions there was the romantic element of *laudatores temporis acti* in the prophets. This element is not altogether absent in the Gospels; but in them emphasis has been shifted from the inherited traditions of the primitive community to new standards of social behaviour – from justice to love. The Gospels are in a sense more revolutionary than the books of the prophets. Their basis is more universal, since their appeal was intended not only for the oppressed classes but for all humanity. Not the elimination of individual abuses but a complete change of man's conduct in society was their goal.

There are also great differences between the teachings of Christ and those of the Greek philosophers. We have already seen that the economic doctrines of Plato and, to some extent, Aristotle derived from an aristocratic dislike of the growth of commercialism and

1 Isaiah, lxi, 1.
2 Luke, iv, 21, 22.

democracy. Their attack upon the evils of the pursuit of wealth is reactionary: it is backward-looking, that of Christ looks forward: it demands a complete change in human relations. They dreamt of an ideal state designed to ensure the 'good life' for the free citizens only and having the boundaries of the existing city state; Christ claimed to speak to, and for, all men. Plato and Aristotle had justified slavery; Christ's teaching of the brotherhood of man and of universal love was, in spite of the views later advanced by Aquinas, incompatible with the institution of slavery. The Greek philosophers, concerned only with the citizens, held very rigid views of the varying worthiness of different kinds of labour; and they regarded the menial occupations, with the exception of agriculture, as fit only for slaves; Christ, addressing Himself to the labourers of His time, proclaimed for the first time the worthiness both in a material and a spiritual sense of all work.

But the same factors which made Christianity more revolutionary also made it more Utopian. The slaves and the poor peasants, fishermen, and artisans, among whom were the earliest and the most eager disciples of Christ, were unable to find the conditions in their own society which could have made it possible to transform that society. In the main social struggle of the time, that between the plebeian and the patrician (complicated by the conflict between the peoples of vanquished colonies and their imperial conquerors), the slaves and the urban proletariat had little part. But the plebeians, the only possible alternative rulers, were unable to acquire economic power since industry was undeveloped. The basis of the plebeians' wealth was predatory: colonial exploitation, usury or monopoly. The struggle between plebeians and patricians, therefore, led not to the establishment of a new ruling class but to the decay of Roman society. The slaves and 'proletarians', in so far as they embraced the new religion and its social doctrines, had to abandon the hope of any material improvement of their condition. The spiritual aspects of the new teaching grew stronger; an apparent opposition between it and the material economic problems of the time developed; and in the end little of immediate social relevance was left. But it was during this period that the Church developed as a feudal institution having its roots deep in the economic structure of medieval society.

When we reach the Middle Ages we find that the words of Christ are no longer enough as a basis for the doctrines of the Church, which, embodied in the Canon Law, held sway over the whole of men's conduct. In addition to the ethical precepts in which Christ's social teaching had originally been contained, the doctrines of Aristotle, derived from a different historical background and inspired by different motives, form the foundations of medieval thought.

## The Middle Ages and the Canon Law

Controversies about the time covered by the term Middle Ages are now rare. It is generally considered to cover a period of roughly a thousand years, from the fall of the Roman Empire in the fifth century to about the middle of the fifteenth century. More precise limits are only imposed by historians with some particular thesis to prove and are not necessary to our purpose. From our point of view the period is important only as an indication of the length of time during which a certain form of society and certain social theories held sway. Nor need we side with any one of the different modes of valuation of the quality of medieval life, a subject on which controversy is still alive. To subsequent societies and their theorists it is always tempting to view the past through dark or rose-coloured spectacles. Many liberal economic historians could see in the Middle Ages nothing but stagnation. Impressed with the enormous expansions which capitalism and its political forms had brought about, they could only pour scorn upon the slow-moving economic process of earlier times. Those, on the other hand, whose social views were inspired by a reaction against capitalism, stressed the order and stability of medieval society and ignored the evils which were their indispensable accompaniment. A realistic view must avoid this one-sidedness and appreciate the social structure of the Middle Ages in its entirety, even though it contained many varying elements.

On one point there is now fairly general agreement: the thousand years that lie between the fall of Rome and the fall of Constantinople are now no longer regarded as a complete lacuna in social development. The dark ages of barbarism which overwhelmed Greek and Roman civilization were real enough; but they did not lead to a complete break between the society of antiquity and that of the Middle Ages. The essential features of medieval social structure, those which concern the distribution and regulation of property, particularly in land, had their origin in certain developments which occurred in the latter period of the Roman Empire. Nor is there any break at the end of the Middle Ages: the fall of feudal society was slow and commercial capitalism was prepared in the womb of the medieval world. The impression of stagnation and of historical isolation which is often produced by the Middle Ages is explicable only by the fact that to modern observers, aware of the rapid changes of the last two hundred years, that social order seems to have persisted for a very long time.

The essence of medieval society lies in the class division between lords and serfs which was derived from the structure of the *latifundia* of latter-day Rome. The growing scarcity of slaves had led to a change in the method of administration of the large estates, though landed property itself still retained its attraction. Instead of working these estates themselves by means of large numbers of slaves, the landlords would rent out holdings apart from their own domain to free tenants or to slaves, receiving a rent in kind and money and having their domain cultivated by the tenants. There was in addition the need to settle the frontiers with a military population for purposes of defence, and this also led to the establishment of *coloni*, who possessed certain privileges but were also subject to considerable compulsion. In the fourth century the free tenant was tied to the estate, and the beginning was made of a new system of bondage which in time effectively replaced ancient slavery. The decline of the empire placed more and more administrative power into the hands of the landlord and made his estate the new economic and political unit. This was the forerunner of the medieval manor.

To the social structure which was thus developed the contributions of other peoples made comparatively little difference. Some of them had already developed a similar economic organization of their own, or did so later. Others acquired it through contact with Rome. Even if their experience was at first different, the people of northern Europe, particularly the Germans, did in the end evolve a manorial system. The most powerful factors in this evolution were seizures of land by conquerors, who became kings, and grants of land by them to past or future supporters. From these the system of feudal lordship arose. It was of varying extent and complexity, covering sometimes an empire and sometimes only a few estates; but its quality remained the same: a rigid division of different social classes with different and carefully defined rights and obligations.

Not only on the land, but in trade and industry too, development proceeds without a break from the beginnings made in Rome. The oriental trade of the empire, though limited in scope, was important and was the basis of the medieval commerce of the Italian cities; to this was added the large trade which had developed in the Eastern Empire. And both Northmen and Moslems, who had begun as raiding warriors, ended by becoming merchants. Industry, apart from building and construction, was not highly developed in Rome. And in the medieval world too, at any rate until its later years, industry remains confined to the needs of a small local market or to a few products of outstanding importance in long-distance trade. But already in Rome the regulation of industry was getting into the hands of voluntary associations of all those engaged in the same trade. Both elements of the medieval guilds, of friendly society and of monopoly, are contained in these Roman *collegia*, even though it is impossible to trace an unbroken line of descent.

What was the unifying principle of this medieval society which was so sharply divided into social classes and groups? In the first place, the principle of division was itself regarded as the foundation of society. In the Middle Ages the worldly inequality of men was recognized and accepted without question. The activities of every individual were regulated according to his status. His place in society, his duties, and privileges, were carefully defined with regard to the major political features of his state. Although the organic community of the tribe had gone for good, and inequality and duress had taken the place of the free association of equals, there was as yet no 'atomic individualism'. The group loyalties were merely more numerous and more variegated and were exacted by means of often brutal coercion.

The second unifying principle, closely connected with the first, was provided by the role of the Church. After the fall of Rome the Church had become increasingly institutionalized and had added greatly to its spiritual and material power. In the Middle Ages it had become in its secular aspect one of the most important pillars of the existing economic structure. Its property in land had grown to such an extent that it had become the greatest of feudal lords. But while temporal feudal lordships were widely scattered and lacked any links of national union, the Church possessed a doctrinal unity which gave it a universal power. This combination of secular and spiritual power resulted in a complete harmony between the doctrines of the Church and feudalist society. It is this harmony which explains why the Church could claim to order the whole of human relations and conduct on the earth as well as to provide the precepts which would lead to spiritual salvation. It explains also why the economic doctrines which result from this claim

31

were not inappropriate to the conditions of their time.[1]

Economic ideas were part of the moral teachings of Christianity. Christian dogma, however, was not enough. The medieval world could not give up the ethical quality of its doctrines without losing its spiritual *raison d'être*. But since it also had its roots deep in the economic conditions of feudal society, it combined the teachings of the Gospels and of the early Christian Fathers with those of Aristotle, the philosopher who had tempered his realistic views of the economic process with ethical postulates. We find throughout the canonical discussions of economic institutions or practices a union between the economic ethic, which had been part of the spiritual missions of Christianity, and the existing institutions with all their imperfections. Often this union is an uneasy one, but it does not break until the institutions are beginning to crumble under the impact of new economic forces.

The Canonists accepted Aristotle's distinction between the natural economy of the household and the unnatural form of the science of supply, the art of money-making. Economics to them meant a body of laws, not in the sense of scientific laws, but in that of moral precepts designed to ensure the good administration of economic activity. The part of economics which was in practice very much akin to that laid down by Aristotle rested on a foundation of Christian theology. This condemned avarice and covetousness and subordinated the material advancement of the individual both to the claims of his fellow men, his brothers in Christianity, and to the needs of salvation in the next world. Thus the Church was able sometimes to condemn those economic practices which increased exploitation and inequality and sometimes to preach an indifference to the miseries of this world. In general it defended the inequalities of stations to which it had pleased God to call men.

It is a greater emphasis on this latter point which distinguishes the Canonists from the early Christian Fathers. The Gospels and the Fathers leave an overwhelming impression of opposition to worldly goods. Even where they do not condemn the whole institution of property, they invariably attack many of its manifestations. Christ had condemned the search for riches and Saint Jerome had said, 'Dives aut iniquus aut iniqui haeres'.[2] The whole basis of trade was called in

---

1 Cf. H. Pirenne, *Economic and Social History of Medieval Europe* (1936), pp. 13, *sqq.*, for a detailed account of the reasons which made the Church the most important feudal institution.

2 Quoted by L. Brentano. *Ethik und Volkswirtschaft in der Geschichte* (1901), p. 5.

question, as Tertullian had appreciated, when he argued that to remove covetousness was to remove the reason for gain, and, therefore, the need for trade. Saint Augustine had feared that trade turned men from the search for God; and the doctrine that 'nullus christianus debet esse mercator' was common in the Church in the early Middle Ages.[1]

But in the later Middle Ages these views on property and trade found themselves in strong contrast with a firmly entrenched economic system which rested on private property and with an increase in trade caused by the growth of towns and the expansion of markets. The intransigence of the early Church could not be maintained in the face of this new economic development. Though some of the schoolmen, like the Dominican General Raymond de Pennafort, continued to condemn trade,[2] we find in the most important of them, Saint Thomas Aquinas, a distinct tendency to reconcile theological dogma with the existing conditions of economic life.[3] In regard to property, he did not go back to the unrestricted rights conceded in the Roman law, which was beginning to come into its own again. He found in the Aristotelian distinction between the power of acquisition and administration and that of use an important separation of two aspects of property. The former conferred rights on the individual and Saint Thomas's arguments in defence of it are those which we have already met in Aristotle's attack on Plato; the latter put obligations upon the individual in the interests of the community. Thus not the institution but the manner of using it determined whether it was good or evil. It was the hereafter that mattered; conduct on this earth was only to be judged with reference to ultimate salvation. Saint Thomas did not pretend that wealth was natural or good in itself, but he classed it with other imperfections of man's earthly life which were inevitable but which should be made as good as their nature would permit. Although he was prepared to go so far in his restriction of property rights as to justify theft by the needy, he was well aware of the implications of status in medieval society. He enjoins, for example, the giving of alms, but only in so far as it does not force the giver to live beneath his station in life.

From this view of property a compromise on the question of trade naturally follows. Saint Thomas does not regard it as good or natural;

1 ibid., pp. 6, 7
2 G. O'Brien, *An Essay on Medieval Economic Thinking* (1920), p. 149.
3 For extracts containing St. Thomas's main economic argument, cf. A. E. Monroe, *Early Economic Thought* (1924), pp. 53–77.

on the contrary, he shares Aristotle's view that it is unnatural and he adds that it implies a fall from the state of grace. But it was an evil inevitable in an imperfect world, and could be justified only if the merchant sought to maintain his household and when the object of trade was to benefit the country.[1] The profit realized in trade was then nothing other than a reward for labour. The justification of trade depended also on whether the exchange which was effected was just; whether that which was given and that which was received were of equal value. For this argument Saint Thomas could draw once again on Aristotle, whose analysis of exchange-value was, as we have seen, contained in the discussion of justice. But there was another source. The early Fathers, in spite of their general antipathy to trade, had had to grapple with the regulation of practices which they condemned but could not abolish; and they too had tried to do so by stipulating the principle of the 'just price'. That price was objective, inherent in the values of articles of commerce, and to depart from it was to infringe the moral code.

It is impossible to discover what, in the eyes of the theologians, determined that price or to explain it in terms which would have any similarity to modern economic theories. Saint Augustine, in his celebrated example of the honest buyer, merely says that, though the vendor was ignorant of the value of the manuscript he sold, the buyer paid the 'just price'. Some attempt at a theory of the 'just price' is to be found later in the writings of Albertus Magnus; in a slight reference he develops the ideas of Aristotle by insisting that, ideally, goods containing the same amount of labour and expense should be exchanged. Aquinas too seems to have held some vague cost-of-production theory of exchange-value. Again, it had an ethical form. Cost of production was determined on the principle of justice, i.e. that which was necessary to maintain the producer. In general, however, the idea of the 'just price' expressed little more than that of the conventional price. Above all, it was designed to prevent enrichment by means of trade. Civil law, with its Roman foundations and the natural instinct of man, seemed to encourage men to sell goods for more than they were worth. But this, Saint Thomas showed, was against divine law, which is superior to man-made law; and the common instinct of man often led to vice. Trade could only be justified if it was designed to further the common weal; it must ensure an equal advantage to both parties.

1 A. E. Monroe, *Early Economic Thought*, p. 63.

Apart from these ethical arguments, the idea of a conventional price was not an unrealistic one in the earlier part of the Middle Ages. With its still predominant natural economy, difficulties of transport, restricted trade, and local markets, early medieval society was not a suitable environment for an unrestricted play of the forces of supply and demand. In the confined conditions of commerce, an insistence on the customary price of the 'common estimate' was not unreasonable. Moreover, though inspired by more practical motives, the views and practices of secular authority led in the same direction as Canon Law. Trade was still sufficiently haphazard to make it necessary to enforce regulations which would ensure as steady a supply of goods as possible; rules against *forestalling, regrating, engrossing*, and the fixing of maximum prices were common features of legislation and guild regulation.

Even so, the advance of trade was sufficiently rapid to necessitate a gradual retreat from the position first taken up by the Church. Even Saint Thomas had permitted oscillations round the 'just price' according to some market fluctuations; in particular, he had justified the taking of a higher price where the seller would otherwise incur a loss. And later writers introduced still further qualifications. The cost of transporting goods to the market, miscalculation, and differences in the status of the participants in exchange became valid reasons for departing from the 'just price'. In time, even variations of supply and demand were allowed to affect the market prices; and in the fifteenth century Saint Antonio, while still insisting on fairness, introduced so many qualifications into the doctrine that the force of the objective 'just price' was greatly diminished and a beginning was made with the 'recognition of the impersonal forces of the market'.[1]

This decline in the rigidity of canon dogma is even more striking in the case of its other main economic precept, that which related to usury. The teachings of Christ on this point are quite unmistakable. Although the only precept which appears in the Gospels[2] is variously interpreted, even an absence of specific condemnation could not alter the fact that enrichment through the lending of money at interest was regarded as the very worst form of the pursuit of gain. Hebrew law had also prohibited the taking of interest. Exodus (xxii, 25) forbids the 'laying of usury' upon any of God's people; and it has been argued that according to the Talmud the prohibition appears to apply universally

1 R. H. Tawney, *Religion and the Rise of Capitalism* (1929), p. 41.
2 Luke, vi, 35.

and not only as between Jews.[1] Whether Saint Thomas was right or not in claiming that the Bible prohibition implied that a Jew could exact interest from a Gentile, he was aware that this could make no difference to the universal nature of Christian teaching. The Fathers condemned usury, and although some of the schoolmen, notably Duns Scotus, were a little less intransigent, Saint Thomas's own view that usury was unjust was the more generally accepted.

The condemnation of usury was part of the general condemnation of unjust exchange. In the early Middle Ages the Church's own prohibition applied to the clergy only. The absence of any developed money economy and of opportunities for profitable investment of money capital made more general prohibition unnecessary. The Church was the only recipient of large sums of money at a time when feudal dues to lords and kings were still paid mainly in kind. When money was lent it was generally to needy persons for purposes of consumption, and the exaction of interest was then more obviously branded as exploitation and oppression of the weak. When kings and princes had to borrow money they were able to have recourse to Jews, who were deprived of other opportunities of livelihood, and for whom the original prohibition of money-lending, in the absence of a central doctrinal authority, was losing its force.

With the development of commerce and the opportunities for monetary transactions in the later Middle Ages, two tendencies arose. On the one hand secular practice went in the direction of increasing the lending of money at interest and of justifying it by a reliance on Roman law; on the other hand the Church, alarmed by the new development, made its original prohibition more emphatic and universal. At the great Lateran Council of 1179 the first of a series of stringent prohibitions of usury was decreed.[2] And the growth of the religious orders, most of which put a complete asceticism in the forefront of their principles, was another symptom of the same movement.

The basis of Church dogma also underwent a change. In the works of Saint Thomas, the doctrine against usury became founded as much, if not more, on Aristotelian argument as on Scripture. Aristotle's opposition to usury arose out of his theory of the quality of money. Money, he had said, arose as a means to facilitating legitimate (natural)

1 Cf. L. Brentano, *Die Anfänge des Modernen Kapitalismus* (1916), p. 191, quoting Funk, *Die Juden in Babylonien* (1902).
2 W. J. Ashley, *An Introduction to English Economic History and Theory* (1914), vol. i, part i, p. 149.

exchange, that which had as its sole aim the satisfaction of the wants of consumers. Barrenness was thus part of its essential nature; usury, which made money bear fruit, was unnatural. Saint Thomas took up this view and combined it with the doctrine of Roman law which distinguished between goods which were *consumptibles* and those which were *fungibles*. Roman law had not made use of this distinction in reference to the problem of loans on interest at all. It had merely classed goods according to whether they were consumed in use or not. Aquinas and other Canonists, following Aristotle's definition, put money in the first category and concluded that to demand interest in addition to the return of the loan was to seek an unnatural and unjust gain.

In spite of the more determined attitude of the Church and its more sophisticated arguments, the practice of taking interest grew with economic expansion. Lay authority became increasingly concerned with the regulation rather than with the prohibition of interest; and decrees fixing maximum rates became more frequent in the fourteenth century. When we reach the age of discoveries of the fifteenth and sixteenth centuries the channels for profitable investment grow to such an extent that the doctrines of the earlier Canonists become hopelessly out of keeping with economic practice. Important modifications appear in the theory of usury, as they had done in the theory of the 'just price'.

Francis de Mayronis, a disciple of Duns Scotus, had said,[1] 'De iure naturali, non apparet quod [usura] sit illicita'. This, however, was a view very much in advance of its time. The retreat of Canon Law in general was slower and involved the concession of exceptions rather than the abandonment of the principle. Of these exceptions the most important was the doctrine of *damnum emergens*, the suffering of a loss by the lender, which had already led Saint Thomas to modify the rigour of the 'just price'. Where a delay (*mora*) occurred in the repayment of a loan, the lender was entitled to exact a conventional penalty. The Church assumed that a bona fide loss had been suffered or that there had been a genuine delay. But these exceptions opened the door to the taking of interest without much discrimination. The *mora* became shorter until, among the later theologians like Navarrus, the tendency arose to dispense entirely with any period of gratuitous loan.

Still more important in helping to break down the original prohibition was the doctrine relating to *lucrum cessans*. To have lost the chance

1 L. Brentano, *Ethik und Volkswirtschaft in der Geschichte*, p. 17.

of gain through lending money became also a justification for the receiving of interest. The controversies over this principle were prolonged and very involved. But as the growing opportunities of trade made it easier to prove that gain had been sacrificed when money was lent, the final victory of this doctrine could not be prevented. Its triumph was made even more complete by the recognition that a special reward could be claimed by the lender for the risk which he undertook. The *commenda* (partnership), which was often a 'sleeping' one, was another favourite method, particularly in the city of London, for concealing the lending and borrowing of money. And other subterfuges, such as the complicated *contractus trinus*, were devised to weaken still further the barrier by which theological dogma was impeding economic progress. In the end the general prohibition fell virtually into disuse. What we might call genuine investment involving risk of loss as well as chance of gain began to be regarded as legitimate. Only the lending of money for gain without any risk or as a consumptive loan proper made to needy persons remained proscribed.

This development was by no means a continuous one; the history of the discussions on usury from the thirteenth to the sixteenth centuries shows how ideas fluctuated in spite of the existence of a definite trend. We have seen how Francis de Mayronis questioned the general prohibition of usury which was still upheld by Saint Thomas Aquinas and by Canonist doctrine in general. Again, in 1514, the German professor Eck,[1] in a lecture before the University of Ingolstadt, justified the *contractus trinus* and went so far as to say that a merchant who borrowed money might justly be expected to pay 5 per cent interest. But Catholic doctrine of the time was still opposed to the *contractus trinus*.

The same divergences existed even among the leaders of the Reformation, in spite of the fact that Protestant teaching was in general more in harmony with the economic trends of the time. Luther held views which were not very different from those of the Canonists. With regard to trade, he still believed in the 'just price', and his condemnation of usury was as strong as that of any of the schoolmen. Calvin, on the other hand, in a celebrated letter written in 1574,[2] denied that the taking of payment for the use of money was in itself sinful. He repudiated the Aristotelian doctrine that money was infertile and pointed out that money could be used to procure those things which

---

1 G. O'Brien, *An Essay on Medieval Economic Thinking*, p. 211.
2 R. H. Tawney, *Religion and the Rise of Capitalism*, p. 106.

would bear a revenue. He nevertheless distinguished instances in which the taking of interest would become sinful usury, as in the case of needy borrowers oppressed by calamity.

The chronological inconsistencies are perhaps most clearly exemplified by the writings of Nicole Oresme. In his *Traictie de la Première Invention des Monnoies*,[1] written about 1360, he develops a theory of money which reveals a very different approach to economic problems from that of his fellow Churchmen. (The only exception is Buridan, who had already laid the foundations on which Oresme built.) The treatise begins with a detailed account of the origin of money on Aristotelian lines; but it is enriched with a careful discussion of the qualities which make goods suitable for adoption as money. This leads Oresme to distinguish between the proper uses of gold and silver in a system of coinage. Although he concludes in favour of both, his bimetallism is tempered with a realization of the need for ensuring that the proportion of the market value of the two metals should rule the ratio of their monetary value. Not only is this a very moderate view of bimetallism, it is also one which implies that the value of money is ultimately derived from the value of the money commodity – a view which is contained in several later monetary theories.

Oresme holds that the prerogative of coinage should be in the hands of the prince, as the representative of the community who enjoys the greatest prestige and authority. But the prince is not, or ought not to be the 'lord of the money in circulation in his country; for money is a legal instrument for exchanging natural Riches among men. ... Money, therefore, really belongs to those who own such natural Riches.' Such a conception of the function of the monetary authority leads Oresme to an extraordinarily vehement condemnation of debasement of the coinage. The prince has no right, he argues, to tamper with the wealth of his subjects by altering the proportion, weight, or material of which their money is made. Gain derived from debasement is worse than usury; it is extorted from the prince's subjects against their will without even that advantage which the borrower obtains from the usurious lender. Debasement is thus a concealed tax which leads to dislocation of trade and impoverishment. And finally – an anticipation of Gresham's law – when the coin is debased, 'despite all precautions they [gold and silver] are carried out to places where they are rated higher', and so diminish the amount of good money in the realm.

1 For an extract of A. E. Monroe, *Early Economic Thought*, pp. 79–102.

The spirit that breathes through the writings of Oresme is that of a much later age. Trade is taken for granted; in spite of his observance of theological dogma, Oresme's main emphasis is on the problems of the merchant. His concern is to protect the commercial class from the oppressive practices of the prince, a problem which was becoming increasingly real even though it did not as yet attract many other thinkers. Oresme foreshadows both the transformation which the Church's approach to the economic problem underwent at a later stage and the direction which secular thought was ultimately to follow.

As for Canonist doctrine itself, we have seen how its teachings steadily weakened with commercial expansion until it was faced with the complete collapse of its power to regulate economic life. With the Reformation that development enters on a new phase. It seems clear now that whatever the views of the great originators of the Protestant movement, the Church was no longer able to stand in the way of the growth of commercial capitalism. Whether, as has been argued, Protestant and Puritan doctrines were themselves conducive to the development of the capitalist spirit, and, therefore, of capitalism itself, we need not decide here. For with the end of the Canon Law a profound change occurs in the relation between theological and economic thought. The harmony between Church dogma and feudal society, which at the beginning of this section was said to have been responsible for the all-embracing quality of the Canon Law, came to an end with the decline of feudal society. Canonist thought was essentially an ideology, in economic matters it was an illusory representation of reality. It was successful so long as the conflicts of reality had not become very acute. With the sharpening of these conflicts, the antithetical elements in this ideology were seized upon by the contending parties, and the original universal character was lost. Although theological teaching tried to make concessions to the needs of the times, it could not abandon its essential nature. As the gulf between precept and practice widened, the foundation on which the precepts rested could only be saved by jettisoning the claim that they had a direct relevance to practical affairs. A separation was effected by which religious dogma ceased to represent an analysis of existing society as well as a code of conduct. Religion became something apart from other branches of thought, in particular from those concerned with the mundane problems of wealth-getting. Though attempts were again to be made to introduce ethical elements into the main stream of economic thought, it remains henceforth independent of religion. The foundation for a secular science of economy was laid.

# 2

# Commercial Capitalism and its Theory

### *The Decline of Scholasticism*

In the three centuries that elapsed between the end of the Middle Ages and the appearance of *Wealth of Nations*, the classical system of political economy was being prepared. During that period of keen economic discussion the number of writers and writings on economic matters increased rapidly. Until lately this large theoretical output was somewhat neglected; but during the last few decades historians have given it more attention, and it is now possible to have a much clearer picture of the development of economic thought between the end of the fifteenth and the end of the eighteenth centuries. From a technical economic point of view many of the writers of this time deserve to be treated in considerable detail; for our present purpose, however, it is enough to give an outline of the general trend of theoretical development. Pre-classical political economy can be divided into two parts. The first is largely a reflection of the rise of commercial capitalism and is generally referred to as 'mercantilism'; with this, the present chapter is concerned. The second, accompanying the expansion of industrial capital in the late seventeenth and early eighteenth centuries, contains the real founders of the science of political economy; it is treated separately in the next chapter.

Any discussion of mercantilist theory must be prefaced by some account of the changes which led from the particularist, feudalist economy to the growth of commerce between large, wealthy, and powerful nation-states. The story of this change has often been told. A number of factors were operating to sweep away the medieval world. The growth of nation-states, anxious to destroy both the particularism of feudal society and the universalism of the spiritual power of the Church, resulted in a greater concern for wealth and a quickening of economic activity. The loosening of the central doctrinal authority, caused by the Reformation, and the progress of the concept of natural law in jurisprudence and political thought prepared the ground for a rational and scientific approach to social problems; and the invention of printing created new possibilities of intellectual intercourse. Feudalism also became inadequate in its regulation of production. The revolution in the methods of farming destroyed the basis of feudal economy. It led to rural overpopulation, growing commutation of feudal dues, increased indebtedness of feudal lords and their resort to trade or new methods of farming for the market. Another powerful factor is to be found in the maritime discoveries which led to a very great expansion of foreign commerce.

These two developments were closely interconnected. In England, for example, where the development of capitalism can be most clearly observed, the growth of commerce destroyed subsistence farming and caused agriculture to rely increasingly on the market. The enclosure movement, perhaps the most important of the economic phenomena of the later Middle Ages and the early modern era, was thereby greatly accelerated. Sometimes it was designed to give greater scope to improved methods of arable farming; sometimes it converted arable land into pasture with consequences which social historians have often described. In either case, it made farming subservient to the needs of the great markets and the merchant capital which dominated them. The accumulation of commercial capital was accelerated by the growth of foreign commerce. For reasons of profit, political power or merely prestige, this capital was often invested in land while an opposite movement took place from the landed aristocracy. And intermarriage completed the union between finance, merchant capital and the landed interest.

The revolution in commerce was accompanied by changes in the organization of production. A new phase appeared in which the merchant capitalist dominated the productive process, which was carried out by small craftsmen. The merchant's profit was the product of monopoly and extortion. During this phase the dominance of the commercial capitalist was complete. But this phase inevitably evolved towards a primitive form of industrial capitalism: the putting-out, or *Verlag* system. A special class of merchant-manufacturers appeared who employed semi-independent craftsmen, working in their homes. The class was recruited from the merchant capitalists or the craftsmen, and its interests were opposed to those of the 'pure' commercial capitalists, who were monopolizing the wholesale and export trades. The seventeenth century saw the rivalry between these two methods of production: the commercial capitalist and the primitive industrial capitalist. In that century (to some extent there are signs of this even in the preceding one), factory production with the use of inanimate power was beginning and, with it, full industrial capitalism.

The great importance of the merchant up to that stage is shown not only by his function in production; it is also exemplified by the methods of home and foreign trading, and by the social and political status of those engaged in trade. Monopoly was the outstanding way in which the rising nation-states sought to increase trade and to create sources of revenue for themselves. To the merchant who wished to develop a particular manufacture the possession of a monopoly appeared the best possible way. The tradition of medieval thought was favourable to carefully defined privilege, and, what was more important, monopoly itself was a necessary form of trading at a time when both lust of adventure and risk were great. If in the process the crown exacted a tribute, that was regarded as a necessary expense allocated to the strengthening of an institution which would protect the trading interest.

In domestic production and trade the beginnings of industrial capitalism led to occasional anti-monopoly campaigns. But the arguments against monopoly were *ad hoc* arguments directed against any particular interest whose privilege it was desired to supplant. Primitive industrial capitalism was not opposed to monopoly; it was only opposed to those monopolies which were in the interests of the merchant capitalists. The newer interests, having ousted the old, often became, in their turn, defenders of monopoly. Particularly in the first half of the seventeenth century, the anti-monopoly agitation was due to the struggle between the *Verleger* and the bigger merchant capitalists. It was not until the end of the eighteenth century (and then only in England) that industrial capital became fully anti-monopolist. It had no need then of a legal monopoly, since the new methods of production, requiring costlier methods, gave it a decisive competitive advantage. And it was anxious to sweep away all obstacles to the use of new techniques.

In foreign trade the rule of monopoly was even less seriously challenged for a long time. Throughout the sixteenth and seventeenth centuries we encounter the large privileged trading companies which monopolize trade with different regions; they are the first to use extensively the typically capitalist joint-stock organization. The Merchant Adventurers, the Eastland Company, the Muscovy Company, and, most important of all the East India Company, are some of the great trading monopolies of the time. The trade carried on by these companies and by independent merchants was still largely that of middlemen only. They were concerned in the same entrepôt trade that had enriched their earlier forerunners in Genoa, Venice, and Holland. This carrying business shows the quality of commercial capitalism in its purest essence. However, it soon became complicated by a more advanced form of commerce which involved the export of the country's own manufactures.

To mitigate the hazards of trade, colonization became an important weapon. The efforts of the merchants and companies to achieve control over the distant areas with which they traded were seldom sufficient. They had to be supplemented by the exercise of the power of the state, towards the strengthening of which the merchants were contributing in such large measure. The links between the trading interest and the state were thus still further tightened; and the concern of state policy became increasingly concentrated on problems of trade. Symptomatic of this union between commercial capital and the state is the prestige which some of the merchants enjoyed. All the great figures in the trading companies, whom we shall shortly meet as the leaders of the economic thought of their time, were persons with considerable political influence. For example, Cockayne (who was one of the leaders of the Eastland Company and a creditor of James I) was able to use his influence with the king in his attempt to change the regulations governing the trade in cloth so as to ruin the Merchant Adventures. Misselden, a leading mercantilist, became a member of a standing committee to inquire into the decay of trade which was later to develop into the Board of Trade.[1] When Sir Josiah Child defended the East India Company he pointed out that the joint-stock companies had brought aristocrats and merchants together. And when Mun, the greatest of the mercantilists, wrote his panegyric on the activities of the merchant,[2] he was only expressing in extreme form a widely held sentiment.

The economic development which had made the merchant powerful

1 E. A. J. Johnson, *Predecessors of Adam Smith* (1937), p.58.
2 Thomas Mun, *England's Treasure by Forraign Trade* (Economic History Society Reprint 1928), p. 88.

also destroyed institutions and habits of thought which might have stood in the way of commercial expansion. Particularly striking is the change which comes over the remnants of social thought that still derive from religious dogma. Like an echo of the debate of an earlier and more appropriate time, the discussion among theologians and between theologians and lay-thinkers turns once again to the problems of money and of usury. But the difference between the religious and the lay approach widens. The importance of the former declines while that of the latter increases. The emphasis of the debate is shifted; and though, as we shall see, there sometimes appear curiously anachronistic views, the chief protagonists of economic discussion are no longer inspired by the same motives.

As examples of the thought of this period of transition from Canonist doctrine to mercantilist theory may be mentioned Thomas Wilson, Carolus Molinaeus, Jean Bodin, and John Hales. Of these the first two are typical of the last stages of the discussion on usury, and the third and fourth of the progress of humanist thought.

Carolus Molinaeus, a very distinguished French lawyer of the sixteenth century, had shocked his contemporaries with his *Tractatus Contractuum et Usurarum* (1546),[1] in which he defended the taking of interest, provided that a maximum rate was fixed. He thus took up a position little different from that of Melanchthon or of the Catholic Navarrus. But perhaps on account of the heresy hunt to which he was subjected, and perhaps because lay thought was already of greater consequence, his views seem to have been regarded as calling more for opposition than those of the theologians. Thomas Wilson, in his *Discourse upon Usury*, makes one of his characters whom he subsequently converts rely on Molinaeus.[2] Wilson's own views were very violently opposed to usury. He allowed none of the exceptions which by that time were commonly conceded. Only genuine *mora*, he thought, could justify the taking of interest. In his own day Wilson's views seem to have had some influence on jurisdiction, if not on practice.[3] When for different reasons the mercantilists later again opposed interest, Wilson's views were quoted in support.

More important for the history of economic thought than these last skirmishes of a dying battle are the treaties of Jean Bodin and John

---

1 A. E. Monroe, *Early Economic Thought*, p. 105.
2 T. Wilson, *A Discourse upon Usury* (ed. R. H. Tawney, 1925). pp. 343–5.
3 R. H. Tawney, *Religion and the Rise of Capitalism*, pp. 156, 160.

Hales. Bodin, whose influence was of more immediate importance in the field of political thought, is distinguished by a very advanced treatise on money. In his *Réponse aux Paradoxes de Malestroit*,[1] published in 1569, he gives the first elaborate explanation of the revolution in prices in the sixteenth century. He ascribes the rise in prices, of which he quotes several examples, to five causes: the abundance of gold and silver; the practice of monopolies; scarcity caused in part by export; the luxury of the king and the great lords; and the debasement of the coin. Of these, the first is the most important. His statement that 'the principal reason which raises the price of everything, wherever one may be, is the abundance of that which governs the appraisal and price of things'[2] is the first clear statement of a quantity theory of money. Bodin proceeds to describe the increase of money, the cause of which he finds in the expansion of trade, particularly with the South American countries, which had an abundance of gold. The discussion of the different ways in which foreign trade has brought more gold into France is remarkably modern in tone. Equally so, even though it is slight, is Bodin's condemnation of monopolistic price-raising. The third cause of dearness, scarcity of home produce, is only a corollary of the first: the influx of money from Spain and other trading countries.

Bodin does not lay great stress on the fourth cause; but it has some affinity with modern schools of monetary theory. It refers to the inflationary effects of spending as against hoarding. For if the increased gold had been 'saved' the rise in prices would have been much smaller. Bodin's discussion of the fifth is a worthy descendant of Oresme's analysis of the nature and effects of debasement, for with historical and deductive proof Bodin demonstrates that debasement results in a rise in prices. Bodin distinguishes between rises in prices due to general monetary causes and those which are of a more particular nature; in the remedies he suggests he is as much in advance of his time as he was in his diagnosis: at a time when severe restrictions on commerce were thought indispensable, he pronounced the view that trade ought to be free.

Equally modern in tone if different in substance is *A Discourse of the Common Weal of this Realm of England*, published in 1581, whose author, first described as W. S., is now often taken to have been John Hales, a scholar who became a state official. As one of the officers of

1 A. E. Monroe, *Early Economic Thought*, pp. 123, *sqq.*
2 ibid., p. 127.

Protector Somerset's commission on enclosures Hales came into close touch with the social problems of his time. In the dialogues of his *Discourse* he shows himself keenly aware of the discontent which the agricultural revolution was producing. But his solutions are always in the nature of compromises. He is a humanist, though with much less vision than Bodin, and his approach to social questions is rational and practical. He does not condemn the pursuit of self-interest which he regards as an ineradicable trait of human nature. And although he still believes in the medieval virtues of justice in all dealings, his proposals for harnessing self-interest to the common good are of the stuff of which a later age fashioned its doctrines. The state should so devise its laws that self-interest worked along channels which were generally beneficial. Some enclosures, for example those which improve the arable land, were not to be condemned. Only those which cause unemployment by converting arable land to pasture should be prevented by freeing the export of corn and restricting that of wool.

The same practical attitude is seen in Hales's view of imports. He is in advance of his time in discounting the general restriction of imports; but he does not go as far as Bodin, because he is anxious to prevent undue purchases from abroad of 'trifles'. Moreover, he deplores the export of English raw materials to be reimported after manufacture abroad, since it robs the country of work. Like Oresme, Hales ascribes many economic evils to debasement. His own contribution, not so complete or so clear as that of Bodin, concerns the effect of debasement upon the price of imported goods. He does, however, clearly bring out the way in which an inflationary rise in prices affects the distribution of wealth among different classes of the community.

## The Quality of Mercantilism

So far, we have considered the contributions to economic thought of lawyers, scholars, and state officials. But although a Bodin was able to enunciate monetary doctrines of great clarity and insight, the substantial development of economic thought was due to the leaders of economic activity, the merchants. The theories which they evolved were never contained in a body of doctrine such as that of the Canon Law. What has made it possible to speak of mercantilism is the appearance in a number of countries of a set of theories which explained or underlay the practices of statesmen for a considerable time. The precise definition of the term has for long been a matter of considerable controversy. Some writers[1] have argued that certain mercantilist theories begin to appear in crude form towards the end of the fourteenth and beginning of the fifteenth centuries. Others, such as Cannan,[2] have claimed that a distinction must be drawn between 'Bullionism', which existed during a large part of the later Middle Ages, and mercantilism proper, which does not appear until the seventeenth century, with the growing influence of early industrial capitalism which was interested in an expansion of the export trade. As will become clear later, neither of these two views is exhaustive. The first antedates the rise of the ideas which are typical of mercantilism and the appearance of which is dependent upon a certain degree of development of commercial capitalism. The second is correct only in so far as bullionism is identified with a high regard for 'treasure', which, it is true, existed long before the mercantilist era. But although there was a break between earlier and later mercantilist ideas on foreign trade, this break is not deep enough to destroy the essential unity of mercantilist thought.

Some writers have followed Schmoller in identifying mercantilism with state-making. Professor Heckscher in his lengthy treatise readopts this thesis. In his view, mercantilism is to be regarded essentially as 'a phase in the history of economic policy',[3] which contains a number of economic measures designed to secure political unification and national power. The building-up of nation-states is put in the forefront, and monetary, protectionist, and other economic devices are regarded merely as instruments to this end. State intervention was an essential part of mercantilist doctrine. Those responsible for government accepted mercantilist notions and fashioned their policy accordingly, because they saw in them means of strengthening absolutist states against both rivals abroad and the remnants of medieval particularism at home. It must also be conceded that a great deal of mercantilist literature, from Mun, the enlightened English merchant, to Hornick, the Austrian nationalist lawyer and privy councillor, claims to speak in the interests of national advancement.

But a view which makes political unification the end to which both economic practice and theory were subservient ignores the more

---

1 e.g. A. Gray, *The Development of Economic Doctrine*, p. 66.

2 E. Cannan, *Review of Economic Theory* (1929), p. 7.

3 E. F. Heckscher, *Mercantilism* (1935), vol. i, p. 19.

powerful causal influence on political institutions which proceeded from changes in the economic structure. It is not necessary to minimize the effect which the growth of the state had upon commercial development and the theory of economic policy; but it remains true that it was the breakdown of the feudal economy and the growth of trade which caused the decline of the feudalist political structure and the rise of the nation state. The claim may also be made that the same factors were still operating in the sixteenth century and that mercantilist views sprang from the needs of commercial capital, even though they may at times have found indirect expression in the shape of policies devised for reasons of state-making.

It is not surprising that mercantilists should have clothed their views in the garb of a policy designed to strengthen the nation or that they should have looked to the state to carry out their theories. The expansion of commerce brought with it a divergence of individual trading interests. Nearly all these interests looked to a strong central authority to protect them against the claims of their rivals. The waverings of state policy during the long period in which mercantilism held sway cannnot be understood without realizing the extent to which the state was a creature of warring commercial interests, whose only common aim was to have a strong state, provided that they could manipulate it to their exclusive advantage. For this reason most pieces of mercantilist policy that were put forward identified the merchant's profit with the national good, i.e. the strengthening of the power of the realm.[1]

Many mercantilists sincerely believed in such an identity; and it was true that for a time state regulation was an essential condition for the widening of markets beyond their medieval limits. But doubt about the universal beneficence of intervention was by no means unknown. As early as 1550 this had been forcibly expressed by Sir John Masone,[2] and during the next hundred and fifty years these doubts were to grow until they became a storm of protest. Nor were the mercantilists unaware of the divergence between the interest of the community and that of the individual, and in the free-trade attitude of the later mercantilists this awareness finds expression.

The relation then between economic organization and political

---

1 Some examples are quoted by H. M. Robertson, *Aspects of the Rise of Economic Individualism* (1933), pp. 66–8.

2 R. H. T. Rawney and E. Power, *Tudor Economic Documents* (1935), vol. ii, p. 188.

institutions and between economic and political ideas and policies must be viewed as one of interaction. When viewed over a long period of time this relation often reveals an antithetical character. It is generally conceded that mercantile capitalism preceded and prepared the ground for modern industrial capitalism. The latter, as we shall find, saw in the power of the state and in state intervention in economic matters a serious hindrance to its own development. Thus it set itself up in opposition to the political structure which its own forebear had found it necessary to create. The mercantilists demanded a state strong enough to protect the trading interest and to break down the many medieval barriers to commercial expansion. Yet they were equally clear that the principle of regulation and restriction itself – now applied on a much larger scale through monopolies and protection – was an essential basis of that state. For commercial capital required wider and consolidated markets which were yet sufficiently protected to allow of secure exploitation. We know now that monopoly, protection, and state regulation in general did not remain indispensable qualities of capitalism once it reached its full flower. And it is symptomatic of the development of modern industry that the outcry against monopoly begins fairly soon in the field of domestic trade, while in foreign trade mercantilism survives much longer. The spectacle of capitalism, in its liberal age, attacking and destroying that which had given it birth contains a paradox only if one takes a narrow view of the development of economic doctrine.

The contrast between commercial and industrial capital has its earlier counterpart in the development of commercial capitalism itself. The struggle between bullionists and mercantilists is its theoretical expression. Adam Smith began his celebrated critique of mercantilism  by an attack on the popular notion 'that wealth consists in money, or in gold and silver'.[1] But this popular notion is explained by the fact that treasure, i.e. money, is the earliest form of wealth once private exchange and a medium of exchange have become fundamental social institutions. The appearance of such notions and of the practices which are designed to give them effect is an indication of the stage of economic development. The formation of treasure implies a great advance in the process of private exchange and circulation. It is essentially different from the accumulation of wealth in its material

[1] *Wealth of Nations*, Book IV, Ch. i.

form; and it becomes possible only when the production and circulation of wealth have become separate processes connected by money and mediated by a special class of merchants. At this stage the concept of wealth becomes separated from the goods which possess use-value, to reappear in the shape of the monetary store of exchange-value. The accumulation of the precious metals of which money consisted was common in the ancient world. In Greece and Rome it was a continual aim of policy to form a metallic hoard which would serve in case of need. And throughout the Middle Ages the pursuit of wealth and power by Church, kings and feudal lords was bound up with the accumulation of treasure.

Commercial capitalism gave a fresh impetus to this view. In the period in which commerce was the dominating force of economic development the circulation of goods was the essence of economic activity. Its end, the accumulation of money, corresponded to traditional ideas of wealth and of the aim of national policy. The search for gold in distant lands is the specific form which commercial expansion first takes. 'Gold', said Columbus, 'is a wonderful thing! whoever possesses it is master of everything he desires. With gold, one can even get souls into paradise.'[1] Luther, who did not share this last sentiment, implied a similar regard for gold in his great attack on trade. He said that the Germans were making all the world rich and beggaring themselves by sending their gold and silver to foreign countries; Frankfurt, with its fairs, was the hole through which Germany was losing her treasure.[2] Hales deplored the loss of treasure occasioned by debasement and the importation of useless trifles. Serra, the great Italian mercantilist, took it for granted that every one understood 'how important it is, both for peoples and for princes, that a kingdom should abound in gold and silver'.[3] Malynes and Misselden, although engaged in a violent controversy on foreign trade policy, could yet agree on the importance of treasure. Malynes said, 'For if Money be wanting, Traffic doth decrease, although commodities be abundant and good cheap'.[4] Misselden, although, as we shall see, he was more advanced in his views on trade, was still anxious to restrict commerce 'within'

---

1 In a letter from Jamaica of 1503, quoted by Marx in *Zur Kritik der politischen Ökonomie* (1930), p. 162.
2 'Von Kaufshandlung und Wucher' (1524) in D. Martin Luther's *Werke* (1899), vol. xv, p. 294.
3 A. E. Monroe, *Early Economic Thought*, p. 145.
4 E. F. Heckscher, *Mercantilism*, vol. ii, p. 217.

Christendom' in order to preserve treasure.[1] And Mun consistently takes it for granted that the aim of policy is to increase the treasure of the realm.

Thus a high regard for money was common to all mercantilists. They looked upon the economic process from the point of view of the primitive stage which capitalism had reached – its commercial phase – and were thus led to identify money and capital. Professor Heckscher has given an interesting account of the 'fear of goods', the almost fanatically exclusive concern with selling which characterized mercantilist thought.[2] In sharp contrast with the aim of securing an abundance of goods, which had characterized earlier state policy, the mercantilists thought, in the words of their greatest German representative, Johann Joachim Becher, 'that it is always better to sell goods to others than to buy goods from others, for the former brings a certain advantage and the latter inevitable damage'.[3] This fear of stocks of unsold goods runs through all their writings, even though it assumes different forms. It underlay Malynes's abhorrence of luxury imports, Misselden's desire for treasure, as well as the arguments on the balance of trade of Mun and of such advanced mercantilists as D'Avenant, Barbon, and Child. Even Petty, the founder of classical political economy, is uncertain about the relation between a country's foreign trade and its wealth.

It was particularly in the sphere of foreign trade that this 'fear of goods' showed itself, and resulted in the mercantilist search for an export surplus. Its essence was a desire to create a surplus of wealth. The only surplus which the mercantilists knew arose if a profit was made in selling. This, it was obvious, could only result in a relative surplus: what one gains, the other loses, as the author of a seventeenth century pamphlet pointed out.[4] Even more clearly, D'Avenant, writing in 1697, argued that in domestic trade the nation in general did not grow richer, only a change in the relative amounts of wealth of individuals took place; but foreign trade made a net addition to a country's wealth.

1 E. Misselden, *Free Trade, or the Meanes to make Trade Flourish* (1662), p. 19.
2 The many examples which he quotes from mercantilist theorists show great similarity to the analysis which is scattered in several of the writings of Marx. Cf., particularly, *Das Kapital* (1922), vol. iii, part i, pp.307 *sqq.*; *Zur Kritik der politischen Ökonomie*, pp. 118–33, 162–4.
3 Quoted by E. F. Heckscher, *Mercantilism*, vol. i, p. 116.
4 *The East India Trade a Most Profitable Trade to the Kingdom* (1677).

This primitive idea of the origin of profits – to be supplanted later by the classical labour theory of value – was widespread in a commercial age in which production was still carried out on a pre-capitalist basis. It serves to explain still further the peculiar views on money and treasure which the mercantilists held. It amounted to an identification of (or, better, a confusion between) money and capital. Examples have already been given of the frequency with which mercantilists spoke of money as wealth. It is not necessary to believe that they considered wealth, as did earlier economists, in the concrete material sense and that they were thus guilty, as Oncken said, of a 'Midas mania'.[1] The term wealth was clearly used in the sense of capital; and the theory of money of the mercantilists was a part of their one-sided view of economic activity.

Such an identification of money and capital has by no means entirely disappeared to-day. The mercantilist era could find striking confirmation of the productive uses of money which had dealt the death-blow to the feudal economy and to the canonical prohibitions of usury. It knew capital only in its primitive monetary form and the confusion which was later so much derided was perfectly compatible with its own economic experience. Nevertheless the mercantilists were led into many notions which are now seen to be erroneous. They ascribed, for example, a definitely active force to money. Trade, they said, depended on plenty of money: where money was scarce, trade was sluggish; where it was abundant, trade boomed. Ironically, however, their high regard for money led them to reject the defences of usury which had been put forward by the precursors of commercialism. They returned to the views of the Canonists and others, who had unconsciously defended the feudal economy against the attack of money-capital. The mercantilists believed that money was productive but, because they were anxious to obtain money-capital, their interests clashed with those of the providers of it. In their fight against what they considered excessive interest mercantilists were not above using the arguments of those who would have condemned no less strongly the merchant's profit.

A striking example is that of Gerald Malynes, who was both an official and a successful merchant. As such he could not condemn the taking of interest entirely, but he drew a distinction between interest and usury. He based himself chiefly on Wilson's *Discourse*, and, in his

---

1 A. Oncken, *Geschichte der Nationökonomie*, part i; *Die Zeit vor Adam Smith* (1902), p. 154.

*Saint George for England Allegorically Described* (1601) and later in his *Consuetudo vel Lex Mercatoria*, first published in 1622, he attacked most bitterly the evils of extortionate usury. Control of interest rates and the establishment of *monts de piété* to prevent the exploitation of the poor were advocated by him as means of avoiding the excrescences of a practice which, as a business man, he knew could not be abolished. Sir Thomas Culpepper, in a *Tract against Usurie*, published in 1621, argued in favour of a decreed maximum rate without entering into the question of the legitimacy or otherwise of interest. Such a maximum, he claimed, would enable English merchants, who were then paying 10 per cent, to compete more successfully with their Dutch rivals, who paid only 6 per cent. To this argument, which is linked with mercantilist ideas on the mechanism of international payments, we shall return presently.

Of the many examples which could be quoted of the mercantilists' attitude to interest, none is more important than that of Sir Josiah Child. In his *New Discourse of Trade* (1669), he replies to the defence of interest put forward by Thomas Manley in his *Interest of Money Mistaken*. He claims to be the champion of industry while Manley, he said, was defending idleness. A low rate of interest was the cause and not, as Manley had argued, the effect of wealth. If commerce was the means of enriching a country and if lowering the rate of interest encouraged trade, could it be denied that a low rate was a powerful cause of wealth?[1] However, since 'the egg was the cause of the hen, and the hen the cause of the egg',[2] he agreed that an increase in wealth brought about by a low rate of interest could in its turn cause a still further reduction of the rate. Like Culpepper, Child was concerned to see the competitive power of English merchants strengthened. He greatly admired the Dutch, thus showing that he saw Holland for what she was: the country of commercial capitalism *per excellence*. There, the power of money-capital had long since been subordinated to the needs of the primitive industrial capitalists – the merchant manufacturers, a victory which English commerce had yet to achieve. The mercantilist attack on high interest rates was natural in an age of great scarcity of liquid funds, undeveloped banking facilities, and growing antagonism between the merchant manufacturers and the goldsmiths and big merchant financiers.

1 Josiah Child, *A New Discourse of Trade* (1694), *passim*.
2 ibid., p. 63.

## Bullionism and Mercantilism

We have so far confined our discussion to those characteristics which were common to all representatives of mercantilist thought; the attitude to selling, the 'fear of goods', the desire to accumulate treasure, and the opposition to usury. These are the essential qualities of the economic thought of the time. Until recently, however, it was more common to lay stress on the differences of opinion of individual mercantilists. Controversies between adherents of different policies were very frequent in the seventeenth century; and the progress of ideas from Malynes to Mun, for example, is certainly an indication of the change in economic conditions and of an appreciation of its significance. In this connection, a distinction is usually made between the bullionists and the mercantilists proper, but it is possible that these names encourage a misunderstanding of the real issue between these two schools. It is sometimes assumed that the desire for treasure was part of the crude doctrine of the earlier mercantilists; while the later mercantilists had discarded the gross error of identifying wealth and treasure, and had adopted instead the more sophisticated mistake of the export surplus. It should be clear now that the desire for treasure was common to all mercantilists for reasons which were connected with the merchant's function in the economic process of the time. What does, however, distinguish those mercantilists who have been called bullionists from the rest is a difference of opinion on the best means of achieving the universally desired end: the enrichment of the country through an increase of its treasure.

The earlier view on this point goes back a long time and was not at first connected specifically with the mercantile interest. It aimed at preserving the stocks of precious metals of a country by a strict regulation of their movements across national boundaries, i.e. by regulation of international monetary exchange. Granted the search for precious metals as the most highly prized representatives of wealth, it becomes an obvious necessity of policy to prevent their export and to encourage their import. Prohibitions of the export of gold and silver date back to medieval times and persisted until the time of mercantilist controversy. By the fourteenth century foreign trade had sufficiently progressed to bring to the notice of rulers the connection between it and the amount of precious metals in the country. An Act of 1339 attempted to compel wool merchants to bring in a certain amount of plate for each sack of wool exported. Richard II, in a reply to a

56

complaint about the shortage of money, included in the Navigation Act of 1381 a prohibition of the export of gold and silver. An inquiry was instituted at which the wardens of the Mint had to give evidence. The most important part of it was the statement made by Richard Aylesbury, an officer of the Mint. He anticipated the later mercantilist argument of the balance of trade with the following advice for preserving the country's stock of bullion: 'Let not more strange merchandise come within the realm than to the value of the denizen merchandise which passes out of the realm.'[1]

But this view did not reflect prevailing opinion or practice. The method generally in use to preserve treasure was still the medieval one of direct control. Prohibitions of the export of bullion and of the import of luxuries were supplemented by the establishment of the office of Royal Exchanger, to whom all exchange transactions were confined. These restrictions and regulations were not, however, capable of holding up for long the development of international trade. The activities of merchants found ways of nullifying the attempts to prevent fluctuations of prices and exchange rates and movements of gold and silver. The growth of trade destroyed the basis on which the rate books used by customs officers were compiled. The bill of exchange became the chief instrument for settling payments and there grew up a new class of financiers specializing in international transactions. These developments made it impossible to enforce measures of state regulation. The disappearance of the staple system made supervision of trade more difficult; and the increasing influence of the privileged companies is seen in the relaxation of bullion export prohibitions to enable them to carry on their trade. For example, the charter of the East India Company of 1600 allowed the export of a specified quantity of bullion on each voyage to the Spice Islands.[2]

Yet the commercial expansion of the sixteenth century, with its problems of national trade rivalries and large-scale movements of the precious metals, was bound to raise once again the question of regulation. Bullionists is the name given to those who proposed the revival of the old export prohibitions, the re-establishment of the office of Royal Exchanger and an increased regulation of foreign exchange dealings.

1 A. E. Bland, P. A. Brown and R. H. Tawney, *English Economic History: Select Documents* (1933), p. 222.
2 W. R. Scott, *The Constitution and Finance of English, Scottish and Irish Joint Stock Companies to 1720* (1910), vol. ii, p. 93.

The most important representative of this school is Gerald Malynes. We have already seen that Malynes had readopted Wilson's view on usury. This he seems to have done as part of a somewhat medieval outlook on social affairs in general, because he believed in the certainty and harmony which only a well-regulated commonwealth could secure. Writing in the seventeenth century, he put the task of achieving these ends into the hands of the state. His interventionism was mainly concerned with economic matters, of which, in addition to usury, he regarded foreign trade and foreign exchange dealings as the most important. In spite of his concern about usury he felt that it was only a symptom of a more deep-seated evil, i.e. the exchange transactions of private financiers, which were often usurious and which, by reducing the volume of bullion in the country, raised interest rates.[1] Indeed, to Malynes foreign exchange was the main economic problem. He approached it with a medieval mind and based his diagnosis and his treatment upon an ethical foundation. Yet by profiting from the monetary controversies of the previous century which had produced Gresham's Law, he was able to enunciate a clear, though limited, analysis of the proximate causes of gold movements and thus to advance considerably the theory of international trade.

Malynes began by admitting the need for domestic and international exchange. Like Hales, he claimed that since trade was inspired by the merchant's self-interest, governments must regulate it in order to insure the general welfare. Money, he argued, was devised as a means of exchange and as a common measure. The bill of exchange was designed as such a common measure in international transactions, but it had been corrupted through the tricks of self-seeking financiers. The growth of illegitimate exchanges had destroyed the true parity of the foreign exchanges. This parity was what is now called the 'mint par of exchange', i.e. the ratio of the values of two currencies which corresponded to their bullion content. Exchanges that took place at this ratio were the only ones to correspond to the *par pro pari* which was the moral foundation of exchange. If the ratio varied, exchange involved an injustice to one of the parties. Moreover, if the exchange rates were stable, no bullion movements would take place. If the exchange rate went in favour of the country, bullion would not flow out; but if it fell below the par, bullion would be drained away.

---

1 G. Malynes, *Consuetudo* (1636), ch. ix, pp. 272 *sqq.*

So far Malynes had given an account of the determination of the equilibrium rate of exchange which was fairly common at the time. He had gone farther by showing the connection between deviations from the equilibrium rate and international bullion movements which was much later to be embodied in the theory of the specie points. His subsequent analysis, however, is less enlightened. He ascribes the possibility of deviations from the *par pro pari* to the existence of two illegitimate forms of exchange transactions. It is not quite clear what exactly his *cambio sicco* and *cambio fictitio*[1] are meant to be. They appear from his examples to be not unlike what would to-day be called accommodation bills (or finance bills, as Tawney has called them) and acceptances. In the case of the former, a merchant borrows money from a financier by being allowed to draw a bill upon the financier's foreign correspondent. Here, although there has been no trade transaction, foreign exchange has come into existence. In addition, extortionate rates of interest can be concealed. In the second case, the credit of a banker and his foreign agent is used to facilitate the trade of merchants of poor standing, who again would have to pay very high interest rates. Malynes's attack upon an operation which is a commonplace of finance today seems to show his lack of understanding of the real nature of foreign trade. It must be understood in the light of the mercantilists' general fight against finance; and it is also an illustration of Malynes's desire to confine trade to the privileged few with whom the small merchant was competing with growing success.

Malynes did not penetrate to the ultimate causes of the variations in foreign exchanges, although he seems to have admitted that they were affected in part by the movements of goods. As his curious theory of the reasons which compel English merchants to sell cheaply abroad shows, his ideas on the connection between exchange rates, bullion movement, prices, and merchandise trade are mistaken.[2] Malynes's remedy is correspondingly retrograde. Exchange transactions should be confined to the Royal Exchanger or some other person authorized by the king. All exchange transactions above or below the *par pro pari* (which was to be publicly declared) were to be forbidden. Exchange under these conditions would be legitimate, the

---

1 G. Malynes, *Consuetudo*, ch. ix, p. 253. See also Tawney's analysis in his introduction to Wilson: *A Discourse upon Usury*.
2 G. Malynes, *Consuetudo*. p. 48.

tricks of the financiers would be defeated, the exchanges would be stable, and the treasure of the realm would be preserved.

Other mercantilists, such as Misselden and Mun, attacked these views and developed their own more advanced analysis. Already Hales had said, 'For we must alwaies take hede that we bie no more of strangers than we sell them; for so we sholde empoverishe our selves and enriche them'.[1] And William Cecil's statement that 'Nothing robbeth the realm of England more than when more merchandise is carried in than is coming forth'[2] was an echo of Aylesbury's evidence of 1381. Bacon, in 1616, when governmental practice was still in the direction of monetary measures, hoped that care would be 'taken that the exportation exceed in value the importation; for then the balance of trade must of necessity be returned in coin or in bullion'.[3] Thus in attacking Malynes's undue fear of financiers, the later mercantilists were able to draw on already existing views, even though these at one time had been used to hamper the development of foreign trade. Misselden and Mun carried the arguments of the bullionists farther so as to explain the ultimate causes of specie movements. Although their polemic, particularly in the form which it took in Misselden's writings, makes them violently opposed to Malynes's way of thinking, they did not deny that there existed a relation between the volume of bullion and the foreign exchange rates. They only made both bullion movements and fluctuations in foreign exchange rates depend upon the balance of merchandise trade.

Typical of this further development are three mercantilist writers: Edward Misselden, Antonio Serra, and Thomas Mun. The first and third were leading English merchants of the period, one a prominent member of the Merchant Adventurers, the other of the East India Company. Of Serra, a native of Cosenza, very little is known.

Misselden (fl.1608–54) contributed two important tracts to the war of pamphlets: *Free Trade, or The Means To Make Trade Flourish, etc.* published in 1622, and *The Circle of Commerce*, published in the following year and noted particularly for the fact that it was the first publication to use the term 'balance of trade'.[4] (Bacon's earlier use of the term did not appear in print until much later.) As with most

1 J. Hales, *A Discourse of the Common Weal of this Realm of England* (ed. Lamond, 1929), p. 63.
2 R. H. Tawney and E. Power, *Tudor Economic Documents*, vol. ii, p. 451.
3 Quoted in Heaton, H., *Economic History of Europe* (1936), p. 368.
4 J. Viner, *Studies in the Theory of International Trade* (1937), pp. 8 *sqq.*

mercantilists, Misselden's immediate motive for theorizing was to provide a background for policies designed to foster the interests he represented. In his first book, self-interest is particularly obvious. He was, as we have seen, anxious to confine trade within Christendom, since the oriental trade drained the country of specie which did not return. This attack on the East India Company did not even remain implied, because Misselden proceeded to blame his trade rival for a good deal of the trade depression.[1] As we should expect from a prominent member of the Merchant Adventurers, he was not opposed to privileged trading companies in general; on the contrary, he thought nothing could be more harmful to the general well-being than unregulated trade. He was equally opposed to monopoly in trade, and he favoured what might now be called oligopoly. In this respect, he shared a view which was common among mercantilists.[2]

Misselden's attack on the East India Company was not carried into his second book; he had become associated with the company in business. It may also be claimed that when he came to write *The Circle of Commerce* he had appreciated better the general interests which he had at heart and ceased to represent a narrow self-interest. Although in *Free Trade* he had still cast his net wide to find explanations for the trade depression, he concentrated in his second tract on the balance of trade. Foreign exchange rates, he claimed, were settled in the same way as the prices of any other goods. There was a price which was determined by the 'goodness' of each commodity. But the price ruling at any time might be greater or less, varying with buyers' and sellers' judgments. Similarly, there were prices of the exchange which were determined by the 'goodness' of the money; this was the mint par. But the rates might fluctuate around this equilibrium point 'according to the occasions of both parties',[3] i.e. according to supply and demand. The exchanges were not the cause of specie movements, as Malynes had maintained, because they were themselves determined by the volume of foreign trade.

Misselden rejected Malynes's remedy. He argued that in order to make sure that trade was beneficial it was necessary to know first the relation of imports and exports. Returns should be made and the nation's trade 'cast into the "Ballance of Trade" which would show us

---

1 E. Misselden, *Free Trade, or The Meanes to Make Trade Flourish*, pp. 13–14.
2 E. F. Heckscher, *Mercantilism*, vol. i, pp. 270–6.
3 E. Misselden, *The Circle of Commerce* (1623), p. 98.

the difference of waight in the *Commerce* of one Kingdome with another'.[1] Once that had been done, the policy of the state should be to secure a favourable, and prevent an unfavourable, balance; for with a surplus of exports the country would receive treasure and grow rich. Exports should be encouraged and the poor be employed in making goods for export. At the same time imports should be discouraged, particularly those of luxury goods, and the fisheries should be developed so as to make England less dependent on foreign supplies of food.

Somewhat similar to Misselden's, and arising also from polemical needs, were the views expressed by Antonio Serra in his *Breve Trattato*.[2] He set out the means by which a country that had no gold and silver mines of its own could obtain a plentiful supply of the precious metals. The first set of means were those peculiar to an individual country, such as a surplus of home products, which could be exported in exchange for bullion, and geographical situation, which might give a country an advantage in the carrying trade. Of the means common to all countries he distinguishes four: 'quantity of industry, quality of the population, extensive trading operations, and regulations of the sovereign'.[3] The first is a significant anticipation of an emphasis on manufacture which was later to become general. Serra said that industry was superior to agriculture because it was independent of the weather; it could be multiplied; and it had a more certain market price because it was not perishable; and finally, the profit from manufacture was generally greater than that from produce. The second, the quality of the population, depended on diligence, ingenuity, and a spirit of enterprise. The third was generally the result of the presence of the particular factor of favourable situation. It made a community embark upon commerce which resulted in much money, because 'commerce cannot be carried on without it'.[4] The policy of the sovereign also could greatly help or hinder the attainment of wealth.

Having given his general ideas on economic matters, Serra proceeds to examine the relation between exchange rates and the amount of bullion in the country. Although his discussion is somewhat involved, he succeeds in demonstrating that the theory that high exchange rates will prevent bullion from coming into the country and will encourage

1 ibid., pp. 116–7.
2 A. E. Monroe, *Early Economic Thought*, pp. 145–67.
3 ibid., p. 146.
4 ibid., p. 150.

its outflow did not give a complete explanation. It is the 'foreign goods needed by the kingdom ... that should be blamed for the scarcity of money, not the high rate of exchange'.[1] Serra rejects the prohibition of the export of money as useless. No one, he argues, exports money without a purpose. If money goes abroad to pay for imports which are re-exported, it will yield a profit and so ultimately increase the stock of bullion.

## Thomas Mun

A similar argument, more lucidly developed, was used some years later by Thomas Mun (1571–1641). A successful London mercer with trade experience in Italy and the Levant, he became, in 1615, closely associated with the East India Company of which he was a director until his death. The company was attacked on account of its privilege of exporting £30,000 of bullion on each voyage (provided that they reimported that amount within six months); to defend his company Mun wrote *A Discourse of Trade from England into the East Indies* (1621).[2] The argument of this book is very primitive compared with the later work which made Mun famous. His special pleading was undisguised. He was only concerned with clearing the East India Company of the charge that it was draining the country of specie; and in the process he made the claim that the East India Company's trade brought in more treasure than all the other trades put together. He pointed out that the company did not export as much specie as it was permitted to do, that it had cheapened the Indian trade by cutting out the Turkish middle-men, and that it was bringing in raw materials for English manufactures. But his main argument on behalf of the company was that its re-exports enabled it to bring back as much specie as it had exported and more. There is in this book still a trace of the fight against the

1 ibid., p. 158.
2 Cf. reprint (Facsimile Text Society, New York, 1930). In a chapter which he contributed to Engel's *Anti-Dühring* Marx attacks Dühring for having made Serra the leader of mercantilist thought. He rightly reserves this place for Mun, whose analysis was not only much cleverer than Serra's but whose second book obtained an immediate and universal authority. Marx is, however, wrong in saying that Mun's *Discourse* appeared in 1609, four years before Serra's *Breve Trattato*. The *Discourse* was published in 1621 and could not have been written before 1615, the year in which Mun joined the East India Company.

financiers which Malynes had carried on, because Mun puts some blame for the loss of specie on the tricks of exchangers.

*England's Treasure by Forraign Trade* was written in 1630 and pub-lished posthumously by Mun's son in 1664.[1] In this work, the ideas of commercial capitalism find their fullest expression. Here the merchant is assigned a very high place in the community. Precepts are given for the perfection of the merchant; and foreign trade is set up as the means for making a country wealthy. Perhaps it was this which led Adam Smith to misquote the title of Mun's book, *England's Treasure in Foreign Trade*. Mun takes up Misselden's concept of the balance of trade, but he adds to it another one which is even more important and which shows his insight into the quality of commercial capitalism. This is the concept of 'stock'. He does not speak any longer of wealth alone, nor does he confuse money and capital. He clearly distinguishes a portion of wealth, which generally takes the form of money, which must be employed as 'stock', i.e. in such a way as to yield a surplus. The way which was typical of the age and the man was that of foreign trade. In a celebrated analogy which Adam Smith singled out for quotation Mun likens foreign trade to a more ancient manner of creating a surplus. 'For if we only behold the actions of the husbandman in the seed-time when he casteth away much good corn into the ground, we will rather accompt him a mad man than a husbandman: but when we consider his labours in the harvest which is the end of his endeavours, we find the worth and plentiful encrease of his actions.'[2] We see here that the special pleading of the East India Company director has become refined and general: it is now an explanation of the place of commerce in the economy.

Stock, Mun argues, is wisely employed in foreign trade when it secures a favourable balance; this is the only means of bringing treasure into England, a country that has no mines of its own. Imports and home consumption of imported goods should be kept down, exports and re-exports should be encouraged. In regard to selling abroad, Mun appreciates the doctrine of 'what the traffic will bear'. For goods in which England has something like a monopoly a high price may be charged; while for others prices should be low enough to compete with rivals. Yet prices should never be put so high as to

1 Cf. reprint (Economic History Society, 1928). An excellent analysis of this work is to be found in E. A. J. Johnson's *Predecessors of Adam Smith* (1937), pp. 77–89.
2 T. Mun, *England's Treasure by Forraign Trade*, p. 19.

discourage sales. Nor is it wise to sell cheaply in order to drive out competitors and then to charge excessive prices. Price-policy should be so devised as to keep out competitors as long as possible. Mun is also well aware of the existence of invisible trade. He urges that English trade should be carried in English ships only, for this will secure 'the Merchants gains, the charges of ensurance, and fraight to carry them beyond the seas'.[1]

*England's Treasure* is a clear synthesis and development of the most advanced mercantilist theories, even though many ideas in it still remain obscure. In his theory of money, for example, Mun did not quite succeed in rising above his fellow mercantilists. Although they had something of a quantity theory of money (inherited from Oresme and Bodin and reappearing in Hales and Malynes), none of the mercantilists ever fully succeeded in developing it further into a theory of international prices. Their great fear of a lack of bullion led them at best to a one-sided appreciation of the relation of the price-levels of different countries to their trade. They knew that a small amount of money in England would make English prices low; so they went on to argue that, in its trade with a country wealthy in money, England might be forced to sell cheap and buy dear,[2] and so lose its mercantile profit and presumably still further diminish its stock of specie. This was the impasse into which the mercantilists were led; it was left to classical economists to connect prices, specie stocks, exchange rates, and the balance of trade in a comprehensive theory of international trade.

Mun seems to have been dimly aware that the high prices which a large amount of money would create might have an adverse effect on the balance of trade. Evidently still anxious to defend the East India trade, he protested that to keep treasure in the country instead of using it in foreign trade was harmful. 'For all men do consent that plenty of mony in a Kingdom doth make the natife commodities dearer, which as it is to the profit of some private men in their revenues, so is it directly against the benefit of the Publique in the quantity of the trade; for as plenty of mony makes wares dearer, so dear wares decline their use and consumption. ... And although this is a very hard lesson for some great landed men to learn, yet I am sure it is a true lesson for all the land to observe, lest when wee have

1 ibid., p. 9
2 E. F. Heckscher, *Mercantilism*, vol. ii, pp. 238–43.

gained some store of money by trade wee lose it again by not trading with our money.'[1] But further than this he did not go; anxious to conciliate the landed interest, he immediately pointed out how trade could bring it advantage too. 'For when the Merchant hath a good dispatch beyond the Seas for his Cloth and other wares, he doth presently return to buy up the greater quantity which raiseth the price of our Woolls and other commodities, and consequently doth improve the Landlords Rents as the Leases expire daily: And also by this means money being gained, and brought more abundantly into the Kingdom, it doth enable many men to buy Lands which will make them the dearer.'[2] In spite of this zigzagging, which finally ends in a blind alley. Mun shows here a much greater insight than other thinkers of the time.

Mun's analysis of the distribution of the world's bullion supply among the different countries is very striking. In chapter vi of the book he discusses the reasons for Spain's loss of treasure and concluded that, apart from war, bullion was leaving Spain because she was importing so much from abroad. It was 'the disability of the *Spaniards* by their native commodities to provide forraign wares for their necessities' that forced them 'to supply the want with mony'.[3] This cause was also operating elsewhere. 'All Nations (who have no Mines of their own) are enriched with Gold and Silver by one and the same means, which is already shewed to be the ballance of their forraign Trade.' Thus, whether countries have mines of their own or not, the balance of their trade determines both 'the manner of getting, and the proportion that is yearly gotten'[4] of the world's stock of specie.

Another sign of Mun's advanced position in contemporary thought is the fact that throughout his book there is evident a much smaller regard for an accumulation of treasure for its own sake than can be found in other mercantilist writings. Mun pays the traditional lip-service to the need for treasure as a reserve for emergencies and as the 'sinews of war', yet he insists all the time on the outstanding importance of trade for which money is only a means. Even in connection with the prince's war chest, he does not fail to point out that this is valuable only 'because it doth provide, unite and move the power of men, victuals, and munition where and when the cause doth require;

1 T. Mun, *England's Treasure by Forraign Trade*, p. 17.
2 ibid., p. 21.
3 ibid., p. 23.
4 ibid., p. 24.

but if these things be wanting in due time, what shall we then do with our mony?"[1]

On other topics, Mun's contributions to economic thought are not considerable. He joins earlier writers in attacking debasement and repeats (in less precise form) Hales's analysis of the redistribution of wealth caused by debasement. He condemns the 'toleration for Forraign Coins to pass currant here at higher rates than their value with our own Standard' as a method for increasing treasure. It would provoke retaliation from foreign countries; it would cause an unjust distribution of wealth; and if the discrepancy is large, it would result in a drain of treasure. Retaliation is also a danger that leads Mun to object to the statute requiring foreigners to spend their proceeds from exports to England on the purchase of English goods. A restriction of this kind imposed upon English merchants, the director of the East India Company points, out, would be disastrous. Like other advanced mercantilists, it is free trade within the limits of regulated companies that Mun really desires.

The few words on the revenue and expenditure of the sovereign which Mun includes in his book are noteworthy only for the views on taxation and on the limits to the accumulation by the prince. The latter, Mun says, is set by the amount of treasure which the favourable balance of trade has brought into the country. A greater accumulation would deprive trade of its capital. 'For if he [the prince] should mass up more money than is gained by the over-ballance of his forraign trade, he shall not *Fleece* but *Flea* his Subjects, and so with their ruin overthrow himself for want of future sheerings. ... All the mony in such a state would suddenly be drawn into the Princes treasure, whereby the life of lands and arts must fail.'[2] On the former point, although Mun regards all taxes as 'a rabble of oppressions', he thinks that they are necessary. He foreshadows a later theory of wages by saying that indirect taxes are not 'so hurtfull to the happinesse of the people as they are commonly esteemed: for as the food and rayment of the poor is made dear by Excise, so doth the price of their labour rise in proportion'.[3]

The only other important point raised by Mun is the difference between 'general' and 'particular' balances of trade. Mun uses it in his

1 ibid., p. 70.
2 ibid., p. 68.
3 ibid., pp. 61–2.

polemic against Malynes's foreign exchange theory. Arguing that the determinant of foreign exchange rates is the balance of trade, he shows that the exchange with any particular country depends upon the balance of trade with that country, while the position of the exchanges in general depends upon the total balance of trade.[1] More significant, however, than Mun's argument against Malynes is the fact that he takes up an advanced position in a controversy which was very important at the time. The aim of earlier systems for regulating foreign trade was to achieve favourable particular balances. England's imports from each country had to balance her exports to it. And attempts were even made to balance the trade of each English merchant. This idea of a 'balance of bargains', as Richard Jones called it,[2] survived into the seventeenth century. As a result of the mercantilist theory increasing attention was given to trade statistics, but policy still remained concerned with particular balances.

The Board of Trade was required by Parliament to consider carefully the balance of trade with each particular country and to advise on means for correcting unfavourable and securing favourable balances. The whole trade policy, with its complicated system of treaties, restrictions, and drawbacks was devised with this end in view. It led to France and Sweden being regarded as bad customers. The former sold to England a large amount of luxury goods, the latter iron and timber; but neither of them bought much from England. Trade with them had therefore to be discouraged. Spain, on the other hand, had a great supply of bullion, and being devoid of industries had to import English goods. Trade with Portugal was regarded with particular satisfaction: wine was exchanged for cloth. Even as late as 1703 this way of viewing foreign trade found practical expression in the Methuen Treaty, which almost excluded French in favour of Portuguese wine.

Mun and Child, with their experience of the East India trade, tried hard to direct attention to the problems of the general rather than the particular balances. Mun's outline of all the things which had to be taken into account in order to draw up the balance of trade, 'the true rule of our treasure',[3] shows that he took a very advanced view of the make-up of international accounts. Child too asserted that the true profit or loss which a nation derived from any particular trade could

1 ibid., pp. 48–9.
2 R. Jones, 'Primitive Political Economy in England' in *Edinburgh Review*, January–April 1847, p. 428.
3 T. Mun, *England's Treasure by Forraign Trade*, p. 83.

not be ascertained from a consideration of that trade alone.[1] But although the exponents of the balance of trade argument had won against the bullionists (the prohibition of the export of specie was abolished in England in 1663), they did not succeed in their other campaign. The balance of trade theory was used for a long time to support rigid trade restrictions, and it was an important part of the theory on which the colonial system was based.

Gradually, however, the basis of trade regulation began to change. Instead of arising from a desire to secure a favourable balance which would bring treasure into the country, the encouragement of exports and the restriction of imports acquired a protectionist character. The creation of work and employment and the nursing of industries, both as ends in themselves and as means of strengthening the country, became the aims of state policy. The transition to this late mercantilist phase was not sudden. Professor Heckscher quotes instances of the work-creation argument for protection in the fifteenth century in Florence and in some English writings of about 1530.[2] Hales, as we have seen, objected to the export of English raw materials since it deprived English workmen of employment. Serra had stressed the advantages of flourishing home manufactures. And in English mercantilist writings the employment argument becomes more frequent at the end of the seventeenth century.

The importance of treasure (already somewhat diminished by Mun) is still further reduced; and though commerce may still be praised extravagantly, the emphasis is slowly shifted to home industry as the real source of wealth. An interesting illustration of this tendency is to be found in the writings of D'Avenant, who, though a mercantilist, was not a merchant himself, and whose writings always contained a mixture of old and new arguments. Having praised the calling of the merchant who enriched the country, he is yet constrained to say, in his *Discourses on the Publick Revenues* (1698), that though gold and silver are the measure of trade, the source and origin of it are everywhere the natural and artificial produce of countries; 'that is to say, what their land, or what their labour and industry produces'.[3]

Even earlier, Child had developed a theory of colonial economy

---

1 J. Child, *A New Discourse of Trade*, p. 153.
2 E. F. Heckscher, *Mercantilism*, vol. ii, pp. 122–3.
3 C. D'Avenant, *The Political and Commercial Works* (1771), vol. i, p. 345.

which was based exclusively on the employment argument.[1] Colonization in general, he admitted, might have harmful effects since it
involved emigration. Like all mercantilists of that period, Child was
very much afraid of a loss of population, a word which seems to have
carried with it the idea of employment. A small labour force in the days
before the large-scale introduction of machinery meant a low output.
And this, at a time when foreign trade was becoming increasingly
dependent on home manufactures, was equivalent to a reduction of
exports. However, the evils of colonization could be mitigated, Child
thought, by compelling the colonies to confine their trade to the
mother country. Once that was done, emigration might, after all, yield
an advantage, because it might create more work at home.

As for the American colonies, Child did not think that they had been
an unmixed evil. It was doubtful whether, even in the absence of the
colonies, those who emigrated there would have stayed in England.
The Puritans would have gone to Holland and Germany. Among the
others, there were many rogues and criminals who, if they had stayed
at home, would have been hanged. What was more important, in the
West Indian plantations one Englishman had ten natives working
under him, thus producing more than he would at home; and the
combined demand of these eleven (of whom only one man was an
emigrant) would keep at least four workmen employed in England.
New England, on the other hand, was not a useful colony because the
emigrants there did not give employment to perhaps even a single
workman at home. Thus the value of colonies depended on their
ability to act as exclusive markets for the manufactures of the mother
country, to supply in exchange raw materials and other produce which
would otherwise have to be bought from foreign countries, and to form
a reservoir of cheap labour.

The use of such arguments as these both in relation to colonial
policy and in support of a system of all-round protection shows, on the
one hand, how far commerce had developed and, on the other hand, in
what theoretical difficulties the later mercantilists were to find themselves. From the point of view of foreign commerce alone the mercantilists were, as we have seen, led increasingly to demand a greater
freedom of trade. The decline of the belief in state intervention, which
will be discussed in the next chapter, was already beginning with some
of the later mercantilist writers. D'Avenant, for example, thought that

1 J. Child, *A New Discourse of Trade*, pp. 212–26.

trade was in its nature free and 'Laws to give it Rules ... are seldom advantageous to the Public'.[1] Yet the growth of industry and the changing character of commerce made them supply arguments which led to an increase rather than a decrease of state regulation.

In the practice of governments at the end of the seventeenth and throughout most of the eighteenth centuries all-round protection and state regulation is in evidence. In that period, the foundations of modern industry were being laid. The methods used were tariffs or embargoes on imports, prohibitions of the export of tools and skilled craftsmen, the encouragement of the import of raw materials or of their production at home, the supervision of the quality of products, and subsidies to those who were developing new industries. There might still be concern with purely commercial problems. Navigation Acts might still claim not only to strengthen the king's navy but also to increase the country's mercantile profit by confining the carrying trade to the country's own ships. But the real meaning of the growth of industrial and commercial regulation on a national scale in the hundred years preceding the *Wealth of Nations* is to be found in the rise of industrial capitalism. Mercantilist theory and policy had done their work. They had abolished medieval restrictions and had helped to produce unified and strong nation-states. These in turn became powerful instruments for fostering trade until early capitalism developed into mature industrial capitalism. In such countries as England and France where this process was first completed state power was at once turned to a new use. It had to help industry to achieve economic supremacy. But earlier mercantilist ideas did not disappear. Down to the present day they all reappear from time to time in various guises, sometimes even to be welcomed as rediscovered ancient truths curiously apposite, it is thought, to modern conditions.

1 Quoted in Heckscher, *Mercantilism*, vol. ii, p. 322.

# 3

# The Founders of Political Economy

### *The Political Philosophers*

In the eighteenth century the development of modern industrial capitalism was greatly accelerated. Its theory, embodied in the works of the classical economists, comes to maturity in the period of forty years that separates Smith's *Wealth of Nations* and Ricardo's *Principles*. But its roots reach back almost two centuries. At least three streams of thought accompany the transition from commercial to industrial capitalism, and, together with that economic development, help to mould classical theory. The first of these is philosophical: the development of political thought from its canonical origin to philosophic radicalism. We have already seen the beginnings of the second; it is the progress of English economic thought from the later mercantilists onwards. The third foundation of political economy is of French origin, the physiocratic system which was developed by a number of thinkers in eighteenth-century France. The first of these contributions has been expounded so frequently and its history is available in so many textbooks that it is not necessary to give more than an outline of it here.

The freeing of thought from the dominance of the Church was conducive to the growth of mercantilism, although it was ultimately to be turned against mercantilist theory and practice. We have seen that economic progress had destroyed the authority of the Church in worldly matters. Economic activity was less and less carried on according to the theological laws of what 'ought to be'. And although economic thinking also tended to become positive, the earlier mercantilists were still anxious to preserve the normative element; in their writings the analysis of what is and the precept of what ought to be are still inextricably bound together. In the field of political thought, however, the emancipation from theology is more radical.[1]

Some thinkers to whom this emancipation is due were also concerned with economic matters. Bodin, for example, whom we have already met as an enlightened economist, was one of those who made 'the relation of man to man, instead of the relations of man with God, the foundation of social enquiry'.[2] But the main impact of the new modes of thought fell on the theory of the state. The foremost influence in this direction was that of Machiavelli. He was able to observe the decay of medieval society in what was perhaps the most favourable environment, that of sixteenth-century Italy. There, the substitution of secular for ecclesiastical authority and the struggle for national unity took the most violent forms. Political leadership became dependent upon an unscrupulous use of all the means of worldly power. Only brute force combined with intrigue and opportunism could give power to a prince and enable him to maintain it. Although it was an experience which every one was sharing, it was the genius of Machiavelli which made the political development of his day the starting point for a new method of approach to social and political questions. In an oft-quoted passage he decried those who had endeavoured to build an ideal republic of their fancy. One had to be aware, he argued, of the great difference between man as he was and as he ought to be; to try to be virtuous in a world inhabited by so many who were without virtue was to court ruin. In his study of the actions of a wise prince, therefore, Machiavelli said that necessity not virtue was to be the guide.[3] Machiavelli was guilty of many errors. He had little idea of the complex forces which fashion history; social development was to him exclusively the work of great men. His protest against the ethical was so violent that it was bound to lead to a reaction. He minimized the power of traditional ideas of right conduct and thought exclusively in terms of the princes of Renaissance Italy. He could not foresee the rise of a new, non-theological, ethical discipline which was to continue to exercise some influence on economic thought. Nevertheless his influence, in spite of initial opposition, was immense. Henceforth social philosophy was based upon a rational and positive foundation.

1 See Christopher Hill, *Puritanism and Revolution* (1958) and *Society and Puritanism in Pre-Revolutionary England* (1964), and C. B. Macpherson, *The Political Theory of Possessive Individualism, Hobbes to Locke* (1962).
2 H. J. Laski, *The Rise of European Liberalism*, p. 19.
3 *The Prince, passim*.

Even greater perhaps was the vision of Bodin. He too was impressed with the problem of authority which the decay of Church power, the religious wars, and the struggle of conflicting civil units had raised. In *Les Six Livres de la République* (1576) he laid the foundation for the theory of the need for a central sovereign authority. This he wanted to be secular. In other words, he pleaded for the modern sovereign state which was to be the source of all law and order. Yet Bodin was conscious of the danger of unrestricted authority.[1] Divine law and natural law, Bodin thought, should prescribe the broad limits of the state's power. His emphasis on the rights of private property, as his belief in the beneficence of free trade which has already been mentioned, shows that he was sensing a possible antithesis between state and society and was groping for a theory which would give 'some place for the consent of subjects to the actions of authority'.[2] He was thus a forerunner of liberalism in a much more direct sense than the natural-law philosophers of the seventeenth century.

In spite of important differences, the England of the sixteenth century witnessed a spiritual revolution similar to that of Italy and France epitomized in Machiavelli and Bodin. The forces which had made commerce predominant were freeing men's minds from the fetters of accepted belief and were opening a new era of speculation and experiment. In almost every branch of science the new ways of life were presenting new problems. And whether they were inspired directly by the needs of expanding commerce or only indirectly through the general zest of the new empirical rationalism, scientists began to provide the answers. In astronomy, mathematics, physics, and optics, and in the biological sciences and medicine, advance was amazing. Its greatest moment, in spite of all the theological and even mystical interests of its author,[3] was Newton's *Principia*.[4] Lessing has well said of it:

---

1 H. J. Laski, *The Rise of European Liberalism*, pp. 46–8.
2 ibid.
3 See Frank E. Manuel, *A Portrait of Isaac Newton* (1968).
4 Professor Hessen in his article 'Economic and Social Roots of Newton's *Principia*' in *Science at the Cross Roads* (ed. Bukharin, 1931), has made a very interesting analysis of the relation of Newton's discoveries to the economic needs of commercial capitalism with the general thesis of which one may broadly agree. Professor G. N. Clark has, however, been able to show ('Social and Economic Aspects of Science in the Age of Newton', in *Economic History*, vol. iii, pp. 362 *sqq*., and *Science and Social Welfare in the Age of Newton* (1937)) that some of Hessen's conclusions are based on slender foundations.

*Das Alter wird uns stets mit dem Homer beschämen;*
*Und unsrer Zeiten Ruhm musz Newton auf sich nehmen.*[1]

But among the social thinkers of this century and the next, no one expressed better the spirit of the age or was of greater significance for subsequent development than Bacon. He laid the philosophical foundations for experimental science; and he carried the method of rational inquiry from the natural sciences to the study of man and his community. With the same practical outlook as Machiavelli, and sharing his frank pursuit of power, Bacon gave the philosophical imprimatur to the authority of the state. His very tolerance of the Church, which he recognized as a useful instrument in the hands of a strong state, shows the extent to which he had freed himself from the remnants of medievalism. His eulogies of the monarch may have been inspired by the desire for personal advancement; they were none the less a sincere reflection of his fundamental belief in the secular authority. Monarchy, he thought, was a natural institution and obedience to it a natural duty. The doctrine of the divine right of kings was thus upheld and absolutism given a powerful theoretical support. To the absolute sovereign was assigned the role of supreme judge, who would not be fettered by prejudice or laws and who would stand above the warring social factions. Here is the political quintessence of the age; here is the authority that was to take the place of the shattered feudal system.

This change found an even clearer expression in the seventeenth century in Bacon's companion, Thomas Hobbes. Forsaking the concept of the divine right of kings, he gave yet a new and more powerful interpretation to Baconian ideas in the principle of the sovereignty of the state. Although he based his analysis on something like a voluntary association of individuals who agreed that one or more of their number should represent the common will, he laid great stress on coercion as an essential element of state organization. For once the state had arisen, it contained an absolute sovereignty to which complete obedience was due. Kings, however, did not possess their power, no matter how absolute, by virtue of divine right. God was the final judge of their rule, but their power on earth came from the very nature of their office. Any ruler, lawful or otherwise, was possessed of the fundamental attributes of kingship.

Hobbes was more akin to Bodin than to Bacon in his greater freedom from the theological argument for sovereignty; and he worked

1 G. E. Lessing, *Sämtliche Werke* (1836), vol. i, p. 243.

in the same direction of religious emancipation as Spinoza. Like the latter, he was regarded by his contemporaries as a foe of belief. And because he had also given a theoretical basis to the claims of usurpers of sovereignty, Church and king were united in opposing him. What made him equally suspect to the opponents of the king's power was the fact that, unlike Bodin, he continued the Baconian disregard for laws and respect for indivisible and unrestricted sovereignty. Hobbes's belief in a power above the conflicting interests of social classes was both his weakness and his strength. His was a theory which was inevitable in an age when social conflicts were of all-absorbing interest and were for the first time rationally viewed, and when economic forces were pressing for the establishment of a strong central authority. It was limited by its own immediate experience, and within a short time it was to receive a new twist which completely altered its significance.

Yet Hobbes's importance in the growth of the new society and its thought was very great. His basis was individualist. Like Machiavelli, he frankly recognized the individual impelled by self-interest as the unit from which to start. The contract by which individuals had submitted to the terrific stranglehold of sovereign state – Hobbes's Leviathan – was based on this self-interest. The absolutist state was a method of obtaining a greater good than could be provided by the life of primitive man – 'solitary, poor, nasty, brutish, short'. If the Leviathan coerced, it did so in the interests of the ruled themselves. Here, in spite of the central doctrine of state authority (in harmony with the practice of state regulation of economic life), was the beginning of utilitarianism. And in apparent contrast with Hobbes, yet in logical development of the principle immanent in his system, utilitarian philosophy was henceforth to progress.

Its next advance is contained in the work of John Locke. We shall shortly meet him again as an economist of the transition from mercantilism to the classics. In the sphere of political thought his position is more significant. He synthesized and carried further all the elements of past thought that could be made to compose a political philosophy fit for the age when capitalism was already certain of victory. The social contract which in Plato had made men build the city, in Hobbes submit to the Leviathian, and in Bodin had established and set the limits to central authority, is found again in Locke. With it, and again in a significant new guise, is the doctrine of natural law. Beginning in Stoic and Epicurean philosophy, this doctrine had found a place in Roman Law and in the Canonist doctrine of natural justice. Now it was being transformed into a recognition of the 'natural' instincts of the individual; and the social contract that established civil government became dependent entirely on the measure of consent of those who were governed.

Realization of self-interest as the motive force of conduct is inherent in Locke's entire political philosophy. But to him it was not the medieval Church, nor Bacon's king of divine right, nor yet Hobbes's superhuman Leviathan that was to make an orderly body out of the individual atoms. Through his experience as administrator of England's colonial possessions Locke had come into contact with trade. And the orderly voluntary association of merchants in commercial ventures that he had seen in the regulated companies appeared to him the natural form of organization for purposes of government. It was, therefore, in constitutional monarchy that rationalism found its political expression. Freedom, he thought, must only be restricted in the interests of preserving it. Its basis was property, acquired by industry and reason, and entitled to the security which the state could give. Here is a philosophy suited to the new conditions of the economy. It is the embodiment of the victory over the Middle Ages. But it is more than that; it is a symptom of the decline of state power which commercial capital had created at an earlier stage of its war against feudalism. It is a development inherent in the relation between capitalism and its first political expression. It is the first chapter of liberalism, the philosophy of triumphant capitalism.

## The Growth of Industrial Capitalism

The appearance of Locke's philosophy at the end of the seventeenth century shows that the new state was beginning to be seen for what it was: the creature of economic power no less than its master. The change of economic policy was less rapid than that of political philosophy. Nevertheless, at the end of the seventeenth century state regulation of economic life was breaking down. Its decline was by no means uniform in all countries. Indeed, we shall see that mercantilism reappeared with additions and distortions in economically backward countries like Germany, when in England and France it was already a thing of the past. But even in the countries which took the lead in the transition to modern industry the progress of unrestricted individualism was uneven. Freedom from the fetters of the state was achieved in some directions in the last years of the seventeenth century. But more often liberal philosophy did not win its decisive victory until well into the nineteenth century.

Many of the restrictive regulations of domestic industry were abolished in England after the middle of the seventeenth century. Others, regulation of wages, for example, did not finally disappear until 1813. Acts regulating apprenticeships and the conditions of production in many industries became inoperative with the expansion of production and the growth of the factory system; and when Parliament came to abolish them in the nineteenth century it was only registering an accomplished fact. Within the system of guilds considerable changes began to take place. A complex differentiation was growing up which led to the appearance of many conflicts of interests. The older type of export merchant company, descended from the guilds of the fourteenth and fifteenth centuries, was being displaced by the great colonial companies. There were also the newer capitalist coporations, dominated either by wholesale merchants or by semi-industrial capitalists of the *Verleger* type, and their influence was growing. The smaller local urban guilds of small master craftsmen, on the other hand, were declining in importance owing to the competition of domestic industry controlled by the *Verleger*. Local regulation was, therefore, continually diminishing in power in favour of national regulation.[1]

The decline of the regulation of foreign trade took place with a time lag. The trade treaties, which had at one time been protectionist and restrictive instruments, were capable of a different use. Once economic interests were strong enough, treaties were concluded for the purpose of expanding trade between the countries concerned. Free trade suffered many set backs, but over the eighteenth century as a whole it was undoubtedly progressing. The earliest symptom of the new spirit of trading was the decline of the regulated companies. Their monopoly rights were undermined by the growth of trade itself, which gave a scope to independent merchants, 'interlopers' or, more significantly, 'free traders', as they were called. By the end of the seventeenth century the regulated company was ceasing to be the dominant form of organization in international trade. The Eastland Company began to lose its privileges in the Baltic trade in the last quarter of the

[1] G. Unwin, *Industrial Organization in the Sixteenth and Seventeenth Centuries* (1902). Cf, particularly chs. ii and iii.

seventeenth century. The Merchant Adventurers were deprived of their monopoly of the cloth trade within their area in 1689. And most of the other trading companies shared their fate at about the same time. Only the East India Company, which was in a different position from the rest, was able to retain monopoly rights much longer. But even that lost its exclusive trading privilege in India early in the nineteenth century.

Thus the decline of state intervention went hand in hand with the disappearance of monopoly and the growth of competition. The cause which produced both these tendencies and which was powerfully reinforced by them was the growth of industrial production. The changes of what is known as the industrial revolution were of such spectacular character that they have obscured the no less important industrial advances of the seventeenth and early eighteenth centuries. If the latter were slower to develop and much smaller in extent than the former, they were nevertheless at least as important in kind. Professor Nef[1] has shown that there was something like an industrial revolution going on in the sixteenth and seventeenth centuries. By 1700 there were in existence in England a number of flourishing industries (for example, mining, salt, copper, brass, and ordnance, alum and nail-making) run, in part at any rate, on a factory basis and controlled by fairly large capitalists. If, by the end of the eighteenth century, the invention and application of labour-saving machinery and the use of inanimate power were beginning to spread at a staggering pace, it was because the specifically social framework of modern industry had already been built at the beginning of the eighteenth century.

The scientific discoveries of the seventeenth century, which were the allies of commercial capitalism, could not develop without the spread of scientific inquiry in a more general sense. Within a hundred years this was to surpass its narrower utilitarian bounds; though even then it remained essentially practical. In the meantime, however, invention was not dormant; it was only the by-product of industry itself. A large number of improvements of manufacture precede the flood which was the industrial revolution. In the extraction of minerals and the refining of metals, in the production of textiles and the building of ships, new methods were introduced; and wind or water power were increasingly applied in place of human or animal energy.

1 J. U. Nef, *The Rise of the British Coal Industry* (1932), vol. i, pp. 165–89.

The comparative slowness of this development illustrates the complex interrelation of technical and social-economic factors. Technical advance was held up by the restricted markets of the earlier mercantilist era. The 'fear of goods' which characterized it found its counterpart in the opposition of state and public opinion to improvements which might have expanded production. In an age of commercial privilege, vested interests were strong enough to oppose the introduction of new processes which threatened their monopoly. On the other hand, technical imrovement had to wait for a larger market before it became profitable. That larger market was produced by commercial capitalism itself. In the eighteenth century commercial expansion had both undermined existing restrictions of competition and stimulated invention. This, by improving and expanding industrial production, was to destroy the very basis of commercial capitalism. It found wider markets and encouraged producers to produce more, and more cheaply. It also encouraged them to improve their production and then to go in search of greater demand by showing them the latent possibilities of increased sales.

The merchant created the industrialist. Very often he turned manufacturer himself. And his example stimulated recruitment of the *homines novi* of capitalism from the land and from domestic industry. Already in the early eighteenth century the organization of production was changing. It has long been recognized that the *putting-out* system was at that time giving way to the concentrated production of the *factory system*. Every fresh piece of research on that period strengthens the view that this transition started earlier and was more rapid than had earlier been supposed. The form of production of the mercantile era (in which the commercial capitalist took the lead by buying raw materials and sometimes equipment, putting it out into domestic workshops, and selling the products in ever-widening markets) might survive for a long time in some districts, countries or branches of industry. But it was no longer typical; the trend was definitely in the direction of factory production. In mining and brewing, in the manufacture of pottery and hardware, the factory was already leading the way. Wedgwood's Etruria and Boulton's works at Soho are now seen not as exceptions but as the pattern, rare as yet, to which industry as a whole was moulding itself.

The change in the status of labour was akin to this transformation of the merchant into the industrialist. For commercial capital to become industrial capital it was essential for it to find labour, land, and raw materials as purchasable commodities. The last two had been market-able long before the eighteenth century. The sale and purchase of goods, including raw materials, had become habitual before the beginnings of modern industry; and the commercialization of agricul-ture and the breakdown of the feudal system had gradually made land into a marketable good also. In regard to labour the change was slower; and it was in this respect that the eighteenth century completed the most important of the social transformations which capitalism required.

The process by which a class of wage-workers was created is well known. Its beginnings are in the fourteenth century, when the manorial system was breaking down. Serfdom had virtually dis-appeared and was being replaced by a system of small, mainly independent, farmers and a small number of wage-labourers. The enclosure movement made havoc of this system; it deprived farmers and labourers of their land, cottages, and common rights and laid the foundation for the modern working class. The expropriation of Church lands during the Reformation, the commercialization of farm-ing, which coincided with the expansion of trade, and the constitu-tional changes after the Restoration, which set the seal on the disappearance of feudalism and established the modern system of public finance, pushed this development still further. Merchants and financiers viewed this transformation with favour. By destroying the feudal title to property and making the landed interest commercially minded, it helped to establish their own status. By its expropriation of the yeoman, it created a supply of labour which the industry of the later mercantilist period needed.

With the transition to industrial capitalism in the eighteenth century this movement received a fresh impetus. The amount of capital required for industrial enterprise increased with the growing com-plexity of the manufacturing process. Few craftsmen were capable of competing effectively either against the cheaper production made possible by a greater use of capital equipment or in markets wider than their immediate environment. If they did not work on their own material but only to the order of a merchant they became increasingly dependent on him. Sooner or later, when the few tools they owned had become out of date compared with new processes and equipment, they and their apprentices would succumb to the comparative security of being regular wage-earners. They might remain in their own domestic workshop for a time; soon, however, the factory would gather them.

There they would be joined by others recruited from the rural population dispossessed by successive enclosure movements, which by the eighteenth century had acquired parliamentary sanction.

The whole of this process created not only industrialists and wage-earners; it supplied also the market for capitalist industry. The destruction of the domestic workshop of both town and country and the commercialization of farming created the demand which absorbed the products of factory industry. On the basis of this internal market – the growth of which completed the separation of agriculture and industry – industrial capitalism could once again turn to foreign trade, which had been one of the bases on which it developed.

The relation between the capitalist and his wage-worker was at first regulated as it had been during the era which knew only of merchants, master craftsmen, journeymen, and apprentices. Custom, remnants of guild regulation, and wage legislation were the determinants of wages and conditions in the early days of the factory system. But they became too rigid for the needs of expanding industry.

The mercantilists, if they held any wage theory at all, believed in an economy of low wages and in strict wage regulation. This was appropriate to merchants engaged in exporting to markets where they had to meet foreign competition. It was also in harmony with the views of some mercantilists on the need for restricting home consumption. But the reliance on regulation of the labour market became inadequate once competition for labour arose between different industries. Not that industrial capitalism began immediately to act on an 'economy of high-wages' principle. But supply and demand became now the proximate determinants of the relation between capital and labour. The guilds lost what little power they had preserved, customs were discarded, and legislation to regulate mobility of labour, and to some extent wages, tended to disappear. The process was more rapid with regard to mobility of labour; and wage regulation did not disappear entirely until the early part of the nineteenth century. But by then the progress of invention and the enclosure movement had created a labour surplus, and the old regulations were appealed to for the purpose of upholding a minimum wage.

On the whole, however, bargaining between capitalist and worker tended to become the common method of settling the labour contract. It was the result, as we have seen, of a twofold process: one part of it was the concentration of capital in the hands of the industrialist, who owned the more complex tools of production now required; the other was the driving out of the urban and rural worker from a place of independence in the scheme of production, together with his legal emancipation from the ties of guilds and landlords. The worker was now free to enter into a contract; he was also forced by the growing complexity of production to sell his labour in the market in order to earn his livelihood. By the middle of the century the process of establishing a free market for labour had gone far enough for Dean Tucker to describe as 'absurd and preposterous' any attempt by a third person 'to fix the price between buyer and seller'. Regulations could not be enforced if they were not supported by the willingness of the contracting parties. Moreover, no laws could be devised that would allow for 'plenty or scarcity of work, cheapness or dearness of provisions, . . . goodness or badness of the workmanship, the different degrees of skill . . . and the demand or stagnation at home or abroad'.[1]

Side by side with this free market there began to develop the typical modern labour problems. As early as the second half of the seventeenth century there appeared examples of working men organizing themselves in order to improve their position. Sometimes they readopted the outward practices of guilds. They stressed the functions of the friendly society, attempted to regulate quality of production, and maintained an elaborate ritual. But gradually their real character became more obvious. They turned into associations whose main task was to fight the employers on wages and conditions. It was against these combinations, the forerunners of the modern trade unions, that Parliament enacted its Combination Laws.

## Petty

Economic thought soon began to respond to all these changes; though it took a hundred years to become fully aware of the revolution it was witnessing. Corresponding with the change in the quality of capitalism there took place a change in the interests of thinkers. Attention was diverted from trade to production: from the relation of merchant and financier to that of capital and labour. Of greatest significance in this change of approach and content of economic thought is the appearance of a new problem of price and value. Hitherto, this problem was conceived almost exclusively in terms of exchange. With Aristotle and

1 Quoted by H. J. Laski, *The Rise of European Liberalism*, p. 176.

the schoolmen it had been a part of the problem of justice: in what manner must exchange take place in order that there should be a just equivalence? This was the question they posed and answered in the doctrine of the 'just price'.

In the mercantilist era both question and answer were different. With all the obscurities and individual variations, a common approach underlay mercantilist theory on the question of price. The approach was that of the merchant. What is the best means for making the country rich? Because wealth is the same as commercial capital (represented by money) the answer is: by making profitable sales. Profit can only arise *upon alienation*, i.e. in the act of exchange, when the seller sells more dearly than he has bought. All the mercantilist conclusions relating to foreign trade and their limited and distorted view of the relation between money and prices are the results of this approach.

With the growth of industry, production instead of exchange became the chief concern of the economist. The process of production, which in its new form involved a changed social relationship, was seen to be the core of economic activity. It was no longer possible to insist that wealth, in a social sense, was created by exchange, that value (i.e. exchange-value, which is the attribute of social wealth) and the profit by which wealth was increased arose in commerce. The problem of wealth and value was reformulated and answered anew; and, although the precision of both formulation and answer increased only gradually, until they reached their most refined form in the classical system, their quality was now always the same.

This development in economic thought is roughly the same in a number of countries. With minor though interesting variations, the problem of value becomes the centre of analysis in England, Italy, and France, and thinkers of all three countries provide solutions in similar terms. In a larger book than this the ideas of Montanari Davanzati, and Galiani in Italy and of Boisguillebert in France would deserve detailed treatment; and so would those of Benjamin Franklin, who was as astute in economic as in other scientific matters. Their omission may be justified on the ground that it was in England that the seed of these founders bore its finest fruit. That part of the French contribution which is of a somewhat different character will be discussed separately.

The most important, as well as the earliest, English economist who prepared the ground for the classical system is Sir William Petty

(1623–87). He has justly been called the founder of political economy.[1] The son of a poor weaver in Hampshire, he had an extraordinarily varied career which made him in turn cabin boy, hawker, seaman, clothier, physician, professor of anatomy, professor of music, surveyor, and wealthy landowner. The formal education which he had received at a Jesuit college in France and at Oxford was richly supplemented by friendship with the leading scientists and men of letters of the day. Petty was a friend of Pepys and Evelyn, and a member of the company of learned men who met in London and in Oxford and later became the Royal Society. He was a charter member of the council of this body. The story of his life, told by Lord Fitzmaurice and in a short account given by the late Professor Hull in his introduction to Petty's economic works, explains to a large extent the extraordinarily advanced place which Petty occupies in the history of economic thought. His freedom from purely mercantile interests, which distinguishes him from other seventeenth-century economists, his unusually wide experience of men and affairs – particularly through his part in the Down Survey of Ireland and the distribution of land to Cromwell's soldiers – and above all, his association with the leaders of experimental scientific thought, give to his economic writings a zest and breadth of vision which was not to be surpassed for a hundred years.

In his *Political Arithmetick*, written probably in 1672 and published in 1690, Petty states explicitly a new approach to economic inquiry which he knows to be still unusual. 'Instead,' he says, 'of using only comparative and superlative Words, and intellectual Arguments, I have taken the course ... to express myself in terms of *Number, Weight*, or *Measure*; to use only Arguments of Sense, and to consider only such Causes, as have visible Foundations in Nature.'[2] Petty truly adhered to this manifesto of empiricism; and his claim to fame is generally conceived to rest on the part he played in the foundation of a science of statistics. There can be no doubt that Petty is rightly regarded as the first to develop this sister discipline of political economy. Not only did he show by his own practice and precept the manner in which data should be collected and marshalled; he did not neglect the wider functions of statistical inquiry. Throughout his *Political Arithmetick* and

---

1 Both by Marx, in at least three places: *Zur Kritik der Politischen Ökonomie*, p. 33; in Engels' *Anti-Dühring* (1928), p. 247; and in *Theorien über den Mehrwer!* (1921), vol. i, p. i; and by Brentano, *Ethik and Volkswirtschaft in der Geschichte*, p. 32.
2 *The Economic Writings of Sir William Petty* (ed. C. H. Hull, 2 volumes, 1899), vol. i, p. 244.

in his other statistical papers he set factual research in its proper place
n relation to theoretical analysis.

More important, however, and more interesting for our purpose are
Petty's contributions to economic thought. His work in this respect,
apart from some scattered observations in the *Political Arithmetick*, is
contained mainly in *A Treatise of Taxes and Contributions* (1662), in
*Verbum Sapienti* (1664), in the *Political Anatomy of Ireland*, written in
1672 and published in 1691, and in *Sir William Petty's Quantulumcumque Concerning Money*, written in 1682 and published in 1695.
Petty's modern editor has implied that the particular avenues through
which Petty approached economic problems (public finance and the
coinage) distinguish him sharply from the preoccupations of classical
and modern economists. He has also suggested that because Petty was
a disciple of Hobbes (a fact which seems well established by Petty's
insistence on the sovereignty of the state) yet not a mercantilist proper,
he should be classed with the German *cameralists* – the pseudo-
economist advisers of absolute monarchs. Such a judgement is based
on misconception and must seriously interfere with a just estimate of
Petty's position in the history of economic thought.

It is true that Petty shared Hobbes's political philosophy. But the
indirect approach which he adopted to the important economic problems of wealth and value was itself an expression of the changes in
social and political relations that had taken place as an indispensable
part of the evolution of industrial capitalism. His interest in state
finance is conditioned by the fact that feudal methods of raising
revenue had disappeared and had been replaced by a system of
national taxation. To any one not connected with foreign trade who
was anxious to elucidate the principles of economic activity, there was
at that time no more obvious approach to economic problems than that
of the methods of raising and spending the revenue of the state. The
problems which these presented raised the questions of value and
wealth in their most acute form.

The *Treatise on Taxes* seems to be a straightforward discussion of the
sources of public revenue, the forms of public expenditure, and of the
best means of raising the one and disbursing the other. Petty's theory
of public finance is simple and need not detain us. He agrees with
Mun in regarding taxation as inevitable. But he feels that princes ought
not to be extravagant. Though they might be forced to raise more by
way of taxes than they needed, in order to create a reserve for
emergencies, they should not do so too often since they would be

withdrawing money from the productive circulation of their subjects. The money which the king has raised could, if wisely spent, stimulate trade and industry; it would thus return in increased measure to the people's pockets. Petty urged economy in the running of the state's main services, defence, administration, justice, and the 'Pastorage of men's souls'. He condemned expensive wars and the maintenance of supernumeraries, though he was willing to support the expenditure of public money in order to provide for those who would otherwise be unemployed lest, as he said, they 'lose their faculty of labouring'.[1]

Petty's views on the raising of the revenue are much coloured by Hobbes's philosophy. He shows throughout a frank recognition of individual self-interest and a high regard for property as the determinant of status. The state exists to protect the individual's property, and the individual has to be prepared to contribute towards the expenses of the state. That contribution should be in proportion to the property, the benefits of which the people enjoyed under the protection of the state. Petty realized that people were not always ready to recognize the utilitarian nature of taxation. They refused to pay because they thought that the king was extravagant or because they felt that they were unjustly assessed compared with their fellow taxpayers. Taxation should therefore be so devised as to leave the relative distribution of wealth unchanged, for 'let the Tax be never so great, if it be proportionable unto all, then no man suffers the loss of any Riches by it'.[2] It is impossible to institute such a system of taxation if 'for not knowing the Wealth of the people, the Prince knows not what they can bear; and for not knowing the Trade, he can make no Judgement of the proper season when to demand his Exhibitions'.[3] The need for statistics is obvious.

It is from this point that Petty is forced to plunge into the most intricate of all his economic analyses. He sets out to examine the different ways in which taxes may be levied.[4] He rejects the setting aside of Crown lands, from which the sovereign is to draw his revenue. A better way is to levy a tax on the whole of the rental revenue; this would give the king 'more security, and more obligees'. And the only thing to guard against is that the trouble and expense of this method of

---

1 *The Economic Writings of Sir William Petty* (ed. C. H. Hull), vol. i, p. 60.
2 ibid., p. 32.
3 ibid., vol i, p. 34.
4 'Treatise on Taxes and Contributions', ch. iv, *Economic Writings*, vol i, pp. 38 *sqq.*

collection should not be considerably greater than that of administering the Crown domain. Petty had no doubt that in a new country, 'before men had even the possession of any Land at all' (like Ireland, where it was in force), such a system of taxation was the best that could be devised. Future buyers of land would make allowance for the rent tax; taxation would be in just proportion; and not only the owners of the land, 'but every man who eats but an Egg, or an Onion of the growth of his Lands; or who useth the help of any Artisan, which feedeth on the same', would pay his contribution. In old countries, however, great difficulties would arise. New leases would take into account the new tax, while old leases would continue at the old rent. Some landlords would gain and others lose. The consumers would lose in any case, because the prices of produce would rise whether the tenant farmer who produces was paying the old or the new rent; only the farmer would make a large profit. At this stage the analysis of taxation and its incidence peters out and the discussion leads to a theory of value.

It is necessary to piece together a large number of separate statements in order to get a clear picture of Petty's analysis. When it is summarized a logical structure can be built which includes a theory of value and wages, a theory of profit or surplus (which is in effect a theory of rent), a discussion of the value of land, and a theory of interest and foreign exchange. These steps do not follow in this order in Petty's writings. There are difficulties to negotiate and obscurities to ignore. But the final picture does not lack a measure of internal consistency.

Petty's theory of value is contained in a short digression on rent, which follows his theory of the rent-tax, in a discussion of the real and the political price of commodities at a later point in his *Treatise*, and also in some remarks on wages in the *Political Anatomy of Ireland*. For an understanding of this theory it is important to appreciate the emphasis which Petty lays on labour as the source of wealth. Although he was not as explicit on this point as Adam Smith, he did nevertheless leave little doubt that he had travelled a long way from the conception of the mercantilists. 'Labour,' he said, 'is the Father and active principle of Wealth, as Lands are the Mother.'[1] And when in another place he spoke of the 'Wealth, Stock, or Provision of the Nation', he thought

---

[1] ibid., ch. iv, *Economic Writings*, vol. i, p. 68.

of it as 'being the effect of the former or past labour'.[1] Petty also realized that the typical form in which labour appeared in the new social structure was as divided labour. His account of the advantages of division of labour lacks none of the ingredients of Adam Smith's celebrated description. He takes the making of a watch as his example; and he shows that cheapening and improvement of production, which division of labour begets in this particular trade, arise also in the growth of large towns and their specialization in different manufactures.[2]

It is not surprising that this view of labour should have determined Petty's analysis of value and price. He is led to it by the question of what is 'the mysterious nature' of rents. His answer is that the natural and true rent of a piece of land for any particular year is the difference between the proceeds of the harvest and the seed plus what the producer 'himself hath both eaten and given to others in exchange for Clothes and other Natural necessaries'.[3] This, however, becomes not only an explanation of the origin of a surplus but also of the origin of value itself. Petty goes on to ask how much money 'this Corn or Rent is worth'. His answer is that it is worth as much as the money which another man producing money (i.e. the money commodity) can save during the same time, above his expenses of production. The hypothetical case with which he illustrates his proposition is worth quoting. 'Let another man go travel into a Countrey where is Silver, there Dig it, Refine it, bring it to the same place where the other man planted his Corn; Coyne it, etc. the same persom, all the while of his working for Silver, gathering also food for his necessary livelihood, and procuring himself covering, etc. I say, the Silver of the one, must be esteemed of equal value with the Corn of the other: the one being perhaps twenty Ounces and the other twenty Bushels. From whence it follows that the price of a Bushel of this Corn to be an Ounce of Silver.'[4] Petty is well aware of possible minor variations; but he argues that when an average is struck over a long period and covering a large quantity the above analysis will hold.

Although this is 'the foundation of equalizing and ballancing of values'[5] there remains much individual variety. He discusses this later

1 'Verbum Sapienti', *Economic Writings*, vol. i, p. 110.
2 *Economic Writings*, vol. ii, pp. 473–4.
3 ibid., vol. i, p. 43.
4 'Treatise', *Economic Writings*, vol. i, p. 43.
5 ibid., p. 44.

when he draws a distinction between the natural price, or 'true Price Currant', as he also calls it, and the political price. The 'natural dearness and cheapness depends upon the few or more hands requisite to necessaries of Nature. . . . But Political Cheapness depends upon the paucity of Supernumerary Interlopers into every Trade over and above all that are necessary.'[1] Other factors which might influence supply and demand and thus the political price, are customs and manner of living; and because 'all Commodities have their Substitutes or Succedanea, and that almost all uses may be answered several wayes', these factors must be considered as adding or taking away from the price of things.[2]

In spite of all these accidental factors, labour remains the true source and measure of value. This is made even clearer in two other passages which supply the beginnings of the classical theory of wages. In these Petty does not speak any longer of labour time as the measure of value. 'The days food of an adult Man, at a Medium, and not the days labour, is the common measure of Value.' 'That a days food of one sort, may require more labour to produce, than another sort, is also not material, since we understand the easiest-gotten food of the respective countries of the World.' Nor is it material 'that some Men will eat more than others, . . . since by a days food we understand $\frac{1}{100}$ part of what 100 of all Sorts and Sizes will eat, so as to Live, Labour, and Generate'.[3] The last phrase anticipates Ricardo's natural price of labour, which is the one 'necessary to enable the labourers, one with another, to subsist and to perpetuate their race'.[4] And in Petty's statement that a 'Law that appoints such Wages . . . should allow the Labourer but just wherewithall to live; for if you allow double; then he works but half so much as he could have done, and otherwise would; which is a loss to the Publick of the fruit of so much labour'[5] one may see the trend of thought which could lead to the surplus value theory of Marx.[6] But if Petty believed in the existence of a surplus product of labour, and, therefore, in labour's power to create a surplus above its own sustenance, he demonstrated these two categories only in the case

1 'Treatise', *Economic Writings*, vol. i, p. 90.
2 ibid.
3 'Verbum Sapienti', *Economic Writings*, vol. i, p. 181.
4 D. Ricardo, *The Principles of Political Economy and Taxation* (Everyman edition), p. 52.
5 'Treatise', *Economic Writings*, vol. i, p. 87.
6 Marx did so himself: *Theorien über den Mehrwert*, vol i, p. 3.

of production from the land. Rent was the only surplus he knew; and it comprised the whole concept of profit within it.

At the same time Petty was also aware of the differential element in rent. A hundred and fifty years before Ricardo he stated clearly the theory of differential rents. 'For as great need of money heightens Exchange, so doth great need of Corn raise the price of that likewise, and consequently of the Rent of the Land that bears Corn, and lastly of the Land it self; as for example, if the Corn which feedeth *London*, or an Army, be brought forty miles thither, then the Corn growing within a mile of London, or the quarters of such Army, shall have added unto its natural price, so much as the charge of bringing it thirty-nine miles doth amount unto.'[1] And although nothing is said here about differing fertilities as the cause of differential rent (some obscure reference appears elsewhere), other factors are enumerated and the general principle could not be better expressed.[2] It should also be noted that Petty was quite clear that rent was determined by price and not vice versa. Not only is this explicitly stated in the discussion of differential rent quoted above; it is implicit in his discussion of the origin of rent as such, which, as we have seen, led him also to a labour theory of value.

A further conclusion which Petty wishes to draw concerns the value of land. 'The question is', he says, 'how many years purchase (as we usually say) is the Fee simple naturally worth?'[3] The reason for Petty's attention to this problem is interesting and shows the error into which he fell, in spite of his genius. Although he gives ample evidence for his fundamental belief in a labour theory of value, he seems nevertheless to have been uncertain about the part played by land in the creation of value. We have seen that in one place he makes land and labour joint determinants of value. This is probably due to a confusion in his mind between exchange-value and use-value. Where he is concerned with the latter, he speaks of land and labour; where he is dealing with exchange-value (at any rate implicitly) he speaks of labour alone. He was himself aware of this dichotomy. 'All things ought to be valued by two natural Denominations, which is Land and Labour. ... This being true, we should be glad to finde out a natural Par between Land and Labour, so as

1 'Treatise', *Economic Writings*, vol. i, p. 89.
2 ibid., pp. 48–9.
3 ibid., vol. i, p. 45.

we might express the value by either of them alone as well or better than by both, and reduce one into the other as easily and certainly as we reduce pence into pounds.'[1]

We have already seen how Petty determined the value of labour. As to the value of land, he developed a theory of the capitalization of rent or the *usus fructus per annum*. This is clearly a break with his own original dichotomy of land and labour, because he had already determined rent as the surplus product of labour. He is himself unaware of this inconsistency and goes on to ask at what rate it should be capitalized. Since Petty's theory of the surplus is exclusively one of rent, he has no other rate of return to resort to which would help him in the capitalization of the rate of return from land. He discovers an ingenious way out. People, he thinks, will pay a price for land in accordance with the return derived from it and the number of years which they themselves or their immediate descendants expect to enjoy that return. Petty regards three generations as a reasonable estimate. And since 'in *England* we esteem three lives equal to one and twenty years', he computes the value of land at twenty-one years' purchase of its annual rent. This would apply 'where Titles are good, and where there is a moral certainty of enjoying the purchase'. In other countries this will vary according to the titles, the number of people, and the estimate put upon three lives.[2]

This process for computing the value of land can now be used in the reverse direction for discovering the rate of return on money-capital. In other words, Petty does not presuppose a rate of interest which would be used in the capitalization of land, but derives his conclusions on interest from his theory of rent and land values. He states explicitly that he proposes to explain the nature of rent 'with reference as well to Money, the rent of which we call usury'.[3] And the chapter on usury follows immediately after the discussion on rent. Petty's general opinion on usury is simple. He condemns the taking of interest if the lender can call upon the borrower to repay on demand. But if the borrower has the enjoyment of the money lent for a fixed period of time, the lender can justifiably demand interest. The rate of interest, he says, anticipating the physiocrats, is determined by the rent of the land. Where the security of the loan is undoubted, the rate of interest

1 'Treatise', *Economic Writings*, vol. i, p. 45.
2 ibid.
3 ibid., p. 42.

is equal to the 'Rent of so much Land as the money lent will buy; . . . but where the security is casual, then a kinde of ensurance must be enterwoven with the simple natural Interest'.[1] Although interest is thus determined by rent, there are factors which cause it to vary from time to time and place to place and it is, therefore, impossible to fix it by law.

This point is emphasized again in the *Quantulumcumque Concerning Money*.[2] Here Petty finds another reason for expressing a view which is implied in much that he wrote and which is both a plea for freedom in trade and an anticipation of the physiocratic and Smithian belief in the 'natural order'. He makes his discussion of interest the occasion for speaking 'of the vanity and fruitlessness of making Civil Positive Laws against the Laws of Nature'.[3]

On the question of interest, then, Petty held more advanced views than the mercantilist opinions which were still current in his time. As for foreign exchange, about which he said little, he, like the later mercantilists, did not share Malynes's fears, although he made usury analogous to foreign exchange dealings. But he considered that the natural measure of exchange was established by the cost of carrying money in specie from one place to another, though variations might arise 'where are hazards [and] emergent uses for money more in one place than another, etc. or opinions of these true or false'.[4] He accordingly rejected all measures of fixing exchanges by law; and he was also a determined opponent of prohibitions on the export of bullion.

Petty did not go much farther in developing a theory of international payments; and his views on foreign trade in general are still coloured by mercantilist notions. However, his references to this question are slight and scattered; and it may be argued that he was merely taking for granted certain views accepted at the time, without devoting much attention to the problems which they were meant to explain. He seems to have believed as firmly as Mun that 'the overplus whereof [of exported goods], above what is Imported, brings home mony, etc.'[5] And his mercantilist belief in the value of exports is clearly in evidence when he said that 'Ireland exporting more than it imports doth yet

1 'Treatise', *Economic Writings*, vol. i, p. 48.
2 ibid, vol. ii, pp. 447–8.
3 'Treatise', ibid., vol. i, p. 48.
4 ibid.
5 'Political Arithmetick', ibid., vol. i, p. 260.

grow poorer to a paradox'.[1] But his chief interest was clearly engaged in a different direction.

His views on money, at any rate in the earlier writings, were also mercantilist. He laid great stress on treasure as the most desirable form of wealth. And even in his analysis of value he was mostly concerned with the monetary form in which value appeared – a remnant of bullionist thought. Yet his own methods of analysis were constantly interfering with these accepted views. It was due particularly to his statistical work that Petty was able to escape more than any other writer of the period from the common confusion between money and capital. In his studies of Ireland he found that money was only a fraction of the total annual expense of the country; the same was true when he tried to compute the national wealth of England. Although he still regarded money as a very important means for making trade active, he often expressed the view that a country might have too much as well as too little money.[2] And, in trying to discover the right money supply for a country, he used the concept of the 'velocity of circulation' of money which was to play an important part in later monetary theory.[3]

His very method of analysis shows that in spite of inevitable occasional lapses he was far removed from the primitive monetary errors of the mercantilists. Even when he praised the virtues of money and trade (particularly foreign trade), and appeared nearest to the theory of commercial capitalism, he introduced important qualifications. Money and foreign trade were important, he thought, because they helped a country to develop and improve its industry. At the same time a country should endeavour by policy to improve its effiency in the production of the commodities needed for trade. Again and again he laid emphasis on 'art' as an aid in production;[4] and he measured the power of the prince by 'the number, art and industry of his people, well united and governed'.[5]

Petty went even farther in the *Quantulumcumque*, his most mature discussion of monetary matters. He stated categorically that a nation might have too much or too little money, suggested that money was only needed as a help in trade and industry, and gave a computation of

1 'Treatise', *Economic Writings*, vol. i, p. 46.
2 'Verbum Sapienti', ibid., vol. i, p. 113.
3 ibid., vol. i, pp. 35–6, 112–13.
4 For an interesting account of the early history of this concept, cf. E. A. J. Johnson, *Predecessors of Adam Smith*, ch. xiii, in which many of Petty's views are quoted.
5 'Treatise', ibid., vol. 1, p. 22.

the amount of money needed in which the concept of the velocity of circulation was also implied. He repeated his objections to the prohibition of bullion exports and to the legal regulations limiting interest and exchange rates. Existing laws, he said, were perhaps 'against the Laws of Nature, and also impracticable'.[1] If a country had too much money it should melt it down, export it as a commodity where there is a demand for it, or lend it out at interest where interest was high. If there was too little money there should be established 'a Bank, which well computed, doth almost double the Effect of our coined Money'. Once again he stressed his belief in England's ability to capture the trade of the world. (In the 'Political Arithmetick' he had tried to show 'that the Impediments of England's Greatness are but contingent and removeable'.) 'And we have', he said, 'in *England* materials for a Bank which shall furnish Stock enough to drive the Trade of the whole Commercial World'[2] – an expectation which was to be fulfilled only a few years later.

Petty seems to have assimilated all the most refined ideas of his predecessors on the effects of debasement and on the place of bullion in foreign trade. When states debase their coins, he said, 'they are like Bankrupt Merchants, who Compound for their Debts by paying 16s., 12s. or 10s. in the pound; Or forcing their Creditors to take off their Goods at much above the Market rates'.[3] Old unequal money ought to be new coined at the expense of the state; but the difference between the value of the new and the old money must be borne by those who hold the latter, since otherwise poeople would be tempted to 'clip their own Money'.[4] The new coinage would make little difference to foreign trade. In an argument reminiscent of Mun, Petty showed that merchants would still carry abroad either commodities or specie with which to buy foreign goods according to relative prices. England need not be impoverished if they took specie since the commodities they brought home would probably yield a profit.

Although Petty does not discuss specifically the relation between money and prices, he makes a few statements on the subject which are lucid and illuminating. A reduction in the silver content of the coin, he said, was bound to diminish the amount of goods which people were willing to give in exchange for it, except among 'such Fools as take

1 'Quantulumcumque', *Economic Writings*, vol. ii. p. 445.
2 ibid., p. 446.
3 ibid., p. 443.
4 ibid., p. 440.

Money by name, and not by its weight and fineness'. If one had more shillings coined out of the same amount of silver one would not be any richer. This was most clearly demonstrated in the case of goods made of the money metal. A goldsmith would not give his silver vessel 'weighing 20 ounces of wrought, for 18 Ounces of unwrought Silver'. The same was true of other commodities, 'though not so demonstrable as in a Commodity whose Materials is the same with Money'.[1]

With this we may take our leave of Petty. The space devoted to him may appear excessive compared with the short account of a number of other pre-classical writers which is to follow. But because Petty's significance as the most important of the forerunners of Smith and Ricardo has so often been neglected, it seemed necessary to redress the balance.

## Locke; North; Law; Hume

Economic thought in England developed briskly in the first half of the eighteenth century, and there are a large number of writers whose contributions are of interest. In general, however, these contributions are only refinements of points originally raised by Petty or changes of emphasis of varying significance. From these many writers a few may be chosen for brief treatment. John Locke and Sir Dudley North are selected as immediate followers of Petty; and Sir Dudley North also as the most important free trade advocate of the time. John Law's monetary theories deserve mention and so does Sir James Steuart's comprehensive work. Cantillon, who has been rediscovered this century, shows the closest affinity to the French physiocrats; and David Hume's economic writings, whose merit may have, at times, been exaggerated, are important as a synthesis of economic thought prior to Adam Smith.

Locke and North are best discussed together both in their relation to mercantilist thought and to the theories of Petty. With regard to foreign trade, their views differ considerably. Locke was largely influenced by mercantilist notions. He still insisted that a country grew rich by exporting more than it imported. North, on the other hand, in his *Discourses upon Trade* (1691), took up an intransigent free-trade attitude. He made a devastating attack on protection, in particular on the prohibition of trade with France. It was he who expressed, for the

---

1 'Quantulumcumque', *Economic Writings*, vol. ii, pp. 441–2.

first time, the view that the whole world was as much an economic unit as was a single nation. All trades he regarded as profitable because no one would continue in an unprofitable occupation. And he identified public good with private good in a manner that would be fit for a nineteenth-century utilitarian writer. His vigorous pamphlet was not well received, naturally at a time when foreign trade restrictions were still the rule. But as it expressed views which were in harmony with the trend of economic development its theoretical influence was great.

The views of these two writers on the fundamental problems of economic analysis were of more immediate importance. Both Locke and North took up some of the points in Petty's theory of rent, interest, and money. They shared his views on debasement; and Locke, in particular, gave a very good analysis of the effect of debasement on prices in his *Some Considerations of the Consequences of the Lowering of Interest and Raising the Value of Money* (1691). Like Petty, they both opposed the laws for the limitation of interest. Locke followed Petty closely in deriving his theory of interest from an analysis of rent. He still regarded rent as the only surplus, and inquired how money, which was by nature barren, could have the same productive character as the soil, which did produce something useful. His conclusion was that just as the unequal distribution of land enabled those who had more than they could cultivate themselves to take a tenant from whom they obtained rent, so the unequal distribution of money enabled its owners to obtain a tenant for it from whom they could receive interest.

North went further. He seems to have been the first to have a clear idea of capital, which he called stock. He made the lending of stock-in-trade, by those who lack the ability to use it or shunned the trouble to do so, equivalent to the letting of land. The interest which lenders received was a rent of money akin to the rent of land. Landlords and 'stocklords' were the same. North preserved no traces of the mercantilist love for treasure. No one, he thought, could get rich, by having all his possessions in the form of money. Only those increased their wealth whose possessions were bearing fruit all the time by either being lent out or employed in trade.[1] Nobody wanted to keep money; everybody was anxious to dispose of it in such a way as to make a profit.

Both Locke and North, but particularly the former, were led to discuss value, price, and money by way of their discussion of the nature

1 D. North, *Discourses upon Trade; principally directed to the cases of the Interest, Coynage, clipping, increase of Money* (1691), p. 11.

of interest. North said little about value itself, though he discussed price. Locke's views on value are not easy to discover, because his statements on the subject are few and do not occur in the same place as his main economic discussions. In the *Two Treatises concerning Government* (1690) he seems to share Petty's view of the origin of value. In a discussion concerned mainly with property he stated that the earth belonged to all men in common. Private property, however, was justified in so far as a human being had mixed his own labour with the gifts of nature. Legitimate property was limited by the amount which anybody needed for his own maintenance. Property in land was equally limited by the amount which an individual could cultivate and the produce of which he could use. Labour was the main source of value. Nearly the whole value of the products of the soil were due to labour; the rest was a natural gift.[1]

However, in none of these statements does Locke reach Petty's conclusion that labour is also the measure of value. He seems to have confined himself to use-value and to have endeavoured to show the importance of labour in its production. Consciously or not, he avoided the issue of the origin of exchange-value and made an analysis which has been classed as a supply and demand theory of price.[2] That analysis appears in the *Consequences*, but is prefaced by a statement on money in *Government*. Locke made money possess a purely imaginary value which was created by common consent. Because money was not perishable, one of the limits to its accumulation in private hands (that no one should own more of anything than he needed for himself) disappeared. Great inequalities in property were thus made possible, though there still remained one limit to the amount that might legitimately be held, namely, the amount of the individual's own labour which enabled him to acquire profit at all.[3] In the *Consequences*, however, Locke went on to give money a 'double value'. One arises from the ability of money to supply a yearly income (akin to rent); the other is the same as that of any other 'Necessaries or Conveniences of Life' which money can procure in exchange. Locke falls thus into the mercantilist error of identifying money and capital – an error which North had avoided.

It was, however, Locke's emphasis on the medium of exchange

1 J. Locke, *Two Treatises concerning Government* (ed. Morley, 1884) pp. 203–16.
2 Cf. the interesting discussion of Locke's views in R. Zuckerkandl, *Zur Theorie des Preises* (1936), pp. 125–31, 223–4.
3 J. Locke, *Two Treatises concerning Government*, pp. 215–16.

function of money which was the starting-point for his further discussion. This was based on the quantity theory of money, already outlined in connection with the problem of debasement. Against the prevailing mercantilist view that a low rate of interest would raise prices, Locke pointed out that prices were determined by the amount of money in circulation. This view was based on a supply and demand theory of price. Although the 'vent' of anything 'depends upon its Necessity or Usefulness',[1] yet the quantity sold at any time was determined by the 'part of the running cash of the nation designed to be laid' out on it.[2] The amount available and the amount sold and the number of buyers and sellers settled the market price. In the case of money, sale was always certain; therefore, 'its quantity alone is enough to regulate and determine its value, without considering any Proportion between its quantity and vent, as in other commodities'.[3] A number of other passages could be quoted to show that Locke, in spite of occasional inconsistencies, held the view that changes in the amount of money were bound to affect prices.

The greatest inconsistency in regard to the quantity theory occurs in Locke's application of it to international prices. He had to reconcile his quantity theory with his mercantilist desire for an export surplus which would bring in treasure. Like Petty, he brought himself to say that any quantity of money might be enough to carry on the trade of a country; yet he emphasized even more than Petty had done that it was desirable that England should have more money than her trade rivals. His way out was ingenious. Because countries traded with one another, he said, the amounts of money they needed were no longer a matter of indifference. The prices of all goods in terms of bullion must be the same in all countries. If, however, a country had less money than others its prices would be lower. It would, therefore, be forced to sell cheap and buy dear, a state of affairs which all mercantilists dreaded. Locke is thus led by different reasoning to a position not unlike that of Malynes, and one which had already been abandoned by Mun.[4]

But these mercantilist vagaries are unimportant compared with the chief use which Locke made of the quantity theory of money. On the problem of interest his position was clear. He avoided the errors of

1 J. Locke, *Some Considerations of the Consequences of the Lowering of Interest and Raising the Value of Money* (1692), p. 48 and *passim*.
2 ibid., p. 44.
3 ibid., p. 70.
4 ibid., p. 76.

Child and Culpepper and regarded interest as a consequence, and not as a cause, of the amount of money seeking employment. North expressed this view more clearly still. The rate of interest, he said, would fail if there were more lenders than borrowers. A low rate of interest did not make trade; on the contrary, with an increase in trade the volume of money (stock) would increase and the rate of interest would fall.[1] He went even farther and adopted Mun's view of the distribution of the precious metals through international trade. Whatever the amount of money brought from foreign countries or mined at home, anything in excess of the requirements of trade was nothing more than an ordinary commodity to be treated as such. This view shows again North's freedom from mercantilist superstition.

The importance of Locke and North lies in the social and political significance of their attitude towards rent and interest. Their economic theories were not the result of a deliberate attack upon the landed interests (this was not as yet an important issue); but taken in conjunction with Locke's whole political philosophy they show a change in outlook which was to have great significance later. Although the produce from land was regarded as the only form in which a surplus could appear, and although interest was, analytically, derived from rent, the conclusions were unfavourable to the landowners. Their net effect was to undermine still farther the claim to special status made by landed property and to help in the creation of private property *per se* as an institution of capitalism. Moreover, the attack upon the limitation of the rate of interest was to the disadvantage of the landowners to whom a low rate of interest meant a high rate of capitalization of their rents, i.e. high land values. We shall shortly find a similar development, though in a somewhat different form, in the work of the physiocrats.

Of the remaining writers John Law is more famous as a business man than as an economist. But he made one contribution to the theory of money which deserves mention, because it contains the beginnings of an idea which was to be developed by certain monetary theorists. Law did not, as has sometimes been supposed, believe that paper money was equivalent to metallic money. He did, however, share the mercantilist belief that money possessed an active power and that a good supply of it was necessary in order to create employment. His main contribution to mercantilist thought was to depreciate reliance on an export surplus (created by import prohibitions) for obtaining a good

[1] D. North, *Discourses upon Trade*, p. 4.

supply of money. In its place, he suggested the issue of paper money, a proposal which was often, though less consistently, made at the time and which Law was able to put into practice with disastrous results.[1] As a good mercantilist he desired the state to have a stock of treasure, and he hoped that his notes would take the place of metallic money in the transactions of the public and that bullion would then accumulate in the state's treasury. The inflation in which his policy resulted was one of the severest of modern times; and it caused, together with Law's own ruin, the destruction of many speculative industrial ventures. It was Law's fortuitous merit that he contributed to the creation of those conditions which inspired physiocratic thought. For the only sort of property which appeared to have remained intact during the post-inflationary slump was land. This fact, together with the subsequent increase and improvement of agricultural enterprise, explains much of the trend of thought of the French economists of the eighteenth century.

Law has also been claimed as the founder of a subjective theory of value, with special reference to the value of money.[2] He definitely rejected the idea that money had an imaginary value. Nothing had any value, he argued, except for the use to which one put it. The same was true of the money commodity, even in relation to its monetary uses. The service which it rendered as money was no different from its other services or from the service of any other commodity.[3] With this theory Law becomes a forerunner of the Austrian school.

Although David Hume's fame rests mainly on his work as a philosopher, he is also well-known by his work in economic theory. In recent years the tendency has even arisen to regard him as the most important of the pre-Smithian economists. This may be due partly to the greater emphasis which has been given to his friendship with Adam Smith and to the more searching analysis of Smith's own writings which recent editorial work that also covers his correspondence (including that with Hume) has encouraged. Certainly, Hume's own *Treatise of Human Nature*, which he regarded as 'capital or centre' for the study of the social sciences, bears a strong intellectual resemblance

1 Cf. E. F. Heckscher, *Mercantilism*, vol. ii, pp. 234–6.
2 L. Mises, 'Die Stellung des Geldes im Kreise der wirtschaftlichen Güter' in *Wirtschaftstheorie der Gegenwart*, vol. ii (1932), p. 310.
3 J. Law, 'Considérations sur le numéraire et le commerce' in *Économistes financièrs du XVIIIième siècle* (ed. Daire, 1851), pp. 447 *sqq*.

to Smith's *Theory of Moral Sentiments*. Hume's discussion of the well-springs of human action is used, as it is in Smith's *The Wealth of Nations*, in the elaboration of the economic analysis. In his *Political Discourses* (1752), he included a number of economic essays of which *Of Money*, *Of Interest*, *Of Commerce*, and *Of the Balance of Trade* are the most important. They are all clearly written and often contain an excellent summary and synthesis of the ideas of his predecessors. In that respect, however, Cantillon's *Essai sur la nature du commerce en général*, published in 1755, but written probably over twenty years previously, is superior.

As an original thinker in the economic field Hume cannot be regarded as highly as in the field of philosophy. Sometimes he repeated mercantilist errors which had already been discarded and which certainly did not reappear in Adam Smith. His praise of the merchants as 'one of the most useful races of men' and as the motive force of production sounds strange after the writings of Petty, Locke and North.[1] Occasionally he praised the uses of money in stimulating trade and urged the desirability of treasure. Yet he adopted and emphasized Locke's view that money was only a symbol and that the amount which a nation possessed was of no importance. On the quantity theory of money he based the belief that the balance of trade argument was wrong, because the movements of specie would affect prices and therefore merchandise trade. The balance of trade of a country could not be permanently favourable or unfavourable. In the long run a balance would be established in accordance with the relative economic conditions of the countries concerned. Hume therefore ranged himself on the side of the free-traders; but his advocacy of free trade was no stronger than that of North.[2]

Hume's most interesting contributions to economic thought relate to money, prices, and interest. He revealed in his views a mixture of arguments that both supported and opposed Locke. In his theory of money and in the view that prices were determined by the amount of money, he followed and was even more consistent than Locke; in the theory of interest, on the other hand, he opposed him in certain

1 D. Hume, 'Political Discourses' in *Essays, Moral, Political, and Literary* (ed. T. H. Green and T. H. Grose, 1875), vol. i, p. 324.
2 Marx claims that Hume's statements on all these points were only repeating the views expressed earlier by Vanderlint in *Money answers all things* (1734) (*Anti-Dühring*, p. 254). I have not been able to check this assertion which Marx uses to disparage Hume; but it seems, in any case, irrelevant to an assessment of Hume.

respects. Like Locke, he regarded the value of money as fictitious only. Money represented commodities, and its value in the process of exchange was determined by the relation between its quantity and the quantity of goods for which it was to exchange. It followed that changes in the volume of circulating money would affect the prices of goods. Hume had in mind the great changes in prices caused by the increased output of precious metals from the newly discovered American mines. But he drew no distinction between changes in the value of the money commodity itself and changes in the exchange relationship between money and goods caused by an increased volume of circulating money. His view of money led him to believe that the prices of commodities would always be proportioned to the quantity of money. The absolute quantity of the latter did not therefore matter: a point which he demonstrated in a celebrated illustration.[1]

Nevertheless, he thought that changes in the quantity of money were of importance, since they could alter the habits of people. Prices might not change if the changes in the amount of money were accompanied by alterations in habits which affected the volume of trade and the demand for money. If, however, these rose following an increase in money, there would be beneficial effects because industry would be stimulated. On this point Hume's analysis was particularly lucid. In tracing the path which an increased amount of money would travel and the gradual manner in which it would affect prices, he developed a theory which was later used by many economists.

Increases in the quantity of money were only beneficial owing to the time-lag with which their effects appeared. 'It is only in this interval or intermediate situation, between the acquisition of money and rise of prices, that the increasing quantity of gold and silver is favourable to industry.' Prices of different goods are affected in turn and the increase of money will 'quicken the diligence of every individual, before it encrease the price of labour'.[2] In other words, Hume described what Keynes later called a *profit inflation*, which was taking place at the expense of labour.

In his essay *Of Interest* Hume began by stating the well-accepted doctrine that a low rate of interest was the surest sign of the flourishing state of a country's trade. But having paid his respect to the doctrine of Culpepper and Child, he went on to show, as Petty, Locke,

---

1 D. Hume, 'Political Discourses', *Essays, Moral, Political, and Literary*, vol. i, p. 333.
2 ibid., pp. 313–14.

and North had done, that a low rate of interest was not a cause but an effect. He joined them, therefore, in opposing state regulation of interest. But he went farther than Locke by rejecting the view that a low rate of interest was the result of an abundance of money, although he admitted that both occurred together. Among the factors which determined the rate of interest he distinguished first of all, as North had already done, the supply and demand of borrowers and lenders. A high rate of interest would, he thought, be caused by 'a great demand for borrowing' and 'little riches to supply that demand'. Both these were in their turn the results of a small amount of industry and commerce. Following North's view of the profit-creating quality of capital, Hume added a third determinant of the rate of interest: the profits arising from commerce. Profits and interest he regarded as interdependent. 'The low profits of merchandise induce the merchants to accept more willingly of a low interest.' On the other hand, 'no man will accept at low profits, where he can have high interest'; and low profits and low interest were both the result of great commerce.

Although he repeated that land was the source of all useful things, Hume showed, as Adam Smith did after him, that he had little love for the landed interest. He pointed out that landowners who received incomes without any exertion of their own were inclined to be extravagant; and that they would diminish rather than increase the amount of available capital, thus helping to raise the rate of interest. The commercial classes, on the other hand, were constantly working in the interest of the nation by creating both an abundance of capital and low profits. 'Among merchants, there is the same overplus of misers above prodigals, as, among the possessors of the land, there is the contrary.' For his lucrative employment will give the merchant a passion for gain and he will know 'no such pleasure as that of seeing the daily encrease of his fortune'. Commerce, then, creates frugality, helps accumulation and increases the number of lenders. At the same time a highly developed commerce produces competition: 'There must arise rivalships among the merchants'; and this diminishes profits and consequently interest.[1]

1 D. Hume, 'Political Discourses', *Essays, Moral, Political, and Literary*, vol. i, pp. 320–30. Many of Hume's views on interest are also to be found in an anonymous publication, *An Essay on the governing causes of the natural rate of interest: wherein the sentiments of Sir William Petty asnd Mr Locke on that head are considered*, which appeared in 1750, two years before Hume's essays. Marx attributes it to one J. Massie, without, however, giving any documentation. Karl Marx, *Theorien über den Mehrwert*, vol. i, pp.23 *sqq.*

Whatever his merits as an original thinker, Hume's place as one of the foremost exponents of the new economy is clearly established. His views on the landed interest and his recognition of self-interest and the desire for accumulation as the driving forces of economic activity in his time helped to consolidate the forces that were on the point of achieving economic supremacy and had already gained much political power.

## Cantillon; Steuart

Richard Cantillon's *Essai sur la nature du commerce en général* (1755)[1] is the most systematic statement of economic principles, before the *Wealth of Nations*. Since its rediscovery by Jevons its prestige has steadily risen until there is now a danger that the justifiable pride of his foster-parents may have given Cantillon too high rather than too low a place in the history of economic theory. It must be emphasized, however that Cantillon was not only responsible for a lucidly written and well-planned treatise, and for elegant reformulations of ideas already in existence, but that he also made some original contributions on individual points of economic analysis.

The *Essai* begins with a definition of land as the source of wealth, labour as the power which produces it, and all material goods as its constituents. It goes on to discuss the economic structure, wages, value, population, and money. The second part of the book is taken up mainly with problems of money, exchange, and interest; and the third part deals with foreign trade, the mechanism of the foreign exchanges, banking, and credit. It is in the last two parts that Cantillon excels in original analysis and description. For it is here that he is able to combine his insight into economic principles with his own commercial experience and to write sentences which can take their place with any modern work on these subjects. He has none of the difficulties about the mechanism of foreign payments which had troubled Locke. If a state, he says, has an export surplus for any considerable time and is drawing specie from other countries, 'the circulation will become more considerable there ... money will be more plentiful there, and

---

1 An excellent reprint edited by H. Higgs and containing an English translation and articles on Cantillon and his work was published by the Royal Economic Society in 1931. All subsequent notes on Cantillon refer to this edition.

consequently Land and Labour will gradually become dearer there'.[1] This will at once redress the balance of trade.

The analysis of the effects of an increase in the circulating medium is more fully worked out than in Hume. Assuming an increased gold output from the mines, Cantillon is able to show how the benefits of the increased purchasing power that has become available are distributed. The owners, smelters, refiners, and other workers will be the first to be able to increase their demand for food, clothes, and manufactured goods. The suppliers of these commodities will in their turn be able to increase their expenses. But the share of commodities that goes to other people in the state must of necessity be diminished, because they do not participate at first in the wealth of the mines. The path of rising prices and the ensuing changes in the distribution of wealth are then carefully traced; and even international effects are not ignored. Altogether, this argument remains an excellent demonstration of an important aspect of monetary theory.[2] Cantillon was also aware that the effects of an increase of the money commodity and those of paper money were only apparently the same. Ultimately an abundance of 'fictitious' money would vanish 'at the first gust of discredit' and would precipitate disorder.[3]

On the question of foreign exchanges, too, Cantillon was able to express clearly the principles which underlie economic practice. He showed better than any previous writer the relation between merchandise trade, speculation and specie movements; and he showed also their interaction with exchange rates and price-levels in the mechanism of international payments. Particularly lucid was the explanation of the causes which raise or lower the exchange from parity and the way in which such movements can be foreseen and discounted.[4]

The central questions of value, wages, and price are contained in part one of Cantillon's *Essai*. His treatment of these is not always strikingly new. He owes more to his predecessors, and he gets less far ahead of them than he does in other matters. In particular, the analysis of value lacks some consistency; though it is perhaps for that very reason that Cantillon may be taken as one of the early representatives of the eclecticism which became a characteristic of English economic thought. His theory of value is in origin a labour theory but it is

1 R. Cantillon, *Essai sur la nature du commerce en général*, pp. 157–9.
2 ibid., pp. 163–7.
3 ibid., p. 311.
4 ibid., pp. 257–9.

transformed into a cost-of-production theory and it also contains some admixture of a supply and demand theory. The first strand of thought is derived largely from Petty, the second from Locke.

We have seen that Cantillon repeats in different words Petty's theory of the origin of wealth. In chapter x of the *Essai* he goes on to develop a theory which is summarized in the title of that chapter, 'The Price and Intrinsic Value of a Thing in general is the measure of the Land and Labour which enter into its Production.'[1] The meaning of the subsequent analysis amounts to this: if two goods are produced by the same amount of land and labour of the same quality, they will have equal value. But the proportion in which land and labour will determine the value of particular goods will vary. In some cases – a watch-spring, for example – 'Labour makes up nearly all the value'. In others – for example, the price of 'a Wood which it is proposed to cut down' – land is the chief determinant.[2]

Besides making cost of production (wages of labour plus cost of material) determine value, Cantillon also distinguishes between the intrinsic value and the fluctuating price at which goods are sold in the market. A rich man who has spent much money on beautifying his estate will not necessarily get its intrinsic value when he comes to sell it. Nor will farmers get the expense of the land and labour which have entered into the production of corn if they have produced more than is necessary for consumption. The ensuing excess of supply over demand will depress the market price below the intrinsic value. Intrinsic values never alter. But because it is impossible always to apportion production among the different commodities in perfect harmony with consumption, variations in market prices will occur.

The supply and demand forces are again mentioned in connection with the problem of money. Cantillon agrees with Locke's quantity theory, but corrects it by pointing out that commodities destined for export must be excluded when the mass of commodities is compared with the volume of circulating money. He does, however, disagree with Locke's view of the value of money. Like Law, he rejects the definition which gives money an imaginary value. It is true, he said, that common consent has given gold and silver value; but so it has to everything which cannot be regarded as an absolute necessity of life. The precious metals have a value which is determined in exactly the same way as that

1 R. Cantillon, *Essai sur la nature du commerce en général*, p. 27.
2 ibid., p. 29.

of any other commodity, namely, by the land and labour which enter into their production.[1]

Cantillon develops this point at some length. He gives a theory of the value of money, and of money's function as a measure of value, which is based on the labour theory of value. 'The intrinsic Value of Metals', he said, 'is like everything else proportionable to the Land and Labour that enters into their production', though their market value, like that of other goods, might vary according to supply and demand.[2] As for acting as a measure of value, money 'must correspond in fact and reality in terms of Land and Labour to the articles exchanged for it'.[3]

Like Petty, Cantillon was troubled by his dual source of value; and he proceeded to inquire, in chapter xi, whether 'some relation might be found between the value of Labour and that of the produce of the Land'.[4] This inquiry into the Par, an expression taken from Petty, resolves itself into a discussion on wages which leads to results somewhat similar to those of Petty. The clue to the Par is to be found in the amount of subsistence required to produce a given amount of labour. From that, the amount of land which has to be allotted to this purpose can be deduced, and an equivalence between land and labour is thus established. Cantillon uses a number of examples covering slaves, serfs, craftsmen, and others; and he concludes that the intrinsic value of labour is found in the amount of land needed to support the labourers' sustenance *plus* an equal amount for the rearing of two children up to the age at which they can work. Cantillon speaks of two children, since he accepts Halley's calculations that half the children that are born die before the age of seventeen.

Cantillon's argument in this chapter is as clear as any formulations of the classical theory of wages. It possesses also the distinction of having been quoted by Adam Smith.[5] To complete Cantillon's theory of wages it is necessary to add that he anticipated much of Smith's reasoning on the difference of wages in different occupations.[6]

---

1 R. Cantillon, *Essai sur la nature du commerce en général*, p. 113.
2 ibid., p. 97.
3 ibid., p. 111.
4 ibid., p. 31 *sqq.*
5 Adam Smith, *Wealth of Nations*, ed. W. R. Scott (1925), vol. i, p. 69.
6 R. Cantillon, *Essai sur la nature du commerce en général*, pp. 19–21.

Finally, he can be said to have anticipated ideas on population which were made famous by Malthus.[1]

The last of this series of immediate forerunners of Adam Smith is Sir James Steuart. Although he is the most voluminous writer of them all, he adds comparatively little to the body of doctrine. In some respects he represents a step back to the mercantilists, though in others, notably in the theory of money, he is in advance of Hume. Steuart's main work, his *Principles of Political Economy*, published in 1767, bears a title which has become the standard one for comprehensive treatises, although Steuart was not the first to use the term 'political economy'. It is not, however, a comprehensive work and it falls far below Cantillon's *Essai* as a systematic exposition of the subject.

The mercantilist remnants in Steuart's thought concern mainly the origin of profit, or the surplus. Steuart still spoke of a profit which arises in exchange, i.e. when a commodity is sold above its value. But he went further and admitted that such profit did not really create new wealth. He distinguished, therefore, between positive profit and relative profit. The latter represented only 'a vibration of the balance of wealth between parties'; it did not add to the existing volume of stock. Positive profit, on the other hand, did not cause any one any loss; it arose from a general increase in labour, industry, and skill, and it added to the public good.[2]

He carried a similar distinction into his explanation of value. Developing a cost-of-production theory of value, he distinguished between the real value of commodities and the profit upon alienation obtained in their sale. Real value was determined by three factors: first, the amount of it which a workman could on an average produce in a given period of time; secondly, by 'the value of the workman's subsistence and necessary expense, both for supplying his personal wants, and providing the instruments belonging to his profession'; and thirdly, by the 'value of the materials, that is the first matter employed by the workman'. Given these three amounts, the real value of a good is determined. Anything above this is the profit of the manufacturer and depends on the conditions of supply and demand.[3] The

---

1 *Essai sur la nature du commerce en général*, pp. 67 and 83.
2 *The Works, Political, Metaphysical, and Chronological of the late Sir James Steuart* (edited by his son, Sir James Steuart, 6 volumes, 1803), vol. i, pp. 275–6. An excellent new edition was published in 1966, edited by Professor Andrew Skinner.
3 ibid., pp. 244–6.

significance of this analysis is twofold. In the first place it makes the manufacturer's profit arise only in exchange and thus represents a consistent application of the mercantilist theory of the surplus. In the second place, it leads Steuart to develop a supply and demand theory of price which was very elaborate for his time.

This theory[1] can be summarized as follows. Prices are in equilibrium when demand and work balance. (Steuart's own theory of real value shows that he thought of the harmony between market prices and intrinsic value in the same terms as Cantillon.) This balance may be disturbed and the price will vary. Steuart enumerated some of the factors which would cause discrepancies between supply and demand, among which the purchasing power of the buyers and the degree of competition were the most important. He explained the mechanism of 'double competition' which would be brought into play by discrepancies between work and demand. If demand was lower than supply, sellers' competition would reduce the price, destroy profits, and even cause losses. If demand exceeded supply, buyers' competition would raise prices and profits. In the case of merchants engaged in regular trade this mechanism would work sufficiently well to make real value effective, and only variations in profits would occur. But bigger changes must not be allowed to affect equilibrium; in these, as in many other cases, Steuart was a firm believer in the desirability and efficacy of state intervention.

Steuart also tended to mercantilist views in the theory of money, and his statements on the value of money and the balance of payments are often obscure and contradictory. He was nevertheless able to correct a number of errors in the analysis of Locke and Hume. In particular, he avoided their mechanical juxtaposition of the mass of commodities and the quantity of money in circulation. He took up the view, which had been expressed before by Petty, that the circulation of a country could only absorb a definite quantity of money. Money, he thought, was needed within a country for two purposes: to pay the debts one owed and to buy the things one needed. The state of trade and manufacture and the habits of the people determined the demand for money; this a given quantity could satisfy. Following North, he said that any metal over and above that required for monetary purposes would be hoarded or converted into plate. Should, on the other hand, the amount of gold

1 *Works of Sir James Steuart*, p. 289.

and silver be insufficient to sustain a country's circulation the difference would be made up by symbolic money.[1] The result is that
'whatsoever be the quantity of money in a nation, in correspondence
with the rest of the world, there never can remain, in circulation, but
the quantity nearly proportional to the consumption of the rich and to
the labour and industry of the poor inhabitants'.[2]

To give the true picture of Steuart's position it is necessary to add a
few words about his views on the wider issues of economics. Steuart's
attitude to the economic process was old-fashioned and somewhat
reactionary. His work breathes little of that air of unbridled self-
interest and freedom of trade that was common at the time. But it is
perhaps because of this attitude that Steuart was able to give an
interesting account of the development of capitalism. He began with
the origin of society (this incidentally led him to an anticipation of the
Malthusian theory of population somewhat similar to that of Cantillon)
and traced its structure through changes in methods of production and
relations of classes. He stressed the fact that labour was the only
source of an increase in the supply of the means of subsistence and
developed the concept of an agricultural surplus, the division of classes
and rise of industry. Finally, he brought out clearly the difference
between particular forms of labour which created specific use-values,
and labour as a social abstraction which created exchange-value. He
called industry that form of labour which by alienation created a
universal equivalent.[3]

## The Physiocrats

The body of economic theory to which the name 'physiocracy' is given
developed in France in the eighteenth century. Although based on
different experience and put in a different form, its effects on the
development of economic thought were very similar to those of the
English economists discussed above. The two contributions are united
into a single system in Adam Smith. With the physiocrats we enter the
era of schools and systems in economic thought; and it is not surprising to find that they have been the subject of a great many studies.

1 *Works of Sir James Steuart*, pp. 165–6.
2 ibid., pp. 403–8.
3 ibid., Book I, *passim*.

It is unlikely that an inquirer will today be able to discover any hitherto neglected aspects of their teaching, or to add anything of importance to what has already been said about individual points in their system. What remains is to give a brief summary of that system and to assess its significance.

There has been some misunderstanding about the essential qualities of physiocratic thought. Adam Smith criticized their emphasis on agriculture and to this day the merits of the physiocrats are often depreciated by the same criticism. Again, the relation between the general political philosophy of Quesnay and Turgot and their specifically economic ideas is often wrongly stated. The belief in the natural order, which was the characteristic of their philosophy, is either left unconnected with their analysis of the production and circulation of wealth; or it is regarded as the underlying principle on which their economic doctrines were built. Only recently has it been suggested that physiocracy was a rationalization of certain specific political aims;[1] and whatever truth there may be in psychological or sociological explanations of this kind, it certainly appears that the political philosophy of the physiocrats was a logical development of their economic ideas.

The physiocrats share with the more advanced pre-classical English economists, such as Petty and Cantillon, the merit of having finally discarded the mercantilist belief that wealth and its increase were due to exchange. They transferred to the sphere of production the power of creating wealth and the surplus which might be available for accumulation. The central point in their analysis was the search for this surplus, the celebrated *produit net*. Having discovered its origin in a manner which was an advance on the English mercantilists, they went on to add, in Quesnay's 'Tableau œconomique', an analysis of its circulation among the different classes of society.

The starting-point is a division of labour into two classes, that which is productive and that which is sterile. The former consists of labour which is capable of creating a surplus, i.e. something over and above the wealth which it consumes in order to be capable of producing. All other labour is sterile. This division is to be found in the whole classical system; and the definition of what did and what did not

[1] Norman J. Ware, 'The Physiocrats: A Study in Economic Rationalisation' in *American Economic Review*, vol. xxxi, pp. 607–19. See also an earlier analysis of the social implications of physiocracy by Marx, *Theorien über den Mehrwert*, vol. i, pp. 33–49.

constitute productive labour was one of the most important subjects discussed by Smith and Ricardo. The physiocrats tried to discover the actual form of productive labour. They had no clear idea of the distinction between use-value and exchange value; and they thought of the surplus entirely in terms of differences between use-values which had been consumed and those which had been produced. The *produit net* was not a surplus of social wealth in the abstract (exchange-value), but of concrete material wealth of useful goods. It was this technological approach which led the physiocrats to single out one particular branch of production as the only really productive one.

The difference between goods produced and goods consumed is most easily seen in agriculture. Here the amount of food consumed by the labourer *plus* what is used as seed is on the average less than the amount of produce raised from the ground. It is the simplest and most obvious form of surplus. Smith and Ricardo were able to show the appearance of a surplus in industry as well. But there the process was complicated by exchange, and therefore by the problem of exchange-value. The physiocrats concentrated on agriculture and thus were able to ignore the problem of exchange-value altogether.

By adopting this approach, the physiocrats did not achieve as penetrating an analysis of the conditions which made the creation of a surplus possible as they otherwise might have done. Clearly, a surplus product appears only at a certain stage of man's development, i.e. when human beings can wrest from nature something more than their bare subsistence. But whereas Steuart had proceeded to show not only the origin of an agricultural surplus but also the development on the basis of it of industry, the physiocrats did not go so far. They realized that the number of those engaged in industry and trade depended ultimately on the amount of subsistence which those who worked on the land could raise above their own requirements. In other words, they understood that that degree of productivity of labour which made a surplus possible made its first appearance in agriculture. But because they did not go beyond agriculture they regarded this surplus as a gift, attributable not to the productivity of labour but to the productivity of nature.

However, this very limitation implies an advance. It shows the physiocrats as the first school of economic thinkers to employ consistently the scientific methods of isolation and abstraction; though they themselves were unconscious of this contribution which they were making to the methods of economic analysis. And as we shall see, they managed to surpass their own limitations in their discussion of the process of circulation. On the basis which they laid, later economists were able to build, notably Smith and Ricardo, who could use consciously, as an analytical tool, what in the hands of the physiocrats had been the whole content of the discussion.

The analysis of the circulation of the *produit net* between the different classes of society forms the most spectacular part of physiocratic doctrine. The attempt to show the whole process of circulation in the simplified form of a table is one of the earliest examples of the rigorous application of a scientific method to economic phenomena. The genius which inspired Quesnay's 'Tableau œconomique' (first printed in 1758 and discussed and popularized by a great number of other economists) was at once recognized by the more discriminating thinkers of the time. It was regarded by many as the most penetrating piece of economic thinking to date; and Mirabeau the elder went even so far as to class it with the invention of writing and of money as one of the most important discoveries of the human mind. The 'Tableau' has often been misunderstood and is still sometimes regarded as nothing but a literary curiosity.[1] But given the basis of the physiocratic system and the method of abstraction which Quesnay employed, it is perfectly simple and logical.

The 'Tableau' is based on the existence of a certain social structure, the implication of which we shall discuss later. The land is owned by landlords, but cultivated by tenant farmers, who thus become the really productive class. The *produit net* which they create has to serve not only for the satisfaction of their own needs above their subsistence, but also for the needs of the proprietors of the land (including the king, the Church, the public servants, and all others who are dependent upon the income of the landowners), and for those of the sterile class (the artisans, merchants, etc.). The 'Tableau' sets out to show two things: first, how the *produit net* circulates between the three classes; and,

---

1 e.g. A. Gray, *The Development of Economic Doctrine*, p. 106. Gide and Rist give a good account of the doctrine. Interesting analyses of the 'Tableau' can also be found in Marx, *Theorien über den Mehrwert*, vol i, pp. 85–125, and Engels, *Anti-Dühring*, pp. 263–70. It should, however, be noted that Marx's knowledge of the physiocratic literature seems to have been very limited. Indeed it is likely that he was only familiar with the first volume of the Daire edition of the works of the physiocrats and relied a good deal on a second-hand source, i.e. Blanqui's *Histoire de l'économic politique en Europe* (1875). For an interesting study of the various graphical presentations of the 'Tableau' see R. Suaudeau, *Les Réprésentations Figurées des Physiocrates* (1947).

secondly, how it is reproduced each year. The 'Tableau' ignores circulation within each class and it assumes constant prices and reproduction each year of the same *produit net*.

A very simplified account of the analysis in Quesnay's 'Tableau' would be as follows: we start with an annual gross product of five thousand million livres. Of this, two thousand million are at once deducted in kind as the necessary expenses of reproduction (the farmer's food, the seed, etc.). The *produit net* is three thousand million, of which we assume two thousand million to consist of food and one thousand million of the raw materials of manufacture. In addition to this *produit net* in kind the farmers also hold the total amount of the nation's money, say two thousand million. How they have obtained this, the subsequent development of the process of circulation will show. The proprietors hold nothing, but have a claim upon the farmers for rent to the amount of two thousand million livres; while the sterile class possesses two thousand million livres' worth of manufactured goods produced in the preceding period.

The farmers now pay the proprietors their two thousand million livres as rent. The proprietors buy one thousand million livres' worth of food from the farmers, who thus receive back half the amount of money they had paid out. The proprietors then spend the second half of their rental revenue on the purchase of manufactured goods from the sterile class, who spend the money thus received on buying food from the farmers. The farmers now spend one thousand million livres in buying manufactured goods from the sterile class, who send the money back in return for raw materials. The process is now completed. The farmers are left with two thousand million livres in money, which will serve to set the whole process going again in the next period. The food part of the *produit net* has gone to the proprietors and to the sterile class, the raw material part to the latter alone. The manufactured goods originally held by the sterile class have been divided among proprietors and farmers. And in return the sterile class has one thousand million livres' worth of food and the same amount of raw materials, which combine to create for the next period manufactured goods to the value of two thousand million.

Quesnay's own 'Analyse du Tableau œconomique'[1] (and even more

1 F. Quesnay, *Œuvres Économiques* (ed. A. Oncken, 1888), pp. 305–78. A very handsome facsimile edition, with translation, new material, and notes was edited by Marguerite Kuczynski and Ronald L. Week for the Royal Economic Society and the American Economic Association in 1972.

so the above summary of it) is a very simplified account of the process of circulation and reproduction. But within its limits it is consistent and lucid. It never departs from its fundamental postulate, that agriculture alone can yield a surplus; and it shows how the surplus is distributed. Part of it (in the 'Tableau' it is one thousand million livres which the farmers spend on manufactured goods) is kept by the farmers themselves. The other part goes to the proprietors and to the sterile class. The significance of the appropriation by the farmer we will discuss presently. As for the sterile class, they are given a share in the surplus product merely because they are servants of the producers and proprietors. They cannot create any value themselves; they only transform the value created in agriculture into manufactured goods, which are consumed in addition to the necessities of life.

Although the 'Tableau' operates with sums of money and purchases and sales, it is not in effect concerned with the process of exchange. Its essence, behind the monetary form, is a circulation in kind; and its main concern is with the distribution and reproduction of the use-values of the *produit net*. The physiocrats started a train of thought which was a powerful stimulus to the development of a labour theory of value and surplus-value. They did not, however, develop such a theory of value themselves. What attention they gave to the problem of exchange-value and price produced results of an altogether different character. Thus although one of their contributions finds its continuation in Smith and Ricardo, and, in a distorted form, in Marx, the other leads to the supply-and-demand and utility theories of value.

Quesnay himself, the founder of the school, did not treat the problem of value in a systematic way. He held a cost-of-production theory of price, as far as manufactured goods were concerned. We have already seen that he regarded manufacture as incapable of creating new values; it only added up existing values. When manufactured goods were exchanged, he said (consistently with his theory of the *produit net*), only equivalents were exchanged. No profit (or surplus of value) could arise in exchange. The natural price of manufactured goods was explained by a number of other prices: those of the expenses (*dépenses* or *frais*) of the producers and of the merchants who brought them to market. At the same time competition among buyers and sellers would settle the right amount of expenses which producers would incur. Competition was a very important factor in the explanation of price; it settled a price which was independent of buyers and sellers. Although these were actuated by self-interest and were trying to buy cheap or sell dear, the interplay of their actions compelled them to sacrifice some of their interests. Neither could have their own way completely.[1]

The role of competition was, however, developed entirely in relation to the subjective factors in the minds of buyers and sellers. The emphasis on the power of competition in determining the price was designed to answer the problem which arose from a consideration of the estimates of buyers and sellers. Quesnay admitted that the valuations of individuals had something to do with exchange. They provided the motive for exchange but did not influence the terms on which exchange took place. These were settled by a sort of general estimate independent of the estimates of the individual parties.

Turgot, who was the most mature, and politically the most important, of the physiocrats, went ever farther in introducing a certain dualism into the theory of value and price. He did not depart from the main physiocratic tenet that only labour in agriculture could create a surplus. But in at least one of his writings he gave an important place to subjective elements in the determination of exchange-value.[2] He made a list of the different factors which an individual took into account in forming a judgement about a particular good. Its ability to satisfy a want, the ease with which it could be obtained, its scarcity, and other considerations would together form what he called the *valeur estimative* of a good. From this exchange-value was derived. Turgot called it *valeur appréciative* and said that it was determined by the average of the *valeurs estimatives* of the parties to the exchange.

Turgot provided a somewhat tenuous link between this theory of exchange-value and the theory of the function of labour. For he said that the individual would apply portions of his labour to obtain the goods he needed according to his valuation of them. On the other hand, this evaluation was itself 'le compte qu'il se rend à lui-même de la portion de sa peine et de son temps, ... qu'il peut employer à la recherche de l'objet évalué'.[3] This appears to be circular reasoning; but it bears some resemblance to the relation between subjective valuation and cost of production which was to be developed by the subjectivist school in the theory of opportunity cost. The apparent inconsistencies in the explanation of value by the physiocrats were due

1 F. Quesnay, 'Dialogue sur les Travaux des Artisans', *Œuvrtes Économiques*, pp. 538 *sqq.*
2 A.-R.-J. Turgot, 'Valeurs et Monnaies' in *Œuvres de Turgot* (ed. M. E. Daire, 1844), vol. i, p. 75 *sqq.*
3 ibid., p. 83.

to the fact that, although they made labour the exclusive creator of the surplus (nature being its source), they thought of value in this connection as use-value only. Thus when they came to consider exchange they were forced to adopt a different explanation.

The theory of exchange-value was, however, not the most important part of the physiocratic system. It was from the concept of the *produit net* that they drew both their political philosophy and their precepts for policy. Because agriculture was the only form of surplus, the mercantilist measures of Colbert, designed to foster industry, were useless. It was against these that the physiocrats raised their battle-cry of *laissez-faire, laissez-faire passer*. Industry created no values; it only transformed them. No regulation of this process of transformation could add anything to the wealth of the community. On the contrary, it was only likely to make production more cumbersome and less economical. Intervention in every form was, therefore, to go. Similarly in the sphere of taxation, the most powerful instrument of state intervention, industry and trade were to be freed from all contributions. The only branch of production on which taxes could rightly be levied was that which created value – agriculture. To tax industry was only to tax the land in a roundabout and therefore uneconomical way. A single tax on the land was the financial maxim of physiocracy.

These views were embodied in an elaborate system to which many books were devoted. Quesnay himself wrote one of its principal expositions.[1] The chief concept of that system was that of the 'natural order'. Human society, according to the physiocrats, was ruled by natural laws which could never be altered by the positive laws of statecraft. These laws, established by a benevolent Providence for the good of mankind, were so clearly in evidence that it should require only a little reflection to recognize them. Quesnay seems to have thought that reflection would not be enough, for he advocated that the natural order should be taught, with the 'Tableau' forming presumably an important part of the instruction. The essential aspects of the *natural order* were the right to enjoy the benefits of property, to exercise one's labour, and to have such freedom as was consistent with the freedom of others to follow their self-interest. The *natural order* was an anticipation of utilitarianism at a time when the economic and political conditions were not yet ripe for it. It is this fact which explains the contradictions of the physiocratic system, itself and of the theoretical

1 F. Quesnay, 'Le Droit naturel', *Œuvres Économiques*, pp. 359–77.

and practical conclusions that were drawn from it. There is an almost feudal air about the physiocratic attitude to land which is reinforced by their passionate defence of landed property. Yet because land was regarded as the only source of wealth, the practical conclusion was one which was against the landed interest – the single tax. This, together with the non-interventionist policy with which it was related, became a powerful help in the development of industry, although the physiocrats themselves never designed it for that purpose.

Even on the question of property the analysis made by the physiocrats was capable of being turned against their own political beliefs. Many of their supporters saw in the physiocrats only defenders of feudalism. Their views on landed property and their frequent defence of an enlightened despotism[1] endeared them to those who were fighting a rearguard action on behalf of feudalism. But when it came to the discussion of economic problems the physiocrats were already forced to look through capitalist glasses. For them the owner of the land had already become a capitalist who employed the labourer.

Particularly in the writings of Turgot is this development made clear and thereby the subsequent development of capitalist industry anticipated. He began with a consideration of the *produit net* in its most primitive form.[2] In a discussion which is very reminiscent of Steuart he showed that the surplus created by the cultivator of the soil was the only fund from which the other members of society could draw their subsistence. Once he had produced a surplus the cultivator could realize it by buying the labour of others. Those employed in industry became *stipendiés* of the cultivator.

The time comes, Turgot went on to say, when the *cultivateur-propriétaire* ceases to be the only one concerned in the appropriation of the *produit net*. Proprietors are separated from cultivators when all the available land has passed into private hands. Those who own no land must become hired labourers either to the *stipendiés* in industry or to the owners of the land. In the latter case the proprietors cease to cultivate their own land: the work is done for them by wage-labourers. The juxtaposition of capital and labour has now appeared in agricultural production and with it the problem of wages and profits. The

---

1 e.g. F. Quesnay, 'Maximes générales du gouvernement économique d'un royaume royale', *Œuvres Économiques*, pp. 329–37.
2 A.-R.-J. Turgot, 'Reflexions sur la Formation et la Distribution des Richesses' (1766), *Œuvres de Turgot*, vol. i, pp. 9 *sqq*.

wage of the labourer, said Turgot, will be determined by the subsistence he needs (the *strict nécéssaire* which occurs in physiocratic writings). But the bounty of nature will return to him more than that; and the surplus will become the proprietor's rent. It is out of this rent that accumulation takes place. Capital is created; and advances for the growth of industry and for the improvement of agriculture become habitual.

The physiocrats themselves were innocent of any desire to use this kind of analysis for the purpose of attacking the landed interest. But the analysis was capable of being used in that way. The practical effect of their teaching, like that of their English contemporaries, was, thus, to help in the further removal of the obstacles that stood in the way of capitalist industry. In retrospect the physiocrats must be given a high place among those who prepared the ground for the French Revolution.

# 4

# The Classical System

## *The Quality of Classicism*

The last quarter of the eighteenth century is full of events which seem
to herald the founding of a new era in economic and political organization. In the field of production it witnesses the beginning of the
Industrial Revolution, which was to open up vast possibilities of expansion to the recently established mode of industrial capitalism. The
partnership of Matthew Boulton and James Watt, concluded in 1775,
brought about a union between the captain of industry and the scientist
which may be taken as symbolical of a new alliance. A year later the
American Declaration of Independence brought to a close the exploitation of one of the most important colonial areas and withdrew a
powerful prop from the old colonial system on which so much of
mercantilist thought was built. In the same year was published the first
volume of Edward Gibbon's *Decline and Fall of the Roman Empire* and,
above all, *An Inquiry into the Nature and Causes of the Wealth of Nations*,
by a Scottish philosopher turned economist, which was destined to
become the *fons et origo* of economics for subsequent generations. And
the fate of what remained of medieval society was sealed a few years
later by the French Revolution.

We have already seen that the beginning of this new era could be
placed almost a hundred years earlier. Industrial capitalism is older
than the Industrial Revolution; mercantilist policy begins to wane some
time before the end of the eighteenth century; and at any rate in
England, the most advanced capitalist country, the political structure
had begun to change in accordance with the ideas of liberalism long
before the French Revolution released its stimulus for the forces of
liberalism everywhere. Economic theory too had acquired a new content and new methods long before Adam Smith appeared on the scene

to make it conscious of its own changing character.

Yet there is justification for the view that the fifty years around the turn of the century mark a profound social change. New forms of production, of social relations, of government and of social thought, which in their struggles against the old had been slow and often hesitant, were now advancing triumphantly; and because of their spectacular progress the earlier battles were easily forgotten. The reflections in the realm of ideas of economic and political changes show an even more striking difference than those changes themselves. Social thought becomes self-conscious; it shows a more complete awareness than hitherto of the quality of the social other which was being erected before its eyes. It becomes capable of seeing the whole structure of that order and the complex interrelation of its component parts. The individual social disciplines become integrated into a comprehensive social philosophy; and each one is itself systematized. Scattered fragments are collected, refined, and pieced together to make a body of doctrines possessing internal consistency.

In the realm of economic thought this process is clearly in evidence. What the century had so far produced had been confused and haphazard. There had been brilliant anticipations, such as North's defence of free trade. There had even been treatises which displayed a marked insight into the economic process, such as Cantillon's *Essai* and Steuart's *Principles*. There had been Petty, whose genius had succeeded in stating the central problem of value. And from the controversy on money and interest certain common views were arising. But in spite of all this the achievement was limited and much confusion remained. Petty's preoccupation was with public finance, and his order contributions were hidden beneath a mass of less important material. Steuart's title was a misnomer: he lacked the understanding of the inner laws of social processes. And even Cantillon's *Essai* was hardly systematic enough to present to the world a coherent picture of the economic mechanism.

It was the supreme achievement of Smith and Ricardo to bring order into the still chaotic state of economic inquiry. To this order the name of the classical system has been given. Different schools of thought among later economists have chosen this name for different reasons. Sometimes the term 'classical' is applied to the doctrines of the system in order to describe the unquestioned and widespread authority which they enjoyed. Sometimes it is used to add a special significance to the consequences in the realm of policy which flowed from these doctrines. Sometimes, again, the system is called classical in order to distinguish it from the critical schools (for example, the romantic) which developed after it and which to many economists signify a certain decadence.

If we were to summarize the distinguishing characteristics of the economic analysis contained in the *Wealth of Nations* or in Ricardo's *Principles*, we should have to put first the insight which it reveals into the economic mechanism of modern society. With great rigour the analysis lays bare the principles which underlie the working of the capitalist system, together with the historical development which produced it. To this Ricardo also added an attempt to discover the trend of the system's future development. Its second claim to distinction lies in the fact that it was the first to recognize explicitly that social phenomena, including their historical development, had laws of their own which could be discovered. It was this appreciation of an inner *Gesetzmässigkeit*, as compelling in the individualist capitalist economy as had been the outward forms of regulation of feudalism, which gives to the work of Smith and Ricardo its scientific imprint. That they were limited, as later critics have pointed out, in their technical analysis and in their views about the validity of the particular laws they had discovered does not diminish the greatness of their achievement. They showed to subsequent economists the need for a unified principle of explanation of economic phenomena which related each to the others. Building on the foundation of the physiocrats, they tried to give a complete picture of the economic process – abstract, it is true, yet containing the essence of reality. And even though parts of the picture had to be redrawn, the pattern remained.

It is not easy to define the chronological limits of the classical system. Provided that we bear in mind the spadework of the earlier eighteenth-century economists in England and of the physiocrats in France, we can make its starting-point coincide with the work of Adam Smith. The determination of its end is more difficult. Indeed, some economists would claim that it never ended and that its tradition has lived on through the work of the leaders of modern economics. Nevertheless it seems unwise to ignore entirely the change that comes over economic thought in England, the citadel of classicism, after the first two decades of the nineteenth century. It is true that the attempt made by Malthus to destroy the foundations of the Ricardian system failed and that the chief tenets of classical political economy continued to enjoy considerable authority. Those that were easily popularized quickly passed into the public consciousness. In England, and to a less extent in other countries, the general conditions were extremely favourable to the reception and survival of many of the classical ideas, and their influence on policy was for a time very great.

In the field of thought, however, signs of change began to appear, and James Mill's *Elements of Political Economy*, published in 1821, is the last expression of unquestioning faith in the Ricardian school. But already this work points to the impending dissolution of the system. After that, evidence of declining authority becomes more abundant. In England and in France economists reared in the classical tradition begin to be disturbed by real or imaginary contradictions in inherited doctrine and by some of its implications; and they begin to strike out on new paths. In both countries too, but especially in England, the influence of classical political economy makes itself felt in an unexpected quarter: the infant working-class movement; and, as a reaction, a powerful apologetic strain makes itself felt in the growth of an economic orthodoxy. Yet another new development, particularly striking in Germany, is a romantic reaction from classical teaching in which mercantilist theories show a sudden revival. For nearly half a century it is no longer possible to speak of a single school of economic thought which commands universal authority. It is only with the advent of the marginal utility theory in the seventies that some unification takes place and that it becomes possible once again to regard one doctrine as the most generally accepted. But even then authority is no longer unquestioned, nor is it universal. Its hold is secure only over academic thought and its impact upon policy cannot be compared with that of the classical theory.

The building up of the classical system was so much the work of two men that it seems best to concentrate entirely on their work in these pages. The only writer to be considered in this chapter besides Smith and Ricardo is Malthus, but only for that part of his work which entered into the classical tradition. We shall meet Malthus again in the next chapter as an important critic of some of the vital conclusions of Ricardo.

It may appear odd to make Smith and Ricardo jointly responsible for the founding of the classical school. When Smith published his chief economic work Ricardo was only four years old. It was forty-one years later (twenty-seven years after Smith's death) that Ricardo himself published a comprehensive treatise. Again, while Smith started as a philosopher, Ricardo came to economic thought as a successful business man who later turned politician. Although the definitive edition of Ricardo's works runs to ten volumes, his chief work is a slim book compared with Adam Smith's bulky treatise. Nothing could be more different than their plans, methods, or styles. Yet with all these differences, their agreements are so fundamental that their names must for ever remain linked in the history of economic thought.

## Adam Smith

*The Sources.* Adam Smith was born in 1723, the son of a Scottish Judge Advocate and Comptroller of Customs. He was educated at the universities of Glasgow and Oxford and became professor first of logic and then of moral philosophy at Glasgow. After thirteen years of academic teaching he travelled for two years in France as tutor to the young Duke of Buccleuch, from whom he afterwards received a substantial pension which enabled him to devote himself entirely to his writing. In 1778, however, he accepted an appointment as Commissioner of Customs, which he held for the remaining years of his life. He died in 1790.[1]

These chief facts of his life may provide some explanation of his method of approach to economic inquiry. Adam Smith was the first academic economist; and his career is not altogether different from that of many economists since then. From his time onwards most of the progress of economic thought is bound up with the work of academic teachers of the subject, many of whom had, like him, been philosophers. The academic influence on Adam Smith is seen in the much higher degree of systematic thinking which he was able to

---

1 Much was written and many conferences were held when the two hundred and fiftieth birthday of Adam Smith was celebrated in 1973 (see *inter alia* Roll, *The Wealth of Nations 1776–1976* in Lloyds Bank Review, January 1976, reprinted in *The Uses and Abuses of Economics* (1978)). On the occasion of the bicentenary of the publication of the *Wealth of Nations* a magisterial new edition of the works of Adam Smith (the Glasgow Edition 1976) was published. It runs to six volumes (of which *Wealth of Nations* itself covers two) and is edited in a meticulously scholarly manner by I. R. H. Campbell and A. S. Skinner. It will surely be the standard work for scholars and specialists for as long ahead as one can see. The quotations in this chapter, however, continue to be from the Scott edition.

The bicentenary of Adam Smith's death in 1990 provided yet another opportunity for commemoration, scholarly (including a conference attended by a number of Nobel Prize winners) and otherwise. On the recent manifestations of a tug-of-war over the intellectual inheritance of Adam Smith see below.

achieve as compared with those who preceded him. A certain detachment from affairs (with a knowledge of them) would almost appear to have been necessary at that stage of development of economic thought in order to complete the transformation of the subject into a science. Nor is it surprising that it should have been a moral philosopher who effected that completion, for at that time this subject consisted to a very large extent of political philosophy, political science, and jurisprudence. And already in his first great work, *The Theory of Moral Sentiments* (1759), Adam Smith had indicated both some of his special interests in the problems of human conduct and the methods of treatment which were to distinguish his later work. It appears that some of his ideas on economic subjects were formed even before he was appointed to a chair at Glasgow.[1] At any rate, it is evident from lecture notes which were edited by Cannan[2] that between 1760 and 1764 his lectures on moral philosophy contained a great deal of economic material. And if it were not otherwise known, internal evidence would show that the *Wealth of Nations* took many years to complete.

Adam Smith absorbed many influences during the twenty-five years or more in which his economic views were maturing. Although the *Wealth of Nations* contains few references to earlier writers and hardly any acknowledgement of inspiration received from others, it would be easy to show that none of its main features is original. The social philosophy which underlies it was widely held at the time, and Smith's teacher, Francis Hutcheson, was one of its chief exponents. It was from him that Adam Smith derived his faith in the natural order. The naturalist school of philosophy to which he belonged had had an unbroken tradition from the later Greek Stoics and Epicureans onwards. It reappeared in the works of Roman Stoics like Cicero, Seneca, and Epictetus, received an enormous stimulus in the Renaissance and Reformation, showed itself again in a modified form in Bacon, Hobbes, and Locke, and came to full flower in the writings of Smith, the physiocrats, and the later radicals.

In spite of their sharp distinctions, these schools can be regarded as representative of a single trend of thought. Its essence is a reliance on what is natural as against what is contrived. It implies a belief in the existence of an inherent natural order (however that may be defined)

---

1 Dugald Stewart, *Biographical Memoir of Adam Smith* (1811), pp. 90–101.
2 Adam Smith, *Lectures on Justice, Police, Revenue and Arms* (ed. E. Cannan, 1896).

which is superior to any order artificially created by mankind. It claims that all that wise social organization need do is to act as nearly as possible in harmony with the dictates of the natural order. At different times this involved different action; and the policies urged by the protagonists at different stages appear contradictory in retrospect. Their common characteristic, however, is the principle from which they claim authority: the superiority of natural over man-made law. We have already seen in the works of the physiocrats in what particular direction the philosophy of natural law was tending at the end of the eighteenth century. We shall find a similar trend in Adam Smith.[1]

The influence of physiocratic economic doctrine on Smith is more difficult to establish. He was certainly acquainted both with the writings of the school and with many of its leaders. The *Wealth of Nations* has references to at least two eminent physiocrats, Quesnay and Mercier de la Rivière, and the final chapter of the fourth book is devoted to a critique of physiocracy. Moreover, in spite of his own belief to the contrary, Smith held many views which were very similar to those of the physiocrats. Both in his adherence to naturalism and in his interest in the problem of the surplus, his path is parallel to theirs. On the other hand, it is known that the main outline of this analysis was ready before he had an opportunity of acquiring any considerable knowledge of physiocracy. We must conclude that the general outlook of the founders of French political economy were not fundamentally different from those of Adam Smith which is not surprising, in view of the essential similarity in the political and economic climate in which they worked.

The debt which Smith owed to earlier English economic thought cannot be in doubt. In his onslaught on mercantilism, for example, he had often been anticipated. We have already seen that there were many conflicting views among the seventeenth-century writers themselves; and the slashing attacks on protection by North could not have been bettered by Smith himself. In the theory of money – which he does not

---

[1] In a work distinguished, as always, by erudition, urbanity of argument and a felicity of style not always found in the literature, Robbins has shown that there is a fundamental difference between utilitarianism and the philosophy of the natural order (Lionel Robbins: *The Theory of Economic Policy in Classical Political Economy* (1952), particularly pp. 46 *et sqq.*). The main thesis of that book is that the Classics were neither as naive (in regard to state action) nor as callous (in respect of the condition of the people) as they have often been painted. I think that Robbins, though not enamoured of the principle of state intervention as such, amply proves this case. See further below.

treat at length or with great success – Smith was much indebted to Hume, Locke, and Steuart. From the last he seems also to have been inspired in his historical interests, though instead of using Steuart's conjectural method he effectively employed realistic illustrations. From Petty and Steuart, to mention no others, Smith took over not only the problems of public finance, but also some of the solutions. An indication of the celebrated four canons, for example, may be found in Petty's *Treatise*. Finally, and perhaps most important of all, Smith's treatment of the question of value and of all the problems that flow from it, owes much to the whole body of economic thought which had already developed. Petty, Steuart, and Cantillon, in particular, must be mentioned at his forerunners.

No recital of Smith's debt to others can diminish the importance of his own achievement. He wove together the separate strands of thought which he had found and in the process transformed their significance. And on at least one point – a fundamental one – his work meant a revolution of economic thinking.

In order to summarize Smith's work in a few pages it is necessary to divide it in some way. It seems best to distinguish two aspects, having due regard to their interrelation. These are: the underlying social and political philosophy and the precepts of economic policy which are derived from them; and the technical economic content. Opinions differ on the relative importance of these constituent elements of the *Wealth of Nations*, but the view here adopted is that the latter is more significant than the former.

*The Political Philosophy.*　The philosophical elements are not present on the surface of Smith's analysis. The work is divided into five books dealing respectively with problems of production, distribution, and exchange, with capital, with different economic policies pursued at various times by different nations, with previous systems of political economy and, finally, with public finance. With the exception of the very short second chapter of Book I, there is no special section set aside for a discussion of the scope of economic inquiry in relation to the study of human conduct in general: nor is there any explicit mention of the system of philosophy from which Smith's economic principles are derived. Yet this system is very much in evidence. It pervades the whole book even more than it does the work of the physiocratic writers. Again and again Smith will make a particular argument the occasion for emphasizing the supreme beneficence of the natural order and for pointing out the inevitable imperfections of human institutions. Take away artificial preferences and restraints, he says, and 'the obvious and simple system of natural liberty' will establish itself.[1] Again, 'that order of things which necessity imposes ... is ... promoted by the natural inclinations of man'. Human institutions only too often thwart these natural inclinations.[2]

We must not forget that the author of the *Wealth of Nations* was also the author of the *Theory of Moral Sentiments*; and we cannot understand the economic ideas of the one without some knowledge of the philosophy of the other. Human conduct, according to Smith, was naturally actuated by six motives: self-love, sympathy, the desire to be free, a sense of propriety, a habit of labour, and the propensity to truck, barter, and exchange one thing for another. Given these springs of conduct, each man was naturally the best judge of his own interest and should therefore be left free to pursue it in his own way. If left to himself he would not only attain his own best advantage, but he would also further the common good. This result was achieved because the different motives of human action were so carefully balanced that the benefit of one could not conflict with the good of all. Self-love was accompanied by other motives, particularly sympathy; the actions resulting from it could not but involve the advantage of others in one's own gain. It was his belief in the natural balance of human motives which led Adam Smith to make his celebrated statement that in pursuing his own advantage each individual was 'led by an invisible hand to promote an end which was no part of his intention'. Indeed, Smith doubted whether the individual did not in this way promote the interest of society more effectively than if he had set out to do so. 'I have never known', he says, 'much good done by those who affected to trade for the public good.'

The consequence of this belief in natural order is that Government can rarely be more effective than when it is negative. Its intervention in human affairs is generally harmful. Let it leave each member of the community to seek to maximize his own advantage and, compelled by natural law, he will contribute to the maximization of the common good. The natural system knows only proper duties of government which, though of great importance, are 'plain and intelligible to

---

1 Adam Smith, *An Inquiry into the Nature and Causes of the Wealth of Nations* (ed. W. R. Scott, 1925), vol. ii, p. 206.
2 ibid., vol. i, p. 385.

common understanding'. The first is the duty of defence from foreign aggression; the second, the duty of establishing an exact administration of justice; and the third, the duty to erect and maintain such public works and institutions as would not be maintained by any individual or group of individuals for lack of adequate profit.[1] Peace at home and abroad, justice, education, and public enterprises, like roads, bridges, canals and harbours, are benefits which government can confer. Another important duty must be added; the management of the currency – which would today be called monetary policy. But generally beyond these the 'invisible hand' is more effective.

What Smith says on this point is worth quoting as it is indicative of his general attitude to the limits of the legitimacy of individual freedom in economic matters. The specific reference is to a proposal to prohibit small notes: 'Such regulations may, no doubt, be considered as in some respect a violation of natural liberty. But those exertions of the natural liberty of a few individuals which might endanger the security of the whole society are, and ought to be, restrained by the laws of all governments ... The obligation of building party walls, in order to prevent the communication of fire, is a violation of natural liberty, exactly of the same kind with the regulations of the banking trade which are here proposed.'

When Smith applies these rules of the natural order to economic matters he becomes a strong opponent of any general state inter-ference with the ordinary business of industry and commerce. The natural balance of motives is most effectively at work in economic affairs. Every individual is most anxious to obtain the greatest profit for himself. But he is a member of a commonwealth and his search for profits can only lead along paths ordained by the natural social order. Through division of labour man increases the productivity of his labour, but he also ceases to be independent of others. Man as a member of society has almost constant occasion for the help of others and it is vain for him to expect it from their benevolence only. He must, in his desire to achieve his own ends, appeal to the self-love of others and not only to their sympathy. 'It is not from the benevolence of the butcher, the brewer, or the baker, that we expect our dinner, but from their regard to their own interest.'[2]

Exchange makes possible this simultaneous satisfaction of two

1 *Wealth of Nations*, vol. ii, p. 206.
2 ibid., vol. i, p. 15.

individual interests. Every individual in using his property or labour for his own benefit has to produce for the purposes of exchange, i.e. for purposes determined by all other members of the community. Whether he wishes to do so or not, he is obliged by his very membership of the social order to confer a benefit in exchange for the one he receives. Every one is obliged to bring the results of his efforts 'into a common stock, where every man may purchase whatever part of the produce of the other men's talents he has occasion for'.[1]

Smith saw particularly in foreign trade the same inherent order which ruled the simplest acts of barter. In the different branches of home trade, in foreign commerce, in the relation of industry and agriculture the principle held good that order would arise spontaneously and that interference would result in a diminution of benefit. 'It is the maxim of every prudent master of a family, never to attempt to make at home what it will cost him more to make than to buy. . . . What is prudence in the conduct of every private family, can scarce be folly in that of a great kingdom.'[2] It follows that if goods could be bought abroad more cheaply than they could be made at home it would be unwise to put obstacles in the way of their importation; for this would direct industry into channels which were less remunerative than those which it would find for itself.

Again, domestic measures designed to favour one trade or suppress another, to encourage agriculture as against industry, or vice versa, were unwise. Encouragements which drew more capital into an industry than would naturally go to it, and restraints which were designed to repel some or all capital from an industry in which it would otherwise be employed, were generally ill conceived. They did not promote the social good for which they were designed, for, by stultifying the individual search for maximum profit, they also diminished the common profit.[3]

Smith becomes thus a champion of a general policy of *laissez-faire* of even greater force than the physiocrats, because he applied the principle without basing it on the view that agriculture occupied a specially exalted position. The universality of the theory gave it its peculiar strength. Smith was not content to state an abstract principle: his aim was to destroy the actual conditions which conflicted with the

1 *Wealth of Nations*, vol. i, p. 17.
2 ibid., p. 457.
3 ibid., vol. ii, pp. 205–6.

principle. To apply the principles of Naturalism to economic policy involved a struggle against the still substantial structure of mercantilist foreign trade policy, against the mass of industrial regulation which had been left from preceding centuries, and against any attempts to add fresh monopolies and privileges to them. That struggle was, in fact, based on the more general effort which was gathering increasing force and pace for individual political liberty.

Among the forces which freed English foreign trade from regulation, which removed prohibitions, excessive import duties and restrictive trade treaties, Adam Smith's work occupies a prominent place. A substantial part of his work was devoted to an attack upon what he called the mercantile system. Although Smith was not always correct in his analysis of the views of mercantilist writers his critique of mercantilist policy was most penetrating and lucid. One by one he examined the methods which had been, or were still being used to manipulate foreign trade in the interests of an individual country, and found them all ineffective and harmful. Bounties and restraints, the colonial system and trade treaties, these and all other measures to secure a favourable balance of trade and a large stock of bullion, were quickly disposed of. They were all shown to have been productive of no common benefit, however much they may have enhanced the profits of individual sections of industry or trade.

Similarly, regulations concerning wages and apprenticeship and all other aspects of production were condemned, but not because Smith was in favour of low wages. On the contrary, he thought that no society can be flourishing of which by far the greater part of the members were poor and miserable. Government should refuse to set up any special economic privilege; and it should take positive action to destroy any monopolistic position, whether of capital or of labour, which men by concerted action might have obtained. Preservation of free competition, if necessary by state action, was the principal duty of economic policy. Only complete competition was consistent with natural liberty; and only complete competition could insure that everybody obtained the full reward of his efforts and added his full contribution to the common good.

The results which followed Smith's efforts were amazingly rapid and complete. The impact of the *Wealth of Nations* upon business men and politicians alike was very great. But although the apostle of economic liberalism spoke in lucid and persuasive terms, his success would not have been so great if he had not spoken to an audience that was ready to receive his message. He spoke with their voice, the voice of the industrialists who were anxious to sweep away all restrictions on the market and on the supply of labour – the remnants of the out-of-date régime of merchant capital and the landed interest. Moreover, the industrial capitalists were not yet matured enough to have acquired respectability. Smith presented them with a theory which supplied what was still lacking. By analysing economic activity against a background of naturalist philosophy, this theory gave to the conduct of the prospective leaders of economic life an imprint of inevitability. They recognized in the self-interest which he put at the centre of human conduct the motive which inspired their everyday business life. And they were delighted to know that their pursuit of profit was now to be regarded as unselfish. Gone was any lurking suspicion that trade might be sinful or beneath the dignity of gentlemen. These remnants of platonic and canonist thought were swept aside; the business man now became in theory what he already was in practice – the leader of the economic and political order.

By basing economic policy on a natural law which implied nonintervention by the state, Smith also gave theoretical expression to the essential interests of the business class. The industrialists saw enormous possibilities of expansion of production and trade which were being frustrated by irksome restrictions. To abolish state regulation and monopoly might have been destructive of sectional privilege, but it was in the interests of the most progressive class of the community, and indeed of the community as a whole. When Adam Smith inveighed against corrupt politicians he was only censuring a state of affairs well known to business men. When he showed that most of the actions of government were designed to impede economic progress he was expressing a truth of which his readers were aware. When he said that 'in the mercantile system, the interest of the consumer is almost constantly sacrificed', and production not consumption is regarded 'as the ultimate end and object of all industry and commerce,[1] he could again claim that he was only stating what was obvious to all. Competition, unrestricted by the state or any other agency, was the first condition of economic expansion and, therefore, ultimately of an increase in the satisfaction of the wants of all members of the community.

The account here given of Adam Smith's social and political philosophy, and more particularly of his theory of economic policy is

1 *Wealth of Nations*, vol. ii, p. 177.

designed to establish his position in the intellectual as well as the economic and political climate of his day. There can be no doubt that, like all great thinkers, he used analytical techniques and reached many theoretical and practical conclusions which transcend the time frame and have universal validity as stepping stones in scientific advance.

It is, however, necessary, especially in the area of what Bentham later called the 'agenda' of state action, to distinguish clearly between what is principle and what is specific practical application, which may vary according to historical circumstances. As we shall see later, this is extremely important when considering certain contemporary tendencies which try to make a doctrinaire ideology of Adam Smith's general preference for absence of government intervention in economic matters and wrongly claim his authority not only for the arguments for and against propositions which he could not possibly have been aware of, but even for those which his own words (some of them quoted above) contradict.

It has often been said that Adam Smith represented the interests of a single class. This is undoubtedly true. We shall see that, in spite of his usual mildness of expression, Smith used very heavy invective against the unproductive members of the community. Although he included many in that category, he could have been under no illusion that his main attack was directed against the privileged position of those who were the most formidable obstacles to the further growth of industrial capitalism. But the success of his advocacy of a particular interest was due to the fact that it coincided with a defence of the common good. This, in itself, is not a guarantee of beneficence. Partisanship had often appeared under the guise of universal bene-volence and justice; but this time the coincidence of interests was not only skilfully worked, it had also a solid basis of truth. Economic progress was dependent upon the establishment of the independence of the industrial capitalist. In helping to create an economic structure in which alone enterprise could flourish, Adam Smith could rightly claim that he was furthering the welfare of the whole community.

Whether the same was true at that time of other countries is another matter. We shall see that it took a long time for similar schools of thought to arise elsewhere and to achieve a substantial following. There is good ground for saying that the full doctrine of economic liberalism which was elaborated by Smith did not as quickly take root in other countries as it did in England. For the peculiar conditions of England on the eve of the Industrial Revolution were not completely reproduced in other countries. When Smith wrote, England was already the most advanced capitalist country in the world. With a large accumulated capital, she was preparing to acquire and to consolidate industrial leadership over the rest of the world. Although it was not until the middle of the subsequent century that England could truly be called 'the workshop of the world', she was already beginning to establish that position for herself in Smith's day. And the policy which Smith advocated was one which was designed to quicken that trend. The attack on monopolistic practices at home, made in the interests of industrial expansion, became part of a general fight against privilege, in harmony with much contemporaneous political thought. The attack on protection could similarly be developed as being in the interests of consumers who desired cheaper goods, although it was also dictated by the interests of manufacturers who desired low costs of production which would enable them to gain export markets.

The identification of particular and general interests was embodied in a theoretical system which claimed universal validity and which involved its adherents in a special view of society and of the state. In particular it implied that there was a harmony of interests of individuals and classes which could only be disturbed by the acquisition of privilege. And this privilege was made to result not merely from any social institutions but from action contrived in defiance of the natural law, i.e. political intervention. The state was thus placed in part outside and above society. Its intervention on behalf of a sectional interest was something artificial. If it intervened to create a privilege, it had been illegitimately manipulated. Its real function was to be impartial. It was a piece of machinery designed for those ends which the interests of society as a whole required. That machinery should not be allowed to get into the hands of any one section of the community.

Adam Smith himself was under no illusion about the desire of individuals, including business men, to create privileged positions for themselves. But he nevertheless believed in the harmony of interests, because he thought that these privileged positions could only be maintained with state support. Without the intervention of government to help them and given an active policy to preserve competition, those in search of monopoly were powerless. Fundamentally, he, like most later liberal philosophers, was an optimist. The social evils which he saw around him he ascribed to past mistakes of government; past history was only a record of misconceived attempts to buttress sectional privilege; sweep them away, and all would be well. Smith's whole work implied great faith in the possibility of freeing the state from the incubus of individual or class influence. Once this emancipation was achieved the natural social harmony would be manifest to all.

The belief in the natural order led Smith to be critical of much intervention. He did not, however, doubt the compatibility of social harmony with the institution of private property. He knew well the relation between property and the development of government. Civil government, he thought, was primarily needed for the protection of property. It was unnecessary in primitive communities, because there was hardly any property that could excite the envy of the poor and create a sense of insecurity in the rich. But once property increased government became essential to safeguard it, 'Civil government, so far as it is instituted for the security of property, is in reality instituted for the defence of the rich against the poor, or of those who have some property against those who have none at all.'[1] Smith also believed that property was the chief cause of authority and subordination; and that birth, the most important of the other causes, was founded upon original differences of wealth.

Yet he did not fear that any disturbance of natural harmony could result from the existence of private property, but he did not favour great inequalities in its distribution. In an opulent and civilized society and in one in which state action was devoted to the avoidance of privilege, great fortunes, he thought, need not create oppression and exploitation. Nobody was dependent upon the benevolence of others; for everything that one got from anybody one gave an equivalent in exchange. Moreover, the free play of natural forces would be destructive of all positions that were not built upon continued contributions to the common good.[2]

Other political philosophers and economists were later to refine and elaborate these views of Adam Smith. And for a long time the theory of harmony and an optimistic view of social development were to remain essential qualities of classical economic thought. However, Adam Smith's own attempt to link his economic analysis with his social

1 *Wealth of Nations*, vol. ii, p. 233.
2 For a brilliant dismissal of the more extravagant claims for the 'invisible hand', see an unpublished paper by Professor James Tobin presented to the Adam Smith Bicentenary Celebration in Edinburgh in July 1990: 'The Invisible Hand in Modern Macro-economics'. For a highly penetrating detailed re-examination of the political and social ideas of Adam Smith, especially valuable at a time when extreme versions of his political philosophy are being propagated, see Donald Winch, *Adam Smith's Politics: An Essay in Historiographic Revision* (1978).

philosophy was not altogether successful. His economic theory, which formed the basis of the classical position, contained elements which, in other hands, were made to support a different view of society and different political precepts. Already, in Ricardo's formulation, Smith's theory loses some of its optimistic and harmonious implication. Potential conflicts begin to appear which, seized upon by critics, particularly the Ricardian socialists turned the theory against the very interests which it had been Smith's task to champion.

*The Theory of Value.* The great advance in economic thought which is due to Smith is the emancipation from mercantilist and physiocratic fetters. For two hundred years economists had been searching for the ultimate source of wealth. The mercantilists had found it in foreign trade. The physiocrats had gone further and had shifted the origin of wealth from the sphere of exchange to that of production. But they had still remained confined within one particular form of production, agriculture. Adam Smith, building on the foundations of Petty and Cantillon, effected the final revolution. With him labour as such becomes the source of the fund which originally supplies every nation 'with all the necessaries and conveniences of life which it annually consumes'.[1] Smith still spoke of wealth in the sense of useful material objects, as his English predecessors had done, but, by making it result from labour in general, he was led to inquire into the social rather than the technical appearance of wealth. The wealth of a nation, he said, will depend upon two conditions: first, the degree of productivity of the labour to which it is due; and secondly, the amount of useful labour, that is to say, labour productive of wealth, which is employed. The examination of the first of these factors leads Smith to the discussion of the division of labour, exchange, money, and distribution, to which the whole of the first book is devoted. The second involves an analysis of capital; and this is made in the second book.

Smith begins his analysis with the division of labour because he wishes to find the principle which transforms particular concrete forms of labour, which produce particular goods (use-values), into labour as a social element, which becomes the source of wealth in the abstract (exchange-value). Division of labour becomes for Smith the principal cause of the increasing productivity of labour. After giving his

---

1 *Wealth of Nations*, vol. i, p. 1.

well-known account of its quality and consequences,[1] he proceeds to inquire into the causes which produce it. It is here that he makes division of labour depend upon the propensity to exchange, which he regards as one of the principal motives of human conduct. There can be little doubt that on this point Smith confused cause and effect. However true it may be that exchange cannot exist without division of labour, it is not true, at least in theory, that division of labour requires the existence of private exchange. It is logically demonstrable that a certain social organization (for example, the economy of a patriarchal tribe which lacks the institution of private property) can have a technology using division of labour without exchange. And communities of this type can be shown to have existed. Adam Smith was guilty of making the characteristics of the society of his own day valid for all time; he regarded as a natural human motive and made into a universal principle of explanation, a feature of the contemporaneous social order which was historically conditioned.[2] But Smith's purpose was propagandist. He emphasized the influence of the market on productivity in order to demonstrate that trade had to be freed as a prerequisite to the development of productive power, and not merely to the full use of the existing powers of production.

He proceeds to analyse how the degree of the division of labour is determined and concludes that it is limited by the extent of the market. He elaborates points made originally by Xenophon, and later by Petty, and gives what has since been regarded as the classic description of the relation between the circle of exchange and the division of labour.[3] He shows that when these have reached a certain stage of development the dependence of each individual upon the rest of the community is very great. Every man becomes then 'in some measure a merchant, and the society itself grows to be what is properly a commercial society'.[4] The efficiency with which this society carries out its now habitual exchanges must remain seriously defective so long as exchange is in kind. The well-known disadvantages of barter lead to the adoption of a generally accepted medium of exchange, money. Smith describes how the precious metals came to be chosen as the commodity of which money should be made, and briefly traces their progress through history. But this is only incidental. The important point to which the

1 *Wealth of Nations*, Book i, ch. i.
2 ibid., ch. ii.
3 ibid., ch. iii.
4 ibid., vol. i, p. 23.

short discussion of money leads is the question of 'the rules which men naturally observe in exchanging [goods] either for money or for one another. ... These rules determine what may be called the relative or exchangeable value of goods.'[1] In this rather roundabout way Smith reaches the central problem of his economic inquiry. But the problem was inherent in the very fact that he had started by abandoning the mercantilist and physiocratic concern with particular forms of wealth and proceeded to examine wealth in general as a social phenomenon.

Before beginning the analysis of value Smith distinguishes two uses of the word. One, he points out, signifies the utility of some particular object, and this he calls *value in use*; the other refers to the power possessed by an object of purchasing other goods: this he calls *value in exchange*. He mentions a paradox in terms which have since become famous. Some of the most useful commodities, such as water, he says, have scarcely any *value in exchange* while others, such as diamonds, although of little use, can command a great deal of other commodities in exchange. It was this paradox which was to provide the starting-point for the theorizing of economists of the later nineteenth century which finally led to the marginal utility doctrine. Smith himself was not interested in elucidating the intricacies of use-value. He puts the distinction of the two meanings of the term 'value' at the end of his chapter on money in order, so it seems, to get it out of the way before beginning the really important work, the analysis of exchange-value. This resolves itself into three parts: what is the measure of the exchange-value of commodities or, as Smith also calls it, their real or natural price? what are the constituent parts of this natural price? and, finally, how do variations of the market price of commodities from their natural price arise? To these questions, chapters v, vi, and vii of Book I are devoted.

It is not easy to give a summary account of Adam Smith's ambiguous and confused theory of value. Subsequent economists have found two or three different strands of thought which Smith did not separate sufficiently clearly. He developed the labour theory inherited from Petty and Cantillon; but he also added to it certain elements of the supply and demand analysis of Locke. And in his struggles with the difficulties of the concept of capital and its place in the economic process he abandoned his own labour theory of value and bequeathed

1 *Wealth of Nations*, vol. i, p. 28.

to later generations what became mainly a cost of production theory. According to their predilections economists have stressed one or the other of these different principles. But not even adherents of the same school can agree on their interpretation of Smith's theory. One writer, for example, is anxious to show the progress of the theory of value towards the subjectivist school to which he belongs; and he criticizes Adam Smith for having concentrated on the exchange-value (or purchasing power) of goods to the exclusion of their utility, which, to this writer, is the real cause of value.[1] A later writer, on the other hand, who is also a follower of the subjectivist school, finds in Adam Smith traces of the beginning of that school. She thinks that Adam Smith, by adopting the consumer's concept of wealth, raised the problem of the connection between production and demand. It was due, she says, to Smith's indecision in the treatment of this problem and to the subsequent victory of the Ricardian school that the demand aspect was neglected in England, and that that part of Smith's tradition was left to flourish on the Continent.[2]

It is true that Adam Smith's theory is inconsistent. But although he involved himself, as we shall see, in many contradictions, he made considerable progress in the explanation of value. And, in the end, his theory rests on what Ricardo singled out as the basis for his own analysis; the labour theory of value. However inconsistent Smith may be in his exposition of it, he keeps to it most strictly in one important application of it – in his discussion of the surplus which formed the basis of all profit.

It seems established that the earliest theory which Adam Smith held regarded labour as the sole source of value and the quantity of labour embodied in each commodity as the measure of that value. But here, already, confusion begins. His discussion of exchange-value in the *Lectures* is little different from that of previous writers who had adopted a similar explanation. Like Petty, Steuart, and Cantillon, he considered the value of a commodity to be determined by the cost of producing the amount of labour necessary for the production of the commodity. This cost included not only the subsistence of the labourer himself but also allowances for education and reproduction. Like his predecessors, he admitted the influence of demand which determined the distribution of labour in such a way as to make value and cost of labour equal.[3]

1 R. Zuckerkandl, *Zur Theorie des Preises*, pp. 65–6.
2 M. Bowley, *Nassau Senior and Classical Economics* (1937), pp. 67–8.
3 Adam Smith, *Lectures on Justice, Police, Revenue and Arms*, ed. Cannan, pp. 173–82.

In the *Wealth of Nations* the theory is elaborated, but becomes less clear-cut. In the first place, the scope of the labour theory becomes limited and an additional theory is developed in order to explain a further range of value phenomena. In the second place, the exposition of the labour theory itself, even within the limits in which Smith still admits its validity, is very confused. The explanation of exchange-value in chapter v begins with an analysis of the quality of exchange-value derived from the social facts of division of labour and private exchange. A man is rich or poor, he says, according to the amount of useful things which he can obtain. When division of labour has taken place his own labour can provide him with only a few of these things, and his wealth will come to depend on the amount of other people's labour which he can command. The value in exchange of any commodity which he possesses will then be equal to the amount of labour it can command. Smith concludes that labour 'is the real measure of the exchangeable value of all commodities'.[1]

There follows immediately another account of the origin of value and its measure, which Adam Smith evidently intended to be only a version of the first but which is quite different. For he goes on to measure the value of a commodity not only by the amount of labour which it can command in exchange (or as he now puts it, the *value* of a certain quantity of labour), but also by the amount of labour which its production requires. These two explanations now persist side by side; and the confusion between then is well illustrated by the statement that a man's 'fortune is greater or less, precisely in proportion to ... the quantity either of other men's labour, or, what is the same thing, of the produce of other men's labour, which it enables him to purchase or command.'[2] In the first half of this statement the exchange-value of labour is made the measure of the exchange-value of other commodities; in the second half that measure is given by the amount of labour embodied in a commodity. Ricardo was later to take over the second explanation. On the other hand, this part of Smith's theory served also as the starting-point for a psychological cost theory of value which relies a great deal on the concept of 'disutility' and forms an important part of many later explanations of value.

The cause of Smith's confusion lies in his desire to emphasize the importance of the division of labour and the changes which its

1 *Wealth of Nations*, ed. W. R. Scott, vol. i, p. 30.
2 ibid., p. 31.

introduction brings about. 'Labour', he says, 'was the first price paid
... for all things.'[1] But once division of labour is introduced it is no
longer the product of one's own labour that determines wealth but the
amount of other people's labour which this product can command, i.e.
the quantity of labour in general which one can buy with the quantity
of labour contained in one's product. In other words, what Smith was
here doing was to develop again, but in other words, the concept on
exchange-value as such, a concept which only arises so far as the
labour theory of value is concerned when labour has become a social
factor. For through division of labour and exchange the products of the
labour of different individuals must somehow be equated. But Smith
applied this concept in a way which involved an equation not only
between the products of labour but also between the product of labour
and labour itself; and it was the difficulty inherent in this which finally
led him to develop a different theory of value.

Before he proceeds to that Smith once again discusses money. Here
too he is involved in some confusion. He now speaks of labour as the
measure of value not in the sense of what is inherent in exchange-
value, but in the sense of a yard-stick with which the value of commodities is compared. In this sense, he finds labour to be an inefficient
measure. Commodities, he says, are seldom exchanged with labour
(here the above-mentioned confusion is again apparent) but with other
commodities. The exchange-value of commodities is, therefore, more
commonly estimated in terms of quantities of other commodities,
which are 'plain and palpable' objects, than in labour, which is 'an
abstract notion'.[2] Once money is used, every commodity is most
frequently exchanged for it; and this now becomes the commonly used
measure of value. Through his confusion of the exact significance of
the term 'measure of value', Adam Smith sets up money as being of
equal status with labour. Or almost so, for he proceeds to search for
something which possesses constant value and which can therefore be
used as an efficient measuring rod. He dismisses gold and silver, the
most widely used money commodities, as being subject to fluctuations
in value, i.e. in the amount of labour which is necessary to produce
them, or (again the confusion) in the amount of labour which a
quantity of them can command. He returns therefore to labour whose
own value, he says, never varies and which remains 'alone the ultimate

1 *Wealth of Nations*, ed. W. R. Scott, vol. i, p. 30.
2 ibid., p. 32.

ADAM SMITH

and real standard by which the value of all commodities can at all times
and places be estimated and compared'.[1] Labour becomes the *real* and
money the *nominal* price of commodities.

We see that the confusion between amount of labour and value of
labour has persisted. Adam Smith himself seems to be aware of a
difficulty for he admits that the value of labour (which he has just
regarded as unchangeable), although always the same to the labourer,
appears to vary for the person who buys it; for sometimes a larger and
sometimes a smaller volume of goods will purchase the same amount
of labour. Smith sidetracks the problem by saying that it is not labour
which is cheap or dear, but the goods which buy it. To the terms 'real'
and 'nominal' price, he now gives a different meaning: the former is
the amount of necessaries and conveniences of life, the latter the
amount of money which we are given in exchange for anything,
including labour. The distinction is nowadays familiar; it is often used
in economic analysis as, for example, when real wages are distinguished from money wages. Smith does not pursue the question of the
real price of labour at this stage, but, after some discussion of coinage,
the changing proportions of gold and silver and the fluctuations in the
value of the commodities, he proceeds to expound still further his
theory of value.

*The Theory of Capital and Distribution.* The difficulties he encountered
in the beginning make him limit the validity of the labour theory to
primitive societies. At the beginning of chapter vi the determination of
the exchange-value of commodities by the amount of labour necessary
to produce them is said to hold only in 'that early and rude state of
society which precedes both the accumulation of stock and the appropriation of lands',[2] i.e., in pre-capitalist times. The celebrated beaver
and deer example is given to show that, in a society of hunters,
commodities will exchange in the same ratio as the labour spent on
their production. Smith points out that in that stage of social development the whole produce of labour belongs to the labourer. The parties
to the exchange are then all owners of commodities which embody a
certain amount of the labour of their owners. These amounts are
equated in the process of exchange.

When product A and B are exchanged at their value, a double

1 *Wealth of Nations*, vol. i, p. 33.
2 ibid., p. 47.

143

equivalence is established. In the first place, there are exchanged two equal amounts of labour embodied in the commodities. In the second place, a commodity can procure for its owner an amount of labour of another person equal to the amount of labour which he has spent on the production of his commodity. In other words, Smith rightly sees that in the conditions he has stated (i.e. when the labourer is the owner of the whole product of his labour), there is not necessarily a confusion between the two determinants of exchange-value which he has used. The value of labour (the quantity of a commodity which can be bought with a given quantity of labour, or the quantity of labour which can be bought with a given quantity of a commodity) can be regarded as the measure of value just as much as the amount of labour embodied in a commodity.[1]

But once the postulated conditions are absent, the situation changes. When stock has accumulated in private hands its owners will employ it to set to work 'industrious people whom they will supply with materials and subsistence in order to make a profit by the sale of their work'.[2] When goods are sold they must fetch not only enough to cover the wages of these 'industrious people', but they must also bring in something by way of profit for their employers. If he did not get a profit, the owner of the stock would have no interest to employ it; nor would he employ a greater rather than a less amount of stock unless his profits bore some proportion to that stock.

Smith dismisses the idea that profits may be merely a special type of wages, the reward for a special kind of labour: they bear no relation to the labour of inspection and supervision which their owner expends, but only to the size of his stock. Profits, Smith says, are a quite separate constituent of the value of commodities. The labourer must share his product not only with the owner of the stock but also with the landlord who draws rent. The real value of all commodities must, therefore, resolve itself into three component parts: wages, profit, and rent. That, however, means that the original theory of value is no longer applicable. For although Smith begins by saying that the value of every commodity 'resolves' itself into these constituents, he soon adopts a terminology that amounts, in effect, to enunciating a new theory of value. He still claims that the real value of each constituent of price is equal to the amount of labour it can command. But wages, profit, and

1 Karl Marx, *Theorien über den Mehrwert*, vol. i, p. 129.
2 *Wealth of Nations*, vol. i, p. 48.

rent are not only the sole sources of the revenues of the different classes of society, i.e. the forms in which the value of commodities is distributed; they become also 'the three original sources ... of all exchangeable value'.[1] In these words Smith has stated a primitive cost-of-production theory of value.

The discussion remains now on this basis and proceeds to deal with the difference between the natural and the market price. The former is a price which is neither more nor less than the sum of the natural prices of its component parts. The second is determined by supply and demand. The excesses or deficiencies of supply will cause the component parts of the price to be below or above their natural rates. This will bring about a diminution or increase of the supply in accordance with the demand. Market price will constantly tend to equality with the natural price. The latter itself varies with the natural rates of wages, profit, and rent, and it is to these that Adam Smith devotes his next chapters.

Before we follow Smith in his further analysis it is necessary, at the risk of some repetition, to show why he apparently abandoned the labour theory of value. Smith's difficulty was to explain the origin of any revenue other than that of labour. He saw that when there existed capital and private property in land the exchange of a product brought its owner (i.e. the capitalist) something above what he had laid out in the production of the commodity. How did this surplus arise? Unlike the mercantilists or Steuart, Smith did not regard it as a profit upon alienation. He did not believe that a surplus arose because a commodity was sold above its value. This value merely resolved itself into two parts, one of which went to the owner of the stock. Like the physiocrats, he believed in the existence of a *produit net*. Unlike them, he regarded it as the value added by the workman to the materials, i.e. as the product of labour and not as a gift of nature. But the existence of the capitalist and his profit made it difficult for him to maintain that labour was the sole source of value and its inherent measure. Nor in the conditions of capitalist production were the quantity of labour embodied in a commodity and the value of labour no longer identical. It was to escape these difficulties that Marx took refuge in the additional concept of 'surplus value' theory. Smith himself never quite abandons the labour theory; indeed, in his discussion of the origin of the surplus he continually makes use of it. On the other hand, he finds

1 *Wealth of Nations*, vol. i, p. 53.

himself unable to apply it to his theory of distribution and he has to have recourse to other methods of explanation.

A part of his theory of the revenues of different classes of society is consistent with his own original theory of value. Here he distinguishes only two kinds of revenue: one the subsistence of the worker, the other the deduction, as he calls it, from the value produced by the worker which is appropriated by either the landlord or the owner of stock, or by both.[1] This deduction under the name of surplus value became later the central point of the Marxian analysis. It is important to emphasize this relationship since Adam Smith's influence on Marx is generally neglected in favour of Ricardo's. In effect, Smith was the first to develop this concept and to stress the fact that it was bound up with capitalist production. Ricardo, on the other hand, avoided Smith's inconsistency in regard to the determination of value itself.

But although this aspect of Smith's theory of distribution may be regarded as being more definitely and rigorously in a direct line of logical descent from his premises, it is not the one to which he devotes most attention. He starts from the statement that wages, profit, and rent are the three original sources of exchange-value and then examines the manner in which they are determined. In regard to wages, he enunciates partly a subsistence, or labour, theory and partly a cost-of-production theory. In the former he regards the natural value of labour as determined by what is necessary to maintain the labourer plus an allowance to enable him to rear a family and maintain the supply of labour. This theory is not much different from that of Petty or of Cantillon, whom Smith quotes. He adds a discussion of the influence on wages of supply and demand (which is not incompatible with the subsistence theory), and he analyses the causes which alter them. But he is not able to escape entirely from the vicious circle of the cost-of-production theory.

In the discussion of the profits of stock the departure from the labour theory is even more marked. Although he has defined profit as that part of value which the capitalist appropriates after he has paid the wages of his workmen, Smith makes the size of profits depend upon the size of the total stock which the capitalist employs. He admits the difficulty of speaking of profits as such (i.e. of an average rate of profits) because they are subject to great variations of time, place, and type of business. And he says that the interest on money can provide a

1 *Wealth of Nations*, vol., i, p. 66.

clue to the rate of profits. The rate of interest, Smith implied, was determined by the rate of profits; the maxim was 'that wherever a great deal can be made by the use of money, a great deal will commonly be given for the use of it', and vice versa.[1]

Having examined different periods and countries, he concludes that generally wages and profits are inversely related. An increase of stock, by increasing competition among its owners, will tend to lower profits; on the other hand, it will increase the demand for labour and thus tend to raise wages. Profits must always be at least 'something more than what is sufficient to compensate the occasional losses to which every employment of stock is exposed'. They can never be higher than what 'eats up the whole of what should go to the rent of the land and leaves only what is sufficient to pay the labour of preparing and bringing them [the commodities] to market, according to the lowest rate at which labour can anywhere be paid, the bare subsistence of the labourer'.[2] Though profits may fluctuate between these limits, they will tend to fall with the progress of society. The accumulation of stock will lead to increasing competition, and (a point Ricardo was to elaborate later) as new countries become more peopled, less fertile soil has to be taken into the cultivation and the profits of the stock employed on it declines.[3]

Smith develops a separate theory of rent. He had originally made rent a deduction from value. Later, it had become a constituent element of price akin to wages and profit. But in the chapter devoted to rent (Book I, ch. ii), both these views are abandoned in favour of a third. Rent, he says, 'enters into the composition of the price of commodities in a different way from wages and profit. High or low wages and profit are the causes of high or low price; high or low rent is the effect of it.'[4] In other words, rent does not enter in the determination of price at all; it is not a cause but an effect. And it is an effect which only appears if the price is higher than what is sufficient to pay wages and profit. Rent is purely differential. If the price of the produce of land is only just enough to recompense the capitalist, the land will bear no rent; if it is higher, the landlord, being a monopolist, will be able to take the excess from the capitalist. The price will depend on demand. For some products of land there is always a demand which

1 *Wealth of Nations*, vol. i, p. 91.
2 ibid., pp. 98–9.
3 ibid., p. 95.
4 ibid., p. 151.

makes their price higher than what is sufficient to bring them to the market; for others there is not. In spite of certain inconsistencies, this is the beginning of Ricardo's theory of rent.

To complete the summary of Smith's view contained in the first and most important book of the *Wealth of Nations* a few words will suffice. He makes certain very interesting contributions which arise incidentally in the confused discussion of the central themes of value and distribution. His treatment of competition, for example, both in its relation to the price of commodities and to wages and profit, is most lucidly worked out and full of apt historical and hypothetical illustrations. Here he is on the solid ground of experience and is speaking with the authority of the new economy behind him. These parts are, therefore, probably the most living ones of his whole analysis.

Particularly successful is the examination of the differences of wages and profits in different employments. Little of this analysis has had to be thrown overboard by later economists; and what has been added has been in the nature of refinement. The whole theory of net advantages and non-competing groups derives from chapter x of the first book. Here Smith clearly shows that competition among capital or labour which is seeking employment will tend to equalize not profits or wages but net advantages; and he classifies and analyses the non-monetary advantages which are taken into account in determining the relative attractiveness of different employments. Smith's description is now a part of every economic textbook and need not, therefore, be outlined here. Nor is it necessary to say anything about his description of the way in which restriction of competition produces inequalities of wages and profits, except to point out that as an opponent of state action he is concerned only with rigidities in the competitive mechanism which are deliberately contrived by policy.

Other sections of the book have been less free from subsequent criticism and emendation, but they still contain important contributions. There are, for example, glimpses of the theory of population already found in earlier writers and full expounded by Malthus.[1] Again, in developing a theory of rent in anticipation of Ricardo, Smith makes differential rent depend on differences of fertility and position.[2] In some respects Smith's analysis is even superior to that of Ricardo, for he works out very carefully the different conditions under which

[1] *Wealth of Nations*, vol. i, pp. 81, 152.
[2] ibid., p. 153.

private property in land can lead to the receipt of rent. The whole discussion is lucid and takes one step by step through different branches of agriculture, through the extractive industries, and through building land. Smith concludes his chapter on rent by saying that the progress of agriculture and the growth of population which follow on an increase in the wealth of the community will tend to increase the share of the product which goes to the landlord in rent. Increased population will increase the demand for, and the price of, agricultural produce; more stock will be employed in agriculture; the produce will increase, and so will rent, because, with improvements in cultivation, no more labour is required after price has risen than before. 'A smaller proportion of it [labour] will, therefore, be sufficient to replace, with the ordinary profit, the stock which employs that labour. A greater proportion of it must, consequently, belong to the landlord.'[1]

Book II is an elaboration of the ideas expounded in the first book and contains two very important ideas. It deals with the nature of stock and contains Adam Smith's ideas on the accumulation of capital and his very important distinction between productive and unproductive labour. Of minor importance is the discussion on money. The introduction of the book attempts to explain the reason for the accumulation of stock. Smith is not altogether successful here. He begins by saying that where there is no division of labour no stock need exist, because each individual endeavours to supply his wants as they occur. Once division of labour has been introduced and everybody has become dependent on everybody else, there must be a stock sufficient to maintain people until they have made their tools and the product itself and have succeeded in selling it. On the other hand, he immediately goes on to say that accumulation must precede the introduction of division of labour and he never in fact makes up his mind on the exact sequence.

This indecision appears also in another place, when the accumulation of capital is discussed in connection with the increase of production. In his critique of physiocracy he says that an increase of the annual produce of society can result only from an improvement of the productive power of labour or an increase in the quantity of labour. The former depends on increased skill and greater use of machinery; the latter on an increase of the capital of society which must, in its turn, be 'exactly equal to the amount of the savings from the revenue, either

1 *Wealth of Nations* vol. i, p. 262.

of the particular persons who manage and direct the employment of that capital, or of some other persons who lend it to them'.[1] Here Smith claims that an increase of produce depends on increased productivity. This depends on increase of capital, which must wait on an increase of produce. Again, an increase of produce can be brought about by using an increased quantity of labour; but this can only be done if there is more capital. Although Smith does not resolve this problem, he has meanwhile introduced a new factor which becomes in effect the chief source of accumulation, namely, saving.

The rest of his analysis of accumulation, the classification of capital, and the discussion of money depend entirely on Smith's distinction between productive and unproductive labour. This distinction, which began with the physiocrats and was implied in mercantilist thought (it is inherent in any search for the 'causes' of wealth), remained one of the most important parts of classical thought. Although it was later often thought of as a mere piece of scholasticism, it was an integral part of the theory of value and the surplus. The confusion to which it subsequently gave rise was due to the nature of Smith's own exposition of it.

Throughout chapter iii of the second book, two separate definitions of productive and unproductive labour are intermingled. At the very beginning, both these definitions appear: 'There is one sort of labour which adds to the value of the subject upon which it is bestowed: there is another which has no such effect.' Immediately, as if by way of amplification of this statement, there follows: 'Thus the labour of a manufacturer adds generally to the value of the materials which he works upon, that of his own maintenance, and of his master's profit.'[2] Productive labour is thus defined both as labour which creates value and as labour which creates a surplus for the employer. With this confusion there is mixed up another. Smith also defines productive labour as that which 'fixes and realizes itself in some particular subject or vendible commodity', and this leads him to regard as productive those activities which result in material goods and to exclude all services.

We have thus three definitions which are not necessarily compatible; one is linked with the output of material goods, another with the creation of value, the third with the production of a surplus. The third

1 *Wealth of Nations*, vol. ii, pp. 194–5.
2 ibid., vol. i, p. 335.

is consistent with Smith's own original analysis of exchange-value and capitalist production. It is also the one which follows and develops the trend of thought of mercantilism and physiocracy. The former had stressed foreign trade by which a country could increase its stock of bullion. This created an inflationary movement which encouraged industry at the expense of labour, owing to the time-lag in the rise of wages. The physiocrats had gone further and had spoken of the *produit net* which went to the proprietors of the land. Smith extended the concept to cover all labour which created a surplus which could go to recompense the owner of stock.

Accumulation of capital can only take place through the employment of productive labour in the above sense. And capital is only that part of stock which is used to set in motion productive labour, i.e. labour which will replace and increase the original outlay. Unproductive labourers, on the other hand, are maintained by revenue.[1] The reason why Adam Smith was led away from this definition into the other two was probably his desire to controvert the physiocratic emphasis on agriculture. His very advance from the view which regarded those engaged in industry and trade as sterile led into contradictions which were only gradually overcome. Smith's further insistence on the material quality of the result of productive labour is a remnant of the early bullionist notion which confused wealth and money.

Smith, however, largely maintains his first definition. On it is based his division of stock into capital (that part which is destined to produce a revenue) and the remainder, which is reserved for immediate consumption. The former is again divided into circulating and fixed capital, according to the manner in which it is employed to set productive labour in motion. The distinction is not worked out carefully enough to avoid confusion. The same definition of productive labour is also implied in Smith's treatment of foreign trade and of the relation of money and capital. This is particularly so in regard to the former. If gold and silver are used to purchase from abroad luxuries such as foreign wines and silks, prodigality is promoted and production is not increased. If, on the other hand, they are used to bring back materials, tools, and provisions for the employment of productive labour, industry is stimulated and, although consumption is increased, the value of that consumption is reproduced with a profit.[2]

1 *Wealth of Nations*, vol. i, p. 337.
2 ibid., vol. i, p. 295.

The remainder of the *Wealth of Nations* need not detain us. Books III and IV, which contain an historical account of the progress of wealth, of different economic policies, and the critique of mercantilism and physiocracy, are noted mainly for the free-trade views which have already been dealt with. Book V deals with public finance, and in it Smith develops his ideas on what are the legitimate items of public expenditure in conformity with his general view of the functions of government. There are many interesting observations in these sections, which are not, however, so important for our purpose as the general philosophy which underlies them. Smith's discussion of the ways in which public revenue is to be raised has formed the starting-point of all subsequent liberal theory of taxation. Here, he sets out his celebrated four maxims of taxation; equality, certainty, convenience, and economy. He shows that all taxes (and, therefore, all those supported out of the proceeds of taxation) must ultimately be paid out of the three revenues of society or, consistently with his original analysis of value, out of wages or surplus value. He examines in turn rent, profits, and wages. If the price of provisions and the demand for labour remained unchanged, direct taxes on wages, he thought, would be paid by the capitalist. The capitalist would endeavour to recoup himself by charging a higher price to the consumer. If this was impossible the demand for labour would fall.

Smith does not appear to favour taxation of profits. The element of profits which is interest was not, he thought, as suitable an object of taxation as the rent of land, because the quantity of stock which a man owned was very difficult to ascertain and because stock could easily be removed by its owner if the tax was burdensome. As for that part of profit which was a compensation for risk, it was unsuitable because it was generally only a moderate amount and because no capitalist could pay such a tax and continue to employ his capital. He would endeavour to shift the incidence which would ultimately fall on the consumer, on the landlord, or on those who had lent the money at interest. This leaves only the tax on rent. There can be little doubt that, like the physiocrats before him and Ricardo after him, Smith favoured a tax on the revenue of land. 'Both ground-rents and the ordinary rent of land are a species of revenue which the owner, in many cases, enjoys without any care or attention of his own. Though a part of this revenue should be taken from him in order to defray the expenses of the state, no discouragement will thereby be given to any sort of industry. . . . Ground-rents and the ordinary rent of land, are, therefore, perhaps the species of revenue which can best bear to have a peculiar tax imposed upon them.''[1]

The above account of the work of Adam Smith has concentrated on the core of his analysis, and this was found to contain a number of contradictions. But in spite of these, perhaps even because of them, the subsequent development of economic thought would have been impossible but for him. He mapped out the field of economic inquiry in such a way that all subsequent thinkers were guided by those landmarks: production, value, distribution. The structure of economic science was firmly established.

But in addition to this achievement Adam Smith's work possesses a deeper significance which rests on its social philosophical implications. We have already seen that he gave the first systematic statement of the harmony of social interests and that he implanted a utilitarian tradition in economic science. His economic analysis, however, also showed where and how conflict of social interest might arise. Smith did not directly attack the landed interest: opposition to the landlord was still not the supreme issue which it was to become in Ricardo's day. The main objective of Smith's attack was still the merchant monopolist. He lived in, and thought in terms of, that transitional eighteenth-century society which had its industrial capitalism, but in which industry was not sufficiently developed to be preoccupied with cheap labour and, therefore, cheap food. The labour theory of value and the theory of the surplus which run through the first two books of the *Wealth of Nations* reveal a possible cleavage between different classes; and this remains in spite of Smith's subsequent exposition of a cost-production theory which could be used to establish equal claims to revenue for all classes by making them all into sources of value.

This dichotomy persists in two post-Smithian schools of thought: one carries on the tradition of harmony and distinguishes three co-operative factors of production; the other develops a theory of exploitation. It is true that both can claim authority for Smith. He did not develop a consistent theory of value. It may be argued that at that stage of economic development the movement of the revenues of the different classes of society was not yet the central economic problem. It was not necessary to have a theory of value to answer the sort of questions which Smith was asking. He was, therefore, content to state a few empirical generalizations which show the factors which are

1 *Wealth of Nations*, vol. ii, p. 373.

relevant to a complete theory. But his formulation could later be interpreted in different ways. If he wrote of an invisible hand which made every one contribute to the common good, he also belied his theory of harmony by his attacks upon the economic status of 'unproductive' labourers. He wrote most savagely of the prodigality of princes and ministers. And although he did not attack the institutions which maintained the whole apparatus of government, justice, and education, he made no bones about his opinion of their economic significance. 'The sovereign,' he said, 'with all officers both of justice and war who serve under him, the whole army and navy, are unproductive labourers. ... In the same class must be ranked, some both of the gravest and most important, and some of the most frivolous professions: churchmen, lawyers, physicians, men of letters of all kinds; players, buffoons, musicians, opera-singers, opera-dancers, etc.'[1] The new view of the social structure could not be more consistently expressed. Capitalist production is the foundation of society; everything else rests upon it.

On one occasion at least Smith allows himself to discuss directly the interests of different classes and of their relation to the good of the community as a whole.[2] He has a low opinion of the quality of intellect and character of landowners. They get their income without any labour (on another occasion, he says that they 'love to reap where they have not sowed'[3]); and they are, therefore, often ignorant of their own interest and incapable of understanding the consequences of any piece of policy that may be proposed. Nevertheless, their interests cannot be opposed to the interests of the community as a whole because rents rise with the general increase of wealth. The interest of the labourer is also bound up with the interests of society, even though he may not be capable of appreciating it. The interest of those who live by profit, on the other hand, may often conflict with the common advantage, because profits tend to fall as society becomes more wealthy. The capitalists are at the same time better able than any other class to judge of their own interest, and their attitude to public policy is therefore always to be suspected. Any proposal coming from them 'comes from an order of men whose interest is never exactly the same with that of the public, who have generally an interest to deceive and even to

1 *Wealth of Nations*, vol. i, p. 356.
2 ibid., pp. 261–5.
3 ibid., p. 50.

oppress the public, and who accordingly have upon many occasions, both deceived and oppressed it.'[1]

Ricardo was to elaborate these disharmonious elements which Smith had sketched out into a theory of economic development with strong possibilities of a conflict emerging between opposing interests.

## Ricardo

*Ricardo and Smith.*    Adam Smith has been dealt with at length for two reasons. He is universally acknowledged as the founder of classical political economy, and disciples and critics alike have based themselves on him. He was also the first to develop all the categories which form the content of subsequent economic controversy, and later economists can be more easily discussed in reference to his work. At the same time it is important not to allow the detailed exposition of Smith's theory as against the summary treatment of Ricardo which follows to lead to unfavourable comparisons.

David Ricardo is without doubt the greatest representative of classical political economy. He carried the work begun by Smith to the farthest point possible without choosing the road which led out of the contradiction inherent in it. Perhaps for that reason recognition of his importance has sometimes been withheld and has often been grudging. Jevons was convinced that Ricardo had given economic inquiry a wrong twist; the American economist, Carey, regarded the *Principles* as the source of inspiration of agitators and disrupters of society; and a modern writer, who gives abundant praise to Smith, has even gone as far as to call Ricardo's literary work 'the production of an unliterary Jewish stockbroker' distinguished by a certain inherited 'Jewish subtlety'.[2] Such judgment is hardly based on evidence. Ricardo, writing fifty years later than Smith, showed a greater insight into the working of the economic system; but as for subtlety (whatever demerit there may be in that!) the Scot does not lose by comparison with the Jew. In the opinion of his own contemporaries at home and abroad,

---

1 *Wealth of Nations*, vol. i, p. 265.
2 A. Gray, *The Development of Economic Doctrine*, p. 172. Gray seems to have been following Alfred Marshall, who, in his Inaugural Lecture on *The Present State of Economics* in 1885, acknowledged Ricardo as a 'masterful genius' (though adding he 'was not an Englishman') but said: 'The faults and the virtues of Ricardo's mind are traceable to his Semitic origin; no English economist has had a mind similar to his.'

Ricardo was acknowledged the leader of the science. His great opponent, Malthus, his disciple, James Mill, and the latter's son, John Stuart Mill, speak with the greatest respect and admiration of the man and his work.

David Ricardo (1772–1823) came of a Dutch Jewish family which had settled in England, though he himself seceded from the Jewish faith early in life. Like his father, he became a stockbroker, and, after acquiring a large fortune in a short time, he became a landed proprietor and a member of Parliament. Virtual retirement from business enabled him to embark on intellectual pursuits at an early age. Although he died young, he gave to the world the chief results of his studies. His most important work is *The Principles of Political Economy and Taxation*, first published in 1817, of which the third edition (1821) is the definitive one. In addition, he wrote a large number of essays (of which *The High Price of Bullion* (1810) is the best known), letters, and notes, which all contain important contributions. The complete edition of his works has made a considerable amount of new material available, without, however, leading to a fundamental alteration of one's view of Ricardo's contribution. It only increases one's admiration for the man's scope (for example, Vol. V, containing the parliamentary speeches).[1]

Ricardo lacked all the advantages for a scholarly career which his great predecessor had had. As a result, the *Principles* have not the polish of the *Wealth of Nations*, nor are they so clearly part of a comprehensive social philosophy. Ricardo's writing is more condensed and demands a greater attention from the reader. His exposition is rarely relieved by those historical digressions and philosophical disquisitions which comfort the readers of Adam Smith, even though they may help their author to sidetrack analytical obstacles. Smith's manner of presentation was such that his book could eventually be read and enjoyed by educated people who were not specialists in economic discussion. Ricardo, unschooled in the academic manner, was more strictly a scientist. He wrote for his fellow economists; and it is on them that his influence was greatest.

A change of method seems to have been necessary in order to make a step forward in the discovery of the laws underlying the economic system. The rigorous deductive method which is often ascribed to

1 *The Collected Works and Correspondence of David Ricardo*, ed. P. Sraffa (1951–55), 11 vols.

Ricardo replaced the less austere mixture of deduction and history which Smith had practised. There is plenty of *a priori* reasoning in the *Principles*. There is the assumption of the economic man always striving to achieve his maximum advantage; there are postulates about the social framework, such as the existence of competition; and illustration is generally hypothetical rather than historical. Altogether, the reader of the book breathes a highly rarefied air of abstraction.

Nevertheless, the approach had not really changed much. The economic man leads as lively an existence in the pages of Smith as in those of Ricardo. Even in Smith's demonstration the working of the invisible hand gradually loses its providential basis and comes to depend on the social fact of competition. And if Ricardo reverted to the method of 'let us suppose', he did so because the essential economic categories, which Smith and his predecessors had laboriously endeavoured to extract from the sum total of historical development, were now available in their abstract form. Moreover, with all his apparent abstraction, Ricardo was essentially a practical thinker: in the sense that his theorizing was always about his contemporary world, which he knew well.[1]

The main achievement of Ricardo is to be found in the theory of value and distribution. He begins with value and to it he devotes his longest chapter. Nor does he leave any doubt about his interest in distribution. In the preface to the first edition he begins with the statement that the whole produce is divided among the three classes of the community, that the proportions of this division vary in different stages of society, that 'to determine the laws which regulate this distribution is the principal problem in Political Economy', and that hitherto there has been given 'very little satisfactory information respecting the natural course of rent, profit, and wages'.[2] He makes this point even more emphatically in a letter to Malthus. Against the latter's definition of political economy as an inquiry into the nature and causes of wealth, he urges that 'it should rather be called an inquiry into the laws which determine the division of the produce of industry amongst the classes who concur in its formation'.[3]

Ricardo was interested in the problems which Smith had raised

---

1 Cf. S. N. Patten, 'The Interpretation of Ricardo', in *Quarterly Journal of Economics*, 1893, pp. 322–52. This is also well brought out by a study of his numerous contributions to contemporary public and parliamentary controversies.

2 D. Ricardo, *Principles of Political Economy and Taxation* (Everyman edition 1926), p. 1.

3 *Letters of Ricardo to Malthus, 1810–1823* (ed. J. Bonar, 1887), p. 175.

without succeeding in elucidating them. He wanted to discover the relations of the different classes of society, and the dynamics of the economic system. He found the clue in the most striking phenomenon of the economic system, exchange-value. His analysis of the causes of value had the same purpose as physiocratic theory: the discovery of the origin of the surplus product, and a consequent classification of different activities and classes of society and of various policies in relation to the production, accumulation, and distribution of that surplus product. The structure of the *Principles* is not in harmony with Ricardo's own interest. The argument is often ill arranged. The distinction between use-value and exchange-value which is quickly discussed in chapter i occupies, in different form, the whole of chapter xx. Chapters ii and iii, which contain Ricardo's famous theory of rent, are supplemented by several later chapters which controvert the views of Smith and Malthus. The discussions on price, supply, demand, and foreign trade spread over several non-contiguous chapters. Wages and profits, discussed in chapters v and vi, are further elucidated in the last chapter but one (added in the third edition) which deals with machinery. And a disproportionately large number of chapters are concerned with the subsidiary problems of taxation.

*The Theory of Value and Distribution.*    In view of this absence of a logical plan, it is convenient to describe Ricardo's theory under the following headings: first, the theory of value; second, the theory of wages, profits, and rent; third, the theory of accumulation; and, finally, the theory of economic development. To complete the picture there must also be added a few words about Ricardo's theories of money, banking, and international trade.

To understand Ricardo's development of the theory of value it is important to remember the position in which Smith had left it. He had wrestled with the determination of value by labour (i.e. the actual time of labour used to produce a commodity) and its determination by the value of labour. In pre-capitalist production this dualism did not matter because the two factors could be shown to be identical: the value of an amount of labour embodied in a commodity was equal to the value of command over the same amount of labour. But in capitalist production the value of the labour which the capitalist bought was greater than the amount of labour embodied in the wages which he gave for it. Thus a surplus appeared which was appropriated by the capitalist. On this basis one could argue that in capitalist production the postulated identity disappeared and that in the exchange of capital and wage-labour capital received a greater value than it gave. This argument was chosen by Marx.

Smith did not develop such an exploitation theory; instead he had recourse to an explanation which recognized other factors, additional to labour, as productive of value. Ricardo was faced with a similar difficulty and his solution represents an advance over Smith which avoided the conclusion of Marx. He is in advance of Smith because of his greater consistency. He refuses to limit the validity of the labour theory of value to pre-capitalist times. He deliberately states it as the fundamental and universal principle and proceeds to examine how far the different aspects of capitalist economy are compatible with it.

He begins by referring to Smith's distinction of the two uses of the term value. He admits that utility is essential if a commodity is to possess exchange-value, but dismisses it as a measure of that value. Exchange-value is derived from scarcity or labour. Rare statues or pictures have a value which is not measured by the amount of labour originally bestowed upon them. But these are comparatively unimportant commodities in a capitalist system. The vast bulk of commodities used by man are capable of almost limitless multiplication. In primitive societies their value is determined 'almost exclusively' by 'the comparative quantity of labour expended on them'.[1] Ricardo uncovers the confusion in Smith's statement of the theory and concludes that it is 'the comparative quantity of commodities which labour will produce that determines their present or past relative value, and not the comparative quantities of commodities which are given to the labourer in exchange for his labour'.[2]

But Ricardo is not free from confusion himself. He says that the determination of this relative value of commodities helps to determine how changes arise in the ratio in which commodities exchange, and he speaks in another place of the comparative values of commodities. However, relative value, as he calls it, may change equally for two commodities if the amount of labour necessary to produce them alters at the same rate, thus leaving their comparative value (the ratio of exchange) unchanged. Ricardo seems to be unaware of this double meaning. He claims that his interest is in the variations in the relative value of commodities and not in their absolute (or real) value. Yet it is clear that his own labour theory of value refers precisely to that

1 D. Ricardo, *Principles* (Everyman edition) p. 6.
2 ibid., p. 6.

absolute value. It is this confusion between (labour-determined) value and the ratio of exchange which was later to be used by Bailey in his attack on Ricardo.

Ricardo tries to show that labour creates value in capitalist as well as in primitive conditions of production. In section 3 of the first chapter, he states that not only present but also past labour, embodied in implements, tools, buildings, etc., determines value. The equipment which is used in production represents so much stored-up labour which enters into the value of the product as it is used up. The question of ownership, i.e. of the particular social conditions of production, does not affect the result. Value remains determined by current and stored-up labour, whether the latter belongs to the labourer or not. The only difference is that in the latter case the value of the product which is appropriated by the capitalist is divided into two parts, one which pays the wages of the labourer, the other which is the capitalist's profit.

In this way Ricardo plunges at once into the problem of profit and into the question of wages; and he is brought face to face with the dilemma which has made Smith retreat from the labour theory. The way in which Ricardo deals with these questions is obscure and ill arranged. His solution depends on his theories of wages and profits; but although these are not dealt with until later, he already anticipates their results in the sections of the first chapter which deal with the law of value in capitalist production. The ostensible purpose of sections 4 and 5 is to show how changes in the value of labour (i.e. wages) cause changes in the value of commodities owing to the use, in different proportions, of capital of different degrees of durability and to the differing periods of turnover of capital. In other words, he is here dealing with certain modifications in the law of value the possibility of which he had, in controversion of Smith, denied at first, but which he appears to have regarded with increasing concern and to which he gave more and more space in successive editions of the *Principles*.

Whatever his original intention, Ricardo does not show in these sections that these variations in value have in fact anything to do with changes in wages. He does, however, demonstrate that assuming an average rate of profits and an average level of wages (both established according to laws which he developed subsequently), the existence of differing capital structures (proportions of labour and capital), together with the other factors mentioned, will lead to the need to modify the law of value. Some commodities will exchange at a higher, some at a lower, value. Value, as determined by quantity of labour necessary in production, is no longer identical with market price; this is equal to the wages paid by the capitalist and the average rate of profit which he has to earn if he is to continue to employ his capital. What Ricardo in fact does is to pose a fresh problem which he never solved. Marx, basing himself on the Ricardian theory, took this problem up again and evolved the distinction between values and price of production. This, however, as we shall see, did not remove the contradiction and, therefore, offered no solution.

On this point must be added the statements of chapter iv, 'On Natural and Market Pirce', and of chapter xxx, 'On the Influence of Demand and Supply on Prices'. They show again Ricardo's confusion between value (determined by labour) and price, which depends on the averaging of profits. A difference arises between the two owing to differences in capital structure. But the fluctuations with which Ricardo is concerned are those of the market prices due to the changes in supply and demand. This particular failure to show how discrepancies arise between prices and value persists through the theory of rent. It is no doubt due to the influence of Adam Smith, against whose views of the problem of value in capitalist production Ricardo was struggling. It explains why many later economists claimed to see in Ricardo's work nothing but a cost-of-production theory, and why it was possible for them to eliminate the labour theory of value altogether.

Ricardo's theory of wages and profits contains also a mixture of confusion and achievement. In the chapter on wages Ricardo regards labour as a commodity whose value must be determined in the same way as that of any other commodity. Its 'natural price' is that which is 'necessary to enable the labourers, one with another, to subsist and to perpetuate their race, without either increase or diminution'. This in its turn depends 'on the quantity of food, necessaries, and conveniences which become essential to him from habit'.[1] This, in other words, is a subsistence theory into which the social and historical factor of habit has been introduced. The market price of labour may differ from the natural price in accordance with supply and demand; but it will always tend to the natural price, which is determined by the customary level of subsistence.

The principle that population tends to increase with an increase in the means of subsistence, which had been fully developed by Malthus,

1 D. Ricardo, *Principles*, p. 52.

underlay the Ricardian theory of wages. If wages remained above the natural price for any length of time the supply of labour would increase and bring them down again. A steady improvement in wages depended on a continually increasing demand for labour and that could only be brought about by perpetual accumulation of capital. Here is one way in which the Ricardian insistence on accumulation could be made palatable to labour; though, in the factor of habit, Ricardo had introduced a new variable which required further elaboration if the system was to stand. Ricardo himself did not pursue this point; his theory becomes, however, a part of his view of economic development.

In spite of a mixture of arguments Ricardo determines wages fairly consistently with his own theory of value. The value of the labour brought by the capitalist, he says, is determined by the quantity of labour embodied in the commodities that form the labourer's subsistence. But at once he has to face Adam Smith's difficulty. According to the labour theory of value the exchange of commodities involves the exchange of equal quantities of labour embodied in them. This equivalence seems to disappear when capital and labour are exchanged. The real wages paid to the labourer (i.e. the commodities which he buys) possess a smaller value than the commodity which he produces for the capitalist. Ricardo had clearly pointed out that Smith had come to grief through continuing to use as equivalent the terms 'amount of labour' and 'value of labour' when, as in capitalist production, they were no longer equivalent. His own way out is simply to say that the value of labour is itself variable, 'being not only affected, as all other things are, by the proportion between the supply and demand, which uniformly varies with every change in the condition of the community, but also by the varying price of food and other necessaries, on which the wages of labour are expended'.[1]

But this is not a complete solution. It does not explain the origin of the capitalist's profit; and it also involves leaving a serious gap in the structure of the labour theory of value in so far as the value of labour (as Ricardo calls it) is itself concerned. In capitalist production wage-labour is a commodity like any other; indeed, its existence as a commodity is an essential condition of capitalism. To establish a theory of value and then to make it inoperative in its most important application was a contradiction in Ricardo's work which his opponents soon

1 D. Ricardo, *Principles*, p. 8.

discovered and used to destroy the whole theory. Ricardo's formulation made it impossible for him to solve the problem. We shall see later by what device Marx endeavoured unsuccessfully to get out of Ricardo's difficulty without abandoning the labour theory of value.

Ricardo tried to maintain the labour theory without allowing it to lead to a theory of exploitation, as Marx was later to do. By making the value of commodities depend on past, equally with present labour and by saying that the value of labour varied (this involved abandoning his original theory of wages), he thought to incorporate capital into his system and to have found an explanation for profits. At the same time he thought that he had avoided Smith's admission of capital as a productive agent. But when he came to deal with profits he tacitly accepted much of Smith's theory.

He seems to have become increasingly aware of the direction in which this theory was taking him and in the end he came very near to saying that capital was productive of value. In a letter written to McCulloch in 1820 he virtually admitted this. 'I sometimes think', he said, 'that if I were to write the chapter on value again ... I should acknowledge that the relative value of commodities was regulated by two causes instead of by one, namely, by the relative quantity of labour necessary to produce the commodities in question, and by the rate of profit for the time that the capital remained dormant, and until the commodities were brought to market.' The theory of distribution, he thought, could perhaps be separated from the theory of value. 'After all, the great questions of Rent, Wages, and Profit must be explained by the proportions in which the whole produce is divided between landlords, capitalists, and labourers, and which are not essentially connected with the doctrine of value.'[1] Here we see once again that the difference between prices and value caused by the existence of different capital structures was leading Ricardo to a cost-of-production theory of value. Indeed, in one place he speaks of a difference in value being 'only a just compensation for the time that the profits were withheld'.[2] The only additional point of importance that Ricardo makes in connection with profits is to demonstrate how competition tends to establish a uniform rate of profits, by attracting capital into channels which yield a rate above the average and repelling it from those in which profits are below the average. It is only when he comes

1 *Letters of David Ricardo to J. R. McCulloch* (ed. T. H. Hollander, 1895), p. 72.
2 D. Ricardo, *Principles*, p. 23.

to his dynamics that a concept of profits based upon the original theory of value reappears.

In order to make his rescue of the labour theory from the Smithian dilemma complete, Ricardo had also to exclude land from the creation of value. On the other hand, he had no need to avoid conclusions which were hostile to the landed interest. If it was his purpose (which was also inherent in the *Wealth of Nations*) to imply the productivity of capital, he was also determined far more than Smith to represent the claims of landed property as economically unjustified. The resulting theory of rent reflects these two aims.

The significant features of Ricardo's theory of rent are the denial of absolute rent and the explanation of differential rent. The exclusion of absolute rent was essential if the theory of value was to remain coherent. The very existence of rent seemed to Ricardo to imply that the produce of land exchanged for more than its value as compared with manufactured goods. This he could not admit. What then was the explanation of the undoubted existence of a revenue from landed property? The answer is contained in his well-known theory of differential rent. By building on the foundations laid by Smith he showed that there were conditions in which rent did not exist.

Given differences in the fertility of the soil and in its situation in relation to the market, the cost of production of agricultural produce will vary. The price of that produce must, however, be high enough to cover the highest cost of production (i.e. the cost of production on the worst soil) which, given a certain demand, must be incurred in order to bring forth the necessary supply. Production on the worst land will just cover cost; cost will equal price. On better land a surplus will appear, which will accrue to the owner of the land if he cultivated it himself, or may be exacted by him from the tenants owing to the competition between these for better land. This theory explained not only the existence of rent in certain conditions and its absence in others; it also made rent into a pure surplus and eliminated it from the determination of value. In addition, it explained differences in the amount of rent yielded by different lands.

This way out of the difficulty was certainly more successful than the method which Ricardo had adopted in relation to capital. This theory of rent had the advantage of enabling Ricardo to inveigh strongly against the landed interest.[1] Rent still remained a surplus; and in his

1 D. Ricardo, *Essay on the Influences of a Low Price of Corn on the Profits of Stock* (1185), *passim.*

accounts of changes in the proportions of the revenues of the three classes of society which take place in the course of time, Ricardo concluded that the share which went to rent increased steadily. This theory became in the hands of subsequent writers (and was so to some extent in the hands of Ricardo too) a powerful new weapon against the landed interest. The defenders of rent were henceforth obliged to stress its constituent element, the interest on the capital, spent in the improvement of land which Ricardo had already mentioned. But the differential theory remained, to explain why there were differences in rent even when the capital invested was the same. And this differential theory implied the notion of a surplus and of an unearned increment.

Analytically in the terms of Ricardo's own theoretical system, however, the differential theory was not satisfactory. It was based on the frequent confusion between value (amount of labour) and price (wages plus average profit). Only by identifying the two could Ricardo conclude that on the poorest (no rent) land, on which price equalled cost, the produce sold at its value and the labour theory of value was satisfied. Once the identity between value and price was abandoned, the problem of fitting rent into the labour theory still remained.

*The Theory of Economic Development.* We now have to consider in what way Ricardo applies his theories of distribution and value to the analysis of dynamic problems. His account of the effects of capital accumulation on wages, profits, and rent, although not systematically worked out, has had an even more profound influence on subsequent economic thought than the rest of his work. Apart from the fact that it necessarily involves highly controversial problems of social welfare, it possesses significance also because it has a bearing on the question of economic crises which soon after Ricardo's day begins its chequered career in the history of economic thought.

Indications of a theory of economic development had already appeared in the *Wealth of Nations*. Smith had shown that profits on an average tended to fall with economic progress. Increasing accumulation of capital brought with it increasing competition among capitalists; and this reduced profits. Ricardo does not accept this view. He tries to show that accumulation would only tend to reduce profits in certain conditions. In the first place, he has to find out how profits vary at all. The price of corn, he says, is determined by the 'quantity of labour necessary to produce it, with that portion or capital which pays no rent'. The price of manufactured goods rises and falls in accordance with the amount of labour necessary to produce them. The whole value of manufactured goods and of the corn grown on the no-rent land is divided into two parts only: profits and wages. Then follows a vital passage: 'Supposing corn and manufactured goods always to sell at the same price, profits would be high or low in proportion as wages were low or high. But suppose corn to rise in price because more labour is necessary to produce it; that cause will not raise the price of manufactured goods in the production of which no additional quantity of labour is required. If, then, wages continue the same, the profits of manufacturers would remain the same; but if, as it is absolutely certain, wages should rise with the price of corn, then these profits would necessarily fall.'[1]

Ricardo thus uses his theory of differential rent, his subsistence theory of wages, and his own version of the labour theory of value to show that profit and wages are inversely related. It follows that though competition will tend to establish a uniform rate of profits, the accumulation of capital will reduce that rate only if it is accompanied by a rise in wages. In other words, population must grow more slowly than capital, the demand for labour must increase at a greater rate than its supply, if, as a consequence of the rise in wages, profits are to fall. The theory of population shows that such a permanent excess of demand over supply is impossible. Yet Ricardo maintains that there is a tendency for profits to fall, only for a different reason. Because he regards profits and wages as inversely related, the reason for the fall of the former must still be found in a circumstance which makes the latter rise. Wages, according to this theory, will rise if the value of the commodities which form the labourer's subsistence rises. But the value of manufactured goods must decline with the progressive improvement in the productivity of labour. Thus only food remains; and here the theory of rent is called in to furnish an explanation. It amounts to this, that 'the only adequate and permanent cause for the rise of wages is the increasing difficulty of providing food and necessaries for the increasing number of workmen'.[2]

The theory of differential rent implies that progressively less fertile (or less favourably situated) lands are taken into cultivation as population and the demand for food increase. It was this implication which was expressed in the 'law of diminishing returns' and formed the basis

1 D. Ricardo, *Principles*, p. 64.
2 ibid., p. 197.

of the Malthusian theory of population. It meant that in spite of his references to the rent-lowering effects of some improvement in agriculture[1] Ricardo continued to believe in a progressive decline of the fertility of land and in a continual rise in the price of food. Money wages, he thought, would have to go on rising in order to keep up with the rising cost of subsistence, though real wages need not rise. Rent would rise steadily and profits would as steadily decline.

Ricardo draws a pessimistic picture of the future. What is more, he implicity destroys the harmony of social interests which Smith had been at pains to establish. The interest of the landlord is now opposed not only to that of the labourer and industrialist; it conflicts also with the general interest of society. It requires that the price of food should continually rise while both capitalist and workers desire a low cost of subsistence. 'The dealings between the landlord and the public are not like dealing in trade, whereby both the seller and the buyer may equally be said to gain, but the loss is wholly on one side, and the gain wholly on the other.' Adam Smith, although many of his conclusions were antagonistic to the landed interest, had still identified the interests of the landlord with those of society. Ricardo's theory of rent leads to a more ruthless conclusion. 'The interest of the landlord is always opposed to that of the consumer and manufacturer.' It is to 'the interest of the landlord that the cost attending the production of corn should be increased. This, however, is not the interest of the consumer ... neither is the interest of the manufacturer. ... All classes, therefore, except the landlords will be injured by the increase in the price of corn.'[2]

It is true that this prognosis rested on a fallacious interpretation of the differential theory of rent. Even if poorer lands are taken into cultivation as society progresses, the application of science to agriculture can more than make up for the deterioration of the soil used. The 'law of diminishing returns', on which Ricardo based the theory of rent and Malthus the theory of population, is certainly not applicable to conditions of change. As later economists have shown, it expresses a formal relation in an idealized state of stationary equilibrium, and it contains an element of historical truth only in the very rare cases in which technique does not change. Moreover, the theory of differential rent does not require that the fertility of land should continually

1 D. Ricardo, *Principles*, pp. 40, 42 *sqq.*
2 ibid., p. 225.

decline; it only rests on the existence of lands of differing fertilities. It is possible for general fertility to increase without altering the relative fertilities of different qualities of soil. The price of agricultural produce could, therefore, fall while rent increased. Nevertheless, there are aspects of the Ricardian theory of the rising trend of the price of food which some modern economists have found to have a good deal of validity. Particularly in certain theories about the longer-term trend in the terms on which industrial and agricultural countries trade their products something of the Ricardian system comes to life again.

The other aspect of Ricardo's theory of economic development, the decline of the rate of profits, was also based on an unsound foundation. The tendency for the rate of profits to fall could only be true if profits were indeed inversely related to wages. In his discussion of capital Ricardo himself had dimly realized that two separate categories could be distinguished: the rate of profit which bore a relation to capital, and the surplus, which consisted of the difference between the value of a commodity and the wages paid by the capitalist to the worker who produced it. But he did not work out the distinction and concluded that if wages fell, profits rose, and vice versa, without pointing out that this did not necessarily apply to the rate of profits.

But the analytical faults in Ricardo's theory made no difference to its effect on political thought and action. Ricardo was as ardent a free-trader and believer in competition as Adam Smith. And with his theory of rent he had provided free-trade doctrine with a specific problem to tackle. The interests of society demanded a low price for corn. A rise, however, seemed inevitable particularly in view of the observed rise during the crises of the Napoleonic wars; and the only way to delay it was to secure as large a supply as possible, in particular from countries in which the fertility of the soil had not yet appreciably declined. The abolition of the Corn Laws, in the interests of cheap food and low manufacturing cost, was now based on an economic analysis and became the immediate objective of the free-trade movement.

The doctrine of rent also became not only an important theoretical weapon in the campaign against the Corn Laws; it was to be the foundation of the single-tax and land-nationalization proposals of later social reformers. Moreover, once the possibility of a conflict of individual and common interest and exploitation arising from one form of property had been admitted, it became possible to criticize in similar terms other forms of exploitation. Thus, the post-Ricardian English socialists and Marx started where Ricardo left off, and, to the extent to which they drew their intellectual ammunition from Ricardo, the previously quoted charge by Carey contains at least an element of 'hindsight'.

Two other questions connected with the accumulation of capital have a place in the Ricardian system: over-production and crises. Ricardo's *Principles* do not contain much on either of these points. Writing at a time when capitalism had not reached maturity, he had little to say about crises. He had witnessed the disturbances of the Napoleonic wars and was forced to deal with the problem of fluctuations in economic activity. But he only devotes one short chapter to it, which he significantly calls 'On Sudden Changes in the Channels of Trade'. Here, he ascribes these changes to fortuitous circumstances and not to any cause inherent in the economic system. War, taxation, fashion will alter the relative profitability of different branches of production both in the country in which these factors operate and in the countries that maintain trading relations with it. Labour and capital will have to be transferred and distress will occur until the economic system has adapted itself to the changed conditions. Rich countries, which have large amounts of capital invested in manufacturing industry, will find these sudden dislocations more painful than poor countries. And even agriculture will be affected by wars and the changes in the export and import of produce which they bring about.

Having put these causes of economic fluctuations outside the economic system, it is natural that Ricardo should also claim that that system had no inherent tendencies to disequilibrium. In this respect he was accepting the theory which he attributed to the French economist, Jean Baptiste Say, that there could never be any general over-production or glut of capital in a country. This view became a very important part of the classical tradition. Ricardo's advocacy of it involved him in a controversy with his friend Malthus which is one of the most famous in the history of economic thought. This controversy revealed an important departure from, and criticism of, the classical position and is therefore deferred to the next chapter.

The summary given in the next chapter shows Ricardo to have been on the whole, a faithful supporter of the prevailing theory of the market. However, some important differences between him and his less important contemporaries should be pointed out. We have seen that, according to Ricardo, economic progress, by bringing about a fall in the rate of profit, involves a diminution in the motive to accumulation. This consequence of the theory of economic development is not directly incompatible with the manner in which Ricardo had upheld Say's law. Nevertheless, it leaves Ricardo's complacency on the score that a glut of capital was impossible in a somewhat shaken condition. In Ricardo's version of Say's law we shall find that a fall in the rate of profit as an accompaniment to capital accumulation is only a temporary phenomenon, caused by a delay in the assertion of the principle of population. But we know that he maintains also that there is an historical tendency for such a fall in the rate of profit produced by the working of the principle of diminishing returns. Thus we shall see that Ricardo goes beyond the tautologies of Say and tries to formulate the theory of the market in a way which is more in harmony with the fundamental facts of a capitalist profit economy.

Another of his doctrines which may be mentioned here also has a bearing on the theory of the level, development, and fluctuation of economic activity. This is Ricardo's theory concerning the effects of technical progress. In the third edition of his *Principles*, published in 1821, Ricardo included a new chapter entitled 'On Machinery'. In this he sets down views which contradict theories current at the time and to which Ricardo himself, so he tells us, had previously subscribed.[1] This classical theory from which Ricardo dissented was a close corollary of Say's law of the market. It was a reply to the antagonism which had greeted the spread of machinery in the eighteenth and nineteenth centuries. The fears of the workers, it was argued, were groundless. There would be temporary hardships; but, in the long run, the increase of machinery could only be beneficial. An increase in machinery, it was pointed out, increased the productivity of labour, and thus the supply of goods. According to Say's law, the demand for goods would inevitably increase also. And so displacement of labour could only be temporary; reabsorption of labour, either in the same or in other industries, was inevitable in the long run; and an increase in the total product of industry could be expected as the ultimate consequence of technical progress. This view, with elaborations and refinements, held sway throughout the nineteenth century as far as the main stream of economic thought was concerned. Ricardo however, who clung (though somewhat inconsistently) to Say's law, abandoned this important corollary.

[1] See Sraffa's comments in his introduction to *The Collected Works of Ricardo*, vol. 1, pp. 7–9.

Ricardo's view on machinery may be summarized as follows. He begins by laying stress on the motive force of capitalist production, the individual entrepreneur's expectation of profit. The introduction of machinery, he argues, will be determined by its expected effect upon profit, or, as he puts it, upon the net produce rather than upon the gross produce of industry. With the aid of an arithmetical example, Ricardo shows that an increase in machinery may lead to an increase in the net product with an accompanying decline in the gross product. This means, of course, that a permanent displacement of labour could be caused by the introduction of new technical devices. Ricardo concludes that an 'increase of the net produce of a country is compatible with the diminution of the gross produce', and 'that the opinion entertained by the labouring class, that the employment of machinery is frequently detrimental to their interests, is not founded on prejudice and error, but is conformable to the correct principles of political economy'.[1]

Later economists have pointed out that Ricardo's conclusion only held for the short run. The Swedish economist, Knut Wicksell, in particular argued that in the long run the displacement of workers from enterprises which employed the labour-saving devices would lower wages and would make the continuance of some enterprises with the older methods once again profitable.[2] But the main importance of the whole discussion was shifted to another level by some remarks made by Ricardo himself. As if to sum up and emphasize his earlier conclusion, he added some views which he had taken over from a contemporary work by John Barton, *Observations on the Circumstances which Influence the Conditions of the Labouring Classes* (1817). Returning to his theory of economic development, he argued that 'with every increase of capital and population, food will generally rise'. This must bring about a rise in wages, 'and every rise of wages will have a tendency to determine the saved capital in a greater proportion than before to the employment of machinery'. Thus 'machinery and labour are in constant competition, and the former can frequently not be employed until labour (i.e. wages) rises'.[3] Ricardo thus states that the historical tendency of capital accumulation involves a change in the proportions in which capital is laid out. According to him, 'with every

1 D. Ricardo, *Principles*, p. 383.
2 K. Wicksell, *Lectures on Political Economy* (1936), vol. i, p. 13.
3 D. Ricardo, *Principles*, p. 386.

augmentation of capital, a greater proportion of it is employed on machinery'. As for the demand for labour, it 'will continue to increase with an increase of capital, but not in proportion to its increase; the ratio will, necessarily, be a diminishing ratio'.[1] Ricardo had already admitted that quite apart from the question of an increase in the net product, the manner in which a net product of given size is consumed affected the demand for labour. He urged that the employment out of the capitalists' profit of unproductive labour ('retainers, or menial servants') was to be preferred to expenditure on luxury goods. For although the gross produce would be the same in either case, the disposition of the net produce in the former rather than the latter manner would increase the demand for labour. It seems therefore that if, as Ricardo himself did, we generalize the question so as to bring it into line with the problem dealt with by Say's law and try to ascertain the effects on the demand for labour of capital accumulation, the gross product-net product relation, first emphasized by Ricardo, ceases to be of importance. On the other hand, the door is opened to further exploration of the changes which occur in the occupational structure of the population and the new forms in which demand arises as the economy progresses through the accumulation of capital.

Thus, in this respect, no less than in regard to the original point of the theory of the market, Ricardo left the automatic self-regulation of the classical system in a seriously weakened condition. It has been the fashion in recent years to regard Ricardo's work as the most distinct exposition of the belief contained in the classical theory that the economic system automatically achieved full employment and equilibrium through time, and that fluctuations of economic activity or prolonged stagnation were impossible. Closer examination reveals, however, that Ricardo's analysis, because it penetrated to greater depths than did that of his contemporaries, was by far the least tautologous statement of these classical beliefs. It left open many problems to which subsequent theories could be attached. The theories of over-accumulation and under-consumption propounded by Malthus and Sismondi and by many nineteenth-century writers which broke against the smooth wall of the tautologies of Say and James Mill would have found a less intransigent opponent in the Ricardian theory. Again, many modern theories of technological unemployment or of

1 D. Ricardo, *Principles*, p. 387.

disproportions in the structure of production can be traced back to the views enunciated by Ricardo.

Ricardo's other theories, though important in their special fields, do not affect his general position. A very brief summary must suffice. These theories concern the problems of money and banking and the mechanism of international payments. Ricardo was led to their study by urgent questions of the day. He had witnessed the great currency upheavals connected with the wars and he had seen the suspension of cash payments in 1797, the great depreciation of paper money, and the marked rise in prices which followed it. In *The High Price of Bullion*, published in 1809, on the eve of the issue of the famous report of the Bullion Committee, he explained that these phenomena had been caused by an over-issue of paper money. He developed a rigorous quantity theory of money, applied it to the international mechanism, showed that inflation and depreciation caused an outflow of gold, and proposed that the Bank of England should gradually reduce the amount of notes in circulation until the price of gold had been brought down to its previous level. Ricardo did not advocate the complete abolition of paper money. On the contrary, like Adam Smith, he regarded the use of a substitute for the money metal as an important corollary of economic progress and he urged the complete withdrawal of gold from active circulation. What he advocated was a gold-bullion standard in which there were no gold coins, and banknotes were convertible at a fixed rate, but only in large amounts, into gold bars. The essence of Ricardo's theory was accepted by the Bullion Committee, and subsequent banking legislation, particularly the resumption of cash payments in 1822 and Peel's Bank Charter Act of 1844, reflect strongly the Ricardian influence.

It is necessary to point out that Ricardo's treatment of money is by no means free from inconsistency, for he had himself approached the question of money from the point of view of the labour theory of value. He had said that the value of gold and silver, like that of other commodities, was determined by the amount of labour in them. Given their value, the quantity of currency in a country will be determined by the sum of the values of all goods that enter into exchange. The metals may be replaced in the process of circulation by substitutes (paper money), which must be issued in a proportion determined by the value of the money metal. The essence of this theory of money is that the quantity of currency depends on prices and not vice versa. Here is a clear conflict with the quantity theory.

But it is the latter to which Ricardo has recourse in stating his theory of international payments. His analysis is now a part of accepted economic theory. Briefly, it amounts to this: a rise or fall in prices is due to an excess or deficiency of the amount of currency in circulation. If that currency consists entirely of the internationally accepted precious metals, the fluctuations in the circulating medium (and therefore in prices) will bring about their own correction. If, for example, there is too much gold in circulation prices will rise and imports will be stimulated. This will cause gold to leave the country; the initial excess of gold will disappear and with it the high prices. This movement cannot take place when part of the currency consists of banknotes. It becomes, therefore, an object of banking policy to regulate the issue of notes in accordance with the international movements of gold and so to reproduce the conditions of a purely metallic circulation. This object was accepted by the exponents of the so-called 'currency principle' and became a tradition of central bank policy. Ricardo, who was largely responsible for establishing it, did not work out clearly its consequences for his own theory. He did not realize that it ascribed to the precious metals so great an importance as to be almost reminiscent of bullionist ideas. Nor did he seem to be fully aware of its inconsistency with his own theory of value.

The importance of Ricardo is that of every great scientific pioneer. He succeeded even more than Smith in isolating the chief categories of the economic system. He left to his successors many unsolved problems, but he also indicated ways in which they might be solved. Several streams of thought have their origin in his work. On the one hand the Marxian theory, though in a distorted form, makes use of the imperfections of classical political economy as expressed by Ricardo. At the same time, the disintegration of the labour theory of value begins with Ricardo's immediate followers. His emphasis on distribution raised the question of class relations and directed attention to social and historical factors in economic analysis. It also marked the end of the search for an index to the wealth of a community and shifted emphasis from the problems of absolute quantity to those of proportion. Ricardo's own preoccupation with the problem of relative values stimulated interest in the determination of individual prices, and this became the chief problem of economics in the latter part of the nineteenth century. Thus modern economics with its interest in the problems of equilibrium may still claim Ricardo as its founder.

## Malthus's Theory of Population

Several references have already been made to the work of one whom it is usual to regard as a member of the classical system. But Thomas Robert Malthus has only one foot in the Ricardian camp. His theories of rent and population are important parts of economic classicism. Yet although Malthus achieved great fame as the exponent of a particular view on these subjects, they are not his most important contributions to economic thought. His systematic treatise is noted mainly for its attack on the Ricardian doctrines of capital accumulation and, in a minor way, for its exposition of a dissenting theory of value. Malthus is in these less original than his modern admirers realize; but there is no doubt that in retrospect his criticism of, rather than his acquiescence in, classicism is of importance. However, in this chapter we are concerned with him as a member of the classical school.

We shall see that much of Malthus's opposition to the Ricardian theory of accumulation has certain social and political roots. His views on population and rent were the results of a reaction to his domestic environment. His father, Daniel Malthus, was an educated country gentleman with intellectual interests and liberal beliefs. He was a friend of Hume (through whom he met Rousseau), an admirer of Condorcet, and a disciple of the latter's English interpreter, Godwin. He shared Godwin's optimism about the future and believed with him in the perfectibility of the human race and in the possibility of achieving an age in which reason reigned, and all were happy and equal.

Robert Malthus reacted against these views. He was impressed by the views of population in the *Wealth of Nations* and the works of earlier writers, and by the law of diminishing returns which was in the minds of many economists and which had been stated clearly by Turgot. He combined these fragments into a theory of population, the conclusion of which contradicted the prevailing optimism. In 1798 he published anonymously the *Essay on the principle of population as it affects the future improvement of society*. What he opposed to the optimism of Condorcet and Godwin was the fear of population tending to outrun the means of subsistence. Given the 'passion between the sexes', the need for food, the observed fact that population increased when the means of subsistence increased, and the declining yield of the soil, the point must be reached when the increase of population overtakes the increase in the supply of food.

Malthus expressed this in the formula that population tended to increase in a geometrical progression (1, 2, 4, 8, 16, 32 ...) while subsistence increased only in arithmetical progression (1, 2, 3, 4, 5, 6 ...). It may well be that he regarded this formula merely as an illustration. But its expression in this from helped to make his theory spectacular and to draw upon it support and criticism in abundance. Malthus thought that the only means of keeping population within the limits of subsistence were vice and misery, and he thus disposed of the optimistic view of the future of society.

After the publication of the first edition of his pamphlet Malthus travelled widely and endeavoured to collect inductive proof for his theory. In the second edition of 1803 and in subsequent ones the *Essay* became an elaborate treatise. The progressions were no longer insisted on; historical material was introduced to buttress the thesis; the law was carefully summarized into three propositions; and a new check on the excessive growth of population was introduced. The three propositions are: (*a*) population is necessarily limited by the means of subsistence; (*b*) population increases where the means of subsistence increase unless prevented by some powerful and obvious checks; (*c*) these checks and the checks which repress the superior power of population and keep its effects on a level with the means of subsistence are all resolvable into moral restraint, vice, and misery.[1]

Excess population could be obviated by two kinds of checks: positive and preventive. The former were all those which increased the death-rate, like wars and famines; the latter, which diminished the birth-rate, were vice and moral restraint. As a practical policy Malthus proposed that people should be discouraged form helping to increase the population. They should be urged to exercise moral restraint, by which Malthus meant 'abstention from marriage not followed by irregular gratification'. And the poor in particular should be enjoined to exercise great prudence and not to rush into marriage and the creation of a family without due regard for the future. As a consequence Malthus was a strong opponent of Poor Relief. He advocated that the state should not recognize the right of the poor to receive support; and that it should abolish the Poor Law. Charity, private or public, was no remedy for the improvidence which had caused the misery of the poor. The poor had brought about their own distress (or, at any rate, their parents, who were not schooled in the Malthusian theory, were

1 *Essay on Population* (Everyman edition), vol. i, pp. 18–19.

responsible), and relief only provided an incentive for aggravating the problem.

The real basis of Malthus's theory of population is the one which underlies *An Enquiry into the Nature and Progress of Rent* (1815), in which he expounded a theory of differential rent similar to that of Ricardo. That basis was an application of the 'law of diminishing returns'. Turgot's statement that a doubling of the capital invested in agriculture would not double the yield was naturally understood, at first, as a law peculiar to agricultural production. If, after a time, an increased application of labour and capital to a given piece of land began to produce a less than proportionate increase in yield, more and poorer land would have to be taken into cultivation. Hence the increase in differential rent which Ricardo and Malthus postulated. Hence also the increasing difficulty of providing subsistence for growing population. The dynamics of Malthus and Ricardo require this particular law as a basis.

The facts of economic development after Malthus sufficiently contradicted his prognosis. A modern economist inquiring into changes in population will find that the development of contraceptive devices has made a great difference to Malthus's expectation. But even more important than the changes on the side of population have been those which have affected the food supply. The opening up of new areas of the world and the development of scientific methods in agriculture have increased and made it possible to increase still further the means of subsistence so as to maintain a larger population at a higher standard of living. As a dynamic principle, the 'law of diminishing returns' was clearly disproved; its place in modern economics is that of a law relating to the idealized condition of stationary equilibrium. With the disappearance of this analytical support Malthus's theory of population and the dynamic consequences of Ricardo's theory of differential rent also fell to the ground. There also went with it some of the theoretical superstructure concerning wages, capital and profits which Ricardo had built on his labour theory of value.

We have come to the end of the classical system. In the next three chapters we shall see the reaction and criticism which it called forth and its gradual transformation into a new body of generally accepted economic doctrine.

# 5

# Reaction and Revolution

## The Shortcomings of Classicism

Classical political economy can be viewed as a representation of the economic structure of the time, as a scientific system, as a theory of development and as a theory of economic policy. A study of Smith, Ricardo, and of the lesser writers of the school shows that those who developed classicism looked upon their work as an integration of these four aspects of economic inquiry. Although their effort to build a comprehensive economic theory produced some contradictions, it is a measure of their greatness that the system they built remained substantially appropriate for many generations and, indeed, in a measure to this day. With the exception of Marx's attempt to erect an entirely different structure on classical foundations, no new 'system' emerges from subsequent economic enquiry until the last quarter of the nineteenth century. And, indeed, not until the last twenty years has it become possible once again to synthesize what remains of classicism, the achievements of the marginalist schools and the intellectual discoveries of the most recent past into a new and comprehensive theory of the economy.

The classics were most successful perhaps in their representation of early capitalism. Their abstractions were far more representative of the essence of reality than anything that had gone before. But even some of their abstractions and assumptions became inadequate with changes in the quality of the capitalist system. In this respect, however, the faults which were later revealed were more closely connected with inadequacies in the other parts of their analysis. As a scientific system, too, classicism achieved a far greater degree of perfection than previous economic thought. It attempted to relate every part of its analytical structure to every other and to the whole. And in so far as emphasis on the functional interdependence of its component parts is a characteristic of a scientific system, the classics were the founders of economic science. They certainly did not avoid mistakes; and the inconsistencies which we have noted caused the distintegration of much of their logical structure.

As a theory of economic development classicism was much less successful. Not only did the logical weaknesses of its static system rob it of a basis on which to build an economic dynamic; on many important points its outlook was essentially unhistorical. In spite of their attention to past facts and ideas and in spite of their preoccupation with the future, the clssical writers were generally static in their view of the economic order. Many of their speculations about economic development showed great vision; for example, in spite of their shortcomings, Ricardo's theory of capital accumulation or Malthus's theory of population. But they regarded their categories as inherent in human nature, and, therefore, as possessing eternal validity. And while they saw the absence, in earlier systems, of the manner and motives of human conduct of their own day, they could not bring themselves to envisage the possibility that there might be further change in the course of time.

As part of a political theory economic classicism was consistently successful and long-lived. Some of its characteristics in this regard have already been noted. The labour theory of value had its roots in the theory of property which was part of the natural philosophy as developed, for example, by Locke. Labour constituted the source of, and title to, property in the natural state. The natural state demanded, therefore, freedom from any intervention which would disturb the natural property relations. Here, however, a possible conflict appears. The classical school applied the requirements of the natural order to the facts of the real world. Because in the real world the property relations which had been established in a long historical evolution were by no means equivalent to those of the natural order, it became possible to draw from the classical economic analysis different political conclusions. One trend becomes conservative with regard to the existing social order, the other critical. These conflicting trends, of course, run through classical literature.

Not only the postulate of freedom, but also the assumption of a harmony of interests which underlay the classical school, became the subject of conflicting conservative and radical interpretations after the appearance of utilitarianism. It is not necessary to go here into the details of utilitarian philosophy. But it must be pointed out that in assuming the existence of social harmony, classicism could be held to imply an egalitarian view of society; it considered the poor equally with the rich in calculating a maximum of social advantage. Bentham, the greatest exponent of this philosophy, went so far as to regard as desirable an equal distibution of income, a conclusion which many economists tried to defend later by means of a psychological refinement of Bentham's analysis. At any rate, the egalitarian interpretation of the concept of harmony could claim as much authority as the conservative one.

The criticisms of the classical school can be roughly divided into a technical and a political one. The former endeavours to eliminate logical inconsistencies and analytical imperfections. The latter attacks the political implications of classical economic analysis. These two kinds of criticism cannot be strictly separated. Technical criticism is often inspired by support of, or opposition to, the political philosophy underlying classicism. If this philosophy is accepted, the economic analysis may still be regarded as an insufficient basis. Attempts are then made to buttress it with fresh economic arguments. On the other hand, if the social philosophy is not accepted, criticism fastens on the inadequacies of the economic analysis. It is not always possible to disentangle the two types of attack on the classical school, but some such division must be made. In this chapter we are concerned with theoretical developments which carry with them, explicitly or implicitly, a criticism of the social and political doctrines of the classical school.

## Malthus's Critique of Accumulation

Indeed, the first attack upon classicism does not come as an explicit negation of its general conclusions. It comes in the guise of a highly technical argument which accepts many of the fundamental tenets of the Ricardian school but opposes their application to certain practical problems. This attack is Malthus's theory of gluts. Ricardo, as we have seen, had accepted Say's dictum (which may have been due to James Mill, in the first place)[1] that general over-production was impossible. We shall meet Say again as a Continental popularizer of Smith and as one of the chief critics of the labour theory of value. He is important

[1] M. Dobb, *Political Economy and Capitalism* (1937), p. 41.

here for his theory of the market, the *théorie des débouchées*, which he developed in his *Traité d'Economie politique*, published in 1803. The theory rests on the concept that every supply involves a demand, that product exchanges for product, that every commodity put on the market creates its own demand, and that every demand exerted in the market creates its own supply.

Put in this way, the theorem contains a simple statement about the interdependence of an exchange economy. Its importance lies in its application. If supply and demand are indissolubly bound together one can deny, as did Say and Ricardo, the possibility of a general glut of commodities, of general over-production. Partial over-production may well occur. One cannot deny that from time to time certain commodities are produced in excess of demand, i.e. that costs are incurred in production which price subsequently does not cover. But that only means that the other commodities have not been produced in a quantity sufficient to supply the demand for them. As Ricardo's most faithful disciple, James Mill, put it, 'there never can be a super-abundant supply in particular instances, and hence a fall in exchangeable value below cost of production without a corresponding deficiency of supply, and hence a rise in exchangeable value beyond cost of production in other instances'. Such partial maladjustments must correct themselves. If there be 'from maladjustment, ... super-abundance or defect', the rise and fall in prices would alter the relative profitability of different lines of production. 'There are certain kinds of goods which it is less profitable than usual to produce: and this is an inequality which tends immediately to correct itself.'[1]

'No man', said Ricardo, adopting Say's argument, 'produces but with a view to consume or sell, and he never sells but with an intention to purchase some other commodity, which may be immediately useful to him or which may contribute to future production. By producing, then, he necessarily becomes either the consumer of his own goods, or the purchaser and consumer of the goods of some other person.'[2] If all individual supplies and demands are exactly balanced, demand and supply in the aggregate must clearly also be balanced. If an individual balance is disturbed; if, for example, there is a glut of cloth, because supply has been increased, while demand has remained unchanged,

---

1 James Mill, *Elements of Political Economy* (2nd edition, 1824), pp. 234–6. An excellent edition of James Mill's *Selected Writings*, edited by Donald Winch, appeared in 1966.
2 D. Ricardo, *The Principles of Political Economy and Taxation* (Everyman edition), pp. 192–3.

'there must of necessity be a deficiency of other things; for the additional quantity of cloth, which has been made, could be made by one means only, by withdrawing capital from the production of other commodities, and thereby lessening the quantity produced ... a demand equal to the greater quantity remaining, the quantity of that commodity is defective'.[1] A supply in excess of demand of one commodity is balanced by a supply below demand of another commodity. A general glut of commodities, distinct from the temporary dislocation of equilibrium in the supply and demand of particular goods, is thus impossible.

But Say and the Ricardians drew yet a further conclusion. As general over-production was impossible, it was also inconceivable that there should ever be an accumulation of capital in excess of the use to which it could be put. This was the really important point. Ricardo and James Mill, even more than Smith, were anxious to show that continual capital accumulation was beneficial. One method which Ricardo had used to prove this was to show that a rise in wages depended upon an increase in the capital of the community. But he also wished to demonstrate the stricter theorem that capital accumulation could never be harmful. The proposition he had to prove was that there could not 'be accumulated in a country any amount of capital which cannot be employed productively'. The only cause which could make the motive for accumulation cease was a rise in wages (occasioned by the rising cost of subsistence) to such an extent that profits diminished below the level at which further accumulation was profitable.[2]

The identity of supply and demand (and the impossibility of demand falling below supply) is easy enough to demonstrate if it is assumed that what is produced is also currently consumed. But the accumulation of capital creates a difficulty. Ricardo's proof depended on being able to show that there was as inevitable a balance of supply and demand, as far as capital was concerned, as there was in regard to goods. The distinction between productive and unproductive labour was applied to consumption in order to give this proof.

Following Smith, Ricardo makes a distinction between productive labour and unproductive labour. The former produces a surplus above the wages paid to it; the latter does not. The French economist Sismondi put it in the form that productive labour exchanges for

1 James Mill, *Elements*, pp. 228–9.
2 D. Ricardo, *Principles*, p. 193.

capital, unproductive labour for revenue. Ricardo also distinguishes between productive consumption and unproductive consumption. The former involves spending in order to produce, that is, to set productive labour in motion, by paying wages and providing the instruments of production and the necessary raw materials. Unproductive consumption does not aim at further production. A person consumes unproductively whether he buys wine for his table or employs a footman; though as we have seen, Ricardo also showed that unproductive consumption which consisted in employing unproductive labour was preferable to that which consisted in the purchase of luxuries.

Capital was that which was consumed productively. An accumulation of capital meant a rise in productive consumption, that is a rise in the demand for productive labour. The question then was: could that rise in demand reach an extent which made it permanently exceed the supply? In other words, could there be a glut of capital? The answer was clearly no. 'If capital increased too rapidly for the population, instead of commanding seven-eighths of the produce, they might command ninety-nine hundredths, and thus there would be no motive for further accumulation. If every man were disposed to accumulate every portion of his revenue but what was necessary to his urgent wants, such a state of things would be produced, for the principle of population is not strong enough to supply a demand for labourers so great as would then exist.'[1] Wages would be high, profits low; the incentive to accumulation would disappear and so would the apparent glut of capital. There could be neither over-production of goods nor over-accumulation of capital. There was this connection between accumulation and consumption (or saving and spending) that the more the capitalist accumulated, the less he spent unproductively, and vice versa. Any change in the proportions of the streams of saving and spending involved a change in the amounts of labour laid out on the production of different goods and, therefore, in their exchange-values. This consequential change provided, as we have seen, the equilibrating force.

The significance of Ricardo's argument (which has been greatly simplified here) was this: it buttressed the case for capital accumulation by showing that its pace was self-regulating; it denied the possibility of economic dislocations for reasons inherent in the capitalist

1 D. Ricardo, *Notes on Malthus's 'Principles of Political Economy'* (ed. J. H. Hollander and T. E. Gregory, 1928), p. 159.

system, since that system was shown to be self-adjusting; and it strengthened the distinction of productive and unproductive labour, which had a definite social and political objective. It was an argument which both approved the trends of the existing system and helped to put in its proper economic place the whole structure of unproductive consumers, which had played such an important part in the old social order.

The main purpose of Malthus's attack on the Ricardian theory was to defend the unproductive consumer. Historically, therefore, it was reactionary. Malthus was defending a primitive, Smithian, formulation of the theory of value at a time when capitalism was sufficiently far advanced to require a more consistent theory. Malthus, like Smith, was probably thinking in terms of a permanent social structure having the qualities of the transitional phase of the eighteenth century. He seems to have aspired to a sort of balance between Whig-aristocratic and primitive industrial-bourgeois elements at a time when a decisive victory of the latter was already inevitable. For this reason, Ricardo's theory was clearly superior because it was appropriate to the direction of contemporary economic development. But for his purpose, Malthus had also to show that the capitalist system was not self-equilibrating and thus to appear critical of that system. The interest of Malthus's contribution lies precisely in the fact that a defence of pre-capitalist conditions had to be combined, not only with an approval in general of capitalism, but also with the uncovering of some of its possible difficulties.

Malthus's attempt to prove that capital accumulation could go too far begins with an attack on Ricardo's method and on his theory of value. This attack is not particularly important in itself, but only in its relation to Malthus's main thesis. In his introduction to the *Principles of Political Economy* (1820) Malthus emphasized the difference between the material of economic science and that of the exact sciences; and he warned his readers that the propositions of political economy could never have the same capacity 'as those which relate to figure and number'.[1] In letters to one another Ricardo and Malthus often referred to the differences in method to which their different conclusions seemed to point.[2] Neither, it appears, was anxious to establish one

1 T. R. Malthus, *Principles of Political Economy* (1820), p 1.
2 For a useful summary of the debate, cf. M. Bowley, *Nassau Senior and Classical Economics*, pp. 31–8.

method as superior to another, as such, at all. What they wished to elucidate was the reason why, in spite of their common acceptance of so many fundamental propositions, they reached different conclusions on so important a practical problem as the question of over-poduction. It was this difference which led Malthus to stress the need for supplementary premises drawn from fresh empirical material in the discussion of short-run problems; while Ricardo continued to rely on the long-run process which could adequately be explained by deductions from the intial premises. The controversy was not based on an opposition between the deductive and inductive methods. It was a difference of opinion about the correct application of an analytical apparatus of a particular degree of abstraction. This difference itself, however, was due to more profound difference in ultimate aim.

Malthus's objections to Ricardo's theory of value have a more direct bearing on the point which was really at issue between them. Malthus did not, in fact, develop a theory of value that could seriously rival that of Ricardo. What he did was to take advantage of some of the confusions in Adam Smith and to modify the labour theory, in order to controvert those of Ricardo's conclusions from it which supported Say's theorem.[1] The result, as far as the theory of value itself is concerned, is further confusion. But it enabled Malthus to reveal some of Ricardo's own inconsistencies with regard to the theory of surplus value. Throughout Malthus's work a number of theories of value intermingle. In one of his earlier writings, *Observations on the Effects of the Corn Laws* (1814), he took Smith to task for regarding the amount of labour which a good could command as a the measure of its value. But he himself later used Smith's definition of value as the power to command other goods, including labour. He thought that 'when the value of an object is estimated by the quantity of labour of a given description (common day-labour, for instance) which it can command, it will appear to be unquestionably the best of any one commodity, and to unite, more nearly than any other, the qualities of a real and nominal measure of exchangeable value'.[2]

In other works he also states that the amount of labour, both past and current, necessary for the production of commodities determines their value. Later he develops a cost-of-production theory which is

---

1 Cf. M. Bowley, *Nassau Senior and Classical Economics*, pp. 87–9, and Karl Marx, *Thoerien über den Mehrwert*, vol. iii, pp. 1–29.
2 T. R. Malthus, *Principles*, p. 119.

interesting because it includes profits. By defining value as the amount of stored and current labour plus profits (which, according to Malthus, was the same as the amount of labour which the commodity could command), Malthus shows that he was really trying to get over the Ricardian dilemma of the origin of a surplus. The difficulty which had arisen in Ricardo's formulation is not overcome by including profit in value; but, by his definition, Malthus demonstrated that a commodity commanded more labour than was embodied in it. Thus, he produced an exploitation theory of the exchange between capital and labour which could be made to follow from Ricardo's premises. Malthus was all the better able to do this and so to destroy Ricardo's original theory, because the latter had failed to develop the distinction between price and value which was caused by the existence of different capital structures.

Malthus uses this definition of value to develop the concept of *effective demand*, that is, of demand which is high enough to ensure a continual supply (or, in other words, a continuous process of production). Malthus regarded the effective demand for a commodity as the amount of labour which as a rule it commanded, because that amount represented the quantity of labour plus profit which was necessary to produce it. In other words, production depended on the existence of effective demand, that is, demand which enabled the producer to cover a cost which was defined as the capitalist's advances in the form of wages, material, and capital plus a profit in accordance with the prevailing rate.

It is from this point that Malthus launches his defence of unproductive consumption and his attack on Ricardo's theory of accumulation. The condition for keeping production going is that the producer should be able to sell his product at its value in the Malthusian sense, i.e. at a price which covers outlay plus profit. How is it possible, Malthus asks, to fulfil this condition? Having discovered a possible way out of Ricardo's theory of the exchange between capital and labour, Malthus makes the mistake of regarding all exchange as being similar to that which he had postulated between capital and labour. Following Smith, he regards exchanges between goods and labour as the most frequent form of exchange as such. 'Now of all objects it cannot be disputed, that by far the greatest mass of value is given in exchange for labour either productive or unproductive.'[1] After this beginning, the rest

1 T. R. Malthus, *Principles*, p. 119.

follows quite naturally. The capitalist who buys productive labour pays for it, by definition, less than he aims to get for the product of that labour. But he cannot get a price that will do that from the labourers he employs. By definition again, the sum of the wages they are paid is less than the sum of the values of their products. The demand of the labourers can never be big enough to enable the capitalist to obtain his profit. It can, therefore, never be big enough to ensure continuous production. Nor can exchange between capitalist and capitalist supply that incentive to production. They both sell the product at a price which includes profit, so that, although they may cheat each other occasionally, on balance no incentive remains.[1] A deadlock is reached, if the producer has to rely on the demand of his fellow-producers and of his workers.

Malthus finds a solution in unproductive consumption; it is this which enables demand to remain effective.'It is absolutely necessary that a country with great powers of production should possess a body of unproductive consumers.'[2] These consumers enable the capitalist to get the profit without which he would cease producing and which he cannot get from the market which the combined demand of labourers and other capitalists offer. Another solution would be that the capitalists themselves should consume the excess of products. 'But such consumption', Malthus thought, was 'not consistent with the actual habits of the generality of capitalists', who were always trying to save a great fortune and whose business interests did not give them the opportunity for unproductive spending on a sufficient scale.[3]

The need for unproductive consumers becomes even more apparent when we consider their function in the light of the capital accumulation which goes on in a progressive country. Malthus maintained 'that an attempt to accumulate very rapidly which necessarily implies a considerable diminution of unproductive consumption, by greatly impairing the usual motives to production must prematurely check the progress of wealth'.[4] Rapid accumulation, or saving, diminishes the efficacy of the safely-valve of unproductive consumption. It diminishes, therefore, effective demand and destroys the incentive to

1 T. R. Malthus, *Principles*, Book II, ch. i, section ix, *passim*. For a detailed examination of this argument from his own tendentious point of view, cf. Marx, *Theorien über den Mehrwwert.* pp. 35–47.
2 ibid., p. 463.
3 ibid., p. 465.
4 In a letter of 7 July 1821, quoted in Keynes, *Essays in Biography* (1933), p. 142.

production. Malthus could not deny that it was important to maintain some measure of accumulation in order to improve the productive powers and increase the wealth of the community. But he claimed that accumulation might be pushed to excess and that it was necessary to maintain a proper balance between saving and consumption, though his analysis of the way in which such a balance could be attained was not very detailed.

Malthus went into great detail in enumerating the different classes of unproductive consumers. The landlords come first. Although they extract their rent from the capitalists, they perform a very useful function, because they are able to exercise a demand which is not balanced by production. In addition, there must be a large body of menial servants, statesmen, soldiers, judges and lawyers, physicians and surgeons, and clergymen to add their demand to an otherwise deficient total. They may be unproductive labourers – Malthus did not break with Smith's and Ricardo's classification – but without them there would be no effective demand.

One thing which is striking in Malthus's theory is that the economic system is shown not to be self-adjusting. Unless a large class of unproductive consumers was maintained, periodic over-production and stagnation would inevitably occur. For the first time, in English economic theory at any rate, the possibility of crises arising from causes inherent in the capitalist system was admitted. Even more strikingly than in Ricardo, the opposition of interests between capital and labour was brought out. 'It is indeed most important to observe that no power of consumption on the part of the labouring classes can ever alone furnish an encouragement to the employment of capital.'[1]

But equally striking and more accurate a reflection of Malthus's intention is the new role which his theory assigns to unproductive consumers. It is tempting to see in this argument – the forerunner of many under-consumption theories – an attempt to reconcile the old and new social order. Malthus is in favour of capitalist industry, but he does not like its revolutionary function *vis-à-vis* the remnants of feudalism. He is prepared to accept capitalism because it brings an increase in production. He has seen its virtual triumph in England and he realizes that it is hopeless to attack it root and branch. But he has to find a secure place in it for the classes whom capitalism has relegated to a very inferior economic status. Hence the 'aristocratic clergyman's'

1 T. R. Malthus, *Principles*, p. 471.

protectionism, his tenderness for the landed interest, for its extravagance in maintaining large bodies of retainers, his desire for public works, and his complacency about government debt.

Modern social reformers who acclaim Malthus as one of their forerunners have overlooked more than half of his work. The sort of society which emerges from his writings is not in all respects a pleasing spectacle. The working class is constantly pressing on the means of subsistence. The capitalists pay them wages which are below the value of their products and which afford them little more than subsistence. Society is saved from destruction by a large class of unproductive consumers who, in such a system, are little more than parasites.

On balance, then, Malthus was a reactionary. The particular form which his reaction took was determined by the very high degree of development which capitalism had reached in England. Advocacy of pre-capitalist interests involved at that stage some attack upon capitalism itself; it also involved, if it was to have any effect, a considerable insight into the working of the capitalist system. It is no accident that a similar reaction in the less highly developed conditions of Germany took a romantic and mystical form; while in France, with the experience of the great revolution as a background, economic criticism, formally akin to that of Malthus, assumed a political significance.

It remains, nevertheless, true that from the strictly logical point of view of the development of analytical tools, the Malthusian theory has rightly been rescued from oblivion by modern authors, notably Keynes. Whatever Malthus's own motives or conclusions, his ideas – or, perhaps better, the ideas exchanged between him and Ricardo in their celebrated controversy – show an early wrestling with one of the most important problems of the modern economy: the determination of the level of aggregate demand.

## The German Romantics

*The sources of romanticism: Burke; Fichte.*   The environment in which Malthus lived was that of successful capitalist industry and penetrating economic analysis. His reaction against the classical school shows the power of that environment. Malthus had fought a rearguard action. He had realized that capitalism and utilitarianism had to be accepted. At first, he was still a faithful disciple of the classical school: the arguments of the *Essay on Population* became an accepted part of its tradition. But when he saw that interests which he held dear were threatened by the progress of capitalism he became essentially an apologist for feudalism on a capitalist and utilitarian basis. The English social reform movement (which arose later on the non-interventionist basis of economic classicism) of which John Stuart Mill was the chief exponent is a more successful form of that compromise. In Mill's explicit reference to the influence of Coleridge one may see a further proof of the essential sameness of the movement.

In the Germany of the early nineteenth century neither the practice nor the theory of capitalism was highly developed. Those who opposed the attempt to bring Germany, both economically and intellectually, to the level of its neighbours were not compelled from the start to come to terms with classical political economy and the philosophy of which it formed a part. Like its literary counterpart, the German romantic school of political economy had no need to have any truck with the philosophy of capitalism. The romantic economists were not yet fighting a losing battle against capitalism: they had no need to take much notice of its economic theory. The time-lag in the development of German economic environment accounts for the belated and often distorted reappearance of ideological battles that had already been decided elsewhere. It accounts for the rise of romantic political economy; and it continues at work throughout the nineteenth century.

Compared with Malthus, the romantic movement in economic thought produces work of an altogether inferior theoretical level. It could hardly be otherwise, because its purpose was not the understanding of reality and its representation in a consistent scientific system. As if the works of the leaders did not proclaim it, we are told by a modern admirer of political romanticism that its 'science' rejected logical analysis.[1] It could be argued that any kind of economic and political thought produced on such a basis has no place in the history of the development of economic science. And such an argument could be supported by the fact that the study of economics in those countries in which the liberal tradition is firm hardly ever concerns itself with the vapourings of the German romantics. But though the universities may ignore them, their power or, at any rate, the power of ideas similar to theirs, is far from dead. In their native home they achieved a belated triumph which, even if it has turned out to be short-lived, entitles them

1 F. Bülow in his introduction to a selection of Adam Miller's writings: A. Müller, *Vom Geiste der Gemeinschaft* (1931), p. xvii.

at least to criticism. Moreover, the general tenor of these ideas is peculiarly suited to any kind of political movement which needs to rely on obscurantism in intellectual matters and on totalitarian methods in government. These ideas are, therefore, unfortunately not without relevance to the modern world.[1]

It may be asked at the outset how it is that a body of ideas which freely confesses its lack of logic and its scorn for rational comprehension should ever be able to achieve a wide influence. In fact, romantic social thought has never in the past been able to survive criticism. Even in Germany it was short-lived in the beginning; and after the middle of the nineteenth century a version of English political economy was generally accepted. The disappearance of romanticism then, and its recrudescence from time to time since, suggest that two circumstances (related to each other) are unfavourable to the existence of economic and political illusions. One is economic expansion and a fairly universally rising standard of well-being. The other is freedom of scientific inquiry. About the first little need be said. It is a well-known fact that irrationalism derives a great stimulus from economic depression. Only when men despair about the future are they liable to lose faith in the power of human reason to understand and solve their problems.

The second factor is of a different order of importance. Material despair may make an environment favourable to illusion; but so long as there is some rational thought left illusion cannot persist. Romantic illusion must, therefore, be an implacable enemy of rational thought, not only in theory but also in practice. A condition of the continued existence of political romanticism is that there should not be any rational thought. Reason, scientific inquiry, and the atmosphere of freedom in which alone these can flourish must be abolished in the literal sense if illusion is to consolidate its power over men's minds. The economic development of the nineteenth century which made Germany into an industrialist and capitalist country also liberalized its political and social structure and created the institutional environment which made possible a rational analysis of economic processes. When, in the thirties, that rational analysis went and was replaced by innumerable variants of the romantic illusion, it did so because its existence had been made physically impossible. What remained from the past was driven out by the enormous facilities available to modern

---

1 Further references to certain contemporary tendencies are given below.

propaganda; and into the increasing vacuum the thought of a more primitive age was pumped.

Judged by English and French standards, Germany at the beginning of the nineteenth century was an economically backward country. Its economic basis was a feudalist agriculture. It had only a primitive industry ruled by medieval guild regulations. Politically, the distinguishing characteristic was the multitude of small states ruled by absolute princes. Economic policy reflected these conditions. Obstructionist regulations of trade and commerce abounded. Each individual state had got so far on the mercantilist road as to possess a 'national' currency for its own territory and to enforce a rigid protectionism *vis-à-vis* other German states. As Friedrich List complained, German merchants and manufacturers had to spend most of their time endeavouring to overcome vexatious tariffs and exchange regulations. To the outside world, however, Germany was not a closed economic unit. Central direction was lacking, and foreign goods manufactured in the more advanced conditions of England and France found a ready German market.

The eyes of business men and theorists were turned towards their successful rivals. There was keen discussion about the reasons for Germany's backwardness. The theory and practice of English and French society were eagerly examined in the hope of finding in them features which could profitably be imitated. The economic theories of Smith and Ricardo, the philosophy of the utilitarians, and the political reforms of the French Revolution were beginning to influence people's minds. In them the rising German business class found the expression of its own interests and of those of the whole community. A movement arose, in close alliance with that for national union and political liberalism, which aimed at economic liberalism in theory and in practice. Its immediate form involved measures which were not compatible with English classical economic policy; but in essence it was an attempt to transplant liberal economic theory into a somewhat different environment from that in which it had first grown up.

The romantic movement appears as a reaction against the influence which English economic classicism was beginning to exert. For its economic theory and policy it could draw on mercantilist and cameralist tradition; for a basic social philosophy it constructed from its own view of the Middle Ages a theory which was opposed to the philosophy of natural law and its utilitarian development. The two political philosophers who greatly influenced the romantics were

Johann Gottlieb Fichte and Edmund Burke. Neither of them was really romantic or medievalist; but their views were complex enough to serve as inspiration for opposed schools of thought.

The admiration for Burke which is so striking a feature of the romantic economists is difficult to understand. Burke was essentially in the tradition from which English liberalism developed, the tradition of Locke and Adam Smith. He had the utilitarian doubt about the efficacy of government action. He upheld free trade; and he was liberal in his attitude to India and the American colonies. His whole work breathes the spirit of the English constitution. The *Thoughts on Scarcity*, as has been pointed out, might have been written by Adam Smith.[1]

Yet there is a conservative and aristocratic streak in Burke. In spite of his non-interventionism, he had on practical grounds a greater opinion of the power and importance of state finance than Adam Smith. For the sake of expediency, too, he favoured a wealthy and financially independent Church. The rights of property, which are implicitly safeguarded in all classical political economy, were strongly emphasized by Burke. He did not regard the lower classes as capable of governing; property alone, he thought, was the basis of government; and to landed property he gave pride of place. This emphasis in Burke could be loosened from the capitalist and utilitarian basis on which he had developed it. It could be applied to a reactionary purpose.

The Burke whom the German romantics acclaimed was not the author of the *Thoughts on Scarcity* but of the *Reflections on the French Revolution*. Burke was alarmed by the influence of the French Revolution on English utilitarian thought. He accepted the results of the English revolution of 1688 but feared the effects of the new revolutionary fervour on the domination which the bourgeoisie had now safely established in England. Burke's *Reflections* show more clearly than any other document in the history of political thought the loss of that revolutionary purpose which had inspired liberal thought before its triumph. The utilitarian attitude to government is still maintained in them. Burke did not revert to doctrines which had been disposed of by Locke. He still regarded kings as the servants of the people and their power as having a utilitarian basis. The declaration of the rights of man was not attacked because it was based on a wrong theory of the purpose of government. Burke condemned it because it took no

---

[1] Cf. H. J. Laski, *The Rise of European Liberalism*, pp. 196–205, for a brilliant short account of Burke.

account of political expediency. His anti-democratic attitude was that of the practical statesman who denied that the scribes who had inspired the French Revolution and the political ignoramuses who had carried it out were the best judges of the general interest. Their actions had produced bad results; and the pragmatic standard was the only one which could be applied to political problems. The doctrine of the sovereignty of the people must not be allowed to lead to the same error as that of the divine right of kings. It must not be used to defend actions which those with experience of political leadership judge to be productive of evil. Man acquired advantages or rights by entering society, but he also renounced rights. His power to choose his representatives did not give him power to destroy the whole fabric of government. Stability, tradition, history, says the conservative in Burke, are as important as the abstract rights of popular goverment.

A condemnation of the French Revolution on these grounds was more than welcome to German reaction. Completely ignoring Burke's agreement with the essentials of utilitarianism and capitalism (which was the most important part of Burke), the romantics fastened on to his conservative qualities and rejected individualist liberalism, which saw in the state only a utilitarian institution.

The *Reflections* were translated into German in 1793 by Friedrich Gentz and became at once one of the chief sources of romanticism. Its other great inspiration comes from the political philosophy of Fichte. In 1796 appeared Fichte's *Grundlage des Naturrechts nach Principien der Wissenschaftslehre*, which gave an interpretation of natural law not unlike Burke's conservative reading of utilitarianism. Fichte was also in the tradition of Locke; but, like Burke, he did not draw democratic conclusions from the philosophy of natural law. The experiences of the French Revolution combined with the conditions of Germany to lead him to a view of the state which could be used by the romantics. According to Fichte, the individual became 'Zufolge des Vereinigungsvertrages, ein Theil eines organisirten Ganzen, und schmilzt sonach mit demselben in Eines zusammen'.[1] The state was best described as an 'organisirtes Naturproduct', each particle of which had existence only by virtue of its participation in the whole.[2]

---

1 J. G. Fichte, 'Grundlage des Naturrechts' in Fichte's *Sämmtliche Werke* (1845), vol. iii, p. 204.
2 ibid., p. 208.

This emphasis on the organism of the state became even more pronounced in Fichte's later writings. From an Aristotelian view of the state, he was led to distinguish the state as a special entity independent of the individual members of which it was composed. From this derives the totalitarian view of the romantics.

*Gentz; Müller.*   Mention has already been made of one of the leaders of the romantic movement. Friedrich Gentz (1764–1832) was a politician who began as an ardent admirer of the English liberals and the French Revoltion. Even after he had translated Burke and had become critical of the Revolution, he remained a believer in the liberal as well as the conservative parts of Burke's thought. For some years he continued to advocate freedom of the Press and freedom of trade. He did not think England's supremacy in international trade was harmful to the rest of Europe, as did the later protectionists. Economically and politically, England represented an ideal structure which he thought ought to be carefully studied. He shared Adam Smith's optimism and believed that the triumph of Smith's economic principles would cure political evils and bring peace. He thought that self-interest was the main motive of human conduct; and he was certain that providence made each individual contribute to the common good even when he was only seeking his own. His belief in the possibility of perpetual progress made him disparage the Middle Ages and hail the discovery of America.

However, even at this early stage in his development Gentz did not accept economic liberalism in its entirety. He stressed Adam Smith's abandonment of free trade when defence was at stake. He regarded the development of trade, industry, and scientific agriculture as unnatural, though he could not deny their usefulness. He welcomed the opening up of America, but not because it brought increased opportunities of trade. Not gold and silver, trading monopolies, or greater political power of the mother country were the true benefits derived from colonies, but the tremendous impetus to fresh human activity and intercourse.

But the emphasis on the ideal values of liberalism was soon replaced by a complete rejection of its political and economic precepts. There set in what one writer called a process of 'drying up'.[1] The ambitious

---

1 W. Roscher, 'Die romantische Schule der Nationalökonomik in Deutschland'; in *Zeitschrift für die gesammte Staatswissenschaft* (1870), pp. 51–105.

and able politician in Gentz grew impatient of the constant regard for popular opinion which democratic liberalism demanded. Contact with the powerful Austrian state machine gave him a view of the functions of government which was not compatible with Smith's doctrines. Gentz tried to compromise by stressing the power of public finance in moulding the economic activity of the community as a whole. He was strongly in favour of indirect taxation as an instrument of state policy. Direct taxation, he thought, would constantly have to be changed if it was not to become out of date. From that it was only a short step to Gentz's defence of feudal domains, which, he claimed, set an example to farmers.

The excessive power assigned to the state is much in evidence in Gantz's theory of money. He was a strong upholder of inconvertible paper money and opposed the ideas of Ricardo and the Bullion Committee. Under the influence of his friend, Adam Müller, he expounded the view that it was only the word of the state which made anything, be it paper or metal, into money. This view, which was later elaborated by Knapp into the state theory of money, became a common characteristic of all romantic economic thought.

His increasing belief in the strong state made Gentz turn to the Middle Ages for inspiration; and though he did not go so far as his fellow-romantics, an idealized view of feudalism is more and more marked in his later writings. The influence of Müller grew stronger and his own practical sense gradually disappeared. The one-time admirer of Burke ended by being a complete reactionary. He became friend and confidant of Metternich; and his gifts of statesmanship were devoted to oppression and intrigue. All traces of liberalism left him. He even discarded the idealistic excuses which had served to hide his earlier retreat from liberal principles. He spent the last years of his life in constant fear of revolution; and died an embittered and hated crank.

Gentz was the politician of the romantic school. His friend Adam Müller (1779–1829) was its theorist. Müller was largely forgotten until the search of the German Nazis for theoretical ancestors led to a rediscovery of his doctrines. Müller was born in Berlin, received his main stimulus at the University of Göttingen, and spent some years as literary critic, tutor, and lecturer. He was on friendly terms with many politicians and with the leaders of literary romanticism. He took some part in politics, particularly in giving the aid of his literary talents to the reactionary politics of the landlords who were opposing liberal reforms. Through Gentz's influence with Metternich, he received a number of state appointments in Vienna, where he spent the last years of his life.

In judging Müller's ideas it is important to remember his career. Although he had acquired his dislike for the philosophy of natural law and for liberalism from his teachers in Göttingen, his literary efforts were not unconnected with his political activities. With all their vagueness, their flamboyant style, their 'poetic' quality, Müller's writings were weapons supplied for use in the political struggle. Müller was not in the thick of politics. He had not Gentz's practical experience and wisdom. But he was sufficiently intimate with politics to know what function his articles and lectures were performing. He was entrusted by Metternich with many diplomatic tasks; and it would be wrong to believe that a man who was very ambitious, and who could make the most skilful use of political opportunities to further his own position, had his head in the clouds when he came to write about political theory. Reaction was fighting for all it was worth against the tide of liberalism. It knew the value of an ally on the literary front who could use the fashionable language of romanticism and who could hide the hard facts of oppression behind high-sounding, but ill-defined, words which appealed to people's idealism.

Adam Müller did not begin as a whole-hearted romantic. His first work as a literary critic was a review of Fichte's *Der geschlossene Handelsstaat* (1800). In this work Fichte applied to economic problems his compromise between individualism and the state. The basis of the *Handelsstaat* was still the natural law. But Fichte rejected *laissez-faire* because power was too unevenly divided. This led him to draw up a plan for a Utopia. The function of the state was conceived of in a more than utilitarian sense. It was the duty of the state not only to safeguard the property which each member owned, but also to ensure that each member should have the property which his contribution to the common labour made his by natural law. The state must act positively in order to give its members what they needed; and Fichte described in detail the constitution of the ideal state which would have the ability to do so. In order to have the power to act according to the dictates of natural law, the state must become a closed unit. That is why, in spite of many agreements on fundamentals, Fichte opposed Adam Smith's cosmopolitanism and free trade. It was not only nationalism that made him urge self-sufficiency. The embargo on all dealings with the outside world was regarded as indispensable if the ideal state was to be insulated from the shocks which foreign trade must bring about. Like some of the more sophisticated protagonists of autarky to-day, Fichte regarded foreign trade not only as a source of economic dislocation but also as a cause of national rivalries culminating in wars.

In discussing the best means for closing the state Fichte stressed the abolition of metal money. He took the view that money had no utility: the stuff it was made of was irrelevant; it was only a representative; and the state alone could make it such. Fichte then proceeded to make distinction between *Weltgeld* and *Landesgeld*, the world money which is precious metals and the native money which the state's decree has made generally acceptable. Fichte was sufficiently clear about the nature of trade, price, and money to know the implications of his proposal that there should be no *Weltgeld* in his ideal state. His *Landesgeld* was to have a fixed value. Accepting the quantity theory of money, Fichte realized that this involved fixed prices (his general view of the economic functions of the ideal state led him to revive the notion of the 'just price') and a completely closed economic unit. In this he was more consistent than later adherents of the state theory of money. And he was perfectly clear about the relation of his proposals to existing practice. He emphasized that he was not concerned with the then existing inconvertible paper moneys: his *Landesgeld* applied only to the future ideal state.

Müller's review was a violent criticism of Fichte. It opposed Fichte entirely in the spirit of Smithian doctrines. It accused Fichte of lack of realism, of ignorance of the literature of political economy, and of a narrow parochial attitude. It compared his views unfavourably with Adam Smith's deep insight into economic processes. And in particular it questioned Fichte's praise of the wisdom of the state. The defence of Smith, attributable probably to the influence of Gentz, gave no inkling of the illiberal views which its author was soon to champion.

Indeed, if there is any leading thought running through Müller's later writings, it is that of reaction to Adam Smith. The two most important of these writings are the *Elemente der Staatskunst* (1809) and the *Versuch einer neuen Theorie des Geldes* (1816). They contain the essence of Müller's social and economic philosophy. It is difficult to distil this essence from the chaotic mixture of ideas which Müller propounded. Nor, when one has isolated certain basic notions, is it easy to give them precise expression.

Müller never entirely abandoned his regard for Smith; but he attacked his undiscriminating German disciples. They had, he said, brought over the dry bones of Smith's theory without the master's qualifications; and they had tried to apply the theory without regard for the different nature of the German state. Smith, he thought, had unduly generalized from English experience. He had been excessively influenced by the industrial and urban character of English civilization, and had illegitimately raised the practice of exchange to the status of a natural principle. This had made him look upon the community from the point of view of the selfish interests of the individual. Müller stressed altruism and religion in opposition to what he regards as Smith's egoism and materialism. The state, he thought, must be regarded as an organism; the individuals, who were the cells, could not be thought of outside the totality of the state, the *Volksganzes*. One cannot say more than this about Müller's view of the state. He himself claims that it is impossible to put the nature of the state into words and definitions. Every new generation, every great man gives it a new form and makes the old definition inadequate. Müller spurns dead concepts, as he calls them. 'Vom Staate aber gibt es keinen Begriff' (But of the state there can be no concept); of this exalted subject there can only be an *idea* which is constantly moving and growing.[1]

Müller does, however, proceed to give a definition. 'Every man stands at the centre of civic life: he has behind him a past which must be respected; before him a future which must be cared for. No one can break away from this time chain. . . . Finally, the state is not merely an artificial institution, not just one of the thousand useful and pleasurable inventions of civic life; it is the totality of that civic life itself, necessary as soon as there are men, inevitable. . . .'[2] These are his three fundamental propositions which are meant to explain the relation of the individual and the state. They lead to the conclusion that without the state man cannot 'hear, see, think, feel, love; in short, he cannot be thought of otherwise than within the state'.[3]

The two social sciences are law and wisdom; they include politics and economics; and religion unites them. God must be thought of as the supreme judge and the supreme *pater familias*. Without religion, economic activity loses its ultimate purpose. Production should be undertaken for its own sake, and for God's sake, not for the material reward it brings. The difficulties in economic life arise mainly because men forget divine power. Labour is not the sole source of produce. It is

1 A. Müller, *Vom Geiste der Gemeinschaft*, pp. 15–16.
2 ibid., pp. 21–2.
3 ibid., p. 23.

only the tool to which must be added power (which comes from God) and the material aids of landed estates and already existing capital. This religious emphasis in Müller's writings is very marked. The *Elemente* were published four years after he had entered the Roman Catholic Church; and into all his subsequent writings he infused the kind of catholicism which was so closely bound up with Austrian politics of the time.

Müller's view of the state is an essential part of his economic theories. As the spokesman of the reaction he idealized the Middle Ages. The ideal organic state, in which rights and duties were instinctive in every member of the community, in which status was accepted and the three estates of clergy, noblemen and burghers (Müller never includes peasants) live in harmony, is transplanted to the feudal Middle Ages. How idealized Müller's picture of feudalism was is to be seen in the fact that his predilection for medievalism did not conflict with his desire for an omnipotent state. Nevertheless, it served as the background against which Müller's defence of feudal landownership could be made to appear less reactionary.

Müller's theory of property, wealth, production, and capital is idealist and suitably vague. Property, he says, must be conceived of in such a way as to avoid the unhappy separation between persons and things. The union of these is a characteristic of a happy state; and it is achieved in feudalism. Every man is both person and thing. As the former, he owns; as the latter, he is owned. The state is the person which owns him. Strict observance of private property, such as is implied in Roman Law, destroys the community. The feudal system does not recognize absolute private property, only usufruct. It is necessary to preserve this aspect of property; and Müller proposes marriage of feudal law and Roman-British law. 'Agriculture, landed property and war will constantly advocate feudal relations; industry, trade, moveable property and peace will champion strict private property.'[1] Both must be present in the organic state. Their nexus is made necessary particularly by the needs of war. Trade and industry are impeded by feudal institutions. But because these institutions are based on the principle that the state cannot be thought of without war, their limitation of wealth is compensated by the warlike spirit which they infuse into all peaceful institutions. On the other hand, although feudal law appears to be impeded by the rights of private property, war

1 A. Müller, *Vom Geiste der Gemeinschaft*, p. 117.

obtains a greater ease of operation through the existence of the money interest which depends on strict property rights.

Wealth is also defined in relation to the totalitarian state. Everything has a private and a civic character, and therefore an individual and a social value. Wealth is also both private and nation property. It cannot be defined by reference to things alone: 'it lies in use as well as in property'.[1] The wealth of a nation cannot be estimated in weight and number; these only show that wealth may arise. Its real existence can be recognized only in use. The state must concern itself not only with tangible things but with the totality of material and non-material goods, with persons and relations, all of which constitute its wealth. Production, in the classical economic sense, consists of increasing material goods and private possessions. Adam Smith had argued as if the wealth of a nation was only the sum of the private wealths of the members; he had, therefore, urged statesmen to adopt a *laissez-faire* policy which would give self-interest the greatest scope. The real object of political economy, according to Müller, is a double one: (*a*) the greatest multiplication of all the utility of persons, things and ideal goods; (*b*) the production and intensification of that 'product of all products', the economic and social union of the great community or the national household.[2] The emphasis is on national production, on the *interêt général* rather than the *interêt de tous*; just as the idea of the state is based not on the *volonté de tous* but on the *volonté générale*.[3]

The factors of production are not land, labour, and capital, but nature, man, and the past. The last includes all capital, physical and spiritual, which has been built up in the course of time and is now available to help man in production. Economists, says Müller, have tended to ignore spiritual capital. The fund of experience which past exertion has made available is put in motion by language, speech, and writing; and it is the duty of scholarship to preserve and increase it. All these elements collaborate in all production; though in different spheres the emphasis will differ. In agriculture the stress is on landed property; in industry it is on labour; in commerce on capital, particularly in its monetry form; and in science the accent is on the capital of ideas. But in all of them the other elements are also preserved. Feudalism is praised because its social structure reflected the existence

1 A. Müller, *Vom Geiste der Gemeinschaft*, p. 150.
2 ibid., p. 157.
3 ibid., p. 159.

of these factors of production. Land leads to nobility, labour to the estate of the burgher, spiritual capital to the clergy. As for physical capital, it was at first also attached to the clergy; but the distintegration of feudalism brought a separation between physical and spiritual capital. The concept of physical capital began to invade every other factor and to obtain supremacy over the whole of civic life. Physical capital acquired the strongest influence in all spheres of production and economists began to distinguish land, labour, and capital only.

Müller's attitude to the economic structure which resulted from his political purpose is clearly incompatible with the *laissez-faire* policy of classicism. Müller adopts the views of Fichte, which he had once criticized, and proposes complete autarky. But true to his romanticism, he has to clothe the policy of the absolutist state and of the landed interest in an idealist garb. Economic patriotism, he said, should be neither calculating nor imperative: not mercantilist balancing of the money that comes in against that which goes out, nor the mere closing of the door to foreign goods. A love for home-produced goods must be inculcated into the citizens. The state's duty is to awaken national pride, the feeling of 'oneness' with the national state in the economic sphere. Utility, as an attractive quality of goods, has in every country its own special meaning. The government must develop the national content of wants. Wise economic policy mediates between national production and national consumption; it establishes an equilibrium between them by strengthening the feeling of national power in each citizen. Free trade destroys national cohesion; it makes each member of the state a citizen of the world. Fichte wished his ideal state to be insulated from the shocks of the outside world; Müller wanted it to be a closed unit, because it might otherwise lose the blind obedience of its citizens. Elements of such an anti-cosmopolitan psychology still appear from time to time to assist nationalist economic objectives. And in totalitarian systems they are, of course, an essential ingredient of spiritual and political isolationism quite apart from any economic objectives.

Perhaps the most important application which Müller made of all these ideas was in the theory of money. He discussed money frequently in the *Elemente* and he devoted a separate book to monetary problems. Again it is not easy to extract the main idea from the jungle of verbiage. Roughly, however, the underlying principle is borrowed from Fichte's distinction between *Weltgeld* and *Landesgeld*, or *Nationgeld*, as Müller calls it. He develops a mystical theory of the nature of money which leads to the view that money is only the economic form of the inevitable union of men in the state. Like the state, it binds men together. It is the mediator between the personal and the civic character of persons and things: in so far as they possess social value they are money; but it would be wrong to think that they alone are money. Everything in a state, man or object, might become money. Indeed, it is one of the chief signs of a great and powerful nation that more and more individual persons and things become money by entering into the social relationship which constitutes the state.[1]

But all this symbolism has a purpose. Fichte had said in the *Handelsstaat* that he was not concerned with existing currencies. But Adam Müller, who was later in the pay of Metternich, was very much concerned to eulogize and justify existing inconvertible paper money, particularly that of Austria. 'If I am asked', he said, 'what is money in Austria . . . I say, it is an imperial word, a national word.'[2] Can a theory be evolved to justify inconvertible paper money? Adam Müller is not at a loss for one. Metal money is cosmopolitan; it is of a piece with international trade. It destroys the links which should tie each individual indissolubly to his own national state. Paper money is national; it is patriotic; it is medieval. National money expresses national cohesion and power. Credit too should be viewed as a national factor. National credit is a creative power which is capable of setting in motion the national capital; it must be regarded as another expression of that complete 'Durchdrungenheit, Verschmolzenheit und Einheit zwischen der Regierung und der Nation'.[3]

After all this mysticism what concrete political and economic institutions does Müller advocate? Paper money, protection, no taxation of landed property (to ask 'what is an estate worth', he says, in a typical passage, 'is to look for the momentary equivalent of an everlasting value'[4]), are perhaps the only definite economic suggestions he makes. Politically, the mystic view of the state seems to resolve itself into an advocacy of a marriage of the landed interests with certain capitalist sections and with reactionary professional politicians to form an absolutist state. The reality behind phrases full of false emotive power was not attractive in Müller's day; nor is it at the present time. That reality was seldom allowed to peep out from behind the scenes. In only

1 A. Müller, *Vom Geiste der Gemeinschaft*, pp. 152–5.
2 ibid., p. 154.
3 ibid., p. 195.
4 ibid., p. xliii.

one respect did Müller forsake any concealment of his real purpose, much though he decked it out in fine clothes; and because this is also a purpose of many of his modern imitators which is seldom obscure, it is fitting to close this account of him with a selection of passages which relate to it.

'In the war of one national power against another (not of national insolence against national impotence) the essence and the beauty of national existence, that is, the idea of the nation, becomes particularly clear to all those who participate in its fate.'[1]

'In a long peace, the most tender and intensive quality of social union must disappear, because the eyes of the citizens are turned exclusively to internal affairs. This union can only be re-established afterwards in a long war which involves the necessity of facing the enemy with a social totality.'[2]

'It should have been the first aim of government policy to hold fast to that proud spirit of war, to infuse it into the so-called state of peace, to let it penetrate every single institution of peace and every branch of the administration.'[3]

'Perpetual peace cannot be an ideal of politics. Peace and war should supplement each other other like rest and motion.'[4]

*List.* Before we leave the romantics it is necessary to mention one other writer who is influenced by them, but is not one of them. Friedrich List (1789–1846) was not a romantic, nor did he, like Müller, represent the landed interest. In a sense List is more correctly placed with the classics; for in spite of his opposition to their doctrines he represented in Germany a theoretical movement which had social roots similar to those of Smith and Ricardo. Müller had tried to marry feudalism and capitalism. He had granted the inevitability of industrial and commercial development, but had wanted to make it subservient to feudalist purposes. List, on the other hand, was representative of nascent industrial capitalism. But whereas the greater age and more solid foundation of capitalism in England had made Smith and Ricardo into free-traders, the backward condition of Germany made List the apostle of economic nationalism. List's association with romanticism is attributable to the fact that the nationalism which he

1 A. Müller, *Vom Geiste der Gemeinschaft*, p. 49.
2 ibid., p. 51.
3 ibid., p. 53.
4 ibid.

was forced to adopt brought him into opposition to Smith's doctrines.

In the process, he expressed many views which were reminiscent of romanticism. He rejected liberal cosmopolitianism on the ground that it ignored the nation, without which individuals could not exist. The 'atomism' of Smith took no account of the national bond: in considering man, the producer and consumer, Smith had forgotten the citizen. The individual's position, even as an economic unit, depended on the strength of the national power. That national power was not to be estimated in terms of exchange-value. What was important to a nation and to the individuals who composed it was not so much the actual amount of material wealth which they possessed as their productive power: the ability to replace, preferably with an increase, what had been consumed. A true view of national productive power should take into account all the nation's resources in their mutual relationship. All this, combined with other manifestations of List's nationalism (such as his pan-Germanism and his qualified approval of war), might well have been said by a pure romantic. But List's manner of saying it is of a different kind. It lacks the romantic psuedo-poetical phrase-mongering. And what is more important, the purpose for which it is said is made perfectly clear.

What is essential in List is not his political metaphysic, but his economic policy. List, it should be noted, gave up an academic career for the sake of political activity. He became the inspirer and active leader of the association of German merchants and industrialists which was formed in 1819 as an instrument of agitation and propaganda on behalf of the trading interest. In numerous articles and petitions to the governments of Austria and the different German states List put forward the economic policy which was to remain associated with his name. It has already been mentioned that at the beginning of the nineteenth century Germany was split into a number of independent states which maintained powerful customs barriers against each other, but offered no resistance to the influx of the products of English industry. In 1818 Prussia had made an important change. Customs duties were all imposed at the frontier; on manufactured goods they did not exceed 10 per cent; and most raw materials were allowed to come in duty free. The association of manufacturers, formed a year later, was trying to generalize this reform. Its aim was to create a free-trade area for the whole of Germany which would at the same time be strongly protected against foreign competition.

List had comparatively little part in the first success which the movement for economic national union achieved. As deputy in Würtemberg List took a liberal line which brought him into opposition to the reactionary government. He was thrown into prison, had to seek exile in France, England, and Switzerland, and finally settled in America. When he returned to Germany in 1832 the first step to economic union had been taken. Two customs unions had been concluded, and List entered into the agitation for an extension of the system. Within two years the *Zollverein* was achieved and practically the whole of Germany (though not Austria) was made into a single economic unit, inside which free trade offered a large market to German industry. At first this unit had a low tariff against the outside world; but pressure from certain sections of industry made the question of increased protection more urgent.

It was at this point that List became the theoretical spokesman of protection. In 1840 there appeared his most important work, *Das nationale System der politischen Ökonomie*. In this book he expounded a theory of protection which was particularly adapted to the needs of the youthful German industry. It is in regard to this theory that the difference between List and Müller becomes most striking. Although they were personal friends and both anxious to develop national power, Müller always expressed hostility to modern industry. He spoke of the vicious tendency of division of labour, of factories which were nothing but barracks, and of the slavery to which modern industry subjected everyone. List accepted manufacturing industry. His theory of the importance of productive power led him to postulate as ideal an equilibrium between the different branches of production. Manufacture was an indispensable part of a well-balanced national productive equipment. Both manufacture and agriculture were essential to the strength of a state. Indeed, without manufacture the other parts of the economic structure could never flourish. Industry led to agricultural improvement and to a development of art and science such as no purely agricultural state could ever attain. The balance between agriculture and industry was the true principle of division of labour; Adam Smith's exposition of it was a one-sided one, due to his neglect of the national interest.

Nations could be divided according to the degree of civilization which they had attained. There were the savage, the pastoral, the agricultural, the agricultural and manufacturing, and finally, the agricultural-manufacturing-commercial states. Not all states could reach the highest stage of development. But those which possessed the necessary material and human resources, like Germany, had to aim at doing so. Clearly the equilibrium between agriculture, manufacture, and commerce did not arise spontaneously; the state had to act so as to bring it about. That is why List rejected *laissez-faire*. He thought that it was necessary to maintain a number of favourable institutions; and he did not omit to mention among them the various social, political, and legal arrangements of democratic government. But the most important thing a government could do was to ensure the establishment of manufacturing industry, not only for the purpose of competing at once with the industries of other countries, but also – and this was more important – in order to possess a permanent productive power from which future generations of members of the nation would draw benefits.

Protection should be used to help in the establishment of industry. It should be resorted to only if the nation had a natural basis for industry but was retarded in its economic development owing to the existence of fully fledged foreign rivals. Tariffs were then justified as educative measures. They should be used to nurse infant industries, but only until these industries were strong enough to compete with those abroad. After that tariffs must not be introduced, except when the very basis of the industrial structure of the country was threatened with extinction. Agriculture was excepted from protection. In accordance with the pre-eminent place which he assigned to manufacture, List argued that agriculture benefited greatly from the existence of a powerful industry. Industry, however, required cheap food and raw materials. Moreover, differences of soil and climate gave agriculture a kind of natural protection. Finally, protection was envisaged as a transitional policy which would bring all the suitable nations up to the level of the most developed (which at the time was England), and would then be replaced by a system of universal free trade.

Such, in brief outline, is the protectionism of List. It will be seen that List's theory was by no means of a completely different quality from that of the English classics. It is true that there are many differences of emphasis and markedly opposed conclusions with regard to policy. And also in matters of theory, that is, in the comprehension of fundamentals of the economic system, List cannot be mentioned in the same breath as Smith and Ricardo. But when due allowance has been made for differences in the economic environment, his social and political significance was not unlike theirs. Like them he was essentially a champion of industrial capitalism.

## Socialist Criticism

*The Growth of Socialist Thought.* The progress of capitalism in the early nineteenth century called forth two types of theoretical criticism. That which was in essence backward-looking has been described in the section on the romantics. Some of the reactionary implications of Malthus's theory have also been pointed out. But, in so far as it struggled for the past, it was in the nature of this criticism that it should have to come to terms with the economic system which it opposed. Neither in practice nor in theory was this rearguard action of feudalism able to delay the victory of capitalism and of its political economy.

The other criticism of capitalism which finds expression in the first few years of the nineteenth century is of a different character. It is revolutionary: it is not bound up with the waning privileges of a particular social class: it represents neither the landed nobility nor the clergy. It has no past golden age to long for: feudalism and medievalism mean nothing to it. It does not sigh for the return of something which is gone for ever. If it finds anything to criticize in the new social order it feels itself free to attack it in any way. It has no need to draw its inspiration from an older system of status: the class which it claims to represent is one which has neither gained nor lost any privileges.

The early history of modern socialism would deserve a chapter to itself, were it possible to devote here more space to political and social theory. As it is, our concern with it is limited to its relation to economic thought; and a somewhat cursory treatment must suffice. A separate chapter is devoted to Marx, partly because of his importance in the development of socialist criticism, but mainly because his theories were consciously made to stem directly out of classical political economy. But Marx's theories did not develop in a void. He had his forerunners not only in the classical economists, but also in the early socialist critics of capitalist practice and theory. It is with these that we have to deal in the present section.

The points of contact between early socialist thought and non-socialist critics are to be found in some of the critical theories which

Malthus and other expounded. They had discovered weaknesses and contradictions in the capitalist system and in classical economic theory and had suggested certain remedies. But once these weaknesses were laid bare other remedies could be proposed. We find in fact that some of the early writers whose criticism of capitalism carries a revolutionary message began their attack in terms which are formally similar to those used by the writers already mentioned. But as their socialist purpose becomes more marked this formal resemblance disappears.

Here is not the place to discuss in detail the conditions which led to the rise of the modern socialist movement. This, however, may be said. Socialism launched its attack upon capitalism on two separate fronts. In the first place, it began as a movement of revolt against specific evils of capitalist industry. We have already seen that the creation of capital required the creation of a new social class, and we have noted the process by which the working class, that of the wage-labourers, was brought into the world. This process brought with it much ruthlessness which was even intensified during the first decades of the nineteenth century. The story of the exploitation, oppression, and misery which the working-class suffered during that period has often been told. To the historian, viewing this evolution over a long period its main achievement appears to have been the ability of the worker to enter freely into contracts, to become equal before the law. But in the short run his dependence on the new class of employers was made extreme by the disappearance of his earlier economic place in the community. The power which economic inequality gave to the capitalist often appeared to the worker more than enough to make up for the disappearance of medieval bondage. The mechanism of a market in which bargaining parties were unequal appeared to the weaker of them to be as harsh a ruler as any feudal lord. Indeed, the comparative economic security which, with all his subjection, the labourer had enjoyed contrasted favourably with the threat of unemployment which the rapidly changing complexion of industry kept constantly before his eyes.

To those, like Smith and Ricardo, who could see the inner workings of the system and could, therefore, look ahead, capitalism meant an undreamed of expansion of production, increase of wealth, and economic intercourse between nations, together with all the cultural benefits which those involved. It meant liberalism in politics and the destruction of oppressive regulation and obscurantist restriction. To the workers at the time it seemed that they were being called upon to bear the cost of this revolution. To them early capitalism meant pauperism, unemployment, or at best, hard labour in factories for themselves, their wives, and children. Long hours, dangerous and insanitary conditions, and oppressive supervision were the common lot. The earliest working-class agitation aimed at the abolition of these evils of the factory system. They took the form of combinations of workmen which, by offering a common front to the employer, tried to make up for economic inequality and to resist exploitation. In this way the trade-union movement was born. Through the experience of its struggles against individual symptoms of the system and against individual capitalists, it gave rise to a theory of opposition to the system as a whole. Gradually the working-class movement became imbued with a socialist purpose.

The other aspect of modern socialism is an ideological one. It has its roots in the very liberalism which was the political philosophy consonant with industrial capitalim. It has already been pointed out that the philosophy of natural law, and the utilitarianism which was one of its expressions, could bear a radical as well as a conservative interpretation. Capitalism had been more revolutionary than any previous social system. It had swept away without scruples old institutions and modes of thought, if they were found to stand in its way. And it had done all this, not in the name of some narrow class interest, but in the name of all humanity. Freedom, equality, justice, the greatest happiness of the greatest number, progress, and the rule of reason – these were its watchwords. It had awakened hopes in every one that a new ideal age was being built. And it could not prevent the revolutionary fervour from persisting and turning against the new social order, if that order was found deficient in the light of the promises made. The critical attitude to human institutions which Machievelli, Bacon, Hobbes, Locke, and the utilitarians had founded became a permanent feature of thought. Men began to look upon the state and the economic system with the eyes of reason. They were not afraid to criticize and to agitate for reform, to call capitalism to account, and to work for a better social order. From this movement based on liberal philosophy, socialism received its second great inspiration.

As far as individual critics of economic practice and theory are concerned, it is not always possible to distinguish between the different influences. In all of them a mixture can be found. The inspiration comes from dissatisfaction with the conditions of the working class and from the disappointed hopes of the liberal revolution. The content (at least that which interests us here) is a criticism of certain conclusions of classical political economy. In spite of the mixture, one can in general distinguish between critical economic thought which is more closely in contact with working-class experience and with the rising labour movement, and that which is more directly a product of liberal social philosophy. The difference is clearly brought out in the comparison between English and French socialist thought. In England, with the earlier development of modern industry and of a working-class movement, early socialism takes the critical elements in the classical English economists and applies them to the purposes of the working class. In France, the experience of the French Revolution, the slower pace of industrial expansion, and the importance of the financial interest give early socialist thought its liberal and sometimes romantic flavour.

It is not necessary to deal here with all the writers who can claim to have been socialist pioneers. Nor can any one of them be dealt with at great length. In a history of socialism Saint-Simon, Fourier, and Robert Owen would certainly have to be considered. They have been left out here because their influence on economic thought has not been very great. Sismondi and Proudhon have been selected for France, and Thompson, Gray, Bray, and Hodgskin as representing England. Sismondi is only a little more critical than Malthus in economic theory, though far more so in political intention. Proudhon is a socialist in purpose; but he lacks clarity in his economic analysis. The English socialists are the most closely in contact with classical political econ009omiy and, therefore, the clearest in the critical use which they make of the classical analysis of the capitalist system.

*Sismondi.* There is a great deal in Sismondi (1773–1842) which is romantic; but there is also a feeling of sympathy for those whom capitalism is making suffer, and a genuine attempt to understand the causes, inherent in the system, which are productive of distress. Sismondi's chief works were historical; and his voluminous histories of France and of the Italian Republic were those which earned him fame in his lifetime. But he also wrote two economic works, separated by sixteen years. In 1803 he published *La Richesse commerciale*; in 1819, the *Nouveaux Principes de l'Economie politique*. In his first book he is still a faithful disciple of Adam Smith: an uncompromising free-trader and non-interventionist. He accepts fully not only the theoretical structure of Smith's work, but also its practical conclusions and its political philosophy. *Laissez-faire* is described as the best possible economic policy. Faith is expressed in the natural harmony which made the undisturbed pursuit of individual self-interest the means for achieving the greatest common advantage. Absence of government interference would cause capital to be disturbed among the different channels of employment in accordance with their relative profitability. This would result in the most advantageous use of the whole capital of the nation. But even into this complacent picture of a *laissez-faire* world Sismondi allows certain doubts to enter. He is not completely reconciled to see the labourer's lot remain permanently that of producer of everything and consumer of only a small part of what he produces.

Before he ventured out again with a theoretical work Sismondi did a considerable amount of historical research and travelling. In Italy, Switzerland, and France he came into direct contact with the first crises of the nineteenth century; and he discovered that they had also ravaged England, Germany, and Belgium. This experience left its mark; and when he came to formulate again his economic views little of the indiscriminate repetition of Smithian doctrines remained. Sismondi did not break entirely with the classical school. He always retained his respect for Adam Smith, and he always claimed to have preserved intact the main theoretical apparatus of classicism. Like Malthus, whom he admired, Sismondi objected to the application of classical theory to practical problems, particularly in the way in which this was done in the Ricardian system. Like Malthus, too, he began with a criticism of the classical method, and to this he added an objection to the classical conception of the aim of economic science.

Sismondi makes the often-repeated and ill-founded charge that Ricardo had been too abstract. He holds up Malthus as an example of the careful balance between deduction and induction which, he claims, was more truly in the tradition of Smith. He claims that political economy has so wide a scope that it has to base itself on a wide experience and a knowledge of history in order to comprehend fully the social relations which were the objects of its study. Political economy has a moral purpose. It is not concerned with wealth as such, but with wealth in relation to man. It has to study economic activity from the point of view of its effect on human welfare. For this reason Sismondi regards the problems of distribution as more important than any other economic problems. In this respect he is, oddly, in agreement with Ricardo. This agreement of emphasis brings out also the different approach and purpose of Malthus and Sismondi.

Malthus had begun by stressing consumption, since his purpose was to justify the unproductive consumer. Sismondi stresses distribution, because his concern is mainly with social justice. Thus, although they reach formally similar conclusions their intentions are quite dissimilar.

Sismondi's remarks on the method and object of economic inquiry are not the important parts of his theory. What is important is his rejection of classicism, in so far as it implies optimism and a belief in harmony and in the self-equilibrating character of the capitalist system. Gone is the complacency which characterized his earlier work. The emphasis is now entirely on all that is bad in the contemporaneous scene. Everywhere Sismondi sees an expansion of productive forces, without any equivalent increase in the well-being of the masses of society. Political economy has no reason to describe the system and then to sit back and hope for the best. The outlook for humanity is black and something must be done about it.

Gone too is the harmony of social interests. Sismondi was one of the earliest economists to speak of the existence of two social classes, the rich and the poor, the capitalists and the workers, whose interests he regarded as opposed: they were in constant conflict with one another. His formulation of this class conflict is almost as extreme as that of Marx; and in the *Communist Manifesto* Marx and Engels acknowledged it.[1] Sismondi also emphasizes the disappearance of the small independent workers on the farm and in the workshop owing to the ruthless competition of concentrated capital and large-scale enterprise. Society, he says, is becoming divided into two classes, the owners and the proletariat. Property and labour are separated.

Having thrown optimism and the idea of social harmony overboard, Sismondi proceeds to analyse the causes inherent in the capitalist system which are responsible for the misery of the masses. Sismondi feels that there is something wrong in the conditions of capitalist production. He sees that this form of production is tending to increase the productive powers and the output of goods, but that the more the productive powers increase, the greater become the contradictions between capital and labour, between production and sale. He sees that the growth of production involves as a corollary that the producers (the workers) shall be limited in their consumption to the minimum of

---

1 Marx and Engels, *The Communist Manifesto* (ed. Ryazanov, 1930), p. 57.

subsistence. Like Malthus, he considers it inherent in capitalist production that the workers cannot absorb the whole output of industry. But he is not prepared to accept this as a natural phenomenon and to suggest as mitigation the use of the safety-valve of unproductive consumption.

All this is implied in his work. But his analysis is based mainly on one idea: over-production and crises which arise from competition and the separation of labour and ownership. The latter makes the labourer completely dependent on the capitalist. The workers are at the mercy of the employers. In order to live they have to accept employment at any wage the employer cares to offer. The supply of labour is entirely determined by the demand of the capitalist for wage-labour. Population does not tend, as Malthus had claimed, to outrun the means of subsistence. Population depends on revenue. When the worker is independent he has control over his revenue; he knows his present position and can calculate his future chances; and he can determine whether, and when, to marry and produce children. Since property and labour are separated, revenue is under the control of the capitalist. It depends on the capitalist's demand for labour and this is constantly fluctuating, because it is determined, not by the needs of consumers, but by the need to produce in order to employ capital profitability.

Here the theory is joined to the ideas of competition and over-production. Capital is obliged by its very nature to seek continued increase of production. The classical economists had regarded this tendency with complacency; the Ricardian mechanism had shown where the self-adjusting force lay. Sismondi now points out that this continual increase in production must give rise to periodic excess. The workers' demand is always insufficient to absorb all products; with the progress of machinery periodic unemployment is created which still further reduces the workers' purchasing power. Neither capital nor labour can be easily withdrawn from industries which are faced with a declining demand for their products. Fixed capital will have to stay in the declining industries; the workers will accept longer hours and lower wages; and production will continue to remain excessive. Sismondi condemns competition. Not only does it lead to increased exploitation, because every capitalist is anxious to obtain the greatest profit; it also intensifies over-production. Competition is determined by the profitable employment of capital, not by the needs of the consuming public.

Over-production appears most strikingly in the crisis. According to

Sismondi crises are caused by three things: the competitive character of production which makes it impossible for each producer to know the market, the fact that capital, not want, determines production, and the separation of ownership and labour which increases the revenue of the capitalists, but not that of the labourers who form the mass of consumers. These three factors create disequilibrium. Demand will increase unevenly: that for the products of industries which cater for the mass of the people cannot grow uniformly with producing power, because it is only the revenue of the capitalist which increases proportionately with production. The capitalist will exercise a greater demand for luxury goods; but this cannot make up for the other demand which has shrunk; it only causes changes in the distribution of productive resources which bring about fluctuations in economic activity and aggravate the difficulties of over-production. The progressive concentration of capital aggravates this disparity of demands. The capitalist system has thus an inherent tendency to widen the gulf between production and consumption.

Sismondi's description of the weaknesses of capitalism was extremely acute. His analysis, quite apart from his unorthodox conclusions, was salutary even for the progress of non-socialist economic thought, because it forced economists (more than Malthus had done) to examine the problem of disequilibrium. His influence in both fields was less great than it might have been, partly because of his inability to link his theory of disequilibrium with the corpus of pure theory of Ricardian economic analysis. Sismondi's formulation of most of the fundamental economic concepts was vague or confused. And however much his practical conclusions may have had a basis in reality, they lacked the theoretical background which would have made them significant to economists or, in the long run, even to socialists.

Sismondi's remedies reveal this lack of a unified principle of analysis even more clearly. He considers the cause of economic evil to be the disparity between productive power and the social relations which determined their use. He wavered between a remedy which would replace the existing social order by one which would be in harmony with the productive powers, and a remedy which would limit the expansion of productive powers so as to make them congruous with the opportunities offered by existing social relations. He was, however, certain that the *laissez-faire* policy of the classics was useless. The state must step in to mitigate evils and remove their causes. But when it comes to saying how this could be done, Sismondi hesitated and indeed expressed doubt about his ability to prescribe the correct policy.

He rejected communism, because he was too great a believer in the importance of private interest. He rejected feudalism too, because he regarded it as a restriction of the productive powers of mankind. But his policy did in the end amount to a return to more primitive conditions. He defined the aim of policy as the reunion of property and labour and the re-establishment of equilibrium between production and consumption. This might also have been described as the socialist aim. But whereas most socialist thinkers of the period, particularly in England, came to regard abolition of private property in the means of production as the right method, Sismondi wanted to see a revival of the independent producer, the small farmer and the artisan. Pending this return to the golden age it should be the task of government to prevent the increase in disequilibrium. This could best be achieved by slackening industrial progress. Government should, above all, put a brake on invention and aim at having such a rate of progress that the necessary adjustments could be made smoothly and without causing over-production and misery. Thus, Sismondi is led into an impasse, in which only the retrograde step of delaying material progress based on scientific advance offers the prospects of a solution. With all his historical interest, Sismondi lacked the insight into economic development which would have prevented his sympathy for the oppressed from leading him into a position incompatible with his intention.[1]

*Proudhon (1809–65).* Proudhon is better known than Sismondi and has had a vastly more important influence on socialist thought. He is one of the main inspirers of syndicalist and anarchist doctrine. But his role as political theorist has been more important than as economist;

---

1 There is in the library of the University of Texas at Austin, Texas, a copy of the first edition (1819) of Sismondi's *Nouveaux Principes*, not only beautifully bound and in perfect condition, but distinguished also by the fact that it belonged to J. B. Say, whose name appears on the fly-leaves. It contains numerous notes by Say, with one exception carefully pasted on to the margins of the book so as not to disfigure the pages. I must reserve for another occasion a full description of these notes which are mainly concerned with a defence of Say's theory of the market. On Sismondi's final conclusion, I might quote these two observations by Say: 'Arrêter l'accroissement de l'industrie pour rendre service à la société! *Bone Deus!*' and 'Le fait prouve contre vous, car le fait est que de nos jours, malgré nos progrès tant deplorés par vous, l'ouvrier est mieux nourri, mieux vetu, mieux logé, qui'il ne l'a été à aucune autre époque.'

and because he has been the subject of many specialist studies a short summary of his theories will suffice.

To understand the quality of Proudhon's criticism of capitalism and of other socialist thinkers, as well as his positive theory and policy, it is useful to remember Marx's characterization of him as a petty-bourgeois. He was the son of a small brewer and was born into an environment of small peasant proprietors. He became a printer, and, although he spoke of himself as a son of the working class, his social roots were definitely in the lower middle class. An unquenchable thirst for knowledge made him read and study continually; and although the knowledge he acquired was never fully digested, it was large enough to make him conscious of the importance of learning and somewhat vain and contemptuous of those whom he thought without it.

From an early age he was interested in social problems. He showed himself possessed of a critical mind which was not afraid to attack accepted ideas. At the age of thirty-one he published his first important and perhaps his most brilliant book, *Qu'est-ce que la propriété ou recherches sur le principe du droit et du gouvernement*. This was followed, in 1846, by his other great work, *Contradictions économiques, ou Philosophie de la Misère*, to which Marx replied in his *La Misère de la Philosophie*: a reply which cost him Proudhon's friendship. In these books the influence of his environment is supplemented by his natural bent for philosophical speculation and his love of dialectics. Contact with the working-class movement, which led to his active participation in the revolutionary movement of 1848, determined the critical aspect of his theory. The interest in philosophy determined his love for abstraction and for verbal paradoxes. This factor became even more important when, largely through Marx's influence, Proudhon took up seriously the study of the philosophy of Hegel. Among other ideological influences must be mentioned the Bible (although Proudhon was not religious, he derived his idea of justice to some extent from the Old Testament) and the writings of the political philosophers of the period after the French Revolution, particularly of Fourier, who had stated the view that social development proceeded by way of continual contradiction between what is aimed at and what it achieved.

One moral idea underlies the whole of Proudhon's thought: the idea of justice. Again and again Proudhon speaks of justice as the supreme principle of human life. But how is justice to be achieved in society? Here an Aristotelian concept is used. Justice is the same as reciprocity, equality, equilibrium. Social life, nature itself even, contains irremovable contradictions. The antinomies of Kant, later the thesis–antithesis of Hegel, are Proudhon's inspiration for the theory that contradition is the eternal principle in human affairs. Having raised contradiction to this exalted status, Proudhon's search is not for the political means of changing social institutions, but for the discovery of the right idea which would abolish contradictions in the abstract. That idea is the concept of justice as an equilibrium of opposing forces. Society can only make the fullest use of its powers when 'les forces en fonctions dont il se compose soient en equilibre' (the forces of which it is composed are in equilibrium).[1]

The idea of a reconciliation of opposing forces underlies all his theory and his practical proposals. It is particularly marked in his attitude to property. Even in his first work, which launched into the world the famous definition 'la propriété, c'est le vol' (property is theft), Proudhon's object was not to analyse the different economic relations which underlay different forms of legal property. He did not attack private property as such. On the contrary, he regarded property as an essential condition of liberty. Because he accepted the view that labour was the sole source of wealth and constituted the only title to property, he regarded it as vital that every one should be able to enjoy and own the fruits of his labour. What he objected to was the abuse of property, the celebrated *droit d'aubaine*, the power to exact an unearned tribute which modern capitalist enterprise and its laws gave to the capitalists. Rent, interest, profit, should be abolished, but property should be preserved.

How were the excrescences of private property to be removed? Proudhon made a large number of suggestions for various reforms relating particularly to rent, but he never went so far as to propose common ownership of the means of production. On the contrary, just as he opposed the contemporaneous French socialists such as the Saint-Simonians for being Utopian and for ignoring the laws of the economic process, he also rejected communism, because he thought that it was based on a false analysis of property. In this *Théorie de la propriété*, published posthumously in 1866, he went so far as to propose the retention of private property in its existing form with its power to use and destroy mitigated only by 'equilibrating' guarantees.[2] But his

1 A. Cuvillier, *Proudhon* (1937), p. 253.
2 ibid., pp. 194–5.

ideal was really not unlike that of Sismondi. The balance of contradictions is achieved and the power of exploitation is abolished when property is parcelled out and agriculture and industry are carried on by numerous small producers. Property may then be said to exist no longer for 'les droits et les prétentions de chacun se faisant contrepoids ... le droit d'aubaine est à peine exercé' (the duties and claims of everyone are balanced ... the right of tribute is scarcely exercised).[1] And similar to Sismondi also, in spite of his explicit rejection of Sismondi's view on invention as retrograde, is Proudhon's instinctive dislike of machinery, because he feels that it is incompatible with his small-producers' commonwealth.

The political organization of this ideal society should also reflect the equilibrium of forces, or, as Proudhon calls it, the social 'mutualism'. The state, he thought, must disappear. Anarchy was the ideal form of social living; that is the absence of government as a coercive force, and its replacement by voluntary association for the administration of things, not the rule over persons. This theory was never carefully worked out, and it did not prevent Proudhon from approving some of the most coercive acts of authoritarian government. It did, however, make Proudhon object strongly to socialist and communist theories which seemed to him to involve the maintenance of a coercive state. Proudhon realized that large-scale industry could not be entirely abolished. It had to be integrated with his society of small farmers and artisans. The way to do it was to hand it over to voluntary associations of independent workers which would be free from state interference. The workers should follow the example of the capitalists and form companies for running big industries.

This syndicalist dream comes at once up against the reality of the need for capital. And this leads to Proudhon's most specific economic theory and proposal. The abuse of private property, he had said, consists mainly in the ability to extract income without labour. One of the most important ways in which this is done is through the charging of interest on money. If only everybody were able to obtain loans gratuitously no exploitation would take place. Nor would there be any difficulty in establishing workers' syndicates. Proudhon regards money as merely a medium of circulation. Following the Canonists, he thinks that, like a commodity, it ought to be bought and sold at cost, and not

1 A. Cuvillier, *Proudhon*, p. 72.

lent at interest. Lending at interest enables the owner of money to sell one and the same thing several times over without losing his property in it.

Having confused capital in its monetary form and money as a circulating medium, Proudhon applies the idea of lending without interest to bank credits, the most common form in which loans are made. Nature, he argues, supplies man freely with raw materials; labour, therefore, not capital, is productive. Credit, being nothing but an exchange, should not bear interest. The most important part of Proudhon's economic programme becomes the creation of free credit through the establishment of an 'exchange bank'.

There should be set up, he says, a bank without capital and thus without any interest burden. This bank would issue notes (*bons d'échange*), which, being inconvertible into gold, would cost little to produce. These notes would be issued against commercial bills representing a sale already made or, at least already decided on. If everybody agreed to accept these notes in payment for goods they would circulate in place of money. The bank would run no risk because it would only be discounting genuine commercial transactions. The important point, however, would be that this service would not cost anything. Interest being abolished, exploitation through property is abolished too. Moreover, since the exchange bank enables every worker or group of workers to get free credit with which to buy the means of production, the division of classes would disappear. Property and labour, which, as Sismondi had complained, were separated, would now be reunited. The way to the ideal commonwealth of free and equal producers, to justice, and, therefore, to the abolition of oppressive government is clear.

Thus, Proudhon's socialism becomes an unrealistic dream of a golden age, to be achieved by the abolition of interest. It may be said, however, that Proudhon lived in an environment in which the power of exploitation seemed symbolized in finance. But Proudhon's failure to analyse the principles of capitalist production and to understand the quality of capital and the function of money make his practical proposal as ineffective as his ideal is retrograde. The impetus which he gave to French socialism was marred by the confusion he sowed. His ideas have lived on in anarchism and in the host of ill-considered nostrums that appear periodically during periods of crisis. Proudhon was certainly moved by righteous indignation and reforming zeal. But he combined with it much that was reactionary. What he said about women and about war,[1] no less than the muddle-headedness which is evident in his economic analysis, makes him akin to the romantics. From Proudhon and Sismondi monetary cranks of all ages have drawn their inspiration.

*The Forerunners of Marx.*   The last group of earlier socialist writers, Bray, Gray, Thompson, and Hodgskin did not wrap up their theory in quite so tortuous a philosophy as did Proudhon. They all base themselves on the teachings of the Ricardian school but use the classical conclusions to point a revolutionary moral. They had an opportunity to observe the early energetic trade-union movement and to acquire a more determined socialist theory. What is more important, the development of this socialist theory was an easy transition from classical political economy itself. These writers did not state the existence of a conflict of classes any better than did Smith, Ricardo, and Malthus. A reading of these English socialist writers disposes of the view that Marx invented the idea of the class struggle. As one writer has said, the surprising thing is not that Thompson, Hodgskin, and Marx drew socialist conclusions from the Ricardian system, but that the Ricardians themselves did not do so.[2] As it was, the triumph of the Ricardian school, exemplified by the doctrinal certainty of a James Mill, was accompanied by a flood of writings of authors who were not prepared to accept the pessimistic conclusions of classicism. The authors who are here specifically mentioned are by no means the only ones in this movement.[3] They are selected because they represent the trend in its clearest form.

There are two common features in their writings. They all start from the Ricardian formulation of the labour theory of value. They accept the explanation that the amount of labour embodied in a commodity is the substance and measure of its exchange-value. They rely on the distinction between productive and unproductive labour. And they all develop in one form or another the concept of surplus value. In the capitalist system, they say, the wages paid to the worker are always less than the value of the product which the worker has produced and

---

1 A. Cuvillier, *Proudhon*, pp. 162–6, 254–7.
2 G. Myrdal, *Das Politische Element in der Nationalökonomischen Doktrinbildung* (1931), p. 124.
3 For a discussion of some examples, cf. Marx, *Theorien über den Mehrwert*, vol. iii, pp. 281–313.

the capitalist has appropriated. Hence exploitation, oppression, and misery.

The other characteristic common to all these writers is their revolutionary interpretation of utilitarianism. They all accepted the utilitarian postulate of the greatest happiness of the greatest number. We have already seen that this ideal could be given an egalitarian content and was given it even by some of the non-socialist utilitarians. The early English socialists also accepted the utilitarian emphasis on liberty and the critical attitude to existing institutions which was a natural result of philosophical radicalism. Bentham had shown the way. An existing social structure with all its concepts of law, rights and duties had nothing sacrosanct about it. It had to be judged in the light of the utilitarian ideal. Thus when the socialists came to inquire into the reasons for the absence of the ideal order in which there was no exploitation, because everyone obtained the full fruits of his labour, they were not precluded from finding the answer in existing social arrangements and laws. In particular, they were led to attack the existing property distribution and the whole system of private property.

With the basic ideas held in common, the writers in question laid stress on different aspects of their socialist creed. William Thompson (1783–1833) is very close to the utilitarians; so is John Gray (1799–1850?) in his earlier writings. Later, both he and John Francis Bray (1809–1895), through concentrating on certain practical remedies, were led to put forward proposals that resembled those of Proudhon; but as the authors were English, their theories never became quite so mystical. Thomas Hodgskin (1787–1869) was perhaps the most determined socialist economist among pre-Marxian writers. The germs of many of Marx's ideas are found in his books; and Marx acknowledged, at least partly, his debt to Hodgskin.[1]

Thompson's chief works are *An Inquiry into the Principles of the Distribution of Wealth most conducive to Human Happiness* (1824) and his *Labour Rewarded* (1827), which was a reply to Hodgskin. In the former book, he gives a consistent socialist interpretation of Ricardian economy and Benthamite philosophy. Labour is the sole source of value; the working class should be the only one to receive the product. In capitalist society labour was deprived of a part of what was its due by the claims of capital and land. This meant not only unnatural and unjust distribution which could never achieve the greatest happiness

1 Marx, *Theorien über den Mehrwert*, vol. iii, pp. 313–80.

of the greatest number; it also created the striking contradiction of capitalism: plenty and poverty, and with them all manner of social evils. The remedy was the abolition of the capitalist's tribute. Thompson knew that the capital which was consumed in the process of production added its value to the product. What he objected to was the capitalist's ability to appropriate the whole surplus value which arose through the worker's dependence upon the capitalist who owned the means of production. The policy of socialism is not very clearly worked out; but as an analysis and indictment of the early capitalist system, the *Inquiry* is an important document. In his second book Thompson took up the problem of policy. By this time he had become an out-and-out disciple of Robert Owen and he saw salvation exclusively in a system of co-operation.

A similar process can be observed in John Gray. His first work, *A Lecture on Human Happiness*, published in 1825, was a trenchant condemnation of the existing social order. It was based on the view that labour was the sole source of wealth and it analysed the falsification of natural justice in contemporaneous capitalism. Those who produce all are shown to receive only a fraction of the fruits of their labour, while the unproductive classes lead a parasitical existence. Labour creates the only title to property; and exploitation through the exaction of rent, interest, and profit is the real cause of all social ills.

In two later works, *The Social System: A Treatise on the Principle of Exchange* (1831) and *Lectures on the Nature and Use of Money* (1848), Gray endeavoured to describe the principles of the ideal society. In these he outlined a system which was in many ways similar to Proudhon's plan for an exchange bank. Unlike the latter it consistently applies the labour theory of value. Gray's national bank was to ascertain accurately the amount of labour time necessary for the production of different commodities. The producer would receive in exchange for his product a certificate of its value which would entitle him to receive a commodity in which an equivalent amount of labour was embodied. This system would organize exchange (which Gray regarded as the great need) in such a way as to ensure an equilibrium between production and consumption. It would destroy the tyranny of money as a measure of exchange-value and put in its rightful place the only true measure, labour time. As a socialist policy this could be shown to be Utopian[1] because it lacked a sound analytical basis. What Gray wanted

1 Marx, *Zur Kritik der politischen Ökonomie*, pp. 70–3.

was to abolish private exchange, but to allow the capitalist conditions of production (which involved private exchange) to continue. He never analysed clearly the role of money in the capitalist economy, and was therefore led to isolate the process of exchange as that which needed reform.

Similar ideas occur in Francis Bray's *Labour's Wrongs and Labour's Remedies or The Age of Might and the Age of Right*, first published in 1839. Bray opposed Owenism, as expounded for example by Thompson in his *Labour Rewarded*. Like Gray, he found the source of evil in unjust exchange. Labour time was the true measure of exchange-value; and just exchange was that in which equal quantities of labour exchanged for one another. But Bray went further than Gray. His universal exchanges involved universal labour, that is, the disappearance of private capitalist property and production. But at the same time Bray's method of reaching this ideal state of affairs was somewhat reminiscent of Proudhon. It consisted in the establishment of companies which would be able, through the issue of paper money, to purchase land and capital equipment. The result achieved with the aid of trade-unions and friendly societies would be a sort of syndicalism.

Thomas Hodgskin wrote a number of books, of which *Labour Defended against the Claims of Capital, Or the Unproductiveness of Capital proved with Reference to the Present Combinations among Journeymen*, published anonymously in 1825, is the most important. His influence appears to have been quite considerable. It was exercised not only through books, but also through lectures. Although inspired, as the sub-title says, by the growing trade-union movement and the opposition to it, *Labour Defended* was not merely a pamphlet of momentary political significance. It contained a careful analysis of the economic system. Its aim was to prove that the combinations of working men were justifiable if they were directed against capitalists who exacted an unjust profit. Capital had to be proved to be unproductive. This is done by basing on the Ricardian theory of value a skilful analysis of capital's function in the process of production.

In this analysis, Hodgskin laid the foundation of the distinction, later elaborated by Marx, between the material aids to production, to which economists give the name of capital, and capital as expressive of a certain form of property relation, which makes steam-engines, raw materials, and the labourer's means of subsistence into capital. According to Hodgskin, by using the term indiscriminately to describe both the stored-up labour, which is a material aid and condition of future production, and a social relationship, which gives the capitalist command over current labour, the economists have created for themselves the problem of the productivity of capital. If, says Hodgskin, by the productivity of capital is meant its power to create exchange value; and if it is, therefore, implied that capitalist property is entitled to a share of the product, capital is definitely not productive. He admits, however, that the results of past production, etc., are necessary material conditions for the expenditure of current labour and, therefore, potentially productive. He does not explain this inconsistency in his own reasoning.

Hodgskin does not make very clear the distinction between use-value and exchange-value; but when he speaks of capital as a magic formula which is used to hide the reality of exploitation, he is very near the Marxian theory. According to a by then accepted economic tradition, Hodgskin distinguishes circulating and fixed capital. The former, he says, is nothing but 'co-existing labour'. Capital accumulation is nothing but the storing-up of labour; and the increase of the skill of the labourers themselves is a more important aspect of accumulation than the storing-up of the products of labour. Fixed capital is equally only a form of stored-up labour which becomes useful in production. It is also dependent on current labour for its utilization. Without the skill and energy of existing labour these embodiments of past labour would be useless. Whether they are productive or not depends entirely on whether they are, or are not, used by productive labour. If all these machines, buildings, and so on were left unused, they would only decay. Fixed capital acquires utility not from past labour but from present labour. It brings a profit to its owner not because it contains stored-up labour, but because it enables him to command present labour.

Hodgskin attempts to resolve all the productive qualities usually ascribed to capital into co-existing labour. He does this in order to build up a case against those who transplant these qualities into the material embodiments of labour and so make capital itself productive independently of labour. The capitalist, according to Hodgskin, is the middleman who intervenes between labour and the things with the aid of which labour is exercised; and who appropriates the larger share of the product. The natural social order is one in which this alienation of labour from its means of production and livelihood is abolished.

Hodgskin has not much to say about policy. He adopts to a large extent the anarchist ideal. He was convinced that the magic formula of the productivity of capital had so impressed men's minds that he was sceptical of any other. He doubted the efficacy of government even when it was democratic in form. The progressive enlightenment of the workers and their increasing strength through union would, he thought, make them abolish privilege, obtain the full fruits of their labour, and establish labour as the only title to property. Government would no longer be necessary, because class division would have disappeared. In the end, therefore, the ideal society to which Hodgskin aspires had the same characteristics as that of the other English and French pioneers of socialism. Marx attempted to build a different socialist theory on the same foundations but, as we shall see, while rejecting the conclusions of his forerunners as being Utopian, he ended up with an even more irrational system than theirs.

# 6

# Marx

## Life and Sources

It is a sound tradition which assigns Marx a place in every history of economic thought, but puts him in a separate chapter. Marx is now generally regarded as an economist who worked in the classical tradition. But admirers and critics alike agree that Marx was not only an economist, particularly as that term is now understood. He was a revolutionary who used the study of political economy as an instrument in a political struggle. His own claim was that it was necessary, through a study of political economy, to discover the laws of social development and thus acquire a theoretical weapon, without which he regarded political action as condemned to be impotent. In fact, however, as we shall see, neither logically nor chronologically can Marx's views as to what constitutes the law of social development be said to have been derived from his economic analysis. The relationship is almost exactly the opposite.

Karl Heinrich Marx was born in Trier in 1818. He came of an upper middle-class Jewish family, but his father left the Jewish faith soon after Marx was born. The son was destined for an academic or official career and was sent to study at the universities of Bonn and Berlin. He came into contact with the circle of young Hegelians who represented the most advanced section of German intellectuals at the time. Quite early in his career Marx became dissatisfied with the scope which Hegelian philosophy offered to his energies and, therefore, critical of it in its current form; he began to search for a more practical mode of expression of social criticism. When he realized that an academic career was impossible in the reactionary conditions which prevailed in Germany, he took to journalism as the form of political activity which was most readily available. From that time he never left politics. For nearly a year he worked on, and later edited, the *Rheinische Zeitung*. He left because the strictness of the censorship prevented him from expressing his increasingly revolutionary views. At about that time he wrote his very interesting critique of the Hegelian philosophy of the state, which already shows clearly his infusion of economic factors, or, as he himself called it, of materialism into Hegelian dialectics.

After his experience on the *Rheinische Zeitung*, Marx's long period of exile began. He moved to Paris where, at the end of 1843, he took over the editorship of the *Deutsch-französische Jahrbücher*, of which, however, only one issue appeared. It contained two important articles, one on the Jewish question and the other a critique of the Hegelain philosophy of law. The latter contains one of the clearest statements of Marx's theory of history, of the class struggle, and of the nature of revolution to be found in any of his writings. Here he spoke of the coming union of German philosophy and French socialism, of philosophy as the head and of the proletariat as the heart of revolution. It is an analysis which clearly reflects Marx's own youthful ferment, his search for a new creed, so typical of many of the younger intellectuals of a Germany which was just emerging from pre-capitalist conditions. Much of the later Marx is already there; but the work is still full of the romance and idealism of his youth.

The persecution by the Prussian government extended across the German frontier and succeeded in getting Marx expelled from Paris. At the beginning of 1845 he moved to Brussels. Before that two important and related events had occurred. Marx had become interested in political economy (his first large economic work, which shows many traces of its philosophical antecedents, became available some sixty years ago[1]), and he made the acquaintance of one who was destined to be his lifelong friend and collaborator, Friedrich Engels.

Friedrich Engels came of an old-established Rhenish bourgeois family. His father was a textile manufacturer and he himself entered

---

1 It appears under the title 'Ökonomisch-philosophische Manuscripte' in vol. iii, abt. I, of the *Marx-Engels-Gesamtausgabe*, published by the Marx-Engels-Lenin Institute in Moscow. Another edition with interesting introduction and commentary containing reflections not acceptable to the 'faithful' is: Marx, K., *Der Historische Materialismus* ed. Landshut, S. and Mayer, J. P. (1932). The first complete edition of the works of Marx and Engels in English, planned to run to some fifty volumes, has been in the process of publication for twenty years. More than half the total have so far appeared.

the family business of Ermen and Engels, cotton spinners in Manchester. Engels had become acquainted with English classical political economy and had developed a critique of it which led to results somewhat similar in their political implications to Marx's critique of Hegelian philosophy. Engels had expounded it in a short article, 'Umrisse zur Kritik der Nationalökonomie', which Marx had published in the *Deutsch-französische Jahrbücher*. After they had met in Paris they began to co-operate, and one of the chief fruits of this co-operation was *Die Deutsche Ideologie*, a critical discussion of German philosophy which the authors claimed had finally freed them from Hegelian idealism.[1] Marx left Brussels in 1848 and returned to Germany in order to take an active part in the revolution of that year. Exiled again, he went in 1850 to London, which remained his home for the rest of his life. He died there on the 14th March 1883.

His chief economic writings began in 1847 with *La Misère de la Philosophie*, a reply to Proudhon. In January of the following year, on the eve of the revolution, appeared the *Communist Manifesto*, written jointly with Engels, which presented the theory and programme of the Communist League formed in London in 1847. The next two years were mainly taken up with journalistic work, Marx having started to edit in June 1848 the Cologne *Neue Rheinische Zeitung*. During his subsequent career in London Marx began to study political economy in a systematic way. His researches in the British Museum made him acquainted with the founders of classical economy, and on the basis they had laid he began to develop his own theory.

Political activity never disappeared from his life; it was even intensified. And his interest and participation in contemporary events gave birth to many influential works, such as *The Eighteenth Brumaire of Louis Bonaparte* (1852) and *The Civil War in France in 1871* (published immediately after the Paris Commune). But from our point of view the most important writings of Marx of that period are his economic ones.

1 It has been argued, convincingly, that the quarrel over the 'materialist' or 'idealist' content of the Marxian/Hegelian philosophy is irrelevant, (by Schumpeter in *Capitalism, Socialism, and Democracy*, reprinted in *Ten Great Economists* (1952), p. 12). It is true that Marx reacted violently against the conservative conclusions of Hegel; and since he remained attached to a kind of Hegelian philosophy all his life, he liked to represent this reaction as standing Hegelian philosophy 'on its feet', instead of on its head. But while the philosophical garb in which he clothed his doctrines explains the extent of their influence in Germany and Russia (and the grotesque developments that have grown up around them), it is not significant for what is characteristic in Marx's economic or sociological work.

In 1859 he published his *Critique of Political Economy*, which contains the germ of *Capital*. It is noteworthy particularly because it contains the only systematic statement of Marx's theory of money, a field in which he contributed little. In 1867 appeared the first volume of *Capital*; the remaining volumes of this, Marx's greatest work, did not appear in his lifetime. It was left to Engels to publish them: in 1885 appeared volume ii and in 1894 volume iii. The fourth volume, which was itself in three parts and which gave an account of the history of economic doctrines, was edited, after Engels's death, by Karl Kautsky; it appeared under the title of *Theorien über den Mehrwert* in the years 1904–10.

This account of Marx's life and writings is necessarily brief. But it may serve as some background for his doctrines. To understand them we must be aware of all the forces which exerted an influence on Marx. As far as economic and political conditions are concerned, we must remember that Marx lived at a time when Germany was emerging from a state of economic backwardness and political reaction to join its western neighbours as a capitalist democracy. The lateness of this development made Marx see the German development against the background of the already established new society elsewhere. The whole experience of English industrialism and the trade unionism it had produced, as well as of the French post-revolutionary political struggles, served as inspiration and as a background against which to interpret the social and political conflicts of Germany herself.

Utilitarianism and early English socialism, French socialist thought, and the beginnings of German radicalism were the inspiration of Marx's youth. He breathed an air full of political discussion. All the young intellectuals with whom he came in contact debated the problems of political emancipation. Republicanism, constitutional democracy, freedom of thought and of the Press were the issues of the day, just as they had been a century and more earlier in France and England.

But these matters were discussed by philosophers; the solutions which were offered had somehow to be explained in terms of the philosophy of the day. Here is the second great influence on Marx. Hegelian philosophy aimed at a comprehensive and dynamic view of society by using the dialectical method. Marx was interested in the laws of movement of society, in the principles which determined social change. He rejected Hegel's conservatism; claimed that it was due to his idealism; and tried to maintain the Hegelian dialect while infusing into it those economic factors which he was increasingly coming to regard as the sole determinants of social change.

It is doubtful whether once he came to study classical political economy intensively, Marx ever really made any important use of the philosophical doctrines of his early period. What remained of them became a sociological framework for his economic theories: the economic interpretation of history and the doctrine of the class struggle. There also remained a certain predilection for dialectical formulations. But it was left to his latter-day followers to resuscitate and enlarge these philosophical elements into the so-called system of 'dialectical materialism'; a system peculiarly suited to the casuistic needs of totalitarian politics. It has little to do with an appraisal of Marx's work as a political economist, notwithstanding the occasional references to it in his own work.

## *Method*

Marx himself tells us, in the preface to the *Critique of Political Economy*, how he was led to study the economic structure of capitalist society. The need to define his attitude to current political controversy which had an economic content was one reason. The other was his desire to explain, by way of a criticism of Hegelian political and legal philosophy, the determinants of different state forms and legal institutions. He came to the conclusion that the root of these were to be found in what he called the sum total of the material conditions of social life. From this conclusion he derived the two elements which constitute the sociological basis of his economic analysis: an economic interpretation of history and the theory of classes and the class-struggle. As both these doctrines have become parts of fiercely-held, and as fiercely-attacked, political dogma, it is not easy without becoming involved in doctrinal battles to formulate them in a manner which is understandable and makes some sense. The following brief summary, therefore, follows as closely as possible Marx's own formulation, even at the cost of some clarity. We shall see later how far these ideas can be said to have any validity apart from the particular purpose to which they were put by Marx himself.

Man, Marx said, is a social producer of his means of livelihood. Social production involves certain social relations, the quality of which will depend upon the degree of development of the social productive powers. These social relations constitute the economic structure of society, on which is built a super-structure of political and legal institutions, of ideas and modes of thought, which reflect in the last resort the existing economic structure. To understand these institutions and ideas in their existing form and in their continual change, one has to study the economic structure which has given them birth. Political economy is the study of the anatomy of society, i.e. of the social productive relationships which constitute the economic system.

This statement, Marx claims, points at once to the fundamental principle of society, as well as to the contradiction within it which is the cause of social change. The principle is the social relationship entered into by men for the purpose of social production: a relationship which is appropriate to a given development of production power. It enables society to make the fullest use of these productive powers and to increase them. But this very increase of productive powers brings them into conflict with the social relationship which they had created. The relationship becomes inappropriate: instead of aiding the full utilization of man's ability to produce and reproduce all his material conditions of life, it begins to hamper it. And sooner or later man will change this social relationship in order to allow the expanding productive powers to find their due scope. Political and legal institutions will have to change and so will ideas. Thus, social change involves at some stage a political revolution to complete the preceding evolution: the abolition of an existing political structure and its replacement by one more appropriate to the new economic order.

The productive relationship in society, Marx claimed, can be said to consist in essence of a distribution of the members of society in relation to ownership of the material means of production. In legal terms, it is a property relationship. When there is private property society is divided into classes which can be defined according to their position *vis-à-vis* the means of production. This division determines the place which each class occupies in the process of production, and it is also the basis of all other economic phenomena. The economics structure of society is simply a particular social arrangement of production. It is the ultimate determinant of all social phenomena. Once economic relations have been established the process of production itself makes them subject to change: they become historical categories. 'If, to one period, they appeared as natural conditions of production, they were to another the historical result of production.

They are continually changed within production itself."[1]

It is to capitalism that Marx now applies this philosophy of history, and it is the peculiar manner in which he applies it which distinguishes him so sharply from even those classical economists who had held not dissimilar views on past social evolution. Marx looks upon capitalism not as a never-changing social order, but as one link in a chain. He is not prepared to accept as sacrosanct the existing property relations which are at the basis of capitalist society. He finds them as transient as those that have gone before. This critical attitude is the main distinguishing characteristic of Marxism economic analysis.[2]

If capitalism was subject to change, what was the motive force of that change? According to this philosophy of history it had to be some contradiction inherent in the system which produced conflict, movement, and change. It is the task, Marx argues, of political economy to discover this contradiction. This basic contradiction of capitalism is the increasingly social, co-operative nature of production made necessary by the new powers of production which mankind possesses and the individual ownership of the means of production. It shows itself in the existence of two classes, capitalists and workers: the one owning the means of production (the material conditions of production), the other owning nothing but labour-power (the means of setting production in motion). This inevitable antagonism results in a struggle between the two classes whose interests are incompatible. This struggle between capital and labour, itself the outcome of the antagonistic social productive arrangement, takes many forms, of which the most comprehensive is the political one. To study the economic structure and to show how it reflects the fundamental contradiction in all its parts was for Marx an essential element in the political activity in which his interest lay.

It is important to emphasize the peculiarity of Marx's method of approach. This method is expounded in the *Introduction to the Critique of Political Economy*, and without it, it is difficult to follow the subsequent analysis in *Capital*. Marx first analyses the four departments into which economists have divided economic activity: production, consumption, distribution, and exchange. He distinguishes between the universal qualities of these categories, which possess validity for all

---

1 Marx, *Zur Kritik der politischen Ökonomie*, p. xxxi.
2 The infusion of a critical and historical sociology into economic analysis, though rare in post-classical economics, is not unknown. Among modern economists, two striking examples of a similar attitude are Schumpeter and Keynes.

time, and the historical ones, which are significant only for a particular phase of social development. In the work of non-socialist economists, he claims, these two qualities are continually mixed up, as part of their general error of regarding the capitalist system as eternal. He admits that there is a connection between these four departments. 'Production brings forth the things needed for the satisfaction of wants; distribution shares them out according to social laws; exchange distributes that which has already been shared, according to individual want; in consumption, finally, the product leaves the social sphere, it becomes directly the object and servant of individual want, and satisfies it.'[1]

This, he says, is only a superficial connection. It makes production subject to natural, and distribution to social, laws. It puts exchange in an uneasy place between the two. And it excludes consumption from the economic sphere, except as the end of one process and the starting-point of a new one. Marx goes on to show what he regards as the natural, that is the universal, connection between production and consumption. First, there is productive consumption, which is the use of the product in a new process of production, and consumptive production, which is the reproduction of human life itself. Secondly, production supplies the material for consumption, consumption the want, that is, the purpose of production. Finally, they are both parts of each other. Consumption is the final act of production; through it alone the product fulfils its function as a product. Production is part of consumption because it creates wants.

But, he argues, the identity of production and consumption exists only if we ignore the social relationship which mediates between them. This mediation is distribution. Superficially, distribution means distribution of products. But before it can be that, it has to be 'first, a distribution of the means of production and secondly (which is only a further quality of the same relationship), a distribution of the members of society among the different branches of production'.[2] Production must, therefore, presuppose such a distribution. And distribution in the conventional sense is determined by distribution as a social element in the process of production. Ricardo, according to Marx, was getting near the truth when he made distribution, rather than production, the subject of political economy. He erred in thinking that the laws of distribution were natural and not historical. Exchange, finally,

1 Marx, *Zur Kritik der politischen Ökonomie*, p. xx.
2 ibid., p. xxx.

is a part of production and is entirely determined by it. There can be no exchange without division of labour (a productive factor); and the quality of exchange depends on the quality of production (for example, private exchange arises from private production). One has, Marx says, to keep in mind the interaction between these elements in order to become aware of the historical–social relations which lie behind their superficial universal connection.

Marx makes a similar analysis of the method of economic inquiry. It would be natural, he said, to approach the economic phenomena of society in their concrete reality. This is how economic inquiry began. It took as its starting-point 'population, nation, state ... and ended by having discovered in its analysis certain determining, abstract general relations, like division of labour, money, value, etc.'[1] Once these abstractions had been made, political economy took them as its starting-point and worked its way up to concrete reality. Although this is the correct scientific method, it has its dangers. It reverses the order in which reality itself proceeds. One must, therefore, always remember that even the most abstract economic concept presupposes an existing concrete reality of which it only represents a single element. Simple economic categories may have had an actual historical existence in their abstract simplicity; but they do not acquire their full significance except in a highly developed economic system.

Political economy must study the most abstract categories in relation to the anatomy of capitalism. Marx endeavours to relate elementary concepts such as value, labour, money, etc., to the conditions of capitalist production. He also traces the historical development which leads up to modern capitalism; and he shows the earlier more primitive form of existence of these economic concepts. This method makes *Capital* very different from the majority of economic treaties after Ricardo's. Some formal resemblance to this method may be found in three other works, *The Wealth of Nations*, Steuart's *Principles*, and Marshall's *Principles* in that they are attempts to combine economic theory, economic history, and the history of economic doctrines. A similar approach, in a more limited field, underlies Schumpeter's *Business Cycles*; and Keynes's *General Theory*, though less systematically presented, shows the same scope.

---

1 Marx, *Zur Kritik der politischen Ökonomie*, p. xxxv.

## The Labour Theory of Value

The simplest concept which relates to man's activity of producing his means of livelihood is human labour. Labour may be viewed in its natural (universal) form and in its social (historical) quality. The former is a 'purposeful activity directed to appropriating natural objects in one form or another'. As such, 'labour is a natural condition of human existence; a condition of the metabolism of man and nature which is independent of all social forms'.[1] Labour in this sense produces objects which satisfy human wants, in other words, objects which possess use-value. Use-value is inseparable from the object's concrete qualities: different use-values coincide with differences in the material qualities of commodities. As use-values these commodities realize their purpose in consumption. Labour, viewed as a producer of use-value, is not the sole source of value; for this labour cannot be exercised without some natural material. Different use-values embody different proportions of labour and nature; but the latter element must always be present.

There are two further aspects of labour in this form: particular labour, and the sum-total of the individual labours of all members of society which produces the sum-total of use-values which society requires. In its second aspect, labour acquires a social significance. As soon as man produces socially, use-value becomes part of the social network and the quality of use-value becomes independent of particular individual labour. Use-value becomes the product of a fraction of the total labour of society. This means further that individual labour has become generalized: it has become a part of social labour. Some social arrangement has been found for apportioning the labour of all individual members of society to the production of all the use-values required.

As far as use-values are concerned, it is a matter of indifference on what particular social arrangement their production has been based. The material qualities of commodities (which constitute their use-value) are not thereby affected. 'We cannot say from the taste of the wheat, whether it was raised by Russian serf, French smallholder or English capitalist.'[2] But it is clear that some social productive relations must exist. 'Every child knows that a country which ceased to work . . .

1 Marx, *Zur Kritik der politischen Ökonomie*, pp. xxxv–xlv.
2 ibid., p. 2.

would die. Every child knows, too, that the mass of products corresponding to the different needs require different and quantitively determined masses of the total labour of society. That this necessity of distributing social labour in definite proportions cannot be done away with by the *particular form* of social production, but can only change the *form it assumes*, is self-evident. No natural laws can be done away with. What can change, in changing historical circumstances, is the *form* in which these laws operate.'[1]

The way in which the transformation of the individual labour into a fraction of social labour takes place will depend on the relations in which ₁the labour of each individual is apportioned to the social order itself. In a patriarchal peasant family, for example, which satisfies all its own needs by producing corn, animal products, yarn, linen, and clothing, the social relations of the members imply a social planning of production in accordance with the total needs of the family and its productive powers. The labour of every one is exercised only as 'an organ of the common labour power of the family.'[2] Similarly, Marx argues, in a typically over-simplified analogy, in an association of free men who communally own the means of production, each one would 'consciously expend his individual labour-power as a part of the labour-power of society'.[3]

There are, however, societies in which the identity of individual and social labour has to be specially achieved. The characteristics of capitalism are private property in means of production, individual enterprise, and private appropriation and exchange. How is social labour apportioned in such a society? The way in which it 'generalizes labour', is to make commodities into carriers, not only of use-value, but also of exchange-value. 'The form in which this proportional division of labour operates, in a society where the interconnection of social labour is manifested in the *private exchange* of the individual products of labour, is precisely the exchange-value of these products.'[4]

In capitalist production every commodity has a double character: use-value, because of its material qualities, and exchange-value, because a portion of social labour has been expended upon it. A commodity may have use-value without having any exchange-value at all, e.g. gifts of nature. But exchange-value presupposes use-value.

1 Marx, *Letters to Dr. Kugelmann* (no date), p. 73.
2 Marx, *Das Kapital*, vol. i, p. 45.
3 ibid.
4 Marx, *Letters to Dr. Kugelmann*, pp. 73–4.

The qualities which give a commodity use-value are, in the capitalist system, the 'material carriers of exchange-value'.[1] The exchange-value of a commodity is nothing but a fraction of 'abstract human labour'; its measure, 'the amount of value-forming substance, i.e. labour, which it contains'. That amount itself can be measured by the labour time spent on the production of the commodity. This labour time must not be regarded as the time spent by a particular labourer on that particular commodity: one must not think that 'the lazier or less skilled a man is', the more valuable will be his product. The measure of the exchange-value of a commodity is the 'socially necessary labour time' embodied in its production. 'Socially necessary labour time is the labour time necessary to produce any use-value with the given normal conditions of social production and the social average degree of skill and intensity of labour.'[2]

In capitalist production labour too has a double character. It is productive of both use-value and exchange-value. As the former, it is concrete, particular labour; as the latter, 'it is abstract, general, and equal labour'.[3] To the variety of use-values in society corresponds a variety of human labour. This can exist without private exchange. But in capitalism, in which there is private exchange of products, there appears also the phenomenon of exchange-value which ignores the individual material differences of commodities as use-values and creates a general equivalence of them. Similarly, labour in such a society, in so far as it results in exchange-value, is an abstraction from the different forms of useful labour: it is 'expenditure of human labour power'.[4] In relation to use-value, the labour embodied in a commodity has only a qualitative significance; in relation to exchange-value, only a quantitive one. The existence of different types of labour and different skills does not matter; each type of labour can be expressed in terms of the simplest, least-skilled form of human labour. In a given time the more complex, more highly skilled types of labour produce commodities with a higher exchange-value than the less-skilled ones. They can be reduced to multiples of the simplest form of labour. Such a reduction does in fact take place all the time: different types of labour are reduced in the economic process to a universal equivalent.

By formulating the labour theory of value in this way, Marx has

1 Marx, *Das Kapital*, vol. i, p. 2.
2 ibid., p. 5.
3 Marx, *Zur Kritik der politischen Ökonomie*, p. 13.
4 Marx, *Das Kapital*, vol. i, p. 10.

made one important departure from the classical economists: if the exchange-value of a commodity is nothing but the expression of the socially necessary labour time used in its production, labour itself can have no value. 'To speak of the value of labour, ... is equivalent to speaking of the value of value; or to wish to determine, not the weight of a body, but the weight of weight itself.'[1]

The twofold character of commodities and of the labour which produces them creates two difficulties. One, Marx called, in a celebrated phrase, 'commodity fetishism'. He argued that if we looked on a commodity merely as a use-value there was nothing mysterious about it. Nor was exchange-value, looked at by itself, difficult to understand. It is not difficult, he claimed, to think of social human labour in the abstract, as expenditure of brain, nerve, and muscle; nor to think of its quantity, as distinct from its quality. The trouble is the contradictory nature of the commodity: it is use-value and exchange-value at the same time. This shows itself in three ways: the equivalence of human labour leads to the equivalence of the exchange-values of the products of labour; the expenditure of human labour, in terms of time, appears in the form of the measure of the exchange-value of products; finally, the social relation of the producers takes the form of a social relationship of products.[2] The commodity reflects the social character of labour. The producers do not see their own social relationship: it seems to them as a social relation of their products. Exchange-value is nothing but a relation between persons; 'but it is a relation which is concealed behind things'.[3] The social relation of producers – which, as we have seen, Marx regards as the essence of the economic structure – appears as a relation of commodities.

The second difficulty inherent in the contradictory character of the commodity is this: a commodity must have use-value, but not for its owner; for if it had, it would cease to be a commodity. For him, it is only exchange-value: it is a means of exchange. To acquire use-value the commodity has to meet the specific want which it can satisfy. There has to take place a general process of exchange between all commodities before they can all become use-values. In this process each commodity leaves the possessor for whom it has no use-value and gets into the hands of one for whom it has. It does not alter its material

1 F. Engels, *Herrn Eugen Dühring's Umwälzung der Wissenschaft* (1928) p. 212.
2 Marx, *Das Kapital*, vol. i, p. 38.
3 Marx, *Zur Kritik der politischen Ökonomie*, p. 10.

qualities, but it alters its relation to man. 'In the hand of the baker, bread is only the carrier of an economic relation'[1] ... in that of the customer it becomes use-value, i.e. food.

In the process of exchange commodities also become exchange-values. Exchange-value is only a theoretical concept until the moment when the commodity changes hands. Marx concludes, therefore, that in the process of exchange commodities become use-values and exchange-values. This means that the relation between commodities which is established in exchange has to be a double one: a relation of exchange-values and of use-values. As exchange-values commodities are all of equal quality, they only differ in quantity; but as use-values they are all qualitatively different. One and the same exchange must therefore be an equivalence of things which are embodiments of the same quantities of labour time; it must also be a relation of specific use-values, designed for different wants. Exchange appears as an equivalence and a non-equivalence.

The difficulty is that 'in order to become exchange-value, ... a commodity has to be disposed of as use-value ... while its disposal as a use-value, presupposes its existence as exchange-value.'[2] The difficulty, Marx says, is solved by making one commodity into the universal equivalent. This commodity is given something in addition to the limited capacity of a specific use-value, namely, the ability to represent embodied social labour. By excluding one commodity from the rest and giving it that ability, it acquires, in addition to its own specific use-value, a new general one which is the same for everybody. It becomes the carrier of exchange-value. Once that is done, different commodities (which are only different amounts of socially necessary labour time) appear as different quantities of one and the same commodity. This universal equivalent is money. 'It is a crystallization of the exchange-value of commodities which they themselves produce in the process of exchange.'[3]

It is not money which makes commodities commensurable. 'On the contrary, because as exchange-values all commodities are embodied human labour and, therefore, inevitably commensurable, are they able to measure their value in the same specific commodity and to transform this into the common measure of value, money.'[4] In a system of

---

1 Marx, *Zur Kritik der politischen Ökonomie*, pp. 20–1.
2 ibid., p. 23.
3 ibid., p. 28.
4 Marx, *Das Kapital*, vol. i, p. 59.

commodity production, that is, in a system based on private property and exchange, 'money as a measure of exchange-value is the form in which the immanent measure of the value of commodities, labour time, of necessity appears.'[1]

So far what Marx has done is to develop a theory of production in certain specific social circumstances. Much space has been given to it, partly because it has been the most controversial part of Marx's 'pure' economic theory; and partly also because it represents the most persistent elaboration of the classical theories of Smith and Ricardo into something like a logical structure. That structure is not, of course, a theory of value in the modern sense. In spite of the elaborate pseudo-philosophical garb in which it appears, the theory says little more, and says it less well, than what Smith had said more than 150 years earlier. We shall see later that it has no use as a tool of economic analysis. To Marx, its real purpose was to serve as a basis for his theory of exploitation.

## Surplus value

Marx summarizes the possible objections to the labour theory of value under four heads.[2] In the first place it may be argued that labour itself is a commodity and has, therefore, exchange-value, a conclusion which Marx rejected. Secondly, 'if the exchange-value of a product equals the labour time contained in it', then the exchange-value of a given amount of labour time, say 'of one day's labour, must be equal to its product'. In other words, 'the wages of labour must equal the product of labour'.[3]

The question why the exchange-value of labour is less than that of its product is, therefore, another one which requires an answer. Thirdly, the market price of commodities is constantly fluctuating. How can this fact be reconciled with the labour theory? Finally, if labour creates, and labour time measures, exchange-value, how is it to be explained that there are commodities, i.e. things which possess exchange-value, on which no labour has been expended? In other words, how can one account for the exchange-value of the gifts of nature?

Marx claims to have provided the answer to these questions in the

1 Marx, *Zur Kritik der politischen Ökonomie.*
2 ibid., pp. 44–6.
3 ibid., p. 45.

remaining parts of his theory: questions one and two in his theory of wage-labour and capital, question three in the theory of competition, and question four in the theory of rent.

The first problem is how to explain wages on the basis of the labour theory of value. Coupled with it is the second problem, namely, the emergence of a surplus. Marx treats them together in his analysis of the wage-labour capital relationship, which leads to the concept of surplus value. The starting-point is the analysis of capital. We have already seen what happens to the commodity in the process of exchange and we have traced the emergence of money. The process of circulation of commodities in its simplest form is $C - M - C$: a commodity is sold for money and with that money another commodity is purchased. But there also develops a different form of circulation, $M - C - M$, in which there is the purchase of a commodity with money for the purpose of selling it again for money. In this form money first acquires the character of capital. The purpose of such a circulation is clearly that the second $M$ should be greater than the first. Thus the quality of the second form of circulation is essentially different from that of the first.

In the first form, the final result is the spending of money on a commodity which serves as use-value. In the second form money is only advanced; it has to return to its starting-point. In the first form, use-value is the aim; in the second, exchange-value. This is what differentiates the circulation of money as capital from its circulation as money. While the first process is based on a qualitative difference between two goods, the second process must be based, if it is to have any purpose at all, on a quantitative difference between two sums of money. There may be quantitative differences in the first form too, in the sense that one commodity is sold above, and another below, its exchange-value. But such a difference is only accidental. The circulation of money as capital, then, involves buying a commodity in order to sell it for a larger amount of money.

But does not the appearance of money as capital contradict the equivalence which, according to Marx, is established in the process of exchange? As far as use-values are concerned exchange does not rest on equivalence. On the contrary, it is just because the use-values of two commodities differ for the two parties that exchange can take place at all. But the original form of exchange must involve an equivalence of exchange-values. Therefore, exchange of commodities itself cannot be the source of the surplus. There is yet a further difficulty. Although a surplus cannot arise in exchange, it is impossible for it to arise any-where else. Exchange-value is not realized until exchange takes place.

The problem seems more difficult than ever, for we have concluded that the surplus, or 'surplus value', as Marx calls its, cannot have its origin in the process of circulation of commodities; and yet that it is only in that process that surplus value can appear. The problem is solved in this way. In the process $M - C - M'$ (where $M'$ is greater than $M$) the increase of the original amount of money cannot take place in the second half of the transaction: in it, 'the commodity in its natural form is only re-transformed into its monetary form'. The increase must therefore take place in the first half of the transaction, i.e. in the purchase of $C$ by $M$. But the increase cannot be due to the exchange-value of $C$; the increase must be due to the use-value of $C$. Now, if the owner of money (which he uses as capital) could find on the market some commodity 'whose use-value had the peculiar quality of being a source of exchange-value', the solution of our problem would be at hand. Such a commodity would, when consumed, create exchange-value. But that, according to Marx's theory of value, can only be a commodity whose consumption results in the embodiment of labour. Such a commodity does in fact exist: it is human labour power, which in capitalist conditions of production can be freely bought and sold in the market.[1]

Marx analyses how the exchange-value of labour power is deter-mined. Like that of every other commodity, it is formed and measured by the amount of socially necessary labour time which is required for its production: it is determined by the amount of socially necessary labour time embodied in the labourer's means of subsistence, i.e. in their exchange-value. These means of subsistence are historically determined, they will contain a traditional element. The means of subsistence will also have to be large enough to ensure the perpetu-ation of the labouring class by allowing the labourer to raise a family.

By consuming the commodity which he has bought, the buyer appropriates its use-value. The capitalist who has bought labour power consumes it in the process of production. The capitalist sets the worker to work. He makes him embody his labour in commodities whose exchange-value is then determined by the amount of socially necessary labour time which they contain. The product belongs to the

---

1 Marx, *Das Kapital*, vol. i, pp. 129–30. See also vol. ii, part i, p. 119 in which Marx explains this doctrine in relation to Ricardo's difficulty over the same problem.

capitalist who has employed the producer and who has made him expend his labour on materials and means of production which contain embodied labour. The exchange-values of these materials, etc., form part of the exchange-value of the finished product. To this must be added the labour time spent on its production measured as the necessary social average. This is the use-value which the capitalist has bought in buying the commodity labour power. But what he has paid for it is its exchange-value, determined by the socially necessary labour time embodied in the labourer's means of subsistence. Human labour power can be expended in a longer time than that which is required to produce it. It is on this ability that surplus value depends. If, for example, the time necessary to produce the labourer's means of subsistence for a whole day were four hours, that would measure the exchange-value of one day's labour power. But the capitalist who buys it obtains its use-value, which may be any portion of that day, for example, eight hours. It is out of this difference that surplus value arises.

The capital which the capitalist employs can be divided into constant capital, which includes raw materials and machinery, etc. and variable capital, which is the part spent on the purchase of labour-power. The former is called constant because it does not alter its value in the process of production: it only adds it to the commodity that is being produced. The latter, however, alters its value: it produces its own equivalent and the surplus value which is itself a variable magnitude. The distinction is, as we shall see, in the Marxian system, of vital importance.

Marx now distinguishes a further concept: the 'rate of surplus value'. This is the proportion of the increment of capital which appears at the end of the process of production (surplus value), to the variable capital. If $C$ is the total capital, $c$ and $v$ its two component parts, and $s$ the surplus value, the whole process will be one in which $c + v$ result in $c + v + s$. The rate of surplus value will be $\frac{s}{v}$. This rate expresses, according to Marx, the 'degree of exploitation' of labour by capital. The part of the product which represents surplus value is the surplus product – the physiocratic *produit net*, but in a different guise. Just as surplus value is expressed in terms of variable capital only, the surplus product is also measured in relation, not to the total product, but to that part of it which represents the socially necessary labour time for creating the labour power used. Marx also distinguishes between the simple rate of surplus value $\frac{s}{v}$ (the, as it were, ratio between 'paid' and 'unpaid' labour) and the annual rate of surplus value $\frac{sn}{v}$ where $n$ is the number of turnovers of the variable capital in a year. It is this which is relevant for the relation between surplus value and rate of profit.

Marx proceeds to examine the different factors which determine the rate of surplus value and the relative size of the surplus product. These chapters, particularly the sections on the struggles over the length of the working day, are, like all the historical chapters in *Capital*, much more interesting and readable than most of the rest of *Capital*. From a theoretical point of view they produce one or two new concepts. Rate of surplus value is distinguished from the total mass of surplus value. The latter depends on the former and on the amount to variable capital used. It can vary with both; and it follows that if one determinant declines, the other will have to increase more than in proportion if the mass of surplus value is to increase. It follows also that although the total capital used by different capitalists will be divided in different proportions into constant and variable capital, the amount of surplus value produced by different amounts of capital must, other things being equal, be in direct proportion to the amount of variable capital they contain. This last consequence is important because it seems to contradict the common experience of every capitalist, who knows that he does not obtain a smaller profit if he uses a relatively small amount of variable capital.

Marx's attempted solution of this contradiction is bound up with the problem caused by the divergence of market prices from value and is dealt with later. Marx points out, however, that if we look at the total capital of society that is being used in production, the total mass of surplus value which it will obtain will depend upon the average length of the working day and the number of the labouring population. The total surplus value created in capitalist society thus conforms to the rules he has set out, even though when it is divided out among individual capitalists the rules do not seem to be observed.[1]

Marx also draws a distinction between absolute and relative surplus value. There are, according to his theory, two possible ways of increasing the surplus value produced for the capitalist by an individual labourer. One way of increasing it is to lengthen the working day. The surplus value which depends upon this factor Marx calls 'absolute surplus value'. The other way is to reduce that part of the working day which represents the labour time required for the worker's subsistence

---

1 Marx, *Das Kapital*, vol. i, pp. 270–1.

and to lengthen that which is embodied in the surplus product. The surplus value which depends on such an alteration of the proportions in which the working day is divided, Marx calls 'relative surplus value'.

An increase of relative surplus value depends on an increase in the productivity of labour. In particular, in order to reduce the exchange-value of labour power it is necessary to reduce the socially necessary labour time embodied in means of subsistence. The productivity of labour must increase in those branches of production which turn out 'wage goods'. But any increase of productivity will raise surplus value for the individual capitalist who applies this increase, for he will produce more units of a commodity with the same amount of labour power. The exchange-value of the unit product declines; but if the labour time embodied in the particular commodity by other producers does not diminish, the socially necessary average will fall less than the labour embodied in the product of the first capitalist. He will, there-fore, obtain an increased surplus value. This increase can also be regarded as an increase of relative surplus value, for the increase in productivity (even though it did not necessarily apply to the means of subsistence) has altered the proportions of the constituents of the working day.

Because relative surplus value is directly proportionate to the pro-ductivity of labour it provides a powerful stimulus to the individual capitalist to improve his technique. Competition, however, forces his rivals also to adopt the new methods of production; thus individual excesses tend to disappear. This means a continual stimulus to each capitalist to increase productivity and thus to reduce the exchange-value of products (including that of labour power), because in the process he increases his relative surplus value. The aim, according to Marx, is all the time to reduce the part which the worker works for himself in order to increase that part which he works for the capitalist. At this point, this therorem becomes involved, in Marx's general theory of economic development.

Once capitalist production is established, the difference between absolute and relative surplus value explains the means for increasing the rate of exploitation which are adopted in different conditions.[1] In one sense surplus value has a natural basis. It appears as soon as a worker is able to work more than is necessary to support himself, and can therefore be made to support others. But the crucial point for

1 Marx, *Das Kapital*, vol. i, pp. 482–93.

Marx is the fact of exploitation by which 'the surplus labour of one man becomes the condition of existence of others'.[1]

In the last sections of his discussion of the capital/labour relationship, Marx deals in greater detail with the problem of wages. It is necessary to mention here only one of his points. The main emphasis is on the fact that wages represent the value of labour power. Marx maintains that the wage-contract helps to hide the real nature of the exchange between the capitalist and the worker, because wages appear to represent the value of labour, and not that of labour power; and he develops this in relation to different methods of wage payment.

## The Theory of Capitalist Competition

The preceding analysis shows Marx's answer to the first two problems which the labour theory of value has raised: the value of 'labour' and the origin of surplus value. The next question concerns the fact that in reality the prices of commodities do not vary according to any changes in the socially necessary labour time embodied in them. We may couple with this problem another one which has arisen: what is the relation of the profit which each individual capitalist makes to the surplus value appropriated by the total capital of society? Marx's answers to both these questions are best summarized in conjunction.

His first step is to draw a distinction between the rate of surplus value and the rate of profit. We have already seen Marx's analysis of the origin of the former. But what interests the individual capitalist is not which particular portion of his total capital is responsible for his increment. He is bound to employ constant as well as variable capital; and both parts of his capital appear to him indispensable for the creation of surplus value. So what concerns him is the rate of his increment to this total capital, that is, not $\frac{s}{v}$ but $\frac{s}{c+v}$. This rate is the *rate of profit*. The distinction can be illustrated by an example. There are two capitalist factories A and B. A has a constant capital of £250,000 and a variable capital of £50,000. Let the proportions in B's case be £150,000 and £50,000. Let the surplus value be £50,000 in both. Then the rate of surplus value is 100 per cent in either case; but the rate of profit is 16.6 per cent for A and 25 per cent for B. The rate of profit is thus shown to vary with the proportion in which the two

1 Marx, *Das Kapital*, vol. i, p. 476.

kinds of capital are united. The ratio of $c$ and $v$ is called by Marx the 'organic composition of capital', the higher it is, the lower the rate of profit.

The distinction can be made clear in this way. When the individual capitalist sells a commodity, he wants to get back what it has cost him to produce, that is, its share of the constant and variable capital which he employs (this Marx calls the 'cost price'), plus an increment which is its share of the surplus value. This he calls 'profit'. Profit is thus nothing but surplus value, but 'in a mystified form'; it appears as 'the offspring of the total capital advanced'.[1] The rate of profit is then the form in which the capitalist becomes aware of the rate of surplus value. But the rate of profit is, as we have seen, not the same as the rate of surplus value; though there is a relation between them. This can be expressed by the formula

$$p' = s' \frac{v}{c + v}$$

where $p'$ is the rate of profit and $s'$ the rate of surplus value. The rate of profit is thus directly proportional to the 'rate of exploitation'; but inversely proportional to the organic composition of capital. We shall see presently what use Marx makes of this conclusion.

One consequence of the preceding analysis is that the rate of profit will differ in different enterprises according to the organic composition of their capitals. But such difference cannot persist because of competition. This will produce a tendency for every capital, regardless of its organic composition, to earn the average rate of profit. Competition, in other words, tends to make each capitalist receive only a proportion of the total volume of surplus value (or volume of profit) which is equal to the proportion of his capital to the total capital. But this tendency involves something else. It means that every capitalist must sell his product at the same price as every other capitalist in the same industry. Because capitalists produce with different organic compositions of capital, their products cannot all have the same exchange-value. The averaging of the rate of profit, and, therefore, the reduction of the price charged by every capitalist to the same level, involves a discrepancy between normal price, which Marx calls the 'price of production', and value. The former is cost price plus average rate of profit. The latter is the socially necessary labour time embodied in a commodity.

We can summarize Marx's doctrines on value and price at this stage

1 Marx, *Das Kapital*, vol. iii, part i, p. 11.

as follows. Three concepts must be distinguished:

1 Value, which is measured by the amount of socially necessary labour time embodied in the commodity. It can be represented as $c + v + s$ (where $c$ is the commodity's share of the constant capital, $v$ the 'paid' amount of labour, or variable capital, and $s$ the 'unpaid' amount, or surplus value).

2 Price of production which can be expressed as $c + v + p$ (where $p$ is the average rate of profit). This may be greater or smaller than $c + v + s$, depending on differences in the organic composition of capital.

3 Finally there is the market price, which represents short-period fluctuations round price of production caused by the working of supply and demand within a given branch of production.

Marx distinguished two types of competition,[1] one with a particular branch of production, the other between all branches of production. The former tends to equalize market price with price of production. The latter, through the averaging of the rate of profit, reduces values to prices of production. There may be temporary excesses, therefore, both of the rate of profit of an individual firm in an industry over the average rate of profit in the industry, as well as of the average rate of profit in a whole industry over the general average rate. These excesses give rise to two kinds of 'surplus profit'. The normal tendency of competition is continually to eliminate these surpluses. If either kind of competition is impeded, as it is in the case of agricultural production, surplus profits may continue to exist. We shall shortly see the application of this line of reasoning to the problem of rent.

Meanwhile it may be noted that one of the most vigorous controversies round the Marxian doctrine has centred on the relation between the labour theory of value, as expounded in volume i of *Capital* and the prices of production theory of volume iii, published posthumously by Engels. Marx has been charged with logical inconsistency and with a last-minute attempt to rescue the labour theory of value from collapse. Thus formulated, these charges are not wholly justified: there are many indications of the prices-of-production theory in Marx's early work; and within his own analytical system, at any rate, a link can be shown to exist between the two theories. This, of course, is quite separate from one's view of the usefulness of the whole doctrine as an analytical tool – of which more later.[2]

1 Marx, *Theorien über den Mehrwert*, vol. ii, part i, p. 14.
2 On the particular point under discussion see L. von Bortkiewicz: 'Wertrechung und

Another difficulty is that of explaining the behaviour of the individual capitalist in relation to the whole process in which surplus value is created. It can be argued that if variable capital alone produces surplus value, it would be in the interests of each capitalist, once he has recognized how surplus value is created, to keep the organic composition of capital as low as possible. This clearly conflicts with observed behaviour. The organic composition of the capital of individual capitalists, and of all capitalists together, is continually rising. And every capitalist knows that such a rise is not accompanied by a decline in his profit. The explanation of this fact can be found in the desire of each individual capitalist to increase his share of surplus-value. Under the stimulus of competition, every capitalist tries to be the first in the field with an improvement in the productivity of labour, because so long as that improvement has not become general, his individual relative surplus value will increase. Now, improvements in the productivity of labour generally involve an increased use of constant capital. They also lower the exchange-value of the product below the social average and thus increase the individual capitalist's profit.

An example given by Marx himself will illustrate this.[1] There are four enterprises with different organic compositions of capital, but with the same rate of surplus value. The following table shows their capitals, the values of their products, and their individual rates of profits. For the sake of simplicity we assume that the whole of the constant capital enters into the value of the product at once.

|  |  |  |  |  |  | *Value of the product* | *Rate of profit per cent* | *Rate of Surplus Value per cent* |
|---|---|---|---|---|---|---|---|---|
| 1 | C80 | + | V20 | + | S10 | = 110 | 10 | 50 |
| 2 | C50 | + | V50 | + | S25 | = 125 | 25 | 50 |
| 3 | C70 | + | V30 | + | S15 | = 115 | 15 | 50 |
| 4 | C90 | + | V10 | + | S5 | = 105 | 5 | 50 |

Capital 400        Profit = 55

Competition will tend to establish a uniform average rate of profit which will be $13\frac{3}{4}$ per cent. The effect of this will be that the total

---

Preisrechnung im Marx' schen System' in *Archiv für Sozialwissenschaft* (vols. xxiii and xxv), which completely disposes of the theory.
1 Karl Marx and Friedrich Engels, *Correspondence, 1846–1895*, p. 130.

surplus value will be shared out among the four capitalists in proportion to their share of the total capital. But in order to achieve this each capitalist will have to sell his product, not at its value but at its price of production, which is $113\frac{3}{4}$. Capitalists 1 and 4 will sell their products above value; while capitalists 2 and 3 will sell theirs below value.

It is, therefore, clearly to the advantage of the individual capitalist to increase the organic composition of capital before any other capitalists have done so. But since every one does so, the result is a general urge for improving the productivity of labour and cheapening the products; and thus to a general increase in the organic composition of capital. We shall have to discuss the further consequences of this tendency in the dynamics of the Marxian system.

Only one important point remains in this section. Marx's final problem in the labour theory of value concerned the origin of the exchange-value of gifts of nature. Marx discusses this in relation to rent. He points out[1] that there are four possible theories of the rent of land. The first he calls a monopoly theory; it is one which is implied in the views of many socialist writers, such as Proudhon and Sismondi. According to this theory rent arises from the monopoly price of agricultural products; and that monopoly price from the existence of landed property. It means that the law of value does not operate in the case of agricultural products. Their price is always higher than their value, because their supply is always lower than the demand for them. The only possible explanation of this constant deficiency of supply is the theory that agricultural land is continually becoming less fertile, i.e. it involves the law of diminishing returns in the form in which it appears in the Ricardian theory of rent.

Ultimately, therefore, the first theory coincides with the second one, that of differential rent. We have already seen that this theory involves an identification of price of production and exchange-value on the marginal land, which Marx rejects. He also rejects the third theory, which regards rent as identical with the interest on the capital invested for the improvement of the land. This theory admits differential elements, but like the Ricardian one it denies the existence of absolute rent. But it is incapable of explaining the rent of land in which no capital has been invested. Marx characterizes it as an attempt to save rent from the attack of the Ricardian analysis by making it identical with a 'legitimate' capitalist revenue.

---

1 Marx, *Theorien über den Mehrwert*, vol. ii, part ii pp. 2–4.

There remains then his own theory, which, Marx claims, joins with the first theory in saying that private property in land has something to do with rent; and it allows also for the existence of differential rent. Its distinguishing features, however, are that it does not base differential rent on declining fertility and that it allows for absolute rent. This is made possible if the identity of price of production and exchange-value is abandoned. In the Marxian system products sell above or below their value because competition, given different organic compositions of capital, makes them sell at a uniform price of production. The existence of rent need not, Marx claims, invalidate the labour theory of value. It becomes only an example of what he called 'surplus-profit', i.e. a surplus above the average rate of profit, which can arise in two ways.

Owing to competition the same price will be paid for the same product, whatever the conditions in which it was produced. If the price of production of an individual capitalist is lower than the average price of production of the product, then (since it is assumed that demand is high enough to allow him to participate in the market) he will obtain a surplus over and above the average rate of profit. The difference depends on the individual cost price, the average cost price, and the average rate of profit. Given the average rate of profit, it is therefore determined by the difference between the productivity of labour in the individual enterprise and the average productivity of labour in the whole branch of production. The higher the individual productivity of labour compared with the average, the lower is the individual exchange-value; the lower the individual cost price, the greater, therefore, the individual rate of profit compared with the average rate. (It will be seen, incidentally, how far in this explanation Marx is forced to go towards a 'supply and demand' theory, and what little relevance is left to the labour theory of value.)

Differential rent is a form of this kind of surplus profit. But there is an important difference from other forms. The increased productivity which is the cause of surplus profit tends, normally, to become general. Provided that the source of the increased productivity is freely available, the competition of capitalists will tend to cause that source to be generally adopted. It will continually tend to remove surplus profits by equalizing market price and price of production. But in the case of certain gifts of nature, a waterfall or particularly fertile land, for example, the condition of increased productivity is not available to all individual entrepreneurs in that branch of production. It is monopolized; and the surplus profit can be appropriated by the owner of that monopolized piece of nature in the form of rent.[1]

The same line of argument is used to explain absolute rent. Here, however, Marx considers not an individual enterprise but a whole branch of production. Competition will tend to average the rate of profit not only in all enterprises of a given sphere of production, but also in all spheres of production. It does this by transforming the exchange-values of commodities into prices of production. Suppose we have two spheres of production, industry and agriculture, of which the average organic composition is respectively $80c + 20v$ and $60c + 40v$. We assume that the rate of surplus value is the same, i.e. 50 per cent, so that the value of industrial products will be 110 and the rate of profit 10 per cent; while the value in agricultural products will be 120 and the rate of profit 20 per cent. We know that competition would normally tend to even out the difference between the two rates of profit, and to force all commodities to sell at the price of production. This would involve forcing agricultural produce to be sold below its value.

But in the case postulated, this tendency comes up against a barrier. The existence of landed property is an obstacle to competition, because it restricts the free employment of capital in all branches of production. It prevents the smoothing out of surplus value to an average rate of profit and appropriates a part or all of the excess, according to supply and demand as well as to the historical and legal relations between landowner and capitalist.[2] 'The landowner intervenes and extracts the difference.'[3] Absolute rent disappears only when the organic composition of capital in agriculture is the same as that in history. When that occurs, the landowner, though legally able to do so, is economically unable to extract absolute rent.

Marx, thus, allows for only two basic revenues in capitalist society, wages and surplus-value. Rent is only a part of surplus value. He also eliminates interest as an independent revenue and shows it also to be a part only of surplus value. He argues that money is lent as capital in a double sense. The lender expects it to come back to him with an increment; and the borrower takes it as a commodity whose use-value consists in its ability to procure surplus value.[4] Money which is lent as

1 Marx, *Das Kapital*, vol. iii, part ii, pp. 184–6.
2 ibid., pp. 292–5.
3 Karl Marx and Friedrich Engels, *Correspondence*, p. 132.
4 Mark, *Das Kapital*, vol. iii, part i, p. 328.

capital has some analogy to the commodity labour power, as far as the industrial capitalist is concerned, because it is a use-value which embodies itself in an increased exchange-value.[1]

Lender and borrower regard the same sum of money as capital; but only the borrower – the industrial capitalist – makes it function as such. That capital cannot bring in double profit. Profit is only made once, that is, where the capital is in fact used as capital. The sum of money can appear as capital to both parties only if the profit which it makes is shared between them. The share which the money capitalist gets is interest. It is expressed as the price of the commodity, money capital; but since, according to Marx, interest is only a part of profit, its upper limit is the amount of profit itself. There is no definite lower limit.

The proportions in which surplus value is divided will vary with a number of circumstances, in particular with the size of the rentier class (which increases with the progress of the community) and with the development of different financial forms of enterprise and of banking and credit.

## The Theory of Economic Development

The final part of the Marxian analysis is that which refers to economic development. It is not added to the main body of theory, but is claimed to be an integral part of it. It is impossible to distinguish static and dynamic Marxian theory because even the concepts of what might appear as static analysis are conditioned by the dynamic purpose of the whole theory, in particular that which is implied in the sociological framework in which the economic analysis is placed. The prognosis of the development of capitalism which arises from his analytical concepts is the most spectacular part of Marx's work and the one which has had a far more dramatic appeal than the laboured analysis of the theory of value. Yet it is not presented in a self-contained section of his writings. The main parts, contained in *Capital*, are the discussion of accumulation, in volume i, and the theories of the falling tendency of the rate of profit, and of crises, in volume iii. These must be supplemented by the analysis of crises in volume ii of the *Theorien über den*

1 Marx, *Das Kapital*, vol. iii, part i, p. 336.

*Mehrwert* and of the problem of reproduction in volume iii of *Capital*. The following is a brief summary.

The first condition of movement is reproduction. This condition operates in all forms of society. Social production must include reproduction; and the particular conditions which determine the one also determine the other. Capitalist production involves, therefore, capitalist reproduction. This means that the capital which is employed for the purpose of obtaining surplus value must be re-employed in the same way. The surplus value increment must appear periodically; if it is entirely consumed by the capitalist there will be simple reproduction.

Accumulation then is transformation of surplus value into capital. Surplus value exists, in the first place, as a part of the value of the product. Once the product is sold and its value realized, surplus value appears as a sum of money, capable of being used as capital, together with the original sum which was so used. But to be used in this way (rather than to be entirely consumed by the capitalist) there have to be available additional material means of production and additional labour-power. Both these are produced in the previous process of production. A part of the surplus value which the capitalist commands has been employed in producing additional means of production and means of subsistence, i.e. machinery and wage-goods, and following the Ricardian theory, it is assumed wages have to be high enough to enable the labouring class to multiply. Thus, there is a 'spiral' of increasing reproduction. The degree of accumulation will depend on a number of factors, the first of which is the proportions in which surplus value is consumed and transformed into capital. The former Marx calls revenue (he uses the word in two senses: to denote the periodic appearance of surplus value; and also that part of surplus value which is consumed by the capitalist). Given the total amount of surplus value, and other things being equal, accumulation will be inversely proportioned to revenue. Marx rejected the different variants of the 'abstinence' theories of capital based upon 'saving' by the capitalist, since he regarded them as inimical to his own exploitation theory according to which the capitalist merely had to decide how much of the surplus-value he had gained he was to employ for fresh gain. The capitalist's decision about these proportions does not remain, he thought, the same at different stages of capitalist development. In the early stages restriction of consumption is the rule; in the later, the tendency is to enjoy more revenue. In any case, there is always a conflict in the capitalist's mind between the desire for accumulation and that for increased consumption.[1]

Other factors which determine the degree of accumulation are the rate of surplus-value and the productivity of labour. The former is the chief determinant of the total mass of surplus value. And longer hours, more intensive use of labour power, and reduction of wages are all means by which the possibilities of exploitation may be increased. These possibilities grow also with increases in the productivity of labour. Improvements in the productivity of labour increase the mass of products in which a given amount of value (and surplus value) is embodied. The surplus product increases; the capitalist's consumption can grow without impinging on accumulation. Labour power also becomes cheaper, and the same amount of variable capital can set more labour power in motion. Means of production have also increased; and accumulation can proceed faster than before.[2]

What are the results of accumulation? Marx described them in his celebrated general law of capitalist accumulation. The most important factor in progressive accumulation is the organic composition of capital. Accumulation must involve an absolute increase in variable capital. If we assumed that the organic composition of capital remains unchanged, accumulation will involve an increased demand for labour power. The increase in demand may at times surpass the increase of supply and raise wages. But the important thing is that enlarged reproduction, i.e. accumulation, involves an increase of labourers, and an increase in the number or 'size' of capitalists. In the condition assumed (unchanged organic composition of capital), Marx was forced to admit that accumulation brought some advantages to the working class.

But the condition, Marx claimed, cannot continue to exist. An increase in the productivity of labour is one of the most powerful means of accumulation. An increase in productivity is an increase in the material means of production on which a given amount of human labour-power can be employed. One part of the increase in the means of production is a cause, the other a consequence, of increased productivity. Increased productivity involves a change in the technical composition of capital; and this is accompanied by a change in its organic composition. Variable capital declines relatively as accumulation progresses. Another consequence of accumulation which follows

1 Marx, *Das Kapital*, vol. iii, part i, pp. 542–62.
2 ibid., pp. 562–73.

from the above is the concentration of capital. Competition forces capitalists to cheapen their products. This involves greater productivity and larger capital. Accumulation goes hand in hand with the squeezing out of small capitalists. More and more branches of production are run by large capital. The development of joint-stock companies and of banking and credit facilities fosters concentration and enables it to go on much faster than it otherwise would.

The relative decline in variable capital results in the creation of what Marx termed the 'industrial reserve army'. Accumulation and concentration involve both absolute increase and relative decline in variable capital. This requires a certain elasticity in the size of the labouring population. Population has to grow to keep pace with accumulation; but as different branches of production adopt improved methods and so reduce relatively their variable capital, their demand for labour power will suffer a relative decline. There is relative over-population. These continual fluctuations in the demand for labour power result in the creation of a reservoir from which labour power can be drawn when needed. The relative size of this reserve army increases as capitalism develops. It is available when necessary. It exercises a pressure on wages in times when less labour power is demanded. It prevents wages from rising unduly when the demand for labour power goes up. This function is particularly important in the ups and downs of capitalist activity which constitute crises.

This relative over-population shows itself, according to Marx, in the fluctuating employment of industry, in the relation between industry and agriculture, in the existence of a large mass of casual labourers, and in the 'submerged' class of paupers. The higher the degree of capitalist development, the greater the wealth of society, the greater is the industrial reserve army in all its branches in relation to the total labouring population. This is 'the general law of capitalist accumulation'. It means that the greater the volume of means of production which society possesses and the greater its productive power, the more precarious are the conditions of existence of the working class. To Marx, it reveals the fundamental antagonism inherent in capitalist production. Capital accumulates, wealth increases, and is concentrated in fewer hands, but over the whole field of capitalism there is also an accumulation of misery.[1] This is the celebrated law of the 'increasing misery' of the working-class under capitalism.

1 Marx, *Das Kapital*, vol. iii, part i, pp. 576–613.

One consequence of accumulation, the increasing organic composition of capital, will through the force of competition gradually appear in all branches of production. But since the rate of profit is inversely related to the organic composition of capital, accumulation produces an inevitable tendency for the average rate of profit to decline. Marx comes thus to a conclusion which appears similar to that of Ricardo. But whereas Ricardo's explanation of the falling tendency of the rate of profit rested ultimately on his belief in the declining fertility of the soil (that is, in a natural factor), Marx claims to develop his theory from conditions inherent in capitalism.[1]

The falling tendency of the rate of profit can be counteracted and delayed by a number of factors, such as increased degree of exploitation, reduction of wages below the value of labour power, cheapening of the materials which constitute constant capital, increase in the industrial reserve army, foreign trade and more complex financial organization of capitalist enterprise. Marx discusses these points very summarily,[2] and some indications are also to be found in a fragment of Engels which he was writing at the time of his death.[3] But it was left to some of their followers to make an attempt at reconciling the basic theory of accumulation with the observed facts of historical development which were in violent contrast to the tendencies postulated in that theory. We shall revert to this presently. In Marx's own work, the theory leads on to a theory of crises.

Marx discusses the ways in which these contradictions unfold themselves. The purpose of capitalist production is the creation of surplus value and the transformation of a part of it into new capital. This process depends only on the size of the working population and on the rate of exploitation. But the creation of surplus value has to be completed by a process in which surplus value is realized. The product which contains surplus value has to be sold. And if it cannot all be sold or if it can only be sold at prices which are below the prices of production, the process of exploitation will be left uncompleted. The capitalist will not realize his surplus value; he may even lose a part of his capital. The conditions for realizing surplus value are not the same as those for creating it. The former depends only on the productive power of society; the latter on the consuming power of society and on

---

1 Marx, *Das Kapital*, vol. iii, part i, pp. 191–212.
2 ibid., pp. 212–22.
3 F. Engels, 'Supplement to Volume III of *Capital*', *Engels on Capital* (1938), pp. 94–9.

the proportion between the different spheres of production. The consuming power of society however, is limited by the urge for accumulation which is inevitable because of the continual changes in productivity and the competitive struggle which forces every capitalist to try to keep pace for fear of being eliminated from the race. The result is a continual increase in social productive powers which involves a progressive intensification of the conflict between production and consumption, between the creation of surplus value and its realization.[1]

Marx, thus, did not ignore the underconsumption aspect of crises. On the other hand, he strenuously opposed the idea that the essence of capitalism could be explained in terms of a simple conflict between consumption and production. He regarded such a conflict as one aspect of crises only and, like other aspects, as a part of the contradictory nature of the whole capitalist system of production. These other aspects were the disproportion between different branches of capitalist production which are revealed in crises and the falling rate of profit and the tendencies counteracting it.[2]

Crises were to Marx violent solutions of a whole series of conflicts in the capitalist economy. They re-established equilibrium; but they were only temporarily effective. They were violent means for establishing a precarious harmony of production. The ordinary processes of competition try to establish a balance between consumption and production in individual spheres of production, and between the different spheres of production. They aim at establishing what Marx calls in one place a 'capitalist communism'.[3] But since these processes include accumulation, rising organic composition of capital, falling rate of profit, and all their mutually conflicting results, the establishment of balance creates the conditions for increasing the disturbance of the balance.

Crises are regarded by Marx as more drastic means for re-establishing harmony. They annihilate the value of part of existing capital in an effort to arrest the fall of the rate of profit and to encourage fresh accumulation. But they cannot overcome the barriers

1 For a schematic representation of the process of reproduction and accumulation, cf. in particular Marx, *Das Kapital*, vol. ii, pp. 483 *sqq*. For an attempt to weave together all the elements to be found in Marx's various dicta on crises into something like a consistent theory, cf. M. Dobb, *Political Economy and Capitalism* (1937), ch. iv.

2 Marx, *Das Kapital*, vol. iii, part i, pp. 225–6.

3 Karl Marx and Friedrich Engels, *Correspondence*, p. 243.

which capitalism imposes. In crises the conflict between productive power and the productive relations which constitute capitalism is most striking. 'The contradiction, in general terms, is this: capitalist production contains, on the one hand, a tendency to develop absolutely the productive powers regardless of value and the surplus value it contains, regardless also of the social relationship in which capitalist production takes place. On the other hand, capitalist production aims at maintaining existing capital values and increasing them at a continually growing pace.'[1] The end of capitalist production is creation and accumulation of surplus value; the means, continual expansion of the productive powers of society. The means, according to Marx, are bigger than the end: capitalism is involved in an insoluble contradiction.

What then did Marx regard as the future of this system? The more capitalism fulfils its historic task of developing man's mastery over nature, the less is its social basis capable of carrying its productive apparatus. The concentration of capital and the increasing social character of labour become incompatible with the continuance of individual appropriation of surplus value which arises from private property in the means of production. Capitalist production brings about the expropriation of individual producers whose private property was based on their own labour. But if the productive powers of society are to go on developing, capitalism in its turn disappears. Capitalist private property is expropriated, and a system of production is established which is based on the common ownership of the means of production.[2] Thus, at the end of his economic analysis, Marx returns to his sociological theory, his view of social change.

## An Appraisal

It is not easy to appraise briefly the work of which a summary has been given in the preceding pages. The scope of that work, which goes far beyond economics proper, the vast interpretative literature to which it has given rise, the militancy with which its message has been propagated, and the vehemence with which it has been criticized, all combine to make the task difficult and hazardous. What has always made

1 Marx, *Das Kapital*, vol. iii, part i, p. 231.
2 ibid., vol. i, pp. 726–9.

an objective assessment of Marx's work difficult has been the almost inseparable interrelation between an attempt at scholarship and irrepressible politics in his own work, and the wholly political uses to which that work has, in the event, been put.[1]

Marx himself would have brushed aside the accusation that in using scientific inquiry for political ends he was infringing the injunction that scholarship should be impartial, that knowledge should be sought for its own sake. His philosophy made him impatient of the assertion that science could be ultimately pure, not only in the sense of being divorced from practical use but also free from political implication. His theory was that social science had to become as exact and as penetrating a study of society as the natural sciences were of natural conditions. The latter, by making man aware of the laws which underlie natural phenomena, enabled him the better to master them. The former by uncovering the laws of society made man able to master the problem of social relationship.

Insistence on a practical aim would, by itself, hardly lead to objections. Even when they have been loudest in proclaiming the 'purity' of their science, economists have never denied that in the last resort it had a practical significance and therefore, potentially political application. Nor could Marx's economic theory by itself explain the hostility which it has called forth. If one takes individual elements of the Marxian system, one might say that there are comparatively few that cannot be found in classical doctrine. Nor can Marx be blamed for wanting to erect a system in which economic analysis, political philosophy, and policy are integrated. As we have seen, it was precisely this integration which was the distinguishing feature of the classical school. Nor is this aim in itself contrary to canons of scholarship.

Yet there is no doubt that in scholarly circles the reaction to Marx has been generally wholly negative. How is this to be explained? The reason must be found not in the details of Marx's economic ideas, nor in those of his sociology, but in the particular quality of the connection which he tried to establish between them. The economists should, perhaps, have been best able to judge with cold objectivity. But the Marxian interpretation of classical theory (derived from his pseudo-sociology rather than from that theory itself) clashed so violently with the prevailing ones (based on quite different premises) that

---

[1] For an interesting and wide-ranging study, see Leszek Kowalkowski's *Main Currents of Marxism*, 3 vols., 1978.

unprejudiced consideration was for a long time impossible. As has been well said, Marx laid bare a certain conflict in economic classicism.

The existence of this conflict between the conservative and the radical interpretation of classical doctrine was well calculated to make economists uncomfortable. Marx increased the discomfort by carrying classical doctrine to one extreme though distorted conclusion. To make economists face up to these classical contradictions resulted in irritating them.[1] The outcome of this irritation was often to abandon objective judgment.

The possibilities of serious and balanced assessment of Marx's place in social science have varied with the interplay between the progress of the science itself and the surrounding social situation. The development of new analytical tools in economics proper has thrown new light on Marx's concepts and enabled one to judge the extent to which they might have analytical value, and the flux of broad social and political movements has influenced the economist's interest in the sister sciences with whom Marx's economics are intermingled.

Today the chance of an objective summing-up seems greater than it has been for a long time, not because new material on Marx himself has become available, but because developments of recent years, both theoretical and political, provide a better and more complete frame of reference for the serious student. As far as the economic elements in Marx are concerned, the developments of the last thirty years enable one to see in broader perspective the relations between classicism, marginalism and the present body of general economic theory; and, therefore, to evaluate Marx's own position which is aside from, though connected with, the main stream of thought. The other elements, as before, are more troublesome. Here, too, however, a clearer view is now possible. The ultimate consequence to which the militant political faith (which is the most active ingredient of Marxism) must lead are now clear beyond any shadow of doubt; and a sharper separation of what is akin to real contributions to the body of scholarship about society and what must remain in the underworld of irrationalism (no less powerful, if menacing, an element) is possible.

First, then, let us take the sociological framework which Marx built for himself before, and independently of, any economic study. The two main parts are his interpretation of history and, closely allied with it,

1 G. Myrdal, *Das politische Element in der Nationalökonomischen Doktrinbildung*, pp. 123–4.

his theory of classes and the class struggle. The former, at least in its more supple forms (which Engels, at any rate, was increasingly obliged to give it) is, explicitly or implicitly, one of the most widely accepted working hypotheses in historical research. It is, of course, far from being Marx's exclusive creation; nor has it anything in common with the long-exploded view that the fiction of the 'economic man' is a valid representation of the springs of human action (Though, in Marx's theory of classes the 'economic interest' fallacy reappears.) But the propositions (a) that the conditions in which men produce their livelihood are extremely powerful, and, in the ultimate, possibly the most powerful single (though by no means the exclusive) determinants of the development of social organization; and (b) that these conditions of production are themselves subject to certain laws of development, have time and again been proved to be valuable tools of historical research.[1] Nor is it difficult to find many scholars who would accept as an extremely useful working hypothesis the related propositions that these conditions of production are also very powerful influences upon the body of ideas, etc., which form the structure of thought of given societies – notably in that part of it which is concerned with the very stuff of the conditions of production, i.e. the economic. The odium which has come to attach to these propositions must rightly be reserved to those extreme and one-sided formulations of them which are to be found in Marx's own works, and which have, above all, been indispensable to his followers who have been primarily concerned with building articles of unquestioning faith and tools of political propaganda. To be valuable in historical research, a process of interaction must be allowed for in this theory. Furthermore, it must be admitted that the history of ideas, institutions and ideologies itself shows remarkable examples of longevity, notwithstanding radical changes in most of the characteristics of the social process of production. Beyond, therefore, the more obvious connections, and, particularly, if one

---

[1] Examples are extremely numerous and three (very different ones) must suffice to show how in the hands of great writers the 'economic factor' finds its rightful – and most fruitful – application: Cairnes, J. E., *The Slave Power: its character, career and probable designs* (1862), De Tocqueville, A., *L'Ancien Régime et la Revolution* (1856), and, finally, a modern American work unfortunately not as well-known as it should be: Webb, W. P., *The Great Plains* (1936). Free from any political 'taint', in no way based upon propositions that are peculiarly those of Marx, this work gives a most illuminating account of the development of the American South West in terms, largely, of the economic conditions of the area.

considers a sufficiently long time-span the subject of speculation necessarily shifts to the 'conditions of man', and away from the 'social conditions of production'. Though this is a point of view which Marx would not have admitted – at least after he had reached, say, his thirties.

Nor is a theory of classes without some respectability as an analytical tool. Most of the best historical and sociological scholarship makes much use of the notion of different social and economic classes or groups with conflicting interests, and shows how the rivalries of these classes constitute a very powerful engine of social change. What is important in each theory, including that of Marx, is how classes are defined, and how this definition is related to the interests by which these classes are supposed to be motivated. Marx's definition – in terms of ownership in means of production – may have some value in describing *some* important characteristics of *some* societies. But it has been shown to be grossly deficient if it is to be regarded as a uniquely important definition; and this deficiency becomes completely destructive of the postulated pattern where modern, complex societies are concerned. Moreover, there is little, if anything, in Marx to explain the actual fluctuations in the arrangement of individuals, families, or groups into the classes he has postulated. In other words, while his definition may be an interesting though primitive and, therefore, often misleading, abstraction for describing a class stratification that had emerged at some stage in history, e.g. the early days of industrial capitalism, it does not show how the members of these abstract classes have been recruited and how the process of recruitment and expulsion continues.

It is at this point that the other major deficiency of the Marxian scheme appears. It is not enough that the abstraction of 'class' should be based on distinguishing characteristics that are of special significance, it is also essential that the classes should act according to interests that are uniformly perceived and perceived in a manner which corresponds to the roles which the author has prescribed for them. In Marx this second condition is postulated rather than proved: antagonism between classes, and solidarity within each class (leading to 'class consciousness') are merely taken for granted; though subsequently an attempt is made, through the theory of surplus-value to provide an economic foundation. It is clear that there was some force in these postulates, in relation to the conditions of mid-nineteenth century industry; and this, in part, accounts for the extent to which they were accepted as doctrines for political action. But in their precise form they have lost a good deal of their initial power; while as scientific categories they are at the very least seriously inadequate when we consider complex industrial communities. This becomes particularly evident, as we shall see presently, in relation to the theory of the 'increasing misery' of the working-class.

The assessment of the economic part of Marx's work is easier, and the whole history of the economic ideas after Marx which we shall traverse in the following pages serves to show up the limits of his theories. Let it be said at once that the complex of basic economic theorems: labour theory of value and the theory of surplus-value, the theory of capital, the theory of competition (with the allied doctrine of the relationship between value and prices), the theory of capitalist development including the declining tendency of the rate of profit, the theory of concentration and crises, contains a certain measure of internal logical consistency, indeed probably higher than most other early post-classical schools. This is not to say that there are no logical weaknesses in it. The theory of the value of labour-power, for example, lacking either the extreme formulation of the subsistence theory of wages to be found in the so-called 'iron law', or a Malthusian type of population theory as a substratum, could not by itself stand up as an explanation, either of the manner in which wages are determined at any moment, or of their historical trend. These theoretical weaknesses carry forward into the theory of surplus-value and its development over time as a result of competition and technical improvement and innovation. The role of increasing productivity, the relation between the motives and actions of the individual capitalist (the 'firm' in later Marshallian terminology) to the industry or to the whole economy are not satisfactorily explained. Nor is there in Marx, para-doxically enough, a satisfactory theory of capital. The distinction between constant and variable capital follows, of course, with rigorous logic from the theory of surplus value. It was quite a useful tool compared with those fashioned by his predecessors; and the theory of the increasing organic composition of capital (together with the theory of industrial concentration) have rightly been described as brilliant anticipations. But the whole structure does not amount to an adequate theory which relates wages, capital, profits and interest either in stationary conditions or, through the introduction of dynamic ele-ments, over time. This is, perhaps, not a major criticism that can fairly be levelled at Marx: the subject had to wait for decades, if not generations, before there was progress beyond the elementary analysis of Ricardo; and it remains, to this day, perhaps the least rounded part of general economic theory.

This weakness of the dynamic parts of Marx's theory shows up particularly clearly in the doctrine of the 'increasing misery' of the working class. Based on the dubious device of the 'industrial reserve-army' which he had taken over practically unaltered from Ricardo's extreme example (his celebrated 'strong case') of the effects of the introduction of labour-saving machinery in a firm, the doctrine has come up against most stubbornly contradictory facts. Later attempts, made by Marx's disciples in the face of improvements in the working-class standard of living not dreamt of in Marx's day, to make the theory apply to the relative rather than the absolute economic position of the working-class have not served either to buttress it theoretically or to make it more conformable to observed fact. Hence latter-day followers of Marx have been obliged to introduce increasing sophistication by evolving a theory of colonial exploitation which at one and the same time, it is claimed, explains how the decline of the rate of profit is delayed (and the breakdown postponed) and how the tendency to increasing misery may be – temporarily – alleviated. It would take us too far afield to examine these theories. We may merely note that not only is it clear that observed fact supports them no more than it does the earlier version, but it is also certain that these sophistications take the whole doctrine into quite other realms in which nearly all that is essential to the basic Marxian doctrine, notably the theory of the class struggle, becomes damaged beyond repair.

In the theory of crises, Marx undoubtedly made interesting contributions which could with advantage have been generally followed up by economists sooner than they were. For example, much that appears in Marx's work of actual quantitative evaluation and description of the process of fluctuations in economic activity may be classed with the achievement of the pioneers of the subject. In theoretical formulations, too, particularly as regards the relations between consumption and accumulation and between profits and capital values, there are many individual ideas which might well have been taken up. Similarities have been found between them and certain modern theories.[1]

As for the labour theory of value itself, the heart and core of

---

1 E.g. J. Robinson, 'Marx on Unemployment', *Economic Journal*, June–September, 1941.

Marxian economic theory, it will be sufficiently clear from the summary which has been given of it here, that it represents the logical culmination of one element of classical thought, whose antecedents go back as far as Aristotle. Attempts could be (and have been) made to represent it also as a possible expression of the more 'orthodox' theory of value, i.e., one of relative prices, of the kind that Ricardo himself appears to have espoused towards the end of his life. And it can then be shown that, on such a basis, the labour theory of value is nothing more than a highly primitive theory of prices in the very specialized conditions of stationary equilibrium under perfect competition. It is, therefore, inadequate as a general theory, even if it were completely satisfactory in logic for the conditions postulated. But there can be no doubt that Marx was not concerned to write a theory of relative prices and he is, therefore, not entitled to the benefit of doubt on this score. His search for the 'substance' and 'cause' of value (even if shorn of any metaphysical or ethical connotations) was designed to discover the manner in which production (and all that Marx claimed to be determined by it) is arranged in certain specific social circumstances. In this sense, however, it must be clear that the theory amounts to no more than (*a*) the original Smithian formula of labour being the source of the fund which originally provides all the means of livelihood (i.e. what Marx himself would have called a 'universal' statement); (*b*) a statement that exchange-value as an economic phenomenon can only arise when there exists an exchange economy with the social and legal conditions appropriate to it; and (*c*) that in such an economy exchange-value (i.e. the price mechanism) rather than some form of 'central planning' determines how production will be arranged. It follows also from this that the basic concept of the surplus product or value simply means that human labour is able to wrest from nature more than the bare means of human survival; that all progress (and civilization itself) depends upon the size of this surplus; and that the division of this surplus between consumption and accumulation and among the various members (or 'classes') of the community is a central economic problem determining, to a major extent, the development of the economy itself.

Thus formulated, it is not necessary, or indeed possible, to quarrel with any of these propositions; nor need one denigrate the contribution which they made to the progress of economics becoming conscious of itself.[1] But beyond that, they contribute nothing to our understanding of

---

1 It must be stated in fairness, however, that credit for formulating these basic proposi-

the economic process. In the outcome, Marx proved himself incapable of fashionable other tools with which to tackle the increasingly complex phenomena of a modern economy. Thus, his whole system has proved essentially barren. No economic contribution of significance has come from his followers. But the major problem of Marxism arises not in regard to the basic economic concepts themselves, but in the use to which they are put by Marx for the purpose of his economic dynamic and his political faith. It is, however, of importance to a true assessment of Marx to realize that these dynamic and political elements are not inherent in these primitive economic concepts themselves; they are derived from a sociological postulate: the Marxian theory of the class struggle. There is no logical connection between the two.

On general methodological grounds one need not reject as necessarily illegitimate or possibly unfruitful the attempt to combine sociological principles, or doctrines of historical development, with the theorems yielded by 'pure' economic analysis. What is, however, quite unacceptable, even from a logical point of view alone, is the illegitimate transfer in the Marxian system of unproved postulates from one branch to the other, whose syllogisms are then made to serve as rationalizations of what had been postulated in the first place. Nevertheless, it is precisely this wholly illegitimate combination of two disparate orders of ideas and methods of analysis which has constituted the peculiar fascination of the system and has made it so curiously impervious to the criticism of ordinary logic. It is this which makes out of a primitive economic analysis, out of a useful working hypothesis of historical research (though one which must be employed with the greatest caution) and out of an extremely amateurish sociology, a comprehensive and intransigent *Weltanschauung*. It is this combination which, in the end, makes the heritage of Marx no different, either in scholastic barrenness or in political repulsiveness, to that of the romantics.

---

tions which mark the emergence of economics from its pre-scientific stage, belongs to Smith and Ricardo. The enthusiasm that accompanied their 're-discovery' by Marx is perhaps a typical experience of the auto-didact. It is interesting to speculate what would have happened had economics continued to occupy itself, as it did in the classics, with the problems of the aggregates of the economic process (without, of course, the Marxian pseudo-sociology). However, as we shall see in subsequent chapters, the science had to pass through a long period of preoccupation with the mechanism of price determination (fashioning, in the process, some invaluable analytical tools) before it could fruitfully turn again to the larger problems of the balance of the economy as a whole.

One cannot deny that there is a a certain grand audacity in the method; nor, given the individual elements of partial truth to be found in both the sociology and the economics, given the way in which they are fused into one in the fire of a *saeva indignatio* over the evils of society and at the same time related to a vision of the future, is it difficult to see why the theory should have had so persistent and so strong an influence. For whatever each individual part may look like under the microscope of scientific analysis, the amalgam is something quite different from the sum of these parts: it has all the attributes of a militant faith, above all it possesses the peculiar characteristic of combining the action of super-human forces (which are supposed inevitably to produce a certain destiny) with the necessity for a certain individual belief and conduct in order to obtain salvation. It is idle to speculate, as some have done, whether Marx willed this result or whether his was the role of the sorcerer's apprentice. But in this case the biblical 'by the fruits shall you know them' is peculiarly apposite; and what is certain is that, in spite of his insistence on the scientific character of his system, Marx bequeathed to posterity not a political or economic science but a political idolatry. In spite of his scholarly gifts, in spite of the tradition of rationalism with which be began his studies, Marx has left behind an irrational and, indeed, an anti-rational legacy. Its viability has, therefore, been only partially affected by purely logical argument. To his disciples – and, it would seem, increasingly to himself as he grew older – it appeared to offer at once an explanation of all the most baffling problems of society. But its economics relied, in the end, on arguments which must be adjudged essentially tautological; and it has, therefore, proved itself incapable of further development in any scientific sense. Indeed, it is significant that such developments as there have been, have eschewed the painstaking methods of economic enquiry (statistical and deductive) Marx himself had used in the beginning, and have taken their inspiration from the phantasmagoria of 'dialectical materialism'.[1] As developments in the Soviet Union and the countries of central and Eastern Europe have shown, it was, appropriately, the failure of the economic system supposedly based on Marxist principles together with the, in the end, no longer supportable political and intellectual dictatorship which had created and sustained that system

---

1 Of which George Orwell's nightmarish 'newspeak' and 'doublethink' can be taken as the grotesque and monstrous, but by no means incredible, offspring.

which caused it to collapse, rather than its logical inadequacy.

As its epitaph, one may well use these words, first applied by a great writer to other forms of anti-rationalism and not without relevance to certain extreme modern formulations of the macro-economic theory mentioned later: '... whenever the doctrine of exclusive salvation is generally believed and realized, habits of thought will be formed around it that are diametrically opposed to the spirit of enquiry and absolutely incompatible with human progress. An indifference to truth, a spirit of blind and at the same time wilful credulity, will be encouraged, which will multiply fictions of every kind, will associate enquiry with the ideas of danger and of guilt, will make men esteem that impartiality of judgment and study which is the very soul of truth, an unholy thing, and will so emasculate their faculties as to produce a general torpor on every subject.'[1]

---

1 Lecky, W. E. H., *History of the Rise and Influence of the Spirit of Rationalism in Europe* (New York, 1876), vol. i, p. 404.

# 7
## The Transition

*The Classical Heritage*

It is proposed in this chapter to discuss the main writers and ideas in the period of transition from the early classics to the rise of modern economics in the last quarter of the nineteenth century. The emphasis is on tendencies rather than on individual contributions; so that many writers are dealt with summarily or omitted altogether.

In the last two chapters we have traced the romantic, the critical, and the revolutionary attitudes to classical political economy. The former was not a serious threat; the latter was more formidable. In its formulation by the English socialists and by Marx, based as it was on the classical postulates, it assumed a form which was dangerous to the continued acceptance of the classical conclusions. Marx could and did claim to be in the direct line of descent from Smith and Ricardo. And he had a plausible case for saying that he had taken the essence from Smith and Ricardo; that he had ignored only their errors and confusion; and that he had pushed their analysis to its logical conclusion. This conclusion was hostile to the capitalist system, though, as we have seen, it did not spring from the economic analysis itself; nor was it an inevitable outcome even of the theory of history which surrounded that analysis. Moreover, in its outcome it was no different from the romantic school.

But at the same time there developed a theoretical movement which, starting from the classics, went in the opposite direction. This movement criticized the classical theory in certain parts and developed a new theoretical analysis which provided a firmer basis for the main political and practical conclusions of classicism. It was the task of this movement to show the critics as being guilty of an abuse of classical theory, or, at least, an erroneous interpretation of it. Classicism had to become the basis for a new tendency. The classical theory did in fact contain many elements which contradicted those which the critics had taken as their starting-point. It was only necessary to take these elements and develop their implications. The resulting theory could then claim to be what Smith and Ricardo had been groping for but had been unable to reach.

The course of this movement during the nineteenth century was by no means smooth. It assumed various guises (particularly in different countries). And it was not until towards the end of the century that a body of doctrines was evolved which, with many minor differences, had dominated economic thought and teaching to the present day. What follows is a survey of the fifty years after Ricardo's *Principles* which, in retrospect, appear as a period of transition.

The classical system remained for a long time supreme in its country of origin. In England the legacy of Ricardo was considered sacrosanct; and even as late as 1848 John Stuart Mill regarded himself in matters of theory as little more than an exponent of pure Ricardianism. To assess correctly the reasons for the supremacy of classicism, its extent, and its decline, it is necessary to distinguish carefully between its theoretical and political content. Once this distinction is made, a glance at the ideological and political scene in the England of the first half of the century will suffice to show that classicism was accepted as much for the theory of economic policy it contained as for its analysis of the economic structure. It was the strength of its case for *laissez-faire*, rather than the purely theoretical analysis on which that case rested, that gave the classical school its authority.

The theory of Ricardo had become something like an institution. It was often embodied in dry and dogmatic textbooks and popularized in tracts, articles, and stories which pointed an economic moral. Ricardo's first and most faithful disciples, James Mill and McCulloch, are witnesses to the fact that much of the vigour of economic speculation had gone. The master's words are often repeated parrotlike; and if his uncertainties have been removed, his brilliance has disappeared also. In the hands of the disciples the theories of Ricardo have become 'the faith of a sect'.[1] Both the elder Mill and McCulloch take as their 'raw material, not reality, but the new theoretical form in which the master had epitomized it'.[2] Their writings have, therefore, comparatively little

1 E. Halévy, *The Growth of Philosophic Radicalism* (1928), p. 343.
2 Marx, *Theorien über den Mehrwert*, vol. iii, p. 94.

theoretical interest. In them the inconsistencies and confusions of Ricardo are either repeated, glossed over, or left out. Their main function, apart from the mere popular exposition of Ricardo's doctrines, was to defend the Ricardian theory of value against the critics who had fastened on to its contradictions. We shall see later in this chapter that their defence was unsuccessful. When John Stuart Mill expounded a watered-down version of Ricardo, there was already in existence – both in England and elsewhere – a theory of value which had only a very attenuated connection with that of the classics.

But these forerunners of a new economic theory did not seriously disturb the harmony of post-Ricardian economics in that aspect of it which was alone of importance to the world of affairs: its underlying political philosophy. The disintegration of the Ricardian theoretical structure was accompanied by the complete triumph of liberalism. No country and no sphere of thought or action was free from its impact.

Political practice in particular seemed to be giving expression to the most important parts of the liberal doctrine. And political economy, though still divided between the conservative and the egalitarian interpretations, claimed a utilitarian descent. During the earlier and longer part of our period of transition the conflict between these two tendencies within liberalism itself was still of small importance. The exact attitude of economists to these tendencies is a debatable matter. There were, no doubt, considerable differences of opinion on specific issues of economic policy. No doubt, also, some economists had transcended the narrow confines of doctrinaire *laissez-faire*. But attempts to portray the whole post-Ricardian school, as social reformers whose interest in *laissez-faire* was only that of opponents of monopoly and privilege have not been generally successful.

James Mill, McCulloch, and others were certainly opposed to the abuses of monopolies, and had they seen all the possibilities in their own day they might well have expressed concern. Senior certainly objected to some of the attempts at rigging of the market which he had an opportunity of observing. It is also true that some of the disciples of classicism in England believed in a 'distributist' society, in a liberalism which recognized private property, but wanted the state to take positive measures for preserving competition and for ensuring equality of opportunity. But it is undeniable that the economists' most bitter attacks were reserved for the associations of working men, who were creating 'monopolies' of their own, and for the state when it was interfering with the free play of economic forces through social legislation. Capitalist interests were more tenderly treated. This is a strong general impression left by a study of the literature of the period; and it was during that period that economics, not altogether unjustly, got its bad name as a rationalization of and apologia for the evil conditions in which the vast majority of the population were obliged to live.[1]

It must, moreover, be remembered that in England the virtues of economic liberalism could be shown to have a strong basis in the facts of the economy. Opposition to any restriction of competition, which itself rested on an effective monopoly of the world market, could successfully appeal for support to the great economic laws of the classical school. Everybody could agree that the greatest happiness of the greatest number was the ultimate aim of wise government. In the continually expanding English economy, it could also be urged without fear of contradiction that individual enterprise and free competition were the best means for achieving that aim. A closely knit theory and a wealth of practical illustration could be used to demolish opposition.

No English economist of note ever spoke again of the invisible hand. But for fifty years, at least, no economist who was not a socialist, or at least a social reformer, denied the beneficence, at least in the sphere of production, of liberty in the sense of unrestricted competition. Ricardo had expressed doubts about the effects of such liberty in the sphere of distribution. But the gloom which he cast on the future of the labouring classes was not allowed to interfere with the belief in the ultimate harmony of interests which all liberals retained. It was no longer a providential harmony; indeed, now and again there is a suspicion that it is a harmony for the wealthier classes only. But the development which intensified the socialist challenge also made England the workshop of the world; and a measured optimism based on economic expansion was able to survive the hungry 1840s. It was not until the later years of John Stuart Mill that the working-class movement made its converts in the liberal camp and forced liberalism itself to review many of its doctrines.

The special historical circumstances which gave English liberalism something of a universal appeal, which made it realistic, and ready in the last resort to compromise, were not, as we have seen, repeated elsewhere. In France the appearance of capitalism is marked at once by

1 For an excellent defence of classicism on this score see Robbins, L., *The Theory of Economic Policy* (1952).

a strong critical current which has the recent memory of the Revolution to feed on. The protectionism of the romantics and, much more so, the socialism of the revolution were such powerful currents that economic liberalism had at once to be more intransigent and less realistic than it had been in its native country. We might recall that the law of the market, that true and yet not always useful conclusion of classical theory, received its most dogmatic and arid formulation in France and not in England. And the eagerness for completeness and consistency which had made Say bowdlerize Smith found its fullest expression in the revival of a providential harmony by Bastiat. The optimism which is characteristic of his work has not the solid foundations of English classicism; nor has his campaign for free trade the firm practical basis which had made Cobden and Bright successful. The absurdities to which he reduced all the attempts at protection may delight present-day liberals exasperated by the excesses of contemporary economic nationalism. But they had little effect on policy in the France of Bastiat.

Only in one other environment could the undiluted faith of the early classics in infinite progress and natural harmony appear with all the intransigence of a Bastiat and yet have a realistic foundation. But it is significant that Henry C. Carey, the American apostle of optimism, was also a strong protectionist. Carey and Adam Smith, Bastiat and Ricardo: the economic doctrines of the classical school could clearly be made to mean many different things.

As for Germany, we have already noted (in Chapter 5) some of the conditions which created an unfavourable soil for economic liberalism. Indeed, although the romantic movement had soon spent its first force and only remained as a muddy under-current of anti-rationalism, it was not replaced by Ricardianism. There was no more attempt from that quarter to challenge the inevitable victory of capitalism. But List and the romantics, the exigencies of national union, the tradition of authoritarian government, and, underlying all these, the weakness of German industry compared with that of its rivals made it impossible for economic liberalism to become the orthodox doctrine. The first substantial independent contribution of German economic thought was of a different character. Though no longer of importance itself, and although chronologically not altogether in place here, it is best treated immediately after other reactions from classicism.

## *The Historical School*

The historical school was for nearly forty years the most influential school of economic thought in German-speaking countries. Its reign dates from 1843, when Roscher's *Grundriss* appeared. It was not successfully attacked until 1883, when Carl Menger published his *Untersuchungen* and ousted it from its place of pre-eminence. The historical school represents a striking example of the difficulty of survival of the pure classical doctrines once it was faced with new economic developments, or, as in this case, with a different national environment. It is, moreover, interesting because it contains the same conflicting interpretations which we have already met in the immediate reaction to classicism. One part of it is in a line of descent from romanticism: this gives the school its anti-individualist tendency. But by the time the historical school was in full swing, capitalism was already advancing rapidly and *Historismus*, therefore, never became anti-capitalist in a reactionary sense. In fact, one part of it represented a socialist criticism of capitalism, though it never became explicitly so in Germany. It gave rise to a specifically German variety of the social reform movement, the so-called *Kathedersozialismus*. When its influence was later transplanted into other environments – the America of Veblen – the radical implication became more marked. A somewhat similar post-Ricardian tendency can be found in England in the work of Richard Jones.

Thus the historical school is not to be regarded as exemplifying theoretical trends which are essentially different from those which have already been discussed in Chapter 5. Its claim to special consideration rests on the fact that it embodied these trends in a discussion of a particular problem of economic inquiry: its method. Concern with economic history was by no means new. Many theorists had also contributed to historical scholarship, and some of the most important works of the classical schools, the *Wealth of Nations*, for example, were distinguished by their use of both historical and theoretical methods. But what makes writers like Roscher, Knies, Hildebrand, and Schmoller into a school is the overwhelming importance which they assign to history in the study of the economic process. There is some disagreement among historians of economic thought about the exact classification of the writers of the school and about the essence of their ideas. Gide and Rist in their *Histoire des Doctrines économiques*,[1] take the more

---

1 C. Gide and C. Rist, *Histoire des Doctrines économiques*, pp. 450–85.

widely accepted view that the historical school had an older and a younger branch: the former represented by Roscher, Knies, and Hilderbrand, the latter by Schmoller. Professor Schumpeter, in his *Epochen der Dogmen- und Methodengeschichte*, claims that the older of these schools is not strictly speaking to be regarded as historical; the younger school under Schmoller is truly historical in its insistence on detailed, realistic, historical research. Menger, however, does not make Schumpeter's distinction (to which we shall presently return). The opinion of the most determined and successful opponent of *Historismus* is of considerable importance and happens to be more in harmony with the exposition already given here of the antecedents of the historical school.[1]

The first incentive to the formation of this school came from sources that were related to those from which romanticism had sprung. Menger draws a distinction between the historical school of jurisprudence of Savigny, with its conservative political conclusions, and the school of political historians, who taught at the end of the eighteenth and the beginning of the nineteenth centuries at Göttingen and Tübingen, and who were liberals. To the former, he adds, correspond the romantic economists (like Müller); to the latter, the historical school.[2] It is quite true that the members of the historical school in economics were not medievalists and reactionaries. But this, as has been claimed, can be explained by the different stage which the development of capitalism had reached. A similarity of attitude remains.

The first economist of the historical school was Wilhelm Roscher (1817–94). He was trained in history and political science in the tradition of Göttengen. Like his teachers, he regarded historical empiricism as the foundation of wise politics. In 1843 he published his *Grundriss zu Vorlesungen über die Staatswirtschaft nach geschichtlicher Methode*. In this work and in his later writings, notably his *System der Volkswirtschaft*, he claims to base himself on the methods of Savigny's school of jurisprudence. Although he was a liberal and not anxious, as Savigny had been, to use historical research for the purpose of finding justification for existing institutions in their past development, Roscher

---

1 C. Menger, *Untersuchungen über die Methode der Sozialwissenschaften und der politischen Oekonomie insbesondere*. Collected Works, vol. ii (London School of Economics Reprint, 1933), pp. 209–31.
2 C. Menger, *Untersuchungen über die Methode der Sozialwissenschaften und der politischen Oekonomie insbesondere*. Collected Works, vol. ii (London School of Economics Reprint, 1933), pp. 212–3.

laid great stress on the need for infusing the historical spirit into economic inquiry. He did not go so far as to reject Ricardo's deduction, but he claimed that empiricism was an essential adjunct to it. He was not quite clear in his own mind about methodological issues. Sometimes he gives the impression of advocating merely the collection of historical material for purposes of illustration and for the inspiration which it can supply to theoretical study. At other times he regards history as important, because it alone can provide the historical sense which enables statesmen to solve political problems wisely. Sometimes, again, he seems to suggest that description of economic institutions and conditions exhausts the fields of economics.

Much more elaborate and consistent an opposition to classicism comes from the pen of Bruno Hildebrand (1812–78). In 1848 he published *Die Nationalökonomie der Gegenwart und Zukunft*, in which he explicitly rejected the claim of the classical school to have found, or at any rate to be searching for, natural economic laws which would be valid for all time and for all countries. He opposed the idea – which occasionally appeared in Roscher – that it was possible to discover a 'physiology' of economic life. He also separated – which Roscher had failed to do – the practical questions of economic policy from theoretical analysis, and concentrated attention on the latter. His great inspiration was historical philology. What one ought to study, he said in a programmatic article which he wrote for the first number of his journal, was the change in the economic experience of mankind. Economics had to examine carefully the development of individual peoples and of mankind as a whole. It had to produce an economic history of culture; it had to work in close collaboration with other branches of history and with statistics.[1] There is little mention in this programme of discovering the great laws of economic development which Hildebrand had earlier set before economics. In fact, he never produced the positive work which he had promised; and on the occasions on which he left criticism for specialized historical statistical study, he seems to have taken most of the classical conclusions for granted.

The last of the three founders of the school, Karl Knies (1821–98), was more precise in his formulation of the methodological issues than were his predecessors. His *Die Politische Oekonomie vom Standpunkte der geschichtlichen Methode* (1853) is now less well known than his *Geld und*

1 *Jahrbücher für Nationalökonomie und Statistik* (1863), pp. 145 *sqq.*

*Kredit.* The latter, although containing historical material, has very little trace of Knies's adherence to the historical school. In the former, however, Knies appears as a more determined opponent of the classical school than either Roscher or Hildebrand, both of whom he also opposes. Knies sees Roscher's confusion; he knows that Roscher was not clear about the relation of the scope, method, and object of different branches of economic inquiry. He objects to Roscher's modified approval of the classical method. And he finds even in Hildebrand an incomplete realization of the mission of *Historismus.* He thought that Hildebrand's laws of development were still too much a concession to pure theory. With complete consistency Knies claims that historical study is the only legitimate form of economics. It cannot yield laws in the sense in which the physical sciences can be said to do so. It may discover certain regularities in the actual sequence of social development and suggest analogies. The programme which he sets before economists is to avoid asserting the superiority of the historical method and to produce works which do, in fact, deal with economic problems from an historical point of view.

Knies himself did not act up to his own precept. It was the founder of the younger historical school, Gustav Schmoller, who really set in motion an active movement of economic historical research. It is interesting to note that, in the hands of Schmoller and his followers, the original aim of the historical school was beginning to disappear. They no longer denied the existence of laws of society. Schmoller, in one of his later works, *Grundriss der Volkswirtschaftslehre* (1904), admitted that economic life had its laws, but he expressed doubt about the ability of the classical method to discover them. He was more than sceptical about the laws of human development and he rejected the search for a philosophy of history. What Schmoller and his disciples in fact produced was economic history. This, one would have thought, made the threat of *Historismus* to theoretical work much less formidable. Yet it was not until the 1880s, when less was heard of the more ambitious aims of Roscher and Hildebrand, that the great controversy over method broke out. Because this controversy was not due to the claims of the historical school, its causes must be found elsewhere. They are closely connected with the rise – to be discussed in the next chapter – of a new theoretical tendency which was itself connected with certain philosophical and logical currents. The quarrel over method was more a means by which the new theory sought to clear its own mind than an attack on the historical school. But it was in the form of the latter that it made its appearance.

The *Methodenstreit*, as it was called, opened with the publication in 1883 of Carl Menger's *Untersuchungen über die Methode der Sozial-wissenschaften und der Politischen Oekonomie insbesondere* and lasted for more than two decades. Menger made an attack on the claims of the older representatives of *Historismus*; and he combined with it a discussion of method in the social sciences in general. To understand the exact significance of Menger's positive attitude, it is necessary to summarize the chief points of the criticism which the historical school had directed against classicism. They concern the approach of classical economists, their often implicit social philosophy, their views on the scope of economic analysis and their method. The historical school objected, in the first place, to the belief that economic laws, established by a development of the implications of a few postulates, could have universal validity. The laws of Smith and Ricardo, they argued, could not be regarded as absolute and perpetually operative either in economic theory or in the practice of economic policy. Economic laws, even if such could be found, must be considered as being essentially relative and variable with time and place. Economic conditions were constantly changing and developing; the conclusions of economic theory could, therefore, never retain their original adequacy.

Although this point was often put in an exaggerated form by the adherents of the school, it helped to draw attention to an important difference, at least of degree, between the physical and the social sciences; it has since been accepted by theorists and was clearly worked out by Menger. It was agreed by theoretical economists that even though their conclusions were not formally different from those of the physical sciences (both being ideal in the sense that they had reference only within a framework of assumed circumstances), there was an important difference in their relation to reality. The conditions within which the physical laws operate more often exist in practice; they and the deviations from them are easily measured; and allowance can be made for divergences from the ideal. Economic laws operate in a reality which contains an ever-increasing number of changeable concrete conditions of which the original analysis has had to make abstraction. These concrete conditions are, moreover, difficult or impossible to measure; and it is rarely easy to discover the exact way in which the tendencies embodied in economic laws are modified in practice.

The criticism of the classical method is closely connected with this first point. The historical school was so impressed with the practical limitations to which economic laws are subject that it wished to abandon the method of deduction altogether and replace it by induction. It had difficulty in distinguishing between the errors which may be committed by deductive reasoning, or any other scientific method, and the place which correct deduction should occupy in a balanced scheme of inquiry. It failed to see that, even though the classics might have been guilty of a wrong choice of assumptions, or of faulty or hasty conclusions from them, the possibility remained of using significant premises and impeccable logic. It did not see that the two methods which were contrasted were not mutually exclusive and had indeed been used together by the greatest of the classics. There is clearly room for serious disagreement about the choice of premises; but it is generally admitted that premises which stand at the beginning of the deductive process are themselves empirical in origin. Induction and deduction are interdependent.

Behind the objection which the historical school made to classical deduction was a disagreement about premises. The classics, said Knies, and many others have said it after him, started with the assumption that man was moved by self-interest only. There was no foundation for such an assumption. The motives of human conduct were numerous and complex; to isolate one, was bound to lead to wrong conclusions. It should be emphasized here that this particular criticism had nothing in common with Marx's charge that the classical school had failed to see capitalism as a transitory phase of human history; and that it had taken the conduct of the bourgeois of their own generation as typical of mankind in all sorts of social environments. The historical school, in spite of its insistence on relativism, did not seriously question the survival of the capitalist system. What it objected to was simply the stress on the motive of money-making which it claimed to detect in Smith and Ricardo. To this charge economists like Menger could, and did, reply that the classics were not ignorant of the existence of motives other than self-interest. Smith himself had taken great pains to study and classify the different springs of action. All that the classics had done was to take that motive which could be regarded as the most persistent and to study its effects. Or, as other economists claimed, the classics had isolated a motive the results of which were most easily observed and measured.

Lastly, the historical school stressed the unity of social life, the interconnection of individual social processes and the organic, as against the mechanistic, view of society. Although not moved by the 'totalitarian' motives of the romantics or of Marx, the historical school was here inspired by considerations similar to those of romanticism. It began by claiming, as Adam Müller had done, that social economic life was something more than the sum of economic activities of individuals. Society, in its totality, had an organic existence apart from that of its members. This view led to a desire for a comprehensive discipline which would understand the entire organism of social life; and it implied depreciation of the efforts of individual social sciences. But this view soon disappeared and all that remained was an emphasis on the intimate interaction between the different branches of social life which made it impossible for one social science to come anywhere near exhausting the field. There also remained the stimulus to detailed historical research. The historical school left as legacy an enhanced desire for a knowledge of concrete reality in all its individual manifestations through time; and this was productive of very valuable work. But it was a desire which, after all, enlightened theorists had always understood and appreciated.

In its native country the *Methodenstreit* gradually petered out for lack of any substantial points of disagreement. Tacitly, the indispensability of both branches of economic inquiry, the historical-realistic and the abstract-analytical, was mutually admitted, even though there remained a difference of emphasis which is still present today. A version of the *Methodenstreit* also reached England; but in the home of classical political economy the controversy somehow never aroused much enthusiasm. In 1857 Cairnes published a methodological work entitled *The Character and Logical Method of Political Economy*, in which the significance of deduction was expounded. This book formed a part of a long controversy between Mill, Senior and Cairnes over the exact relation between the scope and method of economics and other sciences. But this controversy is not important to our present purpose.

It was not until after the second edition of Cairnes's work had appeared in 1875 that the classical methodological tradition was met by the challenge of the adherents of the historical school. In 1879 Cliffe Leslie published his *Essays on Political and Moral Philosophy*, in which all the arguments of the Germans found expression. Others who attempted to influence English economic thought in the same direction were J. K. Ingram and W. J. Ashley. They never made any headway as a separate school; though the historical movement had much influence on some theoretical economists, Marshall for example. Their one positive achievement was to stimulate research in economic history. It is, however, interesting to note that some of the English exponents of *Historismus*, notably Ashley, were also closely linked with the tariff-reform movement. They may be taken as representatives of a new trend in English economic policy perhaps a reflection of the changing position of England in world markets.

In France the impact of the historical school was even less marked. It showed itself again mainly in an increase of historical research; and it found a related trend in the growth of sociological studies which nearly always emphasized the historical point of view.

## *Jones*

Although he was not a contemporary of the historical school, nor yet a real representative of its views, there is one English economist of the first half of the nineteenth century whom it is best to mention here. Richard Jones is seldom given much attention in histories of economic thought. He is generally regarded as 'an isolated representative of the historical method in England in the thirties',[1] Superficially this is true. Jones urged economists to pay greater attention to the historical differences between economic institutions. And he expressed the view that by comparative studies alone would the economists be able to advise on policy. He also stressed the relativity of economic laws. But he made use of history in economic analysis in a much more radical manner than had Roscher and Schmoller. He was unfortunately not able to finish his *magnum opus*; but the indications of what he was aiming at are clear enough in the first part of it, which was completed.

In 1831 Richard Jones published *An Essay on the Distribution of Wealth and on the Sources of Taxation. Part I: Rent.* Two years later appeared his *An Introductory Lecture on Political Economy*, delivered at King's College, London, February 27, 1833. To which is added a *Syllabus of a Course of Lectures on the Wages of Labour*, and finally in 1852, his *Text-book of Lectures on the Political Economy of Nations.* These three works contain an explicit statement of their author's ideas on the method of economic analysis, an implicit use of that method in a discussion of certain major problems of the capitalist system, and a

1 M. Bowley, *Nassau Senior and Classical Economics*, p. 40.

working out of this method in a more detailed study of one particular question, rent.

In the long preface to the *Essay on Distribution* Jones defines his position *vis-à-vis* the classical economists. He traces the origin of political economy in the discussion of mercantilist measures; notes the great advance contained in Smith; and states his belief that the problems of distribution have not as yet been treated satisfactorily. The study of production, he says, has resulted in the enunciation of important laws of universal validity. But in the sphere of distribution economists have only succeeded in stating mutually contradictory opinions. The physiocrats are condemned because they had mistakenly insisted that agriculture was the only source of a surplus from which all classes of society derived their revenue. Praise is bestowed on Malthus for his share in developing the theory of rent and, to a less extent, the theory of population. But Ricardo and others are blamed for having built an illegitimate superstructure on these foundations. Malthus had shown, said Jones, that when capitalist production has become the dominant mode of production, the cost of production of agricultural produce on the worst land tilled will determine 'the average price of raw produce, while the difference of quality on the superior lands measures the rents yielded by them'.[1] But Ricardo had omitted the qualification, which was of an historical character, and had made the principle into one of universal validity. Similarly, in the theory of population, Malthus himself and his followers had overlooked the possibility of important changes in the factors with which they were dealing and had developed a view of the future of society for which there was no justification.

Jones rejected the idea of a 'continuous diminution in the return to agriculture – its assumed effects on the progress of accumulation – and ... a corresponding incapacity in mankind to provide resources for increasing numbers'.[2] He showed that rents were, in fact, highest in countries in which agriculture was very productive and a large population was maintained at a high standard of living; and that the wealthier countries and the wealthier classes everywhere multiplied less rapidly than others. This obvious difference between the theories of the economists and the facts of experience was, he thought, largely responsible for the feeling of distrust in the validity of economic laws

[1] R. Jones, *An Essay on the Distribution of Wealth and on the Sources of Taxation* (1831), p. vii.
[2] ibid., p. xiii.

which had taken hold of the public. People were beginning to think that the subject matter of political economy was too complex to admit of accurate analysis.

Jones did not share the view that it was impossible to discover economic laws of universal validity. He only emphasized the importance of basing all such laws on experience. An historical sense and a wide range of observation (which had become possible to a far greater extent than ever before) had to be the constant adjuncts of economic analysis. 'Truth has been missed not because a steady and comprehensive survey of the story and condition of mankind would not yield truth, even on this intricate subject, but because those who have been the most prominent in circulating error, have really turned aside from the task of going through an examination at all: have confined the observations on which they founded their reasonings, to the small portion of the earth's surface by which they were immediately surrounded.'[1]

This sounds like a straightforward plea for more empiricism, such as might be made by any moderate exponent of *Historismus*. But a study of the way in which Jones followed his own precept shows that he was pleading for a specific form of historical observation. His aim was to study the working of economic principles 'among bodies of men living in different circumstances'.[2] He was anxious to lay bare the distinction between that which was common to all social structures and the different forms in which it appeared as the result of differences in the social structure. Jones distinguished between the different forms of social production which appeared in the course of history. He endeavoured to show their difference as well as their unity. In the *Introductory Lecture* Jones spoke of that relation between production and distribution and of different economic structures as follows. 'Although', he said, 'some wealth must be produced before any can be distributed, yet the forms and modes of distributing the produce of their lands and labour, adopted in the early stages of a people's progress, exercise an influence over the character and habits of communities which can be traced for ages; ... and this influence must be understood, and allowed for, before we can adequately explain existing differences in the productive powers and operations of different nations.' It is not difficult to trace the different methods of distribution. Since the earth can yield its cultivator more than he needs for his own

1 R. Jones, *An Essay on the Distribution of Wealth and on the Sources of Taxation*, p. xxiii.
2 ibid., p. xxiv.

subsistence, the surplus can be appropriated by another class. 'Hence arises a separation of society into classes; and the mode in which the distribution of this surplus takes place, the nature of the class which consumes it, is the first and most influential cause of the future character and habits of the community.'[1] This language is reminiscent of Steuart and Turgot.

The economic structure of society depends on the social forms of labour: the manner in which the labourer obtains his means of subsistence and in which the surplus which he produces is appropriated and accumulated. 'By the economical structure of nations, I mean those relations between the different classes which are established in the first instance by the institution of property in the soil, and by the distribution of its surplus produce; afterwards modified and changed (to a greater or lesser extent) by the introduction of capitalists as agents in producing and exchanging wealth and in feeding and employing the working population.'[2] The whole of the *Introductory Lecture* is a definition of the economic structure as a relationship of different classes, in terms of property in land or capital, and therefore, of function in the economic process. And in emphasizing the social basis of the economic process Jones has also introduced a strong historical point of view.

Jones uses the concept of the 'labour fund', which involves both the manner of appropriation of the product by the labourer and relation of classes to the means of production, although Jones does not distinguish these factors very clearly, they are definitely implied in his analysis. He divided the labour fund into three classes: one, in which the revenue is consumed by its producer; two, in which the revenue belongs to classes other than the labourers and is used by those classes directly for the maintenance of labourers; and three, capitalism, in which there is an accumulation of revenue which is used to obtain a profit. An example of the first class are peasant proprietors; of the second, soldiers, sailors, servants, etc.; of the third, modern capitalism. All three kinds can be observed in actual existence. In England, all but the third are negligible; in other countries pre-capitalist forms of production are still important.[3]

Jones sees clearly, though he does not always express it clearly, that

1 *The Literary Remains consisting of Lectures and Tracts on Political Economy of the late Rev. Richard Jones* (ed. W. Whewell, 1859), pp. 552–3.
2 ibid., p. 560.
3 ibid., pp. 79– *sqq.*

the existence of a surplus product and of accumulation is independent of the particular social forms in which it appears in different phases of history. Capitalism is one such form. When it prevails the labourer is paid out of capital. In pre-capitalist production labour is paid out of revenue. Jones thus carries farther the distinction, made by Smith, between productive and unproductive labour.[1] There are certain inconsistencies, in particular the description of the labourer's revenue in non-capitalist production as wages. But Jones insists that it is the capitalist's saving which is the activity by which the labour fund is provided under capitalism and his whole analysis proclaims the historical form of accumulation. Jones shows that accumulation existed before capitalism, and before the profit motive; and that it is only at a certain historical state that the capitalist – being the one who appropriates the surplus and who initiates production – also carries out the function of accumulation. 'Capital, or accumulated stock, after performing various other functions in the production of wealth, only takes up late that of advancing to the laborer his wages.'[2]

Jones underlines repeatedly the historical quality in his description of economic institutions and functions. Here is a typical example: 'A state of things may hereafter exist, and parts of the world may be approaching to it, under which the laborers and the owners of accumulated stock, may be identical; but in the progress of nations, which we are now observing, this has never yet been the case, and to trace and understand that progress, we must observe the laborers gradually transferred from the hands of a body of customers, who pay them out of their revenues, to those of a body of employers, who pay them by advances of capital out of the returns to which the owners aim at realizing a distinct revenue. This may not be as desirable a state of things as that in which laborers and capitalist are identified; but we must still accept it as a stage in the march of industry, which has hitherto marked the progress of advancing nations.'[3]

This historical point of view underlies Jones's interest in, and treatment of, rent. In the 'Syllabus' which he added to his *Introductory Lecture*, Jones approached the question from the point of view of different social forms of labour. Property was the reflection of these forms. But in his earlier and larger work the procedure is reversed. In

1 ibid., pp. 392 *sqq.*; pp. 414 *sqq.*
2 ibid., p. 457.
3 ibid., p. 445.

the *Essay* Jones starts from the different forms of landed property which can be found in various countries, or which have existed at different times. The origin of all rent he ascribes to 'the power of the earth to yield even to the rudest labors of mankind, more than is necessary for the subsistence of the cultivator himself'.[1] And this power, once land has passed into private ownership, enables the cultivator to pay to the owner a tribute. Unlike Ricardo, he believes in the existence of absolute rent, quite apart from differences in rent due to differences in the fertility of the soil. 'In the actual progress of human society, rent has usually originated in the appropriation of the soil, at a time when the bulk of the people must cultivate it on such terms as they can obtain, or starve. ... The necessity which compels them to pay a rent ... is wholly independent of any difference in the quality of the ground they occupy.'[2]

Jones then traces the actual forms of rent under different systems of land tenure until its final appearance in a capitalist system. He shows that capitalism begins in manufacture and later extends to agriculture. 'Its characteristic is the possibility of moving at pleasure the labor and capital employed in agriculture, to other occupations ... and unless as much can be obtained by employing the working class on the land, as from their exertions in various other employments ... the business of cultivation will be abandoned. Rent, in such a case, necessarily consists merely of *surplus profits*.'[3] Jones does not examine the conditions on which the equalization or non-equalization of the rate of return in agriculture depends. For him rent on the worst soil (the existence of which he admits) is simply due to the existence of private property in a scarce gift of nature – land.

Jones is more concerned with elucidating differential rent and its changes and with controverting Ricardo's explanation. Jones distinguishes three causes which may make rent increase. 'First, an increase of the produce from the accumulation of larger quantities of capital in its cultivation; secondly, the more efficient application of capital already employed; thirdly (the capital and produce remaining the same), the diminution of the share of the producing classes in that produce, and a corresponding increase of the share of the landlord.'[4] Ricardo had only been concerned with the third factor; but Jones

1 R. Jones, *Essay*, p. 4.
2 ibid., p. 11.
3 ibid., p. 188.
4 ibid., p. 189.

shows quite clearly that once rent exists it can rise without any change in the fertility of different pieces of land. (This, Ricardo would probably have admitted.) Reliance on diminishing returns to explain a rise in rent becomes unnecessary. Jones also shows that improvement of agricultural production was not necessarily against the interests of the landowners. It could only be so where it was more rapid than the increase in population and demand for produce. Progress in general is slow: as improvements are introduced, 'every increase of produce occasioned by the general application to old soils of more capital, acting upon them with unequal effect according to the differences of their original fertility raises rents'.[1]

Jones's great achievement in the theory of rent was that he brought out clearly the social basis which underlay Ricardo's theory. In doing so he was able to point out Ricardo's mistaken belief in a progressive deterioration of the soil, and to develop a theory of rent which shows considerable advance on the doctrine prevailing at the time. But his merit goes beyond this. His explanation of the historical evolution of different economic structures, and his extraordinarily penetrating distinction between the universal categories of economic activity and their varying social expressions put him in the select group of those who were able to combine rigorous deductive analysis with an understanding of the broad sweep of history.

## The Break Up of the Labour Theory of Value

*France*   Socialist criticism of classical political economy passed, if not unnoticed, certainly without any lasting positive influence on the development of economic thought. Its influence was negative. The pressure of the problems associated with the rise of the working class, and their theoretical expressions in the writings of socialists and others was strong enough to lead to some modification of the classical doctrine. Slowly the classical analysis was freed from the direct political implications of liberal economic theory. This process starts from the difficulties involved in the formulation of the theory of value by Adam Smith since the labour theory of value could not, in the end, be maintained without the introduction of some non-economic postulate, such as a doctrine of exploitation. Instead of continuing the attempts to

1 ibid., p. 212.

preserve the labour theory through the complications of a developed capitalist system, a number of economists in France, Germany, and England chose a different path. They did not try to show that, in spite of certain modifications, the labour theory of value held good, even where large capital equipment was used in production; nor did they continue to use the concept of the surplus in the explanation of the capitalist's profit. They gradually abandoned the labour theory of value in favour of a different principle of explanation which eliminated the idea of the surplus – in so far, at any rate, as it implied a theory of exploitation. In technical terms this involved the development of a utility theory of value and, as a corollary to it, the admission of the productivity of capital.

The beginning of this process, which was by no means continuous, is most obvious in one who was an immediate and most faithful disciple of Smith. Jean Baptiste Say (1767–1832) always regarded himself as an interpreter of Adam Smith. His *Traité d'Économie politique*, first published in 1803, claimed to be little more than a systematic exposition of Smith's main ideas. But it was much more (and much less) than that. In the process of selecting and refining, Say gave to Smith's doctrines a twist which was, in effect, an alternative to the development which they had obtained at the hands of Ricardo. Say's own contribution – apart from his already noted development of the theory of the market – consists in his emphasis on utility as the determinant of value. From this sprang his theory of the value of the factors of production, his critique of physiocracy, and his theory of the functions of the entrepreneur.

Say's utility theory of value had a certain tradition to rest on. There had been a number of eighteenth-century Italian economists who had emphasized utility. And in 1776 the Abbé Condillac had published a book, entitled *Le Commerce et le Gouvernement considérés relativement l'un à l'autre*, which contains one of the earliest statements of the utility theory. Condillac regards value as the central problem of political economy. The source of value, he say, is utility, but not in the ordinary sense of the word. With Condillac, as with the modern subjective theory of value, utility as an economic concept is no longer a physical quality of goods; it is the significance which an individual attaches to a good for the purpose of satisfying a want. Utility is, therefore, a relation; it rises and falls with want. Condillac appreciated the importance of explaining the effect of varying quantity on the value of goods, and he tried unsuccessfully to connect utility and quantity. He said that, while value rose and fell as the result of scarcity and abundance, it could only do so because utility was also present. He added that a more highly felt want would give goods a greater value than a less-felt want, and that, 'therefore', value rose with scarcity and diminished with abundance.[1] But it was left to later economists to elaborate that 'therefore' into the marginal analysis.

Condillac applied the utility theory fairly consistently to the problems of exchange, price, and distribution. The utility approach was clearly incompatible with the physiocratic ideas on productive and sterile labour. These ideas necessarily involved a denial that value could be created in the process of exchange. If the value already inherent in commodities was increased in exchange, this could not be due to anything more than a fortuitous and temporary cheating of one party by the other. Condillac claimed that both parties to the exchange gained, since they exchanged only if their judgements of the values of the commodities to them differed. In effect, each party gave up something which had less utility for something which had more utility. If followed, therefore, that all activity – agriculture, industry, and trade – which adapted the resources of nature to the satisfaction of wants was creative of utility and was productive. Agriculture was dethroned from its physiocratic preeminence. Land, capital, and labour were regarded as partners in the productive process. Their revenues were prices, determined, like those of other goods, by supply and demand; and their prices represented their shares of the co-operative product.

In spite of obscurities and inconsistencies, Condillac must be regarded as one of the most definite forerunners of the modern subjective school. His influence made itself felt indirectly through Say. The tradition of Condillac and the still existing need to eliminate what remained of physiocracy account for the peculiar interpretation which Say gave to Smith's doctrines. Say completed the emancipation from physiocracy by a radical application of the utility principle.

The details of Say's analysis of value and price are not of great importance. He started from Condillac's principle that value depended on scarcity and utility. Value in exchange was an expression of subjective estimates of utilities in terms of quantities. Cost of production influenced price only through changes of supply. It formed a lower limit above which utility was the determinant. Say thus laid the

1 E. B. de Condillac, *Le Commerce et le Gouvernement considérés relativement l'un à l'autre* (1776), part i, ch. i.

foundation for the functional relationship between cost, price, and consumer's preference which we shall find as a characteristic feature of all variants of modern theory. What was of immediate importance was the use to which Say put his theory of value in developing a theory of distribution.

In the first place, he rejected entirely Smith's distinction between productive and unproductive labour. But he did so by considering exclusively the material criterion which Smith had used occasionally, and by ignoring the other distinction made by Smith (and the physiocrats) between labour which was productive of surplus and that which was not. This made it easy for him to show that, because value depended on utility, the productivity of labour must be judged by utility standards and not by reference to the material or non-material nature of the product.

It was thus possible to regard as productive all activities which create utilities as evidenced by their ability to command a price in the market. Logically, this was a more satisfactory position than the 'material' criterion. But in the process of avoiding what later economists have sometimes regarded as Smith's scholasticism, Say also eliminated the preoccupation with the surplus; he also removed the historical basis of the revenues of the different classes of the community which, explicitly or implicitly, had been the chief feature of English and French classical political economy. The meagre hints of Condillac on the connection between distribution and value are fully developed by Say. It is clear that, once the search for the origin of the surplus is abandoned – and this follows from the elimination of the labour theory of value – Condillac's notion of production as a co-operative process in which all factors have equal status, though varying shares, is the only logical alternative. This in fact, is what Say's theory of distribution states.

The central features of this theory are the concepts of the 'productive services' and of the 'enterpreneur'. Labour, natural resources, and capital have value because they supply productive services, i.e. means for creating utilities. As one of the first of a long line of economists, Say stated the principle that the value of the factors of production was derived from the value of their products. All factors possessed both qualities necessary for the creation of value: scarcity and an indirect utility. How is the connection between the value of products and the derived value of factors established? Say did not give a complete answer to this question; but he gave the first indications of it. The entrepeneurs provide the connecting link between product and factor markets. They are 'the intermediaries who demand the productive services required for any product in relation to the demand for the product'.[1] The factors of production, actuated by a variety of motives, offer their productive services; a market is established and a price, fluctuating with supply and demand, results. Say did not agree with Ricardo in assigning a special place to rent, at any rate in the short run. He regarded the prices of all factors as dependent upon the prices of their products, thus ultimately on consumers' demands. Although he did not, perhaps, express it very clearly, Say seems to have had in mind the sort of functional connection between cost, price, wages, rent, interest, and profit which was to be developed later by the equilibrium school.

Say's groping after an equilibrium analysis of the economic process is even more in evidence in his methodological views. He was one of the first economists to emphasize the positive element of economic method. He objected to the pre-classical concern with practical policy; and he thought that even Adam Smith had been too ready to regard economic science as destined to supply guidance for the statesman. In Say's view, economics established the broad principles inherent in economic activity. It described the manner in which wealth was produced, distributed, and consumed, not by amassing facts – that was the function of statistics – but by discovering the laws which governed the relations of these facts. These laws were inherent 'in the nature of things; one does not decree, but discover them; they govern legislators and princes, and they are never violated with impunity'.[2]

To discover these laws one had to apply the Baconian method, which had been so successful in other sciences. The essence of this method was 'to admit as true only those facts which by observation and experiment have been shown to possess reality, and to admit as constant truths only those conclusions which can naturally be drawn from these facts'.[3] Economics was akin to physics. It aimed not at a complete collection of facts, but at the discovery of the cause and effect relationship between them. Physicists could employ experiment; economists could not. Say was not clear about the way in which this discrepancy was to be overcome. He never seems to have quite abandoned the idea that economics was similar to the physical

---

1 J. B. Say, *Traité d' Économie politique* (6th edition, 1841), p 349.
2 ibid., p. 13.
3 ibid., p. 3.

sciences, even though it could not use the experimental method.

What Say was pleading for was that economists should start only from premises which were general and complete. One had to take 'essential and truly influential facts'; one had to draw correct conclusions from them; and one had to be 'assured that the effect ascribed to them was really due to them and not to other causes'.[1] Given correct deduction, the validity of the conclusions depended on the completeness of the premises. In the methodological controversy between Malthus and Ricardo, Say took Malthus's side. He believed that in ignoring certain aspects of reality Ricardo had left out, not minor modifying influences, but indispensable portions of the necessary premisses. Say did not, however, agree with Malthus in applying this methodological difference to the question of accumulation and gluts. He was too successful an entrepreneur himself not to see the significance of Malthus's advocacy of unproductive consumption. But he did apply it to the problem of rent.

In England over-population and increase in the cost of subsistence seemed real dangers which might militate against continued industrial advance. In France they did not. And Say was able to wave aside Ricardo's theory of rent as having no significance in the short run, even though it might be logically valid in the distant long run.

The importance of Say's work is this: he was the first economist to cut loose entirely from the labour theory of value and all that it involved in the theory of distribution; he was also the first to stress the positive approach in economics. Say can, therefore, be regarded as one of the chief founders of the formalist, equilibrium analysis which is the essence of present-day value theory.

Say was not alone, however. In France, as well as in Germany and in England, there appeared a number of writers who, partly under the influence of Say, partly independently, were developing a utility theory of value and a productivity theory of capital. In his native country Say had an almost immediate influence in setting up a tradition. No important French economist after him returned to the Ricardian theory of value. The utility theory remained as one part of the foundation; the theories of capital developed in England – partly under Say's influence – were another. If space permitted, some of these writers would deserve to be dealt with. One of them, Jules Dupuit, must be named here as an important pioneer of the utility theory and of the

1 J. B. Say, *Traité d' Économie politique*, p. 10.

geometrical method. His discussion of price discrimination, in particular, must be regarded as one of the important contributions to the theory of monopoly. His most important writings are now available in an excellent edition.[1]

Among the individual French writers who carried on Say's tradition one is so important that he must be mentioned separately. Augustin Cournot (1801–77) was not a direct descendant of Say's school; nor has he secured a place among the most important founders of modern economics by any contribution to the utility theory of value as such. Cournot did not inquire into the causes of value at all. In his *Recherches sur les principes mathématiques de la théorie des richesses* (1838) he concentrated attention on exchange-value, which he regarded as the sole foundation of wealth in the economic sense of the term. He refused to discuss the relation between exchange-value and utility – for which he thought there was no fixed standard – though he did not imply that the utility assigned to different things by different people had nothing to do with the formation of exchange-value.[2] But being a mathematician, he saw that relations in the market could be regarded as purely formal relations; that certain categories, demand, price, supply, could be regarded as functions of one another; that it was possible, therefore, to express the relations of the market in a series of functional equations; and that economic laws could be formulated in mathematical language.

Earlier economists, said Cournot, had shrunk from the use of mathematical symbols. 'They imagined that the use of symbols and formulas could only lead to numerical calculations, and as it was clearly perceived that the subject was not suited to such numerical determination ... the conclusion was drawn that the mathematical apparatus ... was at least idle and pedantic.'[3] But mathematical symbols, he pointed out, could be used to express the relations between magnitudes without giving these magnitudes numerical values. Exchange-value was essentially a relative concept: it implied 'the idea of a ratio between two terms'.[4] It was therefore a natural field for the application of the calculus.

The results of Cournot's mathematical treatment of the problems of price in conditions of competition, monopoly, and what is now known

1 Jules Dupuit, *De l' Utilité et de sa Mesure* (ed. Marie de Bernardi, Torino, 1933).
2 A. Cournot, *The Mathematical Principles of the Theory of Wealth* (ed. I. Fisher, 1927), pp. 10–11.
3 ibid., p. 3.
4 ibid., p. 24.

as duopoly, remained completely neglected for a long time. It was only in the 1870s, when such writers as Jevons and Walras were summing up, refining, and adding to the accumulated volume of post-classical theory, that Cournot's work was resurrected. Something will be said later about the details of that work in connection with the modern school, from whom Cournot is separated only through historical accident. But it is interesting to point out the relation between Say's and Cournot's parts in the destruction of the labour theory of value.

Superficially, the difference in their approaches is striking. Cournot was concerned with a functional theory of price; Say with a causal-genetic theory of value. Cournot did not inquire into the factors which lay behind the behaviour of individuals in the market as expressed in offers and demands. His starting-points were not what he called the 'moral causes' (utility, habits, etc.), but only the conduct to which they gave rise. He had a fairly clear idea of the 'limited prices'[1] in the minds of the parties to exchange, which were the quantitative expressions of moral causes, and which were the proximate determinants of market behaviour. In other words, Cournot laid the foundation for behaviourist schools of economics which have operated with Walras's concepts of 'reserve prices' with Pareto's 'indifference curves', and, to-day, with the 'marginal rate of substitution'.

Say, on the other hand, goes a stage further back in his analysis. Indeed, he is almost entirely concerned with the force which, in the last resort, determines the behaviour of buyers and sellers. This, to his mind, is utility. He does not examine in detail the problem of price-formation to which that behaviour gives rise. This difference between Say and Cournot is repeated in our day in the differences between the utility school and the 'valueless' mathematical schools. Cournot regarded his approach as opposed to the traditional method of Smith and Say. Today also polemics between the two schools are not infrequent.

But much more fundamental than the difference is the resemblance between these two post-classical currents. It has been said that the development of the mathematical school in France was largely caused by the existence of a tradition of a utility theory of value.[2] This is indeed true in this sense: the break-away from the classical search for the causes which create value led to an emphasis on the conduct of the

1 ibid., p. 47.
2 M. Bowley, *Nassau Senior and Classical Economics*, p. 80.

individual in conditions of competition, i.e. in those of the 'cash nexus'. Both the utility school and the mathematical schools involve such an emphasis. Compared with what divides both of them from the classical economists, the points of disagreement between them, though significant, are minor. They both tend to be positive and formalist; they both avoid all explicit reference to a specific social order; they both claim, first by implication, then explicitly, that the validity of their conclusions is not bounded by the existence or non-existence of what Richard Jones called a particular 'economical structure'. These characteristics of post-classical theory have continued to exist to the present day.

*Germany.*  Germany experienced a development of a similar kind. But none of the authors who were responsible for it was of the stature of Say or Cournot. A number of them attempted to develop Smith's doctrines in the direction of a subjective utility theory. The first, Soden, went so far as to ignore value in exchange entirely and to deal exclusively with utility. In his *Die Notionalökonomie* (1804) he distinguished between positive and comparative value. The latter – the equivalent of exchange-value – was not, according to Soden, value at all. Value was positive value, i.e. the ability of goods to satisfy human wants. It underlay comparative value; but this was also based on other considerations, such as scarcity. It was, therefore, not to be regarded as value.

The next to work on similar lines was Lotz. In his *Revision der Grundbegriffe der Nationalwirtschaftslehre* (1811) and in his *Handbuch der Staatswirtschaftsllehre* (1820) he accepted Soden's definition of positive value, but made comparative value result from a comparison of two positive values. Exchange, or comparative value, depended on two factors: an inner one – the ability of a good to satisfy the want of some one other than its owner; and an external one – its scarcity. If a good possessed utility for more than one person and if the acquisition of it involved some sacrifice, then, and only then, would the good have exchange-value. Lotz went even farther in distinguishing (positive) value and price. He showed that they were connected in the sense that a good which had no value could have no price and that a good with a high value commonly had a high price. But there the connection ceased. Value was the expression of intangibles, human wants; price that of the concrete obstacles to be overcome in the creation of goods.

Hufeland's *Neue Grundlegung der Staatswirtschaftskunst* (1807–13), von Hermann's *Staatswirtschaftliche Untersuchungen* (1832), and Rau's

*Lehrbuch der politischen Ökonomie* (1826) may be mentioned among the fairly large number of other German works of the first half of the century which helped to evolve a subjective theory of value. There was a considerable agreement of opinion among German theorists on the approach to this central economic problem. Exposition was generally based on Lotz's distinction between value and price. A connection between the two was admitted to exist, but its nature was not developed in any detail. This was probably because the main concern of German writers was to elaborate the new concept of subjective value and to show up as clearly as possible how much it differed from the concept of price by which they understood what Smith had called exchange-value. The employment of a concept of exchange-value, as distinct from both use-value and price, was one of the main results of early nineteenth-century German thought. If use-value was based on ability to satisfy wants (i.e. utility), exchange-value was based on ability to exchange. Use-value arose when goods were considered from the point of view of consumption. Exchange-value was the quality which goods had when they were examined for the purpose of exchange. Price was connected with them, but not in a way that made it possible to say that price in any particular instance was determined by them.

It is not important to pursue here the further development of this line of reasoning. Lotz's dichotomy did not satisfy the requirements of a theory of value and his followers gradually departed from it. The separate categories of value persisted (they even appear in the elaborate structure of the early Austrian theory), but they were increasingly regarded as closely related. The tendency was to make the psychological explanation of value less limited in scope – to show that utility was also the ultimate determinant of price. It was one of the leaders of the historical school who first made this attempt. Hildebrand tried to show[1] that utility – in the economic sense – was a function of quantity and that this provided a connection between subjective value and price. Knies also took this view, which must be regarded as a link between the earlier and the later utility schools. Its further development in Germany (largely independent of what had gone before and ignored for a long time by subsequent authors) was due to Gossen. But his work belongs properly to the next chapter.

One other German author of the period deserves to be mentioned here: Johann Heinrich von Thünen. *Der Isolierte Staat* (first part,

---

1 B. Hildebrand, *Die Nationalökonomie der Gegenwart und Zukunft* (1848), pp. 314 *sqq*.

1826; second part, 1850) is the product of a practical interest. As a descendant of an old landowning family and himself an agriculturist, Thünen was above all concerned with problems of agricultural economics. But his approach to them was rigidly theoretical. He was a firm believer in the use of mathematical methods, though not entirely in Cournot's sense. Thünen used the numerical example more than the calculus. Yet his procedure had something in common with that of Cournot, for even when his arguments were expressed in words, they were mathematical in substance. He was most careful to set out his postulates, to define the validity of his conclusions in conformity with his initial abstractions, and to indicate the way which led back from his simplified assumptions to the complexities of reality.

Thünen said nothing about value or about causes of price. His place is nevertheless with the early utility theorists for two reasons. In the first place, Thünen generally took the existence of a certain market price for granted, and he endeavoured to develop a set of conclusions relating particularly to distribution on the basis of an assumed price. That procedure does not in itself suggest that Thünen held a subjective theory of value and price. But it is a procedure which is perfectly compatible with the utility theories which were widely current in Germany at the time. Thünen repeatedly said that he regarded Adam Smith as his teacher in economic matters. And it must be remembered that Adam Smith's doctrines were then being expounded in Germany by adherents of the utility school. In the absence of any explicit statement by Thünen himself, it is not unreasonable to suppose that he had no quarrel with the prevailing trend in the theory of value.

But what is even more important is that Thünen's contributions to the theories of production and distribution were very much in line with similar work of the utility theorists elsewhere, particularly in England. His use of the marginal analysis and his acceptance of the productivity of capital make of his work an important contributory element in the formation of modern economics.

Thünen's ideas can be briefly summarized as follows. In the first part of his book he aimed at discovering the effects upon agriculture and rent of the price of agricultural produce, of the situation of the land in relation to the market, and of taxes. For this purpose he constructed first an isolated state which had these characteristics. A very large town is situated in the middle of a fertile plain which has neither canals nor navigable rivers. At a considerable distance, the plain ends in an uncultivated wilderness. The town draws its produce from the plain, to which it supplies manufactured products. How in the circumstances will the agriculture of the plain be arranged?'[1]

The answer, though obvious, was worked out by Thünen in so careful a manner that he is rightly regarded as a forerunner of the modern theory of the location of industry. He showed that certain products (like strawberries, salads, milk, etc.), which were difficult to transport or could be sold only fresh and in small quantities, would be produced nearest the town. There would follow other forms of cultivation arranged in concentric circles round the town in accordance with the price of their products and the cost of transport. Anticipating the modern opportunity cost principle, Thünen pointed out that the price of milk would have to be such that the land on which it was produced could not be used more profitably for any other product. This he applied to other produce, too. The price for grain, for example, would have to be high enough 'to replace at least the cost of production and transport of the most distant producer, whose output the town still requires.'[2] This price will of course be a uniform price ruling throughout the market of the town. But of that price each circle of cultivation will have to deduct a sum equivalent to the cost of bringing the grain to the market. That cost increases with distance from the market; and it is easy to see that, given a price, the cost of transport will, after a certain point, swallow up the whole price. After that point, cultivation would cease, even if corn could be produced at no cost. In fact, it will cease at some time before that point is reached. Here then it is a statement about the connection between cost and price which is a part of most modern cost theories. Given a certain demand for a product, output will be increased to the point at which price just covers cost of productions.

From this a theory of rent follows naturally. Thünen distinguishes between the rent of land and the payments which are generally added to it and which are in the nature of interest on invested capital. The former is rent in the proper sense of the term, and it arises in this way. Price must be high enough to compensate the least favourably placed producer. In Thünen's words, 'the price of corn must be high enough to prevent rent from falling below zero on that farm which has the highest cost in producing and delivering to the market, but whose output is still required in order to satisfy the demand for

1 J. H. V. Thünen, *Der Isolierte Staat* (ed. H. Waentig, 1930), pp. 11–12.
2 ibid., p. 226.

corn'.[1] Because other producers have lower costs, they obtain a surplus which measures the rent yielded by their land.

Thünen's theory is not substantially different from Ricardo's doctrine of differential rent. Although he speaks of difference in fertility, Thünen does not use this as a factor in his analysis, but elaborates the whole concept in terms of differences in situation and transport cost only. The significance of this method lies in the fact that it leads to a pure 'producer's surplus' concept of rent, which made it much easier for subsequent economists to extend the concept to factors of production other than land. In addition, Thünen uses the concept of the margin even more than Ricardo had done, which again makes possible the linking of rent with the general marginal theory of the remuneration of factors of production.

Thünen himself took the first step in this direction. In the second part of *Der Isolierte Staat*, he applied essentially the same technique to wages and capital. In almost complete anticipation of the marginal productivity theory, Thünen argued that the use of additional doses of capital and labour would increase the yield of agriculture, but would also increase cost. On the analogy of the distance from the market to which cultivation would be pushed, it could be said that the labour or capital employed would be increased up to the point at which their increased cost was equal to the increased yield which they produced. In Thünen's own words, the increase in labourers 'must be continued to the point at which the extra yield obtained through the last labourer employed equals in value the wage which he receives'.[2] 'The value of the labour of the last employed labourer is also his value.'[3] 'And the wage which the last employed labourer receives must form the norm for all labourers of the same skill and ability; since for the same services it is impossible to pay unequal wages.'[4] The same holds true for capital, which Thünen defines as 'accumulated product of labour'.[5] Its yield is determined by the yield of the last particle of capital employed',[6] and all borrowed capital will be paid for at his uniform rate.

Even these few quotations shows that Thünen had a clear idea of

1 ibid., p. 226.
2 ibid., p. 415.
3 ibid., p. 576.
4 ibid., p. 577.
5 ibid., p. 423
6 ibid., p. 498.

the fundamentals of the marginal productivity theory. The whole of Part II of *Der Isolierte Staat* is a detailed examination of the implications of that theory, including even a consideration of the effects upon the remuneration of each factor of an increase in the quantity of the other. It contains also one other idea, which Thünen regarded as his most important contribution, the doctrine of the natural wage. With the aid of a complicated calculation (including the use of the differential calculus), Thünen claims to prove that the natural wage depends upon the necessities of the labourer and the product of his labour (both expressed either in kind or in money), and that if these two factors are $a$ and $p$ respectively, the formula $\sqrt{ap}$ represents the natural wage.[1] Thünen thought sufficiently highly of this formula to have it engraved on his tombstone. But to those among subsequent economists who have come under his influence he will remain noteworthy for his statement of the marginal productivity theory.

*Britain* England, as befitted the home of Ricardianism, was much slower in abandoning the labour theory of value. However, signs were not lacking even in Ricardo's day of a different approach to the problems of value and distribution. The starting-points of this development were the vacillations of Smith in the formulation of the theory of value and Ricardo's attempt to cut free from the contradictions which these vacillations created. Ricardo's solution rested on the admission of exceptions to the labour theory. These exceptions – caused by different capital structures and different periods of capital turnover – were, as Malthus pointed out, the rule. And, as we have seen, Malthus used this weakness in the Ricardian structure to go back to the inconsistencies of Adam Smith's theory of value, which he then used to attack Ricardo's theory of accumulation.

Ricardo's followers were naturally perturbed by the weakness in the labour theory which had been bequeathed to them; and for some ten years after the publication of the third edition of the *Principles* there was keen discussion on this problem. Robert Torrens laid stress on it in *An Essay on the Production of Wealth* (1821). He took for granted the existence of a uniform rate of profit (though he did not show how it arose) and concluded that capitals of equal size put into motion different quantities of current labour, without causing their products to

---

1 J. H. V. Thünen, *Der Isolierte Staat* (ed. H. Waentig, 1930), p. 542–9.

be of different values.[1] He thus stated Ricardo's exception in terms which made it clear that, in conditions of capitalist production, appearances, at any rate, contradicted the labour theory of value. Torrens did not explain this contradiction; instead, he reformulated it. The labour theory, he said, applies to that state of social development in which there has not as yet arisen a capitalist class. But once capitalists exist, it is no longer the quantity of current, but that of accumulated labour, which determines exchange-value.[2] This in effect is a return to a position taken up by Adam Smith.

The same difficulty troubled James Mill. In his *Elements of Political Economy* (1821) he endeavoured to revise the labour theory of value by insisting that capital was only accumulated labour. Profits were thus a reward for hoarded labour.[3] In this way Mill thought to have solved both the problem of the origin of profits and of the 'exceptions' to the labour theory. But he had clearly done nothing of the sort. He had admitted that capital was productive and that it was one of the determinants of exchange-value, but he thought that this made no difference to the labour theory because capital could ultimately be resolved into labour. This attitude of certainty (which contrasts strongly with Ricardo's doubts) involved Mill in many absurdities. He tried, for example, to get over the embarrassing example of the wine which, when left in the cellar, increased in value with the mere lapse of time. Those who had pressed this example had done so in order to weaken Ricardo's theory and to get him to admit as he eventually did, that the turnover of capital had an influence on value, thus creating an exception to the labour theory. Not so James Mill. 'Time', he repeated after McCulloch, 'does nothing. How then can it create value?'[4] Normally, Mill said, when we say that time has added to value, we mean that a certain portion of capital – which was nothing but hoarded labour – was expended. Therefore, he concluded that 'if the wine which is put in the cellar is increased in value one-tenth by being kept a year, one-tenth more of labour may be correctly considered as having been expended upon it'.[5] This was clearly absurd. As Samuel Bailey, one of the most vigorous critics of Ricardo, said, 'in the instance adduced, no human being by the terms of the supposition has

1 R. Torrens, *An Essay on the Production of Wealth* (1821), pp. 28 *sqq.*
2 ibid., p. 39.
3 J. Mill, *Elements of Political Economy*, pp. 70 *sqq.*
4 ibid., p. 99.
5 ibid., p. 97–8.

approached the wine, or spent upon it a moment or a single motion of his muscles'.[1] Mill was only trying to explain something by calling it by a different name.

McCulloch took a similar line. The subterfuges to which he resorted in order to present the Ricardian theory in perfect formal consistency only resulted in an indiscriminate mixture of ideas, which shows a complete misunderstanding of Ricardo's real problem. McCulloch followed Mill in regarding capital as hoarded labour. In *The Principles of Political Economy*, first published 1825, he more or less reproduced Mill's defence of the wine-in-the-cellar case.[2] His statements on value are, to put it mildly, eclectic. He distinguished between real value (defined according to the labour theory) and relative or exchange-value (which arises in the exchange of two commodities). Real value and exchange-value may be equal. Normally, any exchange will be an exchange of equivalent real values. This holds true for exchange between the capitalist and the labourer. To explain the origin of the surplus in spite of this, McCulloch simply falls back on Smith's and Malthus's doctrine that the value of a commodity is determined by the amount of labour which it can command. This is as a rule greater than the real value of the commodity and the discrepancy is profit. Unless such a discrepancy existed, 'a capitalist would have no motive to lay out stock on the employment of labour; for his profit depends on his getting back the produce of a greater quantity of labour than he advances.' This, superficially, sounds almost the identical deduction from Ricardo as Marx's theory of surplus value. Indeed, McCulloch goes on to say, 'when he [the capitalist] buys labour, he gives the produce of that which has been performed for that which is *to be* performed'.[3] And this exchange between 'living' and 'embodied' labour (or between labour and capital) had the peculiar quality of giving rise to a surplus. But this is only a superficial resemblance. For with Ricardo, and even more with Marx, the problem was how to explain the surplus within a labour theory of value. With McCulloch, however, the futile attempt to provide such an explanation was abandoned. The surplus became akin to the mercantilist 'profit upon alienation'.

These difficulties of the post-Ricardians were due to their inability

1 S. Bailey, *A Critical Dissertation on the Nature, Measures, and Causes of Value, etc.* (1825) (London School of Economics Reprint, 1931), pp. 219–20.
2 J. R. McCulloch, *The Principles of Political Economy* (1849), pp. 372–3.
3 ibid., p. 320.

to work out a reconciliation between the phenomena of the market in conditions of capitalist production and the labour theory of value. The attacks upon the labour theory, therefore, derived additional strength from the ineffective defences of such writers as Torrens, James Mill, and McCulloch.

Perhaps the strongest attack at the time was that of Samuel Bailey. *A Critical Dissertation on the Nature, Measure and Causes of Value*, published in 1825, was written, as the sub-title informs us, 'Chiefly in Reference to the Writings of Mr. Ricardo and his Followers'. Bailey was able to uncover many of Ricardo's mistakes, and so to discredit the labour theory of value. He did not himself replace it by another theory of value; but he made the beginnings of an approach that was to be adopted later.

Adam Smith had elucidated the significance of the labour theory by concentrating attention on the origin of the phenomenon of exchange-value. He had, however, failed to push the analysis of the concept to its logical conclusions. Ricardo went to the other extreme. He neglected to discuss the historical bases of the phenomenon and the social quality of the concept. His interest was mainly in the variations in exchange-value, that is in its relative aspect. He did not make clear the distinction between the quality of exchange-value as such, the size of that exchange-value and the relation between the exchange-values of different commodities.

Here Bailey's criticism sets in. He sees that exchange-value appears as a quantitative relation between two things, and he refuses to go any further. For him the whole problem of value is solved by the statement that exchange-value involves, in practice, a relation. In an ultimate sense, he says, value denotes 'the esteem in which any object is held'.[1] It reflects a state of mind of the subject and not a quality possessed by the object. This esteem cannot arise when objects are viewed in isolation. It has its origin in a comparison of two things. The relative esteem to which a comparison gives rise 'can be denoted only by quantity'.[2] Bailey adopts, therefore, one of the definitions with which Adam Smith had toyed, and which identified value with purchasing power.

Two thoughts continue to run side by side in Bailey's book. The more important one is that which makes value into a relation and

1 S. Bailey, *A Critical Dissertation*, p. 1.
2 ibid., p. 3.

nothing more. 'As we cannot speak of the distance of any object without implying some other object, between which and the former this relation exists, so we cannot speak of the value of a commodity but in reference to another commodity compared with it. A thing cannot be valuable in itself without reference to another thing'.[1] The labour theory of value was clearly incompatible with this view.

On the other hand, Bailey himself seems to have regarded the purely relative conception of value as insufficient. His mention of esteem and utility at the beginning of his discussion (which seems to have been due to the influence of Say) shows that he was trying to link up the functional relations which appear in the market with some fundamental causative influence: that he was trying to find a constant. He did not succeed and subsequent utility theorists have criticized him for his failure to trace the connection between utility and exchange-value.[2] Bailey states, it is true, that 'an inquiry into the causes of value is, in reality, an inquiry into those external circumstances, which operate so steadily upon the minds of men, in the interchange of the necessaries, comforts and conveniences of life, as to be subjects of inference and calculation'.[3] But he does not proceed to discuss the implications of subjective valuation. Indeed, he agrees in the end that in the class of commodities which can be increased at will, and in the production of which there is no restriction of competition, cost of production is the determinant of value. The cost of production 'may be either labour or capital, or both'.[4] In other cases, such as monopolies and goods produced under conditions of diminishing returns (for example those requiring the factor land), the analysis must be that of monopoly price.

Bailey's criticism of Ricardo derived from the latter's search for an invariable measure of value. This, in Ricardo, was merely a confused way of seeking an explanation of the phenomenon of value as such. But it gave Bailey an opportunity for saying some very pertinent things on the question of the measurement of value. Here, his 'relativism' had particular significance: it helped to show up the difference between measure of value in the transcendental sense in which the classics following Aristotle had understood it, i.e. of the inherent cause and substance of value (with which Bailey would have nothing to do), and measure of value in the sense of a quantitative relation between two

1 S. Bailey, *A Critical Dissertation*, p. 5.
2 Cf., for example, R. Zuckerkandl, *Zur Theorie des Preises*, pp. 72–4.
3 S. Bailey, *A Critical Dissertation*, p. 180.
4 ibid., p. 205.

goods, in particular, between a good and money. This latter conception leads Bailey to show that changes in value must affect both commodities that are compared. The search for an invariable measure of value is, therefore, illusory. Bailey shows[1] that money fulfils adequately the function of an external measure of value, although it follows from his definition that it cannot itself be of constant value. He uses this point as an argument for severely circumscribing the validity of price comparisons in time. The modern theory of index numbers has taken a similar line.[2] Bailey's object, however, was to show that once the problem of finding an invariable measure of value had disappeared, the problem of discovering the determinants of value as something separate from price had gone too. He thought that he had put another nail into the coffin of the labour theory of value.

In addition to these frontal attacks, the development of alternative approaches to the value problem helped to destroy this part of the Ricardian structure. Already in 1804 the Earl of Lauderdale, in *An Inquiry into the Nature and origin of Public Wealth, and into the Means and Causes of its Increase*, had expressed views which closely resembled those of Say. Lauderdale also based himself on Condillac and infused a utility element into his interpretation of Adam Smith's theory of value. Wealth, he said, is everything that possesses utility; but individual riches possess utility and scarcity. These two elements determine value. They find expression in demand and supply; and an alteration of either will affect value. Lauderdale examined the effects of increases and decreases of demand and supply upon value in something like the same way in which modern economists analyse the elasticity of demand. He rejected the distinction between productive and unproductive labour, and adapted Say's views on the factors of production. He applied his theories in an eccentric way to problems of public finance; but his main claim to notice in the development of English economic doctrine is definitely his kinship with Say.

The subsequent development of the utility analysis seems to have been due to a number of economists who remained neglected for a long time. In 1903 attention was directed to some of them,[3] and since then their part in the history of doctrine has become widely recognized. The assignment of paternity of ideas among these writers is a

1 S. Bailey, *A Critical Dissertation*, chs. v, vi, vii.
2 Cf., for example, G. Haberler, *Der Sinn der Indexzahlen* (1927).
3 E. R. A. Seligman, 'On Some Neglected British Economists', *Economic Journal*, vol. xiii, 1903, pp. 335 *sqq.* and pp. 511 *sqq*; reprinted in *Essays in Economics* (1925), ch. iii.

matter of some dispute; and the sequence in which some of them are here mentioned is not necessarily to be taken as the correct chronological order in which the ideas represented were born.

Richard Whately, who later became Archbishop of Dublin, had occasion to occupy himself with economics during his short tenure (as second occupant) of the Drummond Chair of Political Economy at Oxford, 1830–1. The conditions of the Chair included one which required the publication of at least one lecture a year. The result of this provision was the publication in 1831 of Whately's *Introductory Lectures on Political Economy*. Prior to that, Whately had come into contact with Nassau Senior, who had preceded him in the Drummond Chair and who had written the economic section of an Appendix on 'Ambiguous Terms' in Whately's *Elements of Logic*, first published in 1826. It is difficult to say whether Whately was expressing original views or voicing those which he had heard from others, particularly Senior. At any rate, the *Introductory Lectures* are noteworthy for their emphasis on utility and for a passing but highly influential reference to the relation between cost and value.

Whately reveals his approach at once by suggesting that the best name for economic science would be *Catallactics*, or the science of exchanges, because '.man might be defined as "An animal that makes *Exchanges*": no other, even of those animals which in other points make the nearest approach to rationality, having, to all appearances, the least notion of bartering, or in any way exchanging one thing for another.'[1] For Whately utility and wealth were relative and subjective. And modern subjectivists have often adopted Whateley's term, 'catallactics', in order to stress the fact that they regard choice as the essence of the economic problem.

Whately[2] did not develop a subjective theory of value to any extent. He rejected, however, the idea that labour was essential to create value; and in a passage which has been quoted many times he expressed what he thought to be the real relation between cost and price. 'It is not', he said, 'that pearls fetch a high price *because* men have dived for them; but on the contrary, men dive for them because they fetch a high price.'[3] It has also been suggested recently that Whately was one of those who, in company with Nassau Senior, extended the

---

1 E. R. A. Seligman, 'On Some Neglected British Economists', *Economic Journal*, vol. xiii, 1903, pp. 335 *sqq.* and pp. 511 *sqq*; reprinted in *Essays in Economics* (1925), ch. iii.
2 R. Whately, *Introductory Lectures on Political Economy* (second edition, 1832), pp. 6–7.
3 ibid., p. 253.

rent analysis by making rent arise from immobilities in the factors of production.[1] Otherwise Whately cannot be said to have contributed much.

Whately's successor at Oxford, W. F. Lloyd, was also a representative of the utility school. Again, it is impossible to say whether, as has been suggested,[2] Lloyd was repeating views acquired from Senior. But Lloyd was certainly in the same tradition. Like Bailey, he describes value as being ultimately a 'feeling of the mind'; but he adds the important point that this feeling will show itself 'at the margin of separation between satisfied and unsatisfied wants'. To this clear anticipation of a formulation made famous by the marginalist school, Lloyd added a statement on the connection between quantity and utility which is of a piece with it. For 'an increase in quantity', he said, 'will at length exhaust, or satisfy to the utmost, the demand for any specific object of desire'.[3]

An even fuller anticipation of marginal utility doctrine is to be found in the *Lectures on Political Economy* (1834) of Mountifort Longfield, the first holder of the Chair of Political Economy at Trinity College, Dublin, endowed by Whately after his appointment to the archbishopric. Clearly, the tradition was spreading. Utility, according to Longfield, is the power which an article has 'of satisfying one or more of the various wants or desires of mankind'; a definition which, as he rightly points out, gives the word a wider meaning than that which it has in everyday language. Value, he says, implies utility; for each article they are both proportional to each other, as far as a single individual is concerned. Exchange ensures that a person shall have that combination of goods which 'in proportion to their value be of the greatest utility to him'. In exchange 'each party to it has gained something, by receiving for the article he disposed something which is, *relative to him*, of more utility ...'. As for the measure of value, Longfield shares Bailey's relativism; he considers that labour is often the best measure.[4]

Later, Longfield examines value in detail. Exchange arises because a definite quantity of a particular commodity is sufficient to satisfy the want for it. People are, therefore, induced to part with their surpluses

1 M. Bowley, *Nassau Senior and Classical Economics*, pp. 106, 131–2.
2 ibid., p. p. 108.
3 W. F. Lloyd, *Lecture on the Notion of Value* (1834), pp. 16 and 9, quoted in M. Bowley, *Nassau Senior and Classical Economics*, p. 108.
4 M. Longfield, *Lectures on Political Economy* (1834) (London School of Economics Reprint, 1931), pp. 25–8.

for those of others. Everybody will be anxious to buy as cheaply and to sell as dearly as possible. Competition – which Longfield describes in detail – will ensure an equality between supply and demand. Cost of production will influence price through its effect on supply.[1]

In his sixth lecture he amplifies his statements on value in such a way as to include a reference to the margin. He repeats the statement that price is determined by supply and demand (behind the one is cost of production, behind the other utility), and that it will be an amount which equates supply with effectual demand, that is, demand backed by purchasing power. Then he examines further the influence of demand on price. 'The measure of the intensity of any person's demand for any commodity is the amount which he would be willing and able to give for it, rather than remain without it.' Now while there may be demands which cannot lead to a purchase, they have nevertheless an influence on price. 'Of this an example is, the demand of those who will not purchase at the existing prices, but who would come into the market and purchase, if a slight reduction should take place. Such a demand always does exist, and has an effect in keeping up prices, exactly similar to the bidding at an auction of the person who is next in amount of that of the actual purchaser.'[2]

This leads to the further point that, although intensities of demand differ between different purchasers, they all buy at a uniform market price which equates supply and demand. From this Longfield's most important statement follows. If the price is raised only slightly above the market price, 'the demanders, who by the change will cease to be purchasers, must be those the intensity of whose demand was precisely measured by the former price. Before the change was made, the demand, which was less intense, did not lead to a purchase, and after the change is made, the demand, which is more intense, will lead to a purchase still. Thus the market price is measured by that demand, which being of the least intensity, yet leads to actual purchases.'[3] No modern exponent of the marginal utility theory could object to this formulation.

Applying the doctrine to wages, Longfield makes another anticipation of the marginal productivity theory. He rejected the subsistence theory; and contended that the wages of the labourer depended 'upon

1 ibid., pp. 44–63.
2 ibid., pp. 11–12.
3 M. Longfield, *Lectures on Political Economy* (1834) (London School of Economics Reprint, 1931), p. 113.

the value of his labour, and not upon his wants, whether natural or acquired ...'. The level of subsistence had only influence on population.[1] (Longfield here takes the opportunity to distinguish carefully between short and long run movements, or what he calls 'primary or immediate causes ... and those whose influence is remote and secondary'.[2]) Wages depend on supply and demand. The former is the 'existing race of labourers'. Demand depends on 'the utility or value of the work which they [the labourers] are capable of performing'. To ascertain the wages of labourers one has to apply the principles which – so Longfield specially mentions – have already been stated.[3] 'The share of the article which each labourer will receive, is found by computing how much of the entire value consists of labour, and how much of profit, and then dividing the former share among the labourers, in proportion to the quantity and value of each man's labour.'[4]

This principle is applied to capital with greater clarity.[5] Capital is useful because it advances wages to the workers before the consumer has bought the product. It also helps to make labour more productive. The profits on capital, given its supply, will depend on the demand, that is, on its productiveness. Again, however, competition establishes a uniform rate which 'will be regulated by the portion of it [capital] which is obliged to be employed with the least efficiency in assisting labour. ... This extends to the profits of capital that principle of an equality between the supply and the effectual demand which in all cases regulates value.'[6]


## Senior

Of all the forerunners of the utility analysis, Nassau William Senior has suffered least from neglect. But even he has had to wait until fairly recently for an extensive study. Senior was not quite so striking an exponent of the subjective theory of value as some of the writers

1 ibid., p. 206.
2 ibid., p. 207.
3 ibid., pp. 209–10.
4 ibid., pp. 211–12.
5 ibid., Lecture IX.
6 M. Longfield, *Lectures on Political Economy* (1834) (London School of Economics Reprint, 1931), p. 193.

already mentioned. In particular, his account of the marginal utility analysis is not nearly so elaborate as that of Longfield. Although Senior was influenced by Say and by German writers, his theory of value and distribution aimed less at providing an alternative to that of Ricardo than at reconciling it with the new current of thought. Senior may therefore be regarded as the first important representative of the tendency to compromise and synthesize which has been a characteristic feature of the tradition of English economic thought, best exemplified by John Stuart Mill and Alfred Marshall. Senior's attitude to problems of economic and social policy is also of interest on account of the influence which it had on his views of the scope and method of economics.

Nassau William Senior (1790–1864) was of a type which became more common after his time: that of the economist who takes an important advisory part in the affairs of government. He was twice Professor of Political Economy at Oxford (once as the first holder of the Drummond Chair in 1825–30 and again in 1847–52) and, for a short time, Professor at King's College, London. Most of the rest of his life was occupied with the study of many social and economic questions as a member of government commissions and in other ways. His theoretical views were, therefore, developed in close contact with his experience of practical affairs and against the background of his political attitude. From the ample information about his work which is now available the clear impression results that Senior can claim to share with John Stuart Mill the distinction of having laid the foundation for the theoretical and political compromise which is the great legacy of neo-classical English economics. But while Senior may even claim priority, he was not only a much smaller and less influential figure than Mill, but his writings do not reflect so clearly the problems which the position of compromise involved.

In regard to the theories of value and distribution, Senior endeavoured to reconcile Say and Ricardo. In what is the most complete statement of his theoretical work, *An Outline of the Science of Political Economy* (first published in 1836 as an article in the *Encyclopaedia Metropolitana*), he defines wealth as everything which is susceptible of exchange or which possesses value. Three qualities are necessary to this end: transferability, relative scarcity, and utility. The last is defined in the wide sense, already common at that time, as the power to give gratification of any kind. It is an indispensable constituent of value; but as it is modified by innumerable causes Senior

implies that relative scarcity is, in practice, the most important determinant of value. This limitation of supply is purely relative: that is in
comparison with want. Transferability means that the utility of the
good in question can be appropriated permanently or for a time. The
inclusion of this quality aims at destroying the material criterion which
was a legacy from Adam Smith.[1]

This preliminary account of the determinants of value (and of
wealth) is noteworthy for the inclusion of a reference to diminishing
utility which, although it is not as elaborate as that of some other
forerunners of the doctrine, is quite explicit. 'Our desires', said Senior,
'do not aim so much at quantity as at diversity. Not only are there limits
to the pleasure which commodities of any given class can afford, but
the pleasure diminishes in a rapidly increasing ratio long before those
limits are reached. Two articles of the same kind will seldom afford
twice the pleasure of one and still less will ten give five times the
pleasure of two. In proportion, therefore, as any article is abundant,
the number of those who are provided with it, and do not wish, or wish
but little, to increase their provision, is likely to be great; and so far as
they are concerned, the additional supply loses all, or nearly all, its
utility.'[2]

In the more detailed examination of value, utility is not explicitly
given a prominent position. This no doubt accounts for the fact that
Senior's theory has generally been regarded as an extension of the
cost-of-production theory into which the post-Ricardians had transformed the labour theory. Under the heading of 'Value' Senior does
little more than state that relative utility and relative scarcity will
determine the ratio in which one commodity will exchange for another.
It is only under 'Distribution' that he analyses the determination of
price – as he by then calls it – more closely. He points out that
'comparative limitation of supply . . . though not sufficient to constitute
value, is by far its most important element; utility, or, in other words,
demand, being mainly dependent on it.' Supply is affected by three
instruments of production: 'human Labour and Abstinence and the
spontaneous agency of nature.' Senior takes this classification as a
basic datum before proceeding to examine 'the obstacles which limit
the supply of all that is produced, and the mode in which those

1 N. W. Senior, *An Outline of the Science of Political Economy* (1836; offprint from
*Encyclopaedia Metropolitana*), pp. 131–2.
2 ibid., p. 133.

obstacles affect the reciprocal values of the different subjects of exchange'.[1]

This examination turns entirely on the relation between cost and price. In it Senior did two things with the theory of value as he found it. In the first place, he eliminated Ricardo's exceptions from the labour theory of value by rejecting the idea that the labour embodied in a commodity was the source and measure of its value; and he adopted a definition of cost of production which admitted the productivity of capital under the term 'abstinence'. The represents an attempted solution of the post-Ricardian dilemma of explaining profits while preserving the labour theory. In the second place, Senior limited the influence of cost of production, even as he had defined it, and stressed the influence of demand or utility. This second line of thought represents the influence of Say and of other utility theorists.

Senior begins by stating that 'the obstacle to the supply of those commodities which are produced by labour and abstinence, with that assistance only from nature which every one can command, consists solely in the difficulty of finding persons ready to submit to the labour and abstinence necessary to their production. In other words, their supply is limited by their cost of production.'[2] The latter is defined as 'the sum of the labour and abstinence necessary to production'.[3] The inclusion of abstinence aimed at overcoming the difficulty of James Mill, McCulloch, Torrens, and others who did not know how to make profits a part of the value of commodities. It avoided Mill's absurdity in the wine-in-the-cellar case which made time equivalent to labour; and while it avoided the inclusion of profits as such, it added 'that conduct which is repaid by profits',[4] that is, something which Senior clearly meant to be of the same quality as the exertion which was termed labour.

But this cost of production determined price only in the case of those commodities in the production of which, as stated above, the assistance from nature is one 'which every one can command'; in other words, in which the factors of production are freely accessible to all, in which, therefore, there is free competition. But even in these conditions cost of production is only 'the regulator of price', because in

1 ibid., p. 168.
2 ibid., p. 169.
3 ibid., ch. xx, p. 171.
4 ibid., p. 170.

actual fact the adjustment of supply which brings about equality of cost and price takes some time.

In other situations which were monopolistic, the importance of cost of production was even smaller. Senior distinguished four such cases of monopoly. In the first, 'the monopolist has not the exclusive power of producing, but only certain exclusive facilities as a producer, and can increase, with undiminished, or even increased facility, the amount of his produce'.[1] Here the power of the monopolist (the owner of a patent, for example) is limited. He cannot charge a price higher than the cost of production that would be incurred by those who do not possess his special facility. On the other hand, since he will probably have economies of large-scale production, his price will tend to fall in order to stimulate a wider demand. Although he will still make a large profit, his own interest and that of the public will coincide.[2]

In the second case the monopolist is in complete control of the output, but the size of that output cannot be varied. Cost of production must still form a lower limit to price. But there is no upper limit: price will be determined by demand. The third case is intermediate between the two. The monopolist 'is the only producer, but, by the application of additional labour and abstinence, can indefinitely increase his production'. Here there is again no upper limit; but otherwise the conditions will be those of the first case.[3]

Finally, there is the situation in which 'the monopolist is not the only producer, but has peculiar facilities which diminish and ultimately disappear as he increases the amount of his produce'.[4] This is a situation in which a factor of production of varying quality is used and in which returns diminish. It applies particularly to land; and it gives rise to rent. Senior calls this case one of 'unequal competition'. Price 'has a constant tendency to coincide with the cost of production of that portion which is continued to be produced at the greatest expense'.[5] Those who produce at a lower cost will reap an additional profit.

So far Senior's theory of value is only a consistent development of an already existing tendency. It is a supply-and-demand theory, and cost of production is assigned its place in the determination of supply. On the face of it, the influence of utility is not very marked. Demand is

1 ibid.
2 ibid., p. 172.
3 ibid.
4 ibid., p. 175.
5 ibid., p. 176.

taken for granted and no attempt is made to go into the causes that determine it. There is not the approach that characterizes the writings of the contemporaneous German economists or even of Longfield and Lloyd. The method is that of Bailey, that is, a conscious development on a Ricardian basis but away from Ricardian difficulties.

In his discussion of distribution Senior shows a little more clearly the influence of the subjectivist current. The derivation of the value of the factors from the value of their products was more in the tradition of Say and the Germans. With regard to rent, Senior admitted in the first place that rent would exist so long as a scarce factor of production (for example land) was used, even if every portion of it was equally productive.[1] In the second place – consistently with this view of rent – he extended the application of the concept to factors of production other than land, for example fixed capital and natural talents.[2]

His treatment of wages is somewhat obscure. He did not develop a cost-of-production theory of wages, presumably because in this connection the break with the labour theory of value would have appeared less striking – and he excluded population almost entirely from his analysis of wages. On the whole, he seems to have inclined to a productivity theory – in harmony with the approach of Say and Longfield; but he cast it in the form of the wage-fund doctrine which remained a somewhat troublesome feature of economic theory for some time. The notion that there was a fund designed to be laid out in wages was not new but had been used by Smith and Ricardo. Senior stated the perfectly obvious proposition that, on the average, the real wages obtained by the worker during a year must be the ratio between the amount of commodities set aside during that year for the maintenance of the working population and the size of that population.[3] This, however, he described as the proximate cause of wages; the fund set aside for wages had to be determined next. Senior did not get very far with this problem, but he did indicate the elements of a solution. The first was the productivity of labour, the determinants of which he analysed at some length.[4] The second (which Senior complicated by the addition of others) was the relation of wages and profits.[5] In other

1 N. W. Senior, *An Outline of the Science of Political Economy*, p. 178.
2 E.g. ibid., pp. 166–7; cf. also M. Bowley, *Nassau Senior and Classical Economics*, part i, ch. iii.
3 N. W. Senior, *An Outline of the Science of Political Economy*, p. 193.
4 ibid., p. 201–4.
5 ibid., p. 206.

words, Senior made the theory of wages abut on the theory of capital.

The striking feature of Senior's theory was the admission of the productivity of capital and the introduction of the term abstinence. The latter he defined as 'that agent, distinct from labour and the agency of nature, the concurrence of which is necessary to capital, and which stands in the same relation to profit as labour does to wages'.[1]

Senior did not say much about the determinants of abstinence; although those who wish to do so may see in some of his remarks the beginnings of a theory of time-preference, which was later to be developed by the Austrians.[2] But he examined at somewhat greater length the cause at the back of the demand for capital, namely, its ability to make labour more productive. The account of the place of capital goods (for the creation of which abstinence was an indispensable agent) in the process of production[3] can justly be regarded as a forerunner of the Austrian theory of roundabout production. When read in the light of his treatment of capital, Senior's statement of the wage-fund doctrine is also seen to be more akin to its more sophisticated modern versions than to the truism which was found inadequate by later economists.

The question as to the weight to be assigned to the different ingredients which went to make up Senior's economic theory is futile, and in a sense based on a misconception. The traditional view expressed, for example, by Cannan and Böhm-Bawerk,[4] regards Senior's contributions as mere emendations of Ricardianism still based on a 'real cost' concept, which had become more elaborate than that expressed in the labour theory of value. Senior's more recent interpreter is at pains to show that he had moved farther away from Ricardo than has hitherto been admitted, and that he was working towards a formal equilibrium theory – with a strong subjective element – of the modern kind.[5] Both views contain elements of truth. The discussion of cost of production, for example, with the introduction of

1 ibid., p. 153.

2 N. W. Senior, *An Outline of the Science of Political Economy*, pp. 153, 187. Miss Bowley (*Nassau Senior and Classical Economics*, pp. 148 *sqq.*) admits that Senior did not really develop a time-*diasgio* theory of the supply of capital, but she claims that he was on the way to doing so.

3 ibid., pp. 153 *sqq.*

4 E. Cannan, *Theories of Production and Distribution* (1924), pp. 213–4; and *A Review of Economic Theory* (1929), p. 187. E. V. Böhm-Bawerk, *Capital and Interest* (1922), Book IV, ch. ii.

5 M. Bowley, *Nassau Senior and Classical Economics*, particularly section i, chs. ii and iv.

the concept of abstinence, and the analysis of rent bear the obvious marks of the post-Ricardian controversies between Bailey, Malthus, Torrens, Mill, and McCulloch. On the other hand, it is true to say that Senior's theory of capital amounts 'to saying that the equilibrium rate of profits, or interest, is determined by the equalization of demand, depending on the productivity of capital, and supply at a level just sufficient to pay for the sacrifice involved in saving'; a theory which is similar to that of Marshall.[1]

But there need be no quarrel between the two interpretations. What is important is not whether Senior was closer to the Continental school or to the English post-Ricardians, but how far he had moved from Ricardo himself. Senior's predecessors in England, no less than the Continental authors, had effectively broken with Ricardo before Senior added his contribution. They did so in somewhat different ways, though these ways ultimately coalesced (a coalescence which is already obvious in Senior); but characteristic of both ways is the abandonment of the search for an objective 'real-cost' concept. The one school did it by stressing utility and by deriving from it the notion of productive services; the other by developing a cost-of-production theory in which the productivity of capital is admitted. And once it had done that, it is only natural that it should have incorporated the utility approach. The purpose is the same: to avoid the concept of 'real-cost' and of the 'surplus'; in relation to which the labour, or any other real-cost theory of value alone has significance. True, the cost-of-production theory in Senior's formulation still contains a 'real cost' (with abstinence now allied to labour); but this is quite different from Ricardo's doctrine, because it is now made subjective. In this, and as we shall see, in later English versions of the same theory, the inclusion of profit and interest in cost of production and of its source (under some name or other) in the factors creative of value, destroys the basis of the 'real-cost' theory of value.

In this change may be seen a reflection of the greater degree of development of industrial capitalism. The main factor was no longer hostility from the landowners (hence Senior's generalization of rent, as against Ricardo's treatment of it as a very special form of income). The effect of the new doctrines was to make capital as legitimate a source of income as labour; and whatever attenuations Senior's 'abstinence' suffered at the hands of later economists, he clearly meant the term to

---

1 M. Bowley, *Nassau Senior and Classical Economics*, p. 103.

carry a certain moral significance. With the acceptance of his theory the debate was moved from the ground of class conflict to that of justice. The question was now what should be the proportionate shares of the product of industry that became profits and wages. Monopoly and avoidable exploitation rather than the system as such became the objects that the working class might justly attack. In this development may be seen, on the one hand, the new status of both the capitalist and the labourer (and their opposing interests); on the other, a greater generalization of the theory itself, of which the full flower appears some decades later.

It is not surprising that economic policy should have become an important field of discussion. With the economic order taken for granted, attention was concentrated on the problem of making capital-ism work smoothly. Senior's writings show clearly that the concern with this problem was increasing. It now seems that, on the general question of the scope of government action, he held less rigid views than was at one time supposed. On the allied question of the scope of economics, his views seem to have fluctuated largely in accordance with his own experience of specific problems of policy.

It has been shown[1] that Senior was not an uncompromising advocate of *laissez-faire*. In his earliest statements he limited the sphere of government action to the traditional 'police' duties. But he soon found – significantly, as the result of dealing with social problems of the more backward economy of Ireland – that distress might exist in spite of the tendency of the economic process to create an output and a distribution in accordance with the workers' own exertion and fore-sight. Such distress was properly a matter for government action. It was not only a right, but even 'the imperious duty of Government' to alleviate it. But an overriding consideration for all social services was the maintenance of 'industry, forethought, and charity'.[2] In one place, Senior went so far as to advocate the advance of public money 'to facilitate emigration, and for the formation of roads, canals, and har-bours', together with measures designed to rid Ireland of feudal survivals.[3] The public works were intended to raise the productivity of Irish labour and so to obviate the necessity for the introduction of poor relief. But it is an interesting fact that these measures were suggested

1 M. Bowley, *Nassau Senior and Classical Economics*, section ii, ch. i.
2 N. W. Senior, *Letter to Lord Howick on a legal provision for the Irish Poor* (1831), pp. 11–12.
3 ibid., p. 45–6.

for Ireland, and that Senior never made similar suggestions for England. They should, therefore, perhaps not be regarded as conclusive evidence of Senior's departure from the liberal path.[1]

There were many English social problems on which Senior advised either as a member of government commissions or in a private capacity. The three best-known instances are the Poor Law Reform of 1834, the discussion of the Factory Act in 1837, and the inquiry into the condition of the hand-loom weavers in 1841. It is not necessary to go into the details of Senior's arguments in all these cases. He did not always appear as a doctrinaire upholder of non-interventionism. In fact, one may readily grant that he was prepared to advocate government action so long as he did not regard it as interfering unduly with the free working of economic laws. He opposed the Factory Act with the notorious argument (bitterly attacked by Marx[2]) that the last two hours of the day's labour alone constituted the capitalist's profit. Instead of a limitation of the hours of labour to ten (which would have injured the industrialist), he suggested the improvement of housing conditions (the burden being placed on the landlord).

*The Report of the Commission on the Condition of Hand-loom Weavers* (1841) is not very dogmatic. It accepts, however, the relative decline in the demand for the products of the hand-loom weavers as a consequence of competition, and it resigns itself to the doctrine of the impotence of the state to prevent it. Education, the prohibition of trade unions, limitation on entry into different trades, better housing (again at the expense of landlord and builder), and the abolition of some import duties which raised the cost of living, were advocated as palliatives.

On the Poor Law, Senior's views were perhaps more definitely coloured by the radical belief in the virtues of free competition. He did nevertheless agree with the necessity of relieving the able-bodied poor, provided that a system of administration could be devised which would avoid the evils of the old Poor Law and would not interfere with the free labour market. The principle of 'less eligibility' and the workhouse test represented the compromise between the anxiety not to hamper competition and the necessity to relieve destitution.

Altogether, Senior appears to have been more ready to compromise than has generally been believed. But although this readiness was due

1 M. Bowley, *Nassau Senior and Classical Economics*, pp. 247–8.
2 Marx, *Das Kapital*, vol. i, pp. 185 *sqq. Theorien über den Mehrwert*, vol. iii, p. 566.

to the absence of a dogmatic faith in non-intervention as a principle of politics, it was not the result of any clearly thought-out theory of the relation between economic theory and policy. It has been shown that Senior's views on this relation fluctuated.[1] His earliest position was the traditional one which recognized the existence of a science and an art of economics which were closely connected. But his experiences in practical affairs seem to have led to a much more formal view of the results of theoretical inquiry. In the *Political Economy* (1836) the function of the economist was conceived as purely positive and analytical. The economist might not advise even though he was elucidating principles which the legislator and the statesman would probably have to take into account. The problems of human welfare are solved by reference to many other considerations besides, and even to the exclusion of, economic ones. Finally, during his second tenure of the Drummond Chair, Senior once again distinguished between the science of economics and two economic arts concerned with a study of institutions and of the relation between wealth and welfare. Science and art were closely connected. But because the science was not yet perfected, one could speak on practical issues only on the basis of one's own interpretation of the conclusions of the science. And in any case, decisions are made by men not *qua* economists, but *qua* statesmen.

This general attitude, though indeterminate, was well suited to the practical issues on which Senior and other economists were then being asked to advise. The attack on certain phenomena of capitalism and on capitalism itself, particularly from the working class, was already powerful enough to make it impossible for the defenders of the system to resort to *a priori* non-interventionism. The view outlined by Senior gave the defence a chance to make the best of any individual case. That this best was conceived in terms, not fundamentally different in aim from the earlier, more intransigent, *laissez-faire*, is demonstrated clearly by Senior's conclusions in individual instances. And nothing throws more light on his general attitude than his violent opposition to trade unionism.[2]

---

1 M. Bowley, *Nassau Senior and Classical Economics*, section i, ch. i and section ii.
2 Sidney and Beatrice Webb, *History of Trade Unionism* (1926), pp. 139–41.

# *Mill*

*Political Philosophy* No writer was ever more carefully trained to carry on a tradition than was John Stuart Mill (1806–73). He was intended to be an uncompromising exponent of pure classical economic theory and of liberal philosophy. Today, we can see more clearly that his summing up of the economic and political discussions of half a century was necessary to complete the process of disintegration of doctrines which changing economic conditions had made inadequate. Estimates of Mill's position have tended to two extremes. To many generations of students, his *Principles* were the undisputed bible of economic doctrine. They represented the final synthesis of classical theory and of the refinements introduced by post-Ricardian writers. They were comprehensive, systematic; and, with few exceptions, they presented their theorems without pugnacity which strengthened the impression of assurance and of unquestioned authority.

That authority rested, in part, on the belief that in Mill Ricardianism had found its most complete elaboration. More recently, however, Mill has been seen to stand half-way in the evolution of economic analysis away from Ricardo's doctrines. In relation to what finally emerged, he can hardly be considered to have been pre-eminent among the pioneers. The rise of the marginal school in the last quarter of the century dislodged Mill. From being an indispensable textbook, the *Principles* became an object of largely historical interest. Mill's part in laying the foundations of the new economics was regarded as comparatively insignificant, and his usefulness to modern students as almost negligible. From the point of view of the history of economic theory, interest moved away from Mill to earlier and more obscure writers.

This change of judgment was reinforced by consideration of Mill's position in the development of political philosophy. His economic theory lacks the logical rigour and his social philosophy the unflinching consistency which are the outstanding characteristics of the 'system-builders'. To opponents of government intervention, to believers in pure Benthamism, Mill's abandonment of doctrinaire *laissez-faire* was not only an act of apostasy, but it diminished also his significance as a representative of early nineteenth-century liberalism. And to rigorous opponents of *laissez-faire* Mill's compromise seemed too weak to be satisfactory.

But although he was not original as an economist, and although he did not leave behind one of the great systems of political philosophy, Mill is not to be dismissed as unimportant, as was the tendency during the ascendancy of the marginalist school. His significance lies precisely in the fact that he was able to make eclecticism in theory and compromise in politics into something like a generally accepted system of impressive quality. His greatest influence was admittedly temporary. But the approach of Mill, both to pure economics and to the problems of policy, became a characteristic of the academic English tradition. Mill remains symbolical of eclecticism and compromise. He, more than any other English economist, reflects the time in which early competitive capitalism – accompanied by English leadership in world markets – attained its zenith. But he also reflects the fact that new problems were clamouring for notice. In particular, his work can only be understood against the background of the increasing challenge of socialism.

In his *Autobiography* Mill describes the amazing process of education to which he was subjected by his father. It is clear from it that the son was meant to carry on the joint tradition of Ricardian economic theory in the form in which it appeared in the elder Mill's *Elements*, and the utilitarian social philosophy of which Bentham was the greatest exponent. But in the course of his experience of the world – shaken as it was by Chartism, trade unionism, and the spreading attack of socialist theory – he soon found himself face to face with the dilemma of the radical and the conservative interpretations of economic liberalism. Mill became aware of the necessity of choosing between them, mainly in the realm of political theory and practice. He describes the mental crisis which accompanied his emancipation from the rigours of the Benthamite view of self-interest as the main motive of human conduct, with its corollary of the eternal search for individual happiness.[1] Through the influence both of the romantic and the socialist critics of utilitarianism, he acquired regard for the historical approach, an appreciation of the complexity of social phenomena, and a doubt about the unfailing beneficence of the free play of the forces of self-interest. Although he never abandoned the harmony theory of utilitarianism, or a general belief in the superiority of competitive capitalism over other economic systems, he was, from that time, prepared to consider and advocate reforms of existing institutions, even if these involved government interference with private interests.

1 J. S. Mill, *Autobiography* (1873), ch. v.

In his essay on *Bentham* (written in 1838) he gives an interpretation which begins by stressing the revolutionary implication of Bentham's scepticism. He calls him 'the great *subversive*, or, in the language of Continental philosophers, the great *critical* thinker of his age and country'.[1] But he goes on to reject Bentham's picture of human nature. He regards as too narrow Bentham's belief that human beings are actuated in their conduct by nothing more than 'either self-love or love or hatred towards other sentient beings'.[2] He charges Bentham with the neglect of motives which involve the search for perfection, honour and other ends entirely for their own sakes. He concludes, therefore, that Bentham's philosophy can only 'teach the means of organizing and regulating the merely business part of the social arrangements'.[3] But Mill thought that with all his greatness in this respect – a greatness particularly evident in his continual exposure of self-interest behind the more pretentious guises in which it often presented itself – Bentham was not capable of showing how the means for regulating the material side of life might best be adapted to the task of improving the national character.

This criticism of Bentham was inspired to a large extent by Mill's regard for Coleridge, the other of 'the two great seminal minds of England of their age'.[4] Mill admired what the romantic school achieved when it was – as in the hands of Coleridge – not a partisan movement but a philosophy. He found in it the beginnings of a philosophy of history – the only form in which he thought a philosophy of society was possible – a just emphasis on education, a feeling of loyalty and national cohesion. He regarded conservative philosophy as an essential adjunct to reform. It should, he felt, provide an acid test for every reform proposal by elucidating the good purposes for which existing institutions were first intended. 'What mode', he argued, 'is there of determining whether a thing is fit to exist, without first considering what purposes it exists for, and whether it be still capable of fulfilling them?'[5] Mill saw in Coleridge's conservatism a powerful critical weapon. It pronounced, he thought, the severest satire upon existing evils, and it was more akin in aim to the reform movement than to the political Toryism to which it was thought to belong.

1 J. S. Mill, 'Bentham' in *Dissertations and Disquisitions* (1867), vol. i, p. 334.
2 ibid., p. 354.
3 ibid., p. 366.
4 ibid., p. 331.
5 J. S. Mill, 'Coleridge' in *Dissertations and Disquisitions*, p. 438.

Mill agreed also with Coleridge's strictures on the principle of *laissez-faire*. The '*let-alone* doctrine, or the theory that governments can do no better than to do nothing', he considered to be due to the 'manifest selfishness and incompetence of modern European governments'. As a general theory, however, he thought that 'one-half of it is true, and the other half false'.[1] He was still sceptical of the beneficence of government intervention when it attempted 'to chain up the free agency of individuals'. But he agreed with Coleridge that, having fulfilled its police duties, government could do much directly and indirectly to help to improve the material well-being of the people, and to ensure that the faculties essential to their moral existence were fully developed.[2]

Mill also approved of Coleridge's objection to the commercialization of landed property. Mill believed that ownership of land was in the nature of a trust; that it gave a great power to the owner, which it was the duty of the state to control. Whether in this, as in other matters, Mill was right in claiming the authority of Coleridge, is doubtful. Possibly Coleridge would have disliked as much to be associated with utilitarianism as with political Toryism. It is significant that Mill picked out from conservative doctrine those elements which could be interpreted as critical of existing practices and which did at the same time allow for government action in appropriate cases. There is no doubt that Mill did not accept any of the possible reactionary implications of Coleridge's theories. He never allowed romantic illusion to invade the citadel of industrial capitalism – its economic theory. 'In political economy especially,' he said of Coleridge, 'he writes like an arrant driveller, and it would have been well for his reputation had he never meddled with the subject.'[3]

Another influence on Mill, similar to that of Coleridge, was that of Comte, the founder of positivism. Although he was a disciple of Saint-Simon, Comte was strongly influenced by the romantic reaction to the practical revolutionary results of eighteenth-century philosophy. Reform had, he thought, overshot the mark. He too wanted to reform human society entirely, but he took over from the romantics the dislike of extreme individualism and the respect for authority; instead of medieval theology, however, positive science was to be enthroned as

1 ibid., pp. 453–4.
2 ibid., pp. 454–5.
3 J. S. Mill, 'Coleridge' in *Dissertations and Disquisitions*, p. 452.

the guiding force. We are not concerned here with the details and often fantastic practical consequences of Comte's philosophy. But it is clear that its apparent mixture of rationalism and romanticism was likely to impress Mill at a time when he was becoming dissatisfied with Benthamism. Comte's philosophy led directly to the desire for a new general science of society, and this involved the establishment of a philosophy of history: with both aims Mill sympathized.

Mill's departure from Benthamism was, however, only partly due to the romantic and pseudo-traditionalist influences of Coleridge and Comte. Mill knew the early English and French socialists and seems to have been impressed by their attacks on the evils of early capitalism. His discussion in the *Principles* of their critique of property is generally sympathetic. In the second edition of this work he pointed out that 'attacks on the institution of property' would continue 'until the laws of property are freed from whatever portion of injustice they contain'.[1] In all his discussions of problems of social policy, he takes from the natural law philosophy, which is his background, its potentially radical element. But he makes a criticism of institutions (also made by the early socialists) compatible with the principle of freedom derived from utilitarianism and natural law. The result is a combination of liberal principles with social reform. Before we attempt to trace the consequences of this attitude in his economic doctrines it is worth looking a little more closely at its theoretical and practical results in Mill's political outlook.

In the first place, Mill did not give up the general principles of individual liberty and free competition which he had learnt from his father. His most explicit theoretical statement is that contained in his essay *On Liberty* (1859). The absolute principle that should govern the relations between society and its individual members is here stated in strongly liberal terms. 'That principle is, that the sole end for which mankind are warranted, individually or collectively, in interfering with the liberty of action of any of their numbers is self-protection. That the only purpose for which power can be rightfully exercised over any member of a civilized community, against his will, is to prevent harm to others. His own good, either physical or moral, is not a sufficient warrant.'[2] But Mill's attitude on practical issues was not really

1 J. S. Mill, *Principles of Political Economy* (ed. Ashley, 1923), p. 203. An excellent modern edition in two volumes, edited by Bladon and Robson, appeared in 1965.
2 J. S. Mill, *On Liberty* (ed. Fawcett, World's Classics, 1924), p. 15.

determined by the principle contained in this declaration. He excepted certain matters from his general rule of non-interference. He regarded children, for example, as incapable of judging of their own best interests; education and legislation relating to the employment of children were, therefore, proper matters for government action. Other problems, like prostitution, which concerned adults, were also excepted; though clearly there was a possible conflict here between the utilitarian maxim of the supremacy of individual judgment and conventional ideas of right and wrong, useful and harmful.

In economic matters the principle stated in *On Liberty* was even more difficult to maintain consistently with Mill's desire for reform born of a sympathy with the weak and exploited. Logically, Mill's theoretical position was that no exceptions whatever to the rule of unfettered individual liberty should be allowed. But this led him into difficulties when he tried to reconcile it with his desire to justify certain restrictions of competition. Mill's attitude to trade unions is an outstanding example. Earlier utilitarians had opposed the combination laws because they did not regard state restriction of the right to form trade unions as necessary. Mill sought to strengthen his defence of trade unions not by denying their possible monopoly effects, but by an appeal to the principle of *laissez-faire* itself. To prevent the formation of corporate unions was, he thought, to interfere with a right obviously included in the general rule of freedom of contract.[1]

This piece of casuistry was made inevitable by the inconsistency of Mill's general attitude on *laissez-faire*. Mill's inconsistency is further illustrated by his defence of the state support for one type of voluntary association which aimed at altering the terms of contract which would result in a free market. Among the exceptions to the *laissez-faire* rule which he enumerates in the *Principles* there is the celebrated case of the reduction of hours of labour. If, says Mill, the labourers wanted to reduce hours from ten to nine (and if such reduction did not materially alter their earnings), it is not possible for the reduction to be adopted, unless the labourers combine in order to enforce it. If a voluntary association could be sure of adequate power, all would be well. But it is very likely that in the circumstances assumed no voluntary association could succeed in binding the great majority of the

1 J. S. Mill, *Principles*, pp. 933–9.

labourers concerned. The only remedy, therefore, is to enforce the reduction in hours by legislation.[1]

In truth, Mill's theoretical vacillations shows his search for a theory which would enable him to keep the *laissez-faire* principle and make just those exceptions which he himself regarded as desirable. For Mill had an emotional sympathy with the growing working-class movement which made him anxious to make concessions. He often spoke of socialism with respect. 'It is not to be expected', he said, 'that the division of the human race into two hereditary classes, employers and employed, can be permanently maintained.'[2] 'There can be little doubt ... that the relation of masters and workpeople will be gradually superseded by partnership in one of two forms: in some cases, association of the labourers with the capitalist; in others, and perhaps finally in all, association of labourers among themselves.'[3] Again, in his celebrated discussion of communism, he did not hesitate to say that if 'the choice were to be made between Communism with all its chances, and the present [1852] state of society with all its sufferings and injustices; if the institution of private property necessarily carried with it as a consequence, that the produce of labour should be apportioned as we now see it, almost in an inverse ratio to the labour ... if this or Communism were the alternative, all the difficulties, great or small, of Communism would be but as dust in the balance.'[4]

But against these and similar statements which appear to favour socialism, must be set many others which show that, fundamentally, Mill remained faithful to a generally liberal economy. He tempered his remarks on the probability of a future collectivist system with disquisitions on the desirability of the capitalists treating their workpeople fairly – in their own interests as well as in those of the workers. He did not fail to stress his hostility to one of the socialists' central doctrines: 'I utterly dissent from the most conspicuous and vehement part of their teaching, their declamations against competition.'[5] Nor must it be forgotten that he urged that communism should be compared not with the existing unregenerate state of private property, but with a social order which contained only the best features of capitalism. In other words, he envisaged a state of society in which the existing distribution

1 ibid., p. 963–5.
2 ibid., p. 761.
3 ibid., p. 764.
4 ibid., p. 761.
5 ibid., p. 792.

of property, caused by past conquest and violence, had been corrected, in which inequality of opportunity had been reduced to a minimum, in which legislation was designed to favour the diffusion of wealth, in which there was universal education, and in which population was limited. In such a society 'the principle of private property' would be found 'to have no necessary connection with the physical and social evils which almost all Socialist writers assume to be inseparable from it'.[1]

Mill was thus a radical and a social reformer: the first distinguished liberal with 'Fabian' leanings. He maintained close contacts with the Chartists; and it was with the help of his working-class followers that he secured a seat in parliament. He relied on restriction of inheritance, spread of co-operation, extension of peasant proprietorship, education, and similar measures to remove the evils of capitalism without sacrificing its basis. If Malthus was urging on the industrial capitalist concessions in favour of the landowning class, Mill was pleading for similar concessions to the labourers. In one sense, the appearance of his particular blend of political theory is a sympton of the strength which the working class had attained; it is also a reflection of the degree of economic development which made it possible for concessions to be granted. Capitalism and political democracy in England were sufficiently advanced to allow the working class (though admittedly as a result of continual pressure) a rising standard of living and increasing political influence. It is significant that, as an important factor in social reform, this movement of which Mill is the symbol began much earlier in England than elsewhere. Its equivalent in Germany for example, *Kathedersozialismus*, arose later; though when it arrived after the advance of German industrial capitalism it showed much resemblance to its English counterpart.

*Economics.* It is difficult to trace in detail the same process of compromise in Mill's economic theory. As a type, Mill's importance lies more in the field of political thought. The main work of adapting classical economic doctrine had already been done before him. Senior, who was much less involved in political theory and practice than Mill, illustrates much better the transformation which Ricardianism was undergoing. One cannot find in Mill's theory many propositions that have a direct relevance to his political difficulties. It is rather in a

1 ibid., p. 209.

general eclecticism that his compromise is reflected. Nevertheless, some of his theorems, including the changes they underwent in the course of time, show his appreciation of the need to provide an economics in harmony with his political philosophy.

There are, in the first place, Mill's ideas on the scope and method of the science. He was not ready to abandon the body of doctrine which he had inherited; but in deference to Comte's striving for a comprehensive social science, he was ready to redefine the scope of abstract economics. He regarded political economy as only one department of the sociology which was still to be created. It was to be supplemented by ethology, the science of character, and political ethology – its application to the problems of nations and epochs. He maintained that the method of the science was hypothetical; and in a celebrated passage in his first book on economic matters, *Essays on Some Unsettled Questions in Political Economy* (1844), he described the nature of the principal hypothesis which economics makes. This is the abstraction of the 'economic man'. Political economy, he says, 'does not treat of the whole conduct of man in society. It is concerned with him solely as a being who desires to possess wealth, and who is capable of judging of the comparative efficacy of means for obtaining that end. It predicts only such of the phenomena of the social state as take place in consequence of the pursuit of wealth. It makes entire abstraction of every other human passion or motive. . . . Political Economy considers mankind as occupied solely in acquiring and consuming wealth. . . . Not that any political economist was ever so absurd as to suppose that mankind are really thus constituted, but because this is the mode in which science must necessarily proceed. . . . The political economist inquires, what are the actions which would be produced by this desire, if . . . it were unimpeded by others.'[1]

Mill himself did not keep to this rigid limitation. Indeed, he made it clear by the very sub-title of his main work that he was dealing with economics in a wider context. In 1848 he published his *Principles of Political Economy with some of their applications to Social Philosophy*; and in this work there are not only continual references to factors which modify the working of the forces of competition, but also many discussions which use arguments of a normative character. One of its most interesting chapters is that on 'Competition and Custom' (Book II, Chapter 4), in which competition is shown as a comparatively new

1 J. S. Mill, *Essays on Some Unsettled Questions of Political Economy* (1844), pp. 137–40.

social force, restricted in its operation by tradition. Indeed, it would appear that the rigid definition to be found in the earlier essay was used precisely for the purpose of allowing ethical considerations explicitly to be taken into account, even though this meant enlarging the study from one of political economy to one of social philosophy.

Most characteristic of Mill's political position is his attitude to the different branches of economic inquiry. Senior had already drawn a distinction between the quality of the laws of production and exchange and those of distribution. Mill emphasizes that distinction. 'The laws and conditions of the Production of wealth partake of the character if physical truths. There is nothing optional or arbitrary in them. . . . It is not so with the Distribution of Wealth. That is a matter of human institution solely. The things once there, mankind, individually or collectively, can do with them as they like. . . . The Distribution of Wealth, therefore, depends on the laws and customs of society.'[1] This proposition makes it possible for Mill to plead for the maintenance of free competition in the sphere of production and exchange, and to advocate reforms which would redistribute property and income. He did not see that distribution was closely connected with production and that interference with one involved interference with the other.

The central propositions of Mill's theory – those relating to value and to production – show his endeavour to prove them immutable laws of nature and to cast them in such terms that they have no connection with the laws of distribution. In the sphere of value, this again meant a weakening of the real cost analysis, since the classical real cost theory involved certain propositions with regard to matters that are generally treated under distribution. It led to some differentiation between factors of production and sources of income; and this was followed by the concept of the surplus. We find, therefore, that Mill adopts, without substantial modifications, the theory that was expounded by Senior. He accepts utility as an upper limit to value. He repeats the theory of cost of production which includes 'abstinence', and he adds the capitalist's risk as a further factor. He distinguishes between goods produced under constant returns and perfect competition (where cost and price tended to equality) and different cases of monopoly (in which supply and demand determined market price). Though Mill still admitted a cost element into his theory, his emphasis was much more on the market phenomena of supply and demand. His attention was

1 J. S. Mill, *Principles*, pp. 199–200.

mainly directed to the working of competition in causing and smoothing out the differences between market values and natural value, which
was either a monopoly value or one determined by the cost of production.

As for the cost element, Mill's analysis is not consistent. He sometimes speaks of labour and abstinence in terms of a subjective real cost
theory; that is, he uses them to denote the actual amount of effort and
abstinence embodied in the product. But more often he defines cost in
terms of remuneration paid to labourers and suppliers of capital. This,
of course, means approaching the problem from the angle of the
entrepreneur; and in spite of vacillations Mill seems to have given a
great impetus to this way of looking at cost. His confusion was particularly marked in his inclusion of permanent differences in wage
rates or profits as factors which affect value. He saw that such cases did
exist and that they had some influence on market price. But he did not
realize that this made a considerable difference to the subjective real
cost concept, because such differences in remuneration need clearly
have no connection with the relative amount of effort and abstinence
which they called forth. Cairnes pointed this out, and included the
problem in the theory of non-competing groups.

Mill's theory of production is noteworthy for its emphasis on the
Malthusian theory of population and for the basis on which this theory
is made to rest. In Mill, the connection between the theory of population and the law of diminishing returns is made complete. 'It is the law
of production from the land', he said, 'that in any given state of
agricultural skill and knowledge, by increasing the labour, the produce
is not increased in the same degree.' And this he regarded as 'the most
important proposition in political economy'.[1] From it the danger of
over-population inevitably followed. Nature was niggardly; and even
though every fresh mouth to feed brought two hands, these hands
could not produce as much as the old ones.[2] Mill thought that in the
populous and developed countries the danger of over-population was a
serious one. And although unjust distribution might be responsible for
making the evils of over-population felt early, and although these evils
might be mitigated by emigration and the free importation of food, the
real hope of improvement for the masses of the people lay in restriction
of numbers.

1 J. S. Mill, *Principles* p. 177.
2 ibid., p. 191.

This gloomy view was closely related to Mill's acceptance of the wage-fund doctrine. The proposition that the average level of wages was determined by supply and demand was not new, but in his *Principles* Mill gave it a more complete formulation than it had previously had, and made it into the exclusive explanation of wages. From the point of view of the subsequent development of the productivity theory of wages and capital, Senior's statement of the wage-fund doctrine was more advanced than Mill's. The latter's position is summarized in the following passage. 'Wages, then, depend mainly upon the demand and supply of labour; or, as it is often expressed, on the proportion between population and capital. By population is here meant the number only of the labouring class, or rather of those who work for hire; and by capital only circulating and not even the whole of that, but the part which is expended in the direct purchase of labour. ... Wages not only depend upon the relative amount of capital and population, but cannot, under the rule of competition, be affected by anything else. Wages (meaning of course, the general rate) cannot rise, but by an increase of the aggregate funds employed in hiring labourers, or a diminution in the number of the competitors for hire; nor fall, except, by a diminution of the funds devoted to paying labour, or by an increase in the number of the labourers to be paid.'[1]

Following Senior, Mill adds to this statement an analysis of the objections which might be made to it. But he does not examine in detail the causes which determine the size of the fund set aside for the payment of wages. The chief use to which Mill put this doctrine was to buttress the case for the limitation of numbers and to urge that the capitalists should devote an increasing proportion of their means in advances to labourers. It was this latter desire which led Mill to state, as corollaries of the wage-fund doctrine, the propositions that the portion of capital which is destined to the maintenance of labourers may be 'indefinitely increased without creating an impossibility of finding employment',[2] and that 'demand for commodities is not demand for labour'.[3]

But the wage-fund doctrine was generally used to show that attempts by the workers to raise their wages were futile; and this use made it incompatible with Mills's support for reforms and for trade

1 J. S. Mill, *Principles*, pp. 343–4.
2 ibid., p. 66.
3 ibid., p. 79.

unionism. It is not surprising, therefore, that Mill should have abandoned the doctrine in later life. His famous recantation, contained in a review of a book by Thornton in the *Fortnightly Review* (May 1869), was undoubtedly dictated by a desire to oppose the idea that the efforts of trade unions were doomed to failure by the working of economic laws. He now said that although the amount to be spent on wages could not exceed 'the aggregate means of the employing classes' and that it could not 'come up to those means; for the employers have to maintain themselves and their families', the amount was not fixed. The whole of the capitalist's means was potentially capital (in the Ricardian sense of advances to labourers); and the amount that actually became capital depended on the capitalist's personal expenditure.[1]

But as later developments showed, this recantation was no more (and possibly less) satisfactory than the original position. For not only did Mill fail to analyse the factors behind the supply and demand of capital, he still clung to the notion of capital as 'advances' and did not distinguish between fixed and circulating capital. Nor did he pay attention to the differences between the money streams of saving and investing, and the streams of different types of production and consumption goods. When the wage-fund doctrine was later revived by Taussig and the Austrians these considerations were taken into account in elaborating a new version.

In conclusion, a word may be said about Mill's view of the future of society. On the whole, his dynamic follows that of Ricardo. But he added to it his famous chapter, 'Of the Stationary State'.[2] The increase of wealth, Mill thought, must sometime come to an end and society must enter upon a stationary condition. Improvements in technique, the law of diminishing returns, the accumulation of capital, and the working of competition combine to produce declining profits, rising rents, and, if population is restrained from rising unduly, an improvement in the condition of the working classes. But although advances in technique and the export of capital might ensure a continuance of progress even in highly developed countries, the arrival of the stationary state cannot ultimately be postponed. Mill looks complacently upon this state of blissful equilibrium, in which the competitive struggle has disappeared, in which wealth is more evenly divided as the result both of individual prudence and frugality and of

1 J. S. Mill, *Principles*, pp. 992–3.
2 ibid., pp. 746–51.

legislation. But this vision serves again as an argument for the desirability of restricting population here and now.

Mill's search for a compromise in the field of economic theory was less successful than in the field of social philosophy and public policy. It left far too many logical inconsistencies to serve as an adequate complement to the philosophy of compromise and steady reform. But in spite of his analytical shortcomings, Mill left an extremely valuable legacy in his consistent attempt to combine analysis with policy conclusions: indeed to make the former subservient instruments of the latter. To this day, this has remained the outstanding feature of economic thought in the English-speaking countries. And while it may have given that thought the flavour of eclecticism, lacking in more rigorous logical systems, it has also saved it from a doctrinaire spirit and has infused it with a strong practical concern for human welfare combined with a spirit of tolerance, both of which have stood it in very good stead.[1]

---

1 An interesting interpretation of Mill is to be found in Pedro Schwartz, *The New Political Economy of John Stuart Mill* (1968).

# 8

# Modern Economics

## *The Quality of Modern Economics*

The subject-matter of this chapter is the immediate past of present-day economic thought. We limit ourselves to the body of doctrines which was developed in the last few decades of the last, and the first few decades of the present century. Even so, we shall find ourselves uncomfortably near to the problems which are the subjects of current theoretical activity. The ideas which form our immediate background are still in ferment; and in a following chapter more recent aspects of contemporary theory will be discussed. In the present century we are faced with a very large number of writers whose relative significance cannot as yet be fully assessed. They are too near to us to have gone through the sieve of history. The selection which follows must, therefore, be regarded as tentative. In particular it should be noted that this chapter deals with the main body of economic theory and that it ignores almost entirely many developments which lie outside the academic and professional fields which could later turn out to be significant.

It has been customary to regard the changes made in the apparatus of economic analysis in the 1870s as marking a complete revolution in economics. Classicism, it was said, emphasized production, supply, and cost; modern theory is mainly concerned with consumption, demand, and utility. The marginal utility concept was introduced to effect this shift of emphasis and has since dominated academic thought. It has, however, been looked upon, not only as an addition to the economic 'tool-box', but also as a vital innovation in the method of approach of the science.

Compared with the classical theory of Ricardo the marginal utility schools certainly exhibit marked differences of kind. But the origin of these differences must be placed before the appearance of the marginal utility concept in the works of Jevons, Menger, and Walras. As has been shown in the last chapter, the technical development which culminated in the work of these writers started with Ricardo's successors. The essential elements of the modern technique – the emphasis on demand and on utility and the recognition of diminishing utility – were developed by a number of early nineteenth-century authors. Their work is now known; and the continuity of thought from their time to ours is recognized. If these technical developments involve a significant change of emphasis and approach, it is McCulloch, Say, Bailey, and Senior, rather than Jevons and the Austrians, who were the first to be responsible for it.

But whatever its exact date, the change from classicism is real enough. It marks a major transformation in the development of post-mercantilist economic thought, and its beginning must be placed chronologically in the period which follows soon after the completion of Ricardo's work. It may be admitted that the 1870s bring a considerable refinement and systematization of the subjective approach which had begin in the 1820s. The changes which mark this process of refinement are substantial enough in the evolution of modern economics and are clearly identifiable, even when all allowance has been made for the large number of forerunners of the modern school. This is particularly so in regard to the emphasis upon the new method of examining the effects of small increments and decrements in economic quantities.

One interpretation of the marginal school has proclaimed it as the economics of the rentier class.[1] It links the development of a subjective and 'unhistorical' method in economics (which takes consumption as its starting-point) with the rise of a class of people who live by 'clipping coupons'. This leisure class, it is said, is no longer a part of the process of production and is interested exclusively in the disposal of the income from its investments. It is Veblen's class of absentee owners, and it is natural that it should consider economic activity solely from the point of view of consumption. The lack of interest in the social character of production and in its changing historical forms, and the concentration upon the behaviour of Robinson Crusoe, appear thus to be made a direct result of the structural changes of modern capitalism.

Such an interpretation cannot stand the test of serious analysis. In

1 N. Bukharin, *The Economic Theory of the Leisure Class* (no date).

the face of the vastly increased complexity of theoretical work in the last nine decades, it must be regarded as, at the very least, a crude juxtaposition of economic reality and economic thought. We have seen throughout this book that a direct relation between the two can only rarely be established even for the more primitive stages of economic theorizing. In the 1870s, when there was already in existence a substantial body of economic theory, the further development of which was largely in the charge of a highly institutionalized body of professionals, the description of marginalism as the economics of the rentier must be regarded as a grotesque travesty. This is particularly clear when we remember both the distant antecedents of the new school and the fact that it was identified to a considerable extent with Austria, a country of greatly retarded capitalist development. The truth is that the theory which had broken away from classicism and which had, as we have seen, its roots in the development of nineteenth-century capitalism, made the changes of the 1870s inevitable. And it would be nearer the mark to regard the concern of the new theory with the behaviour of the individual as a sign of the progress of liberal political philosophy.

Before we trace the more recent progress of the utility school, it is worth while to glance at the characteristics of modern economics and to contrast them with those of the classical system. A statement by a modern economist of the problem which he sets out to study might be something like this. The first thing which confronts the economic theorist is an economic reality which in spite of all its complexity is at once reducible to a network of exchange transactions in the market. The surface phenomena are those of supply, demand, and price. Comparatively little reflection is needed to recognize these factors in all the markets which are the theatre of modern economic activity. In regard to the goods and services which individuals require directly for the satisfaction of their wants, the general purchase-and-sale character of individual behaviour is easy to recognize. But even the transactions of the productive process are seen to resolve themselves into the purchase and sale of raw materials, capital goods, money capital, and labour. If, then, we regard the economic system as an enormous conglomeration of interdependent markets, the central problem of economic inquiry becomes the explanation of the exchange process, or, more particularly, the explanation of the formation of price.

Not that the classical economists neglected the more obvious phenomena of the market: some of Adam Smith's most successful analyses were precisely those concerned with the effects of competition in the market. But in all the works of the classics there is, in addition, emphasis on the fact that the mechanism of the market required ultimately to be explained by more fundamental concepts, either relating to human conduct, or derived from a view of society and its historical development. Hence the supply-and-demand explanations were based upon a theory of exchange-value which was of a particular type. The original labour theory of value is the reflection of the aim to provide such a 'fundamental' explanation of the economic process.

We have seen that among the post-classical economists, the labour theory of value was first significantly altered and finally abandoned. Nevertheless many economists still felt the need for an explanation which would go behind the phenomena of supply and demand; and the result was the addition of a psychological substructure which made the post-Ricardian theory of value into a subjective real-cost theory. The introduction of the psychological element is seen in the new emphasis on utility and in the changed view of labour as a determinant of value. Instead of an expenditure of effort – measurable in time-units – which it had tended to be in Ricardo, labour, in the later cost of production theories, became expressive of a subjective sacrifice. Adam Smith's 'toil and trouble' was its inspiration.

The significance of the new theory was this: it was based upon the continued search for something more than a theory of price; but by the transition from the objective to the subjective approach it brought about a major change in the relationship between economic analysis and its sociological antecendents. In nearly all classical literature, economic analysis was allied with an historical view of the structure of society which underlay the whole economic process. In its place was put a view of society as an agglomeration of individuals. The subjective theory of value (even in its earlier cost-of-production form) is only  compatible with an individualist view of society and in some of the more extreme formulations becomes even 'atomistic'.

In a more formal sense, however, the classical and the subjective theories of value show a considerable resemblance. As has been pointed out, they both aim at a fundamental explanation of the exchange process. The one claims to do it by going into the sphere of production and the social relationship which it involves; the other by inquiring into the working of individuals' minds, that is into the psychological processes which result in a certain behaviour in the market. The latter course leads ultimately to the modern marginal utility school, which takes consumption as its starting point. Another resemblance lies in the fact that both schools claim to have developed a universally valid theory. Both the labour and the utility theories of value start from assumptions which can be claimed to be relevant to all social systems: the one from the disposition of resources, on which every society must decide; the other from the subjective valuations of individuals, which must always precede or accompany supply and demand.

There are, however, differences. The classical theory was, in the outcome, based on a somewhat lifeless and mechanical view of a stratified society in which particular social groups were made to correspond to functions in the economic process. This identification (labour – wages, rent – landowners, profits – capitalists) was taken as an implied, but never-changing pattern.

The utility schools claim universal validity for a different reason: because they claim that they develop a theory of value which is independent of any specific social order. Nevertheless it cannot be doubted that in its origins the utility school was often also influenced by a desire to strengthen the potentially apologetic aspects of economic theory. The classical theory was not strong enough to withstand the attacks of the growing working-class movement. The claim that a certain social structure – particularly when, as in the work of Ricardo, this was shown to contain severe conflicts of interests – should be regarded as the end of history could not be logically defended. Nor could existing conditions be made palatable simply by appeal to universal laws. The retreat from the objective labour theory of value was a retreat from this position. It was effected by the introduction of a subjectivism which absolved economists from concerning themselves with a particular social order. Theorems which had been developed on a basis of equal individuals undertaking abstinence and toil and trouble could have nothing to say about the real differentiation of these individuals. But more often they were excellently suited to defending (by a fallacy which systems of thought derived from the philosophy of natural law have often been guilty) an existing reality far removed from the abstract assumptions. That the first use to which the new doctrine was put was to strengthen the idea of productivity of capital by the introduction of the concept of abstinence was, in the circumstances of the time, calculated to create some suspicion that a new rationalization was born.

The subjective real-cost theory was, however, inherently weak. It continued to regard labour as a determinant of value – an idea which it had taken over from a different system of thought. It was difficult to make this concept fully psychological, particularly if the purpose was to have a uniform system of sacrifice that included 'abstinence'. The equation of the abstinence of the capitalist with the labour of the worker was difficult to achieve; though, as we shall see, it was attempted once again by Marshall. The tendency arose, therefore, to abandon the cost approach more completely than had yet been done and to replace it by a more fully developed utility analysis. The rise of the marginal utility school does, therefore, represent a break with its immediate past, in the sense that it draws the logical conclusion from the abandonment of the labour theory of value.

There is one feature of the more recent development of theory which is also worthy of notice at this stage, that is the increase in the number and importance of non-English contributions. Classicial political economy had been an almost exclusively English science. It was developed in the most advanced economic environment that was then in existence. By the end of the nineteenth century, however, England was no longer the only industrial country in the world; indeed, the forces which were ultimately to challenge her pre-eminence were already at work. And although the earliest complete statement of the new doctrine comes from an English economist, its formulation in terms which were particularly significant for further development was the work of Continental writers. Jevons was still influenced by utilitarian philosophy. But Menger, the founder of the Austrian school, gave the new theory a non-utilitarian interpretation and thus provided it with new and, and in the end, more effective methodological credentials.

## Marginal Utility

*Hermann Heinrich Gossen.* The first generation of modern marginal-utility theorists consists of the celebrated trinity, William Stanley Jevons, Carl Menger, and Léon Walras. But there is at least one other author whom one is obliged to mention in company with them. Gossen was not dealt with in the last chapter, because he is an anticipator rather than a forerunner. He exercised no influence in his own lifetime. His book, *Entwicklung der Gesetze des menschlichen Verkehrs und der daraus fliessenden Regeln für menschliches Handeln*, remained completely ignored for many years. Its first edition of 1854 sold very few copies and the embittered author had the book withdrawn. Only after its rediscovery in the 1870s, and the praise which it subsequently earned from Jevons and Walras, was it reissued in 1889. Since then Gossen has not only been recognized as a pioneer, but his theorems have influenced economic thought after their basic ideas had been made known by others.

Gossen's analysis of the laws of human conduct is characterized by these features: determined utilitarianism, a consumption approach, and mathematical method. With regard to the last, Gossen declares in his preface that economics is concerned with results produced by a combination of forces and that it is impossible to determine such results without the aid of mathematics.[1] Gossen begins by stating that the aim of all human conduct is to maximize enjoyment. From this the approach follows. It is necessary to examine the manner in which enjoyment proceeds. From everyday observation Gossen derives certain laws of human enjoyment of which two, now known as Gossen's first and second laws, are the most important.

Gossen's first law states in explicit form the principle of diminishing utility – 'The amount of one and the same enjoyment diminishes continuously as we proceed with that enjoyment without interruption, until satiety is reached.'[2] Gossen illustrates this idea of the satiability of wants with well-known examples, such as the declining enjoyment of successive bites of food. But it was left to later marginalists to expound this principle in more relative terms. Gossen's second law refers to the manner in which the maximum of all enjoyments can be achieved. 'In order to obtain the maximum sum of enjoyment, an individual who has a choice between a number of enjoyments, but insufficient time to procure all completely, is obliged, however much the absolute amount of individual enjoyments may differ, to procure all partially, even before he has completed the greatest of them. The relation between them must be such that, at the moment when they are discontinued, the amounts of all enjoyments are equal.'[3] In this cumbersome way Gossen stated the principle that maximum pleasure will result from a uniform level of want-satisfaction. The second law follows from the

1 H. H. Gossen, *Entwicklung der Gesetze des menschlichen Verkehrs und de daraus flissenden Regeln für menschliches Handeln* (1889), pp. vi and vii.
2 ibid., pp. 4–5.
3 ibid., p. 12.

first and from the additional postulate that it is impossible to obtain full satisfaction of all wants. We shall see presently what part these laws now play in economic theory.

The rest of Gossen's work is an elaboration of these laws. The value of a thing is to be reckoned entirely in terms of the enjoyment which it can procure.[1] Owing to the operation of the first law, individual units of the same good will have different values according to the quantity possesed; beyond a certain quantity a single unit will cease to have value at all.[2] Value must be conceived only in relative terms. 'Nothing in the external world possesses absolute value'; value depends on the relation between the object and the subject.[3] The objects which may possess value can be classified into consumption goods, those which are immediately capable of supplying enjoyment; goods 'of the second class', which are jointly necessary for enjoyment (what are now called complementary goods); and goods of the third class', which are those used in the production of other goods.[4] Labour which creates means of enjoyment is also accompanied by 'pain' (or 'disutility'). It follows that we can increase our enjoyment by labour so long as the enjoyment which results is esteemed more highly than the pain of the labour involved.[5] Exchange must also follow the two laws. Exchange remains of advantage to an individual 'until the values of the last units of the two commodities in his possession have become equal.'[6] Thus Gossen's book contains the main elements of the Jevonian and the Austrian theory. Even the geometric and algebraic apparatus is there. But the conditions of the time were not ripe for so determined a use of the subjective approach. With Jevons, a new reign begins.

*William Stanley Jevons (1835–82).* Jevons did much work in fields other than pure theory. The *Investigations in Currency and Finance*, published posthumously in 1884, contain a number of papers on problems of applied economics which show Jevons to have been particularly interested – and often successful – in the linking of statistical investigation and theoretical analysis. In one of these papers, one of his earliest literary efforts, *The Serious Fall in the Value of Gold*, he traced

1 ibid., p. 24.
2 ibid., p. 131.
3 ibid., pp. 46–7.
4 ibid., pp. 24–8.
5 ibid., p. 38.
6 ibid., p. 8.

the effect on prices of the increase in the supply of gold; and in this and other papers he advanced considerably the study of index numbers. *The Coal Question* (1865) is an elaborate attempt to use statistical information to prove the probability of an early exhaustion of Britain's coal resources. Though not wholly successful in its more remote conclusions, it has certainly drawn attention to a factor which is still operative. On the other hand, Jevons's effort to construct a theory of crises on the basis of empirical material was a failure. The 'sunspot' theory, which established a connection between the rhythm of harvests and trade (the former being traced to periodic meteorological fluctuations), is now abandoned; though somewhat akin to it is Moore's theory of generating economic cycles.

Jevons's work extended, however, beyond the limits of economics, pure or applied. Much though he may have desired to keep to the narrow path of academic theory, he was drawn into discussion of the problems of policy. His contribution is small in volume; his one comprehensive statement is contained in *The State in Relation to Labour* (1882). It is of considerable interest because it shows the continuance and intensification of the difficulties of the *laissez-faire* doctrine which we have already encountered in Mill. Jevons's general position appears at first to be based on the early utilitarian principle of expediency. He thought that 'we can lay down no hard and fast rules, but must treat every case in detail on its merits. Specific experience is our best guide or even express experiment where possible, but the real difficulty consists in the interpretation of experience. We are reduced to balance conflicting probabilities of good and evil.'[1] But all the effects, he argues in the same place, of a 'proposed act must be taken into account'.

Even with this qualification Jevons's position must appear unsatisfactory to a liberal economist who believes in the existence of an economic argument for *laissez-faire* as the general rule of policy. And indeed Jevons himself seems to have been aware of its unsatisfactory nature, because he specifically excepted protection against foreign competition from the general principle of judging each case on its merits. He calls himself 'a thorough-going advocate of Free Trade' and implies that he does not regard this doctrine as inconsistent with those measures of intervention at home which he was prepared to

---

1 W. S. Jevons, *The State in Relation to Labour* (1882), pp. v and vi.

support.[1] But a fundamental inconsistency there clearly was. And its presence reveals the extent to which the claims of the working class were pressing and forcing concessions which had to be justified on thereotical grounds. In the field of foreign trade *laissez-faire* was still the most advantageous policy for Britain; there was, therefore, no need to abandon it in theory. Thus Jevons greatly widened the breach already made by Mill; and we shall later have occasion to refer to the way in which it was further widened by Jevons's successor.

Whatever Jevons's merit as a statistician or his significance in the development of political thought, his claim to notice rests mainly on his contribution to pure theory. It was he who made the scattered fragments of earlier utility analysis into a comprehensive theory of value, exchange and distribution. Already in 1862, in a paper read to Section F of the British Association, Jevons had revealed the trend of his thought. In this sketch of a 'general mathematical theory of Political Economy',[2] he showed both his belief that the laws of economics could be reduced to a few principles cast in mathematical terms and that these principles had to be derived from 'the great springs of human action – the feelings of pleasure and pain'.[3] And in this main work, *The Theory of Political Economy*, first published in 1871, the vindication of abstraction and of the mathematical method, together with the explicit reference to hedonism, is repeated and amplified.

Jevons, himself a statistician, did not deny that empirical studies were an essential part of the total of economic studies; but he urged that the ultimate laws of economics were of so general a character that they could rightly be compared with the laws of the physical sciences, which 'have their basis more or less obviously in the general principles of mechanics'.[4] Economics was closely analogous 'to the science of Statical Mechanics'.[5] This analogy extended to method. Economics had to be as mathematical in character as the physical sciences. The reasons for this are given in terms reminiscent of Cournot (whose work Jevons did not know at the time). 'To me it seems that *our science must be mathematical, simply because it deals with quantities.* Wherever the things treated are capable of being *greater or less*, there the laws and relations must be mathematical in nature. . . . Economists cannot alter

1 ibid.
2 Reprinted as Appendix III of W. S. Jevons, *The Theory of Political Economy* (1924).
3 ibid., p. 304.
4 ibid., p. xvii.
5 ibid., p. vii.

their nature by denying them the name. . . . Whether the mathematical laws of Economics are stated in words, or in the usual symbols, $x, y, z, p, q$, etc. is an accident, or a matter of mere convenience.'[1]

This view of the character of ecomomics did not lead Jevons, as it had led Cournot, to confine himself to the enunciation of the general principles of the relations between demand, supply, and price. He criticized Cournot for his exclusive interest in the system of functional interdependence between these quantities observed in the market. 'Cournot', he said, 'did not frame any ultimate theory of the ground and nature of utlity and value';[2] and, again, 'Cournot does not recede to any theory of utility, but commences with the phenomenal laws of supply and demand'.[3] It was Jevons's aim to provide a mathematical exposition of the laws of the market as well as an 'ultimate' theory of value on which he considered that these laws rested.

The central principle of this theory is the statement that 'value depends entirely upon utility'.[4] Adherence to this central principle appeared to Jevons to mark an innovation in economic thought. It was only in later years that he realized the extent to which he had been anticipated by earlier writers. But when he first expounded his views, the Ricardian tradition – in its attenuated form, it is true – was still strong enough to make him regard himself as revolutionary.

His innovation was substantial enough. The classics and their followers had not ignored utility; Adam Smith, in particular, had stressed its importance. But utility had never been regarded as a proper basis for an explanation of exchange-value, because of the glaring discrepancies between them. The classical theory of value was objective, that is, it referred to the whole of society's economic activity. This being the approach, it was natural that the classics should ignore individual, subjective factors. It is in this respect that Jevons effected an important change which made it possible for the first time to formulate a theory of value based on utility as an alternative to the classical theory. His starting-point was the individual and his wants. And for the study of individual conduct he found ready at hand a complete philosophy whose aim was precisely the establishment of the principles of human action. Hedonist philosophy was, moreover, cast in a form that seemed to make it particularly suitable to mathematical methods.

1 ibid., pp. 3 and 4.
2 ibid., p. xxix.
3 W. S. Jevons, *The Theory of Political Economy*, p. xxxi.
4 ibid., p. 1.

Accordingly Jevons begins with a theory of pleasure and pain based on Bentham's *A Table of the Springs of Action*. Man is here regarded as a pleasure machine; his aim is to maximize pleasure. Utility is then defined as the quality possessed by an object of producing pleasure or preventing pain, 'provided that the will or inclination of the person immediately concerned is taken as the sole criterion for the time, of what is or is not useful'.[1] Utility, in other words, is not an intrinsic quality; it expresses a relation between an object and a subject. Utility, however, can only become a significant concept in a theory of value if the total utility of a commodity is carefully distinguished from the utility which an individual, at a given time, attaches to a portion of that commodity. In a way reminiscent of Gossen Jevons examines the effect of changes in the total quantity of a commodity on the utility to an individual of portions of that commodity, and concludes that successive increments reduce the utility of every unit. Total utility is thus distinguished from degree of utility at any point; and from this the concept of 'final degree of utility' results. This term denotes 'the degree of utility of the last addition, or the next possible addition, of a very small, or infinitely small, quantity of the existing stock',[2] and it becomes the fundamental concept of Jevons's theory of exchange and distribution.

The essence of Jevons's explanation of the formation of exchange-value and price is to be found in what is an adaptation of the second law of Gossen. In harmony with that law Jevons argues that, when a commodity is capable of satisfying wants in a number of different uses, it will be distributed over these uses in such a way that its final degree of utility is the same in every use. From this he passes on, by somewhat clumsy means which had to be refined later, to the conclusion that, when two individuals exchange two commodities, the ratio of exchange 'will be the reciprocal of the ratio of the final degrees of utility of the quantities of commodity available for consumption after the exchange is completed'.[3] In other words, in equilibrium, that is in a position in which neither party can obtain any further advantage by continuing the exchange, marginal utility for each participant will be proportionate to price. From this it follows that 'a person distributes his income in such a way as to equalize the

1 ibid., p. 39.
2 W. S. Jevons, *The Theory of Political Economy*, p. 51.
3 ibid., p. 95.

utility of the final increments of all commodities consumed'.[1]

In the detailed working out of his theory of exchange Jevons was not very successful. It was left to later theorists to produce a more plausible argument to connect the subjective estimates of individuals with the formation of market prices. It has been argued that Jevons himself – in spite of his strong emphasis on utility – abandoned half-way his attempt to give an explanation of the origin of value in terms of utility, in favour of a purely 'functional' theory. He regarded market price as given; and only described its relation to quantities and final degrees of utility when equilibrium had already been reached.[2]

But even Jevons's statement of this relation has been shown to be defective. To elaborate the notion of the subjective valuations of individuals and their attempts to maximize satisfaction (including exchange) into a theory which was valid for social exchange, Jevons employed two very clumsy concepts. These are the 'law of indifference' and the 'trading body'. Different prices, Jevons argues, must be due to different preferences. Because it must be clearly a matter of indifference to a person whether he obtains this or that portion of a perfectly homogeneous commodity, there cannot be two prices in a market for the same article at the same time. As was shown by later economists, particularly by Walras, Edgeworth, Marshall, and Wicksell, this law of indifference only expresses – and clumsily at that – the assumption of perfect competition.

The concept of the trading body is even more open to objection. By this Jevons means any body of buyers or sellers – ranging from a single individual to the sum total of inhabitants in a country. Jevons, without modification, applies his theory of exchange between two individuals to the case of exchange between a multitude of buyers and sellers. But this procedure was unjustified. It completely obscured the problem of competition. As Wicksell rightly pointed out, in Jevons's treatment, competitive exchange is no different from isolated exchange (i.e. exchange between two individuals).[3] And in this situation, which again Jevons did not fully analyse, a number of prices could fulfil the conditions of equilibrium. Edgeworth charitably assumed that Jevon's

---

1 ibid., p. 140.
2 Hans Mayer, 'Der Erkenntniswert der funktionellen Preistheorien', *Die Wirtschaftstheorie der Gegenwart*, vol. ii (1932), pp. 181–2.
3 K. Wicksell, *Über Wert, Kapital und Rente* (1893. London School of Economics Reprints, 1933), p. 48.

trading bodies were in some sense typical dealers.[1] But Jevons clearly meant them to represent the aggregate body of buyers and sellers operating in conditions of perfect competition. It was for this situation that his equations of exchange were devised. He represented the equilibrium of exchange in this way:

$$\frac{\phi_1\,(a-x)}{\psi_1\,(y)} = \frac{y}{x} = \frac{\phi_2\,(x)}{\psi_2\,(b-y)}$$

where $a$ and $b$ are the total quantities of the two goods, $x$ and $y$ the respective quantities which have changed hands ($\frac{y}{x}$, therefore, the price), and the different functions, the final degrees of utilities. But he nowhere explained how these collective marginal utilities were determined. In fact, what he was considering was a case of isolated exchange, in which it is now admitted that the actual ratio of exchange is indeterminate within certain limits. It was left to Walras and others to show the connections between marginal utility, demand, and price under competitive conditions; and their analysis is now an accepted part of the price explanation of the theory of value.

However much Jevons may have fallen short of giving a complete subjective theory, his abandonment of the labour theory is clear cut. He denied that labour could be regarded as the source of value. The labour spent on the production of a commodity was 'gone and lost for ever'.[2] It could have no influence on the price which an article would fetch when brought to the market. Nevertheless, Jevons admitted that because the final degree of utility (on which value depended) could be altered by variations in supply, labour could affect value indirectly. The relation was: 'Cost of production determines supply; Supply determines final degree of utility; Final degree of utility determines value.'[3]

Labour was defined by Jevons in purely subjective terms; and on the analogy of his theory of utility he built up a theory of disutility which is similar to that developed later by Marshall. The English marginal utility school after Jevons for a long time tended to preserve the concept of the disutility of labour, claiming that it helped to determine value through its influence on the supply of labour. In other words, Jevons and his English followers were evidently anxious not to cut

1 F. Y. Edgeworth, *Mathematical Psychics* (1881. London School of Economics Reprints, 1932), p. 109.
2 W. S. Jevons, *The Theory of Political Economy*, p. 164.
3 ibid., p. 165.

adrift entirely from the post-classical tradition. Jevons merely added utility to the already existing apparatus of explanation. The equilibrium relation between labourer and utility was one in which 'the increments of utility from the several employments (of labour)' were equal. To make equilibrium fully determinate another relation was required. This was given in the statement that 'Labour will be carried on until the increment of utility from any of the employments just balances the increment of pain'.[1] As Edgeworth put it, 'utility and disutility are independent variables in that expression, the maximum of which determines economic equilibrium'.[2]

Jevons did not work out a comprehensive theory of distribution. It was his Austrian contemporary who attempted to follow up the implications of the utility theory of value in the sphere of distribution. Jevons adopted without much modification the classicial theory of rent; and this almost led him to a productivity theory of wages. Every worker, he said, 'seeks the work in which his peculiar faculties are most productive of utility, as measured by what other people are willing to pay for their produce. Thus wages are clearly the effect not the cause of the value of the produce.'[3] But he never worked this up into a marginal productivity theory. Indeed, when he came to deal specifically with wages, he abandoned the above explanation in favour of another one. He pointed out that the wage-fund theory was merely a truism; and he also rejected the classical subsistence theory. Instead, he concluded that 'the wages of a working man are ultimately coincident with what he produces after the deduction on rent, taxes, and the interest of capital'.[4] Thus wages are defined as the residual share of the total product. The wage-fund doctrine does, however, come into its own as an explanation of the short-run mechanism of the determination of wages. The capitalists invest capital and buy labour according to the estimates they form of markets. They 'sustain labour before the result is accomplished' and if the result is above their expectations, they will make large profits. But competition will increase and bring these profits down to the average, the previous excess being now appropriated either by the workers in higher wages or by the consumers in lower prices; or shared by both.[5]

1 W. S. Jevons, *The Theory of Political Economy*, pp. 184–5.
2 F. Y. Edgeworth, *Papers relating to Political Economy* (1925), vol. iii, p. 32.
3 W. S. Jevons, *The Theory of Political Economy*, p. 1.
4 ibid., p. 270.
5 ibid., p. 271.

Jevons's theory of capital has a more modern flavour. It is somewhat obscurely expressed in the *Theory of Political Economy*; but the essence of the theory resembles that of the Austrians. According to Jevons, the function of capital is to enable us 'to make a great outlay in providing tools, machines, or other preliminary works, which have for their sole object the production of some important commodity, and which will greatly facilitate production when we enter upon it'. Capital enables us to surmount the 'time elapsing between the beginning and end of work'.[1] And 'whatever improvements in the supply of commodities lengthen the average interval between the moment when labour is exerted and its ultimate result or purpose accomplished, such improvements depend upon the use of capital'.[2] The greater productivity of processes involving a lapse of time – what Böhm-Bawerk was later to call 'roundabout' processes – can only be obtained by the use of capital (which ultimately consists 'of those commodities which are required for sustaining labourers'[3]); and the rate of interest is 'the rate of increase of the produce (occasioned by lengthening the period of production) divided by the whole produce.[4] Jevons preserves the abstinence element; but the relation between the sacrifice of abstinence and the productivity of capital as determinants of the rate of interest is not worked out. Jevons can be said to have stopped on the threshold of the marginal-productivity theory.

In conclusion, it may be worth while referring again to Jevons's failure in the theory of exchange. The primitive – and obviously faulty – device of the trading bodies was an attempt to proceed from the subjective valuations of individuals to the formation of price in competitive conditions. With this technical aim was connected another: the desire to give an economic justification for free competition and *laissez-faire*. Jevons denied, as explicitly as did Wicksteed after him, that the subjective valuations of one individual can be compared with those of another. 'I see no means', he said, 'by which such comparison can be accomplished. . . . But even if we could compare the feelings of different minds, we should not need to do so; for one mind only affects another indirectly. Every event in the outward world is represented in the mind by a corresponding motive, and it is by the balance of these that the will is swayed. . . . Each person is to other persons a portion of

1 W. S. Jevons, *The Theory of Political Economy*, p. 224.
2 ibid., pp. 228–9.
3 ibid., p. 223.
4 ibid., p. 246.

the outward world. .... Thus motives in the mind of A may give rise to phenomena which may be represented by motives in the mind of B; but between A and B there is a gulf. Hence the weighing of motives must always be confined to the bosom of the individual.'[1]

And yet Jevons was unable to free himself entirely from his utilitarian tradition. In spite of his extreme individualist hedonism, he did operate with a concept – the trading body – which implied an aggregate (or average) of many individual scales of subjective values. This operation not only allowed Jevons to skate over a difficult technical problem, it also introduced (by implication rather than explicitly) the idea that free competition maximized satisfaction all round. If exchange between two individuals proceeded according to the second law of Gossen until maximum satisfaction for both was reached, Jevons's statement of competitive exchange implied a social maximization. With the exposure of the error in the technical analysis one might have expected that the implication was destroyed. But it had become too firmly implanted; and many later economists, using a more refined technical apparatus, still clung to a similar implication whenever questions of policy were involved.

*Carl Menger (1840–1921).* Though more important from the point of view of present-day theory than Jevons, Menger can be more briefly dealt with, because his work exhibits just that quality which Jevons's lacked: a high degree of consistency. Whatever one's judgment of the development for which Menger stood, his own contribution to it was marked by a high regard for the requirements of a comprehensive system. And the chronicler has an easy task in summarizing his work.

Menger's contributions to economics fall into three main classes: method, money, and pure theory. The first of these has already been dealt with in connection with the historical school. It is sufficient to add only a word or two about the connection between Menger's methodological position and his analytical work. In his *Untersuchungen* Menger insists that economic method must rest on an individualist foundation. He argues that the economic phenomena of society are not the direct expression of some social force, but are only the resultants of the conduct of individuals, of *wirtschaftende Menschen* (men engaged in economic activity), as he calls them. In order to understand the total economic process one has to analyse its elements, the behaviour of

---

1 W. S. Jevons, *The Theory of Political Economy*, p. 14.

individuals.[1] Like Jevons and Gossen, Menger puts the individual into the centre of the picture. But he does so in a way quite different from these writers or from other post-classical authors who had been influenced by hedonist philosophy. Menger claims that the 'atomistic' approach is a methodological necessity, and that it has no ethical or social-philosophical implications. He was thus the first to attempt to build a subjective theory of value which should be free from any hedonist assumption.

Menger's work in the field of money can be little more than mentioned here. He wrote a number of articles and memoranda in connection with the Austrian currency reform which have remained important contributions to the applied theory of money. His main statement of pure monetary theory is contained in a long article, *Geld*, first published in the *Handwörterbuch der Staatswissenschaften* in 1892.[2] The chief importance of this work lies in the fact that it is the first application of the subjective theory of value to the problems of money. It has served as the basis for much modern work on monetary theory; and it contains one of the best short explanations of the function of money in the process of exchange and in the formation of price.

It is on his subjective theory of value, however, that Menger's claim to fame rests. This theory is developed in his first book, *Grundsätze der Volkswirtschaftlehre*, published in 1871, the same year as Jevons's theory. Menger begins with what he evidently regarded as the two poles of economic activity: human wants and the means of satisfying them. He defines utility in a relative sense, that is as the ability of a thing to be put into a causal relationship with a want. Things which have this ability become goods when the want is present, when the causal relationship is recognized by the individual experiencing the want and when that individual has the power to apply the thing to the satisfaction of the want. These goods may be classified on technical grounds as goods of the first and of the second, third, and higher orders. The former (for example bread) are those which immediately serve to satisfy wants; the latter (for example flour, the mill, wheat, etc.) only satisfy wants indirectly: they are jointly required to produce

1 Carl Menger, Collected Works, vol. ii: *Untersuchungen über die Methode der Socialwissenschaften und der Politischen Oekonomie insbesondere* (London School of Economics Reprint, 1933), pp. 82–8.
2 This, together with his other monetary writings, forms volume iv (*Schriften über Geldtheorie und Währungspolitik*) of the London School of Economics Reprint of Menger's collected works (1936).

the goods of the first order. Their property of being goods at all depends on our ability to dispose at one and the same time of all the (complementary) goods required for a particular purpose.

The aim of this classification is to bring out the technical conditions of production (which later acquire importance in the theories of production and of capital) and to establish at once a relationship between the value of goods of the first order (those of immediate importance to the *wirtschaftende Mensch*) and the value of production goods of all kinds. When he comes to deal with this problem Menger is able to elaborate the productivity view of the factors of production which Say and others had tried to introduce.

The next classification of goods is based on their quantitative relation to wants. Of all the possible relations the most important is that in which the quantity of goods is less than the want for them. These goods are economic goods; the individual has to economize them, since he is aware that no portion of them can be lost or given up without causing a sacrifice of want-satisfaction. This dividing line between economic and non-economic goods is not a permanent one; goods may move from the category of economic goods to that of non-economic goods, and vice versa, with changes in wants, supplies of goods, technique, etc. When they are in the economic class, goods may be said to possess 'scarcity', a term which earlier English writers had never fully assimilated into the system. Auguste Walras, the father of Léon, had used *rareté* in something like the Mengarian sense. But Menger was the first, without using the word, to express precisely this quantitative relation between ends and means to which the word is now applied.

Menger's theory of value follows from his discussion of economic goods. The realization by an individual of the economic quality of a good gives rise to a judgment in his mind which we call value. In Menger's own words, 'value is the significance which concrete goods or quantities of goods obtain for us from the fact that we are aware that the satisfaction of our wants is dependent upon our disposing of these goods'.[1] Value arises from the limitation of goods in relation to wants; and it is this which gives to these goods their economic character. Free goods cannot possess value; for no want-satisfaction is dependent upon the availability to us of any portions of them.

---

[1] C. Menger, Collected Works, vol. i: *Grundsätze der Volkswirtshaftslehre* (London School of Economics Reprint, 1934), p. 78.

How is this subjective value determined? We know, says Menger, that we experience different wants with different intensity: some, those on which our very existence depends, are very intense; others, of a more refined character, are less urgent. But even the same kind of want appears in units of different urgency. Each concrete act of satisfaction has a different significance for us according to the degree of satisfaction that we have already reached. Menger gives numerical illustrations for his argument (which is really a more formal statement of Gossen's first law), but insists on the purely 'ordinal' nature of his comparison of the intensity of successive want-manifestations.

He proceeds to argue that if for each concrete want there were a single good suited exclusively to that want, the determination of the subjective value of that good would be a simple matter. It would be equal to the significance of that want. But in reality the matter is complicated by the fact that we generally deal with a quantity of goods accompanied by a complex of concrete wants. As a result, individual portions of the good will appear to have different significance according to the wants to which they are applied. The individual will use these portions to supply his wants in a descending order of urgency, the last available portion satisfying the least intense want. To discover the value of a portion, we have only to ask ourselves what satisfaction would have to be foregone if that portion were deducted from the total quantity. The answer must be: the satisfaction of the least intensive want. Menger concludes, therefore, that the value to the individual of any portion of the available quantity of goods is equal to the significance attached to the least satisfaction made possible by a single portion of the total available quantity.[1] This is the same as Jevons's 'final degree of utility'. Menger himself never used that kind of phrase; it was Marshall and Wieser who introduced the term 'marginal utility' (though the former made it apply to a slightly different concept).

This subjective value has now to be used as a basis for the determination of price. Menger denies Smith's dictum that exchange is due to a human propensity to truck. It is merely a part of the general activity of economy which is designed to supply maximum satisfaction with available means. And it is simply due to the existence of differences in relative subjective valuations of the same goods by different individuals. 'Whenever – either on account of differences in quantity or for other reasons – A values a unit of X more highly than one of Y and B

[1] ibid., p. 99.

values a unit of Y more highly than one of X, exchange will be possible. When A and B actually exchange portions of X and Y, the relation between the subjective values of the two goods to each individual will alter until this relation is the same for both A and B. At this point exchange will stop, since there will be no incentive to continue.' In other words, in equilibrium, the ratio of the marginal utilities of the two goods will be the same for both parties.

Subjective values will thus determine the limits of exchange and the limits of price. Each individual will, when the occasion for exchange arises, formulate some quantitatively determinate ratio in which he is willing to exchange. This ratio will reflect the ratio of his subjective values; but the subjective values themselves cannot be conceived of as determinate quantities. This, according to Menger and his successor, is the relation between the supply-and-demand theory of the market price and the 'ultimate' theory of subjective values. In the further elaboration of his theory of price Menger examines in turn different situations ranging from isolated exchange, where there are only two parties, to perfect competition. His treatment in this respect has not been modified to any considerable extent by subsequent writers, such as Wieser and Böhm-Bawerk, who adopted a similar approach.

He showed that in isolated exchange, price would be within the limits set by the buyer's and seller's maximum and minimum exchange ratios; and would tend – given equal desire to achieve a maximum advantage and equal bargaining ability – to the average of these ratios. Later economists have generally regarded price as indeterminate within these limits; and although Menger did not say this himself, he did say that variations from the average, due to differences in bargaining strength, would be of a non-economic character. As regards monopoly, Menger concluded that if only one unit was on offer, the limits of price would be set by the offer of the 'strongest', and that of the next strongest (the extra-marginal) buyer; and that within these limits it would be fixed according to the laws of isolated exchange. If more than one unit is offered, the price is fixed again by the offer of the marginal and the first extra-marginal buyer; and all those whose 'bids' are above the marginal acquire their units at that price. Or the monopolist may discriminate, that is make a separate bargain with each buyer. Menger's analysis of the factors which will determine the choice of policy is little different from that to be found in many later textbooks. In competition, discrimination is impossible; nor can any individual seller have an incentive to withhold any portion of the supply. Price is again fixed by marginal demands and offers; but this time there are what Böhm-Bawerk later called 'marginal pairs' of buyers and sellers. After a general summary of changes in the relation of subjective value and price, Menger goes on to discuss the origin of money. His account in the *Grundsätze* and in the article *Geld* begins with the inconveniences of barter, due to the different degrees of *Marktgängigkeit* (saleability, or acceptability) of different goods. Money gradually becomes the most *marktgängig* of all goods, the universal medium of exchange. In fulfilling this function it also facilitates the 'quantification' of subjective values: it acts as a price index, as the medium in which the equivalence of exchange is expressed. Menger examines the problems to which the existence of a unit of account gives rise; and much of the contemporary 'Austrian' theory on the question of monetary policy in relation to prices derives from him.

In the theory of distribution Menger is responsible for posing what is known as the problem of imputation; that is the problem of the value of goods of a higher order. Having adopted a subjective approach, Menger goes on to state that the value of goods of a higher order (including the factors of production) is 'conditioned by the anticipated value of those goods of a lower order for the production of which they serve'.[1] Menger's own solution of the problem of how the shares of the co-operating productive goods in the value of the product are to be determined is not quite clear. He says that the share of any individual factor is to be determined by the loss in value which the product would suffer if that factor were withdrawn from the co-operative combination.[2] But it is only fair to interpret this by inserting 'at the margin'; that is to think of Menger as having held a marginal productivity theory, even if it was of a primitive kind. This view is strengthened by the fact that Menger applied the same analysis to land, labour, and capital. Like Jevons, however, he did not manage to assimilate the problem of cost into his system, though his theory of distribution leads him to the brink of the law of cost, or opportunity-cost principle, which was to be enunciated by his disciple, Friedrich Wieser.

*Léon Walras (1834–1910).* As the last of the founders of the marginal utility school, Walras stands somewhere between Jevons and Menger. Like the former, he bases himself on hedonism; and he uses the

---

1 C. Menger, Collected Works, Vol. i: *Grundsätze der Volkswirtschaftslehre*, p. 124.
2 ibid., p. 142.

mathematical method even more thoroughly than Jevons. Like the latter, he avoids some of Jevons's errors in the translation of subjective values into the prices of a competitive market. Because of this, and in spite of his hedonism, Walras's influence on the modern mathematical school has been more considerable than that of Jevons. Walras was influenced by Cournot, and it was probably this influence which enabled him to combine a utility theory of value with a mathematically precise theory of market equilibrium. In spite, or perhaps because, of the difficulties which he experienced in this task, Walras was increasingly led to enunciate a general, non-'utilitarian' theory of economic equilibrium, expressed in terms of functional equations. He is, therefore, essentially the economist's economist, rather than of the general reader or the politician.

In 1874, three years after Jevons and Menger, but independently of them, Walras enunciated the marginal-utility doctrine in his *Éléments d'Économie politique pure*. This work falls into two parts: one dealing with the theory of exchange, the other (published in 1877) with the theory of production.

Walras operates with essentially the same concepts as Jevons, but he searches continually for solutions of the most general character. Like Jevons and Menger, he bases exchange-value on utility and limitation of quantity. Following his father, he uses the term *rareté*, which he defines as the 'dérivée de l'utilité effective par rapport à la quantité possédée'.[1] In other words, *rareté* is the same as marginal utility. The desire to equalize marginal utilities (according to Gossen's second law) will lead to exchange. And this desire, together with the stocks of goods possessed by each individual, will give a determinate demand or supply for each individual. This can be represented by a functional equation or by a curve.

Equilibrium in a competitive market will be achieved when the price is such that supply and demand are equal. Walras uses a special device for showing how this price results from competition. This is the notion of the *prix crié* – a price called out by an auctioneer. If at this price supply and demand are not equal, a new price will be called out; and this procedure will go on until equality is established. So, by *tâtonnements*, the equilibrium price will be achieved.[2] There is little here that

1 L. Walras, *Éléments d'Économie politique pure* (1926), p. 103. There is now available an admirable English translation, excellently edited by a distinguished Walras scholar: Walras, Léon, *Elements of Pure Economics*, translated by William Jaffé (1954).
2 ibid., pp. 34–71.

is new as compared with other statements of the relation between supply and demand, except the insistence on their functional inter-dependence with price and on their ultimate determination by *rareté*. Walras did not, however, make clear whether he conceived of deals being concluded at the non-equilibrium prices or not. If they are, then clearly the marginal-utility ratios of the participants are changed and so are their demands and supplies. Consequently, the equilibrium price will be different from what it otherwise would have been. If no transactions take place, Walras's equilibrium will arise. But to include this condition in the assumptions one would have to suppose, with Edgeworth, that there is continual 'recontracting', each deal prior to the establishment of equilibrium, being provisional only.[1]

Once we have these equations of supply and demand at equilibrium prices for each good, we can proceed, as Walras did, to the problem of general exchange equilibrium. Here again Walras used a special device of his own, that of the *numéraire*. This is one good which is used as a standard of reckoning. It is not, however, money in the ordinary sense of the word, because Walras assumes that it is merely an accounting unit and that there is no demand for it except that which is bound up with its non-monetary qualities. The use of this device enables us to say that if there are $n$ goods, we have $n-1$ equations of supply and demand (the one for the *numéraire* is derived from the others) and $n-1$ unknown prices to determine. This, Walras said, means that there is a determinate solution for the problem of general equilib-rium.[2] Walras's method of analysis gives a picture of the general system of the interdependence of prices, demands, and supplies; but it is weakened by the already mentioned obscurity in his method of connecting it with marginal utilities.

That Walras was very anxious to preserve this link, on account of the implications which it might be said to have for policy, is clear. Wicksell reports that Walras was led to his economic analysis by a desire to build up a strong case in favour of *laissez-faire*, in answer to an attack by a follower of Saint-Simon.[3] As a result, Walras gives another series of equations which reverses Jevons's procedure and takes prices, rather than quantities exchanged, as independent variables. Walras shows that, given certain prices, each individual will proceed to exchange

1 F. Y. Edgeworth, *Papers* (1925), vol. ii, p. 311.
2 L. Walras, *Éléments d'Économie politique pure*, pp. 109–33.
3 K. Wicksell, *Lectures on Political Economy*, vol. i (1937), pp. 73–4.

until the ratio of the marginal utilities of the two goods is to him equal to their ratio of exchange. This gives us determinate supply and demand functions, a number of equations equal to the number of unknowns, and thus determinate equilibrium.[1] It has recently been urged against this reasoning that, like that of Jevons, it really abandons the causal-genetic problem, that is, the problem of the origin of price from its subjective value roots.[2] This judgment seems justified. It makes Walras an important pioneer of the modern trend which is to abandon the search for the origin of value in favour of a purely formal but completely general theory of functional interdependence. It is claimed that later economists, using very refined and sophisticated mathematical tools, were able to complete the Walrasian model of general equilibrium. The decisive work on this subject was done in the 1950s by two Nobel Prize winners, Kenneth Arrow and Gerard Debreu, to which reference will be made below in connection with the equilibrium and market-clearing theorems of the 'New Classical Macroeconomics'. Briefly, it is argued that what has been proved is that however large the number of inputs and outputs there will always be a set of prices at which markets clear, provided certain conditions are fulfilled. Among the necessary conditions for this mathematically elegant theorem are complete flexibility of wages and prices, no uncertainties which cannot be insured against, no externalities or increasing returns and no monopolies or oligopolies! Its practical value for economic policy purposes seems limited.

Another criticism of Walras's theory is directed against the conclusions which he draws from it. Like Jevons, he was inclined to argue that free competition resulted in a maximization of utility.[3] But as later writers proved, the fact that at a price other than one fixed by competition some parties might wish to continue to exchange, while others would not, does not entitle us to say that on balance there is a sacrifice of satisfaction. We have no standard of comparison by which this could be scientifically established. But common sense supports Wicksell's view that since changes in the distribution of property might clearly be to the advantage of some people (in some cases, of a majority of the people), intervention in competition which alters price and, therefore,

1 L. Walras, *Éléments d'Économie politique pure*, pp. 72–106.
2 H. Mayer, 'Der Erkenntniswert der funktionellen Preistheorien', *Die Wirtschaftstheorie der Gegenwart*, vol. ii, pp. 188–99.
3 L. Walras, *Éléments d'Économie politique pure*, p. 99.

the distribution of property, might also produce an advantage to a majority.[1]

Walras's theory of production is an attempt to apply his general equilibrium analysis to the problem of the pricing of factors. It is, therefore, only a special case of his theory of value. By a different path (the details of which are not important to our present purpose) he reached a position not unlike that of the later Austrians. His solution was one of the earliest statements of the opportunity-cost principle and of the modern marginal-productivity theory. The other part of the theory, that concerned with capital, was sketchy and incomplete.

## The Second Generation

*Alfred Marshall.* After the passing of its founders, the marginal utility analysis becomes the accepted basis of economic theory. What follows is almost entirely a process of refinement. Some of the writers who have been responsible for this process during the last seventy-five years might almost be counted amongst the founders, and the work of others is a part of the raw material of the theorists of today.

In what might be called the second generation of the marginal-utility school three broad groups may be distinguished: the English, the Austrian and that of Lausanne. They represent three versions of a common doctrine rather than three separate schools of thought. From a technical point of view the differences between them are not negligible. But seen in a wider historical perspective their agreements are their more obvious features. They all begin with Menger's *wirtschaftende Mensch*, they all accept Gossen's laws as the fundamental characteristics of individual conduct, they all think in terms of infinitesimal increments and decrements (that is, they accept the concept of the margin) and they all analyse the conditions which are required to satisfy an equilibrium situation. The differences that remain relate to formulation and emphasis.

The English school is represented by the work of Alfred Marshall (1842–1924). In one way Marshall belongs to the first generation. He began his economic studies in 1867, after a mathematical training and the awakening of an interest in metaphysical and ethical problems, that is, at a time when Mill was still alive and when Menger, Jevons, and

1 K. Wicksell, *Lectures on Political Economy*, pp. 77–8.

Walras were not yet on the scene. It is known that by 1871, the year in which Jevons's *Theory* and Menger's *Grundsätze* were published, Marshall had already developed a similar approach. Under the influence of Cournot, von Thünen and Bentham, and of his own mathematical background, Marshall was beginning to translate many of the theorems of Ricardo and Mill into diagrammatic language. He adopted the utility view of value; and he seems to have reached the conclusion that 'our observations of nature . . . relate not so much to aggregate quantities, as to increments of quantities',[1] independently of Jevons. But his first substantial contributions to economic theory were not published until a few years after those of Jevons. The two papers on the *Pure Theory of Foreign Trade* and the *Pure Theory of Domestic Values* and the *Elements of Economics of Industry*, in which he had collaborated with Mrs Marshall, were published in 1879. His chief work, the *Principles of Economics*, appeared in 1890.

It is not easy to give a brief summary of Marshall's ideas. But the following may be mentioned as special characteristics of his system of thought. Compared with the Austrian and the pure mathematical economists, Marshall's break with the English tradition appears much less marked. He was himself a mathematician who could, and did, employ the algebraic or geometrical technique to show the precise relationships between different variables in certain well-defined situations. But there can be little doubt that Marshall was never fully satisfied with the study of the pure mechanics of abstract forces working in isolation. His *Principles* might well have carried a sub-title similar to that of Mill's treatise. For Marshall was a realist, keenly aware of the complexity of economic life, anxious to use to the full any scientific apparatus which he could develop, but convinced that there must remain a residuum of fact which could not, as yet, be satisfactorily assimilated by that apparatus. He was also anxious to expound the results of scientific inquiry in terms which could be generally understood. For he was, above everything, determined to see that economics continued to be regarded as productive of fruit: as able to give counsel and to influence policy. His apparatus of analysis was designed to preserve this contact between theory and policy.

Compared with the work of many of his contemporaries, Marshall's

---

1 A. Marshall, *Principles of Economics*, Preface to the first edition (8th edition, 1927), p. x. The definitive (ninth) and *Variorum* edition was edited by C. W. Guillebaud and published in 1961.

system appears eclectic, or even lacking in internal consistency. But this is an impression produced by the very elaborate quality of his system. Marshall was far from averse to formal analysis. But he aimed at preserving and linking up a series of normal analyses, each on a different level of abstraction and each relating to a different set of real tendencies. As a connected whole they would, he thought, present a true and fairly detailed picture of economic reality. Marshall's formulation of the theories of value and distribution, together with a host of subsidiary theories, which might impress one by their eclecticism, all involve a technique (based on the use of a special time element) which is derived from three closely connected aims: comprehensiveness, realism, and significance for economic policy.

Marshall's central doctrines of value and distribution reflect these aims. They combine marginal utility with subjective real cost. The forces behind both supply and demand, according to Marshall, determine value. They are to be conceived of as the two blades of a pair of scissors: it is useless to ask which does the cutting. Behind demand is marginal utility, reflected in the demand prices of buyers (the price at which given quantities will be demanded); behind supply is marginal effort and sacrifice, reflected in the supply prices (the prices at which given quantities will be forthcoming).

The novelty of this view, compared with the Austrian version, is that cost of production comes into its own once more as a determinant of value. Marshall distinguishes between real cost of production and expenses of production, though he does not always adhere strictly to the latter term.[1] The former consists of the disutility of labour, together with the sacrifice involved in providing the necessary capital. Marshall abandons Senior's term abstinence, which was too suggestive of an apologetic intention, in favour of the term 'waiting', that is the mere abstention from consumption in the present. But since he also speaks of it as the postponement of gratifications which involved sacrifice and for which interest was the reward,[2] he clearly had in mind something similar in kind to the toil and trouble of labour. Both elements which made up real cost were thus subjective.

Marshall guarded himself against the suggestion that if the money costs of production of two commodities were the same, their real costs were the same also. 'If it be given', he said, 'that twenty minutes' work

1 A. Marshall, *Principles of Economics*, p. 339.
2 ibid., p. 587.

by a physician, or two days' work by a watchmaker, or four days' work by a carpenter, or a fortnight's work by an agricultural labourer, can be bought in a given market for a guinea, and that the sacrifice involved in the loan of twenty guineas for a year can be bought by a guinea, then these several efforts and this abstinence are equivalent to one another for the purposes of the machinery of exchange. . . .' But when we speak of the ratio of the cost of production of two commodities, we must remember 'that one aggregate of diverse efforts and abstinences does not bear a ratio to another'. We are, therefore, forced to assume the existence of 'an artificial mode of measuring them in terms of some common unit, and refer to the ratio between their measures'.[1] 'These various efforts and abstinences . . . are certainly not equal to one another. But they would all exert an equal influence upon value; because their economic measures, the *expenses which would have to be incurred by anyone who would purchase them*, are all equal.'[2]

The same caution is evident in Marshall's view of the relation between money demands and marginal utility. He did not go the way of Cournot or the later mathematical theorists and sever the link between subjective states (wants and their satisfaction) and the objective phenomena of demands in the market. But he was aware of some of the difficulties involved in maintaining this connection. On the analogy of the relation between real money cost, he said that 'it cannot be too much insisted that to measure directly, or *per se*, either desires or the satisfaction which results from their fulfilment is impossible, if not inconceivable. If we could, we should have two accounts to make up. . . . And the two might differ considerably. . . . But as neither of them is possible, we fall back on the measurement which economics supplies, of the motive or moving force to action: and we make it serve, with all its faults, *both* for the desires which prompt activities and for the satisfactions that result from them.'[3]

One of the most characteristic Marshallian concepts, that of 'consumer's surplus', follows from the above view. This term expresses the surplus satisfaction derived by a consumer whenever he can buy a good at a lower price than that which he would be willing to pay rather than

---

1 A. Marshall, 'Mill's Theory of Value' in *Memorials of Alfred Marshall* (ed. A. C. Pigou, 1925), p. 125.

2 A. Marshall, *Principles*, pp. 92–3 (footnote).

3 A. and M. P. Marshall, *The Economics of Industry* (2nd edition, 1881), p. 97, quoted by C. Guillebaud, 'Davenport on the Economics of Alfred Marshall', *Economic Journal*, March 1937, p. 26.

go without the particular good. The notion follows directly from the difference between total and marginal utility. This is not the place to examine it in detail; but it may be said that those who have attacked the concept have urged that no measurement of the surplus satisfaction implied in consumer's surplus is possible. Marshall never suggested that it was, except on the very abstract assumption that the marginal utility of money was constant. The concept was used by him rather as a counterweight to the more usual analysis of producer's surplus. He used it to demonstrate the effects of taxes on commodities with elastic and inelastic demands. With it he tried to show which kind of government intervention was desirable. The whole field of 'welfare economics', of which Marshall's disciple and successor, Professor Pigou, is the founder, really rests on considerations of which the consumer's surplus doctrine is the intellectual ancestor.

Apart from his formulation of the connection between utility and demand and disutility and cost, Marshall's special contribution to the problem of value and price lies in his analysis of the equilibrium between supply and demand. This is based on his distinction between the different periods of time over which the forces tending to establish equilibrium are conceived to be operating. Marshall distinguishes four cases. First, there are the *market* values equating supply and demand, when supply is assumed to be fixed. Secondly and thirdly, there are the *normal* values, which may relate to short periods or long periods. In the former category we conceive of supply as the amount which can be produced at the given price with existing equipment and labour; in the latter, supply means 'what can be produced by plant which itself can be remuneratively produced and applied within the given time'. Lastly, we can widen our field of vision so as to include the changes in the economic 'data': population, tastes, technique, capital and organization; we shall then be having in mind the slow, secular changes in normal values.[1]

Marshall's apparatus is elaborate because of the purpose for which it is devised. By making possible the distinction of different degrees of adjustment, it becomes capable of application to concrete problems. This 'step by step' or 'partial equilibrium' method was not perhaps different in kind from the general equilibrium analysis of Walras. But it was designed for different, more realistic aims. It was also a method which was well adapted to the task of generalizing the propositions of

1 A. Marshall, *Principles*, pp. 378–9.

ɔf value. In Marshall's treatment, the principle of substit-
..ɪ at the margin became the operative principle of economic equilibrium. Like the equations of Cournot and Walras, it was used to
make clear the functional relationship of all economic categories. The
special place given to the distinction between adjustments over different periods of time also helped to join together the problems of
supply, demand, and price of goods with those of the supply, demand,
and price of the factors of production. Exchange, production, and
distribution became thus closely interrelated; and it depended on the
period of time taken into account whether the tracing out of the path to
equilibrium involved the factors appropriate to one or more of them.

Long-period equilibrium, though still a partial equilibrium (in the
sense that it does not imply a position of equilibrium as between the
industry examined and all others), tended to bring about prices proportional to the expenses of production. In this position, 'the earnings
of each agent are, as a rule, sufficient only to recompense at their
marginal rates the sum-total of the efforts and sacrifices required to
produce them'.[1] But Marshall was careful to point out that even in the
long run the earnings of the factors of production were not identical
with their real costs of production. That could only be true when
general equilibrium has been reached, that is in the unreal world of the
'stationary state'. The forces making for equilibrium in the long run
must be conceived of as continually tending towards the position
implied in the stationary-state concept. But in the real world this
position would never be reached.

This particular form of equilibrium analysis was productive of many
concepts which are now in general use. The notion of 'elasticity of
demand', and the 'principle of substitution' for instance, have become
accepted parts of the theory of exchange. The distinction between
'prime' and 'supplementary' costs has been an important aid in the
theory of production. Other concepts, however, such as that of the
'representative firm' and of 'external' and 'internal economies', have
been found less clear-cut and useful than Marshall took them to be.
They have nevertheless helped to clarify the conditions of equilibrium.
And the recent developments of the theory of imperfect competition,
which will be discussed later, have been inspired to a considerable
extent by the problems posed in these Marshallian concepts.

We have noticed that the Marshallian analysis of the equilibrium of

---

1 A. Marshall, *Principles*, p. 832.

value already includes a theory of distribution, since it establishes a series of relations between the earnings, the supplies of, and the demands for, factors and the prices of their products. These relations differ according to whether we assume stocks of goods to be fixed, stocks of factors to be fixed, stocks of factors to be variable but change to occur, or general equilibrium to prevail. Marshall's use of the time factor enabled him to distinguish between factor-incomes that are price determining and those that are price-determined. He showed that this distinction was not an absolute one (except in the case of the rent of land which he regarded as always price-determined), but that it depended on the period of time one had in mind. In the short run, the incomes of many factors are in the nature of rent; they are what Marshall called 'quasi-rent'.

Apart from these considerations, Marshall applied his long-period normal value to both labour and capital. In the long run, Marshall argued, there would be a tendency for the earnings of factors to equal their marginal real cost: interest would tend to be identical with the marginal sacrifice involved in saving, wages with the marginal disutility of effort. Marshall did not discard the marginal productivity doctrine of wages and interest. But he argued that this should be regarded as a part only of a complete theory of distribution – that which related to the forces governing the earnings of factors on the demand side.[1]

In other words, as in the theory of exchange, so also in that of distribution, Marshall was anxious to preserve the dual character of the 'pair of scissors'. The emphasis on real cost was vital for the dynamic purposes of the theory. With its aid, the repercussions of changes in one quantity on all the others could be brought out. As has recently been pointed out, 'the significance of real costs lies in the fact that, whenever important divergencies occur between the trend of actual realized values and the long-period trend of normal value (behind which in turn are real cost elements which influence normal values), then economic forces will be set in motion which will alter the trend of actual values – the change being in the direction of the long-period equilibrium'.[2] It was because Marshall realized that an ultimate cost analysis was an indispensable part of a theory of value that he was always anxious to defend Ricardo against Jevons and his followers.

1 A. Marshall, *Principles*, p. 518.
2 C. Guillebaud, 'Davenport on the Economics of Alfred Marshall', *Economic Journal*, March 1937, p. 30.

...s, however, so cautious in his formulation that almost in ... himself he shows up the unsatisfactory features of that aspect ...of the theory. For the subjective cost factor must always remain quantitively unprecise. And 'waitings' and 'efforts' do not run well in double harness. For this very reason Marshall often speaks of real cost in terms which seem to exclude any reference to ultimate psychological states. His theory then becomes purely 'behaviouristic': the 'sacrifices' of abstinence meaning nothing more fundamental than the desire of demand, and the ability to obtain, a reward for a particular act of choice. This is very much akin to the opportunity-cost principle first enunciated by Wieser. The only difference is that the Austrians, in their formulation of the theory, assumed either that the quantity of the factors of production was given or, at any rate, that it was an independent variable. Marshall, on the other hand, allowed the supplies of factors to be variable and to be in part determined by price, so as to make his apparatus more suitable to dynamic problems.

There thus remains some dichotomy in Marshall's great system. Real cost is preserved, but is given a subjective character. However, it is often robbed of any substantial meaning by the way in which it is formulated. On the demand side, desires and satisfactions are preserved, though they too are hedged round with major qualifications. The reason for this dichotomy is Marshall's spiritual kinship with Mill. In spite of his disclaimer of any utilitarian bias, Marshall was essentially a latter-day utilitarian, that is a liberal social reformer. Though anxious not to abandon any arguments which modern economics could offer in favour of the existing economic system in general, he was also most anxious not to close the door on proposals for specific reforms. His political compromise was similar to Mill's and, like the latter's, often uneasy. But his analytical genius enabled him to build an economic theory sufficiently comprehensive to be acceptable to the greatest variety of political opinion which that compromise could attract. It was, in any case, an economic theory of a most fruitful kind for subsequent development in the apparatus of economic analysis and in the evolution of practical aids to statesmanship.

*Wieser and Böhm-Bawerk.* Compared with Marshall's achievement, the work of the later Austrians, though more rigorous in appearance, is both more narrow in scope and more arid in conception. Menger had two great disciples, Friedrich von Wieser (1851–1926) and Eugen von Böhm-Bawerk (1851–1914). Though both are better known in

English-speaking countries than Menger, their writings do not contain any fundamental changes of the views of their master. In the pure theory of value they merely refine the subjective approach originated by Menger. The individual and his wants is still the beginning and end of the analysis. Utility is still conceived of in the sense of 'significance for conduct'. Wieser and Böhm-Bawerk seem to stress the purely formal character of subjective valuation even more than did Menger. Among innovations in this field may be mentioned Wieser's introduction of the term *Grenzmutzen* (marginal utility) in his *Ursprung und Hauptgesetze des wirtschaflichen Wertes* (1884), and Böhm-Bawerk's more precise statement of the formation of market prices by the bidding of 'marginal pairs' in his *Grundzüge einer Theorie des wirtschaflichen Güterwertes* (1886).

Both Wieser and Böhm-Bawerk were, however, responsible for certain additions to the body of Austrian theory which have given their work a characteristic imprint. Wieser's achievement lives in the theory of cost and distribution; Böhm-Bawerk's in the theory of capital and interest. The early Austrian theory of exchange-value had a gap of which Menger himself was conscious. This consisted of an omission to deal with cost. Here Wieser set in with an analysis which brings him nearly to the Marshallian position. In the *Ursprung* he almost appears to make value depend on both utility and cost. But in reality his solution is different from that of Marshall. Wieser, and all the other Austrians after him, do not use a real-cost concept. Disutility and other sacrifices in the traditional English sense have no place in their theory. Utility alone is the cause of value. And if utility is conceived of in a purely formal sense (that is, as relative preference inferred from observed acts of choice), disutility is merely an unnecessary duplication. All choice can be said to involve sacrifice, in the sense that to choose A involves forgoing B. The disutility of labour and the sacrifice of waiting can, therefore, be adequately explained in terms of preference for income or leisure, and for present or future goods.

In Wieser's view, the formation of value is a circular process. Like Menger, he regards the value of goods of a higher order as being derived from the value of their products. This derived value then becomes the cost element. Once formed, this may be accepted as given; but it is logically secondary. The actions of the entrepreneur are responsible for the continual tendency towards equality at the margin between cost and price. They exercise a demand for raw materials, capital goods, and labour in the respective markets, according to the existing or anticipated demands for the products. Errors are inevitable; but the forces of supply and demand will continually tend to correct errors made in the past. Wieser's 'law of cost' or the opportunity-cost principle, as it was later called, amounts to this: given the quantity of the factors of production, competition for factors in the different lines of employment will distribute them in such a way that the values of their different products allow them to earn the same total amount in every alternative use.

This theory really involved abandoning the search for real cost, which, for reasons already stated, the classical and post-classical economists had regarded as desirable. But it was a theory of great elegance which seemed to make the whole marginal-utility analysis – at any rate in its more formal guise as a theory of choice – comprehensive and self-consistent. With minor variations, it was widely accepted and propagated by economists like Davenport and Wicksteed; and it became one form in which the marginal productivity theory could be stated. Moreover, as noted above, some of Marshall's formulations of the real cost doctrine removed much of the conflict with the opportunity-cost theory, leaving only the formal difference relating to the assumption about the supplies of factors. But this was not a substantial difference: Walras, for example, succeeded in formulating the theory of opportunity-cost on the assumption of variability of factor supply in a way similar to the English real-cost theorists.

Another point worthy of notice in Wieser is his doctrine of natural value which appears in *Der Natürliche Wert* (1889) and in *Theorie der gesellschaftlichen Wirtschaft* (1914). The indirect significance of this concept is considerable. Wieser had perhaps done more than any other economist to complete the transition from the socio-historical approach of the classical theory of value to the individualism of the marginal utility school. His law of cost effected the final breach with the objective real-cost theories. Yet he himself seems to have felt that there were some shortcomings in pure subjectivism. He knew that economics was concerned with a social process, that it had, therefore, to be based on the concept of a social economy. He saw that this concept involved certain institutional assumptions which, if slurred over, might be held to give the subsequent theory an apologetic character. He proceeded, therefore, to make his assumptions explicit. 'Most theorists,' he argued, 'particularly those of the classical school, have tacitly made the same abstraction. In particular, those opinions which regard price as a social value judgement are designed to abstract from individual differences of purchasing power which make price deviate from natural value. Thus, many a theorist has written the theory of value of communism without knowing it. . . .'[1] Natural value is the value which would result in a 'communist' state. Here, owing to the postulated absence of individual selfishness, errors, inequalities of wealth and the presence of a strong communal purpose, the theoretical analysis of the acts of choice of an individual would be applicable to the economy of the community as a whole. Value would be the resultant of the available quantity of goods and of utilities. In the real world, however, natural value is only one element in the formation of price. The existing distribution of purchasing power together with error, fraud, and compulsion is the other.

Natural value, Wieser claims, is a completely neutral phenomenon. Although it would be present in a collective economy, this does not mean that the natural values of interest and rent, for example, need give a right to an income. Whether they do or not depends entirely on the institutional structure of the state. Wieser succeeds to some extent in emancipating himself from the common error of tacitly identifying an implied institutional framework with reality. But he does not remove the political norm altogether. He implies an identity between his system of natural values and the social maximization of utility of hedonist philosophy. Although analytically superior to similar attempts (for example of the American economist J. B. Clark), Wieser's doctrine rests on the assumption common to them all that it is possible to conceive of a subjective social value. Such a concept, it is clear, must be self-contradictory except on the most special assumptions regarding human nature and the springs of human conduct.

Böhm-Bawerk's special contribution lies in his theory of capital. In 1889 he published his *Geschichte und Kritik der Kapitalzinstheorien*, in which he criticized somewhat ungenerously all earlier interest theories. Four years later appeared the *Positive Theorie des Kapitalzinses* in which his own theory was expounded and in which he gave a version of his general theory of value similar to that contained in the *Grundzüge*. A number of influences contributed towards Böhm-Bawerk's theory of capital. The first was the desire to apply more consistently the theory of marginal utility to the problem of interest. The second was derived from the later neo-classical English and German productivity and

1 F. v. Wieser, *Der Natürliche Wert* (1889), p. 60.

wage-fund theories. The third – as an incentive, perhaps the most important – was Böhm-Bawerk's anxiety to destroy the influence of Marx, which had grown considerably on the Continent.

Briefly, the existence of interest and its size are explained on three grounds – the famous *drei Gründe*. These reasons combine both subjective and objective (technical) factors; a combination which was clearly designed to overcome the difficulties of the abstinence theory and the subjective real-cost theory in general. Böhm-Bawerk's doctrine had, however, this in common with the others, that it started from a consideration of the significance of time in relation both to consumption and production.

The first two grounds are psychological and relate to consumption. Böhm-Bawerk argues that individuals faced with the choice between present and future goods normally overestimate future resources and underestimate future wants. Hope is the cause of the former, lack of imagination and weakness of will are those of the latter peculiarity of choice which involve the lapse of time. These two causes operate to increase the marginal utility of goods in the present compared with their marginal utility in the future. They create an *agio*; and to call forth a supply of present in return for future goods, that *agio* has to be paid.

The third factor is of a technical character; it affects production, and it accounts for the existence of a demand price for present, in terms of future, goods. It is a fact of experience that if the original factors of production, labour and natural resources, are to be more productive of consumable goods, they have to be used in an increasingly indirect manner. The whole progress of civilization on its technical side consists, according to Böhm-Bawerk, in the adoption of more 'roundabout' methods of production. From the making of simple tools and instruments to the production of the most elaborate modern machines, progress has meant embarking on *Produktionsumwege*, on the interpolation of more intermediate stages between the original factors and the finished consumption goods.

Roundabout production creates a demand for capital. Means of subsistence are required (either directly or in a monetary form) to maintain the owners of the factors during the time which must elapse before fresh (and more abundant) consumable goods are available. And the great productivity of these 'capitalistic' methods of production enables a price to be offered in order to overcome the time discount between present and future goods. Here, then, was an explanation why interest had to be paid and why it could be paid. And it was put forward to prove that interest was a 'natural' phenomenon – a necessity from which not even a socialist economy could escape.[1] This explanation depended in the last resort on the general marginal-utility theory of value. Although Böhm-Bawerk claimed that any one of his three grounds was alone sufficient to explain the presence of interest, it is clear that the subjective factors were the ones which really created that scarcity of means in relation to ends without which, according to the Austrians, value could not arise. Against these subjective factors a number of objections have been urged. Not only was the existence of this time-preference questioned; even if it exists, it was argued that it has no quantitatively precise significance. In any case, time-preference – as indeed all so-called consumers' preferences – is conditioned by a particular social framework. If, therefore, there is an *agio*, it is due in its concrete form, not merely to human nature, but to social factors such as income distribution. Anything like a 'natural right' to a particular income from capital could not be deduced from the theory without a slurring over of specific social facts.

In a suitably 'purified' form, this theory of capital and interest does not carry these implications. And Böhm-Bawerk's merit was to have provided a starting-point for theoretical work in this field, which can be, and has been, free from any particular socio-historical element, and partakes entirely of the nature of tool-making. It has also served as an important stepping-stone in the theory of economic fluctuations.

*Vilfredo Pareto.* The last of the great writers of the second generation is Pareto (1848–1923). Pareto's interest in economics came after twenty years' practice as an engineer, which had followed a training in mathematics and the physical sciences. This background, combined with a strong and lasting interest in the economic aspects of current political problems, explains much of Pareto's approach to economics. He became interested at an early stage in the application of mathematics to economics, both in the sense in which Cournot had urged such an application, as well as in the use of statistical techniques in empirical studies. This mathematical interest attracted the attention of Walras and caused him to choose Pareto as his successor at Lausanne, thus definitely establishing a 'Lausanne school'.

Pareto's first large work was based on his lectures at Lausanne. The *Cours d'Economie Politique* (1896–7), although much less important for

1 E. v. Böhm-Bawerk, *The Positive Theory of Capital* (1923), pp. 365–7.

present-day theory than Pareto's later writings, is nevertheless indispensable for an understanding of Pareto's intellectual development. It continues the work of Walras by emphasizing the value of the concept of general equilibrium and by setting out what Pareto conceived to be the mathematical conditions of general equilibrium. From the simple mathematical rules concerning the determinancy of a system of equations of *n* variable, Pareto proceeds to show, in the same way as Walras had done, the general interdependence of all economic quantities and the theoretical legitimacy of the concept of a determinate general economic equilibrium. Pareto is not, however, content with theoretical validity only. In the *Cours* he professes the hope that all the variables in his algebraic equations may one day be filled with quantitative values derived from statistical data. Pareto does not seem to have been aware of the methodological difficulty here, the conflict between the conditions underlying the abstraction of an algebraic system and the inevitably historical character of statistics, a difficulty which was forcefully pointed out by one of his early critics.[1] His subsequent development suggests, however, that he had abandoned his hope of ever quantifying his functional equation. Pareto's approach enabled him to emphasize and to elucidate the relationships of complementarity and substitution. In this respect, while he himself may not have gone so far as Marshall in details, at least in his earlier work, his approach appears to have been more suggestive and on it much recent work has been based.

On the general problem of the utility foundation of value, the *Cours* clearly shows, by its confusion, the beginning of an uneasiness in Pareto's mind. The basic approach to the problem of value is still strongly subjective, the individual's *goûts* and *obstacles* being the poles of economic activity. But although Pareto is not clear about the 'ordinal' character of utility (which had been emphasized by Menger), there is already in evidence some tendency to ignore the psychological premiss and to concentrate on the empirical fact of choice. An indication of some awareness of the confusion to which the utility concept is apt to lead is to be found in Pareto's distinction between different types of human action, in particular those which find their *rationale* solely in the observed preference of the individual, and those which can be referred to some objective standard. It was in connection with the

---

1 L. v. Bortkiewicz, 'Die Grenznutzentheorie als Grundlage einer ultraliberalen Wirtschaftspolitik', *Jahrbuch für Gesetzgebung, Verwaltung und Volkswirtschaft*, vol. xxii, p. 1191.

former, which, according to the marginalist school, alone mattered in economic theory, that Pareto suggested replacing utility as the motivating characteristic of the object of desire by the more colourless term *ophélimité*. But his treatment was not sufficiently different from that of the earlier, still hedonistic, utility theorists, and the new term did not, therefore, succeed in ousting the old.

The *Cours* is especially interesting for its many disquisitions on social and political problems in general. Pareto's methodological position is one in favour of an absolutely formal and positive theory and of the purging of economics of all ethical elements. Yet the *Cours* is full, if not of normative postulates, at any rate of categorical statements on matters which, from the point of view of his methodology, Pareto should have regarded as extraneous to economics. There is, first, the already mentioned distinction between types of human action which is made use of for the construction of certain (implied) social norms. Then there are references to broad trends of history, and there is also a consistent attempt to provide some philosophy of social change. Here the chief theoretical concept is a distinction between the *forces coercives* and the *forces automatiques* of society.

Pareto's hypothesis is that human progress involves an increase of the automatic elements in the regulation of social affairs at the expense of the coercive ones. The distinction between the two forces is not made very clear, nor is the hypothesis proved. Indeed, Pareto's definition of what constitute coercive forces was clearly designed for purposes of current political debate rather than as an explanation of the broad movements of the past. Social legislation, for example, is therefore regarded as a retreat from the progress of civilization. Socialism is rejected, not because it could not work in the economic sphere (indeed Pareto believed that it could be shown that a socialist ministry of production might, in theory, arrive at exactly the same economic 'plan' as that which would result from the equilibrating forces of an ideal *laissez-faire* capitalist economy), but because it represented a victory of the coercive forces. A list of past instances of the inefficiency of state action is drawn up and is made into a general indictment of both partial state regulation and socialism. Even the effectiveness of the waging of war (or the preservation of peace) through the machinery of the state is questioned.

Of the problems treated in the *Cours* which are not connected with the central issues of economic theory, there is one which deserves to be mentioned, Pareto's 'law' of income distribution. On the basis of some statistical studies, Pareto concludes that income distribution shows a high degree of constancy for different times and countries. If the distribution is plotted on a logarithmic graph, it will appear as a straight line sloping downward to the right, the inclination of which is extremely stable, and can therefore be regarded as the numerical expression of a law of income distribution.

We cannot pause here to discuss the details of this law or the many criticisms to which it has been subjected. It may be pointed out, however, that these criticisms have been directed both against the adequacy of the statistical evidence as well as against the value of Pareto's special definition of inequality of income. What is more important to our purpose is the use to which Pareto puts this 'law'. In the first place he believes that the constancy of inequality in the distribution of income reflects inequality of human ability, which is a natural and universal category. Even before more numerous statistical tests had been made, it was pointed out[1] that, to prove his point, Pareto would have to show that there is at all times and in all places a definite distribution of human beings according to their ability to earn income, and that the actual distribution of income was exclusively determined by the ability distribution. The *Cours* certainly did not provide such a proof, and subsequent evidence of marked long-period changes in the distribution of income has almost completely deprived Pareto's 'law' of its statistical foundation. Pareto's further conclusion, that a reduction in inequality could only be achieved by a rise in average income (that is, by production growing faster than population), was thus also undermined. This conclusion was, moreover, subject to the further deficiency that it was implied in Pareto's peculiar definition of inequality.[2]

The interesting features of the elaborate income distribution study is its close connection with Pareto's general ultra-liberal attitude as expressed in the *Cours*. The immutable character of inequality and the fact that it could be mitigated only by a rise in production harmonized well with the intransigent *laissez-faire* position which Pareto held at the time. His income study provided an apologia for the inequality which reformers were attacking, as well as arguments against the means which they suggested for curing it.

1 L. v. Bortkiewicz, 'Die Grenznutzentheorie als Grundlage einer ultraliberalen Wirtschaftspolitik', *Jahrbuch für Gesetzgebung, Verwaltung und Volkswirtschaft*, vol. xxii, pp. 1208–9.
2 ibid., vol. xxii, pp. 1208–9.

Pareto's subsequent work shows marked and interesting changes from his original position, both in regard to economic theory and to politics. The chief feature of these changes is that the more traditional treatment of value of the *Cours*, which had gone hand in hand with a strong belief in an economic justification for *laissez-faire*, is abandoned. And together with the development of a new approach to the value problem, there takes place a withdrawal from economic liberalism and an increase in methodological formalism.

An indication of this new approach is given in Pareto's short paper, *Anwendungen der Mathematik auf Nationalökonomie* (1902); but its most complete statement is to be found in the *Manuale di Economia Politica* (1906; French translation, 1909). It has been suggested by many of his followers that in this work Pareto discards the value theory altogether in favour of a theory of price unrelated to subjective factors.[1] Whether this is quite true is a matter for some debate. What is certainly true is that the theory of the Manual is marked by an entirely new view of utility which seems to push towards it logical limits the purely formal quality of the modern theory of value.

The innovation consists in stating that utility was not measurable, but that a purely 'ordinal' conception of utility sufficed for the formulation of a theory of choice. In technical terms, a scale of preferences can be deduced for each individual without the assumption of determinate utility functions. The scale of preferences as exhibited in conduct is the only determinate phenomenon; any number of utility functions could fit it. Actually this change in outlook had been foreshadowed before, not only in the work of Cournot but also in the writings of some of Pareto's contemporaries, like Irving Fisher (*Mathematical Investigations into the Theory of Value and Prices*, 1892) and Gustav Cassel (*Grundriss einer elementaren Preislehre*, 1899). But Pareto's exposition was the one which attracted the greatest attention.

Pareto did not work out a complete theoretical apparatus based on the new view of choice. But he made an important start. He adopted the concept of 'indifference curves', first used by the English economist, F. Y. Edgeworth, in *Mathematical Psychics* (1881), to show the possibility of constructing a theory on the basis of scales of preference only. Pareto takes two goods and shows that a number of quantitative combinations of these goods will all be equally desired by

1 For example, A. Osorio, *Théorie mathématique de l'échange* (1913), p. 302; and P. Boven, *Les Applications mathématiques à l'économie politique* (1912) p. 174.

the individual. All these can be arranged on an indifference curve to which an index can be assigned. Other combinations of the same goods, being either more or less desirable, can also be arranged on curves to which higher or lower indices will be given. An individual's system of preferences with respect to these two goods can be represented by an 'indifference map', which will show, on the analogy of a contour map, different levels of satisfaction. It is then possible to write a number of differential equations which will represent an equilibrium system in terms of indifference rather than of utility functions.

This increasing formalism did not lead directly to a break with the utilitarian justification for *laissez-faire*. At first, Pareto seems to try to buttress this case by the way in which he defines the collective maximum of *ophélimité*. This, he says, will be reached at a point from which no departure giving a gain of *ophélimité* to all participants is possible.[1] As Wicksell pointed out,[2] this is equivalent to saying that perfect competition, given its assumptions, will produce such a collective maximum. But although Pareto gets very near in this place to the subjective social value concept mentioned earlier, he proceeds to examine the possibilities of a collective economy and ends up with a perfectly 'neutral' conclusion. 'Pure economics', he says, 'gives us no truly decisive criterion for choosing between a social order based on private property and socialism. This problem can only be solved by taking into account phenomena of a different character.'[3] On many particular points (notably in the theory of international trade), Pareto went further than this: he opposed policies based on the principles of economic liberalism. And as if to strengthen his conclusion about the 'neutrality' of pure economics, his interest turned increasingly to general social problems. His last substantial work was his voluminous *Traité de sociologie générale* (1917–19).[4] In this, he supplemented the neutral and formal analysis of equilibrium economics with social-psychological theorems which had already made an appearance in the Manual.

We need not stay to analyse these in detail. They show a curious, if perhaps only formal, resemblance to Marx's socio-psychology. Pareto's system distinguishes logical from non-logical actions; and it introduces the notion of *derivations* to describe all those concepts and

1 V. Pareto, *Manuel d'économie politique* (2nd edition, 1927), p. 354.
2 K. Wicksell, *Lectures on Political Economy*, pp. 82–3.
3 V. Pareto, *Manuel d'économie politique*, p. 364.
4 Available in an English translation under the title *Mind and Society*.

beliefs that serve to rationalize (though in an entirely inadequate manner) man's non-logical actions. A further concept is the *residue*, which is the objective determinant of conduct for which the *derivation* supplies the rationalizations. Finally, there is the socio-historical doctrine that all history is a *succession of aristocracies*, which is based upon the theory of the circulation of *élites*, i.e. of minorities in all social classes, especially capable of rising to the top.

Unlike Marx, Pareto did not attempt an explicit combination of his sociology and his economics; the latter remained strictly separate and strictly 'pure'. It is, nevertheless, interesting to recall that when Pareto was faced with an actual political movement of strong impetus, Fascism, he became its intellectual ally.

# 9

# The Beginning of American Economics

## The Background

During the last hundred and fifty years economics has ceased to be as much of an English science as it used to be, and there have been important contributions to the discussion of its central doctrines from many different countries. Some of these early non-English contributions have already been noted in the preceding chapter. We may now add a brief account of one of these contributions, that of the United States of America. In doing so, we shall be concerned only with those authors who bring economic thought up to, rather than beyond, the threshold of contemporary analysis. For, at that point, economic thought can no longer be conveniently classified into national compartments. In particular, in the English-speaking countries interchange and coalescence become the rule. Nevertheless, we shall have occasion, even later, to note certain important features of present-day economics which owe their existence largely to an American impetus. Indeed, it can be argued that in the last fifty years or so, America has been the prime source of much new economic reasoning. More about this later.

A word of explanation is necessary to show why the earlier contribution of America deserves separate treatment. American economics is not particularly notable for its part in the introduction of the marginal-utility approach. Its claim to our attention rests on a different fact. The preponderantly English character of classical political economy can in part be explained by the leadership of England in the development of modern capitalism. It is not surprising, therefore, that the relative preponderance of English economic thought should decline once England ceased to be the only important capitalist country. Nor is it surprising that the emergence of the United States as the leading capitalist country should have coincided with a very considerable increase of American theoretical activity. To-day the accumulated and current output of American economic literature is vast; and it is only barely an exaggeration to say that the study of economics, in the form in which we have become accustomed to it during the last hundred years, has its most congenial home in the United States. For this reason, if for no other, it would be necessary to examine the development and present position of economics in the United States. But it is not quantity alone which compels attention. American economics has in several significant respects taken a somewhat different path from that developed in Europe. Where its theory was imported, as in the earlier period, its formulations were altered to fit the new environments. Later, contributions which were wholly peculiar to America began to make their appearance.

This history of American economic thought undoubtedly deserves the long and detailed study a beginning of which has been made fairly recently.[1] A method similar to that which underlies this book can, and has, with great advantage been applied to America. Here, too, the relation between theory and practice make an instructive story. The 'other side' of a colonial economy, the beginnings of modern capitalism, the achievement of independence, the Civil War and the growth of a vast domestic market, and the beginnings of outward expansion are all traceable in their theoretical reflections.

The present chapter has, of necessity, a much more modest aim; it is to add to the story of the preceding pages some of the early contributions made by Americans to modern economics. But even within this restricted field, some further limitation has had to be imposed by virtue of the general plan which underlies this history. Many individual writers are not dealt with if their contribution, however interesting in itself, is not typical of some major new development, or is not to be regarded as being peculiarly American. A considerable amount of American economic literature, particularly at the end of the last and beginning of the present century, is of this character. It consists to a large extent of expositions, elaborations, and refinements of Marshall, Pareto, and the Austrians; and mere mention, therefore, of special American variations on a familiar theme will have to suffice.

The early period of American economic thought shows no specially

1 Joseph Dorfman, *The Economic Mind in American Civilization* (1946).

noteworthy features.[1] A considerable amount of pamphlet literature fills the hundred years from the last quarter of the seventeenth century to the achievement of independence. It is generally concerned with immediate problems and is almost wholly ephemeral. And much of it reproduces debates that had exercised public men in England and France many decades earlier. There are, of course, interesting individual variations on familiar themes. Roger Williams formulates most skilfully through his concept of 'corporate freedom', the already established compromise between divine command and the needs of commerce. William Penn, friend and follower of Petty, had many interesting remarks to make on the essential quality of a colonial economy and its relation to that of the metropole. During this period, too, with Penn and others a theme emerges which was thereafter to run through American thinking as a recurrent *leitmotiv*: monetary reform, and reliance on credit and paper money. But by common consent there is only one writer in that period who is worthy to be mentioned in the company of the early political economists of Europe – Benjamin Franklin (1706–90). Franklin does not rank very high as an original economic thinker. His main claim to fame rests rather on the broad scope of his interests and on his enlightened views on many political as well as scientific problems. His general position in economic theory is not unlike that of Petty, with whom he shared his experimental bent. The chief indications that more than sixty years separated their writings are the greater evidence of physiocratic concepts and formulations and a more systematic mode of expression in Franklin's books. His first work, *A Modest Inquiry into the Nature and Necessity of Paper Currency*, published when he was twenty-three years old, contains a statement on the determination of value which is almost identical with that given by Petty in his *Treatise*. However, with a later tract, *Observations Concerning the Increase of Mankind* (1751), Franklin joined the ever growing circle of writers who are now known to have anticipated Malthus's views on population. Franklin wrote a number of economic works on a variety of topics. In all of them he shows himself possessed of an extremely astute mind and of a great respect for that pragmatic criterion which has to this day remained a special feature of American social thought.

Much of the immediate post-Revolutionary literature was still of the

---

1 The reader should in addition to Dorfman's work consult E. A. J. Johnson, *American Economic Thought in the 17th Century* (1932) for a detailed treatment.

pamphlet type, and this state of affairs continued until the end of the first quarter of the nineteenth century. The fiscal and monetary difficulties of the Confederation gave rise to much discussion and to an increasing literary output. Alexander Hamilton and Albert Gallatin, Jefferson's Secretary of the Treasury, are probably the best-known names among the authors of that period. Jefferson himself, however, though he was, of course, of gigantic stature in political and social philosophy generally, made only very few pronouncements on economic matters.

It was not until the third decade that anything in the nature of systematic discussions of the economic process began to appear. It was not until then that the predominant agricultural economy of the country was modified by the kind of industrial development which had been taking place in England for at least a hundred years. Smith was republished several times, and American editions of Ricardo and Say were printed. It was, however, some years before there was much general interest in the work of the classics. But with the growth of industrialization in the Atlantic states and the opening up of the West from the 1830s on, there is added to the discussion of individual problems of policy the beginning of a systematic study of political economy by specialist scholars in colleges and universities.

The few systematic expositions of economic principles which date from the pre-Civil War period are not very important. They generally reproduce the worst features of the post-Ricardian era of mediocrity, lack of penetrating thought, and a pedestrian regard for neatness in the exposition of the theories of the masters. All the early academic exponents of the subject fall into this class. The rare exceptions are to be found among the protectionists, who, whether they were writing voluminous treatises or slender tracts, were all pamphleteers by nature. John Rae's *Statement of Some New Principles on the Subject of Political Economy, etc.* (1834) deserves mention for its attack upon the free-trade doctrines of the *Wealth of Nations* and for its sociological theory of capital. Another protectionist pamphleteer of this time (although much of his work falls into an earlier period), Mathew Carey, may also be listed, if only for the reason that his name was to be perpetuated by his son, one of the few important American economists of the early nineteenth century.[1]

---

1 For a detailed account see E. Teilhac, *Pioneers of American Economic Thought in the Nineteenth Century* (1936).

Henry C. Carey (1793–1879) began as a disciple of the English classical school and as a free trader. Like Fichte and List, he was soon forced by his environment to change his views. In his *Principles of Political Economy* (1837–40) and in his other works he held a labour theory of value and stated his belief in the possibility of a continual improvement of the position of the labouring classes. His analytical abilities were not very great, but his insight was acute enough to make him appreciate the disharmonious implications of Ricardianism. As is not surprising for one who was writing in the days of the pioneering settlers, he rejected the Ricardian theory of rent, which was later to be taken up by another important nineteenth-century American writer, Henry George. The problem of land scarcity did not exist for him: he was not afraid, as were the witnesses of the industrial revolution in England, of an ever-increasing tribute exacted by the land-owning class. His optimism and nationalism led him along a path which was parallel to that taken by List. However, it should be remembered that the 'nationalist school' which Carey founded, as well as Carey's later ideas, shows that he had much more in common with various Utopian European social reform schools than with List and with the protectionism which later became so important in America.

The end of the Civil War inaugurated an era of rapidly increasing economic development and theoretical activity. Economics became a more and more popular subject in university curricula, and the number of its professional practitioners and of books on it grew at a fast rate. The 'second American revolution' finally cleared the ground for the expansion of manufacturing industry and for the full establishment oif modern capitalism. It created a large class of industrial wage-earners, opened up a vast home market, and speeded up the development of the West and the rapid exhaustion of the pioneering possibilities of the frontier. It ushered in an era full of the problems which Europe had been experiencing for a long time. It also greatly increased the range of economic activity of the government and the problem of economic policy.

From that time economics becomes an institutionalized discipline. But although the number of university professorships devoted to the subject grew rapidly, it is to be noted that from that day to this, the practice of theoretical economic inquiry in America always maintained much closer and continuous ties with business and government than it did in England. The period between the end of the Civil War and the end of the century is marked by a division between the 'old' school and the new, and by an increase of socialist activity and literature. To the old school belong a number of economists who had much in common with the post-Ricardians, against whom Jevons and his fellow-marginalists were inveighing in England. Few of them have achieved any fame that went beyond the frontiers of America; Francis A. Walker (1840–97) being the only one of the group in the realm of general economics. Walker worked in a number of fields in all of which he distinguished himself by a considerable energy and by the vigorous espousal of definite views. In monetary matters he was a strong opponent of the views of the banking school, and a faithful upholder of the quantity theory of money. He did a considerable amount of work in statistics for which his experience of public office gave him the opportunity. In pure theory, one of his main ideas was to insist upon the distinction between interest and profits and to emphasize the similarity of profits and rent.

But Walker is probably best known as one of the chief opponents of the wage-fund doctrine, already abandoned at that time in its primitive form by most of the English economists. He replaced it by a residual theory of wages which was designed to emphasize the interest of the working class in continual progress and accumulation. These views are expounded in a number of writings of which the earliest, *The Wages Question* (1876), contains perhaps the most incisive statement. The general structure of Walker's theories seems to make him most akin to the early nineteenth-century Continental writers, particularly the Germans of the Lotz, von Hermann, Hufeland group, mentioned in Chapter 7. He showed, however, a much more marked awareness of the pessimistic possibilities of the classical school, as witness his rejection of the wage-fund doctrine. And he was also much more influenced *per oppositionem* by the growing American socialist movement. His *Political Economy* (1883), a widely used textbook at the time, is now perhaps most noteworthy for the robust language which it uses in dismissing the rapidly growing number of writings critical of the existing scheme of things, including the single-tax proposals of Henry George and the Utopia of Edward Bellamy. It also contains a somewhat pathetic plea for a 'new Adam Smith, or another Hume', which was to be answered a few years later by the appearance of John Bates Clark.

Walker is reported to have had a strong sense of fairness and to have avoided an intransigent belief in *laissez-faire*. But his lack of knowledge of European theoretical developments and his strong antipathy to anything savouring of the radical are apparently in strange contrast with his acceptance of the first presidency of the American Economic Association. For this body was founded in 1885 as the organization of the new school. The paradox disappears, however, when the character of this 'new school' is examined against a background of the circumstances existing at the time of its establishment. The beginning of the new school can be placed in the 1870s, when the rapidly growing number of university professorships was filled by young men who had received their training in Germany. These men had come under the influence of the leaders of the German historical school and of the incipient movement of *Kathedersozialismus*. The American Economic Association was launched under the impact of these two influences and appears to have been closely modelled on the *Verein für Sozialpolitik*. Its opposition to the Ricardian tradition, its emphasis upon the need for historical studies, and its interest in social reform brought it into conflict with the mode of thought prevailing among the academic economists of the older generation.

The hostility of the conservative economists was intensified by the fact that they were engaged in an attempt to stem the rising tide of socialist writings. The period was one in which the United States began to experience the disorders that always seem to mark the rise of industrial capitalism. The growth of the American working-class movement was accompanied by a mass of literature which faithfully reflected the confusion and the gropings for a consistent critical theory of capitalism which England and continental Europe showed some decades earlier. Its similarity to the European development is so marked that it is not necessary to examine it here. Once again it consisted of the most diverse mixture of theories and proposals ranging from monetary reforms to quasi-Marxian ideas.

Mention must, however, be made of one writer of this group who achieved world-wide fame and who is fairly typical of a large part of the critical literature of the time. He was, moreover, the most frequent object of attack by the orthodox. The writings of Henry George (1839–97), although still enjoying a wide circulation, have ceased to command much attention or to be an important force in the world of today. They are no longer even considered so dangerous by the academic economists as to be worthy of vituperation or rebuttal. And in the working-class movement they have long since been superseded by other theories. Henry George's life gives some clue to his ideas. With due allowance for the difference in time and place, his background is somewhat reminiscent of that of Proudhon. George too came from a lower middle-class environment, and throughout the vicissitudes of a hard, varied, and poverty-stricken life, he always remained what may be best characterized as a petty-bourgeois. He never really belonged to the wage-earning class which had already been formed and was rapidly expanding in his day. His connection with the working-class movement came from outside; he presented it with a panacea.

George, too, fastened upon one strikingly visible symptom of economic disorder, although one which was different from that which had absorbed Proudhon's attention. His long residence in California may have helped him to the conviction that it was monopolization of land which kept men poor. A strong religious background, a certain native arrogance, an easy style, and a journalistic career may have combined with the experience of grinding poverty to give him the missionary zeal for the propagation of this idea. It would seem that its first exposition, in *Our Land and Land Policy* (1871), was made without benefit of any extensive study of classical political economy. After this first manifesto, however, George read the works of the classics and was delighted to find in the Ricardian theory of rent, in Ricardo's advocacy of free trade, and in his theory of economic development, a more rigorous demonstration of theories on which his own proposals were based.

*Progress and Poverty* (1879) is George's most famous work. That and the posthumous *Science of Political Economy* (1897) contain more detailed expositions and show the effect of George's greater acquaintance with the literature. But the essential core is still the same. Everyone, says George, has a natural right to apply his labour to the cultivation of the land. Private ownership and monopoly of land stultify this right. Moreover, as the community progresses, an ever-increasing toll is exacted by the landowners in the form on increased rents. Hence the paradox of progress and poverty. The remedy was to be found in the taxation of land values. And the movement inspired by George became increasingly concerned with the single-tax proposal, although George himself often embodied it in more comprehensive reform proposals, particularly on the occasion of his various election campaigns.

It should be remembered that this theory was not original with Henry George, and that its influence remained confined to the single-tax movement as such. The theory itself may be traced to the physiocratic notions which were fairly common in a number of countries in

the eighteenth century. Its application to the purposes of a programme of economic policy may also be found among such early
writers as the immediate followers of Ricardo and their French contemporaries. James Mill, Cherbuliez, and others were inclined toward
a similar utilization of the Ricardian theory of rent.

It is not easy to appraise George himself. It is undeniable that he
had a powerful, though rather short-lived, influence of a critical and
radical character, at any rate in the realm of thought. It may be
mentioned, for example, that Veblen is known to have accepted
George's ideas in his early years.[1] There is, however, no evidence of
any influence to be found in Veblen's later writings. Nor was
George's impression on the working-class movement very profound.
The mixture of oracular presumption, insistence on a single idea, and
muddle-headedness on economic problems in general is sufficient to
explain the meteoric rise and almost equally rapid exhaustion of his
power. George seems to have had a good share of the blindness
induced by an *idée fixe*. Although he directed his attentions to the
problems created by industrial capitalism, it never occurred to him to
note that these problems were no less acute in the United States than
in Europe, although the land situation in which the growth of capitalism took place was, from the point of view of his theory, very much
more favourable on the American side of the Atlantic. The agitations
of the 'no-renters' in New York in the 1830s and 1840s ought also to
have influenced his thought, but that does not seem to have been the
case.[2]

George's importance from the point of view of the development we
are here tracing is that of a symbol. He can be regarded as symptomatic of the mass of 'unsound' doctrine which was so upsetting to
the economists of the last quarter of the nineteenth century. The
more short-sighted ones among those reared in the tradition were
ready to regard the new school as another accession of strength to
unorthodoxy, all the more dangerous because it affected academic
thought and teaching itself. It may have been accident or real far-
sightedness which made Francis Walker ignore such scruples and
join the new Association. His daring was justified. It was not long

1 J. Dorfman, *Thorstein Veblen and His America* (1934), p. 32.
2 For an interesting if tendentious estimate of Henry George, see the introduction to the
American (1887) edition of Friedrich Engels, *The Condition of the Working Class in
England*.

before both sides showed a more conciliatory spirit.[1] The socia
emphasis of the Association was abandoned; the new school, or.
the product of the historical influence of Germany, turned to t
with a new zest; and marginalism in the United States was born.

## The Marginalist School

It is a thankless task to review the American version of the marginal-
utility doctrine. Much of the earlier literature is subject to a serious
disability from the point of view of the plan which underlies this book;
it is not sufficiently distinguishable from earlier English or continental
work to deserve extended treatment. As for the later developments in
the field of pure theory which stem from the doctrines evolved in the
last quarter of the nineteenth century, they are too detailed or, from a
broad historical view, of too minor a character to be dealt with at any
length. As a result, it is inevitable that the work of many authors will
have to be given scant attention.

Marginalism in the United States is in part an indigenous growth,
in part an import from Austria and from England. Its spontaneous
appearance on the American continent is almost entirely the work of
one writer, John Bates Clark (1847–1938). This brief survey must give
him pride of place, because he can be said to have evolved independently the marginal-utility principle and, moreover, to have given it an
application to the problems of production and distribution which is
historically of great importance. Clark has spent two years in Germany
as a pupil of Roscher and Knies; and much of the ethical and teleological flavour of his work may be traced to this influence. However, when,
at the age of thirty, he started his teaching and writing career, he
quickly revealed his theoretical interest.

Between 1877 and 1882 he wrote a series of articles for the *New
Englander*, which were revised and republished in 1885 as his first
book. *The Philosophy of Wealth*. This work shows at one and the same
time his first formulation of the marginal-utility principle and his
antagonism to some of the tenets of classical political economy,
acquired, no doubt, while studying under the German historians.

---

1 Frank A, Fetter, *Present State of Economic Theory in the United States* (manuscript), p. 2.
Printed in German in vol. i of *Die Wirtschaftstheorie der Gegenwart* (ed. Mayer, Vienna,
1926).

Clark had three complaints against the classics. He argued that by postulating an economic man they ignored the higher motives of human behaviour, which were, in fact, extremely important. Another false basic datum of classical theory was the belief in competition. In the first place, competition was visibly passing away. In the second place, it had to be emphasized that competition existed only by permission of moral forces. It was controlled and tempered by the moral values of society, which were ultimately the most powerful. Finally – and here the influence of German *Historismus* is very obvious – classical theory had not realized that society was an organism.

The new philosophy of wealth which Clark was propounding was designed to remedy these defects. His book was, in a sense, a manifesto of the new school, regarded by the author himself as a part of the widespread revolt against 'the general spirit of the old political enemy'. Clark abandoned the limitations of the economic man by dropping the distinction of the classics between productive and unproductive labour and by defining wealth in a very broad way. As for competition and the 'organic' conception of society which the classics had brought to the fore, Clark believed that an ethical spirit in trade, the growth of voluntary co-operation, and an increase in the communal use of the 'inappropriable' goods, such as works of art, would effect the necessary improvement. Of Clark's most outstanding later contribution to economic theory, the marginal-productivity doctrine, there is no evidence in this early work beyond the statement that both wages and interest had their source in the product. But he did give expression to the marginal-utility theory. Value, he said, is a measure of utility; but a distinction has to be drawn between 'absolute' utility and 'effective' utility, the latter being measured by that alteration in the subjective conditions which would be occasioned by either the disappearance or the addition of some object. The essence of the whole marginalist approach from Gossen to Menger is contained in this definition.

The *Philosophy of Wealth* is also noteworthy for the introduction of Clark's concept of 'social value,' which was designed for the purpose of infusing into economics that organic view of society which was lacking in the classics. This doctrine is not unlike that of Wieser, although it is not so carefully or so consistently developed as the latter's 'natural value'. Clark's theory amounted to saying that although effective utility appears to be a subjective, individual phenomenon, it was society which made the estimate of utility which constituted value in the market. Similarly, disutility can be looked at from a social point of view, thus producing something like a psychological formulation of the labour theory of value. Although Clark's social value concept gave rise to a considerable literature, it has now lost all except historical significance. It is interesting as an indication of the kind of thing which troubled the early exponents of marginal utility. On the one hand, there were the purely theoretical needs of linking the new theory to the old, of 'quantifying' and 'socializing' the intensive, individual valuations. (Of this Wicksteed's theory of the communal scale is perhaps the most ingenious example.) On the other hand, there was the desire to preserve some of the socio-ethical elements in economics which the historical and social reform schools had stressed so much. Clark's own concern with these elements did not last very long, even though some trace of it remained in all his writings. In his later work he adopted an entirely different attitude to many of the problems with which he was concerned.

A large number of articles in the years following the *Philosophy of Wealth* indicated the direction of Clark's interest and thought. But the final formulation of the ideas expounded in those articles did not appear until 1899, when Clark's most important book, *The Distribution of Wealth*, was published. This book was the first major American work in the modern manner. It was systematic, and it showed a considerable advance upon the work of Clark's contemporaries in the degree of theoretical consistency which it achieved. It contained, moreover, an important extension of the marginal principle (which was already fairly generally accepted by that time) into the field of production and distribution analysis.

The exposition of the marginal-productivity principle is undoubtedly the most significant part of Clark's chief work. But it is worth while glancing at the more general aspects of the book. Clark restates the postulates of economics which he considers common at the time and adds certain others to them. The accepted postulates, according to him, are certain basic assumptions about human behaviour and about the social framework. These data are private property, individual freedom, a limitation of government activity to those fields which Adam Smith had laid down as proper to it, the mobility of capital and labour according to the stimulus of varying remuneration, and, finally, the desire of the individual to satisfy certain objective wants. It would be difficult to question Clark's sense of the significant in his choice of these five assumptions as being basic to the contemporary corpus of economic analysis. But Clark felt dissatisfied with their range, and he added three others to them. These are: first, society is an organism; second, a distinction must be drawn in economics between a static and a dynamic analysis; and third, the laws of economics are only valid if the moral sense of the community approves of them. The first and third of these additional postulates are clearly remnants of the influence of the historical school, and they reveal Clark's strong interest in the ethical. The second point is of a different character, and from the point of view of pure economic theory it has perhaps been Clark's most fruitful contribution.

The ethical interest finds a curious outlet. It impels Clark to stress the need of discovering the laws of distribution, because it is ethically important to find out whether men receive all that they create.[1] On the other hand, he states that the question whether the existence of some of the basic data, such as private property, is justified, must be regarded as an ethical problem,[2] the implication being that it is not to be questioned by an economist. However, it is clear from this statement of Clark's own initial approach that he himself at least worked out his theory of distribution essentially as a contribution to the problems of social justice. Subsequent writers have claimed that there is no necessary logical connection between the marginal-productivity explanation of how the distributive shares are determined and any political or moral justification of the results of the pricing process in the market. But it is well to remember that the authors most responsible for the original formulations of these theories were equally interested in the 'what is' and the 'what ought to be'.

On methodological matters, Clark continues by dividing economics into three parts. One states universal laws: it is concerned with isolated man. The second and third are concerned with social economic phenomena. The former is static: it assumes no change in the basic data of the economy. The latter is dynamic: it allows for a change in the fundamental assumptions of the analysis. We shall see presently what these changes are which, according to Clark, make the economy into a dynamic one. His main analysis of distribution, however, was confined to a static situation. Its basic assumptions were four and may be summarized as follows. In the first place, it was assumed that the principle of diminishing utility was operating, and this principle was defined in terms which made it almost identical with the second law of

1 J. B. Clark, *The Distribution of Wealth* (1899), p. 3.
2 ibid., p. 9.

Gossen. In the second place, Clark assumes that production is carried on under conditions of diminishing returns, defined both physically and in terms of value. Although he gave this law an extremely prominent place in his system, he made a number of analytical errors in his statement of it. Not only was he confused in his exposition of it, but he failed to state it in the logically impeccable (if not very fruitful) manner in which it usually appears in modern expositions; namely, as a description of a condition obtaining in a state of competitive equilibrium with optimal distribution of productive resources. Clark's formulation was so extreme as not even to allow for any possibility that increasing returns may operate for a time before diminishing returns begin to be felt. As an entirely illegitimate way out, Clark proposed to regard changes in the combination of the factors of production which brought about increasing returns as being of a dynamic character and, therefore, as being *ipso facto* excluded from the analysis.[1]

The third postulate is that there is a division between goods for present consumption and goods applied to the purpose of creating wealth in the future. But it should be noted that the existence of capital which Clark stipulated was combined with an emphasis upon the limitation of the stationary economy. Capital, according to Clark, is created by abstinence, by an exchange of present consumption in favour of a creation of wealth in the future. But a stationary economy is one in which there is a given degree of abstinence; that is, one which allows for a uniform flow of capital goods sufficient to maintain existing equipment. In stationary conditions there is no net new abstinence.

As a final assumption, Clark states that production is directed, equally with consumption, by the principle of marginal utility. Given these postulates, some physical and some psychological, competition (in which, by this time, Clark was placing very great faith)[2] would distribute the factors of production until no advantage could be gained by any further movement. When this adjustment – which goes right through to the smallest sub-group – has been achieved, there can be no profit. As we shall see, the possibility of a return other than that to capital and labour is reserved for a dynamic economy. In the stationary state wages and interest are the only normal returns.

It may be well to see at once how land is treated. Clark removes rent

1 J. B. Clark, *The Distribution of Wealth* (1899), p. 164.
2 See, for example, ibid., p. 77.

as a separate return by denying that land is distinct from any other impersonal factor of production. The classics had treated land as distinct from capital by stressing two properties possessed by it: the fact that its supply is fixed, and that it differs in quality. According to Clark, these are not special characteristics of land, but are qualities common to all capital goods. In a stationary economy, one may assume all physical capital goods including land to be fixed in quantity. Moreover, the stipulated mobility of capital (which is necessary for the achievement of competitive equilibrium) is also true to a significant extent of land. Differences in the quality of different portions of the supply are again a characteristic common to all capital goods. Thus Clark argues that any differential element in the return to land is not peculiar to land, but may be found in the return to all kinds of capital.

The most important part, however, of the whole theory is the determination of the two 'normal' returns, wages and interest. It is here that the marginal-productivity theory really takes shape. Clark was not the first to enunciate it. We have seen its roots in many forerunners, notable examples being Longfield and Thünen. And the other early exponents of marginalism particularly Marshall, are also to be credited with some development of this doctrine. But in Clark's work the theory of marginal productivity occupied a very central position. It did, moreover, achieve special fame, or notoriety, because of the manner in which it was formulated.

Clark's argument can be summarized as follows. In perfect competition, a productive service will be employed up to the point at which the addition to the product of the last unit employed is equal to the cost of that unit. The stipulated condition of perfect competition ensures that the entrepreneur will have to pay the productive service which he employs an amount equal to the value of the product which that service creates. Thus, because the return to the last employed unit of productive service cannot fall below the value of its addition to the product, we may say that the wage of the marginal man will equal the marginal product.

By the principle of indifference it may be further stated that the wage of every unit of labour employed will equal the marginal product of labour. At this point a question arises which Clark poses explicitly. Does the equality of the wage paid to every worker with that of the marginal worker mean that the entrepreneur obtains a surplus – a producer's surplus similar to the consumer's surplus to be found in some types of diminishing-utility analysis? In other words, Clark asks himself whether the theory provides a new proof of the exploitation of labour. His answer, however, is in the negative. In the first place, he makes the well-known point that, assuming complete interchangeability of labour (an assumption which one is obliged to make according to the basic postulates of the theory), the loss of any one labourer always means the loss of the product of the marginal man.

The second argument leads directly to the theory of capital. According to Clark, capital always adjusts itself to the amount of labour employed, with the result that, whatever the productive combination, each unit of labour works with the same amount of capital as every other. The 'specific' product of each unit of labour is therefore the same as that of every other. Thus, although the marginal product of labour is greater when there are fewer labourers employed and less when more units of labour are used, these variations in the marginal product are due to the variation in the amount of capital employed in the productive combination. By this 'specific' productivity theory of wages, the possibility of exploitation is removed. Spoliation is excluded by the theory itself.[1]

It must again be pointed out that subsequent writers have been at very great pains to remove this ethical connotation of the marginal-productivity theory of wages. Some of the general problems involved in the relation between marginalism and politics are discussed elsewhere in this book. But it is impossible to deny that Clark himself was only too anxious to make his theory into a defence of the *status quo*. Many of his contemporaries must have felt uneasy about it, and a number of objections were raised. Some, like that of F. W. Taussig, were analytical.[2] They made the subsequently well-established point that the notion of a separate specific productivity of one factor was an abstraction and could have no bearing on so realistic a problem as the justification of a particular rate of remuneration. The product is the joint result of factors employed in combination, and the statement that wages equalled the marginal net product of labour had to be regarded as only one of the elements in a theory of wages. Other authors – Professor F. A. Fetter, for example – argued in effect that problems of ethics and those of abstract economics were entirely distinct and that no ethical judgment could result from an economic analysis. On the former point, the theory has long since been considerably refined and

---

1 J. B. Clark, *The Distribution of Wealth* (1899), p. 324.
2 F. W. Taussig, *Principles of Economics* (1911), vol. ii, pp. 213–14.

made into a part of general equilibrium analysis. As for the latter argument, the discussion, which appears to have been quite strenuous at the time, has by now lost its savour. It is interesting to note, however, that it was those American economists that came most strongly under the Austrian influence who were most anxious to sever the nexus between ethics and the market. The Austrian version of the theory of distribution, at least in its earlier form, was, of course, much easier to defend against the accusation that it was apologetic. For a theory of 'imputation' of shares in the product can be much better defended as a 'neutral' description of the working of the competitive market than can a theory which by its very name suggests that the labourer gets the value which he produces.

Clark's theory of capital and interest may be summarized quite briefly. We shall see that the theory of interest is broadly the same as that of wages, but it is in many respects analytically far superior, partly, perhaps, because it is freer from the suggestion of ethical justification. Clark's discussion of the concept of capital is one of his rather special contributions to economic theory. It has, moreover, a peculiarly American flavour. It grew out of discussions which were going on in the last two decades of the past century, and many American economists since Clark have shown a special interest in it. As early as 1887 Clark had emphasized the ambiguities in the post-classical use of the capital concept in a small book, *Capital and Its Earnings*. The social environment in which the discussion – which continued for decades – took place, was the same as that which had produced Carey and his rejection of the Ricardian theory of rent, in which there had arisen Henry George's single-tax doctrine, and out of which Clark himself had derived his ideas on land and on rent. For in the young and expanding economy of America, it was difficult to subscribe to the idea that land was the one scarce factor of production. In the same way it was apparent to all economists that property in land was an important form of capital investment and accumulation, and an important source of income.

Clark began by showing, as many social economists before him had done for a different purpose, that the term capital was used to denote two separate and distinct things: the concrete goods which were employed as means of production, and 'an abstract quantum of productive wealth'.[1] The former was a concept covering certain technical

1 J. B. Clark, *The Distribution of Wealth* (1899), p. 119.

data; the latter was an abstract value concept which was peculiar to the realm of economics. On the American continent this distinction between the concrete form of the agent of production and the abstract source of a flow of income was particularly obvious in the case of land. The whole of Clark's theory of production and distribution is thus logically consistent.

However, Clark's distinction of two kinds of capital was not entirely happily formulated. In the first place he identified the concrete capital goods with 'material' goods, thus falling into the unnecessary difficulties which Adam Smith had been unable to remove. In the second place, having made the now obvious distinction between means of production and the capitalized values of a series of future incomes, he unnecessarily combined it with a statement concerning the method by which capital, in the abstract sense, is maintained, increased, or consumed. Capital goods, he said, not only may be destroyed, but must be destroyed if their value-creating property is not to be lost. Capital, on the other hand, is permanent, in the sense that it must be maintained if the community is not to suffer a disaster.[1] It is clear that this formulation is misleading and has really no necessary connection with the logical and terminological distinction between capital and capital goods. It is misleading because capital is not 'permanent' of itself, but only as the result of a certain specific direction of the process of production. For that reason, too, it is confusing to make a distinction between capital and capital goods by defining them in terms of permanence and impermanence.

The Austrian theory of capital associated with the name of Böhm-Bawerk was not in harmony with this American trend which Clark had started. Böhm-Bawerk's theory of roundabout processes of production and of the subsistence fund inevitably involved an emphasis on the concrete aspects of capitalistic production. Its main concern appeared to be with concrete capital goods – that is, with the produced means of production – and the distinction for which Clark was pressing was not relevant to the Austrian theory. At the same time the Ricardian theory of rent was kept substantially intact in Böhm-Bawerk's structure; and this again contributed to a sharp divergence between the two branches of the marginalist doctrine. Thus we find the odd phenomenon that, on this particular point, the older so-called Ricardian, economists in America were on one side, but those of the younger school, who were

1 J. B. Clark, *The Distribution of Wealth* (1899), p. 117.

otherwise much influenced by the Austrians, were on the other. Among those who shared and developed Clark's concept of capital in the value sense may be mentioned A. T. Hadley, Irving Fisher, and F. A. Fetter. The last, although in some ways much influenced both in economic analysis and in policy by the Austrian school, laid particular stress in his *Principles of Economics* (1904) upon the distinction between capital as a financial investment relating to all kinds of concrete goods (including land) and wealth, which consists of concrete (though not necessarily material) goods, which is impersonal, and which is therefore to be defined in terms of economic qualities rather than property and individual acquisition. Fetter also emphasized that 'psychic income' may consist of quite different things from those which constitute concrete wealth. Irving Fisher evolved an allied approach first in a series of articles in the *Economic Journal* in 1896 and 1897, later expanded in a number of books, notably *The Nature of Capital and Income* (1908) and *The Rate of Interest* (1908). Fisher shared with Clark and Hadley a recognition of, and emphasis on, the value aspect of capital. His special concern, however, was to distinguish between income as a flow of goods and services through time, and capital as a stock of goods at a given moment, both consisting of the same concrete things.

Fisher's theory of interest, although in sharp disagreement with the doctrine of roundabout processes, is substantially in agreement with the explanation of the existence of interest which Böhm-Bawerk gives. It regards interest as the result of time-preference, a preference for present psychic income (satisfaction) over future income. Clark's theory is largely the same in so far as the explanation of the ultimate origin of interest is concerned. But it contains an elaborate statement of the marginal-productivity doctrine. Interest, according to Clark, is, in the last resort, due to the existence of a time-preference. But its rate is determined by the marginal productivity of capital in the same way in which the wages of labour are determined by the marginal productivity of labour. The main difference is that in the case of capital there is no 'zone of indifference' such as is to be found in the case of labour. For there can be no labourless employment of capital. The specific productivity analysis is, however, the same as that for labour. Clark emphasizes that when we conceive of additions being made to capital, we must remember that the whole quality of the structure of capital goods employed changes. Thus the final increment, which measures marginal productivity, is to be regarded from the point of view of the interest rate as an increment of capital rather than of capital goods. Although it is a unit of a concrete good, its effect is qualitative rather than quantitative. Its disappearance would cause an unfavourable re-arrangement of all the remaining units which constitute the total amount of capital employed; 'this final increment of the capital is not one that can be physically taken out of it'.[1] Thus the marginal product by which the rate of interest is measured is always the marginal product of capital rather than that of capital goods.

Only a few minor points need be added to complete this brief outline of Clark's contribution to economic theory. One of these is the disagreement between Clark and Böhm-Bawerk on the problem of capitalistic production. This controversy, in which Clark was joined by Fisher and Fetter, deserves mention because it is another example of the smouldering disagreement between the American exponents of the doctrines of the Austrian school and the Austrians themselves.

The main criticism of the Böhm-Bawerkian theory is based on the role which the distinction between capital and capital goods plays in Clark's theoretical structure. He points out that Böhm-Bawerk's doctrine of production is true for concrete capital goods, but that it does not hold where capital is concerned. And it is capital, rather than capital goods, with which the theory of production and distribution deals. Because capital, according to Clark, is permanent, its maintenance must be taken for granted. In a stationary economy there is a given structure of production which relates consumption and production. Given that structure, it may be a technically important fact that some capital goods must pass through a certain period of production before they result in finished consumption goods. From an economic point of view, however, this does not matter, because it is assumed that the structure of production is such as to keep a certain level of consumption continuously in being. Synchronization of production and consumption is inevitable, and it is preserved in the capitalistic process of production. In a stationary economy, the flow of consumable goods is uniform over a period of time. When there is net new abstinence, capital is created and the flow of consumers' goods is altered. But, although it may be possible 'to add to the units of capital that are to exist through the ages, . . . it is not possible to add to the ages through which capital exists.[2]

1 J. B. Clark, *The Distribution of Wealth* (1899), p. 251.
2 ibid., p. 138.

There was a fairly solid front of opposition among the leading American economists of the time against Böhm-Bawerk's 'third ground'. Clark, Fisher, and Fetter attacked it and made a considerable impression upon contemporaneous theoretical opinion. Perhaps the only exception to this trend which deserves mention here is F. W. Taussig's *Wages and Capital*. In this work an attempt was made to revive something like the post-classical wage-fund doctrine. But it was so modified in form that it became in effect a theory of capitalistic production not much different from that of Böhm-Bawerk in so far as such elements as the subsistence fund, the rate of interest, and the effect of changes of the length of the productive process are concerned. Because of its divergence from the current thought of the time, Taussig's theory exerted very little influence. That of Böhm-Bawerk, on the other hand, persisted through a powerful oral tradition and finally became the basis for an important contributory strand in the modern theory of crises.

Another aspect of Clark's theory of a stationary economy which may be mentioned is his theory of cost. Here Clark shows himself as much less of an innovator. His theory of value and cost is slight. On the whole he tended to accept the kind of cost-of-production approach which became common after John Stuart Mill. He certainly approved of Mill's theory of prices.[1] But being a marginalist with a hedonist bent, he accepted the subjective utility approach and the pleasure-pain calculus of the psychological real-cost theory. To him cost was, in the last analysis, pain; utility was pleasure, Pain, in turn, was either labour or abstinence. And the determination of their rewards was explained in the marginal-productivity theory of wages and interest.

The last part of Clark's theory which should be mentioned is his definition of a dynamic economy. A stationary economy is one in which the fundamental data of the economy do not change. Conversely, a dynamic economy is defined as one in which some of five possible types of changes occur: population, tastes, capital, technique, and the forms of industrial organization, Clark's own discussion of the effects on the theoretical conclusions produced by the assumption of changes of this kind is slight. Nevertheless this explicit introduction of a body of dynamic doctrine and its distinction from and relation to economic statics was in itself a major achievement. It is one which gave American economics a characteristic flavour from that day on. The main specific

---

1 J. B. Clark, *The Distribution of Wealth* (1899), p. 230.

significance of the widening of the terms of reference is in the bearing upon the theory of the profits of the entrepreneur. Clark argued that in a stationary economy profits could not exist. The two normal returns are wages and interest, and rent is a differential return to be found in the income of all impersonal factors of production. But in the conditions of change which characterize a dynamic economy it is possible for profits to appear. In stationary conditions, the entrepreneur is merely a supervisor, a labourer whose remuneration is not distinct in kind from that of other recipients of wages. But when data change, the entrepreneur is faced with new problems in his task of co-ordinating capital and labour. And the measure of his success in this process of readapting the productive process to the changed conditions is the measure of his special reward, profits.

This theory has often been criticized, although there has been a persistent tendency – observable notably in Marshall and his disciples – to eliminate profits from stationary equilibrium and to make change responsible for the entrepreneur's income. The criticism which may most appropriately be mentioned here is that of another American theorist of today who is in many ways a disciple of J. B. Clark. Professor F. H. Knight in Part Two of his *Risk, Uncertainty and Profit* (1921), although admitting that without change there would be no profits in the theoretical sense, has argued that it is not change as such, 'but the divergence of actual conditions from those which have been expected and on the basis of which business arrangements have been made' that causes profits. It is ignorance of the future, caused by the fact that economic data are continually changing, which brings about a special entrepreneurial income.

This short review of American marginalism has been almost wholly devoted to the work of J. B. Clark. Such a weighting could hardly be avoided. For in the earlier period of American marginalism – say up to the beginning of the third decade of the present century – Clark's work both leads and typifies American economic thought. On the other hand, at the present time American contributions, just like those of any other country, are scarcely identifiable by the national label. Some of the other outstanding exponents of the new doctrines have already been mentioned in connection with the theories of Clark. In general, we may say that the contributions of these writers have helped to turn American economics in the same direction as the work of their European contemporaries; that is, away from the hedonist formulations with which early marginalism was so closely associated. American theory has been distinguished by a strong 'psychological' but non-utilitarian flavour. This quality is well exemplified in the work of Fetter; it is marked in the mathematical theories of Irving Fisher, which parallel, and in some respects anticipate, Pareto; and it appears even in the more orthodox, Marshallian doctrines of Taussig. One important aspect of it was the development of the concept of opportunity-cost in which H. J. Davenport took so prominent a part. Here we find American thought joining with the English contribution of Wicksteed and (in spite of Davenport's failure to recognize this) Marshall, and with the later Austrian contribution of Wieser. Perhaps the most complete and concise expression of the final form of marginalism in the field of value theory is to be found in the work of an American. Part Three of *Risk, Uncertainty and Profit* by F. H. Knight contains perhaps the best exposition of the theory of choice as it emerged at last from the successive refinements of a generation of marginalists.

## *Veblen*

No present-day economist has had so fluctuating a career in the estimation of contemporary opinion as Thorstein Bunde Veblen (1857–1929). Among the many vicissitudes of his life, not the least was the resistance of the majority of his professional colleagues to his ideas and his consequent lack of advancement as measured by the accepted standards of the world in which he lived. Towards the end of his life, his influence both inside and outside the universities had become great enough to afford him ample moral consolation – had he desired such – for the material disappointments of a lifetime. Today the power of his thought is widely admitted, and his influence is sometimes acknowledged in the most unexpected quarters. Indeed, what most forcibly strikes anyone approaching the study of Veblen is the virtually unanimous chorus of admiration which his work now evokes, and the surprisingly large measure of approval which is joined to it.

Even a rapid and superficial survey of his work, from his article on Kant's *Critique of Pure Reason*, published in 1884, to *Absentee Ownership* and his last article on economics, published within six years of his death, puts one at once in the presence of an exceptional mind. It is not difficult to agree with those who have come to regard Veblen's work as an outstanding American contribution to political economy. By all the criteria of originality, range, and profundity of thought there are few others who have such a high claim to be included in the extremely select company of those who during the last 250 years have added to the yeast in the thinking on economic and social problems.

One must, of course, guard against exaggeration. Veblen cannot be grouped with the classics, Smith and Ricardo; with Mill, in the combined fields of social philosophy and economics; with Marshall in this as well as in the field of that economic analysis which is peculiarly applicable to policy; and, in our own day, with Keynes, pre-eminently the author of the political economy of the twentieth century. As measured by the immediate influence of giving a new direction to the main stream of economic thought, his work must also be accounted as much less effective than that of the founders of marginalism. Nevertheless, if by some system of proportional representation, in which originality, not to say uniqueness of contribution, was the decisive quality, an American had to be chosen for inclusion among the great economists, there are few who would be so well qualified for this purpose as Veblen. He has this in common with most of the great thinkers in this field, that the individual components of this thought are to be found in the writings of many other, less distinguished authors; but that in spite of his indebtedness to earlier writers, the sweep of his work gives it the hallmark of originality.

It will be necessary later to examine the character of the influence which Veblen has exercised. But it may be said at once that it is impossible today to point to any one distinct school and show that it carries on an undiluted Veblenian tradition. Nor are there more than a very few individual economists who would claim to be wholly faithful disciples. It is doubtful whether, in spite of the large number of those who claim to be Veblen's disciples in some manner or other, there are many Veblenians in the sense in which there are Ricardians, Marxians, Marshallians, or Keynesians. Veblen's influence is to be sought rather in the way in which his teaching and writing moulded the thought of a few pupils and colleagues who subsequently – for reasons which also form an interesting topic of speculation in the social history of America – were themselves able to exercise a crucial influence.

Veblen was very much a product of his time. A detailed study[1] of his life and work and the environment in which he moved shows clearly

1 J. Dorfman, *Thorstein Veblen and His America* (1934).

how much he absorbed from, and entered into, the America of his day. The critical and radical attitude towards the problems of society which he revealed at a very early stage never wholly left him. It was somewhat obscured in his middle years, but it broke out again in full force towards the end of his life. It does not require adherence to any very fanciful 'sociology of knowledge' to see that this attitude was largely formed by and in the Mid-western farm environment of the 1870s which was then being subjected to the stress of a modern industrial and financial economy. The circumstances of the Norwegian family of which he was a member, and the religious, cultural, as well as economic, strains to which it was subject in the years of his adolescence, can be made to explain his manner and his idiosyncrasies. The foundation of Veblen's scepticism and of the critical and amused outlook of the spectator which characterizes much – although by no means all – of his work was laid in that environment. The explanation which he later gave of the intellectual pre-eminence of Jews in modern Europe is applicable to him also. He was the intellectual wanderer, freed from the shackles of 'the scheme of traditions and conventional verities handed down within the pale of his own people',[1] and questioning with an open mind the scheme of things which he encountered in strange lands.

Native talent and personal background were the predisposing influences to unorthodoxy. But the economic changes of the last quarter of the nineteenth century which Veblen witnessed, often uncomfortably closely, explain much of the formation of the substance of his views. All the major American economists worked at a time when the American economy was undergoing a profound structural development. Yet he is the only one who allowed this development to affect his conscious thought and in whose intellectual preoccupation the maturing of American capitalism is clearly mirrored. In his youth he witnessed the tremendous upsurge of feeling of the mid-western farm community against the 'business interests' – the railroad boom, the rise of the Granger movement and the monetary controversies which were intimately linked with the East-against-West, farm-against-factory struggle. He saw the vast increase of mass production and the drive toward the 'intensive' frontier, the growth of the large modern corporation, and the emergence of finance capitalism and absentee

1 T. Veblen, 'The Intellectual Pre-eminence of Jews in Modern Europe,' in *Essays in Our Changing Order* (1934), p. 227.

ownership. He also saw, and depicted with an unequalled incisiveness, the growth of an American leisure class, built upon a foundation of capitalist industry, yet indulging in manners of life established by leisure classes of other, older economic structures. These changes formed the raw material of Veblen's thought.

Veblen's work is distinguished by great extent and range. The volumes – some of them collections of previously published individual articles – number more than ten. A brief glance at Veblen's bibliography shows the great width of his active interest and the fact that his many-sidedness did not diminish with the years. Here one finds reviews of German philosophical and socialist books, essays on philosophy, translations from the German and the Icelandic, articles and books on technology, economics in the narrow sense, anthropology, war and peace and innumerable other subjects. Not even the most ardent admirer of Veblen would claim that these writings are of equal merit. In subjects which were on the margin of his main interest, the problems of society, Veblen dos not appear to have been able always to recognize lacunæ in his knowledge or judgment. But, in general, the quality of his discussion of so many different subjects remains exceptionally high.

For the purpose of this brief survey it is not necessary to pay attention to the writings which are not concerned with social matters. These may be divided into writings which deal with problems in political economy (which are mainly critical), those which develop positive elements of a theory of modern industrial organization and its relations to society (which include discussions of what might be called *Kulturkritik*), and, finally, those of a narrower political character. It is neither possible nor necessary to deal with all which properly belong within the above categories. It is necessary to select the most typical ones which reveal the essential quality of Veblen's thought. For such selection, a better division is not so much along the lines of subject matter as along method of treatment.

We may, therefore, distinguish the critical writings, those with a positive theory, and those which reveal Veblen's political attitudes.

The first category contains, among others, works which are of most relevance to the interest of the economist. Much – if not all – of Veblen's economics consisted of a critique of what it is usual to call in the United States by the somewhat misleading title of Neo-classicism. Indeed, it would not be a violent distortion of the truth to say that Veblen's contributions to economics proper consist solely of a critique of the content and method of marginalism combined with what was meant to be an exposure of the alleged invalid premises of classical economics. These two attacks were closely connected. Veblen himself began with the preconception (which was a misconception) that marginalism and classical political economy were essentially identical. It is interesting, but idle, to speculate on what he would have written had he realized that there was not only similarity but also contradiction between the theory of Ricardo and that of Jevons. As it was, his critical concentration on marginalism (caused, perhaps, by his closeness to its most important American exponent) seems to have blinded him to the less obvious but more important differences between the new school and its classical antecedent.

It is, fortunately, easy to summarize Veblen's critique of 'orthodox' economic theory, both because it rests on a few simple principles and because it is contained in a small number of articles written in his earlier working years. The following, in particular, give a clear statement of their author's attitude: 'Why is Economics not an Evolutionary Science?' (*Quarterly Journal of Economics*, 1898); 'The Preconception of Economic Science' (a series of three articles published in the *Quarterly Journal of Economics*, 1899–1900); 'Professor Clark's Economics' (*Quarterly Journal of Economics*, 1908); and 'The Limitations of Marginal Utility' (*Journal of Political Economy*, 1909). All these articles have conveniently been included in the volume *The Place of Science in Modern Civilization* (1919), which may be regarded as one of the best single sources of information on Veblen's thoughts.

Even one who wishes to approach Veblen's critical work sympathetically needs to have considerable patience in the face of frequent pomposity and prolixity of style and a certain repetitiveness of argument. Veblen begins with the oft-heard criticism that economics is out of date as compared with the natural sciences, in particular the biological disciplines. Here we find the adoption of the modern evolutionary point of view; there a preoccupation with classification of certain principles of a 'normal' economic situation, a taxonomy based upon 'natural rights, utilitarianism, and administrative expediency'.[1] It is a characteristic of evolutionary sciences (and even of the modern form of so non-evolutionary a science as inorganic chemistry) that the question which their practitioners ask is always, 'What takes place next, and why?' The theory which these scientists produce is always a theory of a

1 T. Veblen, *The Place of Science in Modern Civilization* (1919), p. 57.

genetic succession of phenomena.¹ Economic theory, on the other hand, is formulated from the standpoint of 'ceremonial adequacy'. Its laws are based on the preconception that there is a tendency for things 'to work out what the instructed common sense of the time accepts as the adequate or worthy end of human effort.'² This teleological basis of economic theory is clearly in evidence in physiocracy and in classical political economy, both of which rely strongly on the philosophy of the natural order. Classical political economy joins to this teleological and meliorative view of the social order a utilitarian psychology.

Hedonism, with its unrealistic abstraction of the 'economic man' whose action always results from a balancing of pleasure and pain, is the other great vitiating preconception of economic theory as currently taught. Incapable of becoming evolutionary because of its natural-law basis, economic science is also continuously led into false conceptions of the economic process through its translation of all human activity into terms of pecuniary gain. On this latter point, the example which Veblen was fond of using repeatedly waas that of the 'classical failure to discriminate between capital as investment and capital as industrial appliances'.³ The quotation suggests an approach somewhat similar to that of the Ricardian socialists and of Marx. However, Veblen does not pursue the argument in quite the same terms. With him, the distinction between the technical (universal) qualities of the instruments of production and their social (transient) implications was not made the foundation-stone of a theory of exploitation. It became a minor part, serving as an illustration of the basic distinction between the technical or industrial, and the pecuniary or financial elements of the current economic scene.

The distinction, around which the whole of the positive part of Veblen's economic theory revolves, thus begins to show itself already in his critical analysis of orthodox economics. It arises logically from Veblen's insistence on the vitiating effects of the classical hedonistic and utilitarian 'preconception'. It is interesting to note here a distinction between the ways in which Marx and Veblen attack the foundations of classicism. Marx also rejected the economic man as the basic datum in the analysis of the economic process, and he has much to say about the classics' readiness to fashion man 'in the image of the

1 T. Veblen, *The Place of Science in Modern Civilization* (1919), pp. 84–5.
2 ibid., p. 65.
3 ibid., p. 141.

bourgeois' of their own day. But he was not nearly so impressed as Veblen with the significance of this assumption in the structure of classical theory, and, hence, with the attention that should be given it in a critique of economic orthodoxy. Marx is, therefore, never led into a theory that is concerned primarily with human motives and instincts except in his disembodied 'classes'. Veblen, starting with a somewhat inflated idea of the importance of the hedonistic assumption in the theory of the classics, was forced to very elaborate theorizing on the subject of instincts and motives. Marx's theory thus became institutional only in the sense that it operated with entirely abstract social categories fashioned by their author to lead to the conclusions he had resolved upon to start with: a theory in which private property and its changing forms and the state and its changing forms are the principal categories. Veblen, on the other hand, although the founder of a school which is known as Institutionalist, was in fact primarily concerned with human motives in general.

Indeed, such explicit definitions as Veblen gave of institutions[1] show this psychological approach. Institutions are defined as principles of action about the stability and finality of which men entertain practically no doubt. Thus the principles of marginal utility find such ready acceptance among the uncritical because they appear to be so much in conformity with the institutions – the habitual, conventional modes of behaviour – of a pecuniary culture. Once it is understood that Veblen's and the Veblenians' definition of social institutions is in ideal terms, there should be little room left for some of the perplexing questions which inevitably arise about the relation of Veblen to Marx. Veblen's institutionalism rests on a foundation of what might be made into a general social psychology, while Marxism is founded upon an *a priori* view of the main motive force of history in which a specially chosen definition of social class was the essential element. Veblen is concerned with phenomena which in the Marxian scheme of social analysis belong to the 'superstructure'. The Veblenian institutions are the religious, aesthetic, literary, and other complexes of ideas. Probably their closest intellectual relations are the Paretian *derivations*.

This peculiar interest of Veblen's is evident in every one of his writings. It enabled him to make numerous acute and memorable observations on certain aspects of capitalism – our pecuniary culture,

---

1 See, for example, T. Veblen, *The Place of Science in Modern Civilization*, pp. 239, 241, and 250–1.

as he significantly called it. But it is difficult to avoid the feeling that he was much more interested in the mental processes which accompany the working of our present economy, in the rationalizations of behaviours which it produces, and in the habits of thought in which it is enshrined, than either its precise working or in the social relations which underlie it or arose from it, and the purposes of human progress which it served. His most popularly succesful works are precisely those which deal explicitly with these epiphenomena of capitalism: first and foremost among them being *The Theory of the Leisure Class*. Here, his psychological interest, his critical method, his ironic style, and his anthropological approach combine to perfection to produce a great book. It does not matter that the style is in places almost unbearably stilted and that the book has that air of audacious charlatanism which pervades so much of Veblen's writing. Nor does it matter that many of the premises upon which the argument is built are of the flimsiest (for example, the acceptance as axiomatic of a barbarian distinction between 'exploit' and 'drudgery' which conceals a world of problems). Within the real limits of the study (namely, the analysis of the functional attributes of a modern leisure class) Veblen's touch is always sure. His exposure of the utterly fictional character of most of the social functions of the leisure class is all the more merciless because of the subtle and yet deliberately transparent pretence of dispassionate objectivity with which it is made. Its categories, such as 'pecuniary emulation', 'conspicuous leisure', and 'conspicuous consumption', have proved their power by their incorporation in the language of social analysis.

*The Theory of the Leisure Class* has, however, only very limited relevance to the problems of political economy. The closest approach to economic theory is to be found in those parts in which it returns to something like the classical analysis of the productivity of labour. Even though its conclusion has little in common with Adam Smith's 'material' criterion, it does help to dispose of the circular, all-embracing definition of productive labour of the modern marginalist schools, which is sometimes obscurantist and often lifeless. But the chief import of Veblen's analysis is cultural. It derives its criteria from axioms taken over from other realms, whose dubious character is concealed beneath such glib phrases as 'instinct of workmanship', which even if they should prove sound, are unsuitable for the specific needs of economic analysis. One has only to compare Veblen's discussion with the definitions of productive labour with which Smith,

Ricardo, Malthus, and, in a different way, the modern school wrestled, to see for what purpose such an instrument of definition has to be fashioned in the field of economic analysis. Veblen gave up the search for an explanation of the working of the modern economy of which this forms a part, in favour of the more entertaining but less fundamental description of the mode of behaviour by which a leisure class maintains its separate cultural identity.

This part of Veblen's work, the critique of a pecuniary culture, is without doubt his greatest original achievement. His style was peculiarly adapted to it; and he produced not only some delightful aphorisms,[1] but also many profoundly penetrating analyses. The immediate interest of the economist is, however, not well served by work of this kind. When one asks what it was that Veblen put in the place of the classical political economy which he rejected, one is left with something which claims to be a theory of economic development. This theory, it is true, is nowhere systematically expounded, but in that respect Veblen may claim to be in the company of many great writers. We may piece it together, first from the critique of economic classicism itself, then from a number of works which deal somewhat more explicitly with the subject, and finally from writings in which Veblen makes some special applications, economic or political, of this theory of economic evolution. Veblen's critical views have already been discussed. Among the large number of other works from which a theory of economic development can be distilled, *The Instinct of Workmanship*, *The Theory of Business Enterprise*, *The Engineers and the Price System*, and *Absentee Ownership* may be mentioned. For the application of his central ideas to a number of specific topics, one may have recourse to *Imperial Germany and the Industrial Revolution*, *An Enquiry into the Nature of Peace and the Terms of Its Perpetuation*, and the extremely interesting articles, written for *The Dial*, which are published in *Essays in Our Changing Order*.

The central theme of Veblen's theory of economic change is, at first sight, startlingly similar to that of Marx. Like Marx, Veblen stresses change and movement; like Marx, he builds his system round a conflict between two opposing forces. Technology is one pole of Veblen's process. It is to be regarded as the sum total of knowledge, skill, and technique available in the community at any moment of time. It is to be

---

1 For a typical example see the definition of snobbery: *The Theory of Business Enterprise* (1904), p. 388, n. 2.

thought of in terms of 'tangible facts or workmanship', the sole aim of which is to make production more efficient and more abundant. Technology is continually developing. It is driven by that 'sense of economic or industrial merit' inherent in all men, which is 'an impulse or instinct of workmanship; negatively it expresses itself in a depreciation of waste'.[1] The development of technology is the most potent cause of changes in institutions. We have already seen Veblen's definition of institutions. To repeat, they are made up of biological instincts and reflexes, and they are the result of conditioning and habituation. Technology, by changing the way of performing the material operations of living, makes certain habits and modes of thought (institutions) out-of-date and stimulates the creation of new ones. Here is a powerful cause of conflict, not unlike the conflict between the 'forces of production' and the 'social relations of production' of Marxian theory, though, as we have seen, placed in the ideological sphere. The chief manifestation of that conflict in modern times is the antagonism between 'business' and 'industry'. The former is made up of the ways of thinking of the business community, the absentee owners and their retinue, who are far removed from the essential quality of the machine process. They have made pecuniary gain the touchstone of their behaviour and have erected an elaborate apparatus for testing everything by that criterion. 'Industry' has other criteria. It is concerned with the material improvements of the productive process; and the engineers, inventors, skilled workers, and – though far behind and only dimly discernible in Veblen's theory – the industrial working-class generally, are its protagonists.

It is not possible within the scope of this survey to deal with the problems raised in the Veblenian philosophy of history. Its relation to that of Marx has already been touched upon.[2] Nor is this the place to discuss the political moral which Veblen seemed to point in his *Engineers and the Price System* and which some of his more exuberant followers made into the technocratic creed with its dubious, if not pernicious, implications. As a theory, Veblen's view of historical change is, to put it mildly, full of unexplained assumptions. It is strikingly subject to the charges which he himself levelled against classical economics. But in his own hands it became a useful

1 T. Veblen, *Essays In Our Changing Order* (1934), p. 81.
2 For an interesting and well-informed comparison, see A. Harris, 'Economic Evolution Dialectical and Darwinian', *Journal of Political Economy*, vol xlii, pp. 34 *sqq*

instrument for the discussion of specific historical problems. Much of *Imperial Germany* is wrong-headed and obviously full of the most amateurish psychology and anthropology. But the bulk of it is, to this day, a magnificent analysis of the delayed impact of capitalism upon German feudalism, over the acuteness of which one may well forget its author's preconceptions. The same is true of all Veblen's writings which deal with war and peace, not only the *Nature of Peace*, but also the smaller articles written at the time of World War I and after. One has only to read the half-forgotten review of Keynes's *Economic Consequences of the Peace Treaties*[1] to see that at least in Veblen's own hands his theory could be made to yield interesting results

From the point of view of economic theory proper, however, the use of the Veblenian dichotomy is quickly exhausted. Its main application may be found in the distinction between pecuniary capital and industrial capital, and the Sismondi-like consequences for employment and crises which Veblen draws from it. Veblen argues that there is no necessary connection between the physical means of production employed in industry and the value of capital assets, the pecuniary capital with which the absentee owner is concerned. These values are capitalized 'on the basis of their income-yielding capacity to their owner'.[2] They are enshrined in assets – titles – which are intangible and which serve no materially productive purpose. Here, then, is another manifestation of the basic conflict of our economy which has shown itself in a variety of forms, becoming ever more marked in the course of history.

The development of credit and the growth of the modern corporation have accentuated this conflict. Through modern corporation finance there is brought about a rapid increase in the gap between 'business capital ... the volume of business, as counted in terms of price, etc.' and 'the volume of industry ... the aggregate material apparatus of industry'.[3] There is no reason to suppose that every time capital funds are increased there will be a corresponding increase in the 'physically useful goods ... back of these funded savings'.[4] There is, in fact, a strong presumption against such correspondence. And out of this disparity Veblen fashions his two most specific economic theories: the relation between advancing technology and the structure

1 Included in *Essays in Our Changing Order* (1934).
2 T. Veblen, *The Place of Science* (1919), p. 359.
3 T. Veblen, *The Theory of Business Enterprise* (1904), p. 99.
4 ibid., p. 87.

of business organization, and the explanation of crises.

These two theories are very closely related to one another and may best be summarized together. Two opposite tendencies may be observed. The increase in the value of pecuniary capital is cumulative. Pecuniary capital grows partly as the result of the increasing complexities of corporate organization and banking, and partly in response to every external stimulus such as an armament race or a war. On the other hand, the progress of technology is constantly tending to reduce the value of capital assets. Technology introduces new means of production, increases efficiency, and increases the rate of obsolescence of existing capital equipment. It is this which is continually causing a decline in the value of existing capital assets, because this value must ultimately be based on earning capacity. From the pecuniary point of view, the point of view of the absentee owners whom our economy has placed in charge of the process of production, the progress of technology is a hostile force. It undermines the value of capital, and it is continually tending to create business depressions.

Veblen's explanation of the business cycle follows logically from this argument. Fluctuations in economic conditions are simply the expression of the excessive inflation or deflation of capital values above or below the income-earning capacity of the assets which these values are supposed to represent. The tendency is for capital values to be increased out of all proportion to physical assets. Crises are the inevitable consequence of such inflation. A process of liquidation, of 'writing down', must follow, which, because of the highly artificial and tenuous relation between physical and pecuniary capital, will again tend to go too far. This may, in itself, produce a turning-point and so start a fresh upward movement of business conditions. It would be interesting to follow out these suggestions as to the possible place of successive movements of inflation and deflation in the history of economic growth and decay, perhaps in combination with Keynesian concepts (indeed some hints are to be found in Keynes's *General Theory*). Veblen himself, however, was too pre-occupied with his institutions and their historical role to trouble about the strictly economic conclusions to which his theory might lead.

Nor was he a believer in a perpetual wavelike motion of economic activity. He thought that there was an historical downward tendency, that business would find it increasingly difficult to lift itself out of the trough of depression. The tendency for technology to improve was very powerful; it did moreover call forth important changes in the structure and practices of business which were themselves tending to perpetuate a state of depression. Advances in productivity brought about by technological progress have 'forever threatened to lower the cost per unit and to increase the volume of output beyond the danger point – the point written into the corporation securities in the shape of fixed charges on funds borrowed for operation under industrial conditions that have progressively grown obsolete'. The 'custodians of absentee-credit' must therefore engage in a 'business-like sabotage, a prudent measure of unemployment and curtailment of output'.[1] The monopolization of industry and the complexities of modern finance capital, which are a part of the development of the inherent qualities of absentee ownership, must also be regarded as a response to technological development, which results in keeping business in a perpetual state of semi-depression. But technical progress does go on, notably in the industries producing capital goods. It gives a differential advantage to new investors at the expense of the old, and it revives competition at the same time as it calls forth an intensification of the defensive monopolization and financial elaboration of existing concerns. The conflicts inherent in the system are thus bound to grow progressively more acute.

In *The Theory of Business Enterprise*, and even more so in *Absentee Ownership*, the possible outcome of this conflict is pictured in very pessimistic terms. In the earlier book the choice is still left open. Business enterprise, it is true, is regarded as a transient phenomenon, a biological sport. It is bound to disappear and to be followed either by the development of a society consciously based upon the logic of modern machine technology – an industrial republic – or by a complete reversion to the dark ages of feudalism. The rapid shrinking of the world because of technical advance and the aggressive imperialist national policies which are, according to Veblen, the inevitable corollaries of modern business enterprise make the ultimate clash and the ultimate choice inevitable.

*The Theory of Business Enterprise* in the end leaves it a 'blind guess' which tendency would prevail. In his last book, however, Veblen seems to have made up his mind that the more pessimistic of the two possibilities was the more probable. In *Absentee Ownership* there is a suggestion of despair on the part of the author over the continued readiness of the 'underlying population' to bear the burden of the

---

1 T. Veblen, *Absentee Ownership* (1923), p. 97.

control of its destinies by the 'money power'. Out of this despair grows something of a conviction that business enterprise is irrevocably embarked upon the course of becoming increasingly feudal. An ultimate collapse of civilization is therefore far from improbable. Here is yet another important difference between Veblen and the nineteenth-century socialists who were both more partisan and more optimistic . A quality of despair in the future is present in nearly all of Veblen's later writings, and this may well be the outcome of the 'objective,' somewhat cynical, attitude to social problems which Veblen cultivated in his middle years.[1]

The summary just given of this unique American social thinker's work is far from exhaustive. But enough has been said to show the quality of his thought. It only remains to add something about the influence which he left behind. Veblen was a controversial figure during his lifetime, and to some extent he remained so after his death. As a result, one might expect that he would have had a militant following which would ultimately create a definite school of thought. On the face of it, that is precisely what appears to have happened. An 'institutionalist' school did make its appearance on the American theoretical scene, and for some time its tenets formed one of the most popular subjects of debate in the field of economic methodology. It is not necessary to re-examine this debate and the voluminous literature in which it is embodied; for, in the form in which it first appeared, it is now almost completely dead. The reason is probably to be found in the fact that the most prominent of Veblen's followers subscribed to only one part of his work. It is true that there are a number of writers who uphold one or the other 'institutionalist' interpretation of social development. They either stress legal forms and modes of thought as the essential fields of economic study, or they repeat the Veblenian insistence on a conflict between technology and institutions. But some of the most influential and active among the economists who acknowledged their debt to Veblen have pitched their theory on an entirely different level. They have made a distinguishing characteristic out of the emphasis upon the importance of empirical studies in the field of economics. Veblen's works do not contain very many or very weighty pronouncements on the worth-whileness of quantitative, statistical

---

1 A somewhat similar result is reached by Schumpeter in *Capitalism, Socialism and Democracy*. In spite of entirely different arguments, these two authors (so different in antecedents and method, though similar in the range of their interests) reach similarly pessimistic conclusions about the long-term viability of capitalism as we know it.

work. But those who partake of the oral tradition insist that an emphasis on the importance of inductive studies of modern business is the chief precept which their contact with Veblen has impressed upon them.

There can be no doubt about the results of this supposed Veblenian influence. Perhaps the greatest contributions of American economics are, as we shall see later, those in the statistical and descriptive branches of the subject. These contributions have come from the universities, and to an even more important extent from the interplay between the Universities, Business and Government, which is so striking a feature of American economic thought. The construction of indices of production, the statistical studies of the national income, and the successful quantitative work in regard to international balances of payment may be cited as examples of the progress achieved along these lines. The rise of special research institutions and the vast endowments for empirical work in economics are, in some ways, the outstanding features of the present state of economics in the United States; and many of Veblen's disciples have been prominently associated with this development. Very few of them have preserved traces of their master's preoccupation in the field of ideology or his radical attitude to the present economic order. Indeed, the observer is struck by the curious paradox that strong conservatism marks the attitude of many American economists who claim spiritual descent from Veblen.

Even if one were to accept the interpretation that Veblen's chief legacy is an emphasis upon statistical studies, one could yet point out that Veblen's own writings were almost wholly theoretical in the same sense as the works of the classics are theoretical. There can be few reasonable economists today who would deny the importance of factual statistical work. On the other hand, as Veblen's own work so well shows, nothing worth while has ever been achieved in any science by a perpetual amassing of facts without the guidance of theory. It is, therefore, not to be wondered at that 'institutionalism' was very short-lived as a serious methodological issue.

This is not to say that a Veblenian type of amalgam or juxtaposition of analysis of the facts of modern business enterprise with the main categories of classical or neo-classical economics has not found its talented practitioners. These have usually fashioned out of this amalgam some highly critical propositions relating to both contemporary economic organization as well as to conventional theory. The work of Keynes, which will be discussed later, has often lent itself particularly well to this kind of theorizing, no doubt because of its own critical approach to much of classical theory. Galbraith (see below) is perhaps the most important example of this tendency; and one very distinguished Japanese economist, Shigeto Tsuru, has argued persuasively in favour of a revival not so much of institutionalism as understood some sixty years ago, as of the infusion of institutional analysis into the corpus of economic theory.[1]

1 Shigeto Tsuru, 'Economics of Institutions or Institutional Economics'. Keynote address at Tokyo Round Table Conference of the International Economic Association (September 1987) published in Proceedings of the Conference, 1989.

# 10

# The Inter-war Years

## *Theory and Reality*

The two decades from the end of the First World War to the outbreak of the Second were economically and politically very turbulent. The re-drawn map of Europe, the emergence of the United States as the leading economic and (at least potentially) military world power and her continued involvement in European affairs, and the Russian Revolution and its counterparts elsewhere clearly signalled the disappearance of much of the old social and political foundations. The *pax britannica* maintained by the British navy had disappeared and the *aequilibrium britannicum* – a gold standard managed from London – was disappearing; and no new clear framework for the world's economic activity had emerged. Economic theory remained strangely untouched by the cataclysm; its central doctrines, at least as taught to generations of students, were much the same as they had been for some decades. But in another sense it entered the post-war world badly bruised and battered. For its relation to the world of reality, to the pressing problems of the day, was now everywhere and at all times called in question. Refinements of the theoretical structure continued; but the gap between it and the daily preoccupations of the public, of statesmen, and even of some economists themselves became ominously wide.

The thirties saw a fresh impetus. There appears evidence of a fresh consolidation of academic economic thought, of a resumption of the process of internationalization of its doctrines, and also of a measure of co-ordination between the problems of reality and the economists' literary output. But one would have to be very bold indeed to say that by the time World War II broke out economics had completely shaken off the inertia of earlier years.

It is impossible in a few pages to deal in detail with the work of this period. The scope of the chapter must be severely circumscribed. To mention all the authors who made contributions would reduce this account to a mere catalogue of names. As for the subjects that are to be discussed, they are limited by the structure of this book, which excludes many branches of economic thinking. One interesting part of the thought of this period will have to be omitted, the discussions of the non-professional practitioners of economics. It is easy to ignore the more 'popular' contributions to the subject made in the past. For example, in a short review, the interesting ideas of Thomas Atwood or the bimetallist controversy may be readily omitted. But it is a little more dangerous to exclude from consideration the stuff of which contemporary economic discussion in newspapers and magazines is made. The heterodoxies of today may, at a future date, appear as indispensable tributaries to the main stream of economic science.

During the inter-war period, there arose a widespread belief that economic theory was not designed to grapple with the new problems created by the war. The First World War itself, of course, gave a strong impetus to government regulation of economic life. This created a crop of new specific problems in the field of economic policy and at the same time weakened the extra-academic influence of economic theory, because this was still overwhelmingly non-interventionist. The problem of achieving an increase of social welfare by appropriate economic measures was also given greater attention. This was partly a direct result of the responsibilities which governments had been forced to acknowledge in war time, and partly a consequence of social and political upheavals which war and revolution had created. In this respect, too, the supposed indifference of accepted economic theory caused an impatient public to lose much of its faith in that theory.

Even if there were many ways in which economic theory could, with justice, still be shown to be relevant, new problems seemed to be demanding new methods. This was obviously the case in two of the most important technical problems of the post-war period: international trade and monetary policy. The dislocation of customary channels of trade, the change in the relation of international debtors and creditors, and the new national entities which embarked upon policies of extreme economic nationalism put a strain upon the pre-war mechanism of international trade and payments which that mechanism was unable to bear. Many economists argued that economic theory could hardly be said to have been underminded by problems which were the result of practices which took no account of the conclusions of economics. Nevertheless, the net effect of the concentration of attention upon practical problems was to make the gap between theory and policy even wider, because these problems were not posed in such terms as to make established doctrine relevant to their solution.

One important result of this development was an increasing separation of the economists themselves into those who continued to refine the central doctrines of the theory of choice and of production, and those who plunged into the world of affairs and devoted themselves to the problems of monetary stabilization, of the business cycle, or of the policy of the state toward the monopolistic organization of business. The bulk of the literature of the twenties, both learned and popular, was concerned with questions of the latter kind. Monetary reform ideas were particularly abundant. Nineteenth-century doctrines were revived and a whole host of new schools of monetary 'heretics' made their appearance. They ranged from comparatively restricted proposals, which often had some sanction from 'respectable' economic opinion, to far-reaching programmes of reform, more reminiscent of the notions of Proudhon and of similar nineteenth-century social critics. In a different kind of book these theories would well deserve detailed treatment. In particular, the social and political roots of the monetary doctrines of Major Douglas, of the mystical views on wealth and debt of Professor Soddy, of the 'free land' and 'free money' agitation of Silvio Gesell, would form interesting subjects of analysis. At any rate, the keen discussion which those views evoked and the many adherents which they could claim, particularly in the years immediately after the Great Depression, were both a symptom and an aggravating cause of the decline of relevance and of authority of economic theory.

It is not suggested that economic theory in the proper sense was unaffected by the changes in the world around it. But the theoretical reflections of the economic and political upheavals of the period were slow in appearing and, as we shall see later on only became fully discernible after the Second World War.

The most direct effects are to be found in the large volume of work carried on in the twenties and thirties in the closely related fields of monetary and business cycle theory and in that of international trade. In addition, and not unconnected with these developments, the early thirties witnesses a lengthy controversy on the theory of a planned economy as well as a re-examination of the methodology of economics itself.

A detailed examination of developments in business cycle theory would go beyond the scope of this book. A few words must suffice to describe the very intensive work in this field which took place between 1925 and 1935. The most striking feature of that decade is the gradual combination of different strands of thought, in particular of the monetary and non-monetary schools. In each, separately, much work had taken place. Under the leadership of Hawtrey, Keynes and Robertson the study of the relationship between prices and monetary and credit policy and the consequences of changes in both on business conditions was increasingly refined.[1] Historical research and governmental enquiries added much material to an understanding of both the domestic and international implications of monetary disturbances.[2] The resulting body of theory, though more sophisticated, shows a clear family resemblance to traditional English doctrine as it emerged from the controversies that followed the Napoleonic wars.

Meanwhile, building on the foundation of the Böhm-Bawerkian theory of capital, a number of authors, notably in Scandinavia, Austria and Germany, and to some extent also in the United States, had developed a theoretical apparatus for analysing changes in the structure of production following upon fluctuations in the general level of business activity. In the resulting theories, special emphasis was placed upon the disproportions which arise between different branches of production, particularly between, on the one hand, those concerned with construction and the production of capital goods and, on the other, those producing consumer goods.[3] These theoretical enquiries were strongly supplemented by a very large increase in

---

1 It is perhaps invidious to mention only one work from among a vast literature, but Professor Robertson's *Banking Policy and the Price Level* (1932) must be regarded as the outstanding contribution in that field during the period.

2 As an example of the former J. Viner's classic *Canada's Balance of International Indebtedness 1900–1913* (1924); as one of the latter the report of the 'Macmillan Committee', *Report of the Committee on Finance* (1931) may be mentioned.

3 Professor Hayek's *Prices and Production* (1931) may be cited as the typical work of that school and as one which gave rise to a great deal of controversy. While it is not appropriate to go into the details of this controversy, certain aspects of the disagreement between the 'Austrian' approach, that of the traditional Cambridge school, and the later Keynesian innovations, are dealt with later.

statistical studies. In this field, the United States assumed a lead which it has never relinquished since.[1]

The full fruits of this activity are best seen in the final work of Keynes: in retrospect, much of this activity can be regarded as having prepared the way for the appearance of the *General Theory*. But already in the early thirties a considerable coalescence of various schools of thought was perceptible. Increasingly, the content of economic fluctuations was seen in shifts in the use of resources between consumption, stocks, and investment; while to monetary factors was assigned an important (though not the exclusive) role in either generating or propagating such changes. The sharpness of earlier controversies between the different schools was tending to disappear, and in the period immediately following the Great Depression, which, at the outset, had exacerbated the debate, a more tolerant and eclectic attitude became a prominent characteristic of economic thought on these matters.

Less quickly composed was the methodological debate which broke out in the thirties, partly no doubt again under the stimulus of depression and unemployment. One aspect of it was concerned with the economics of 'planning'. In purely economic terms, the discussion ranged round the question how far a rational distribution of resources could be achieved without the use of the price mechanism; or, conversely, how far and in what form pricing would need, and could continue, to be used in an economy in which the majority of productive resources were collectively owned. In its purest form, this discussion had its origins long before the first world war, with Wieser's concept of natural value as its theoretical starting point. The debate received a strong impetus as a result of revived attention to the problem of state intervention, itself provoked by the economic fluctuations of the interwar years; and some added interest was given to the problem by the experiments in authoritarian economic planning in Russia. On the one side, a number of attempts were made to show how far the pattern of the use of a community's resources could be laid down from above without involving complete regimentation, not only of the material factors of production but also of human labour. On the other side, this kind of interventionism was criticized on the ground that 'partial planning' was not possible and would necessarily involve progressive

---

[1] Wesley Mitchell's *Business Cycles and Unemployment* (1923) may be mentioned as perhaps the most typical example.

authoritarian direction leading to the 'servile state'. It was also argued that even if, *per impossibile*, planning could stop short of serfdom, it could ensure neither as rational nor as stable a distribution of resources as the market economy'[1]

The debate soon took a different form based on the possibilities and limits of action by the public authority associated with the Keynesian school, and on the actual experience of government action in war time. Another effect of what was in essence a re-examination of the economic case for *laissez-faire* (which was to reappear in a very virulent form in the seventies) was the renewed attention which it directed to the scope and method of economics generally. In this respect, the most striking development of the period immediately preceding the Second World War was the appearance of a new and more intransigent economic formalism. This may be regarded as, in part, a revolt against the open or implied acceptance of interventionism of much of the contemporaneous work in the field of monetary and trade cycle theory, reinforced by the evident failures of many restrictionist and nationalist governmental policies of the twenties and thirties. In part it was a consequence of the refinements of the logic of economics brought about by the greater use of mathematical methods. Briefly, the doctrine amounted to a proclamation of the neutrality of economics *vis-à-vis* the ultimate ends of human conduct. This view was much influenced by the new *Wissenschaftslehre* based on neo-Kantian philosophy and developed by such writers as Heinrich Rickert and Max Weber. Their work was designed to define the material of economics in a way which strengthened the formal quality of theoretical results. It was, perhaps not unnaturally, in the home of Menger that the significance of the new methodological development was first realized. We can regard as its manifesto Weber's essay, *Die Objektivität sozialwissenschaftlicher und sozialpolitischer Erkenntnis* (1940) in which not 'the material relations between things, but the intellectual connection between problems' is made the criterion by which the fields of the sciences are defined.[2] According to Weber, the function of social science is to provide 'concepts and judgments which are not empirical

1 The subject has a vast literature, more voluminous and thorough on the anti-planning than on the pro-planning side. The most comprehensive work of the non-interventionist school is Mises, L., *Die Gemeinwirtschaft* (1932). For a balanced, but at the same time highly sceptical assessment of the possibilities of planning as seen by some economists at that time, see Hall, R. L., *The Economic System in a Socialist State* (1937)

2 Max Weber, *Gesammelte Aufsätze zur Wissenschaftslehre* (1922), p. 166.

reality, nor pictures of it; but which allows us to arrange it intellectually in a valid manner'.[1] This attitude was presented most clearly to the English-speaking world in Lionel Robbins's *Essay on the Nature and Significance of Economic Science*. The essence of its message is in the sentence, 'there is no penumbra of approbation round the concept of equilibrium, equilibrium is just equilibrium.'[2]

This sentence must not be taken to mean that those who hold these views do not also have something to say on particular problems of public policy. Indeed, Robbins, for one, was one of the most active commentators on many practical issues. But, methodologically speaking, it would be argued, such comments can only in part be derived from the theorems of economics (which, given adequate data, can at best demonstrate the implications of different actions). In part they are based on a number of practical judgments for which the economist may be especially well-informed but which he makes essentially as citizen and not as economist. It could be contended that such an attitude is not fundamentally in conflict with the liberal element contained in the tradition of economics. In the physiocrats and in the forerunners of the English classics, the political elements in economic reasoning had an obviously metaphysical character. But already in Adam Smith, and particularly in Ricardo, the providential quality of the natural order could be said to receive little more than lip service. A development which finally frees economics from its philosophical antecedents could, therefore, be said to be a consistent development of the trend towards basing precepts regarding public policy on utilitarianism in its strictly pragmatic sense.[3]

But even this more thorough heartsearching on the part of some economists did not have any lasting effect. In England and America where theoretical activity was greatest, the traditional reluctance to delve too deeply into the more philosophical aspects seems to have made economists hesitant explicitly to take up the challenge of the new ideas. Moreover, energies were engaged on the many immediate practical problems left in the wake of the depression. In an indirect way, however, the new view of the role of economic science in the real world influenced at least one of the more important developments in pure economic theory, the new formulations of the theory of equilibrium.

1 Max Weber, *Gesammelte Aufsätze zur Wissenschaftslehre* (1922), p. 113.
2 L. Robbins, *An Essay on the Nature and Significance of Economic Science* (1935), p. 143.
3 See Robbins's work, already referred to: *The Theory of Economic Policy in Classical Political Economy* (1952).

This, most striking, specific theoretical development, to which we may now turn, did not appear until the middle thirties. As an aftermath of crisis and depression there was a marked speeding-up of activity on the theoretical front. It concerned at first the more recondite branches of economic thought, and was closely related to the new methodological discussion which has already been mentioned. Some particularly delicate refinements were soon afterwards made in the theory of choice. Later, the more obviously realistic branches of theory, those dealing with competition and production, began to share in the renaissance. Later still, the larger problem of classical political economy – the determination of the general level of economic activity – was once again put in the centre of theoretical discussion. Indeed, it is at this point that the gap between economic theory and economic practice again began to be closed.

## The Theory of Equilibrium

The central core of modern economics, the theory of consumers' choice and the theory of equilibrium of exchange and production, was cast substantially in the same mould in the twenties as it had been before World War I. Some differences of formulation existed, but the general tendency was for unification. In England some traces of the real-cost, disutility approach persisted until the thirties. This was, no doubt, due to the overwhelming influence of Marshall, whose work never succeeded in cutting adrift completely from its nineteenth-century antecedents. Both in Marshall and in many of his followers there is also to be found an often deprecated, but evidently ineradicable, liking for implicit ethical postulates which left English theory with a characteristic Victorian flavour.

In America, as has already been pointed out, the non-utilitarian interpretation of marginalism had more quickly gained the upper hand; and had Wicksteed been writing in the New World rather than in the Old, his *Commonsense* would not have remained isolated and forgotten, to be resuscitated only in the thirties. In Austria, too, hedonism was abandoned; and under the influence of Menger and Wieser (with the proximity to Lausanne acting perhaps as a contributory factor) the ordinal view of utility and the mutual relationship of cost and value, embodied in the opportunity-cost principle, became accepted doctrines.

The mathematical expression of economic relationships, at first associated with the Lausanne school, also became more widespread. Obviously, the purified utility concept, the opportunity-cost doctrine, and the marginal-productivity theory of the productive shares are more appropriate to the neutral language of functional equations than were the doctrines of John Stuart Mill. And although it was not until the thirties that a substantial increase took place in the literature of mathematical economics, there can be little doubt that mathematical formulations of widely accepted doctrines were an important factor in the spread of a certain degree of eclecticism and in the internationaliz-ation of theory in the first three decades of the present century. This eclecticism and this disappearance of national doctrinal barriers are well exemplified in one of the best expositions of the economic theory of yesterday, Knut Wicksell's *Lectures in Political Economy* (1901). Although published before the period we are now discussing, the first volume of this work remained probably the best single synthesis and exposition of marginal-utility economics for more than a quarter of a century. In some respects, notably in the marginal-productivity theory, it contains many original contributions. But its outstanding quality is the skill with which it fuses elements from many divergent authors (for example, Walras and Böhm-Bawerk) into a single structure and the facility with which its author combines literary and mathematical methods of analysis and exposition.

The mathematical method proved to be the one to produce the most clear-cut developments and refinements. These developments are by no means the most significant; and in point of time they are later than other recent changes which have more profoundly affected the general status of economic theory. But they represent the most logically consistent advance from the position reached by the second generation of marginalists; and it may therefore be appropriate to sketch them first. The most elaborate refinement stems directly from the work of Fisher, Edgeworth, and Pareto, and, in a special sense, Marshall, in the theory of consumers' behaviour; and from Walras and Pareto in the general theory of equilibrium. These, of course, are not the only antecedents. The basic concept of substitution which is involved in the present theory of consumers' choice is to be found in substantially identical form, though expressed in words rather than in curves and equations, in the writings of Wicksteed and Knight. And in the latest versions of the theory, the influence of Marshall is very clear.

An early attempt at a new formulation based on the Paretian

technique is to be found in a paper written in 1915 by a Russian author, E. Slutsky.[1] The best-known later version has been mainly the work of English economists. It was first expounded in an article by J. R. Hicks and R. G. D. Allen;[2] and a more expanded statement of it was given by one of these authors, Hicks, in his *Value and Capital* (1939). The first and second parts of this work set out to provide a definitive exposition both of the theory of subjective value and of the theory of general equilibrium. It has also the advantage over the earlier state-ment of showing up more clearly the contacts between the new for-mulation and those of Pareto, Marshall, and Walras. It may be convenient to give a summary of it here as an indication of the direction in which marginal utility has been evolving.

Briefly, the new formulation attempts to do two things: first, to demonstrate the deficiencies of the older version, particularly that of Marshall, and to show how the Paretian approach enables one to overcome these deficiencies; and secondly to develop and complete the Paretian indifference curve method itself. In Marshall, it is asserted, the theory of consumers' behaviour amounts to a comparatively simple expansion of Gossen's second law. A consumer with given tastes and a given money income, when confronted by prices formed in a competi-tive market (which he must take as data) will, if he wishes to maximize total utility, ensure that 'a marginal unit of expenditure in each direc-tion brings in the same increment of utility'.[3] This means that in equilibrium marginal utilities will be proportional to prices, a con-clusion which is emphasized not only by Marshall, but by Wicksteed, Wicksell, Knight, and many others. Indeed, it has become a standard theorem of the textbook.

Hicks claims that Marshall's theory suffered from its continued reliance on the concepts of utility and diminishing utility. For, despite the work of Menger and the frequent subsequent denial of the measurability of utility, the Marshallian version still implied a given utility function – that is, a given absolute intensity of desire for a collection of goods – thus re-introducing measurability by the back door. At this points, it is argued, Pareto comes to the rescue. The

1 E. Slutsky, 'Sulla Teoria del bilancio del consummatore', *Giornale degli economisti* (1915).
2 J. R. Hicks and R. G. D. Allen, 'A Reconsideration of the Theory of Value', *Economica* (1934), pp. 52–76, 196–219.
3 J. R. Hicks, *Value and Capital* (1939), p. 11.

indifference curve approach offers the solution of supplying a determinate equilibrium system with less data than seem to be involved in the marginal-utility approach. If we wish to represent graphically in the Marshallian manner the principle of diminishing utility for two goods, we would have to draw a three-dimensional diagram, the quantities of the two goods being plotted in two dimensions and their corresponding utilities in the third. A 'utility surface' can then be drawn connecting all the points which represent the utilities of different collections of quantities of the two goods. The transition to Pareto's indifference curves is then quite simple; it is the transition from a relief model to a map. Utility is thus eliminated, because we are left merely with a series of more preferred, less preferred, and indifferent combinations of quantities of two goods.

It is claimed that this linguistic and expository change involves a major methodological improvement, because it makes it possible to start from the assumption that an individual prefers one collection of goods to another without inquiring into the extent to which he prefers it. If the claim were to be confined to saying that the notion of relativity and immeasurability of utility – which Menger first stressed – only achieves precision when the concept of utility functions is dropped and the theorems are stated purely in terms of preferred positions on the indifference map, one could accept it. But the more extravagant suggestion that this change produces either novel basic concepts or that it is 'a positive change in the foundation of the theory'[1] can hardly be maintained. The relative 'greater or less' notion of utility has always been an accepted part of modern marginalism, and it is not easy to see that one formulation produces any substantial improvement over the other where the difficulties which inevitably arise in the process of 'quantification' of subjective desires are concerned.

Some interesting expository consequences follow when the new terminology is substituted for the old. Diminishing marginal utility disappears with utility as such. In their place we have marginal rate of substitution. This is not the place to define these new terms, or the uses to which they are put. But nearly every Marshallian theorem now finds its counterpart. Thus proportionality of marginal utilities to prices becomes the tangency of the price line to the indifference curve. In other words, the theorem now states that the marginal rate of substitution between two classes of goods (which is expressed by the

---

1 J. R. Hicks, *Value and Capital* (1939), p. 21.

slope of the indifference curve) must, in equilibrium, be equal to the ratio of prices. Diminishing marginal utility is replaced by diminishing marginal rate of substitution, or, in other words, by the condition that the indifference curve must be convex to the origin. But diminishing marginal utility and the convexity of the indifference curve are not identical propositions. For it is conceivable that in the case of certain goods (competitive or complementary ones) the relation of the marginal utilities may be such as to offset the direct effects resulting from increases or diminutions in the quantity, thus producing, at times, an increasing rather than a diminishing marginal rate of substitution; that is, a concave curve. Further conditions must therefore be stated, and this leads the authors of the new technique into an elaborate discussion of complementarity.

Another interesting 'translation' of Marshallian doctrine is to be found in the manner in which the law of demand is derived from the theory of choice. In Marshall this derivation requires the addition of a simple assumption, constancy of the marginal utility of money. Given this condition, it follows that the ratio between marginal utility and price must be constant; that is, that quantity demanded and price must be inversely related. Hicks proceeds to show that this Marshallian assumption amounts to ignoring the effects of changes in income upon the demand of any commodity in relation to changes in that commodity's price. By an extremely skilful separation and subsequent union of the analysis of the income and price effects upon the demand of a commodity (including the case when that commodity is the inferior of a pair of substitutes), Hicks presents a law of consumers' demand which is more flexible. At the same time he demonstrates that for the major part of the probable cases Marshall was right in ignoring income effects, in concentrating upon substitution effects of price changes, and thus in deducing his general law of the downward sloping demand curve. The discussion then proceeds to cover the special case of the seller and to show the existence of an asymmetry between the law of demand and that of supply in the sense that the 'exceptional' cases, in which the curve slopes in a direction opposite to that postulated in the general case, are more probable on the supply side than on that of demand.

A further interesting aspect of this re-examination of static economics (the only part of Hicks's important work which can be dealt with here) is the analysis of the equilibrium of exchange. In general, this bases itself largely on Walras; and it repeats the condition for the determinacy of a system set down by Walras, namely, that the number of equations should be equal to the number of unknowns. The mathematical (and economic) inadequacy of such a simple condition has repeatedly been pointed out,[1] but it is not possible to discuss here the simplifying assumptions which, so it is argued by the critics, have to be made before the Walrasian determinacy condition can be said to hold. Hicks, having concluded that the Walrasian theorem is adequate, proceeds to show that it can be adapted to the indifference curve terminology in all cases in which indifference curves can be drawn for the individuals concerned, independently of prices. There must, therefore, be excluded speculative markets, the Veblenian examples of conspicuous consumption, and the markets for the factors of production (where demand must depend on anticipated prices of the product). For other cases, the one where personal services are exchanged being perhaps the case *par excellence*, a determinate system is said to be demonstrable.

Hicks then turns to the question of the stability of such an equilibrium.[2] A number of refinements are introduced to the well-known laws of supply and demand. Some of them, such as the special use of the new term 'excess demand' and the drawing of an excess demand curve, seem entirely pointless. Others, particularly the ones in which the previous separation of income and substitution effects of price changes are taken up again and combined with the analysis of the different position of the buyer and seller, are designed to make the analysis relevant to a larger number of possible situations and, therefore, to increase its 'realism'. The upshot of the discussions of the stability conditions is, in Hicks's words, that the 'existence of stable systems of multiple exchange is entirely consistent with the laws of demand', that the 'conditions of stability are quite easy conditions', and that 'instability can only arise from two causes: strongly asymmetric income effects, and extreme complementarity'.[3]

1 See O. Morgenstern, 'Professor Hicks on Value and Capital', *Journal of Political Economy* (1941), pp. 368–77, where reference is made to the work of J. von Neumann, 'Über ein ökonomisches Gleichungssystem, etc.', and A. Wald, 'Über die eindeutige positive Lösbarkeit der neuen Produktionsgleichungen', *Ergebnisse eines mathematischen Kolloquiums* (1938 and 1935 respectively), see also A. Wald, 'Über einige Gleichungssysteme der mathematischen Ökonomie', *Zeitschrift für Nationalökonomie* (1936).

2 J. R. Hicks, *Value and Capital*, pp. 62–77. For comparison, it is amusing to see the formulation in Henderson's *Supply and Demand* (1922).

3 ibid., p. 72.

This reassuring conclusion is, however, hedged round with qualifications: it is reserved for the static part of theory; it excludes certain types of exchange; it is not, at this point, concerned with production; and above all, it is based on the overriding assumption of the existence of perfect competition. It is true that the intellectual path by which the conclusions are reached is smoother than previous ones. The whole formulation is more elegant; and it has taken its place in the current body of the general theory of price and equilibrium. It is thus a useful new intellectual tool, and like other recent ones is free from the 'natural order' implications for public policy from which earlier versions of marginalism suffered.

In the theory of production Hicks devotes about thirty pages of his book to an extension of his analysis of the equilibrium system to the problem of production. A situation other than perfect competition remains excluded, and Hicks has little difficulty in replacing the consumer by a producer and the consumer's indifference curve by a production curve (which relates amount of factor employed to amount produced). He then proceeds to establish the conditions of equilibrium of production. Similarly, he examines the conditions under which such an equilibrium system will be stable, finds them not to be difficult of fulfilment, and concludes that we 'may satisfy ourselves that a perfectly stable system of production equilibrium is a reasonable hypothesis'.[1]

However, a very interesting passage in this section treats, in passing, the difficulties which arise when the assumption of perfect competition is dropped. The whole question is disposed of in less than two pages. One cannot blame the author, who has explicitly limited himself to the assumption of perfect competition. But it is indicative of the limitation of static economics that even so elaborate and refined a restatement of it remains untouched by what is undoubtedly one of the two most important modern developments in economic theory, the theory of monopoly and imperfect competition. It may serve as a useful introduction to a brief summary of this development to show the way in which Hicks gets round the difficulty he has raised by his reference to the problem of competition in relation to the equilibrium of production. He points out that the equilibrium conditions include the postulate that at the point of equilibrium both marginal and average cost must be rising. But because at the point where marginal cost is at a

---

[1] J. R. Hicks, *Value and Capital*, p. 104.

minimum, average cost must necessarily be higher than marginal cost, it is possible for marginal cost to be rising while average cost is still falling. If price equals marginal cost (a condition of equilibrium), then in that range, price will be below average cost. In other words, the producer will be selling at a loss, a situation clearly incompatible with equilibrium. This dilemma can, of course, be overcome by abandoning the assumption of perfect competition; for in a monopoly price may be higher than marginal cost to an extent determined by the degree of monopoly. But this step, as Hicks points out, has 'very destructive consequences for economic theory'; because in a situation of monopoly the stability conditions, so neatly established, become indeterminate, and this 'wreckage is that of the greater part of economic theory'.[1] The somewhat weak solution which Hicks decides to adopt is to assume that the degree of monopoly is so slight that the postulate of perfect competition does no great violence to reality. Although admitting that this may mean a serious limitation upon the problems to which the technique may be applicable, he expresses the doubt whether the problems which are thereby excluded are 'capable of much useful analysis by the methods of economic theory'.[2]

The post-Keynesian economics of recent years, or what may still, despite the 'counter-revolution', which will be discussed later, be called mainstream economics has greatly enhanced the role of J. R. Hicks in the elaboration of the corpus of economic theory.[3] This enhancement is only in part due to higher assessment given to his earlier work, whose stimulative quality was quickly recognized. He continued to add to it right up to his death in 1989 with a series of writings which showed – somewhat unusually – a broadening rather than a narrowing of interest with advancing age, though it was his earlier work that earned him the Nobel Prize.

It is not possible here to go into any detail as far as others of his writings are concerned, but the following may be mentioned: *Capital and Growth* (1965), *A Theory of Economic History* (1969), *Collected Essays on Economic Theory* 3 vols (1982) (Volume II, *Money, Interest and Wages*, contains a particularly useful collection of essays on Keynes and post-Keynesian theoretical development); and, published in the year of his death, *A Market Theory of Money* (1989).

1 J. R. Hicks, *Value and Capital*, pp. 83–4.
2 ibid., p. 85.
3 A short, but brilliant appreciation is to be found in an obituary (May 1989) in the *Independent* newspaper by Lord Peston.

One of the most vigorous trends in recent economic literature has been based, at least by implication, on the belief that dropping the postulate of perfect competition was an important basis for further theoretical advance. Probably the major part of the literature of 'pure' economic theory since 1926 has been concerned with the theoretical reformulations which are necessary once the assumption of perfect competition is dropped. The discussion took some time in starting. It derived almost wholly from Marshall, and arose out of the fact that there were many loose ends in the Marshallian system of equilibrium of supply and demand. Marshall's time analysis, his concept of the representative firm, the place of increasing and diminishing cost in his theory, and the doctrine of external economies, were found to have been used in an ambiguous manner. An extensive literature grew up out of the attempt to clarify these concepts.

These developments in the theory of the market and of the individual firm exemplify particularly well both the interplay between theory and practice and the development of theory itself. It would not be accurate to conclude that the writers who have been most responsible in recent years for the development of the new theorems have been directly led to the study of monopolistic situations by the growth of the large corporation in the real world. It was not Standard Oil, AT&T, or Imperial Chemicals, or the growth of the proprietary article which precipitated the discussion. Nevertheless, it was reality that caused dissatisfaction with the Marshallian doctrine. A simple, obvious fact of experience contradicted the conclusions of the traditional supply and demand analysis. In a large number of cases experience showed that a threatened onset of diminishing returns was not the real obstacle to an expansion of production by the individual firm. On the contrary, more often than not, the individual producer found that average cost was still diminishing at the point at which he stopped expanding his output. It was the market – that is, the extent to which he was able to dispose of this output without either lowering price or incurring special costs – which formed the barrier. A barrier of this nature is, of course, well known and has been studied extensively in the theory of monopoly.

This pointer in the direction of monopoly theory was paralleled by the rediscovery (through increased attention to mathematical theory) of the work of Cournot. The possibilities of cut-throat competition through individual increasing returns, already envisaged by Marshall and powerfully supported by the actual history of large areas of modern business organization, also led back to a renewed study of monopolistic situations. Thus the two trends mutually reinforced each other.

There were a number of important forerunners of the great debate on the Marshallian heritage. The first to question its full relevance to the problems of the real world was J. H. Clapham who, in an article in 1922, asked economists whether their various boxes labelled 'Diminishing Returns', 'Increasing Returns', and so on, had any content.[1] The discussion was not, however, continuous, and it had to wait for a further powerful stimulus four years later from an article by Piero Sraffa which remains to this day the best statement of the problem, particularly from the point of view of the history of economic doctrines.[2] It is therefore best to give a brief summary of Sraffa's argument in order to see the setting in which the discussion began. Sraffa begins with a statement of the place which, historically, the laws of returns have occupied in the theory of value. It is not necessary to recapitulate this at any length. We know that in classical theory the relation between unit cost and size of output was not given much attention. Diminishing returns were considered mainly in relation to rent; and because they affected the cost of all things, the classics, with their interest centred on relative prices, ignored them. Increasing returns were considered as a part of the doctrine of division of labour. The modern and Marshallian modification of this classical position was to generalize the two laws and to make them a part of the theory of value, where they provided the basis of the theory of supply. Diminishing returns, as is well known, were generalized to cover all factors with fixed supply; and increasing returns were made to consist, for this purpose, of what Marshall called 'external economies'. This later restriction was necessary, because internal economies of scale were found to be incompatible with a stable competitive equilibrium.

Sraffa points out the unsatisfactory character of the laws in this form. We have here an analogy to the indifference curve's independence of prices, stipulated by Hicks. For it is essential in the theory of supply and demand that the conditions of each should be capable of statement independently of one another. Applying this essential criterion to the laws of returns, we find that such independent

---

1 J. H. Clapham, 'Of Empty Economics Boxes', *Economic Journal*, 1922.
2 P. Sraffa, 'The Laws of Returns under Competitive Conditions', *Economic Journal* (1926), pp. 535–50.

formulation of the conditions of production and demand is possible only in a very small number of cases. According to Sraffa, it is confined to those cases in which the production of an individual commodity uses the whole supply of a scarce factor, and to those in which there are economies which are internal to a whole industry, but external to the individual firm within that industry. Thus we reach the same point as that which presented a dilemma to Hicks. Sraffa, however, proposes that it should be met boldly by the abandonment of the assumption of competition, and by the application of the well-tried methods of monopoly analysis. These are precisely applicable to a situation in which the individual firm finds the market, rather than its conditions of production, the limiting factor.

Sraffa makes a most successful beginning with such a reformulation of the theory of market equilibrium. And on the foundation which he laid, others, notably E. Chamberlin and Joan Robinson, have built an imposing structure of new theory.[1] Sraffa's beginning has now become an established part of the history of economic thought. Briefly summarized, it runs as follows. The starting-point is the position of the individual seller. It has already been pointed out by Marshall that 'when we are considering an individual producer we must couple his supply curve, not with the general demand curve for his commodity in a wide market, but with the particular demand curve of his own special market'.[2] Now this 'individual demand curve' – or better 'sales curve', as it has recently been called[3] – is downward sloping in the cases we are considering; that is to say, the individual seller is forced to reduce price if he wishes to sell more. Alternatively, he has to incur special sales costs (advertising, and the like) which may succeed in shifting the whole of his sales curve to the right or in reducing its slope.

The latter method involves breaking down in practice what is an essential part of the assumption of perfect competition; namely, the indifference on the part of buyers as to the seller from whom they

---

1 E. Chamberlin, *The Theory of Monopolistic Competition* (1933); J. Robinson, *The Economics of Imperfect Competition* (1933). The extensive discussion, which ran through the *Economic Journal* from 1926 to 1933 and in which Professor Pigou, G. F. Shove, Allyn Young, and many others took part, should be consulted. Two articles in this group may be mentioned specifically: Viner, J., 'Cost Curves and Supply Curves' in *Zeitschrift für Nationalökonomie* (1931), and Robinson, J., 'Rising Supply Price' in *Economica* (1941). Both should be read in conjunction with Sraffa's article and both are reprinted in *Readings in Price Theory* (1953).

2 A. Marshall, *Principles of Economics* (Book V, xii, 2).

3 R. Triffin, *Monopolistic Competition and General Equilibrium Theory* (1940), p. 5, n. 3.

purchase. Or, in other words again, it involves the creation of heterogeneity among the products offered for sale by competing producers. If this can be established, the single market of competition becomes subdivided into a number of special markets for the products of each firm, separated from one another by more or less strong and more or less stable insulating walls of special buyer's preferences. In that situation, as Sraffa pointed out, each firm has to consider the demand of two kinds of marginal buyers: those who are marginal in its own special market, and those who are marginal to all the related 'monopolistically competitive' markets. Theoretically, its policy may be either one of price reduction to attract buyers away from the competitors, or one of buttressing its monopoloid position by maintaining the thickness of the insulating wall between it and the others through the continued expenditure of sales costs.

The upshot of Sraffa's analysis is to show that in many cases where there are a large number of sellers (and where, therefore, one would normally think of the existence of competition), and where internal economies are present but not excessively marked, the second alternative policy will be chosen. But this means that a determinate equilibrium – a monopolistic one – is possible in spite of the existence of conditions which make the apparatus of competitive equilibrium analysis inappropriate. It will not necessarily be an equilibrium with a single price, although that may be the case where the internal economies and the degrees of buyer's preference have become slight and where the individual firms are fairly similarly placed. In such a case, the resulting price will tend to the level which would obtain under a single monopoly; and the competition of the individual firms will have as its object the securing and holding of as large a share of the total market as possible.

There have been many elaborations and refinements of this line of reasoning. Most significantly, perhaps, the case of perfect competition has, since Sraffa, been increasingly analysed in precisely the same terms as that of monopoly or of the imperfect competition with which Sraffa's theory was concerned. In Professor Chamberlin's work, for example, we find a very ingenious restatement of the laws of supply and demand, including the theorem that in competition the equilibrium price equates demand and supply, in such new terms as average and marginal revenue which, had they been in use before, would most certainly have been reserved for the theory of monopoly.

A word may, however, be added on the more general position which

Sraffa now occupies in the modern history of economics, particularly since the appearance of his highly advanced and difficult *The Production of Commodities by Means of Commodities* (1960). He was for many years known almost entirely only to fellow academic economists, and even today, almost a decade after his death in 1983, he is still virtually unknown to a wider public, except in his native Italy, and more there perhaps by reason of his political inclinations than his strictly economic writings. Thanks largely to the work of Professor Roncaglia of the University of Rome (see for example his article 'Piero Sraffa and the Reconstruction of Political Economy' in the *Quarterly Review* of Banca Nazionale Del Lavoro, December 1983) his work is increasingly used in the literature. To mention only some examples, there is his contribution to equilibrium theory, his ingenious re-formulation of Ricardian principles and the theories of circular flows of the *Tableau Economique* or of Marx. Professor Samuelson – who had paid tribute to Sraffa at an early stage – has contributed an important article on 'Sraffian economics' to the *New Palgrave Dictionary of Economics*, a work which also contains a very useful, more general, article on Sraffa by John Eatwell and Carlo Panico. Curiously, Sraffa's aim to return to the classical pattern, away from the Marshallian utility and partial equilibrium concepts, bears some superficial resemblance to the Walras/Arrow/Debreu pattern, but only in a formal sense. It will be interesting to see how future theoretical developments deal with the 'true' return to classicism of Sraffa against the supposed novelty of the New Classical Macroeconomics! These theoretical refinements cannot be dealt with in any detail here. However, some special features of the new analysis may be mentioned. For example, the theory of competitive supply and demand equilibrium forms, in the new version, an interesting solution of the expository difficulties which troubled Jevons and Walras. As we have seen, the former was led to using the clumsy expedient of the 'trading body' and to misapply the concept of the 'law of indifference'. The latter employed the more subtle but still unsatisfactory procedure of the *prix crié* and the *tâtonnements*. In the present theory, these difficulties are to a considerable extent overcome. The laws of supply and demand are restated in terms which make the position of the individual buyer or seller in a competitive market much clearer. Chamberlin's formulation, in particular, is a simple and clear statement of the implication of the assumption of perfect competition. He uses the neat device of two graphs: one with composite curves representing the total demand and supply in the market; the other an enlargement, as it were, of that infinitesimal portion of the total market which the single buyer or seller occupies. This enables him to use geometrical propositions and terms to give precision to the conditions of a competitive market; the horizontal individual 'sales curve' becomes the expression both of the postulated conditions of equilibrium (absence of buyer's preferences and absence of individual influence over total amount supplied) as well as of their consequence, the infinite elasticity of demand for the product of an individual seller at the ruling market price.

It is unnecessary to go through all the reformulations which this approach makes possible. The aim of profit maximization can be more precisely worked out; and the individual cost curves can be treated in this same way as their equivalent on the demand side, the individual sales curves. The scale of production in competitive conditions of the individual firm can then be analysed, as can that of a whole industry.[1] Needless to say, exactly the same technique can be used for monopoly or monopolistic competition, because the initial impetus to the reformation of the theory of the market came precisely from the realm of monopoly. The final outcome, in both Chamberlin's and Joan Robinson's theory, is a statement of the conditions of market equilibrium which is of such generality that it can be applied equally to competition, to monopoly, or to any intermediate situation.

One important consequence follows, and it is this which was uppermost in the conclusions at which Sraffa was hinting. Because the conditions of equilibrium are now stated in similar terms for all market situations, it becomes possible to compare the results (in terms of price, output, and remuneration of the factors of production) to which each one leads. This aspect of the new theory is not very prominent in Chamberlin's work, but it plays an important part in that of Joan Robinson. It is only fitting that this should be so, because it is to the Cambridge school and the Marshallian tradition that one must look for the elements of significance for practical policy to be distilled from current academic theory. The whole theory of Pigou with its distinction between private and social marginal net product forms an obvious bridge between Marshall and the conclusions of the theory of imperfect competition. Again, a detailed exposition of this part of the theory

1 See, for example, E. A. G. Robinson, *The Structure of Competitive Industry* (1931). Written before the new terminology became generally accepted, this book shows, nevertheless, the influence of the new approach and the refinement which it represents over the Marshallian theory.

would not be in place here, but it may be worth emphasizing that the newer refinements have only underlined the criticisms of what one may call the 'optimal distribution of resources prejudice' of economic theory, which were implied in Sraffa's article. Output-restricting and price-raising tendencies inherent in the monopolistic and imperfectly competitive market have long been obvious to the observer of the structural changes in modern industry. These now have their theoretical expressions.

The precise extent to which such comparisons may be taken is still a matter of debate. And it is not yet evident how much of an advance the new theories represent, particularly in regard to the precepts of policy which may be deduced. But it is significant that a number of policy conclusions have already been drawn from them. These show an unmistakable affiliation with the social reform tradition in English economic thought of which Marshall, and especially Pigou, are the chief twentieth-century representatives.[1] The technical apparatus now available is more refined than that by which the 'smoke nuisance' was analysed. And opportunities for testing them have been more frequent in the last decade than before. For example, the theorems concerning the extension or restriction of monopoly and the regulation and the control of varieties of products have proved helpful in war-time and since to governments faced with the need of restricting the supply of consumers' goods and of controlling the allocation of scarce resources.

The ultimate direction, as far as public policy is concerned, in which these theoretical developments are tending is still somewhat obscure. What is, however, certain is the profound change which they have produced within the bounds of theory itself. This change is undoubtedly in the nature of an advance; for by broadening the theory it makes it present a better picture of reality. One important consequence of this is that the natural order incubus hitherto vulnerable mainly to heterodox argument can now be more easily exorcized with means provided by orthodox theory itself. More is said about this aspect of the theory later. But it is already clear that when Hicks spoke of the possible wreckage of the greater part of economic theory, he was at least right in so far as the *laissez-faire* tradition of the old market analysis was concerned. For the spontaneous tendencies of the market

---

1 The most interesting example in what is in essence a textbook of the trend which has been called forth by these new theoretical developments is to be found in J. E. Meade, *An Introduction to Economic Analysis and Policy* (1936).

can now be shown as by no means inevitably leading to an optimal distribution of scarce resources. And one would have to be very bold indeed to speak nowadays of 'consumer's sovereignty', in any 'natural order' sense, where the contrived variety of products in an imperfectly competitive market is concerned.

The revived interest in the analysis of monopoloid situations, first developed by Cournot, has led to very similar results. Here the consequence has been not so much to undermine the 'optimal' prejudice of marginalism as to raise a serious doubt about the ability of the market to produce spontaneously a stable equilibrium. Cournot thought that there was a determinate solution of the duopoly problem, the problem of two sellers. He showed that, after successive reactions to each other's policy with regard to the individual amounts put on the market, the two sellers would reach a position from which it would not be in the interest of either to depart. Subsequent writers have questioned this solution in the case both of duopoly and in the more general situation of oligopoly when there are few enough sellers to make the assumptions of competition inapplicable. The debate has gone back and forth with contributions coming from many distinguished economists, and two schools of thought seem to have developed: one which maintains the Cournotian result of derminacy; and the other which follows Cournot's critics, Bertrand and Edgeworth, in regarding the duopoly case as being essentially indeterminate. The history of this debate, though interesting, is of too special a character to be outlined here.[1] It is, however, possible to point out that the determinacy solution either requires very special assumptions or, alternatively, that fairly realistic cases can be constructed in which an indeterminate situation is the more probable. In the first place, many of the post-Cournot duopoly theories which have yielded determinate results have been based on the assumption of 'asymmetry' in the positions, intentions, and policies of the two contending parties. Such assumptions, which one German economist has called *wirtschaftsfriedlich*, are not satisfactory solutions from the point of view of pure economic theory, because the postulated conditions are restrictive and do not, therefore, have any priority over other assumptions that might be made about the behaviour of the duopolists. Clear agreements among the rival sellers must also be excluded from the assumptions that are open, because

---

1 An interesting brief résumé is to be found in H. von Stackelberg, *Marktform und Gleichgewicht* (1934).

they transform the initial duopoly situation (which is the one to be analysed) into one of a monopoly with special subsidiary features. The product-differentiation solution is on a different footing. It may be regarded as a legitimate postulate for the achievement of a determinate market equilibrium in cases of duopoly and oligopoly. But although it removes the disequilibrating effects of the pure duopoly situation, it reveals the socio-economic implications which we have already met in the post-Marshallian theory of imperfect competition.

Thus we find that these two parallel developments in the theory of the market have, in effect, constituted a twin attack upon two cherished traditions of economic theory. Special assumptions about the real world must now be made if a theoretical market situation is to produce a determinate equilibrium, and if it is to be described as leading to the best possible distribution of resources. Indeed, a substantial portion of conjectural market situations – certainly the majority of those which have the most likeness to the contemporary economic scene – cannot, on *a priori* grounds, be said inevitably to produce these.

Substantially this trend of development came to an end around the time World War II broke out.[1] Since then the subject was largely dormant until it reappeared in the seventies and eighties in new formulations of market behaviour and theory.

## Keynes

The next few pages will be concerned with a major development in contemporary economics which is largely associated with the name of one man. However, this section must not be regarded as an essay on Keynes. It would be very interesting to trace the evolution of his ideas, which have continued to be a powerful force in economic theory and practice for the quarter of a century since his death. To some extent this has been done in R. F. Harrod: *J. M. Keynes* (1951), the first full-length biography.[2] But this most interesting and readable book has

1 An excellent summary, which contains much material for a further advance, is R. Triffin, *Monopolistic Competition and General Equilibrium Theory* (1940).

2 A new biography by Robert Skidelsky of which the first volume has so far appeared takes the story of Keynes only up to 1920. For a book containing some interesting biographical reflections and character analyses as well as descriptions of the intellectual atmosphere of Cambridge in the thirties and after the war (in the case of the former with some admitted traces of a Canadian 'chip on the shoulder' which add to their charm) see

not been designed primarily to serve the purposes of *Dogmengeschichte*. Excellent studies are also to be found in S. Harris (ed.) *The New Economics: Keynes's Influence on Theory and Public Policy* (1947) and in L. R. Klein *The Keynesian Revolution* (1949). But these two are concerned, in the main, with Keynes's last, and greatest, achievement; and it must still be left to the historian of the future to assess his work as a whole.[1]

The following very brief account of his life and work leading up to the *General Theory* is not intended to anticipate future judgment on his intellectual development. It is merely a short introduction to the marked change in the approach to the major economic problems which was initiated by his last work. The change, as we shall see in the next chapter, is so great that it has opened the door for the reintroduction of a new political economy concerned, as was that of the classics, with the problems of the economy as a whole, and not only with those of the individual consumer.

John Maynard Keynes was born in 1883 and died in 1946. During forty out of these sixty-three years, that is, from his leaving the University to his death, he was continually active as an economist, in every form which was open to him: as thinker, writer, teacher business man, public servant, and statesman. Thoroughly grounded in Marshallian economics, as well as mathematics, possessing a philosophical bent and the widest literary and artistic interests, Keynes also acquired early in life a considerable knowledge of business and public affairs. Thanks to these accomplishments and at least as much to an extraordinary vigorous and attractive personality, Keynes exerted an influence on economic theory and policy unequalled since Smith and Ricardo. Indeed, in his later years, Keynes's connection with the affairs of state was such that he had a unique opportunity, not enjoyed by any other great economist before him, to make his ideas impinge directly upon the formation and conduct of public policy.

Though rooted in the Marshallian version of neo-classical economic doctrine, Keynes's own theories showed, almost from the beginning, a strongly original, not to say heterodox, tendency. He himself was conscious of a break with his tradition only as far as his last, and greatest, work is concerned. But to the observer, now that he can look

---

Harry and Elizabeth Johnson's *The Shadow of Keynes* (1978). It is moreover a valuable addition to the Canon.

1 This has been made easier since the publication of his collected works, which has now been completed: *The Collected Writings of John Maynard Keynes*, ed. by E. Johnson, 30 vols. (1971–89).

back upon it, the evolution of Keynes's ideas can be seen as a continuous process of renovation and reformulation of established doctrines and, in the end, of their transformation into something wholly new.

It is not surprising that the full significance of what was happening was lost upon author and public alike. The main emphasis, from the *Economic Consequences of the Peace* (1919) to *A Treatise on Money* (1930) was almost always on issues of practical policy. True, there were many theoretical articles in learned journals intermingled with more popular books, pamphlets and articles, but even these were on topics arising out of issues of policy: German reparations and the transfer problem, the return by Britain to the gold standard, the reform of the British Currency issue. Not until the *Treatise* is there even the beginning of an attempt by the author to absorb all this work into a theoretical system. But this work, in spite of brilliant essays on individual topics,[1] turned out to be prolegomena to a major theoretical work, rather than that work itself. Keynes's great task, to draw the lesson of his struggles with each practical problem and to produce a new theoretical framework, was yet to come. It was not until the *General Theory of Employment, Interest and Money* (1936) that this task was consciously undertaken and triumphantly completed. For the author, therefore, it was the writing of this book that represented 'a struggle of escape' from old ideas; and so it did to its readers at the time. But in retrospect, the struggle was a continuous one, the *General Theory* only its successful conclusion.

It is not easy to summarize adequately Keynes's contributions to economics before the *General Theory*. For our purpose, it must suffice to indicate briefly his main preoccupations which were to find their fullest expression in that work. Keynes's first work, published when he was thirty, was *Indian Currency and Finance*. Apart from a highly successful analysis of the specific subject with which it dealt, it is noteworthy for a classic exposition of the gold-exchange standard. Some writers also profess to see in that exposition (and in the book as a whole) a predilection for monetary management which was later to become so characteristic of Keynes's attitude to economic policy. There is, however, nothing in the book to indicate any departure from the prevailing mode of Marshallianism.

His three next major works, leaving aside the *Treatise on Probability*

---

1 These, incidentally, are well worth re-reading in the light, particularly, of recent debates on international monetary problems.

(1921),[1] are concerned with the economic settlements after the war, with their aftermath, and with the monetary problems of the immediate post-war period. *The Economic Consequences of the Peace* (1919), and *A Revision of the Treaty* (1922) – especially the former – gained Keynes a world-wide reputation as a publicist on politico-economic matters and as a writer of literary accomplishment exceptional in this field. To the student of Keynes's economic ideas, these books are important primarily for the insight they throw on Keynes's general political and social attitude. They clearly demonstrate his strong rationalism and humanitarianism, his deep concern for international amity and peace which, notwithstanding a passionate attachment to the interests of his own country, remained with him throughout his life; and, above all, his ineradicable belief in the power of reason to find solutions to the most difficult problems and in the power of persuasion to make these solutions generally acceptable.[2]

But it was the third of these works, the *Tract on Monetary Reform* (1923) which came nearest to being a systematic statement of the author's views on the means of economic policy. To those who wish to seek early indications of the theories that were later to appear in the *General Theory*, the *Tract* is the most rewarding source. In it will be found, above all, the clearest possible demonstration of Keyne's abiding interest in the objective of stabilizing the level of business activity. Later, during the years of depression and unemployment, this interest found even more striking expression in the semi-political pamphlets on the means for curing unemployment. These inevitably led Keynes into a reappraisal of the agenda of the State and a consequent modification of the doctrine of *laissez-faire* (not an abandonment as the title of his best-known pamphlet, *The End of Laissez Faire* (1926) might suggest). The same objective, a high and stable level of economic activity; the same framework within which means of policy must be considered ('the next developments of politico-economic evolution will emerge from new experiments directed towards determining the appropriate spheres of individual and governmental action'), are present throughout his subsequent work.

1 Although recent studies have shown a closer relation of his approach in this book to his economic theory than might appear at first sight. Indeed, in a highly interesting study, *Keynes's Vision* (1988), Arthur Fitzgibbons presents a very plausible interpretation of the ethical and idealistic foundations of Keynes's economics in which the theory of probability plays a much greater part.

2 In this respect, though in hardly any other, he showed great affinity to one of his great contemporaries, Jean Monnet.

The *Treatise on Money* (1930), though similar in many respects to his earlier work and containing much that was to be further developed in the *General Theory*, was sufficiently different in conception and execution from the rest of his life's work not to fit readily into an appreciation of the continuous nature of Keynes's intellectual evolution. To the ordinary reader it was too technical a work: erudite (though characteristically patchy in knowledge of non-Anglo-American literature), with a difficult and largely new terminology, and interspersed with what appeared to be a series of monographs; to the student brilliant and rewarding, but of a highly specialized character. The general public, therefore, was largely unaffected by the book. As for the economist, he had barely managed to keep abreast of the flood of specialized (and controversial) articles which followed the appearance of the earlier book, when he learned (a year or more before its publication) that a new, and more revolutionary, statement of Keynes's theory was about to be made available.

The theories which were first presented to the world in a systematic form in Keynes's *General Theory of Employment, Interest, and Money* (1936) were not worked out in such detail as to present by themselves a fully-fledged new general corpus of economic analysis. But they were such as to open a path to further advance of 'pure' economic theory, as well as to the more fruitful study of the problems with which they were explicitly concerned, including, above all, the problems of policy. It should be pointed out that Keynes's theories grew in a field of enquiry, the study of the business cycle, which had for many decades been separated from that of general economic theory. The doctrines which Keynes expounded in the *General Theory* are directly descended from earlier ones which were developed in the course of his search for an explanation of sudden changes in the level of economic activity. Some writers have been able to show without much difficulty that there is a clear line of descent from Keynes's earlier works, notably *The Treaties on Money*, to the new work. But his own sense of a change in the approach was soon shared by his readers. And the wider terms of reference of the *General Theory* were soon generally appreciated. It was realized that what Keynes was now trying to do was to re-examine the determinants of the general level of economic activity.

Keynes himself appeared quite self-conscious about the novelty of this attempt and regarded it as being in sharp contrast to what he conceived to be the main purpose of the classical economists. Keynes defines the classical tradition as comprising not only Ricardo and his direct followers, but also the more distant descendants of his school, including John Stuart Mill, Marshall, and Pigou. Such a definition is different from that which underlies the analysis of the decline of Ricardianism presented in these pages. But this issue may be left to one side here. What is important is the *differentia specifica* which Keynes detects in the classical tradition and which makes that tradition unacceptable to him.

Classical political economy, Keynes argues, was concerned with the distribution of the social product rather than with its amount. In support of this contention, he quotes Ricardo's famous statement made to Malthus that political economy is not an enquiry into the nature and causes of wealth but 'into the laws which determine the division of the produce of industry amongst the classes who concur in its formation'.[1] Classicism, in other words, tried to explain the determinants of the relative shares in the national income of the different factors of production, rather than the forces which determine the level of that income (which may also be called the level of employment or of economic activity in general). The implied assumption of the classical system (which becomes explicit in the law of the market developed by James Mill, Say, and, to some extent, Ricardo) is that the economic system spontaneously tends to produce full employment of given resources.

Keynes's theory is built upon a rejection of this assumption. But before we examine the consequences of this rejection, it may be well to recapitulate briefly the classical attitude to this problem. The classics, as we have seen, virtually ignored the problem of crises. They also failed to analyse specifically the possibility that there may be different levels of economic activity with the same amount of resources. So far Keynes's appraisal of classicism is undoubtedly right. But when the classics developed their theory of value and distribution for what Keynes calls a special case, that of full employment, they did so because they thought that their analysis of the mechanism of exchange and their theory of capital accumulation had already proved that the economic system invariably tended toward full employment. This tendency, which was implied in the inevitable correspondence between supply and demand, is most dogmatically expressed in Say's law. But this law only continues a long line of reasoning, expressions of which can be found in both mercantilist and physiocratic literature. In the writings of many seventeenth- and early eighteenth-century authors

---

1 *Letters of Ricardo to Malthus, 1810–1823* (ed. J. Bonar, 1887), p. 175.

there is a clear recognition of the mutual creation of demand and supply, of the fact that A's income, when spent, becomes B's income, and so on in a continuous chain. This interdependence is stated by Say in its most tautological form, to the point of excluding overproduction by definition. Although, as we have seen, it is not quite fair to name Ricardo side by side with James Mill and Say as an intransigent opponent of the possibility of general overproduction, it is nevertheless true that, apart from the disharmonious implications of his theory of economic development and his views on machinery, there is nothing in Ricardo that can be regarded as an analysis of the economics of less than full employment.

So far, then, Keynes is on solid ground when he places himself in opposition to the classical tradition by deliberately rejecting any initial assumption about the 'normal' level of employment. Keynes acknowledges many anticipators among the mercantilists and among the under-consumptionists from Malthus to the present day.[1] The discussion of the relation of earlier, nineteenth-century critical views of Keynes's own system is interesting, and would well deserve a special study. It is, however, important to point out that there are similarities as well as contrasts between Keynes's approach and that of the classics. Keynes is concerned, as were the classics, with aggregates: income, consumption, saving, and investment, rather than with the determination of individual prices which formed the core of economic theory as it developed from the latter part of the nineteenth century. The discussion of the determinants of the general level of economic activity, though fragmentary and soon forgotten among the orthodox, formed the most important flare-up of classicism before its vigour was finally lost. What we have seen of the direction which Ricardo's views were taking at the end of his life shows that Say's law of the market, like so much of post-Ricardian economics, stopped the classical impetus rather than propelled it still further (notwithstanding a revival of interest in Say's law after the appearance of Keynes's *General Theory*, and some ingenious attempts to connect them intellectually).[2]

1 For an excellent comparison of Keynes and Malthus see Klein, L., *The Keynesian Revolution* (1949).
2 Don Patinkin's *Anticipation of the General Theory* (1982) is a particularly interesting study, coming as it does from one of the outstanding neo- or post-Keynesians (according to taste), of the intellectual tributaries that went into the making of the mainstream Keynesian flood. See also Pascal Bridel, *Cambridge Monetary Thought: The Development of Saving-Investment Analysis from Marshall to Keynes* (1987).

However, Keynes drew a quite specific distinction between the direction of actual employment, which he thought the existing system broadly speaking achieved reasonably well, and the total volume of actual employment, where the system, from time to time, went seriously wrong. He wanted to establish the bases on which policies could be erected that would create the right macroeconomic environment for market forces to operate so as to secure 'the full potentialities of production'.[1]

In other words, Keynes was not concerned to destroy the very bases of microeconomics but rather to set alongside them the new and even more basic foundations of macroeconomics. Yet another way of putting it is to say that when Adam Smith argued (in regard to what one would nowadays call public policy) that 'what is prudent conduct in the master of the family can scarce be folly in that of a great Kingdom'. Keynes, by implication, denied this identity; but there remained the desire to reconcile the classical system (as Keynes understood it) with his new view of the economy as a whole, what Samuelson has called 'the neo-classical synthesis'. This comes out very clearly in one of his last utterances, the speech he made in the House of Lords in December 1945, defending the Anglo-American Financial Arrangements: 'The outstanding characteristics of the plans is that they represent the first elaborate and comprehensive attempt to combine the advantages of a freedom of commerce with safeguards against the disastrous consequences of a *laissez-faire* system which pays no direct regard to the preservation of equilibrium and merely relies on the eventual working out of blind forces. Here is an attempt to use what we have learnt from modern experience and modern analysis, not to defeat, but to implement the wisdom of Adam Smith'.[2]

The opinion may, therefore, be ventured that Keynes's approach represents, above all, a return to the fundamental preoccupations of classical political economy, and to that extent a departure from that concentration upon the implications of individual choice which had for so long been the distinguishing characteristic of the central part of modern economic theory. It is as such a departure in economic methodology in general, rather than as merely a contribution to the study of economic fluctuations, that the Keynesian system acquires its greatest significance.

1 J. M. Keynes, *General Theory of Employment, Interest and Money* (1936), p. 379.
2 J. M. Keynes, *Collected Writings*, vol. xxiv, p. 621.

The following brief outline must not be taken as a summary of everything to be found in Keynes's *General Theory*. In the first place, there are far too many issues raised in that work which have only a secondary, even if important, bearing on the main theme. In the second place, the Keynesian ideas have been refined and developed since they first appeared; and some of these developments are continuing today and will, no doubt, do so into the twenty-first century. What follows is therefore a distillate of the main essence of the new theory. The starting-point of the new approach – at least in its origin – is the Malthusian concept of effective demand, resuscitated and modified by Keynes. Effective demand is defined as 'the aggregate income (or proceeds) which the entrepreneurs expect to receive, inclusive of the incomes which they will hand on to the other factors of production, from the amount of current employment which they decide to give.[1] It can be represented as a point on an aggregate demand curve which is obtained by relating 'various hypothetical quantities of employment to the proceeds which their outputs are expected to yield'.[2] A similar supply function can be established, relating the aggregate supply price of the output obtained by employing a variable number of men with that number.[3] The point of intersection of the two curves gives us that value of demand which Keynes calls effective demand. This is an extremely important point, because it is at that point that the entrepreneurs' expectations of profit will be maximized. It is the point, therefore, which will show the equilibrium amount of employment.

In this way, the volume of employment is translated into terms of demand for goods, and the question which can now be posed is: what determines that volume? To answer it, the Keynesian theory set up a system of functional relations which, although not wholly novel in regard to the elements which it comprises, shows these elements in a highly original connection and makes an original use of their relationship. The system is, roughly, as follows. We have already seen from Keynes's definition of effective demand that the ultimate determinant of the volume of employment is to be found in the degree to which the entrepreneur judges such employment to be profitable. Total demand, in terms of money, for goods and services determines profitability. This total amount of money which comes on to the market ready to

1 J. M. Keynes, *General Theory*, p. 55.
2 ibid.
3 ibid., p. 25.

exercise a demand is, however, nothing more than the total money income created within the economy. Because payments and receipts are the same thing, national expenditure (that is, total money demand) is identical with total national income. We have thus gone a stage further and have now connected employment with national income.

Having found that employment depends upon the size of the national income, we are now in a position to embark upon the next part of the analysis and to ask such questions about income as, what determines its level, and what are its characteristics? At this point, Keynes, revealing some vestiges of influence of the orthodox tradition, brings into play a psychological law which explains people's behaviour in regard to changes in their incomes. In the first place, we must go back somewhat on our previous statement that income and expenditure are equal. In one sense it is true enough that what one man spends another receives, and vice versa. But we must remember that income is spent in different ways, one of the most important divisions being that between expenditure on current consumption and saving. Can we say anything about this division of the expenditure of the total income stream? Keynes answers in the affirmative. He asserts that there is a definite law concerning the changes consequent upon changes in the size of the income, in the proportions in which income is divided between the two forms of expenditure.

The term which is now introduced for the purpose of expounding this law is 'the propensity to consume'. This is a term which expresses the relation between total income and aggregate consumption. Keynes leaves to one side changes in the psychological proclivities of people (resulting from individual as well as social causes) as being unlikely to change in the short run except in 'abnormal or revolutionary circumstances'; and he also decides to ignore as unimportant certain objective factors which might be said to influence the propensity to consume. He is, therefore, left with the doctrine that the propensity to consume may be regarded as a fairly stable function of aggregate income. What, then, is the nature of this function? Keynes's answer is something like this. Apart from the poorest, people do not spend the whole of their income on current consumption. And although they increase their consumption as their income increases, they do so less than in proportion to the rise in income itself. A higher income thus means a relatively lower consumption and vice versa. This law holds both when we are thinking of short-period changes in the level of income, as well as when we are comparing two absolute levels of income. The 'marginal propensity to consume' (a term which Keynes uses inter-changeably in two technically distinct meanings) shows how an incre-ment of income will be divided between current consumption and saving.

A very important consequence flows from Keynes's fundamental psychological law about the propensity to consume. Because total income must be equal to total expenditure and current consumption does not in any fairly advanced and fairly wealthy community absorb all income, total income must equal expenditure on current consumption plus some other expenditure. This, of course, we call investment. Thus we have the simple relationship that income equals consumption plus investment, or, in the symbols that are now commonly accepted:

$$Y = C + I$$

The same relationship can now be expressed in another way which is really identical to the previous one, but which has more meaning from the point of view of our objective. We have found that the volume of employment is determined by the level of income. We can, there-fore, say that the volume of employment is determined jointly by the level of consumption and by the level of investment. What appears, at first sight, as merely a terminological change which uses the same concepts, has come to be regarded as an extremely revealing statement of a vital relationship in the real world. In Keynes's phrase, the marginal propensity to consume now 'tells us how the next increment of output will have to be divided between consumption and invest-ment.'[1]

The important thing about this formulation is that it enables us to make some very important statements about the functional relations of employment, consumption, and investment, given a certain marginal propensity to consume, and that it enables us to attack again the problem of the equilibrium level of employment. It shows us that a certain level of investment is necessary if certain levels of income and consumption are to be maintained. If, starting with a given level of income, consumption, and investment, we suppose investment to dis-appear, it is clear that total expenditure would decline and that income (and therefore employment) could not be maintained at the previous level. Consumption too would decline, though not as fast as income itself. But this would lead to a further fall in consumption, and the

[1] J. M. Keynes, *General Theory*, p. 115.

downward movement would go on until income and consumption had fallen to that low level at which they were equal; that is to say, at which all income was consumed. This low level of income and employment could be regarded as an equilibrium level, because there is no inherent economic reason for it to change. The qualification should at once be added that this is so because at this stage of the analysis we have met no factors which would indicate the process by which income could spontaneously rise again. The analysis is incomplete in other respects too; but we shall presently see some of the complications which have to be added. For the moment, however, we may recapitulate that, given the marginal propensity to consume, we have found an important connection to exist between employment, consumption, and investment.

The equilibrium level of income and consumption, which we discovered when we reached the position of zero investment, can now be generalized. For since the three items which made up our equation mutually condition each other, and because we assume a constant factor of relationship (the marginal propensity to consume) between two of them – namely, income and consumption – there must be an equilibrium level of income for every possible level of investment. Every level of income has its corresponding level of consumption. If that level of consumption and the existing level of investment do not add up to the total of income, that level of income cannot be maintained. It will have to rise or fall (with consumption rising or falling less) until the equality of $Y = C+I$ is restored again. We thus get a series of values of income, consumption, and investment which are of such a nature that they can mutually maintain each other; these are equilibrium values.

So far, Keynes's system has merely established a completely closed, circular system of relationship, without, at this stage, any clear indication as to which variable in the equation is to be regarded as the independent one; that is to say, which element in the system could be chosen for purposes of policy. Nevertheless, we can already discern one major consequence of these doctrines. By approaching the problem of aggregate employment in the way he does, he avoids committing himself to any preconception concerning the level to which employment will 'normally' tend. Indeed, the main initial conclusion is to show the theoretical possibility of different levels of income (and employment) which would all be equilibrium levels. It now remains to fill in this outline in three stages, the first of which is to introduce a number of other determinants of the level of income, consumption, and investment. In the second place, it will be necessary to see how Keynes analyses the combined operation of all the determinants in bringing about different levels of income and employment, and in particular how he explains the existence of prolonged periods of under-employment. Finally, we shall have to examine the policy conclusions which he draws, both as regards economic techniques and policy in the wider social-philosophical sense. The following summary will concentrate on the main structure of the system.

So far we have met only one ultimate determinant in Keynes's system, the psychological factor which he called the propensity to consume. There are two others which play a vital part: 'the psychological attitude to liquidity and the psychological expectation of future yield from capital-assets'.[1] The second of these is concerned with one of the determinants of the volume of investment. When a man invests, Keynes argues, 'he purchases the right to the series of prospective net returns which he expects to obtain from selling' the output of the capital asset in which he has invested 'during the life of the asset'.[2] Keynes calls the relation between the above-mentioned prospective yield of one more unit of that type of capital asset and the cost of producing that unit, the 'marginal efficiency of capital'. We can conceive of different marginal efficiencies for different types of capital assets, and the greatest of these marginal efficiencies 'can then be regarded as the marginal efficiency of capital in general'.[3] Keynes further points out that an increase in investment will tend to reduce the marginal efficiency of capital, both because prospective yield will fall and because the cost of producing more of the capital asset will rise. It is possible, therefore, by relating rates of investment to the corresponding marginal efficiencies of capital which these rates will establish to arrive at a schedule of the marginal efficiency of capital (or the investment-demand schedule).

Without going into a rather elaborate discussion, we may roughly liken Keynes's schedule of the marginal efficiency of capital to the rate of profit in the classical system, because it is designed to play much the same role. And it is clear that the schedule of the marginal efficiency of capital is one of the determinants of investment, because it influences the inducement to invest.

1 J. M. Keynes, *General Theory*, p. 247.
2 ibid., p. 136.
3 ibid., p. 135.

What other factors influence investment? Here again we must leave out many aspects of the Keynesian analysis and of the refinements to which it has been subjected and confine ourselves to the outstanding points. The chief of these relates to the attitude of people in regard to the holding of money. Keynes's analysis of this point provides both important clues to his ideas on policy and to his opposition to certain traditional economic theories, as well as a link with the theories of economic fluctuations with which Keynes himself had been associated. Money, in the new theory, is essentially 'a link between the present and the future'.[1] From this point of view, its outstanding property in our economic system is that it is an 'asset for which the liquidity premium is always in excess of the carrying costs',[2] or, in other words, that a relatively high liquidity premium attaches to it.

We need not, in this context, discuss the problem why there is such a thing as liquidity preference, although Keynes devotes a part of his analysis to the factors which create an incentive for people to hold a part of their assets in liquid form. But this part of his doctrines is not particularly novel, because the problem of the demand for money as a 'store of value' is a standard aspect of all monetary theory. What is important, however, is the use to which the concept – with its new name of liquidity preference – is put in the theory of employment. In Keynes's system it is promoted to a central position in the theory of interest. Keynes opposes both of the prevailing doctrines on the subject, which, following his general and somewhat misleading practice, he calls classical. What may be called the long-run marginalist doctrine states that the rate of interest is determined by time-preference; that is, by people's preference of present over future goods. Keynes rejects this view as well as that relating to the short run; namely, that the rate of interest, like any other price, is fixed at the level at which the demand for capital equals the supply of loanable funds. Interest, in his view, is essentially a monetary phenomenon. It is not a reward for 'waiting', but one for not hoarding; that is, for relinquishing liquidity. Therefore, argues Keynes, unless we introduce data about the amount of money and the state of the liquidity preference, we are not in a position to know what the rate of interest will be.

We can amplify this point somewhat and introduce another Keynesian notion in the following way. According to the traditional

1 J. M. Keynes, *General Theory*, p. 293.
2 ibid., p. 239.

view, the rate of interest equates what Keynes calls the investment-demand schedule with the supply of saving: in short, it equates investment and saving. Now, in Keynes's system, investment and saving are always of necessity equal. Saving can be defined as income minus consumption:

$$S = Y - C$$

We have already seen that $Y = C + I$. Therefore, $I = S$; investment equals saving. This argument has been the subject of much discussion. It has been attacked on the ground that to establish a relationship by definition is hardly fruitful. Considerable work was, however, done on this point subsequently and this led to a fairly wide acceptance of the Keynesian doctrine, though in a modified form. The so-called 'period analysis', largely associated with the name of Robertson, by which a distinction is made between income in one period and expenditure in the next (which itself becomes income in the subsequent period), has been used in partial explanation of the savings and investment problem. Similarly, the distinction introduced by a number of Swedish authors between planned and realized investment (*ex ante* and *ex post*) may be called into play. This matter will not be pursued here; but the important point is to realize the interdependence in the Keynesian scheme of investment and saving via income which makes it impossible to regard them as the determinants of the rate of interest. Or, to put the point in another way, Keynes's criticism of the traditional theory is that it assumes income to remain stable when either of two schedules, that relating investment or that relating income to the rate of interest, shifts. But such an assumption, he points out, is unwarranted, because it would mean that neither schedule could be assumed to be changing independently of the other. A shift in either of them means, as a rule, a shift in income. On the analogy of the argument about the supply curves and the laws of return developed by Sraffa, we may, therefore, say that the traditional analysis breaks down. If, however (according to Keynes), we introduce new data which between them determine the rate of interest, then we are in a position to know how one curve will shift in response to a shift in the other. These additional data are the liquidity preference and the quantity of money.

There are many points in this analysis which may be, and have been, criticized. In particular, it has been argued that the rate of interest, even if it is defined as the price paid for liquidity, is not independent of the level of income. And because the level of income is determined by investment and saving, the rate of interest must not be regarded as independent of these two variables. However, the important point is that Keynes's emphasis on the monetary determinants of the rate of interest is an indispensable part of his whole system without which neither his explanation of depressions nor his suggested means for curing them could be maintained. To these aspects we must, therefore, now turn.

In the first place, we are in a position to summarize the 'general theory' of employment. We have already seen that different levels of equilibrium are theoretically possible. We can restate the determination of these equilibrium levels in the following way. We make the (reasonable) assumption about our present economy that consumption is less than one hundred per cent of income. The establishment and maintenance of any particular level of employment demands that it should be profitable for the entrepreneur to offer that amount of employment. That, in turn, means that there must be an amount of investment 'sufficient to absorb the excess of output over what the community chooses to consume when employment (income) is at a given level'.[1] As we have seen, unless this is so, the amount of income (that is, expenditure or entrepreneurs' receipts) will fall, and so reduce the profitability of the original volume of employment. We thus come back to the point that, given the propensity to consume, the level of investment will determine what the equilibrium volume of employment will be. There is no evidence in the analysis thus far that this level of investment will be such as to produce full employment as its corresponding equilibrium level. Only one particular level of investment will produce that, and it must now be shown how such a level can be achieved and what are the chances of this being done by the automatic action of the economic system. The level of investment is determined by two things, the marginal efficiency of capital and the rate of interest. Unless these stand in such a relationship as to create exactly the 'right' volume of investment, equilibrium may be reached at less than full employment. It may be added that more than full employment is not possible, because it would involve inflationary price rises with subsequent reductions in the community's real income. This point is not pursued in Keynes's own work. It is, however, extremely important, both theoretically and in many a conjuncture of real circumstances. We shall have to revert to it later.

1 J. M. Keynes, *General Theory*, p. 27.

Keynes turns at this point to examine the behaviour of the relationship between the marginal efficiency of capital and the rate of interest. One situation which is particularly revealing is to be found at the time when, after a more or less prolonged period of depression, investment is beginning to revive again. In the course of the depression, replacement of capital equipment has been neglected, and now a point has been reached when business, perhaps aided by some extraneous factor, is once again beginning to take a more optimistic view of the prospective yield from current investment. The marginal efficiency of capital rises. But a rise of investment beyond a certain point will (perhaps again with the aid of some extraneous factor) cause the marginal efficiency of capital to fall. Thus a continuous variation in the level of investment, caused by the ever-fluctuating marginal efficiency of capital (the rate of profit) seems to be inherent in the very nature of the concept in the Keynesian system. What is even more important, Keynes believes that there is a long-run tendency for the marginal efficiency of capital to decline.

The extent of the fluctuations in employment which follow upon fluctuations in investment will depend upon what Keynes calls the multiplier, a concept first developed by R. F. Kahn.[1] The multiplier is simply a term to describe in a slightly different form the relationship expressed in the propensity to consume. The marginal propensity to consume is the ratio between an increase in consumption and an increase in income: algebraically $\frac{\Delta C}{\Delta Y}$. Because an increase in income must equal an increase in consumption *plus* an increase in investment ($\Delta Y = \Delta C + \Delta I$), it follows that with a given propensity to consume any increase in investment will be followed by a determinate increase in income. The factor by which income will be increased is called the multiplier. If we denote it by the symbol $k$, we can write $\Delta Y = k\Delta I$; and because $\Delta I = \Delta Y - \Delta C$, we can write $k = \dfrac{\Delta Y}{\Delta Y - C}$ or $\dfrac{1}{1 - \dfrac{\Delta C}{\Delta Y}}$

In other words, the multiplier equals the reciprocal of one *minus* the marginal propensity to consume. Thus, for example, if two-thirds of income is consumed, the multiplier will be 3; that is, every increase in

[1] 'The Relation of Home Investment to Unemployment', in *Economic Journal*, June 1931. The late Lord Kahn has left in his *The Making of the General Theory*, the Rafaele Mattioli Lectures, 1984, a most interesting account of the intellectual conception and gestation of the Keynesian theory.

investment will lead to a threefold increase in income (or employment).

In addition to these fluctuations in employment (which follow upon changes in investment and the extent of which is determined by the psychological factor of consumption habits), there is, according to Keynes, a long-term trend in the marginal efficiency of capital. A wealthy community 'will have to discover much ampler opportunities for investment if the saving propensities of its wealthier members are to be compatible with the employment of its poorer members'. But in a wealthy community, 'owing to its accumulation of capital being already large, the opportunities for further investment are less attractive'.[1] So we find that in the course of economic progress, not only does the marginal propensity to consume become weak (the multiplier diminishes), but the inducement to invest, or the marginal efficiency of capital, declines. There is thus a continual downward pressure upon investment as well as a continual decline of the extent to which fresh investment is capable of creating employment.

So far, however, we have only looked at one of the factors influencing the level of investment. The rate of interest, as we know, is another determinant. It must be clear that a sufficient downward movement in the rate of interest in times of depression and as a long-run trend might offset the unfavourable effects upon investment caused by the declining marginal efficiency of capital. It is Keynes's belief that theoretical considerations, as well as observation of the past behaviour of interest rates, show that the rate of interest will not fall sufficiently fast or sufficiently far to maintain that level of investment which can ensure full employment. The reason for this belief flows from Keynes's definition of interest as a monetary phenomenon. The rate of interest is primarily determined by the quantity of money and by liquidity preference. And the conditions influencing these two factors can be shown to be unfavourable to a fall in the rate of interest to the extent necessary to ensure a 'full employment' rate of investment. Investment will tend to be pushed to the point at which the marginal efficiency of capital and the rate of interest are equal. The long-run tendency would be for investment to increase and for the marginal efficiency of capital to decline. But the 'stickiness' of the rate of interest frustrates this tendency and restricts investment. Hence, not only is it theoretically possible that equilibrium will be achieved at less than full employment; the balance of the numerous factors involved is

1 J. M. Keynes, *General Theory*, p. 31.

so delicate that the automatic achievement of full employment must be regarded as the lesser probability.

The preceding is an extremely brief and necessarily incomplete account of a very elaborate theory. This summary has omitted among many other aspects any mention of the international complications of Keynes's system and of his doctrines on the relation of money wages and real wages to employment.[1] Later developments of these ideas have been designed to clear up certain obscurities in formulation, or to link the new theory to some of the earlier doctrines concerning economic fluctuations. Some of this work has resulted in the elimination of controversies on points now seen to be either unimportant or resolvable in more general formulations (such as the problem of the equality of savings and investment). Other refinements have explored problems which will remain peculiar to the theory of cyclical fluctuations. Among these may be mentioned the question of the 'upper turning point'; the causes which may make for a spontaneous recovery out of the trough of a cyclical depression and the relation between the multiplier and the 'principle of acceleration' which connects changes in consumption with changes in investment.

Probably the single most important theoretical advance in more recent years (stimulated in part by the monetarist critique of Keynes, dealt with later) has been the use of the so-called *IS–LM* analysis. These concepts can be represented graphically respectively in a downward and an upward sloping curve, with interest rates on the vertical and real output on the horizontal axis. The former (IS) curve shows the relation between interest rates and output at points at which planned saving and planned investments are equal; the LM curve relates output and interest rates at points at which the supply and the demand for money are equal. The point of interrelation is that at which there is equilibrium. This new theoretical tool has been used to determine the best fiscal policy and monetary policy mix in different circumstances; and in terms of dealing with 'models' some of the writers representing the 'new synthesis' mentioned in a later chapter have done highly interesting work. It cannot, however, he said that the issues faced by policy-makers and by those economists who habitually comment in the media on current problems have become less contentious or less fiercely argued.

1 These are referred to later.

# Macroeconomics and Economic Management

## *From War to Peace*

In the preceding chapter we have looked at the initial impact of the Keynesian doctrines. Their first expansion was under the stress of war which also began their flowering into a general theory of the economic process. There were three elements that contributed to bring about this result. In the first place, we have seen that the initial impulsion that led Keynes to challenge the view, explicit or implicit in the traditional body of economics, that there was an inherent tendency for the economy towards a full employment equilibrium, came from the observed facts of the depression (and later the needs of war-time economics) and his own close involvement in the formulation of economic policy. However, for Keynes the economic theorist as well as the economic statesman, memoranda on how to cure unemployment, or on how to pay for the war, were not enough. Even though the first objective was to find the means to raise the level of economic activity, to reabsorb unused material and human resources, and later to allocate them in the most efficient way to war-time purposes, there was also the need to derive these means from an intellectually acceptable source. This aim was very quickly impounded in the more general one of restating the basic principles of economic theory in a manner more consistent with observed facts. Once this seed had been sown, the inherent forces of intellectual analysis took over; that is to say, the concepts first enunciated in the *General Theory* became the raw material for the next generation of theorists. Each one was examined and further developed both in width and in depth; and in the process the theory inevitably became even more one designed to account for the economic process in general. We shall presently look at some of the main ones of these theoretical developments, that can be said to have had their origin in the original Keynesian analysis.

Another factor that must be mentioned as having operated in the same direction was the increasing concern of government with the economic system and particularly with its performance as regards both the stability of the level of employment and the total output of goods and services through time. There is a clear resemblance here with the period after the Napoleonic wars of the stimulus provided to economic analysis both in the facts of the economic situation and in the needs of government (be they emphasis on the stability of the currency and of the banking system or on the maintenance of full employment) which saw the Ricardian system brought to full flower. The process cannot be compared in directness with what might take place in the physical sciences, where a specific need would lead to quite specific research. Nevertheless, in economics, too, however indirectly, the requirements of policy, for example in regard to countercyclical measures, to the whole field of welfare economics (increasingly intertwined with the problem of the maintenance of full employment) or to national or international financial management (equally so connected), the analyst in the field of pure doctrine was, and is, constantly receiving new impulses for further elaboration and research. Some of the outstanding developments in this field, are due to the first post-Keynesian generation.

There is, however, one contributory stream to the Keynesian revolution which needs to be briefly looked at, because it was designed to provide an essential empirical element that was missing; because it was, in point of time, more definitely contemporaneous with the initial emergence of Keynesianism; and also because it becomes, at this point, a much more closely integrated part of the general body of economic analysis than ever before, even giving rise to a new subdivision of the science, *Econometrics*. To this, the statistical contribution, we must now turn.

## The Statistical Contribution

So far in this book, there has not been occasion to say much about either the development of statistics in its application to economic facts, or about the relation of the progress of statistical enquiry to the development of economic thinking. It might be tempting to relate Petty's pioneering efforts in vital statistics, Quételet's *homme moyen*, and the nineteenth-century English blue books, for example, to the appearance of new tendencies in pure economic theory. It is, however, unlikely that even with great ingenuity close affinities could be established or elaborate theories of family relationship evolved. In particular, much of the statistical work of the century preceding the Second World War was carried on virtually in isolation from economics, even though, on occasions, individual practitioners worked in both fields. This is not to say that the need for a close link was not recognized (e.g. by Jevons), or that examples of cross-fertilization could not be found. The mercantilists' views of the foreign trade mechanism owed much to, admittedly rudimentary, attempts at collecting foreign trade statistics; while their precepts of policy, in turn, suggested new directions for statistical activity. In Petty's own day, economic theorizing was much influenced by data on public finance. Throughout the nineteenth century the collection of statistics on, for example, earnings and hours worked, or, later, on monetary matters, was undoubtedly in part stimulated by the search for quantitative proofs of theoretcial propositions. Senior and Marshall certainly derived much valuable material from their experience on various Commissions of Enquiry and other public bodies. In turn they brought their theoretical equipment to bear upon the problems with which they were confronted.

Nevertheless, these examples remain isolated. Jevon's recognition of the need for a systematic link between the two branches of enquiry went unfollowed beyond its formal acceptance in the more broadminded textbooks on 'method'. A somewhat more determnined attempt to forge such a link followed the rise of the institutionalist school in the United States, and the very great impetus given to quantitative work by early followers of this school must be acknowledged.[1] Much of it was purely statistical, in the sense that it was accompanied by only a general hope that a greater knowledge of the facts of the economic system would, in the end, enrich thought by

1 As a good example of outstanding pioneer work in this category might be mentioned the construction of an Index of Production. See Walter W. Stewart, 'Index of Production' in *American Economic Review* (1921). Other examples of pioneering statistical work to be recorded are E. E. Day, 'Measurement of Variations in the National Real Income' in *Journal of the American Statistical Association* (1921), and the path-breaking studies on the balance of payments of the United States by J. H. Williams beginning with 'The balance of international payments of the United States for the year 1920' in *Review of Economic Statistics* (1921).

providing a test for old hypotheses or by suggesting new ones. In one field, however, a more self-conscious attempt to make new statistical discovery subserve the evolution of theory was made: that of the business cycle. Here the outstanding name is that of Wesley Mitchell.[1] Under the influence of Veblen, he not only made major contributions in this particular field, but also for many years, largely through his direction of the *National Bureau of Economic Research*, stimulated fresh factual work in all branches of economics to a quite unprecedented degree. It is a matter for debate how far Mitchell (and others who worked on similar lines) really succeeded in the search for a synthesis between the deductive and the empirical approaches. But even on a generous interpretation of the amount of theoretical innovation contained in his work,[2] it is at least true to say that a considerable process of 'distillation' still remained necessary before his quantitative work could be made to yield major generalizations.

It is, however, significant that problems arising from the general course of development of the economy (at least in the short run) first led to a deliberate effort to combine statistical and theoretical work. Even in the early stages these efforts were fairly successful; and, several years later, the signs of a successful synthesis of the greatest significance begin to appear.

Yet another major element went into this synthesis: the growth of 'national income' analysis. The concept of the national income or 'national dividend', though appearing under different names and with somewhat varying meanings, was not a novelty in the history of economic thought; neither was discussion of changes in its distribution, nor of the factors causing fluctuations in the total. From the circulation process of the Physiocrats, through Adam Smith's annual fund and Ricardo's relative shares of the factor of production, a study of the national income has in fact been co-terminous with the central enquiry of economics as such. What is new, however, is the application of mathematical techniques and statistical data to these basic concepts,

---

1 His first important volume being *Business Cycles* (1913). Three others that should be recorded are: W. C. Mitchell, *Business Cycles: The Problem and its Setting* (1927); W. L. Thorp, *Business Annals* (1920) and A. F. Burns and W. C. Mitchell, *Measuring Business Cycles* (1946).

2 For a somewhat over-zealous interpretation see M. Friedman, 'Wesley Mitchell as a Theorist' in *Journal of Political Economy* (1950). On the other hand, this is a convenient place to record Wesley Mitchell's highly stimulating contributions to the history of Economics: *Types of Economic Theory*, ed. by J. Dorfman (1969).

the transformation of the concepts themselves to make them more appropriate to the actual facts of a changing, complex, economic situation, and, finally, the application of both the statistical technique and the apparatus of theory to problems of policy.

Some indications are to be found here and there in the earlier literature of an appreciation of the specific problem involved in this synthesis. Irving Fisher in his *Nature of Capital and Income* (1906) explicitly set himself the task of evolving concepts suitable to economic accounting.[1] In the Marshallian system, too, the national dividend and the causes which produce changes in it are at the core of the analysis. This is still more obvious in Pigou's *Economics of Welfare* (1920) in which particular policies are examined almost exclusively in relation to their effects upon, first, the distribution and, second, the total size of the national dividend.

It was, however, from the side of specific factual studies that the greatest impetus was to come. The pioneers were actuated primarily by the desire to perfect the statistical material available on changes in the total income of all the individuals of a country and changes in its distribution among different classes of income-earners. These studies went hand in hand with attempts to obtain more accurate and complete series of data over time of production and of expenditure, since it was clear from the outset that, expressed in terms of money, they provided alternative, but equivalent measures for the same magnitudes.

The pioneering work in this field took place in England. The first attempt at a comprehensive estimate relating to the year 1911 was that of Bowley in *The Division of the Product of Industry* (1920). A more elaborate version appeared in 1927 in Bowley and Stamp, *The National Income in 1924*. Later still (1932) Colin Clark published a study which went further than earlier attempts by setting out in a connected fashion the material over a number of years (*The National Income 1924–31*). In this period falls also the first comprehensive study of national expenditure, Feavearyear, A. E., 'Spending the National Income' in *Economic Journal* (1931),[2] a belated sequel to the pioneering work of the nineteenth century German statistician Engel. By this time, other statistical series had been much improved and greatly assisted work on the national income. A good deal of what in the comprehensive studies had

---

1 In a recent work: *A Review of Economic Doctrines 1870–1929* (1953), p. 274, Mr T. W. Hutchinson has rightly drawn attention to Fisher's pioneering effort in this respect.
2 Followed by 'National Expenditure 1932' in the *Economic Journal* 1937.

had to be based on fairly loose estimation could now be drawn from accurate time series. The *British Census of Production* first published in 1924, the American Production Index already referred to, the increasingly accurate and vastly enlarged statistical material in both Britain and the United States on earnings, prices, and hours worked, may all be mentioned in this connection.

From the thirties on, the subject of national income studies in both its quantitative and conceptual aspects was vigorously taken up in the United States and for some years the major contributions came from that country.[1] Again it was the National Bureau of Economic Research which took the lead.[2] Though this movement derived at first from what might be termed pure factual curiosity and a desire to improve statistical techniques, it is clear that the onset of the great depression had a considerably stimulating effect. In the face of changes in profits, prices, employment, savings, investment and all the other national economic variables unprecedented in their rapidity and magnitude, the machinery for gathering data and arranging them in a manner which was meaningful for 'clinical' observation was greatly improved. The various new agencies set up in the United States under the New Deal programme such as the Agricultural Adjustment Administration and the National Recovery Administration, the Social Security programme and the various relief projects, all found that their successful operation depended on a much greater knowledge of certain areas of the economy than existing statistical material or technique made possible. Greatly expanded statistical activity, strongly fostered, or directly pursued, by government, followed. The remarkable co-operation and co-ordination of activity between government, the universities, various research institutions and learned foundations and business which ensued was not only most productive at the time but has remained a characteristic feature of the American economic scene.

At the centre of economic policy, too, the depression years greatly stimulated the amassing and systematic use of statistics. For the

---

1 The Canadian contribution must, however, not go unrecorded. In 1919 there appeared R. H. Coats, 'National Wealth and Income of Canada' in *Monetary Times*, January 3, 1919, and from 1931 on the Canadian Dominion Bureau of Statistics, responsible for much pioneering work in other fields, has produced statistics of national income.

2 W. I. King, *The National Income and its Purchasing Power* (1930). An earlier work by the same author should also be mentioned: *Wealth and Income of the People of the United States* (1915).

purpose of making decisions, first and foremost in the traditional field of fiscal policy, government needed to have information on total income and its utilization. This was essential if it was to be able to judge the effects of different courses of action in the field of taxation and government expenditure. A fresh impetus was thus given to work on the central problems of national income analysis and to the organization of suitable governmental machinery for securing it. Developments in this regard in the United States were closely paralleled in Britain. In 1930 there was set up an Economic Advisory Council whose duties included a 'continuous study of developments in trade and industry – and in the use of national and imperial resources, of the effect of legislation and fiscal policy at home and abroad, and of all aspects of national, imperial and international economy with a bearing on the prosperity of the country'. It is immaterial at this point to judge how effective this new instrument was;[1] what is significant is the comprehensive and mutually related manner in which the various factors that make up the state of the economy are here expressed and the explicit recognition which is given to the collection and meaningful arrangements of facts in the formulation of policy.

Nor did recovery from the depression slacken the impulse that had thus been given. Emphasis, however, was shifted from consumer expenditure with its effects on prices, profits and employment, to investment by business, either in fixed capital or in stocks. These were essential data for the formulation of correct decisions, not ony in fiscal policy but also in money and credit control, the tasks of which were naturally changing once the upturn had begun.

Considerable progress in all these directions had already been made by 1939. The war put the existing statistical machinery to the test and provided a most powerful stimulus to its improvement. In those aspects of national economic policy directly concerned with the war effort, major advances in statistical activity were recorded. They included

---

1 The reader is referred to Sir E. Bridges's Stamp Memorial Lecture: *Treasury Control* (1950), pp. 13–15, for one assessment. A full study, *The Economic Advisory Council 1930–1939* (1977), has been produced by Susan Howson and Donald Winch. Apart from being a detailed account and critical description of the attitude of politicians and professional economists to the first halting steps towards the creation of a governmental economic advisory service, it is also a fascinating analysis of the subtle interplay between the preoccupations of economists and the needs of the politicians. As such it should be compulsory reading for anyone interested in this important subject; it carries moreover a valuable lesson to this day – and beyond.

estimates of prospective supplies and requirements (food, raw materials, munitions) and forecasts of manpower and output and in each the technique of drawing up 'budgets' was greatly perfected. But more significant for the principal theme of this account are the improvements which took place at the centre: the refinement and speed with which estimates of the aggregates of the economic system, that is of statistics of the national income, were made and presented to those responsible for decisions on policy. Once more, Britain took the lead. In 1941, there was set up in the Cabinet Office a Central Statistical Office, which had the task, apart from providing a higher degree of co-ordination than hitherto of the statistical activities of different government departments, of producing the central statistics of national income and product without which it was recognized that a war in which all the nation's resources were engaged could not be successfully prosecuted. It is not only a tribute to the steadfast judgment of those who were responsble for this decision, but it is also a symptom of the recognition given to the significance of this type of analysis for economic policy that in the days of greatest physical danger work of, at first sight, so academic a character should have been vigorously pursued. From 1941, annual estimates of national income and expenditure, showing each time greater scope, refinement, and accuracy, have been published by the British Government. In the United States a similar development took place. A *National Income Unit* was set up in the Department of Commerce and each July the *Survey of Current Business* (a publication of the United States Department of Commerce) produced data for the preceding year.

In other countries, too, a similar development can be traced, though usually with a time-lag. In Western Europe, and in a number of countries of the British Commonwealth, these developments go back to the twenties and thirties, and in many of them the war gave a special impetus. In few, however, is the availability of the material as great, the technique as refined, or the organization as perfected as it is in Britain and the United States. In the most recent past, however, far-reaching and surprisingly successful attempts have been made both to improve matters in this regard in countries where development has been slow and to increase the international comparability of national income statistics.[1]

1 Some reference will be made below to the growth of international economic co-operation since the war and to its effects on economic thinking and policy. Much

The great improvement in statistical technique which has been traced above also led to important refinements in the concepts used and in the theoretical structure into which the quantitative material was fitted. The American economist Kuznets, in particular, was responsible for enquiries in which statistical research went hand in hand with major advances in the theoretical apparatus. In a short article written in 1933 he set out with great clarity possible definitions and classifications of the various items entering into the national accounts. Moreover, the discussion of terms was closely associated with fundamental propositions in economic theory relating to wages, profits, capital and interest.[1] In a later work a wealth of historical material was provided.'[2]

Just before the war, the impact of the Keynesian analysis of the relation between income, consumption, saving and investment began to be felt. Statisticians endeavoured now to direct their researches to the discovery of time series for these aggregates that would best fit the Keynesian scheme and thus provide appropriate quantitative tests. The war accelerated this process.

In Britain, the other countries of the Commonwealth, and in the United States, the question had to be answered what size of war effort could be mounted. At the same time the problem was to ensure that the financial flows were appropriate to the balance sheet of use of resources, that is, to ensure that there was no inflationary gap. In Britain, the work of the Central Statistical Office already referred to was consciously directed to this task and valuable improvements in technique resulted. New terms appeared: gross and net national income (depending upon the treatment given to allowance for depreciation and amortization); national income at market prices or at

---

pioneering work had already been done by the League of Nations; and in recent years the United Nations and its specialized agencies have a remarkable extension and improvement of economic statistics to their credit. Special mention may be made of the work of the Organization for European Economic Co-operation and its National Accounts Research Unit in influencing the improvement of national income statistics and analysis. Among the many publications of this body which deal with, or have a bearing on, this point may be mentioned: *A Simplified System of National Accounts* (1951) and *A Standardized System of National Accounts* (1952).

1 S. Kuznets, 'National Income' in *Encyclopaedia of the Social Sciences* (1933), vol. XI. This article remains indispensible to this day.

2 S. Kuznets, *National Income and its Composition 1919–1938* (1941). The path-breaking achievement of this author, who has been honoured with the Nobel Prize, can be fully appreciated now, in the perspective of five decades of intellectual history.

factor cost (depending upon whether or not prices paid by consumers, i.e. including indirect taxation and 'transfer payments' generally are taken as the basis); gross as against net national product (including the output not only of the business sector of the economy but of government as well); and so forth.

Undoubtedly many obscurities and disagreements remained.[1] The expression in monetary terms of the various magnitudes involved raises many acute problems in the field of index numbers. The comparison of the estimates of different countries aggravates this problem by introducing the issue of exchange rates as expressing (or not expressing) true purchasing power or balance of payments parities. Moreover, the treatment of foreign balances in the accounts is still a disputed subject particularly on the question of how changes in terms of trade are to be allowed for. Nevertheless, a very large measure of agreement on the general techniques to be employed in this field was quickly reached and virtual unanimity as to the purpose for which these statistics are designed. This purpose is best described in the following terms taken from an official publication: to provide 'a measure of the goods and services becoming available to the nation for consumption or adding to wealth'; to provide 'a series of "social accounts" ... tracing every important money "flow" from its origin in one account to its destination in another', 'or ... of expenditure between different groups of commodities', and to analyse 'movements in figures of expenditure on goods and services between changes in quantity and changes in price.'[2]

There was also a considerable measure of agreement of how, beyond this immediate purpose, the construction of social accounts can be made use of both for diagnosis and prescription in economic policy. In war time this further purpose became plainly apparent. The planning of production so as to avoid both bottlenecks and unused capacity, the channelling of production into war-essential industries, the restriction of personal consumption and its direction into channels

---

1 For a more detailed account of the various ways of measuring and presenting these data the reader is referred to: M. Gilbert and G. Jaszi, 'National Product and Income Statistics as an Aid in Economic Problems' in *Dun's Review* (1949), J. E. Meade and J. R. N. Stone, *National Income and Expenditure* (2nd ed. 1948); the July 1947 issue of the *Survey of Current Business*; R. Ruggles, *National Income Accounting and its Relation to Economic Policy* (1949); Central Statistical Office, *National Income and Expenditure 1948–1951* (1952) (this gives a particularly useful account of method).

2 Central Statistical Office, *National Income and Expenditure 1948–1951*, p. 3.

appropriate to the total war effort, and, perhaps most important of all, the measures needed for financing the war effort, all these could be sensibly devised and administered only in relation to the kind of total picture of the economy which national accounts analysis provided.[1]

Since the war, further studies in this direction have been made. This is not the place to go into the technical details of these developments. What is interesting for our general theme are the directions in which these developments lead from the point of view of economic analysis and economic policy. In that perspective the two most important aspects of the further refinements of national accounting have been, first in regard to theories of growth and second for conjunctural diagnosis and policy, that is to say, in relation to short-term cyclical economic movements. Both these will be touched upon in the next chapter when we examine growth theory, and more particularly the recent tendencies to look critically upon economic growth as an end of policy as far as the advanced, developed countries are concerned, and, at the same time to lay greater stress on certain features of the development of the less advanced countries different from those which can be measured by national income statistics. On the other hand, the use of statistical measurements (derived essentially from national accounting concepts) in connection with short-term economic management has come under critical examination in the measure that economic management itself is now viewed more sceptically.

At any rate, while there may not be any fundamental change in concept or in the methods of data collection and presentation, the statistics published by the major advanced countries were by the beginning of the seventies certainly vastly more elaborate, more quickly available and more fully analysed than they had been twenty years earlier.

This development continued for some years, particularly in the United States, and the advances achieved in the English-speaking countries generally stimulated similar developments elsewhere, notably in France and Germany (where, for example, the 'Monthly Reports' of the *Bundesbank* provide, as does the 'Quarterly Bulletin' of the Bank of England, particularly useful series of monetary and financial statistics). In the mid to late eighties, however, some disquiet was

---

[1] For a succinct demonstration of how, in this respect, a simple theoretical scheme can be successfully linked with statistical data see Meade, J. E. and Stone, J. R. N., *National Income and Expenditure*, pp. 42–44.

caused by a tendency in what was the home of modern statistics, the United Kingdom, to put a brake on further developments and, indeed, to retreat from territory already gained. This seems to have been due in part to economy and so-called efficiency objectives in public expenditure and administration but seems partly also to have been the result of a general prevalence in the administrations then in office of a non-interventionist attitude leading to the curious belief that, if the government were not to take an active part in economic management, it need not know quite as much about the actual course of the economy as before. This did not, however, prevent frequent changes in the method of compilation of certain politically sensitive statistics, such as those of unemployment. Even in the Reagan years this was not the view that prevailed in the United States. (However, since writing this last sentence, at least one example of a similar decline in the United States – concerning the census – has come to light. In *The New York Times* of 10 January 1990, Professor Leontief complains bitterly about the deterioration.)

## Underemployment or Employment Economics?

Keynes's *General Theory*, the main features of which were briefly summarized in the preceding chapter, has stood, chronologically and doctrinally, at the centre of a discussion which has been going on for five decades even though the emphasis has changed from time to time. It is reminiscent of that of the Ricardian era. There are striking similarities in the circumstances of periods of post-war adjustment which provided much of the stimulus for the debate, as well as in the chief problem – the determinants of the level of economic activity and the consequential policy options – round which controversy raged. As has already been said, Keynes saw his contribution as a major methodological departure, not only away from the previous concern of economists with individual price-formation (including the relative shares of the factors of production), but also away from past preoccupation with sudden changes in the level of employment. It was the word *general* in the title of his work which most clearly expressed its author's purpose.

Nevertheless, the birthmarks of the new theory remained obvious for a long time. It was conceived during the depression, and born in a time when underemployment of resources was still the rule. It is not surprising, therefore, that this new doctrine remained for some time – particularly for the political practitioners who used it – essentially a theory of underemployment. A more general approach to the problem and particularly a more comprehensive attitude regarding the means of economic policy could be derived from the book. But for some years the problems on which Keynes's disciples concentrated their attention were, first, those connected with short-period fluctuations in business activity, second, the means for getting out of a depression and, finally, the alleged long-term trend of the economic system towards stagnation. Applied for a limited time, therefore, the description of Keynesianism as 'depression economics' was not altogether unjust.

It is particularly significant that the main theoretical advances from the Keynesian position came to a considerable extent from the United States.[1] Largely under the leadership of Professor Alvin Hansen of Harvard, although his original review of Keynes's *General Theory* was unfavourable, a number of able young American economists began to develop different parts of the Keynesian system. It is not necessary to mention many of the detailed contributions in this field. Some were concerned with the conditions required to ensure full employment in the longer term (thus also leading to advances in the theory of economic growth). Here, the outstanding example is the Harrod–Domar model, so named after the two economists who produced it (independently of each other) as well as the later work of Solow and Kaldor. Others were directly concerned with the technical apparatus of the *General Theory*, particularly the means by which changes in one of the major aggregates are transmitted to the others and, thus, to the level of activity as a whole. As typical of work of this kind (and particularly fruitful in 'rounding-off' the theory) may be mentioned the doctrine of the 'relation' between the *multiplier* and the *principle of acceleration*, which connects changes in consumption with changes in investment.[2] Similarly, a considerable literature arose on the foundation of Keynes's discussion of the relation between money wages and real wages, both in regard to the underemployment equilibrium which was

1 It is perhaps during this period – the late thirties and forties – that the United States became the pre-eminent home of modern economics.

2 The pioneer work in this field is P. A. Samuelson 'Interactions between the Multiplier Analysis and the Principle of Acceleration', *Review of Economic Statistics* (1939), pp. 75–78, reprinted in *The Collected Scientific Papers of Paul A. Samuelson*, ed. Joseph E. Stiglitz (1966) vol. i, pp. 1107–10. Five large volumes of this important collection had appeared by 1986.

so important a postulate in the Keynesian system, as well as to the more direct problem of wage negotiations.[1] Much work was also devoted to the elucidation of the steps by which periods of high activity come to an end and the downward turn is brought about and to the mechanism by which the economy is lifted out of the trough of depression. Here the field was not new, for the mechanics of change, at the top and the bottom of the business cycle had been an important part of the literature of the subject for a considerable time. However, the discussion was henceforth in terms made familiar by the *General Theory*.

The least immediate impact of the *General Theory* was on the theory of international economic relations. It is surprising, in view of his life-long interest in this subject (to which he devoted the greatest volume of his writings) that Keynes had practically nothing to say on it in the *General Theory*. One may see in this yet a further symptom of the deliberate escape from past modes of thought of which he spoke, or a further proof of his return to the classical system, in which international economic problems tended to be treated apart from the general body of doctrine. For Keynes's own return to his earlier love we have to wait until the war and the immediate post-war period brought him into direct contact with the pressing issues of international economic policy. It should, however, be mentioned that among Keynes's followers an active discussion ensued about the relationship of the new theory of employment to international equilibrium including the transmission across national frontiers of the business cycle. Here, the principal point of contact was the Keynesian multiplier theory. An expansion of economic activity in one country produces, *inter alia*, an increased demand for imports, thus stimulating the export industries of one or more other countries and, through them, the general level of economic activity. It was the aim of subsequent analysis to show how this *foreign trade multiplier* effect worked itself out and under what conditions, and at what levels, international equilibrium was restored.[2] But is it true to say that in this field, too, the earlier

1 Among a very large literature (mainly in journals) may be mentioned: J. Dunlop, 'The Movement of Real and Money Wage Rates', *Economic Journal* (1938); J. Keynes, 'Relative Movement of Real Wages and Output', *Economic Journal* (1939); L. Tarshis, 'Changes in Real and Money Wages', *Economic Journal* (1939); and A. Smithies, 'Effective Demand and Employment' in *The New Economics* (ed. Harris) (1947).

2 The following may be mentioned from among a large literature: R. F. Harrod, *International Economics* (from 1939 edition on); W. A. Salant, 'Foreign Trade Policy in

work tended to be primarily concerned with the prevention or cure of short-term lapses from full employment caused by events outside the national frontier. We shall have to revert to this point presently but it may be said that for some years – and indeed into the early post-war period – a major preoccupation of policy as well as an important part of the activity of many of the Keynesian theorists was how to maintain full employment in a closed national economic system; that is to say, the search in the field of international economic policy was for means of insulating the domestic economy from fluctuations in the rest of the world while, at the same time and with Keynes himself in a leading role, attempts to reconstruct the international economic fabric were getting under way.

The most striking effect, however, of early 'Keynesianism' was on the general direction of public policy in the late thirties, and on opinion regarding the long-term tendencies of the capitalist economy. In both these respects, the effects of the new doctrine were more striking in the countries of adoption, notably in the United States, than in their original home. It is interesting to speculate why this should have been so. Schumpeter has suggested,[1] no doubt with some general doctrine of 'cultural transplantation' in mind, that 'practical Keynesianism is a seedling which cannot be transplanted into foreign soil: it dies there and becomes poisonous before it dies'. There is, of course, some truth in this. Away from the oral tradition, from close knowledge of its author's many-sidedness and essential consistency in the midst of an apparent eclecticism, the new theory easily luxuriated in a most startling fashion. There were other contributing factors. In Britain the depression had been mitigated by certain international effects, notably an improvement in the terms of trade, while at the same time the economy's dependence on foreign trading and financial transactions (realization of which, though not always wide, has always been deep) limited the scope of experiments in domestic policy. In the United States the experimenters found a substantially closed system, vast potential resources, and a relatively virgin field as far as large scale

---

the Business Cycle' in *Public Policy* (ed. C. J. Friedrich and E. S. Mason) (1941); F. Machlup, *International Trade and the National Income Multiplier* (1943); League of Nations, *Economic Stability in the Post-War World* (1945); R. Nurkse, 'Domestic and International Equilibrium' in *The New Economics* (ed. Harris) (1947); and S. Laursen and L. A. Metzler, 'Flexible Exchange Rates and The Theory of Employment' in *Review of Economic Statistics* (1950).

1 J. A. Schumpeter, *Ten Great Economists* (1952), p. 275.

national government expenditure was concerned. The conditions of underemployment postulated in the *General Theory* could hardly have found a better realization.

It would be wrong to find a direct family relationship between Keynes and Roosevelt's 'New Deal'. It could well be argued that much, if not all, of the policy of the 'New Deal' was evolved in a purely *ad hoc* manner and primarily by men little versed in economic theory of the Keynesian or any other variety. Indeed, there is direct evidence that the principal author of the policy found little intellectual contact with the principal author of the theory, and that the latter had much to criticize (often from a very 'orthodox' point of view) in the actions of the former.[1] There is nevertheless a strong coincidence between Keynes's prescription for getting out of a depression and the policy pursued by the 'New Deal' in the essential realms of government investment and deficit financing. As Seymour Harris has pointed out, 'more money, lower rates of interest, loan expenditure, measures to raise the propensity to consume, some freedom from dictation from abroad – all of these were the ingredients out of which the New Deal cocktail was made.'[2]

More significant, perhaps, as signs of the transplantation of these ideas, was the volume of literature on public economic policy which appeared in America, by way of rationalization or criticism of policies adopted in Washington and in conscious evolution of the theoretical principles of the *General Theory*. Here the main theoretical development was a much greater confidence in the ability of government, by means of monetary and fiscal policy, to influence, if not to determine, the level of economic activity. In particular, much attention was devoted to the manner in which, through government expenditure, underemployment might be cured in the short tun by bringing into play the multiplier and acceleration effects. Founded on the principal Keynesian proposition that investment and the propensity to consume together determine income and employment and drawing on the observed insufficiency in times of depression of private investment as

---

1 For an interesting discussion see S. E. Harris, *The New Economics* (1947), pp. 15–22. Harris rightly points to the inconsistencies between American and British policy in relation to Keynes's ideas, particularly where exchange rates are concerned. Interesting light on Keynes's ideas on American problems (both before and after the *General Theory*) is shed by his letters to *The New York Times* (December 31, 1933) and the London *Times* (January 3, 1938).

2 S. E. Harris, *The New Economics*, p. 18.

well as of consumption, many varieties of taxation and/or government loan, investment and interest policy could be evolved to fit, in theory, different conditions of underemployment.[1] These views were substantially unchallenged while large-scale unemployment existed and policies based upon them were seen to make an appreciable impact upon employment. And it was not until they came up against the stubborn economic and financial problems, of the war and post-war period that their theoretical one-sidedness and inadequacy were fully realized.

Their longer-term implications proved more immediately controversial. Although many individual dicta of a contrary nature could be found in the *General Theory*, the overwhelming impression left upon his disciples was that Keynes was pessimistic about the longer-term ability of our economic system to maintain full employment. The theory of the declining marginal efficiency of capital, the advocacy of lower interest rates, the reference to a possible '*euthanasia* of the rentier' as well as the direct doubt cast upon the likelihood of the private investor to play his part in maintaining a steadily rising level of income and employment, led many of Keynes's followers to develop a theory of 'declining investment opportunity' or of the 'mature economy'. Such a theory led to certain views as to the proper spheres of private enterprise and government action and therefore tended to enter more directly into the field of quasi-political controversy. It is probably true to say that it was on this point, rather than on the refinements of the theoretical apparatus itself, that the 'New Economics' was, initially at least, most hotly debated.[2]

The theory of declining investment opportunity[3] can be briefly

1 The most distinguished, and most comprehensive, work in this field is undoubtedly that of Alvin Hansen, of whose many books the following two may be mentioned: *Full Recovery or Stagnation* (1938); *Fiscal Policy and the Business Cycle* (1941).

2 As we shall see, this is, indeed, the issue on which the argument between Keynesians and anti-Keynesians has continued to erupt from time to time, it is again particularly virulent today not only as a theoretical subject fit for analytical disputations but very much as a major issue in practical politics and not just over the range, provision and funding of public services, but also, under the name of 'privatization', over the advantages, disadvantages as well as the techniques to be employed in moving from state-owned to privately owned, and run, industrial and commercial enterprises.

3 It may be called this, or the theory of the mature economy, or the theory of secular stagnation. The essential features are the same. Its most distinguished exponent was Alvin Hansen. For useful short discussions see S. E. Harris, *The New Economics* (1947), 'Introduction', and A. Sweezy, 'Declining Investment Opportunity'; also P. A. Samuelson, *Economics* (1952), pp. 402–8.

summarized as follows. Keynes himself had stated that while during the nineteenth century population growth, invention, the frequency of war, the opening of new lands and the state of confidence had produced a marginal efficiency of capital which kept employment relatively high and interest rates reasonably acceptable to the owners of wealth, 'today, and presumably for the future, the schedule of the marginal efficiency of capital is, for a variety of reasons, much lower than it was in the nineteenth century.'[1] The reasons for considering some of the advanced Western countries as having reached a state of 'mature economy' must thus be that the three chief dynamic elements of investment, namely increases in population, rapid technical innovation, and settlement of new territory, had lost their impetus. The first and the third of these require little explanation (particularly when one remembers that it is not absolute increases but rates of growth that are involved). As for invention, Hansen and others believed that whereas in the part, and particularly in the nineteenth century, invention was primarily labour-saving, it would in future tend to have mainly a capital-saving character (e.g. atomic energy, or air transport). Such views were often combined with some pessimism arising from the belief that business savings will tend to be at least adequate, and possibly excessive, to finance business investment for replacement and capital expansion, thus leaving fairly stable, if not rising, personal savings to have a depressing effect on employment. It must be emphasized that few who held these views considered that invention and productivity would not continue at least at the same rate as hitherto. But it is easy to see how, on the basis of the Keynesian categories, they reached the conclusion that, if no action were taken by government to counteract this tendency, the level of investment, in the long term, might, at the levels of savings and consumption likely to exist, be inadequate for full employment.

Such views could easily be exaggerated (or misrepresented) into a full-scale attack on the existing economic system and as a plea for state enterprise *à l'outrance*. Counter arguments were, therefore, not slow in forthcoming. There were first the objections formulated in terms of theory even though much of the attack was initiated by business interests,[2] which, under the still live rancour produced by the New

---

1 J. M. Keynes, *General Theory*, pp. 307–8.
2 See G. Terborgh, *The Bogey of Economic Maturity* (1945) and *The American Industrial Enterprise System* (1946). The former is a particularly acute analysis by an able economist,

Deal, felt themselves threatened by the new tendencies. The first argument of this group was, however, of an empirical character. It was argued that if the American or any other advanced economy was to be considered senile in the late thirties, one would expect symptoms to have become apparent much earlier. Yet until 1929, that is until the onset of the depression, no one would have seen anything but signs of continuing growth and expansion. This argument is particularly important in relation to the population factor. A decline in the rates of growth had been evident for many decades; there is, therefore, no particular reason to base gloomy general forecasts on this tendency. Again, while a decline in the rate of increase of population may have depressing effects on investment, it also reduces savings; and the two movements may be sufficiently compensatory. As regards the opening up of new lands, this tendency again can be shown to have been operative for a long time (in the United States, for example, many historians have long regarded the period after 1890 as marking a shift from the 'extensive' to the 'intensive' frontier). The argument is, therefore, necessarily forced back upon the questions of industrial innovation and the propensity to consume. As to the former, the opponents of the theory of the mature economy, attacked the optical illusion of a few, dramatic, inventions which are supposed to have made the industrial revolutions of the last three centuries. They point instead to the importance of a 'total flow of technological development',[1] and mention a large number of new industries of rising importance which perhaps only decades from now will be recognizable as the 'carriers' of the great industrial advance of this era. Thus, it is argued, the idea of a technical insufficiency of investment opportunity is a bogey. And if, in truth, actual investment tends to be inadequate to take advantage of the opportunities that are present, the reason must be sought in aspects of economic, financial, or political policy which tend to have a discouraging effect.

There is, of course, another factor in this argument which must not be overlooked. In the Keynesian scheme it is not only the volume of investment but also the schedule of consumption which determines the level of income and of employment. We have already seen that some believers in a chronic tendency towards underemployment base

---

marred only here and there by a polemical attitude which exaggerates the views ascribed to the author's opponents.

1 G. Terborgh, *The Bogey of American Maturity*, p. 89.

themselves on an insufficiency of investment. Others (even if they are prepared to grant that investment opportunities might not fail) believe that as consumers' expenditure is fairly rigidly linked to income, another tendency to secular unemployment may be found in the relative stability of individual savings. Against this it has been argued that the propensity to consume is by no means as stable as the Keynesians have assumed. In particular, changes in total income are bound to affect its distribution (quite apart from changes in distribution deliberately brought about by taxation, etc., as a result of changing social and political ideas); and modifications in the distribution of income have a very marked effect on the propensity to consume. But once the possibility of changes in the consumption schedule (and changes in investment) are admitted, there is no longer a uniquely determined level of income or employment. There is only 'a complex cumulative movement, not a movement toward some fixed position.'[1]

Attempts have been made to test these opposing views by means of statistical research. Indeed it is perhaps one of the major achievements of the 'stagnation school' that it re-awakened interest in the longer-term trends of the economy and greatly stimulated factual studies in this field – for example, in America, those of the National Bureau of Economic Research. But the evidence of the years during which the seeds of these controversies were planted – the two decades between the wars – does not clearly support one theory or the other.[2]

The war produced an important change in opinion, even though this change did not become fully discernible until somewhat later. Keynes himself was able, under the stimulus of wartime financial problems with which he had already become thoroughly acquainted in the first war, to combine much of his earlier analysis and prescription with the new concepts and terminology. In *How to Pay for the War* (1940) he presented an ingenious mixture of theoretical arguments, founded on doctrines derived essentially from his study of the conditions of under-employment equilibrium, with sound practical advice drawn from the experience of earlier war and post-war inflations. In the monetary field, the policy advocated was not essentially different from his earlier notions. These were based on the view that no measures for raising the revenue necessary to prosecute the war could be successful, if policy

1 A. F. Burns, *Economic Research and the Keynesian Thinking of our Time* (1946), p. 10. This short paper, a report of the National Bureau of Economic Research, contains an excellent discussion of the subject.
2 ibid.

was not directed to raising the level of national income. Thus a monetary expansion was an inevitable prerequisite and only thereafter did taxation and borrowing come into their own. This view was not fundamentally different from Keynes's earlier descriptions of that 'virtuous war-finance' which had, in the end, prevailed during the First World War. But there were some significantly novel features which could rightly be traced back to the new theoretical apparatus of the *General Theory*. For the first time the notion of the 'inflationary gap' made its appearance, clearly a child of the new analysis which operated with economic aggregates. Keynes argued that when taxation, borrowing, direct controls such as price control, allocation and consumer rationing (none very efficient but each in a measure indispensible in the existing situation) had been used to the full, there would still remain a gap, an excess of spendable funds in relation to available supplies, which only a radical system of deferred pay could bridge. Such a system of post-war credits would have the additional advantage of providing a reserve against a post-war slack of purchasing power.

The influence of these ideas on policy, particularly in Britain, was great. What is even more important from the point of view of intellectual history is the fact that they were taken up with zest by many writers, in whose work both the general problem and its individual components were further developed. A spate of articles and books on the problems of economic and financial policy in war time appeared. It would be wrong to ascribe to Keynes the exclusive role in directly stimulating fresh work in price control, rationing techniques, exchange, interest, or fiscal policy. In the long run, however, a great affinity between this work and his general doctrine became apparent. Most of the work on these particular subjects was increasingly set into a framework of analysis concerning the economy as a whole, thus showing a much greater awareness of the effects of measures in one department on others, of the inadequacy of individual policies in the absence of a suitable balance of the economy as a whole.

Most significant of all was the emphasis placed on the avoidance of inflation, the closing of the 'inflationary gap'. Some critics have claimed to see in this development a reversal of Keynes's earlier views. The disciples, on the other hand, have been able to quote many passages from Keynes's earlier writings, as well as from their own, to show that the dangers of monetary expansion had always been present in Keynes's mind, and that the problems of full employment were as capable of being tackled by the tools of the *General Theory* as were those of underemployment. As far as Keynes himself is concerned, it is, no doubt, true that his purpose was to evolve a theory of employment rather than of unemployment, and to discover the means by which the level of economic activity could be maintained over long periods at a high level rather than only those by which it could be lifted out of the trough of depression. The war was, nevertheless, an intellectual watershed in this respect, and the doctrine of the 'inflationary gap' its clearest expression. It was from this point on that it became possible to free current theory from excessive attention to the problem of underemployment and to generalize it in the direction originally perceived by its chief exponent.

## The Macroeconomic System

For those who have learnt their economics since the end of World War II and to whom the currently used terms and the concepts to which they relate are commonplace, it is almost impossible to imagine the sense of emancipation bordering on revelation with which the generations that preceded them greeted the emergence of what became known as the 'New Economics'. But looking back on what must now be called the first generation of post-Keynesian economists, it is not surprising to find that it provided a solid foundation for an exceptional upsurge of new theoretical activity. For it is now easier to see the 'great divide' that separates the economics of the period up to the thirties from what came after.

To those who were actively engaged in the discipline at that time, there seemed to be a great deal going on, even if one ignores the continuous stream of writings on specific economic issues particularly in the then growing field of industrial or business economics. The post-Marshallian type of general and partial equilibrium analysis was in full swing and so was the whole body of welfare economics which, following Pigou,[1] was being built on it. It is, however, worth noting that the field of 'Public Economics' as now understood was still in its infancy and that there was relatively little work concerned with the pricing of public goods or with the economics of nationalized

[1] For an interesting and sympathetic brief appreciation of the often rather neglected significance of Pigou see Harry Johnson obituary in *Canadian Journal of Economics and Political Science*, vol. 26.

industries as distinct from very general and, in retrospect, somewhat arid debates on 'planning'.

In the well worked-over field of the theory of value, as we have seen, important advances were being made to eliminate the last traces of hedonist philosophy, and if ever it was justified to say that 'there is nothing in the laws of value ... to clear up', it was after the work of Hicks and Allen rather than after that of John Stuart Mill. In price theory as distinct from value theory, or more broadly, in the theory of the market, the old rigid and relatively unfruitful divisions between perfect competition and monopoly theory were giving way to the much more flexible and subtle theorems of monopolistic and imperfect competition; and empirical studies of actual price-making soon showed evidence of the beneficial effects which this theoretical work was having on realistic investigations.

Not surprisingly, in the theory of money and in what was then still called the trade cycle, even contemporaries could find little ground for satisfaction. Keynes's *Treatise* ought perhaps to be excepted as having, in part at least, the character of prolegomena to his later work. Of course, much else, even if not immediately fruitful to the enlargement of our understanding or directly helpful in fashioning policies to deal with actual problems, can be found as an ingredient of later, more successful work. This is true of the work linking monetary policy with the explanation of business fluctuations, or that which applied capital theory to the same end. But the characteristic feature of the period, at least in retrospect, is the great concentration of effort on what today would be called the microeconomic problem, the behaviour of the firm or the individual in certain, usually less rather than more, realistic situations, combined with an almost complete failure to explain the behaviour of the economy as a whole, let alone to find effective means for dealing with its gross misbehaviour. The total impression must, therefore, be qualified as one of stagnation of the subject. Writing some years later, Professor Samuelson justifiably spoke of 'the unmistakable signs of decadence which were clearly present in economic thought prior to 1930'.[1]

The 'New Economics' to continue to give it this name began, as we have seen, precisely at this point. Very soon, certainly in the early post-war period, the argument whether it was biased towards

---

[1] P. A. Samuelson, *Foundations of Economic Analysis* (1947), p. 4.

situations of underemployment died out. The bias, in so far as it had existed, tended to give way under the impact of war-time scarcity of resources. While the balance between over-full employment and underemployment continued to be discussed – and, as we shall see later – became particularly important in the late sixties, this did not engage economists in debates as far as the main body of theory was concerned, which was soon recognized as being a general one.[1] Similarly, the controversy over declining investment opportunities was soon forgotten. For several years, 'stagnationists' and 'anti-stagnationists' were virtually silent. In particular, the unprecedented ease with which the immediate post-war conversion was achieved and the great opportunities which new technological advances were opening up, seemed to indicate that the economic system was fundamentally resilient and belied the earlier fears of an inevitable slowing-down of economic advance. Again, this is not to say that these longer-term speculations were silenced for ever. Indeed, we shall later see that questions about economic growth made their reappearance before too long, though in a somewhat different form.

What then, apart from its immediate relevance to certain policy problems, particularly the cure of unemployment, is the characteristic feature of the new approach to economic reasoning or, perhaps more accurately, of this particular branch of economics? The title now generally given to it, Macroeconomics, is a useful indication and also effectively demarcates it from the Microeconomics mentioned earlier. The name itself derives from Ragnar Frisch, a distinguished Norwegian economist.[2] A useful description of what it is concerned with is one given in one of its most widely-used textbooks. It is a branch of Economics 'concerned with the problems of unemployment, economic instability, inflation and economic growth'; and it can also be described as 'income and employment analysis'.[3] Professor Samuelson, about

---

1 Of course, this did not happen all at once and when some of Keynes's followers, in circumstances very different from those which obtained when the *General Theory* was written, advocated 'prudent' social or monetary policies, they were accused of inconsistency. It was left to Alvin Hansen to point to the consistency of a man who wears an overcoat in winter and a straw hat in summer: 'Keynes on Economic Policy' in S. E. Harris, *The New Economics* (1947), p. 207.

2 The first economist to be awarded (jointly with the Dutch economist, Jan Tinbergen) the Nobel Prize for Economics. Professor Frisch must also be credited with the term 'Econometrics', an area of study in which he made outstanding contributions.

3 Gardner Ackley, *Macroeconomic Theory* (1961), p. 3. For those who can follow a fairly

whose work is said more below and who is a principal founder and certainly the 'codifier' of the New Economics defines Macroeconomics as 'the study of the aggregate performance of the whole GNP and of the general price level'.[1]

As a system of thought on economic matters and in the chain of historical development of the subject, Macroeconomics, as already pointed out in the section on Keynes, is only in part based on a rejection of classical theory. In so far as there was an assumption in classicism of full employment equilibrium as a norm to which the economy tended, the New Economics rightly rejected it. Whether, and to what extent, this blind spot could be imputed to the whole of classical economics is a moot point. On the other hand, in so far as the classics, and this covers all the major economists at least up to and including John Stuart Mill, were in the main concerned with the aggregates of the economic system, total output, income, consumption, saving, investment, the shares going to capital, land and labour, the movement of the total economy through time as a result of the balance between these various elements of it – in that sense the New Economics, or Macroeconomics, represents a return to the origins, a turning-away from the preoccupations of Microeconomics. It should, however, not be forgotten that in one vital respect – in relation to policy – this return to the approach of the classics (at least as formulated by Adam Smith) was not complete but, on the contrary, involved a radical break. For what Keynes showed was that the Smithian doctrine of 'what is prudence in the conduct of every private family can scarce be folly in that of a great kingdom' could at times be the exact opposite of the truth. The qualification 'at times' is, however, important: as Keynes himself pointed out, what one had to do was to attempt to use what we have learnt from modern experience and modern analysis, not to defeat but to implement the wisdon of Adam Smith'.[2] Whatever the primary impetus that moved thinkers in this direction, even if it was wholly the immediate preoccupations of politicians, this return to the

---

advanced mathematical treatment, Sir Roy Allen's *Macro-Economic Theory, A Mathematical Treatment* (1967) contains probably the most complete available statement. An excellent elementary exposition of the central core of the new theory can be found in Charles L. Schultze, *National Income Analysis* (1964).

1 P. A. Samuelson, *Economics* (8th edition, 1970), p. 193.

2 In a speech in the House of Lords on the Anglo-American Financial Agreement on December 18, 1945.

economics of Ricardo or of Quesnay must be judged to have been wholly salutary.

Before we go further to consider what are the main elements of the present-day body of macroeconomic theory and with what categories it operates, which are different from those which had been the basic ones in economics for nearly one hundred years before Keynes, there is one subject, perhaps tangential to the main theme, that must be touched upon. For one hundred and fifty years after the *Wealth of Nations*, economics had been essentially a British science. This is a statement of bare fact, and no particular theory of the history of ideas is being invoked here to explain this fact. This is, of course, not to say that there were not important contributions forthcoming from other countries, or that great economists are not to be found elsewhere.[1] In earlier chapters the various examples of economic theorizing that emerged in other countries after the appearance of Adam Smith have been described. In particular, a special account has been given of the rise of economics in the United States. This has shown that from the latter part of the nineteenth century onwards, the American contribution assumes an increasingly important role; and a specialized history of economics in America would find a great deal more to say about the work of the second generation of American neo-classicists, such as Frank Knight and Irving Fisher.

What is, however, striking about the last three or four decades, is the virtual supremacy which American economics has achieved. Schumpeter may have been partly right in his stricture on the 'poisonous' nature of transplanted Keynesianism in the United States in the early period, but had he lived longer and been able to continue his *History* beyond 1949, he might well have changed his view. For both the elaboration of the new macroeconomic analysis on Keynesian foundations and the later scepticism as to its validity (dealt with in the next chapter) are very largely the work of American economists.

This is by no means to say that economics has now become an exclusively American science. There are major figures on the contemporary scene still to be found in Britain and elsewhere – though France and particularly Germany have yet some way to go as far as the theoretical side of modern economics is concerned. But no country

---

1 Indeed, Schumpeter considers a non-British economist to have been the greatest of them all, Walras, though it must be added that this judgment stems from a very special definition of economics.

can compare with the United States in either the volume or the quality of its output. It would be interesting to speculate why this is so. No doubt, the wealth of the United States and the amount of resources it has been able to devote to scientific research has had its effect in this area as in so many others; and much of the work in economics for which the United States is rightly renowned has been accomplished by European scholars who have either had to leave the inhospitable climate of their own countries or who have been attracted by the far greater opportunities available in America.

This, however, cannot be the sole explanation. To some extent, a future historian may well conclude as far as Britain is concerned, that the handicap was self-inflicted. For during the thirties when – certainly as far as the availability of economists of the highest ability was concerned – Britain had every opportunity to move forward, the bulk of her creative efforts in this field were diverted into sterile controversies, sometimes of the most scholastic kind. In part, the powerful tradition of earlier days when its own economic schools were supreme imposed heavy burdens on anything new (mirroring much of what was happening in industry and the economy generally). Thus, the stirrings of something new – particularly in the work of Keynes and his immediate collaborators – was not at once made welcome in its own home of Cambridge; and at the same time, Cambridge itself was being engaged in what can now be seen to have been idle controversy with the newly-found enthusiasm at the London School of Economics for the latest versions of Austrian economics. The more orthodox views in Treasury and Central Bank circles also greatly delayed the objective examination of new ideas since these were inevitably involved in current debate on economic policy and in politics.[1] Perhaps, in the end the more exuberant welcome (criticized by Schumpeter) which Keynes's ideas found in the America of the New Deal and post-New Deal period,[2] combined with the wider exposure to public debate of

[1] An extremely interesting analysis, not specifically written from the point of view of the bearing of the events it describes on the evolution of economic thought, but casting much light on it can be found in Robert Skidelsky, *Politicians and the Slump, The Labour Government of 1929–1931* (1967).

[2] An interesting example, though it does not mention Keynes, but was very influential in its day is: *An Economic Program for American Democracy* by seven Harvard and Tufts economists (1938). This today almost forgotten little booklet is particularly illuminating as one of the earliest expressions of a tendency which continues to exhibit the more interventionist and meliorative aspects of the 'New Economics'. Twenty-eight years separate it from the more formal statement by a Chairman of the American Council of

government policies which has always been characteristic of the United States, proved in the end to provide a more fertile ground for new ideas. Once they had taken root, the economies of scale of American Universities and research institutions began to make their influence felt,[1] just at the time when Britain was completely absorbed in war-time tasks (though in economics, one must acknowledge that these produced some beneficial 'fall-out').

To describe in any detail the *corpus* of Macroeconomics as a major branch of present-day economic theory would involve virtually the summing-up of one of the current textbooks. An adequate idea can, however, be got by looking at the structure of the presentation of economics in manuals and classes as it has become broadly accepted today. Since one of the most widely used and comprehensive of these if Professor Samuelson's, this may be an appropriate place to say something more general about his work, to which a number of references has already been made.

*Paul Anthony Samuelson's*[2] career is not untypical of that of many members of the present generation of economists. A strict grounding in pre-Keynesian economics of the austere, mathematical kind common in the Chicago of his day was followed by a spell at Harvard and subsequently, off and on (with a fairly lengthy off period in the fifties) by periods of close experience in governmental and non-governmental public affairs. His first major work, written at a very early age, was based on a Prize Essay at Harvard and was published in 1947: *Foundations of Economic Analysis*. This book is, in the first instance, notable for its method. It is mathematical in conception and uses *pace* the author's claim of using only elementary mathematical tools, more, and more advanced, mathematical methods than had hitherto been applied with any frequency to so wide a range of economic problems. At the same time it is an economic work (and the author is justified in saying that his interest in mathematics is secondary); and it presents a skilful

Economic Advisers, Walter Heller – mentioned below – but the intellectual relationship is perfectly clear.

1 The 'community' of Cambridge (Mass.) comprising Harvard, MIT and a number of other institutions of higher learning was and remains an outstanding example of these economies of scale in the breadth and diversity of the contributions which its members have made.

2 Professor Samuelson of the Massachusetts Institute of Technology, the second winner of the Nobel Prize in Economic Science (and the first American to achieve this distinction) continues at seventy-five to be reckoned among the half-dozen or so most distinguished and influential economists working anywhere in the world today.

blend of literary and mathematical method. The book was designed, and has served, as a source of 'meaningful theorems', that is of propositions which could 'conceivably be refuted, if only under ideal conditions', in 'diverse fields of economic affairs'.[1] It has certainly been a source book for a great deal of subsequent economic work, including, not least, the author's own.

Thereafter, he turned his attention, on the one hand to the elaboration of certain aspects of the Keynesian system and, on the other, to improving the teaching of the subject. As regards the former, mention has already been made of a pioneering article of 1939 which, by linking the multiplier and acceleration effects of the Keynesian analysis greatly enriched and generalized the system. It is impossible to do justice in a brief space to Professor Samuelson's subsequent work in this and related areas. A collection of his scientific papers already runs to five volumes[2] quite apart from the wealth of more popular articles which Samuelson has produced.[3] In 1958, he also collaborated in the production of another major work in mathematical economics.[4]

Samuelson is, however, best known as the author of the widely used and translated (including into Russian) modern textbook in Economics. It first appeared in 1948 and has since been regularly revised, the edition at this time of writing being the thirteenth and the second to be written jointly with William D. Nordhaus. The book was at once a success. It marked a complete break with the traditional structure and substance of expositions of the subject, not only reflecting the influence of Keynesian ideas but also greatly helping the establishment and further development of the macroeconomic analysis which it presented. Leaving aside a final section on current economic problems (many of which also fall into the macroeconomic sphere), about half the analytical exposition of the book (significantly the first half) was devoted to the nature of the national income, its determination, how incomes, job opportunities and levels of prices fluctuate and how fiscal

1 P. A. Samuelson, *Foundations of Economic Analysis* (1949), pp. 4, 5. A new, enlarged, edition appeared in 1983.

2 *The Collected Scientific Papers of Paul A. Samuelson*, ed. Joseph E. Stiglitz (1966), an invaluable collection of articles already referred to, often very difficult to trace in their original form.

3 To mention only two which ran for many years in the American magazine *Newsweek* and in the *Financial Times* of London.

4 Robert Dorfman, Paul A. Samuelson and Robert M. Solow, *Linear Programming and Economic Analysis* (1958).

and monetary policy 'can keep the aggregate system working tolerably well'.[1] The other half, devoted to Microeconomics, deals with the question of what determines the relative prices of particular goods and the quantitative breakdown of the aggregates of the national income into various goods and services. The distinction could not be put more clearly, nor can the break with the older tradition (which made value and price theory always come first in any textbook) be more emphatic.[2]

In Professor Ackley's text, already referred to, which is virtually exclusively concerned with Macroeconomics, the central core of the book, after an initial description of the main categories, is occupied by an exposition, first of classical macroeconomics and, second, by that of the Keynesian system. This is a particularly useful juxtaposition. We are shown, first, the postulates of Say's law, its relation to the quantity theory of money, and then the complete classical full employment equilibrium theory. This is described in modern terms, i.e. by means of a series of equations (production function, profit maximization postulate, the quantity theory, the supply of labour) which makes easier – and more striking – the subsequent contrast with the model elaborated by Keynes, which is of a more generalized character since it introduces concepts which as we have seen make it possible to explain the existence of less-than-full employment equilibrium and also lead to a new understanding of the possibilities of inflation.

Of the many specific applications to which this schema has been put, two deserve special mention: one which is at the heart of the policy implications of Macroeconomics, fiscal policy in relation to employment and stability; and the policy prescriptions as far as international payments equilibrium is concerned. On both these, Samuelson again provides the clearest and simplest guide. The idea that the national budget is not to be viewed as a family household budget writ large, but that, over and beyond the canons laid down by Adam Smith, the conduct of the national finances have a positive part to play in shaping the whole of the nation's economy in the aggregate (quite apart from its 'microeconomic' effects on individual supply, demand and price situations) is the outstandingly novel feature of the new economics. The detection of the likelihood of inflationary or deflationary gaps, i.e. over-full employment with inflationary consequences for prices and

---

1 P. A. Samuelson, *Economics* (8th edition, 1970), p. 357.
2 Reference will be made later to the change in the balance between different areas of interest of the author which is evident in the successive editions of this book.

wages, or under-employment of resources, is the signal for an attempt by fiscal policy, that is by action on either or both the revenue and expenditure side of the national budget, to influence total demand in such a way, as, through the operation of the various national income aggregates, to correct the prospective situation.

From this simple proposition, many refinements both of concept and of policy have been derived. To mention only a few, there is the notion of 'fiscal drag' or 'fiscal dividend' and the related concepts of full-employment budget-surplus or deficit; the latter two measuring what would be the budget position, if, given a certain pattern of taxation and public expenditure, the economy were at full employment. In the one case fiscal drag, in the other fiscal dividend may produce a situation which is different from the apparent budget situation. We cannot pursue these points further here,[1] but much work is continuing on these lines, including, in particular, detailed efforts to assemble more data, and by empirical studies to refine and modify the theoretical apparatus. Nor have these theories remained confined to the broad question of the effect of fiscal policy on employment and inflation. They have also been increasingly applied to the question of influencing specific problems of resource allocation where, for a variety of reasons, the uncontrolled results of the market-place may be expected to lead to unsatisfactory results.[2]

1 Though it is worth pointing out that quite apart from the macroeconomic management aspect of fiscal policy, the New Economics has also beneficially influenced the general area of public finance. It is more than doubtful whether a book such as Joseph A. Pechman's *Federal Tax Policy* – latest (fifth) edition 1987 – could have been written before Keynes, even if one ignores the relatively short part devoted to taxation and economic policy. While Pechman's main work was in the area of fiscal policy (both in its theory and in its application to problems of statecraft, which he himself practised as an adviser to government), it also extended over a very wide field of practical economic policy issues, particularly during the twenty-one years when he was director of economic studies at the Brookings Institution. One of that distinguished institution's most effective products, an annual volume called *Setting National Priorities*, was edited for seven years by Joseph Pechman and now continues under the editorship of Henry J. Aaron (1991). Pechman's last book, published a few months before his untimely death, is referred to further below: *The Role of the Economist in Government: An International Perspective* (1989). Another book that may be mentioned in this connection is Richard Goode, *The Individual Income Tax* (1964).

2 An interesting recent example is Kenneth J. Arrow and Mordecai Kurz, *Public Investment, The Rate of Return, and Optional Fiscal Policy* (1970). Some of this new literature in Welfare economics is referred to in the next chapter.

The other area to which the new analysis has been applied and which is worth alluding to since it has also played an important part in policy formation is that of foreign trade and payments. Reference has already been made to the foreign trade multiplier and the general discussion of the lapses from, and restoration of, international equilibrium. As stated, the early impetus came from a desire to insulate the domestic economy from fluctuations originating elsewhere. Although this preoccupation did not disappear altogether – indeed in the late sixties and early seventies it became more pressing as a practical matter – the main work of the last two decades has been devoted to broadening the analysis considerably, ensuring that it is fully integrated into the general body of macroeconomic theory, while at the same time studying more deeply and intensively certain specific aspects of the trade and payments problem. There is hardly a segment of international economics that has not been greatly enriched by the very large literature of the most recent past. Not only the basic theory of the 'gains' to be derived from trade and the directions of trade as determined by the original doctrine of comparative advantage, but also the crucial policy questions of 'welfare' economics as related to interventions through different forms of trade policy has been almost entirely overhauled.[1] Needless to say the treatment of the subject at a more elementary, expository, level has also been virtually revolutionized. One has only to compare the relevant chapters in a modern textbook

---

1 Among forerunners might be mentioned, A. Lerner, 'The Diagrammatical Representation of Demand Conditions in International Trade', in *Economica* (August 1934) and the same author's 'The Symmetry between Import and Export Taxes', in *Economica* (August 1936); then, T. Scitovsky, 'A Reconsideration of the Theory of Tariffs' in *Review of Economic Studies* (Summer 1942) and J. Marcus Fleming, 'On Making the Best of Balance of Payments Restrictions on Imports' in *Economic Journal* (March 1951). On the more general relationship between international payments (including their operation under different exchange rate régimes) and national income, a few examples may be mentioned: Lloyd A. Metzler, 'The Process of International Adjustment under Conditions of Full Employment: A Keynesian View' read before the Econometric Society, December 1960 and published in Richard E. Caves and Harry S. Johnson (eds.) *Readings in International Economics* (1968), pp. 465–86; G. D. A. MacDougall, 'British and American Exports: A Study Suggested by the Theory of Comparative Costs' in *Economic Journal* (1951/52); S. Laursen, 'Production Functions and the Theory of International Trade' in *American Economic Review* (1952); J. R. Hicks, 'The Long-Run Dollar Problem' in *Oxford Economic Papers* (June 1953); and, Keynes himself, a posthumously published article, 'The Balance of Payments of the United States' in *Economic Journal* (1946).

with the more traditional statements to recognize the extent of the change.[1]

While a good deal of the work just referred to is concerned with abstract 'models', most of it is either directly devoted to policy problems or has policy implications. At the theoretical level, there can be no doubt that the frontiers of understanding have been greatly enlarged. Much more is now known, for example, about the ultimate effects of tariffs, export subsidies and similar policies on terms of trade, national incomes, investment and consumption of diffeent trading areas; or of the circumstances in which exchange rate changes – or régimes other than those of relatively fixed exchange parities – may contribute towards stabilization of international payments relations and when they may be destabilizing. Similarly, the consequences, in different assumed circumstances, of international investment, for example in developing countries, or of international capital movements both long-term and short-term in general, are now capable of much more refined definition.[2]

It must, however, be emphasized that all these advances have so far remained confined to the theory of the subject and have not yet produced any great coalescence of views (not only among 'practical' men, but even among economists) on the right policy decisions in different conditions that have appeared in the real world. This subject has, therefore, become, as we shall see in the next chapter, one of the main areas in which the disparity between theory and confidence in the efficacy of the practical measures that might be based on it, constitutes a major source of disquiet.

1 Samuelson's *Economics* may again serve. See 2nd edition, part 5, pp. 621–705.
2 The literature on these matters has assumed flood-like proportions in recent years and only a minute (and wholly arbitrary) selection of examples can be listed: J. H. Williams, *Post-War Monetary Plans* (1944), and numerous articles; Robert Triffin, *Europe and the Money Muddle* (1957), *Gold and the Dollar Crisis* (1960), to choose just two out of a voluminous, but consistently important output; Richard N. Gardner, *Sterling-Dollar Diplomacy* (new edition, 1969); Robert V. Roosa, *Monetary Reform for the World Economy* (1965) and *The Dollar and World Liquidity* (1967) from a major participant in these matters who is also a leading theorist; Jaques Rueff, *Balance of Payments* (1967) and Milton Gilbert, *The Gold-Dollar System: Conditions of Equilibrium and the Price of Gold* (1968). Mention must also be made of the continuous contribution made by one of the founders of the post-war system, Edward Bernstein, and of the work of a distinguished theorist, Professor Fritz Machlup, who rendered notable service by bringing together officials, academics and bankers in a series of discussions of world monetary problems which went on for some years.

The Keynesian and post-Keynesian techniques for dealing with the economy as a whole are not, however, the only ones. It is a further indication of the newly recovered interest in the aggregates of the economy that various economists have tried other methods, additional to, or in replacement of, the Keynesian. One which deserves special mention is that of 'Input-Output' Analysis first developed by another eminent American economist, Professor Wassily Leontief, who has been awarded the Nobel Prize. One at least of the inspirations for this work is to be found in the Walrasian system of equations. Leontief tried to give it content, first by making it more manageable through the aggregation of production by industries – beginning with 45, later expanded a good deal – and applying it to the actual data of the United States. He first published his results in 1941: *The Structure of the American Economy 1919–1929: An Empirical Application of Equilibrium Analysis*. Ten years later, in 1951, he brought the work up to date to 1939; and in 1953 he published a more general book, *Studies in the Structure of the American Economy: Theoretical and Empirical Explorations in Input-Output Analysis*. By drawing up tables which represent schedules of uses of the output of different industries which can, thus, become 'inputs' of other industries, a mathematical analysis becomes possible, designed to show the relationships between the different quantities. This analysis can then be applied to discover 'optimal' allocation patterns of different resources, a technique that has been considered applicable to micro- as well as macroeconomic problems. In this way, Leontief was able to integrate into the Walrasian system of general equilibrium the other consideration which appears always to have inspired him, namely precise, empirical investigation, clearly not capable of being as extensive in economics as in the natural sciences, but nevertheless possible to some extent, and certainly highly desirable.[1]

What emerges very clearly from even the briefest review of macroeconomic theory is its inherent affinity with policy questions. It is not surprising, therefore, that the most striking feature of this development of the last thirty or forty years is its intimate involvement in the processes of administration of economic affairs. The resulting

---

[1] In a lecture delivered in 1953, this need to 'look under the hood' is clearly expounded: Wassily Leontief, 'Mathematics in Economics', reprinted in *Essays in Economics, Theories and Theorizing* (1966), pp. 22–44.

'institutionalization' of economics is a sufficiently novel development to deserve separate treatment.

## *Economic Management: the New Orthodoxy*

In considering the relevance of recent developments of economics to policy, it would be wrong to start with the idea that the application of economic analysis to the practical tasks of government is a wholly new development. It has been a major thesis of the account given in this book of the evolution of economic thought, that systematic intellectual enquiry in the realm, of the 'economic' has always been the result of a practical motive; and that notably the economics of the last two hundred years has always – successfully or not – been devised with 'a tendency to use'. One has only to recall the purposes of Adam Smith – and certainly the results which can be directly traced to his theoretical activity – to realize the closeness of the relationship between the most abstract propositions in economics and some highly practical consequences in the legal and institutional environment which profoundly affect the lives of everybody.

The great achievement of classical political economy, as has been repeatedly stressed in these pages, was to complete the sweeping away of the multifarious barriers to trade and industry, to consolidate the rule of the market and, thereby, to help to establish firmly the whole complex of political, social, legal, economic, and indeed, cultural conditions which form the framework within which, in the advanced countries of the world at least, life was thereafter to be carried on.

This process had as a consequence a more or less clear demarcation of the agenda of the state, as against that of the individual, which, despite various national differences, remained valid throughout the countries in which modern industry developed; and, together with it, of the agenda of economic enquiry and the elaboration of economic policy based on the results of this enquiry. The supremacy of the free play of the market (apart from clearly defined exceptions) remained, broadly speaking, the guiding principle throughout the nineteenth and early twentieth centuries. Despite the attempts of the historical and romantic movements in economics, or the variety of social reform and socialist schools, this also remained the principle by which the frontiers of economic theory continued to be defined. It clearly imposed a limitation on the extent to which professional economic advice could be brought to bear on the practical tasks of government, even within the field of economic action itself.

This is not say that some degree of 'economic management' was not present, or that individual economists were not involved, more or less deeply or for more or less long periods of time, in this kind of governmental activity. The areas, however, in which this was particularly true are themselves indicative of the limited scope for this projection of economics into government. The bulk of the direct participation of economists tended to be in the fields of money, banking, and international trade on the one hand and public finance on the other, the latter being understood in the relatively restricted sense in which that subject was defined until very recently. Later, particularly during the first few decades of the present century, some specific problems in what would now be called Welfare economics also tended to be added. But if one takes the example of a modern economist who was involved in tendering advice to government considerably more than the average, Alfred Marshall, and compares with him any one of a large number of present-day economists who have been so involved, the contrast is surely very striking.

The process by which the agenda of the state was gradually changed, the many ramifications of the movement away from the limitations imposed by Adam Smith and his philosophical ancestors and contemporaries has – in so far as it relates specifically to economic matters – been frequently touched upon in these pages. A full description and analysis would require a separate study. What must be clear is that the acceptance of responsibility by governments – elected governments in one or other form of democratic system – for the maintenance of a high level of economic activity, for avoidance of major economic fluctuations, for material growth, perhaps even, at least by implication, for some progress towards greater economic equality, is one of the major turning-points in modern history. We have traced its consequences as far as economic thought in the last forty years is concerned. Equally dramatic have been the consequences for the application of economics to governmental problems and the methods by which this is accomplished.

It is in this context that the word 'institutionalization' has been used at the end of the preceding section to denote an entirely new relationship. Early recognition of this can be seen in the following two quotations, both from administrators, rather than economists. In one, central planning by government is said to rely on 'how much or how little can be had of the necessaries and the good things of this life, given the existing and prospective resources of foreign currency ... an estimate of the national productive resources and a division of the anticipated product between home and foreign markets ... (which) necessarily involves assigning relative values to the main variables of the economy'.[1] In the other, the year 1941 is said to mark 'the date when a new theme was introduced into the making of the Budget, namely the inflationary-deflationary scheme, a conscious attempt to use fiscal measures to hold the balance between the money in people's pockets and what they could buy with it'.[2] These are, of course, descriptions of the central preoccupations of modern macro-economics; and as an early one of the long line of distinguished academic economists who participated in this process put it, when speaking of the role of the economist in government 'the special province of the economist is the economic system as a whole, and the relation between the workings of its different parts'.[3]

Perhaps the most striking immediate sign of the new relationship is to be found in the number of leading economists who have been drawn into the governmental machine. This is particularly so in the English-speaking countries, especially Britain and the United States, though in continental countries, in some of which the occasional appearance – usually for brief periods only – of an academic economist as Minister of Finance or Central Bank Governor was not unknown before,[4] the use of more economists on a regular basis in advisory or administrative functions has also greatly increased.

But in Britain and the United States any list of those who have served, or are still serving, in these positions, reads like the roll-call of some of the most distinguished of modern economists. In the Economic Section of the Cabinet office, as it was first called, during and after the war, later as economic advisers in the Treasury or other central economic departments in London on long-term or *ad hoc*

1 Sir Oliver Franks (now Lord Franks), *Central Planning and Control in War and Peace* (1947), pp. 32–3.
2 Sir E. Bridges (later Lord Bridges), *Treasury Control* (1950), p. 18.
3 Sir Robert Hall (later Lord Roberthall), 'The Place of the Economist in Government', The Sidney Ball Lecture 1954, published in *Oxford Economic Papers* (June 1955), p. 125.
4 It is interesting – perhaps paradoxical in view of what is said above – to note the widespread comment that greeted the appointment of a distinguished academic, George Schultz, to be the first academic economist to hold the position of Secretary of the Treasury in the United States; perhaps even more remarkably later that of Secretary of State.

assignments, we find such figures as Lionel Robbins, James Meade, Robert Hall, Alexander Cairncross, Donald MacDougall, Austin Robinson and Brian Reddaway to name only a few. Again, to list only some of those who have served as Chairmen or members of the American Council of Economic Advisers or as more personal advisers to Presidents, Arthur Burns, Walter Heller, Arthur Okun, James Tobin and Gardner Ackley, quite apart from many others already referred to who have also put their professional skills at the disposal of those in charge of political decisions, is to recognize how totally different has become the scale – and the depth – of the involvement of the highest talent of economic knowledge in practical affairs of government compared with what it was fifty years ago.

Few of those concerned would fail to acknowledge that their economics had benefited from these activities.[1] But it also means that a large part of their work, sometimes perhaps their best work, is scattered through official memoranda and reports and often also impounded in Committee documents where the individual contributions are almost impossible to disentangle. A further feature that is worth mentioning to illustrate the changing climate in which economists now work is the much greater mobility of individual economists between governmental and academic work. This has for a long time been a characteristic of the American scene, but has now become much more general.

An important contribution has also been made by international organizations in the economic sphere which have been generous in their policy of recruiting economic specialists and providing substantial sums out of their budgets for research which is quite frequently of a highly theoretical character. Thus, side by side with the great increase in the number and size of university economics departments, and various research organizations associated with them, the growth of intergovernmental organizations and the development on a substantial scale of national and international research institutes and associations has immeasurably increased the points of location of economic work, the opportunities for economists to pursue their researches, and has greatly added to the economies of scale operating in the subject. One sometimes wonders what an economist like Marshall – whose own

---

1 See, for example, the generous tribute paid by Lionel Robbins: Lord Robbins, *Autobiography of an Economist* (1972), p. 185, Sir Alexander Carincross, 'The Work of An Economic Adviser' in *Public Administration* (Spring 1968), p. 11 and the whole tenor of Lord Roberthall's Sidney Ball lecture already quoted.

output of 'official' work though substantial by contemporaneous standards would be judged meagre by those of today[1] – would say when confronted by the stream of material issuing from, say, the United Nations, the World Bank and International Monetary Fund, the OECD and the European Economic Community, the National Institute for Economic and Social Research and the Brookings Institution, the Central Banks as well as most of the big commercial banks everywhere, and if he was given an idea of the number of academic economists responsible for it!

What does all this activity amount to? Is there some common theme running through it, by which the general terms of the relationship between economic analysis and economic policy as it exists today can be identified and explained? There are three separate strands of possible enquiry to be distinguished here. In the first place, there is the organization, the structure in which this relationship is established and through which it operates. Secondly there are the procedures and methods by which the translation of abstract economic theorems into measurable realistic statements about actual situations is effected, the proper policy conclusions drawn, and the measures thought appropriate applied. Thirdly, there is the effect which this process has on the economists taking part in it : the manner in which they themselves conceive of the nexus thus created between 'positive' economic analysis and policy desiderata, and of their part in it.

The first of these does not strictly belong in the area with which this book is concerned. Structures will depend on constitutional factors, on political circumstances, on traditions and on personalities. They will differ from one country to another, and they will change from time to time in response to changes in the factors enumerated as well as to the pressures of economic necessity. Moreover, as in most matters of political and constitutional organization, the reality and the form do not always coincide; and changes in the balance of power as expressed in practice between different sectors of the machinery take place all the time without necessarily affecting the formal appearance. It must also be remembered that those who have – or share in – the power of making decisions receive advice from very many sources; and the extent to which they rely on, or consider themselves dependent on,

1 *Official Papers* by Alfred Marshall, ed. J. M. Keynes (1926). This volume contains the whole of Marshall's contributions to official enquiries on economic questions with the exception of his work on the Labour Commission.

those who are formally charged with the task of advising them profes-
sionally, will vary a great deal from person to person and time to time.

Nevertheless a good deal of similarity can be observed in the way in
which economic advice is organized in most of the industrialized
countries of the world and nowadays also to a considerable extent –
perhaps simply by way of imitation – in less developed countries; that is
quite apart from the vast amount of advice, solicited and unsolicited,
which these receive from visiting scholars and missions, and the like.
Thus we have a Council of Economic Advisers in the United States
instituted in consequence of the Employment Act 1946, a Government
Economic Service (the current heir to a whole series of differently
named forerunners) at present primarily located in the Treasury in
Britain, a 'Plan' organization in France directly responsible to the
President of the Republic, an Economic Council in Canada, a *Sachverstaendigenrat* in Germany, and so on. All these, and similar organizations are, as has been pointed out, not by any means the only sources of
economic advice in their respective countries, nor are they necessarily
the most potent, but, generally speaking they tend to be the locus of the
most professional economic advice, that is that which is most closely
derived from economic analysis and linked with the work going on in
non-governmental, academic circles.

There are, of course, differences between them. Thus the American
Council of Economic Advisers is formally very closely linked with the
Presidential office, though successive Presidents have tended – in this
instance, as in others – to create a separate focus for advice elsewhere
in the machine or in the White House itself. In Britain, the general
structure of Departments of State and Ministries is rarely bypassed in
any formal sense, and the varying patterns that have existed in recent
years have generally expressed themselves in the creation, amalgam-
ation or elimination of departments, but with the professional advisers
almost always integrated into some regular administrative department,
usually, as now, in the Treasury.[1] In France, the 'Plan' is concerned
mainly with longer-term problems, while economic advice on current
matters comes from within departments, usually the Ministry of
Finance; and in Germany the Council of Experts is a good deal more
independent of government than similar agencies elsewhere. It is safe

1 The existence for a time in the present British Government of a Central Policy Review
Staff directly responsible to the Prime Minister illustrates the fact that the administrative
location of these advisory cells, which usually also indicates their relation to the chief
sources of power, varies as does their life span.

to predict that these patterns will continue to undergo changes – real or apparent – but that in essence the sort of structure that has been built up will continue.

As far as the third aspect of the matter is concerned, this touches, of course, on the whole qustion of the fundamental relation between economic theory and economic policy – not to say Politics – and goes, therefore, much further than an analysis of the manner in which macroeconomics is brought to bear on current economic problems. Some reflections on it will be given in the Conclusion to this book which is more generally concerned with the ends of economics. What may be said at this stage is that a number of the most eminent and experienced practitioners of this new art of official economic advice – being writers as well as thinkers – have, happily for the student of these matters, given us their own reflections.[1] In these there is often a

---

[1] Indeed the literature on the role of economic advisers is already quite a substantial one and only a few examples can be given here. In addition to the lectures by Sir Alexander Cairncross and Lord Roberthall already cited, the following two books by former Chairmen of the American Council of Economic Advisers should be consulted for very complete and frank statements of how they view the relation between economics and policy and their own position in regard to it: Walter W. Heller, *New Dimensions of Political Economy* (1966); Arthur M. Okun, *The Political Economy of Prosperity* (1970). An interesting comparison of the American and German systems is Henry C. Wallich, 'The American Council of Economic Advisers and the German *Sachverstaendigenrat*. A Study in the Economics of Advice' in *The Quarterly Journal of Economics* (August 1968). Those who wish to consider the more traditional function of government in the 'public sector' within the new context of economic management, should consult Sir Richard Clarke's 1964 Stamp Memorial Lecture, *The Management of the Public Sector of the National Economy*; and for a description of a short-lived experiment in a new departmental structure in Britain, see E. Roll, 'The Department of Economic Affairs' in *Public Administration* (Spring 1966). The flow of books and articles on this subject has continued unabated in recent years, not surprisingly in view of the accelerated increase in the number of economists who, in one form or another, are members of the administrative machine. (In Britain, for example, where this development has lagged behind that of the United States, there are now some four hundred economists in the Government Economic Service compared with practically none in 1939). Of the recent literature, the following may be mentioned: Cairncross and Watts, *The Economic Section 1939–1951* (1989); Pechman (ed.), *The Role of the Economist in Government*, An International Perspective (1989); *The Robert Hall Diaries 1947–1953*, ed. by Cairncross (1989–90); Plowden, *An Industrialist in the Treasury: The Post-war Years* (1989). See also Roll, *Crowded Hours* (1985) and *The Uses and Abuses of Economics* (1978). Walter Heller, one of the most distinguished and, in his day, most effective economists who worked in government (Chairman of the American Council of Economic Advisers in the Kennedy/Johnson years) has given a particularly interesting account of the application by the economic adviser of Keynesian Macroeconomics in his *New Dimensions of Political*

mixture of the old and the new, of the traditional definition of economics and of the problems to which it can be applied and a recognition of the new tasks of government. Thus Heller says the economist's 'method is to factor out the costs, the benefits, and the net advantage or disadvantage of alternative courses of action';[1] and Okun echoes, 'the economist looks for the opportunities sacrificed in selecting any alternative'.[2] But the one also says that the economic adviser is involved 'in value choices, in advocacy of Presidential programs, and in balancing what is ideal against what is practicable';[3] and Okun again echoes, that 'when they (economists) come to Washington, they cannot leave their ideologies behind. Indeed, they should not'.[4]

What is, however, more directly germane to our theme is by what means the principles of macroeconomic theory are made to subserve the broad objectives of economic policy, i.e. full use of resources, growth, stability, international balance which continue, at least in theory, to be generally accepted, although there are some fundamental differences of view as to how they can be achieved. Unfortunately, it is not easy to give a succinct account of this and, at the same time one that would have real meaning. A straightforward description of the way in which the statistical material is assembled and arranged so as to show the position actually existing in the national economy, the methods by which forecasts are made over whatever the relevant planning period is, the timetable for the subsequent operations in which not only economists, but also administrators and politicians are involved, would not, of itself, be very illuminating. Moreover, description, let alone analysis of this procedure is very difficult to separate from judgement of its results. Indeed, some of the best accounts are embedded in critical analysis of the records of particular administrations.[5] Furthermore, although there is wide agreement on the broad

*Economy* (1966), already mentioned. This book is, perhaps, the high-water mark of the influence of Keynesian economists in practical policy-making.

1 Walter W. Heller, op. cit., p. 5.

2 Arthur M. Okun, op. cit., p. 4.

3 Walter W. Heller, ibid., p. 18.

4 Arthur M. Okun, ibid., p. 23.

5 See for example Andrew Shonfield, *British Economic Policy since the War* (1958); J. C. R. Dow, *The Management of the British Economy 1945–1960* (1964); Samuel Brittan, *The Treasury under the Tories* (1964), the same author's *Steering the Economy* (1971); and Wilfred Beckerman (ed.), *The Labour Government's Economic Record* (1972). For assessments of United States experience, see the books by Heller and Okun already mentioned.

objectives, there is considerable difference at the margin of choice, for example, on how much a given degree of instability is to be tolerated in return for a given amount of extra growth, and so on.[1]

Nevertheless, a broad pattern can be discerned, both in the operations of the governmental machines as well as in the methods employed by unofficial prognosticators and critics.[2] The core of it is the economic assessment and the economic forecast against the background of the government's acknowledged responsibility for the level of economic activity responsibility which some political groups regard as best met by a high degree of governmental non-activity. This means knowing what the immediate past has been, what the present situation is, and what path the economy is likely to follow in the short-term future *given existing policies*. That the ascertainment of the last-named, dependent as it is on forecasts, may be subject to error is accepted as a matter of course. But even the past and the present are never perfectly known, for they are at best instantaneous photographs of a situation which is in the process of change even while the photograph is taken. Time-lags are, therefore, inevitably involved: the lag between the event and its record; that between the diagnosis, the prescription and the administration of the remedy (if remedy is judged necessary); and the time-lag between policy measures and their visible effect on the economy.[3] Because of these technical difficulties of forecasting as a basis for policy (though sometimes on the more ideological ground that even forecasting involves too much planning), it has sometimes been argued that it should be abandoned. Against this it has been urged that not to act on a systematic forecast is to act on an unsystematic one – since all action designed to affect the future implies a view of what the future would be if no action were taken.

In most countries which have developed this art, the technique of forecasting is concerned essentially with the balance between prospective aggregate demand and aggregate supply. It involves estimates of the likely change in the gross national product and its principal

1 An interesting statement of this difficulty is to be found in Michael Lipton, *Assessing Economic Performance* (1968).

2 For example the methods used by the National Institute of Economic and Social Research – as described in M. J. C. Surrey, *The Analysis and Forecasting of the British Economy* (1971) – are not basically different from the official ones, although the Institute often reaches different conclusions.

3 See the Introduction by C. W. McMahon to *Techniques of Economic Forecasting*, OECD (1965).

constituents, of changes in prices in general (thus yielding forecasts in real terms), of wages and earnings, of productivity, of exports and imports as well as the invisible components of the balance of payments and so on. The aim is, first to arrive at an estimate of the likely pressure of demand – leading to the assessment of potential inflationary or deflationary 'gaps' – on the basis of which a first judgment, of what needs to be 'put into' or 'taken out of' the economy is made. This judgment is then refined, as far as possible by 'disaggregating' the various constituents of the GNP so as to be able to adjust more accurately various policy means available for the desired broad objective (on the fiscal front: action both on taxation and expenditure – and in both cases on the details of each with some reference to sectoral imbalances of supply or demand; on the monetary front: on interest rate and money supply policy). Where balance of payments considerations weigh heavily – as they have done over a long period in Britain – an attempt will also be made to adjust policy accordingly.

Apart from the obvious difficulty inherent in any process of this kind that relies on data subject to the sort of time-lags already referred to, there are two others that need to be stressed. While the broad objective of stabilization by means of demand management can be easily enough understood, it operates not only on aggregates but also on – and indeed only through – the individual elements of the total economy, even if it is not specifically refined so as deliberately to affect these in different desired degrees. Here it inevitably comes up against – and frequently clashes with – existing governmental programmes, the result of past policies devised for quite specific objectives: for example, social or physical infrastructure (hospitals, schools, roads) or socio-political desiderata (improvement of the incomes of certain wage-earners, discouragement of certain types of consumption). There is thus a considerable 'stickiness' in these matters, which makes for a lack of congruence between the broad macroeconomic objective and the specific microeconomic effects which policy must of necessity produce.

The second problem is one of timing, not so much from the point of view of the time-lags already mentioned, but from that of the requirements of the political and administrative process itself. The activity of most democratic governments is bounded by a certain time-span, imposed by the electoral calendar, and moves through a definite cycle of parliamentary, or congressional sessions as well as the inexorable periodicity of executive plans. Almost invariably the annual budget becomes the central focus for major decisions in the field of economic management. This, in turn, imposes a certain life-cycle on the collection of data, their digestion, analysis, presentation, distillation into assessment, projections to form forecasts and judgments as to the necessities of the situation.[1]

It follows from this that energies are almost exclusively focused on refining the process, so as to meet exacting timetables and rigorous requirements of presentation in a form specially adapted to the needs of non-experts who nevertheless must exercise judgements and take decisions, but in a framework which is very largely prescribed and immutable – a translation of analysis into action by means of a highly restrictive and stylized dictionary, as it were. It is a major achievement of the art that this refinement has been taken to a very high level indeed. The form in which the 'budget judgment', the basic assessment of the balance of demand, for example, appears in Britain has certainly reached a high degree of sophistication. In the United States, the process has perhaps been taken even further. There is not, for example, as yet available anywhere except in the United States the sort of speedy, highly computerized series of data that can help diagnose the tendency of the economy for the ensuing phase.[2] The results, of course, are not necessarily generally acceptable even to economic analysts working outside government. Reference has already been made to the independent forecasts of the National Institute in Britain. The Brookings Institution provides through its many publications a running alternative to the prognostications and evaluations of the official machine; and in Canada, the Canadian Economic Policy Committee, set up in 1969 under the sponsorship of the Private Planning Association of Canada, provides regularly its own report, as a counterpoint to those of the Economic Council.

But the process has gone on over at least the last two decades or more, without much concern over the professional criticism of experts, with perhaps some change in emphasis since the arrival at least in the United States and Britain of governments whose views on economic management were based on aspects of the 'revolution' of the 'New Classical Macroeconomics' (see below). Apart from the mechanical requirements of organizing and managing so complex and exacting a

1 As far as Britain is concerned, this process is well described in the books by Dow and Brittan already cited.
2 See Julius Shiskin *Signals of Recession and Recovery, An Experiment in Monthly Reporting* (1961).

series of intellectual and administrative exercises, the main concern has naturally been its success in achieving the basic objectives. On the former front, successes have undoubtedly been scored. There is in existence now in many countries, a more intimate integration of statisticians, economic theorists, economic administrator, administrators pure and simple, and politicians in respect of the tasks of economic management than has ever existed before. 'Decision makers' and advisers have become much more dependent on each other and on the operation of the whole mechanism of which they form a part; and the whole process has inevitably acquired something of the nature of a ritual, in which substance and form are at times hard to distinguish. Given the vast amount of material that has to be absorbed, those who master and operate the machinery (even though they may, in a sense, be its slaves) inevitably become its stout defenders against any criticism, and a new orthodoxy is born, no less potent than that, based on a much more meagre agenda of state action and on quite different relations and procedures between thinkers and actors, which dominated economic thought and policy for so long, and seems for the moment to do so again. This self-consciousness, in the first place of its own novelty, later of its superiority of technique is, of course, a familar phenomenon in the up-and-down of cultural tendencies. In this instance, substantive achievement was certainly also present. Not surprisingly, therefore, the New Economics, in its practical expression as macroeconomic management, acquired a good deal of self-confidence, even complacency. But this, as we shall see, has not lasted very long.

# 12

# The Age of Doubt and a New
# Counter-revolution

## *From Authority to Disaffection*

As we approach the end of the century we have enough historical perspective to look back upon its third quarter and recognize it as a halcyon period in which the New Economics enjoyed an acclaim unprecedented in its spread and intensity. Economics had itself become a remarkable growth industry. Whether as a field of academic study, as a discipline to be applied to a variety of practical activities including business, particularly when combined with training in the vastly increased numbers of schools of business management, or as a source of recruitment of expert advisers to government, economics expanded at an extraordinary rate. As we have also seen, the penetration of central policy-making by large numbers of economists, acting either as such, or having transmuted themselves into administrators, is, of all these developments, perhaps the most remarkable. In many advanced countries of the world a close alliance was created between economists, statisticians, and their hybrid offspring, the econometricians, on the one side and the bureaucracy on the other; and the relationship between this combined group and the politicians on whom rested the task of final decision became closer and more systematized.

As in all these matters where an evolution of a broad cultural nature involving subtle shifts in the relative influence of different groups in concerned, it is only after some interval of time that a major change can be seen to have occurred, even if as a result of a series of small steps, not perceived as very significant at the time at which they happened. It is interesting to compare the relationship between economists and the governmental machine (administrative and political) at the time of the great depression with the situation that existed in the fifties,[1] if one wishes to have an appreciation of the totally different manner in which economic ideas were brought to bear on those political decisions which have an economic content or an economic effect.

This is not to say that many examples cannot be found in a number of countries in the history of the last two hundred years of individual economists who for a variety of reasons had an important, and sometimes decisive, influence on major political developments. Indeed, Keynes himself, with whose name the rise of the New Economics is indissolubly linked, maintained throughout his life a close connection with many politicians and had a continuing concern with public affairs, which led him as a Treasury adviser during a number of critical periods, such as the Second World War and the immediate post-war phase, to become a direct participant in the formal processes of government.

One can, nevertheless, maintain that there is a difference in kind between, say, the early pre-war attempts exemplified by the creation in Britain of the Economic Advisory Council or in the United States in the New Deal Brains Trust round Franklin Roosevelt which drew some economists into the role of economic consultants, and the highly institutionalized pattern now existing in all developed countries. (One may add that the position in the so-called developing countries, though somewhat different in regard to the relationship between advisers and politicians – the former being often indistinguishable from the latter – still testifies to the much enhanced status of economics.) Some details of this pattern have been given in the preceding chapter. There also, the increasing emphasis in economic analysis on policy problems has been pointed out. While it would be difficult to provide a statistical measurement for the output of economists in 'pure' as distinct from 'applied' matters during the last twenty-five years, casual inspection seems to provide very strong evidence for the preponderance of the latter.

One would expect the greater involvement of very much larger numbers of economists in the policy-making machine, together with the closer relationship – often on a customer–contractor basis – of

1 Robert Skidelsky, *Politicians and the Slump* (1967), already referred to, is a fascinating account primarily of the pre-war politics of economic management, but also containing interesting sidelights on the point made above.

government with research organizations in universities and elsewhere, to lead inevitably to greater concern with problems of economic policy.

Another symptom of this development that has already been referred to – which, as one would expect, strengthens in turn the tendency which gave rise to it – is the increasing space (or time) devoted by various communications media to problems of economic policy and the underlying problems of economic analysis. Not surprisingly, the material used to fill this space (or time) is in large measure provided by the more renowned professional economists – who renown is thereby increased – who are often called upon not only to comment upon or to criticize current policy or to give their own prescriptions, but also to provide popular versions of sophisticated economic theorizing that lies behind the policy differences. None of this is wholly new: Ricardo and the post-Ricardians often appeared in the public prints, as did the founders of the Viennese school or the great American economists of the beginning of the present century. But the scale of this involvement in public debate through the daily and weekly press, the radio, and television is such that it can rightly be regarded as a difference in kind rather than degree. Certainly, the appearance for some considerable time, week in, week out, of each three of the most distinguished American academic economists in turn in a popular news magazine is indicative of a new situation.

In addition to the emergence of economists in great number in government and their much more emphatic impact on the formation of opinion by the great public at large, many of the daily practitioners in information and in opinion-forming have themselves become more expert in economic analysis as part of their craft and in relation to their daily occupation as commentators on economic policy. Economic and financial information has also been a growth industry and has attracted to itself some of the best particularly of the younger generation of economists, those who, had they not for whatever reason abandoned the academic world, would certainly have made their mark as economists *sans phrase.*

As has already been said, this process has not been confined to any one country, but with only slight differences traceable to historical factors and the general social and cultural framework, it is common to many countries. In each it helped to give rise to, and in turn was intensified by, a similar development on an international scale. The growth and proliferation of international bodies for specialized or general economic purposes is another striking feature of the period under review. As we have seen in the last chapter, a number of advances in economics, particularly in the fields of econometrics, statistics and monetary economics has been due to, or at least been stimulated by, these bodies. Here the point to emphasize is that by providing large and competitive markets for economic talent, they have greatly widened the outlets for the products of economic faculties.

In short, for at least over thirty years after the appearance of Keynes's *General Theory*, the status of economics, largely of the kind associated with his name and general approach, increased steadily until it reached a position of authority, both as a branch of social science and as a perceived tool for the better ordering of human affairs, unparalleled in its history and unequalled by any of the other of the non-physical sciences. Yet, in the latter phase of this period the authority of the views of economists begin to be doubted, to the point that uncertainty starts to creep into the pronouncements of economists themselves both about practical matters and about the limits of understanding of their whole intellectual apparatus. Certainly, any visitor from another planet going round universities, government organizations – national and international – newspaper offices or business firms in the last few years would find these doubts fairly widespread. There are some economists who would – as did an earlier, more secure generation – blame deficiencies in economic performance on the lack of strict obedience to economic 'laws' rather than on deficiencies in the laws themselves. But many contemporary economists would probably admit that notwithstanding some considerable modern achievements, a perfect congruence between economics and economic management is still a long way off.

How is this change to be explained? What factors have been responsible for this questioning of what had been a new orthodoxy and for this erosion of its authority in the world of action? If we have entered a new age of doubt in economics, what are the reasons for this and what, if any, consequences may one be able to discern for the direction of economic enquiry in the near-term future? For a proper understanding of this new phase in economics it is important to try to separate out different aspects of the new criticism and scepticism as to the forms they take, the extent to which they are in conflict with the general body of economic thought as it emerged from the Keynesian revolution, and as to their wider significance for the continuing, primarily practical, concern of the science: human betterment.

Unfortunately this separation is not easy, partly because different writers are not necessarily easily classifiable in respect of the criticism for which they are responsible. To take one example to which we shall revert: while Professor Samuelson should in one sense not be regarded as a critic at all, but rather as one, who having pushed further the frontiers of the New Economics has also consolidated it in the most complete and effective way, a study of the successive editions of his text-book shows such marked changes in the author's preoccupations as to amount almost to a revolution. A comparison of the first edition of 1948 with the twelfth is revealing – not that the author's basic ideas have changed, or his general approach, but his new edition (the penultimate one) shows by its preoccupation with anti-Keynesian views how the general landscape has changed. On the other hand, Joan Robinson, one of the most distinguished Keynesian pioneers (yet one who from the beginning has harboured certain transcendental doubts about the whole corpus of even the Keynesian form of neo-classicism), later developed a full-scale attack, not so much on Keynesianism as on the preoccupations of Keynesians and anti-Keynesians alike. Yet again, Galbraith has repeatedly struck out on new paths of enquiry without unduly worrying about the status at any moment of time of any one part of the general corpus of economics.

Nevertheless, an attempt must be made to bring some order into these diverse tendencies and the following might serve as a convenient method for analysing them. One possible way would be to distinguish between those developments away from accepted doctrine which were endogenous to the theory itself, that is imperfections in some particular theorem, giving rise to developments in new theoretical directions. While it would be possible to erect an analysis of divergent tendencies on this basis, it would not produce the most significant results from the point of view of explaining either the decline in authority of the new orthodoxy or the essential aspects of the recent critical tendencies, or yet the possible or probable future directions of economics. A comparison with the circumstances in which the Keynesian revolution itself took place may supply an interesting light. For in the twenties economics, while not commanding the authority in practical affairs which it was to do thirty years later, had also grown respectable, established and somewhat complacent. The calm was shattered by the hyperinflations after the First World War, by the great depression and the disruption of the international monetary system, and by mass unemployment and the paradox of poverty amidst plenty, which were the outstanding characteristics of the early 'thirties. It was precisely at this point that the Keynesian revolution occurred, bringing with it above all an entirely new way of looking at the economic system. It discarded the predisposition established by Adam Smith to equate the behaviour of the total economy with the conduct of the individual or the single firm or to derive policy guidance for the one from the cherished traditional precepts for the other. The purpose of this emancipation was a severely practical one (as had been that of the classical revolution a century and a half earlier): in this case, to cope with the underemployment of human and material resources.

If, therefore, we are now faced with a turning away – in different directions – from the new orthodoxy into which Keynesianism had developed, we must seek it again primarily in dissatisfaction aroused by the system's declining ability to cope with practical economic problems. We have seen that the great achievement claimed for the system of economic management evolved on the basis of macroeconomic analysis had been an ability to keep the economy 'on an even keel', that is to avoid, by and large, both underemployment and inflation, to ensure, thereby, continuing growth and to do so, again by and large, while maintaining an international economic and financial system in good order; indeed to enlarge its scope and extend its benefits. Despite the fact that a good deal of the work of Keynes and of later economists was concerned with such questions as divergences between real and money incomes, the policy implications of the new forms of economic management for purposes other than growth, high level of economic activity and absence of inflation, in particular for regulating the shares of the total product going to the different factors of production were not at all worked out. As regards policy means, the emphasis – whether justifiably derived from Keynes or not – was essentially on the fiscal weapon, that is on the annual budget and associated fiscal policies. Monetary policy was not explicitly excluded, but came for a considerable time to play a very subordinate role indeed. Moreover, since fiscal policy is more specifically 'interventionist' than the more general, 'climate-creating', monetary policy, the emphasis on fiscal policy, though it at first excluded other forms of intervention, naturally created a predisposition to seek new means in this direction.

Despite the successes in relation to the stated policy objectives which economic management had to its credit, disappointment began to be felt, certainly by the middle sixties. In Britain, for example, where next to the United States new economic management had been practised with increasing virtuosity there was also increasing awareness of the persistence of certain deficiencies in economic performance. Sluggish growth in periods of markedly rising world trade and fast increasing gross national products in her main competitors, together with recurring balance of payments crises giving rise to recurring bouts of stimulation and restraint – the tools of economic management proving reasonably efficaceous in producing alternating 'stop and go', but not sustained, rising levels of economic activity – began to shake belief in the adequacy of demand management. In the United States, too, demand management, mainly by fiscal means proved to be partially successful only. Here, the limits on total success were further narrowed by the sluggishness with which policy responded to diagnosis and prescription, a sluggishness due to a large extent to constitutional and political lags. Here, after an exceptionally prolonged period of absence of inflation, the conflict between continued stability and full employment showed itself very sharply to be resolved only, as it had been, or was to be, in other countries, by simultaneous unemployment and inflation, together with the unprecedented appearance of a severe balance of payments problem.

It is out of experiences such as these that a turning away from the New Economics had its origins. The disenchantment took various forms. First (not necessarily chronologically) it was the excessive reliance on fiscal policy which was attacked and a full-scale 'monetarist' counter-revolution was mounted. On the other hand, the apparent limitations of demand management led some to seek more direct intervention to stimulate employment either in total or in certain directions leading to various forms of industrial or regional policy designed to provide sticks and carrots for expansion or contraction. This included government attitudes to industrial structure, i.e. to mergers, monopoly situations and the like. The recurrence or persistence of inflationary pressure also stimulated a search for more direct measures of influencing price and wage determination.

In the international sphere, too, the inadequacy of existing forms of demand management coupled with established methods of inter-national co-operation, seemed to be demonstrated by the appearance or persistence of balance of payments and exchange problems. We have seen that it was one of the greatest achievements of Keynes himself and of his school to have been largely responsible for creating the 'Bretton Woods' post-war international financial mechanism. Aided by additional machinery of an *ad hoc* character, such as the Marshall Plan, it had certainly contributed to stimulating and maintaining a high rate of growth of world trade and to facilitate the development of highly refined and effective international money and capital markets. But the easy assumption that demand management could not only reconcile the objectives of growth, stability and high employment but also effect the 'adjustment process' designed to keep the domestic economy in step with the evolution of the international system – as demonstrated by the absence of severe balance of payments problems – could not be justified in the British case and very soon became untenable in regard to other economies, too. Here, then, was another area in which doubt and disaffection were to set in – though as we shall see this involved not necessarily a departure from Keynes, but a reliance on some features, including earlier ones, of his own thinking.

Thus we shall need to examine in the following sections of this chapter, the monetarist counter-revolution, the various new controversies on the international financial system, the suggestion for more direct intervention either into industrial structure or into price and wage determination.

These are not, however, the only areas in which doubt is evident. They all lie, in a sense, within the system. Many of the criticisms to be heard today go beyond these. They can be broadly classified as structural and sociological. The changes in industrial structure together with the new forms of corporate finance and their relation to the industrial process as such have led to new concern with an area of enquiry last cultivated by Veblen. Partly as a result of technological developments new problems have also arisen, such as pollution and other inroads into an acceptable environment including urban congestion and the like. These have stimulated questions about the proper content of economic growth as such. The general malaise that pervades modern society which is perhaps most acutely seen in the difficulties of communication on these matters between the younger and older generations has led to a revived interest in those theories which are primarily concerned with the relation between the individual and society in regard to the economic process. From this stems a revived interest in Marx, though not so much in the economics of Marxism as in the philosophical and sociological ideas of Marx, the young Hegelian. And, finally doubt has been expressed whether economics as a whole is concerned with the right problems.

## Money and the International Nexus

It seems appropriate to link in this section those developments which tended to lead macroeconomic management away from primary reliance on fiscal means with other recent developments concerned mainly with the functioning of the international financial system. This link is not to be seen as reflecting a similarity in the character of these two tendencies as essentially anti-Keynesian counter-revolutions. In so far as Keynes is identified with the post-war financial system (and therefore liable to criticism if this system is thought not to be working perfectly) this is due to his practical involvement in the negotiation of the agreements that shaped the post-war world in this regard. The serious fissures in this system from the mid sixties onwards, leading to near-collapse at the beginning of the seventies, cannot be linked logically with Keynes's own theoretical views in this field, which were different from the practical compromises to which they had to be subordinated in the course of what were highly political negotiations. A search of Keynes's pre-war writings, particularly the *Treatise on Money*, shows many ideas which would certainly have ranged Keynes today with the critics of the system as it has operated recently.

The link, therefore, is rather to be found, first in the fact that many of those who have led the monetarist counter-revolution against fiscal macroeconomic management have also expressed strong views on the proper organization of the international financial system and strong criticism of its present structure. This is not surprising since the smooth functioning of any international economic and financial order requires the maintenance of a certain congruence between fluctuations in a country's economy and that country's position internationally. Consequently both the objectives and the means of economic management on the one hand and the achievement of international balance and the means by which it is achieved on the other, are necessarily closely linked.

The second aspect which makes such a link convenient lies at a deeper level. While the revived emphasis on monetary policy and opposition to fiscal management has taken many forms, what is common to all of them, and most clearly to be seen in the writings of its most distinguished exponent, Professor Milton Friedman, is a basic difference with Keynes over the agenda of the State. Most, if not all, monetarists would, for example, not subscribe to Keynes's statements on these matters in *The End of Laissez Faire*. The reliance on monetary policy stems, in a larger sense, from a desire, again most clearly in Friedman's formulation, to reduce the possibilities of specific intervention by the 'Authority' by introducing a high degree of automatic regulation of those aspects of the social environment which determine fundamentally the operation of the economy. Its protagonists regard such automatism as superior to the wisdom likely to be shown by deliberate human action.

Similarly, in the international sphere many critics of the post-war system would revert to a higher degree of automatism. Here again, the prescription how this is to be achieved varies. In the most consistently worked-out and most cogently argued form, that of Professor Friedman, it takes the form of advocacy of completely flexible exchange rates formed, like any other price, by the free play of the market.[1] As we shall see, other non-interventionists have taken a different view and have argued in favour of a more rigid link of exchange parities with gold; while some others who have been in favour of more flexible exchange rates, paradoxically perhaps, have as a strong bias in favour of intervention in domestic policy drawing a good deal of their inspiration from Keynes. Nevertheless, the pure monetarist doctrine has a particular affinity as far as international aspects are concerned with the argument for floating exchange rates.

What then is the monetarist case, both negatively as an attack on the efficacy of fiscal macroeconomic management, and positively as regards its own prescription for achieving high employment, growth, and absence of inflation?[2] While there are numerous statements by Professor Friedman and other members of the Chicago School, the clearest, simplest, and shortest is to be found in Friedman's *The Counter-Revolution in Monetary Theory*.[3] The essential features of the

[1] M. Friedman: 'The Case for Flexible Exchange Rates' in *Essays in Positive Economics* (1953). Earlier, Friedman had himself pointed out the connection between his views on domestic and international policy: 'A Monetary and Fiscal Framework for Economic Stability' in *American Economic Review* (June 1948).

[2] Professor Harry G. Johnson, himself a member of the Chicago School, has written a highly interesting analysis, both of the Keynesian Revolution and of the Monetarist Counter-Revolution, using arguments not incompatible with those presented here but going much further in developing a theory of how revolutions and counter-revolutions in these ideas arise: Johnson: 'The Keynesian Revolution and the Monetarist Counter Revolution', *Encounter* (April 1971).

[3] A lecture delivered at the University of London and published by the Institute of Economic Affairs in 1970. Of the many earlier and more elaborate statements may be mentioned: Don Patinkin, *Money, Interest and Prices* (1956); M. Friedman and W. W.

views there presented are as follows. The basis of the present monetarist school is the quantity theory of money, a theorem which relates prices and money and which has had a long history, particularly in Anglo-Saxon economic thinking, a number of pre-Smithian economists notably David Hume, being the principal early exponents. Among modern economists, as Professor Friedman rightly claims, Irving Fisher must be regarded as its chief protagonist. In the form in which he expounded it, it can be said to have dominated that segment of economic thought, including to a considerable degree the thinking of Keynes himself, up to the later phases of the Great Depression. Its simplest statement is the traditional equation $MV = PT$, that is the amount of money in circulation multiplied by its velocity of circulation equals the general level of prices multiplied by the volume of trade (or better, the number of transactions). It follows that the general level of prices must always be inversely related to trade and directly related to the amount of money and to its velocity. The latter was generally taken to be very stable or at least influenced independently of the other terms; thus the main determinant of the price level could be taken to be the amount of money, that is to say something dependent on the operations of the monetary authorities. It followed that inflation or deflation were essentially monetary phenomena, the results of particular monetary policies.

Keynes, certainly in his early writings, did not dispute the fundamental relationship expressed in the quantity theory. He did, however, argue that the velocity of circulation was not a constant or independent variable but that it would readily adapt itself, rising or falling in different circumstances to compensate for either an absence of change in the amount of money or of changes in opposite directions, or else to intensify the changes in one or the other direction.

Furthermore, in his 'fundamental equations' in the *Treatise on Money*, Keynes had expressed the necessity of an equilibrium between savings and investment. If this equilibrium is to be achieved – and this is a condition of price stability – the total amount of money is no longer adequate as a critical concept, but rather the uses to which streams of

---

Heller, *Monetary versus Fiscal Policy* (1968) an account of a debate at New York University; the series of essays in Friedman, *The Optimum Quantity of Money* (1969) and the monumental effort to give a historical foundation to the theory, in M. Friedman and A. J. Schwartz, *Monetary History of the United States 1867–1960* (1963). For an early statement of a monetarist view by an author who has had much influence in shaping the views of Professor Friedman, see H. C. Simons, *Economic Policy for a Free Society* (1948).

money of different kinds are put. In particular, what is important is that part of the use of money which is not directly related to current income, namely private and public investment as distinct from consumption expenditure. It is indeed this line of argument which led directly on to the multiplier and acceleration principle concepts and to the other ideas of the *General Theory* for explaining fluctuations in the general level of economic activity.

It is probably fair on the part of the monetarists to claim that some post-Keynesians in applying these concepts to the problems of policy were guilty of an excessive reliance on fiscal policy. The exaggerated 'cheap money' policies of certain post-war governments which did contribute to the generation of inflationary pressures, while they can hardly be taken as evidence that monetary policy had come to be regarded as being of no importance, do show that monetary policy was subordinated to other policies, which may be broadly described as fiscal. Nevertheless, though the combined effects of the policies that were then followed was certainly to make the transition from war to peace infinitely smoother and more conducive to recovery and subsequent advance than had been the case after World War I (thereby avoiding the likelihood of some very menacing social and political developments), it can be argued that the presumption tended to be that monetary policy had little autonomous influence and could be made to fit into any pattern of what was essentially fiscal policy management. This was especially evident to the extent that government financing requirements, mainly in consequence of an expansionary fiscal policy, predisposed the authorities to open market operations designed to keep interest rates low; a situation which certainly existed both in the United States and Britain in the immediate post-war years.

The monetarists also argue that it is not only wrong to neglect the role of monetary policy, but that it is also wrong to assign too effective a role to fiscal policy. In this connection the slowness of the effect of the tax cut introduced by President Kennedy is often cited. Here the monetarists are, no doubt, on much weaker ground in that they tend to ignore the political rigidities, aggravated in this instance by the particular difficulties of a practical nature resulting from constitutional factors, which made action at the right moment impossible. Be that as it may, as a result of disappointments with the efficacy of economic management in either quickly mobilizing under-utilized resources or alternatively preventing inflationary pressures from arising or persisting, the monetarists succeeded first in the United States and, later, in

Britain in influencing opinion in favour of greater reliance on monetary means. In the process, the theoretical and statistical apparatus was much refined and earlier, cruder, methods of defining and measuring changes – particularly increases – in money supply were replaced by more sophisticated concepts, such as Domestic Credit Expansion.

On the other hand, some 'fiscalists' at least have tended to refuse to admit that monetary policy can make any significant impact on the total level of economic activity, or excercise any autonomous influence in the balancing of high activity versus inflation; perhaps, in the limit, even to deny it any contributory influence alongside other policy means. Needless to say both in relation to demand management and in the narrower sphere of management of money and capital markets through interest rate and open market policy, there have been numerous episodes in recent years in many countries which could be cited in support of these views as effectively as they could for the purposes of the monetarists.

In a more specialized study of monetary theory it would be appropriate to pursue further the intricacies of these arguments and the work of a number of economists who have attempted, often successfully, to integrate the two approaches at the theoretical level. What is significant for our theme here is the fact that for the purposes of economic policy, first one school of thought and then the other, over-simplified the argument and put one-sided and excessive emphasis either on the real (and psychological) changes or on the changes in money and credit conditions deliberately produced by the monetary authorities not merely to explain fluctuations in economic activity, but above all, to prescribe remedies to cure unwelcome ones.

For a time, though not for very long, it seemed as if this was to become another celebrated *Dogmenstreit* such as had occurred from time to time in the history of economic, as indeed of other, ideas. The reasons are not far to seek: the subject matter could not have been more important, given that the prosperity of millions of people depended on correct analysis and practice; and there was the further fact that their achievement seemed continuously to escape the grasp of those in charge except for very brief moments. Professor Johnson[1] has given additional reasons why this argument should have become as fierce as it did.

The debate between the two sides which has been particularly

1 In the Richard Ely lecture, reprinted in *Encounter*, referred to on p. 513.

intense in the last twenty-five years is now showing some signs of calming down (though not as yet of disappearing altogether). It may, therefore be less hazardous than it might have been in the very recent past, to attempt to arrive at a balanced view.

It is clear that, as so often happens in the excitement of debate, both sides have tended to state their views in exaggerated fashion: thus 'money does not matter' is said to be the slogan of the fiscalists,[1] while 'inflation is a purely monetary phenomenon' is regarded as the quintessence of the monetarist belief. Equally, when challenged, both sides tend to introduce special qualifications or to seek refuge in semantics by defining their terms in such a manner as to lead inevitably to their (tautological) conclusions. Much fuel is also added to the flames by argument over historical or statistical evidence. On the whole, the fiscalists or neo-Keynesians have generally shown a greater willingness to compromise than have the monetarists. They admit that sole reliance on fiscal policy has been proved inadequate not only in relation to the contribution which monetary policy might have been expected to make, but also in relation to other policies which need to be brought into play (on this, more in the next section). Though they have insisted on the likelihood of monetary changes following rather than causing other, such as fiscal, changes, they have otherwise tended to be less intransigent than their opponents.[2]

The monetarists, particularly those to be found in central as well as some commercial banking circles, have generally been more extreme in their views, resorting to formulations which assign a positive potency to money almost reminiscent of the views held by some bullionists. These have, therefore, in their practical policy recommendations been inclined to urge greater use of monetary policy, relying on delicately balanced changes in the quantity of money to produce the desired stabilization of the economy. In the hands of its master, however, the conclusion drawn from the monetarist analysis is rather different. Professor Freidman does not believe in 'fine tuning', not even by monetary policy means. While continuing to insist that 'inflation' is always and everywhere a monetary phenomenon, he also believes that the relation between money, prices and output is not (or not yet)

[1] A possibly not unreasonable inference from the analysis contained in the 1959 Radcliffe Committee Report (which should be compared with the 1931 report of the Macmillan Committee).

[2] See the debate between Firedman and Kaldor in *Lloyds Bank Review* (July and October 1970) as well as that between Heller and Friedman already referred to.

sufficiently understood to make it possible to predict the precise effects of any particular measure, and that it is, therefore, hazardous to entrust the monetary authorities with the task of keeping the economy on an even keel. He, therefore, concludes against discretionary monetary policy altogether and in favour of a moderate, but steady rate of growth of the money supply as the contribution which monetary policy can make that it most likely to be fruitful for stability.

It seems that any attempt to substitute something like the Fried-manite prescription, let alone the 'fine tuning' by exclusively monetary means has seen its most propitious moment come and go. Given the general disenchantment with economic management as practised in recent years it is highly unlikely that monetarism will suddenly come to be regarded as the panacea. For the debate between the monetarists and the fiscalists must be regarded as merely one symptom, and a limited one at that, of the more general malaise in economic policy when viewed, as we shall view it in the next section, as an attempt to find means for reconciling the four different objectives of economic policy: full employment, growth, absence of inflation and a smoothly functioning international financial system. The quarrel between the fiscal and monetary views merited some mention here not only because it is of significance as a major economic debate of the sixties and seventies in its own right. It also illustrates to some degree certain deep-seated differences of approach to the problems of the economy as a whole between 'interventionists' and 'expansionists' on the one hand as against 'non-interventionists' and 'deflationists' on the other, of which, even though the major debate may now be closing down, some residue can still be found here and there in the differing attitudes of Treasuries (and Finance Ministers) and Central Bankers to specific situations.

On the other hand, it would be quite wrong to accept the facile current labelling of this debate as 'revolution' and 'counter-revolution'; and not only because this now appears to have been a rather short-lived episode in the argument over current economic policy. One cannot seriously equate the onslaught of the monetarists with the truly path-breaking departure from decades (almost centur-ies) of old thinking about economic matters which was associated with the name of Keynes in the late thirties. The monetarists have nothing remotely as important to offer to economic thinking as Keynes's rediscovery that the truth of Adam Smith, that what is prudent in the conduct of the single family cannot fail to be prudent in the conduct of a nation, may only very rarely be the most significant truth. Compared with this central revolutionary change in the approach to the economy – in which the precise role to be assigned to particular fiscal and other policies is not the crucial element – the monetarist debate must be judged as peripheral.[1]

Before we turn to the more general problem of the conflict between the different objectives of economic policy and the means for achieving them of which the monetarist *versus* fiscal argument is only one, a little more needs to be said about the considerable preoccupation of many economists in recent years with the functioning of the international financial system. This is also a highly specialized subject and it would be inappropriate to give it extended treatment here. Some of the reasons for referring to it have already been mentioned. Moreover, like the monetarist debate as such it brings echoes of the great bullionist-currency schools controversy of the early nineteenth century; and it exhibits both dilemmas of economic policy and attitudes of different economists to them which are illuminating in the general context of the current confusion in economic thinking.

The debate concerns a number of interrelated yet distinct issues. These include the nature of the reserves to be maintained by individual countries for the purpose of ultimate settlement of international payments imbalances; combined with this, the process by which the growth of international liquidity – that is the growth in the total of these reserves – thought to be required by the general increase in economic activity and world trade is to be assured; the process by which the domestic economy is to adjust to fluctuations in the international payments situation of a country; and what role international organization is to play in this complex of issues.

The answer which was given to these questions at the end of World War II in the international agreements reached at Bretton Woods was very briefly as follows. Reserve assets were to consist of a mixed package of gold, certain so-called key currencies, primarily the dollar and sterling, and certain credit facilities of which countries could avail

---

1 Professor Johnson in the previously referred to article (see p. 515) judges that the Keynesians chose a politically better issue – unemployment – than the monetarists – inflation – on which to stand. This is, no doubt, true, since, whether willed or not and avowed or not, the fiscal policy emphasis has tended to go together with fear of unemployment and monetary policy emphasis with fear of inflation. The issue goes, however, even deeper than this.

themselves, unconditionally or under certain conditions, in the International Monetary Fund. No clear answer was at first given to the second question, no doubt because the possibility of a deficiency of total world liquidity was not thought sufficiently serious, or the gravity of the problem that would arise if there were to be such a deficiency, appreciated. As for the third question, here again no systematic answer was provided. The classic 'mechanism', by which, under a full gold standard, payments deficits (and surpluses) led to reserve/gold losses (or inflows) which automatically brought about contraction (or expansion) in the money supply and increases (or decreases) in interest rates, thereby altering relative price levels until international payments balance was restored, was clearly inappropriate to the situation existing after the war. The immediate post-war imbalances were so great that any attempt to remove them by these means would have produced violent swings in domestic policies with incalculable social and political repercussions. Moreover, the Keynesian 'revolution' had taken place and had both strengthened the desire for autonomous domestic economic policy and the possibility of conducting it by fiscal means. The very institution of, on the one hand, credit facilities through the IMF and, on the other, the careful articulation of conditions under which various restrictions on international transactions were or were not to be tolerated, testify to the explicit determination to cut away such automatic link between domestic policy and international balance and substitute for it machinery which, while preserving a relationship between the two, would be subject to human intervention through international machinery operating under an international code.

On the final point a compromise was reached. Under a classic mechanism, so long as countries were prepared to accept it, they could be said to have surrendered a part of their sovereignty, that is their autonomy to influence the domestic price level, and domestic economic activity, to the virtually automatic operation of certain international rules. Under the new system, they were preparing similarly to surrender a part of their sovereignty but to a much more complex set of rules which were subject to interpretation, application and enforcement by an international agency of which they were themselves a part. Thus the surrender was on the one hand more deliberate and explicit – because less automatic – yet, in intention at least, less far-reaching and capable of allowing greater scope for domestic action. On the other hand, the reform did not go so far – as Keynes would have wished – as to approximate the international financial system much more closely to a national one by making the IMF into an international central bank, operating as a lender of last resort and controlling credit conditions generally.

During its first twenty-five years this system operated with varying degrees of success and often only as a result of the use, deliberately or fortuitously, of auxiliary motors. The premature and quickly abandoned attempt to introduce convertibility of sterling; the steadily growing role of the dollar as the principal reserve currency and the periodic devaluation of a number of currencies, including particularly sterling, the secondary reserve currency, in terms of the dollar; the Marshall Plan and other forms of aid which sustained world liquidity; the toleration for perhaps longer periods than would have been justified on a strict interpretation of the post-war international codes of restrictive and discriminatory trade practices; the various, finally successful, attempts to regulate the use of war-time sterling balances: all these were among the many features of the post-war period which must be taken into account in judging the efficiency of the Bretton Woods system. Throughout the period, the literature of the subject, too voluminous to be mentioned here in any detail, gives evidence of an undercurrent of dissatisfaction, a sort of constant rumbling of criticism, not surprising in view both of the somewhat mixed nature of the solutions for the four basic problems which the system provided and its questionable strength in absorbing major critical developments.

This undercurrent of controversy covered all the major issues: the nature of reserves and the adequacy of liquidity, the role of the IMF and the adjustment process, or more generally the extent to which freedom of action in regard to domestic policy could be preserved despite membership of the international system. An interesting feature of this continuous debate is the extent to which it was carried on not only by academic economists, but also by politicians, officials and practical men engaged in banking and other business enterprises. Another is the extent to which it was pursued in public. Although not altogether unknown before (for example during the Napoleonic war and post-war periods, or during the nineteen-twenties when in and around the League of Nations a good deal of public discussion took place), the scale on which these very difficult matters were now debated in national and international, official, semi-official, and academic fora, often by mixed groups of officials, academics and bankers, and to a very considerable extent with the public having access to the discussions, was truly unprecedented.[1]

It received yet further stimulus when in the sixties the American balance of payments began to show a series of growing and massive deficits which, while they enabled the world to enjoy still further accretions of liquidity (which was also being enhanced by the creation of additional facilities in the IMF, the Special Drawing Rights), made even more acute than hitherto the dilemma posed by the objectives of national policy within a frame work of international equilibrium. Accordingly, the wide divergence of views became even more marked than it had been. The attitude to gold, for example, became highly polarized with advocacy of early complete demonetization being opposed by pressure for a substantial appreciation of gold in monetary reserves (in terms of all currencies, but especially in terms of the major reserve currency) which would, of course, not only have consolidated the position of gold as a reserve asset but greatly enhanced its importance.

On the other side, the general doubt about the efficacy of macro-economic management as practised for a generation became bound up with the more specific question of the extent to which it should be guided by criteria derived from the closeness of the international nexus, that is to say, being primarily directed to achieving a certain balance of payments result, as it had been for so long, particularly in Britain. From this sprang renewed questioning of the value of a régime of relatively fixed exchange parties – the most obvious element of the existing international financial mechanism. Advocacy of more flexible – or, in the limit, freely floating – exchange rates became more fashionable, though, as already indicated, not only on the part of those who wanted greater freedom to 'steer' the domestic economy according to criteria that might conflict with the international ones. Since all this coincided with, first, the beginnings and, later, a strong upsurge of regionalist tendencies in international economic affairs, notably in Europe, it is not surprising that the debate also became involved in this aspect.

It is not possible to pursue these problems further here. It must, however, be emphasized that they have assumed an importance both in the ordering of practical affairs and in the intellectual preoccupations of economists, the like of which has not been seen for one hundred

---

1 It is also significant that very much of the literature was of a 'collective' kind, that is, the product of official or unofficial groups.

and fifty years or more. The debate of Ricardo's day has some similarity with that of to-day primarily through the fact that the classical economists who were engaged in it were as concerned as are most of those to-day to see the problem in the context of the general behaviour of the economy as a whole. On the other hand, the international aspect was not nearly so acute, given the overwhelming position of Britain in world commerce and finance and witness also the fact that the debate was virtually entirely British.[1] Perhaps the most significant difference is that at the beginning of the last century, notwithstanding the sharpness of the debate, there can be no suggestion that it was a symptom of a more general doubt about the corpus of economic thought. On the contrary, classical political economy was about to enter upon a period of complete acceptance and unquestioned authority. Today, uncertainty about the proper manner in which to construct and operate the international monetary system is a particularly striking symptom not only of the erosion of long-accepted patterns of national and international economic policy, but also of a significant degree of lack of acceptance of the received body of economic doctrine.

## Employment and Inflation

We have seen that probably the most striking feature of the new emphasis in economic thinking after the end of World War II was the open acknowledgement in a number of countries – most explicitly in the United States and Great Britain – of the state's duty to maintain a high level of economic activity: more succinctly, of employment. This was a truly staggering change, not only because it radically redefined the scope of the state's responsibility in relation to the play of market forces, but also because it meant acknowledging a new, principal, preoccupation of policy-makers and economists. When one remembers that barely twenty years had gone by since the tremendous effort of the mid-twenties to conquer inflation and restore internal and international financial stability and that this was accomplished by the only means then available, or at least acceptable, that is by a classic process of deflation, the magnitude of the change can be truly appreciated. That the methods then employed led to depression and massive

1 See J. A. Schumpeter, *History of Economic Analysis* (1963), p. 689.

unemployment with its intolerable social and political concomitants undoubtedly caused them to be discredited, created the seedbed for the ideas of the 'New Economics', and produced the violent swing in concern from inflation to employment.

However, it would be wrong to suppose that inflation was totally forgotten. Among the more conservative economic thinkers, particularly among one section of monetary economists, warning voices continued to be raised throughout the earlier, no less than the later, post-war years. Even in pronouncements in which the emphasis was on the need to maintain full employment, for example, in some British White Papers, such as the 'Economic Surveys' of the period, or the Annual Economic Reports of the American President, the need 'to guard against inflationary tendencies' or 'to maintain internal financial stability' was almost invariably mentioned alongside the need to ensure full employment. These, however, tended to be regarded as little more than ritual incantations, and were perhaps so regarded even by some at least of their authors.

Here and there, more valid signs that inflation as the alternative danger to unemployment was still regarded as real, can be discerned. In some ways the most significant instance, since it was neither the exclusive work of a school of theoretical economists nor of alarmist bankers, is an early post-war report on *Internal Financial Stability* of a working party set up by the Organization for European Economic Co-operation, a body devoted explicitly to fostering high levels of trade and of economic activity. In general, however, the dilemma (or at least apparent dilemma) with which the world was later to become so familiar, of either having full employment or of being spared inflation, was definitely not at the centre of the stage. Apart from the main reasons for this state of affairs which have already been referred to, there were certain contributory factors at work. The most important of these was the fact that for many countries, in particular for all the developed countries of Western Europe, there was another, and more urgent dilemma that had to be faced; that between full employment and international payments balance.

This can be seen particularly clearly in the post-war history of Britain where for many years the limiting factor to the maintenance of full employment and economic growth was a deteriorating balance of payments (or at least the recurrent fear of it) which from time to time put a severe strain on inadequate reserves and led to the application of the brake at regular intervals. This stop-go cycle of the economy, which became so characteristic of the British economy during virtually the whole of this twenty-five year phase, was not exactly paralleled elsewhere in Western Europe. There, the combination of Marshall Aid, the size of monetary reserves, periodic devaluations, a higher threshold of political and social tolerance of unemployment, and perhaps a general social background, including possibly the effect of war, occupation, defeat, producing a pattern of resource allocation more conductive to growth, made the payments equilibrium-employment dilemma less acute. In a number of countries, too, special problems added a complicating factor: underdevelopment of certain regions, such as the Italian south, or the special position of agriculture, as in parts of Germany and France. At the same time, in a number of these countries, perhaps because the memory of the great inter-war inflations was still very intense, the maintenance of internal financial stability was a fairly constant factor in policy objectives, thus producing less dramatic swings in the preoccupations of policy-makers.

In the United States, though for somewhat different reasons, the change in attitude also followed a rather different path, and for a number of years neither the international balance nor the avoidance of inflation can be said to have posed a major problem of principle in relation to the objective of securing full employment. It is rather fluctuations in the vigour with which macroeconomic management was applied and in the timing of specific measures to this end that dominated the scene in the first two post-war decades.

From the point of view of broad intellectual history, however, the picture throughout the Western world is not dissimilar. It is one of a certain degree of complacency not only, as we have already seen, in regard to the potency of economic management itself, but also in relation to the possibility of maintaining employment without engendering inflationary pressures. As always in these matters, the change of emphasis is not easy to time, for, as we have seen, concern over price stability was felt from time to time even when the emphasis was strongly on full employment; and even at the beginning of the fifties practical attempts to contain the wage/price spiral were not absent. Nevertheless, one can say that as far as the general climate of opinion is concerned, it begins to show a marked change from the early sixties, though with slight differences in timing in different countries, as well as in the form which the change took. From that period onwards we can date not only a slow loss of faith in macroeconomic management but also a growing pressure for greater use of monetary policy, a natural concomitant of the then growing fear of inflation.

From the point of view of the evolution of economic thinking proper, the change in emphasis was not so marked. Even earlier a more decided attempt was made to define inflation, to discriminate between different types of inflation, both as to origin and consequences, and to distinguish between different degrees of inflation according to certain levels of tolerance related to the character and speed of spread of its repercussions. The purpose of these refinements from earlier, simpler formulations, essentially of the quantity theory of money type, was to provide a more effective analytical apparatus from which policy prescriptions could be derived.

Much of this work goes back to Keynes's pattern in the *Treatise on Money* which distinguished between 'income inflation' and 'profit inflation' as well as to his attempt and that of some of his contemporaries to analyse wage pressures in terms of demands for real as against money wages.

Two sets of concepts emerged from this work which still play a very important part in economic analysis in so far as it is directly related to policy-making: the notion of the 'full-employment' budget surplus or deficit (as indeed, of the 'full-employment' balance of payments surplus or deficit) which we have already met in our discussion of post-Keynesian economics, and the distinction between 'cost-push' and 'demand-pull' inflation.

It is the latter, in particular, which is of considerable importance in current debate. Interest in both types of inflation was first aroused owing to concern with the relationship between inflation and growth. As long ago as 1922, Dennis Robertson had examined the case for a steady, a falling, and a 'gently rising' price level and had concluded that the latter 'will in fact produce the best attainable results, not only for them' (the controllers of industry whose energies and activities will be stimulated) 'but for the community as a whole':[1] and periodically thereafter, the pros and cons of different price movements in relation to growth have been debated.[2]

1 D. H. Robertson, *Money* (1922), p. 125. This passage survived a number of revised editions, 1924, 1928, 1932, though it would be wrong to forget that the author thought primarily in terms of a 'wink at a little judicious use of the money-pump, while considering it right to stick fairly closely to the obvious decision to keep the price-level stable'.

2 For a useful discussion see N. Kaldor, 'Economic Growth and the Problem of

More recently, the relationship has tended to be studied more in terms of the movement of prices and/or wages starting from a position in which the aggregate quantity of resources available (which is fixed at any one moment of time as is their productivity) is fully employed. If, in this situation, total demand whether through excessive government spending (as in a war or through an over-ambitious social programme), or through exaggerated expectations of future profits by entrepreneurs leading to an excess of private investment, or through a sudden upsurge of private consumption, nurtured perhaps by fear of future price increases, exceeds the total output of the fully employed resources, then prices will risé: they will be pulled up by the excess demand. Wherever this excess demand may first appear the upward pull on prices which it generates will eventually spread through the whole economy. By definition, i.e. through the assumption of full employment of resources, this price rise is not self-correcting, since it cannot engender increased supplies; it can only be brought to an end by a reduction of demand. This is, of course, looking at the economy as a whole and over a sufficient period of time to allow the full effects of excess demand to percolate right through. In the meantime, that is before this state of affairs has been completely attained, individual outputs can be increased through the 'bidding away' of materials, facilities and, above all labour, by some sectors of the economy which, rightly or wrongly, consider themselves better able to offer the higher prices and wages required to allow them to expand their own production. Indeed, as a rule in the course of a demand-pull inflation as just described, wages tend to rise faster than prices in general, thus resulting in an increase in real wages.

To understand the parallel concept of a cost-push inflation, we start from a situation of general price stability rather than full employment and suppose wages in some sector or sectors to be pushed up, for example, as a result of the pressure of an exceptionally strong trade union organization. This will lead to an increase in some prices as the employers at first affected pass on their increased costs. As this movement gathers momentum and as the price increases become more general, it is highly likely that pressure for increased wages to cope with – and indeed to overtake or often to anticipate price rises – will become general.

---

Inflation', *Economica*, August and November 1959, reprinted in *Essays on Economic Policy* (1969), vol. 1. pp. 166–99.

It is not necessary for our purpose to pursue further the paths which either a cost-push or demand-pull engendered inflation will take or their effects on productivity, income distribution and the like. What is important, is to note the debates to which these analyses have given rise among economists as far as they relate particularly to employment and inflation and also as far as the corresponding policy considerations are concerned; for it is these which do not remain confined to economists and have therefore the most profound effect in fashioning both public opinion and the different views of policy-makers.

The earliest of the modern expositions of this subject was given by a French economist, later to become particularly distinguished in the monetary field and, in that, by his rigorous advocacy of a strict monetary policy and continued substantial reliance on gold, M. Jacques Rueff. In 1925 he published tables and graphs showing a close correlation of movements of real wages and unemployment in the years 1919 to 1925; and he supplemented these by further studies published in the *Revue d'Economie Politique* in 1931. These studies were made to enjoy exceptional publicity both in timing and method by being given to the English public by Sir Josiah Stamp (later Lord Stamp) in two articles published in *The Times* at the height of the slump.[1] The theory expounded in these articles was first that there was an extremely close correlation between real wages and unemployment. The conclusion was drawn that flexibility of wages was an essential condition for the avoidance of persistent unemployment. In the second place, it was argued that the failure of wages to decline from 1923 onwards despite the persistence of high unemployment, could be explained by the existence of unemployment benefit which put a floor under wages and thus prevented a decline in unemployment to set in once wages had fallen low enough. While it would be wrong to put too much weight on this particular theory of this particular author, the general point of view which it expressed was very much in tune with widely held opinions at the time on the proper methods to be employed to counter the depression. In fact, a reduction in unemployment benefit was included in the total programme for reductions in public expenditure proposed by the 'May' Committee and adopted by the British 'National' Government a few months after the appearance of these articles.[2]

1 Sir Josiah Stamp, 'Work and Wages', *The Times*, 11 and 12 June 1931.
2 For a handsome acknowledgement of the error of this policy see Lord Robbins, *Autobiography of an Economist* (1971), pp. 152–5.

In the light of both the actual events as well as the history of ideas in the twenty-five years that followed the traumatic experience of the Great Depression, it is not surprising that this group of ideas, at least in their original formulation, remained largely forgotten. It was not until 1958 that a new and rather different attempt was made to link wage and price movements with levels of employment, in the so-called Phillips curve.[1] It is no exaggeration to say that the relationship sought to be established by Phillips has been one of the central points in the economic literature of recent years in so far as it relates to problems of economic policy. Many modification and reformulations have been applied to it in the light of experience but as it deals with one of the most crucial issues of present-day applied economics, it is worth while briefly to state the basic concept and the conclusions first derived from it.

The simple schema of demand-pull or cost-push inflation sketched out above clearly does not correspond to situations likely to be met in reality save in most exceptional circumstances. If demand-pull occurred exactly in correspondence with the theoretical pattern, the attainment of the macroeconomic objective of 'keeping the economy on an even keel' which we considered in the preceding chapter would be greatly simplified. There would still be room for differences of view on the correct 'mix' and timing of fiscal and monetary policy; but, broadly speaking the chances of successful management of the economy to produce *reasonably* full employment with *reasonable* price stability would be encouraging. But the complete flexibility of wages in relation to employment or the complete flexibility of prices in perfectly competitive markets are idealized conditions which do not exist in reality. Similarly, in the conditions postulated in a pure cost-push inflation, namely an increase in wages in excess of any increase in productivity, regardless of any changes in demand, there will inevitably be an erosion of employment unless steps are taken to increase demand by fiscal or monetary means so as to keep pace with a continuing inflation whose first cause lies in the 'independent' upward movement of wages. Superficial inspection, let alone detailed statistical investigation[2] shows

1 A. W. Phillips, 'The Relation Between Unemployment and the Rate of Change of Money Wage Rates in the United Kingdom 1861–1957', *Economica*, November 1958.
2 A very voluminous literature exists from which a few early examples may be cited: J. C. R. Dow, *The Management of the British Economy 1945–1960* (1964), G. D. N. Worswick (ed.), *The British Economy 1945–50* (1952); G. D. N. Worswick and P. H. Ady (eds.) *The British Economy in the 1950s* (1962).

that real conditions tend to be somewhere between the two theoretical extremes and that the most likely situation is one in which it is not easy always to disentangle the influences stemming from the side of demand from those stemming from the side of cost and where, over time, secondary movements are generated from the opposite side of the original ones.

What Phillips tried to do was to show, on the basis of considerable statistical data over a long time-span, what the quantitative relation between employment on the one hand and wage/price movements on the other might be thus indicating possible choices or 'trade-off' which may be available as far as those responsible for decisions in economic policy are concerned. Leaving aside the specific quantitative data derived from the particular time series used, a 'realistic' Phillips curve would be downward sloping within a horizontal axis that measures the level of unemployment and two vertical ones, measuring respectively average prices and average wages, the latter differing from the former only by the amount of the postulated productivity increase. Thus, there is always a 'trade-off' possible, in that unemployment does tend to limit the extent to which wages may increase in excess of productivity increases, and measures influencing demand may affect wage and price inflation.

The practical difficulty is not only to find the appropriate 'dosage' at any one moment of time, but also to determine the politically decisive choice between 'acceptable' rates of unemployment and 'acceptable' rates of inflation. The problem is, moreover, greatly complicated by the fact that both on grounds of theory as well as on the basis of historical evidence, it must be assumed that the position of the Phillips curve may shift over time, as a result of any particular policy itself, at least when this is applied for any length of time, as well as, one must assume, for 'external' reasons. Prolonged unemployment, for example, may produce a curve which shows wages and prices more responsive to changes in unemployment, while prolonged inflation may produce the opposite result causing a lack of responsiveness of the kind many observers have thought to detect in the experience of a number of advanced countries in the late sixties, and early seventies. It is reasonable to assume that other, exogenous, causes may alter the social climate and, with it, economic expectations, and, therefore, the character of the unemployment/inflation 'trade-off'.

The relationship between price and wage movement on the one hand and unemployment on the other, which the Phillips curve set out to establish, has remained a basic part of modern theory on the subject; and the trade-off between inflation and unemployment which it postulated is still accepted as an important theorem to describe possible developments in the short run. In the last two decades, however, a more complicated analysis has been built upon the original concept, designed to encompass more actual economic situations than could the original. These analyses operate with such concepts as the 'natural' rate of unemployment, i.e. that at which price and wage inflation does not have a tendency to accelerate; and with that of an 'inertial' rate of inflation, i.e. one which is expected but from which the actual rate of inflation may differ because of unexpected demand or supply shocks. It is the movement of the actual rate of inflation away from the inertial rate which causes shifts in the Phillips curve in the short run.

In the long run, modern theory states inflation will stabilize when unemployment is at the natural rate. This distinction between the short run and the long run Phillips curve relationship means that while trade-offs between inflation and unemployment are possible, they come up against limits in the long run set by the coalescence of the actual and the natural rate of unemployment and of the actual and intertial rate of inflation. The practical consequences for policy-making of this elaboration of the original doctrine are important up to a point. While they open up the possibility of practical intervention by means of various policy instruments in the fight against either inflation or unemployment, they do not provide ready-made prescriptions for action in specific real conditions, thus leaving open the certainty of substantial and hard-fought differences in the realm of public policy.

Indeed, much of the most recent work in this field has been concerned to establish whether, in fact, shifts in the Phillips curve have occurred and to determine, if possible, the causes of such changes which clearly could have very important policy implications.[1] Much of this discussion, which, like so much else in the area of economics related to policy has flourished particularly in the United States, is of a very high degree of technicality and uses mathematical methods to a considerable extent. Leaving aside some of the more sophisticated and

---

1 Among a considerable literature, a particularly illuminating discussion can be found in the following: George L. Perry, 'Changing Labour Markets and Inflation', *Brookings Papers on Economic Activity* (3: 1970), pp. 411–41. Charles E. Schultze, 'Has the Philips Curve Shifted? Some Additional Evidence', ibid. (2: 1971), pp. 452–67, Robert E. Hall, 'Prospects for Shifting the Phillips Curve through Manpower Policy', ibid. (3: 1971), pp. 656–701.

contentious discussions, there seems to be a fair measure of agreement among a substantial number of economists that there has been 'a shift to the right' of the Phillips curve in recent years, that is that wages and prices have become less responsive to unemployment than seems to have been the case in earlier periods. Another way of putting it is that, from a policy point of view, the achievement of a high level of employment without inflation has become more difficult: the choice between the two objectives is a more acute one.[1]

Assuming these numerical results to be well-founded, the next question is why the shift should have occurred. A good many of the proximate causes have been isolated in recent work. This has consisted in part in disaggregating the statistics of unemployment, for example, by weighting each age-sex group by the relative hours of work and wage levels of that group, as well as by introducing an index measuring the variance of unemployment rates among different age-sex groups. The effects of changes in the structure of the labour market as well as different experiences in regard to the incidence of unemployment on different segments of the labour force can then be traced; and it can be demonstrated how these express themselves in the unemployment/wage-price relationship. But beyond these, as it were econometric, refinements, the problem becomes much more difficult both as regards diagnosis and cure. It is on the one hand a question of determining the more deep-seated reasons for the co-existence of relatively high levels of unemployment and inflation, on the other hand of deciding, either which is the greater evil (in so far as one or the other cannot be wholly avoided), or what additional policy means can be applied to mitigate the sharpness of the choice.[2]

On the former of these questions little 'scientific' work has been done. Here, the debate has tended to be in the sociological realm concerned with such matters as union power, including the balance of power within unions, the practices of large-scale business (who may be much motivated by fear of interruptions of activity and the consequences of these on market shares, cash flow, etc.) in regard to

---

1 In Perry's above-mentioned work, the results seem to show that a 4 per cent overall unemployment rate (NB 4 per cent by US measurements) would produce about 1½ per cent more inflation than would have been the case in the fifties.

2 It is just worth while pointing to the relevance of the difficulties presented by this problem not only to the general problem of macroeconomic management, but more particularly to that of the adequacy, indeed the efficacy, of monetary policy especially in its more extreme form, as preached by the Monetarists.

labour 'hoarding', attitudes to work, particularly of younger workers, and the effects of more substantial social benefits, including unemployment pay on the 'threshold' of unemployment.[1] These are, of course, matters which transcend the pure economic and for which even the neighbouring areas of the social sciences do not offer, as yet at least, much in the way of a systematic theory. Yet these are undoubtedly the sort of questions on which popular views are easily formed and which enter very readily into the consciousness (or, perhaps more dangerously, the subconscious) of 'practical men'.

What is clear is that however inadequate our present intellectual apparatus for analysing the 'trade-off' between employment and inflation may be, its existence as a practical problem that must be resolved in practical terms cannot be denied. The debate, from a policy point of view, concerns (a) the exchange ratio, as it were, between these alternative evils that should be considered acceptable and (b) the means to be employed in order to realize the chosen ratio.

On the first point, there are now relatively few economists who will take either of the extreme positions, that is to reject any degree of inflation, however high the level of unemployment that may then have to be accepted; or to tolerate any degree of inflation that the pursuit of full employment may generate. Those who still take such extreme positions will support them not only by emphasizing the undoubted social evils of inflation or unemployment respectively, but will also use the economic argument of the self-defeating effects of inflation, i.e. by ultimately destroying the bases of growth, or of unemployment by preventing growth of output and often militating against increases in productivity, thus ultimately destroying the bases of more stable prices.

The vast majority of economists, however, now take a middle position, their individual stance differing according to how far they lean to one side or the other. This is not, however, to say that these differences are unimportant. On the contrary, they are, at least from the practical point of view of economic policy, more important than the extreme positions which in advanced modern democratic societies tend almost by definition to be left out of account in the arrangement

---

1 In Britain, in particular, popular and semi-popular discussion in recent years has been much concerned with these points, and has produced curious echoes – *mutatis mutandis* – of the discussions of the early thirties. For an admirably clear and balanced statement of these issues, as indeed of most of the subject-matter of this section, see Gardner Ackley, *Stemming World Inflation* (1971).

of the practical affairs of government or even of business. The different degrees of acceptance of one or the other evil are first reflected in different assessments made by government economists or by independent experts of any existing situation and, then, in the forecasts they produce of the likely future path of the economy in regard to levels of unemployment and inflation. While much of the work concerned with these matters is to be found in articles in scientific journals, a good deal of it has to be gathered from governmental publications, from speeches by politicians (or occasionally by their professional advisers); and as yet, little in the way of a systematic, comprehensive exposition is available. Even a casual look at such publications as the Reports of the American Council of Economic Advisers, of evidence given by officials and academic economists to American Congressional Committees, of British budget speeches and the periodic reports of the Treasury, the Review of the National Institute for Economic and Social Research in Britain and of the Brookings Institution in the United States, to say nothing of the increasingly frequent excursions of academic economists into the more popular public prints, will soon reveal the extent to which this problem has become 'politicized'.

In the two English-speaking countries but also, though not always in the same rhythm, in France and Germany, oscillations can be observed in the relative emphasis placed on each of the twin evils of unemployment and inflation as far as public policy is concerned. The differences in attitude, as has already been indicated in considering changes in the position of the Phillips curve, can be elucidated if not fully explained, by differences in the age and sex structure of the population, income distribution, recent experience, as well as some more traditional attitudes to the 'money illusion', consequently to saving, current consumption, work and leisure and the experience of unemployment or inflation itself. Since politicians must necessarily try to gauge the prevailing mood of their electors (while not being free themselves from acquired attitudes on these matters) it is not surprising to see the general direction of macroeconomic management change from time to time, with sometimes one sometimes the other being taken as the prime objective. Given the relative under-development of the strictly economic apparatus for dealing with these problems (quite apart from the fact that they lie to a considerable extent in areas outside the strictly economic) it is not surprising to find that academic economists – particularly where they have been more directly identified with governmental policies – also tend to 'take sides' rather more emphatically on this than on other issues. The advocacy of a 'gently rising price-level' which we have met as early as 1922 in the work of Dennis Robertson[1] is echoed nowadays by those who, particularly if they accept that the choice presented by an up-to-date Phillips curve is more agonizing than it used to be, are prepared to 'live with' a certain amount of inflation.[2]

When it comes to the means of policy to be employed in achieving the right balance between high employment and price stability, the views of economists tend to be even less specifically derived from economic analysis. In the search for a resolution of the dilemma of employment and inflation, fiscal and monetary policy, in whatever policy 'mix' have – *pace* the extremists on both sides – seldom proved adequate to all the circumstances that may be encountered. In the United States, after years of remarkable price stability, high employment and a respectable growth rate, unemployment, rising prices (and massive balance of payments deficits) appeared simultaneously to plague the economy. In Britain the first two phenomena (and, later, the third) have coexisted far longer than could be considered tolerable on economic or social grounds. While the picture in the main continental European countries has not been so clear-cut, here too the problem has made its appearance from time to time.

No wonder, therefore, that policy-makers have been searching for new means to supplement the instruments of macroeconomic management: if one may so put it, to shift, or to change the shape of, demand and supply curves rather than, as is more usually the case with fiscal and monetary policy, to induce movements along 'existing' supply and demand curves. In this search, governments have so far had relatively little help from advances in economic theory. The areas of manpower

---

1 Another, American, example can be found in the work of Sumner H. Slichter. It should be noted that neither Robertson nor Slichter could in any way be regarded as 'left' economists.

2 See, for example, William S. Vickrey 'Stability through Inflation' in Kenneth K. Kurihara (ed.), *Post-Keynesian Economics* (1955). A particularly trenchant recent statement of this point of view is to be found in James Tobin and Leonard Ross, 'Living with Inflation', *New York Review of Books*, May 6, 1971, pp. 23–6. While clearly more sympathetic to this point of view than to its opposite, a more balanced exposition can be found in Arthur M. Okun, *Inflation: The Problem and Prospects Before Us* (1970) and the same author's, 'The Mirage of Steady Inflation' in *Brookings Papers on Economic Activity* (2: 1971), pp. 485–98.

policy, for example, or regional development[1] or the broad spectrum of 'industrial' policy, i.e. the attempt directly to influence investment or industrial structure, have always tended to be somewhat separate from the general corpus of economic analysis.[2] This is seen particularly in that area of policy which has been most directly concerned with attempts to mitigate the aspects of the choice between employment and inflation: action on prices and incomes. It is unnecessary to trace in any detail the history of attempts in recent times by the 'authorities' to ensure that prices or wages are at levels different from those which would be formed by the play of market forces. As far as individual prices or wages are concerned, such attempts can be found in many countries at many different times. Nor are we here concerned with comprehensive controls of the kind resorted to in war time, though the combination of financial and direct control measures adopted during the Second World War (and which owed much to Keynes and his school), certainly have an intellectual relationship with more recent ideas on price and income policy. Experiments with one or other type of policy – ranging from exhortation to compulsion – designed to make people act differently from the way in which, on the basis of market conditions alone, they would be able to act, have been widespread in the whole post-war period. Examples can be found in Austria, Sweden, Norway, the Netherlands, Great Britain, Canada, and, more recently, the United States, France and Germany. While the precise measures adopted in these countries vary a good deal – as does the extent and duration of their success – they are all eloquent testimony to the seriousness of the employment/inflation dilemma as well as to the inadequacy of macroeconomic demand

---

1 Regional economics is a particularly clear example of a certain lag. Despite the keen practical interest of this subject, and despite the existence of much detailed work on specific areas, for example, the Italian South, the general body of theory of the subject is either impounded in development economics as such or is still largely confined to standard location theory and the theory of interregional trade.

2 This is not to say that there has not been a good deal on certain aspects of public policy of a micro/macroeconomic kind. See, for example, an account of a conference organized by the International Economic Association: J. Margolis and H. Guitton (eds.) *Public Economics* (1969). Other examples in specific fields are Stuart Holland (ed.), *The State as Entrepreneur, New Dimensions for Public Enterprise: The IRI State Shareholding Formula* (1972); C. D. Foster, *The Transport Problem* (1963); Edwin T. Haefele, *Transport and National Goals* (1969).

management through the – by now – traditional means.[1]

A reasonably dispassionate summing-up of the record of these policies[2] would show that they have for a time at least had some favourable results, and even the price or wage rises that have followed the deliberate end of the policies or their practical breakdown, are nor necessarily evidence against the policies as such. However, we are not here concerned with the practical aspects, but rather with the contributions which economists have made and are currently making to the analysis of the problems of price and incomes policy. Here the record to date is meagre. Much of the work has tended to be – as already noted earlier – within the realm of specialists in certain branches of applied economics, such as labour economists who have studied techniques of collective bargaining, manpower policies and the like.[3] Undoubtedly, a great many useful conclusions have been derived from careful study of the experiences of different countries on such practical matters as the relation between voluntary and compulsory controls, the role of independent advisory or executive Boards and Councils, the

1 A good survey of the measures adopted in different countries together with a very good analysis can be found in an OECD publication *Inflation: the Present Problem* (1970). See also E. Roll, *The World After Keynes* (1968), pp. 79–84. The pessimistic view there taken of a dininution of 'the possibility of a conflict arising between expectations of security of employment, the strengthened bargaining position of unions that results from governments' commitment to this objective, the inflationary dangers inherent in that situation, and the claims of satisfying ideals of social justice' remains, alas, justified at this time of writing.

2 Such as the one in the above mentioned OECD report, in Gardner Ackley's previously referred to booklet, *Stemming World Inflation* (1971), pp. 77–83, and in the publication of the American Committee for Economic Development, *Further Weapons against Inflation: Measures to Supplement General Fiscal and Monetary Policies* (1970).

3 A very early statement of the problem by a number of Swedish economists including discussion of the more general economic aspects is Ralph Turvey (ed.) *Wages Policy Under Full Employment* (1952). Although not directly falling within this survey, a few more specific studies may also be mentioned: H. Clegg, *How to Run an Incomes Policy* (1971); Santos Mukherjee, *Making Labour Markets Work: a Comparison of the UK and Swedish Systems* (1972); John Sheahan, *The Wage-Price Guideposts* (1967); Edward F. Denison, *Guideposts for Wages and Prices: Criteria and Consistency* (1968); Robert E. Hall, 'Why is the Unemployment Rate so High at Full Employment' in *Brooking Papers on Economic Activity* (3: 1970), pp. 369–402 and 'Prospects for Shifting the Philips Curve through Manpower Policy', ibid. (3: 1971), pp. 659–701; and Charles C. Duncan MacRae, Stuart O. Schweitzer and Ralph E. Smith, 'Manpower Proposals for Phase III', ibid., pp. 703–34; John Dunlop, 'Guideposts, Wages, and Collective Bargaining' in *Guidelines, Informal Controls and the Market Place* ed. George P. Shultz and Robert Z. Aliber (1966).

relation, both quantitatively and in timing, of measures bearing on wages and those on prices, the question of wage differentials and that of the particularly low paid. On the other hand, there is not anything approaching the amount of more general analytical work in this field that is to be found in modern writings on fiscal and monetary management.[1]

On the whole, the initial reactions at least of most economic theorists to the possibilities of direct intervention in price – and wage – formation was, predictably, closely linked to their general attitude both to interventionism as such, and to the scope of management by the means of the 'New Economics'. It was also to some extent related to their emphasis on fiscal *versus* monetary policy (some degree of affinity here respectively to an interventionist and to a *laissez-faire* attitude has already been noted), and, more generally, to their inclination to regard either price stability or full employment as the most desirable policy objective.[2]

Perhaps here, as in the case of the analytical work itself, another factor which has had some influence in shaping the views of economists has been whether or no they have been involved in government and have, therefore, had direct experience of the practical pressures to which policy-makers are subject to find more effective means to cope with widely held, yet not easily reconciled, aspirations.[3]

1 For example, Gardner Ackley, op. cit., Arthur M. Okun, op. cit., or the treatment given to this segment of public policy in one of the most authoritative statements on modern macroeconomic management, Walter W. Heller, *New Dimensions of Political Economy* (1966), pp. 42–7. See also the references to this problem in the work of another experienced practitioner, Arthur M. Okun. *The Political Economy of Prosperity* (1970) *passim*.

2 For a generally sceptical view see Paul McCracken, 'Economic Policy and the Lessons of Experience' in M. Laird (ed.) *Republican Papers* (1968) and more specifically on prices and incomes policy; Arthur F. Burns 'Wages and Prices by Formula?' in *Harvard Business Review* (March–April 1965). Both these authors express their views, as may be expected, in a restrained manner and it is perhaps fair to add that both statements were written before their authors had assumed very high responsibilities in economic policy-making in their country. Certainly, Dr Burns quite early in his tenure of the Chairmanship of the Board of Governors of the Federal Reserve System became one of the most emphatic and persuasive advocates of an active prices and incomes policy.

3 The wish which was implicit in what I wrote some years ago when speaking of economic policy may not be capable of fulfilment until economics has itself been transformed (if ever but see further below): 'The first economist who develops a general theory ... of how to make these – sometimes massive – changes in the pattern of resource allocation while having regard to traditional rights and aspirations, how to

Although many of the problems with which we have dealt in the preceding sections of this chapter, and which are largely the consequence of the now generally accepted objective of maintaining a high level of economic activity, are also intimately related to economic growth (and indeed hard to disentangle from it), growth as such has in recent years become a particularly actively cultivated area economics. It is, however, far from being a new subject in economic literature. For example, to go back no further than Adam Smith, we already find a detailed discussion of the accumulation of capital in the *Wealth of Nations*; and the theory of economic development is one of the most important parts of Ricardo's *Principles*, which, greatly transformed, was also a crucial part of Marx's *Capital*. The whole of Book IV of Mill's *Principles* is devoted to a discussion of economic development, including the celebrated disquisition in Chapter VI on 'The Stationary State'.

After the great burgeoning of classical and post-classical economics, that is after the middle of the nineteenth century, relatively little new is added to the general body of doctrine on economic development. Schumpeter was clearly right in saying that all the great economists of the second and third post-classical generation, Jevons, Walras, Menger, Wicksell, Clark and even Marshall (who had rather more than the others to say on the subject) continued to treat 'progress', as it was generally called, in much the same way as before, 'all this (what makes for progress) does not go *fundamentally* beyond J. S. Mill or even A. Smith',[1] though Schumpeter's own *The Theory of Economic Development*, first published in 1912,[2] was an outstanding exception from this judgment. What, however, characterizes Schumpeter's own theory is something which is only partly different in kind from earlier theories. Indeed, there is much affinity in a sense with Marx's work. Both give an important place to technological change, but Schumpeter added a

---

balance – in collective terms – the claims of different sections of the community . . . in an environment in which the democratic process itself makes sole reliance on market forces impossible, even if it were desirable, will, indeed, deserve a great prize'. E. Roll, 'The Uses and Abuses of Economics', The Sidney Ball Lecture, 1968 (reprinted in *Oxford Economic Papers* , November 1968, p. 301.)

1 J. A. Schumpeter, *History of Economic Analysis* (1954), pp. 893.

2 The English edition, somewhat revised, was published in 1934. Characteristically it is referred to in his above-mentioned book only in footnotes added by his editors.

wider definition of innovation, so as to include quality and market changes and those in sources of supply. Above all, he also gave a special position in the explanation of the process of evolution to the entrepreneur, that is the man who has the flair to seize upon the possibilities that these changes offer and to translate them into economic reality. These entrepreneurs, having seen new investment opportunities, are responsible for impelling, through credit creation and inflation, the generation of enough (forced) savings to finance new ventures until, eventually, overproduction sets in and recession follows. Thus the progress of the economy through time is linked with a theory of economic fluctuations, as it was also in the work of others writing in the first twenty-five years of the present century, such as Spiethoff and Cassel. Apart from this feature, the essential characteristic of growth theory during that period was that, like classical theory, it was concerned to show what was the probable path of growth in reality rather than to construct abstract models, as became the fashion later.

It is interesting to speculate not only on why this change of approach took place, but, and perhaps even more, on why there has been such an astonishing increase in both the 'realistic' analysis of growth and in the more austere 'model' type of theory in the last fifteen or twenty years. For the general increase in interest in the subject a number of reasons can be advanced though, no doubt, different observers may place a different weight on the various factors. The emphasis on full employment in advanced industrialized countries, combined with much greater sensitiveness to claims based on social justice – that is on greater equality of opportunity, income and wealth – have undoubtedly led to greater preoccupation with the size of the 'cake' to be distributed and with the means to make it bigger. Another factor has probably been the increased awareness of the progress of the economy through time made possible by more refined concepts of national accounting together with better techniques for the presentation of statistical material. It is no accident that one of the foremost economists responsible for modern advances both in the theory of national accounts as well as in the statistical field, Simon Kuznets, should also have been in the vanguard of modern growth theory.[1] The fashion to make international comparisons (to construct 'league tables') – itself

---

[1] See for example S. Kuznets, *Six Lectures on Economic Growth* (1959) and *Modern Economic Growth, Rate, Structure, And Spread* (1966).

made feasible by the progress of national accounts techniques and, no doubt stimulated by quasi-political factors – is yet another cause of the increasing concern with the facts of growth and the explanations for them. The relative performance of countries with different economic, political and social systems has been another focus of interest which has led to this new preoccupation. Yet another powerful inducement to study 'growth' economics has come from the greater awareness of the needs of the less developed, or, more simply, the poorer countries of the world. Perhaps, additionally, some impetus has come from renewed interest in economic history, a beginning of a new realization that the pursuit of undiluted macroeconomic theory can, in the last resort, be less than totally satisfying.[1]

Whatever the reasons, there can be no doubt that the literature of growth has itself been a growth industry in recent years.[2] It would be impossible in a short space to give anything like a full review of what has been done to date nor, given the continuing stream of publications, is it possible to form a confident view of which tendencies are likely to be lasting and which ephemeral. However, a brief classification of the types of investigations that are currently under way, may serve. In the first place, there has been continuing work in what has been described above as the realistic school, that is to say composed of those writers who are mainly concerned to discover the factors operating in the real world which are likely to promote growth or to militate against it.[3] This is in the tradition of the classics right down to Schumpeter, and its most extensive application has been to the problems of the poorer countries.[4] The literature specifically addressed to individual developing countries or to the underdeveloped world as a whole is already

1 It is possibly significant that one of the most austere of modern theorists has ventured into this field with a book which is particularly stimulating in this regard: J. R. Hicks, *The Theory of Economic History* (1969)

2 Another significant straw in the wind is the setting up in 1961 at Yale of an 'Economic Growth Center', 'to further comparative analysis of the structure and development of national economies'. Although, despite its name, not confined to 'growth' problems, the center has been responsible for a very considerable output of important contributions to this subject.

3 Probably the most important single work in the group is Edward F. Denison (assisted by Jean-Pierre Pouillier), *Why Growth Rates Differ, Post-War Experience in Nine Western Countries* (1967), and of the same type, but more specifically dealing with certain particular factors: Richard P. Nelson, Merton D. Peck, Edward D. Kalachek, *Technology, Economic Growth and Public Policy* (1967).

4 A useful survey which – significantly – explicitly excludes the 'model' type of growth

enormous and cannot be usefully discussed here. Attention may, however, be drawn to the surveys prepared by missions sponsored by the World Bank as well as by the many 'Institutes' and 'Centres' now existing in a number of Universities devoted to the study of development problems.[1]

The more general analysis of the 'realistic' school tend, according to authors' predilections, to lean to the sociological/institutional or to the historical/statistical approach.[2] This group tends, therefore, to merge with the pure historical approach, of which more presently. Modern work on these lines has certainly greatly enlarged and enriched the scope of the analysis compared, for example, with that to be found in Schumpeter. More light has been thrown on such diverse subjects as the respective roles of different patterns of income distribution or the state of development of financial markets, and of public expenditure *versus* private consumption in different types of framework of social and political institutions in determining the rates and directions of growth. A good deal of stimulus has also come from enquiries attempting to relate growth to types of general economic policy, including macroeconomic management against a background of cyclical fluctuations.[3] Here the work naturally abuts on the one hand on the more

theory can be found in M. Abramovitz, 'Economics of Growth' in *A Survey of Contemporary Economics* vol. II (1952). For a review of later developments, particularly of more formal theory, see: F. H. Hahn and R. C. O. Matthews, 'The Theory of Economic Growth: A Survey' in *Surveys of Economic Theory* vol. II (1965).

1 The annual reports of the Development Assistance Committee of the OECD and the publications of the British Overseas Development Institute are particularly useful. See also the report of the 'Pearson Commission', *Partners in Development* (1969) produced by a group of distinguished public men. Two books by one author deserve special mention for they combine acute analysis with practical proposals which deserve more attention than they have received; David Horowitz, *Hemisphere North and South: Economic Disparity among Nations* (1966) and *The Abolition of Poverty* (1969). Finally, if, from the extensive and varied output of that most versatile of British economists who was primarily concerned with current policy problems, Thomas Balogh, one area had to be singled out as having the most lasting value, I would choose his work on the problems of the underdeveloped countries, see, for example, *The Economics of Poverty* (1966) and *Unequal Partners* (1963).

2 A good, relatively early, example of a comprehensive treatment of the subject on the lines of the former of these tendencies is W. Arthur Lewis, *The Theory of Economic Growth* (1955); of the latter the already mentioned S. Kuznets, *Modern Economic Growth, Rate, Structure, and Spread* (1966).

3 Interesting examples of a systematic attempt to relate growth and economic policy in general are Thomas Wilson, *Planning and Growth* (1964) and M. Dobb, *An Essay on Economic Growth and Planning* (1960). Professor Kaldor, in addition to his work in the more theoretical field, has written a good deal in this borderland of the 'realistic' and the

formal, model-building theory of growth, on the other, on the whole body of discussion of policies to maintain high levels of economic activity without inflation and so on.

The 'realistic' school, therefore, very naturally leads on, on the one hand to the historical, on the other to the purely theoretical. As far as the historical school is concerned, attempts on the lines either of Marx or of Schumpeter to build comprehensive systems have not been very abundant in recent years. Historiography itself has tended to be chary of 'system-building' and economists have been even more reluctant to venture into this area. Where they have, their concern has usually been, as in the case of Professor J. K. Galbraith,[1] more with economic structure, rather than with growth as such.[2]

One book, however, has attempted to present a broad sweep of historical explanation of economic development as a whole: W. W. Rostow, *The Stages of Economic Growth*.[3] Designed as an 'alternative to Marx's Theory of modern history', this book is based on the distinction of five stages of growth: the traditional society, the preconditions for take-off, the take-off, the drive to maturity, and the age of high mass consumption. It is fair to say that at least in the way they are presented, these stages do not appear as categories distilled from a vast volume of statistical-historical material, but are rather posited in advance of the examination of their application to different countries at different historical points. Though the author may well claim that the pattern is the result of an inductive process in his mind – and though this particular method of proceeding is not unknown (being very much Marx's, for example) – the practical test of the categories is by no means easy. It requires a good deal of broad generalization from carefully selected data; and the acceptability of these generalizations must remain very much a matter of personal taste and temperament.[4]

---

analytical, see, for example 'Capitalist Evolution in the light of Keynesian Economics', 'The Relation of Economic Growth and Cyclical Fluctuations', both reprinted in *Essays in Economic Stability and Growth* (1960).

1 For a more detailed discussion of his work, see below.

2 An early exception to this should be mentioned: C. E. Ayres, *The Theory of Economic Progress* (1944), a brilliant and beautifully written analysis which forms a bridge between Veblen and Galbraith and well deserves to be re-read now.

3 Second revised edition 1971.

4 While there is much that is stimulating in Professor Rostow's wide-ranging study, there is no evidence that his schema has so far proved particularly productive in further research; and a good many of his propositions, for example the definition of take-off, have been criticized as at least arbitrary, and even as tautological. As a contrasting

Indeed, the economist and economic historian have tended increasingly to leave this kind of system-building to practitioners of other sciences some of whom have shown a ready disposition to fall for this temptation.[1] Economists in the strict sense of the term have, as already noted, been reluctant to do so,[2] though occasionally the temptation proves too great even for them. One such is an attempt by Professor Kaldor, on the basis of the so-called 'Verdoorn' Law (which states that a higher rate of growth of output involves a faster rate of increase of productivity and employment) and an analysis of the relation between growth of manufacturing output and growth of gross domestic product as a whole, to reveal the causes of the slow rate of economic growth of the United Kingdom.[3] It deserves special mention here not only because the theory on which it is based happened, temporarily at least, to have a direct and significant effect on the making of policy in Britain in one particular respect,[4] but also because it represents something of an amalgam between the 'realistic' and the 'abstract' growth schools.

As for the latter, the beginning of the modern phase, by common consent, is now placed in 1939 with the appearance of an article by Sir Roy Harrod, 'An Essay in Dynamic Theory',[5] later expanded in his book, *Towards a Dynamic Economics* (1948). As supplemented by E. D. Domar in his article 'Capital Expansion, Rate of Growth and Employment',[6] the Harrod-Domar model can be regarded as typical of a sector of economic work in which nearly all the most distinguished 'post-Keynesians' have participated.[7] The basic ingredients of the

---

example of a simple, robust, explanation of the growth of the American economy which while also operating with some sociological and historical concepts is completely different in tone and treatment, see Paul M. Mazur, *The Dynamics of Economic Growth* (1965).

1 See, for example, C. D. Darlington, *The Evolution of Man and Society* (1969), E. R., Leach, *A Runaway World* (1968) and T. Dobzhansky, *Mankind Evolving* (1962) which show that botanists, anthropologists and biologists are all ready in different degrees to encompass all the social sciences as well.

2 The interesting exception, Sir John Hicks's essay, *A Theory of Economic History* (1969) has already been noted.

3 The title of his inaugural lecture at Cambridge University, November 2, 1966.

4 Generally regarded as not altogether beneficial.

5 *Economic Journal*, March 1939.

6 *Econometrica*, April 1940.

7 A few examples from a vast literature must suffice: P. A. Samuelson's already referred to major work, *Foundations of Economic Analysis* (1947, new edition 1983), particularly part II; P. A. Samuelson and R. M. Solow, 'Balanced Growth under Constant Returns to Scale', *Econometrica*, July 1953; M. Kaldor, 'A Model of Economic Growth', *Economic*

theory are first, the capital/output ratio, i.e. the number of units of capital it takes to produce a unit of output – in the original Harrod-Domar model capital is assumed to be the only factor of production, with which labour combines in fixed proportions, and growth of population affects only per capita increase in income – and secondly the Keynesian saving/investment equality, and an assumption about the propensity to save. The pattern of growth of the economy can then be easily determined mathematically, it being of course emphasized that the model does not pretend to be a representation of reality.

Subsequent work has consisted in modifying the assumptions underlying the original model so as to make it capable of being applied with a greater degree of realism to different situations. Thus, different proportions of capital and labour inputs can be stipulated, or the complication of the effect of different forms of income distribution can be added starting, for example, from the extreme position that all profits are saved and all wages are consumed. In this way income distribution theory can be brought to bear on growth theory and vice versa.[1] Yet another series of variations can be added by attempting to take account – in a 'model', i.e. abstract, manner rather than in the way of the 'realistic' school of the possibilities of technological change, as distinct from the effect of a larger per capita stock of capital. Not surprisingly, a good deal of the discussion that has been generated on this point has been concerned to define technological change, a process that cannot yet by any means be said to have reached finality. It is to be expected that on these matters a fruitful collaboration between those economists who have been mainly occupied in accumulating and evaluating actual data for different countries and various sectors of the economy and the model-builders may become possible. This seems to

*Journal*, December 1957; R. M. Solow, 'A Contribution to the Theory of Economic Growth', *Quarterly Journal of Economics*, February 1956; ; R. M. Sollow, *Capital Theory and the Rate of Return* (1963); P. Sraffa, *Production of Commodities by Means of Commodities* (1960); Joan Robinson, *The Accumulation of Capital* (1956) and *Essays in the Theory of Economic Growth* (1962); Kenneth K. Kurihara, 'Distribution, Employment and Secular Growth' in K. K. Kurihara (ed.), *Post-Keynesian Economics* (1955); R. F. Kahn, 'Exercises in the Analysis of Growth' in *Oxford Economic Papers*, June 1959. For an excellent collection of papers on this general subject edited by Professor Heller and containing a very interesting introduction by him, see Walter W. Heller (ed.) *Perspectives of Economic Growth* (1968).

1 See, for example, Martin Bronfenbrenner, *Income Distribution Theory* (1971), particularly pp. 87–91 and 416–22.

be happening particularly in the study of the underdeveloped countries.[1]

As can be seen, despite these attempts at a greater realism of assumptions, there is still a gulf fixed between growth theory in the strict sense of the term and the preoccupations of those concerned with the application of the advances of economics to the realistic problems of the promotion of economic growth. Curiously, however, the main reaction has not come so much against the austere (and, therefore, tending to be identified with arid) economics of growth as methodology. The real rebellion has taken the form of a questioning of growth as such, or, at least, of certain aspects of material growth. The oddity of this reaction with its frequent fear of 'excessive' growth is in striking contrast with the fears of the late thirties of the 'mature' economy which, it was argued, had reached the limits of growth and was, therefore, condemned to stagnation. Two strands of thought may be mentioned in this connection in the first instance: one which questions the worthwhileness of growth in terms of the 'costs' incurred, the other, the effects of continued growth on at least some of the factors that make growth possible. We might refer to those who take the first view as the 'cost-of-growth sceptics', and to the other as the 'limits of growth alarmists'. Both these schools of thought, though to some extent involved in economic reasoning (particularly the former), not surprisingly also call in aid considerations drawn from quite other universes of discourse. As typical of the first school we might take E. J. Mishan, *The Costs of Economic Growth* (1967), of the second, Donald L. Meadows (*et al.*) *The Limits of Growth* (1972).[2]

The thesis of the former bears some resemblance to one developed several years earlier by Professor Galbraith in his celebrated *The Affluent Society*. (Since the latter forms an integral part of the whole of its author's work, it is dealt with in more detail below.) It is, however, in one sense more general since it arises out of 'doubts about the value

---

1 P. N. Rosenstein-Rodan, 'Problems of Industrialization of Eastern and South-Eastern Europe', in *Economy Journal*, June 1943; 'Notes on the Theory of the Big Push' in *Economic Development for Latin America, Proceedings of a Conference held by the International Economic Association* (1961); H. B. Chenery, 'The Interdependence of Investment Criteria' in M. Abramovitz (*et. al.*) *The Allocation of Economic Resources* (1959).

2 It should, in fairness, be added that while Mr Mishan's book is a work of scholarship by a professional economist fully versed in the techniques of modern neo-Keynesian analysis, the Meadows symposium is essentially a 'public document' designed primarily for the purpose of creating an immediate public impact.

for human welfare of the growing tide of post-war economic expansion'.[1] As one who has worked in the field of cost-benefit analysis and the economics of welfare generally, Mr Mishan uses the apparatus of external diseconomies to a considerable extent to identify the circumstances in which these may outweigh the advantages of growth as they may appear to the individual; and he has little difficulty in showing that these circumstances may occur very frequently indeed in the real world. While undoubtedly more trenchantly expressed and more vigorously applied to certain situations, for example, the problem of built-up areas, than other writings on these topics, these sections are essentially in the general tradition of the body of welfare economics as it has developed from Marshall and Pigou onwards.[2] Mr Mishan's book carries, however, a special impact by virtue of its strong, and strongly expressed, views based on considerations which go far beyond the economic as normally understood and enter the field of what can perhaps best be called, cultural criticism. This is seen, for example, in the exposure of the myth of consumer's sovereignty and the true scope of choice which is supposed to be enlarged by economic growth: 'In all that contributes in trivial ways . . . new models of cars . . . prepared foodstuffs . . . and an increasing range of push-button gadgets, man has ample choice. In all that destroys his enjoyment of life, he has none';[3] and again 'the chief sources of social welfare are not to be found in economic growth *per se*, but in a far more selective form of development'.[4] This theme in a somewhat different form was, as we shall see, also that of Galbraith's *Affluent Society*. It recurs in a number

---

1 E. J. Mishan, op. cit., p. ix.

2 A very useful collection of modern writings in this field can be found in Kenneth J. Arrow and Tibor Scitovsky (eds.), *Readings in Welfare Economics* (1969). Mr Mishan himself has made a number of important contributions, particularly in regard to the concept of consumer's surplus, for example, 'Realism and Relevance in Consumer's Surplus' in *Review of Economic Studies*, vol. 15, also *Welfare Economics* (1969). Special mention must be made of the path-breaking article by A. Bergson, 'A Reformulation of Certain Aspects of Welfare Economics' in *Quarterly Journals of Economics* (1938). For a restatement of the impossibility of reconstructing the GNP index so as to reflect welfare, see Edward F. Denison, 'Welfare Measurement and the GNP' in *Survey of Current Business* (January 1971).

3 Mishan, op. cit., p. 85.

4 ibid., p. 8. That the impulse behind Mr Mishan's views must come at least as much from, shall we say, 'ideological' considerations as from dissatisfaction with the adequacy of economic categories can be seen in his highly emotional reflections on modern youth or pornography in this book and in many other writings.

of economic writers, quite apart, of course, from its continued reiteration in the works of ecologists whose concern for the environment has suddenly caught the imagination of large sections of public opinion. For example, the distinguished Japanese economist, Professor Shigeto Tsuru[1] has also called in question the explicit or implicit equation of growth of GNP with increase in human welfare, mainly on the ground that modern technological development had eroded the assumptions on which this identification was based. He goes on to distinguish five types of 'money votes' which consumers cast and which 'thus enter as components of GNP ... whose welfare significance can be questioned'.[2] They include, for example, high commuting costs due to urban sprawl, excessive dependence on legal advice resulting in a generation of income for services which may be institutionally indispensable, but do not contribute to welfare, depletion of social wealth (which is where much of the environmental damage would be placed), and inefficiency of dynamic adjustment, for example reclamation of coastal lands in Japan as against a change in utilization of agricultural land no longer required for rice production. It can be confidently predicted that these and similarly sceptical views on the constituents of GNP, and, therefore, on growth will go on giving rise to interesting new analytical work in the field of welfare economics. In Professor Tsuru's case, for example, it has meant a return to the use of the capital and income concepts developed by Irving Fisher as being more suitable, as Pigou (who criticized them) pointed out, if we are interested in 'comparative amounts of economic welfare which a community obtains over a long series of years'.[3]

The other type of reaction to modern growth is of a different order. It derives to some extent from concern over the ravages done to the environment, whether natural or consisting of man-created social amenities. Its main concern, however, as the title of its principle manifesto indicates is with the *Limits to Growth*. This particular booklet which has achieved very great publicity to the point of putting this subject on the agenda of public debate, at least for a while, is not the work of a single economist or indeed a single social scientist. It is the collective work of a team of members of the Massachusetts Institute of Technology working in different fields and using for the purpose of

1 'In Place of GNP', in *Towards a New Political Economy, Collected Works*, vol. xiii (the only one in English), pp. 73–93.
2 op. cit., pp. 8 and 9.
3 A. C. Pigou, *The Economics of Welfare* (1932), p. 36.

this study modern computer techniques. The team's work was initiated by a group of private individuals, and in this way is perhaps also typical of a new trend in social enquiry. Briefly, the study tries to establish the interrelation between population, industrial *per caput* output, *per caput* food supply, non-renewable resources, and pollution. By means of the computer, charts are drawn up showing the interrelations between these five variables over the last 90 years and the next 110 years, that is to the year 2100. The main conclusion is a new version of Malthusianism. Population and capital grow 'exponentially' (Malthus's geometric progression) while resources do not (Malthus's arithmetic increase of food). It follows that unless population is stabilized and growth that will exhaust material resources is stopped, population will 'overshoot', and, after collapse, a new equilibrium at very low living standards will be re-established. This is explicitly stated not to be a prediction but it is presented by their authors – and those who have been spreading their ideas – in a manner which carries a high degree of persuasiveness as to the probability of just such an outcome.

While the results are presented in a much more complex manner and deal, in the process, with many environmental and similar problems that are much in the public's eye at this time, the basic thesis is so close to that of Malthus's clash between population and food supply as to make little difference to its economic validity. As critics have pointed out, similar extrapolations made, say, one hundred, or even fifty, years ago would have produced equally startling results which, however, the course of events, both as regards the actual development of population in different parts of the world, as well as the progress of technology, have made unrealistic. That the problem to which the group points is an important one – as was Malthus's formulation – cannot be denied, and policy must clearly take it seriously into account. It can, however, be argued that it is not changed in character simply because it is exhibited in terms of computerized results; and when it comes to the wider, not exclusively economic conclusions of the authors it is far from clear that a wholesale stop on all growth is necessarily either intellectually the right prescription or the best from the point of view of practical politics.

It may be convenient at this point where the ideas discussed above intermingle with wider sociological problems, in particular with those concerning the relation of the individual and society briefly to re-visit Marx, the nineteenth-century economist *par excellence* who aimed to combine *inter alia* a theory of society with an analysis of its economic structure. There is little to add to the detailed discussion of Marx's economic ideas given in Chapter VI. In considering the course – or fate – of Marxian ideas in the more recent past, there are a number of approaches that can be adopted. There is first what might be called the scriptural, that is the continued study of the works of Marx and Engels themselves in order to arrive at a clearer understanding of their own ideas. Naturally, this is primarily the work of those who have accepted Marx's own basic ideas and a steady, though in Western countries not a very large, stream of writings continues. There is, secondly, the work of Marxists to 'continue' the work of the Masters by applying Marxian techniques to new economic data. Outside the Soviet Union and other communist countries, the output in this area is not very considerable. It is very largely inspired by Hilferding's *Das Finanzkapital* (1927), Lenin's *Imperialism, The Last Stage of Capitalism* (1917) of which the first major continuation was Eugene Varga's *New Data for Lenin's Imperialism* (n.d.). Generally this work[1] has tried to show that the essential elements of the Marxian analysis and the predictions as to the future development of capitalism, including its proneness to periodic crises, have not been changed by the structural alterations of modern industrial organization, both on the side of enterprise and of labour, or by changes in the relationship of the state, directly or through various organs, with the industrial machine.[2]

Another area is the study of economic development in those countries which have passed through revolutions inspired by Marx's views of Capitalism, and have installed communist régimes. This is, of course, of quite a different order either from the study of the original 'texts' or from the attempt to prove their continued validity in capitalist countries. Marx's own writings have only a minimum to contribute to the question of how the economy can be organized in a communist (or, as a Marxists would say, in the intermediate, socialist) society. Indeed he explicitly rejected the idea of writing 'recipes for the soup-kitchen

1 Leaving aside purely political pamphleteering literature, one or two scholarly works may be cited: Paul M. Sweezy, *The Theory of Capitalist Development* (1942); Paul A. Baran, *The Political Economy of Growth* (1957); Paul A. Baran and Paul M. Sweezy, *Monopoly Capital, An Essay on the American Economic and Social Order* (1966) and, in a somewhat different vein, M. H. Dobb, *On Economic Theory and Socialism* (1955) and *An Essay on Economic Growth and Planning* (1960), already mentioned.

2 An interesting symposium which explicitly asks the question, rather than assumes and then tries to prove, the answer is Shigeto Tsuru (ed.), *Has Capitalism Changed?* (1961) in which a number of authors, only some of whom are Marxists, give their individual answers.

of the future'. This discussion has, therefore, little to do with Marxism as such and tends to be concerned with techniques of planning, central direction of the economy, regional autonomy and autonomy of individual enterprises, pricing, wage-fixing and so forth. There are a number of technical points of contact here with the preoccupations of economists working in capitalist economies in the field of Public Economics, and dialogues between them and their counterparts in communist countries had become more frequent.[1]

Finally, there is the attitude to Marxian economics of non-Marxist economists. Here one can say that there has certainly been no revival of interest such as occurred in the 'thirties when under the influence of the social and political *sequelae* of the economic depression in capitalist countries and when Soviet planning was scoring some first successes, many economists were drawn to a study of Marx. Broadly speaking the post-Keynesian macroeconomic developments have left Marxism severely on one side. Nevertheless, there are a few instances to show that some modern economists are prepared to treat Marx, the scholar, with considerable respect. One of the earliest, who, though not a Marxist has always been somewhat sceptical about the assumptions of 'orthodox' economic theory and has consequently shown some sympathy for Marxism, is Professor Joan Robinson. As long ago as 1942 she thought that 'hope of progress in Economics' lay 'in using academic methods (i.e. presumably, the techniques of modern economic theory) to solve the problems posed by Marx';[2] and Professor Leontief, one of the most original thinkers in present-day economic theory, while sceptical about 'Marx's analytical accomplishments' emphasized his strength 'in realistic, empirical knowledge of the capitalist system' and thought that 'the significance of Marx for modern economic theory is that of an inexhaustible source of direct observation'.[3] Even

---

1 See two interesting papers and the discussion on them in J. Margolis and H. Guiton (ed.) *Public Economics* (1969), namely V. P. Gloushkov, 'New Methods of Economic Management in the USSR, Some Features of the Recent Economic Reform' and A. Pokrovski, 'Socialist Planning and Capitalist Programming: An Analytical Comparison of the Procedures'. See also, Vladimir S. Treml, 'Interaction of Economic Thought and Economic Policy in the Soviet Union' in *History of Political Economy*, vol. I, no. I (Spring 1969), pp. 187–216, which speaks of a 'Rebirth of Economics' in the Soviet Union and lists numerous examples of the spread of 'Western' ideas and techniques. Light is also thrown on this subject in J. M. Letiche, 'Soviet Views on Keynes: A Review Article Surveying the Literature' in *Journal of Economic Literature* (June 1971).

2 Joan Robinson, *An Essay on Marxian Economics* (1942), p. 115.

3 Wassily Leontief, in a 1937 address reprinted in *Essays in Economics* (1966), pp. 82–3.

Professor Samuelson, the doyen of modern neo-classical economics has on a number of occasions mingled his criticisms of Marx with references to some of his achievements, such as some anticipation of the Leontief input-output analysis and the Marxian schema of expanded reproduction as a forerunner of some modern growth models.[1]

These, however, are all isolated instances. In general, one must conclude, as does a modern economist who has shown considerable sympathy for Marx, the social scientist, 'that objective conditions have been more important than abstract intellectual merit in accounting for both the rises and the declines of Marxian Economics', and he continues to stress two factors which have worked in favour of Marxism: 'embodiment in an impressive system of social philosophy, and the availability of a wide range of effective materials for an equally wide range of intellectual interests and levels'.[2]

Indeed, if there has been a revived interest in Marx in recent years, it is certainly not to be found in intensified study of Marx's economics, but rather in his more general ideas on society; and here it is particularly the young Marx with his passionate preoccupation with the Hegelian problem of 'alienation' to whom the younger generation of present-day Marxists have gone for inspiration.[3] The word and concept originated with Hegel who, in fact, used two words, that can be

---

1 Paul A. Samuelson, 'Marxian Economics as Economics' in *American Economic Review* (May 1967), pp. 616–23.

2 Martin Bronfenbrenner, 'The Vicissitudes of Marxian Economics' in *History of Political Economy*, vol. 2, no. 2 (Fall 1970), pp. 207, 223.

3 It is the so-called 'Paris economic-philosophical manuscripts' that form the basic source. Attention was first drawn to them by Professor Peter Mayer in J. P. Mayer, 'Über eine unveröffentlichte Schrift von Karl Marx' in *Rote Revue* 1931, no. 5, and these were subsequently included in a collection edited by him (with S. Landshut) in *Der Historische Materialismus* (1932). An enormous volume of controversy of a highly esoteric kind has since been generated around the question whether the 'humanistic' concerns of the younger Marx were abandoned later when he became absorbed in the economic analysis of *Capital*, or whether there is an unbroken intellectual line leading from the rebellion against the Hegelian view of alienation to the later theory of capitalist exploitation, crises and final collapse which are all comprised in the materialist interpretation of history. In support of the latter view reference is usually made to another set of Marx's manuscripts written some thirteen years later, *Grundrisse der Kritik der politischen Ökonomie* (1957/58) which, first published in Moscow in 1939 just before the war, remained relatively unknown in the West until the fifties. The above argument is not particularly significant for an appraisal of the ideas themselves, though it naturally excites the different factions among Marx's followers.

translated as alienation and estrangement. The former is the process by which mind becomes conscious of itself by activity, by working on an object. The second denotes the divisions in the mind of man as it confronts its own externalized products. In Hegel, history is the progress of mind through labour, externalization, opposition, i.e. estrangement to final harmony in self-consciousness. Marx, who used the two terms interchangeably, claimed to have stood Hegel on his feet by making this into a material rather than a mental process. Beginning with alienated labour, and an economy consisting of commodities, including labour power with both use-value and exchange-value, he went on to develop his whole theory of the evolution of capitalism. Its ultimate downfall, brought about by 'real' struggles ushering in an era in which alienation of man from man, man from his product, and mind from object will have ceased.[1] It is not difficult to see that emphasis on this approach would carry a special appeal to a generation bewildered by the increasingly (and almost absolutely) impersonal character of the modern economic process and often moved to a total rejection of many of its by-products, not only as far as the individual's relation to the economy is concerned, but also through the directly adverse effects on the environment or through the kind of values it fosters – a point where much of the disillusion of the younger generation joins with the criticism of material growth which we have already met.

But the critical attitude to the modern economy is by no means confined to Marxists on the one hand or to sceptics about the proper evaluation of rising GNP on the other. For more than four decades a steady stream of critical analysis has come from the pen of an academic economist, whose influence on the minds of the present generation has been considerable.

*John Kenneth Galbraith* does not readily fit any conventional description.[2] He has been variously regarded as not an economist at all but as a journalist and politician (despite his tenure of a number of academic appointments including that of a coveted chair at Harvard), as the only original economist working today, as a social prophet, or as an *enfant terrible* out to shock the more conventionally minded. There can be no

---

1 For a recent, sympathetic, account of Marxism with the emphasis on the sociological aspects see Henri Lefebure, *The Sociology of Marx* (1968). For a critical analysis, particularly of the Marxist philosophy, see H. B. Acton, *The Illusion of the Epoch, Marxism-Leninism as a Philosophical Creed* (1955).

2 Though I would certainly class him among the half-dozen 'seminal' economists working today.

doubt about his standing as an economist, unless the term is to be rigorously reserved to those engaged exclusively in the construction of macroeconomic models and using sophisticated mathematical techniques in the process. Perhaps his election to the Presidency of the American Economic Association will finally have laid to rest any doubts that may remain.[1] He began with a primary interest in agricultural economics rather than in pure theory; and it is perhaps not fanciful to suppose that experience in an area of economics in which the traditions of *laissez-faire* have never been particularly potent, and in which the political and the economic tend to be inseparably intermingled, may have contributed to the direction which his subsequent interest has taken. Another factor was certainly his involvement in the practicalities of war-time price-control which must have provided most vivid lessons in the interplay of politics and business and, no doubt, contributed to Galbraith's amused, not to say cynical, attitude to the pretensions of some of the high priests of the market economy. A spell in journalism helped to develop fluency and style. Indeed, as his great counterpart in Cambridge (Massachusetts) at the other end of the spectrum of economic scholarship, Professor Samuelson (himself a stylist), has remarked, Galbraith is an exception to the rule of indifferent writing that seems to prevail among social scientists.[2] Partly because of his style, which has greatly enriched the language by such phrases as the 'affluent society' or the 'conventional wisdom' and which, while carrying an almost self-mocking aura of scholarship, is extremely lucid, partly because of the encompassing nature of his analysis, Galbraith has often been likened to Veblen. There probably is some conscious influence here. In any event, there is no doubt that Galbraith is strictly in the tradition of Veblen (without much intermediation of later Veblenians such as Michell and Commons, though very much akin to Clarence Ayres), a tradition which is peculiarly American; though whether the admixture of a Scandinavian origin in the one case, and a Scottish-Canadian one in the other, is an essential

---

1 For a more detailed analysis of the attitude of the 'profession' to Galbraith see E. Roll, 'What Is Economics, What Is an Economist? The Case of J. K. Galbraith' in Samuel Bowles, Richard O. Edwards and William S. Shepherd ed., *Unconventional Wisdom* (1989).

2 On the general question of economic 'style' see Walter S. Salant, 'Writing and Reading in Economics' in *Journal of Political Economy* (July/August 1969).

ingredient of the particular form in which this tradition is expressed, it is hard to say.[1]

Leaving aside ephemeral pieces, an ambassadorial diary, two novels and the like and also excluding *The Great Crash, 1929* (1950), essentially a brilliant piece of journalism, and *A Theory of Price Control* (1952), the direct result of war-time experience, Galbraith's books on economic subjects, which run to some twenty now, have been mainly concerned with economic structure and, within that subject, essentially with the American economy. *American Capitalism, The Concept of Countervailing Power* (1951) was a first attempt to develop a theory to explain the change in the general climate of enterprise in its relation with the State. Then came, in 1959, *The Affluent Society*, which immediately catapulted its author into world fame, and later (1967) *The New Industrial State*. It is these last two books which are perhaps the two most significant, that show clearly the general direction of Galbraith's economics. In approaching them one must bear in mind that the author is clearly more concerned to influence the opinions of large sections of the reasonably literate public and, through them as well as directly, the politicians, than to carry his professional colleagues along with him. A tendency to overstate a thesis by presenting formulations that are meant to have a maximum impact by omitting carefully balanced qualification, is, therefore, always present. Some measure of misunderstanding of his purpose is, accordingly, a risk that he runs.

The main thesis of *The Affluent Society* is that the corpus of traditional economics and the common understanding which it both reflects and influences, having been worked out in circumstances when wants were chasing goods, is inappropriate when the opposite becomes true, as it has in the advanced industrial countries of the world. Galbraith links the emergence of traditional economics (to become an important part of the 'conventional wisdom') to the circumstances of the upsurge of modern production in the late eighteenth, early nineteenth centuries, after centuries of stagnation; and he shows that the 'tradition of despair' with which modern economics started was not lost even through the more optimistic phase of the late nineteenth century. Today things are different. 'Now goods are abundant, more die in the United States of too much food

---

1 His autobiography, *A Life in Our Times* (1981), is a frank and highly interesting account of his intellectual development.

than of too little';[1] and so it goes right through the list of conventional consumer goods poured out in an ever-increasing stream by a production machine that has become an end in itself. But, this private affluence is matched by 'public squalor', by a neglect of those public goods for collective consumption which could improve the quality of life – a thesis that has since been taken up, as we have seen, by a whole school of sceptics about the contents and quality of material growth.

These Galbraithian views have been criticized on the ground that while they may contain a truth as far as rich countries are concerned, and for the rich in the rich countries, it has no applicability to those who do not yet suffer from a surfeit of goods – from private affluence – be it the poor everywhere, be it, more generally, the poorer countries. There may be some superficial justification for the view concerning the developing world. But one must remember that the book is specifically concerned with the advanced countries, and, more particularly, with the United States; and the occasional references in it to Asia or the Middle East, to say nothing of many of Galbraith's other writings, show beyond a shadow of doubt that he is fully aware of the problem of the less developed areas of the world.

There is no justification whatever for the view that in stressing the problems of affluence, Galbraith ignores the position of the poor, those whose wants remain unsatisfied at a very low level of private consumption. In the chapters on inequality and on poverty ('in the contemporary United States ... it is a disgrace'[2]), he makes his views abundantly clear; and it would be fairer to say that the failure to raise the living standards of the poor and to make a major inroad into inequality are to be counted among the elements of that public squalor which he contrasts with private affluence.

In *The New Industrial State*, the indications given in the earlier book about the structural features of our economy which create and perpetuate the social and cultural blemishes to which he has drawn attention, are set out and examined more systematically. Once again, our language is enriched by striking phrases such as 'the Techno-structure', and 'the Educational and Scientific Estate'. There is also the 'Revised Sequence', the replacement of the old economic proposition of consumers' sovereignty, of wants calling forth produc-tion, by a situation in which the large corporation creates markets and

1 J. K. Galbraith, *The Affluent Society* (1958), p. 97.
2 ibid., p. 259.

determines consumers' behaviour in the interest of maintaining a certain productive rhythm and the financial consequences that that implies. The 'market' – as a category in the economic textbook – is replaced by planning which makes possible 'the organized use of capital and technology'.[1] This is the genius of the industrial system, and Galbraith acknowledges that it performs its tasks with a high degree of competence. What he questions are the purposes which it serves rather than the manner in which it serves them; and, at the very least (recalling again the theme of *The Affluent Society*), its neglect of many other purposes of the human existence, because it is not designed to serve them.

There is probably more in this book than in anything he has written that is reminiscent in its substance as well as in the method of attack, of Veblen, in particular of *The Theory of Business Enterprise* or of *Absentee Ownership*.[2] There are also other strands of a long tradition of American economic analysis to be found here: the sceptical attitude to the big corporation, the fear of monopoly, the concern with realistic investigation of economic structure, which have continued to flourish in the United States side by side with the astonishing increase in the purest of pure economic theory and which may, perhaps, derive a continuous impetus from certain features of the American political structure which provides for a close, continuing, and publicized concern of the legislature with the specificities of the economy on the one hand and the actions of the Executive on the other.

The above, very brief account has concentrated on the two books, here considered the most typical of the author's general approach. This is not to say that the *opus*, taken as a whole, does not contain many other highly valuable contributions. *Economics and the Public Purpose* (1973) and *A View from the Stands* (1986) may perhaps be singled out. The latter is a particularly rewarding collection of miscellaneous writings which demonstrate very clearly Galbraith's wide interests and special talent for witty, and yet at the same time highly instructive writing. His last work on economic topics at this time of writing (*Economics in Perspective*, 1987) is a particularly lively history of the

---

1 J. K. Galbraith, *The New Industrial State* (1967), p. 354.
2 Nevertheless, it is the case that, with all his brilliance, Veblen cannot compare with Galbraith as an economist. Indeed, Veblen was, in a sense, not interested in economics as such, but was essentially a cultural critic. Where he was more clearly an economist, as in *The Engineers and the Price System*, he went – and led – astray.

subject. Its concluding discussion is on the relation between economics and politics, a subject which will be dealt with later.

But interest in the implications of recent economic developments, particularly as they affect industrial structure has not been confined to the United States. A considerable new literature has grown up around the large new corporation,[1] particularly when its operations transcend national boundaries. Much of this is of a specialized nature, but a number of economists have also dealt with the implications of the concentration of economic decision-making into relatively few hands. These concern such problems as the international location of investment and production, with its consequences for the incidence of employment in different countries and for the long-run currents of trade as well as international payment balances. Other implications, too, cannot be ignored and call for the re-examination of a number of factors that have traditionally played a part in economic analysis, such as the profit motive, or the significance of enterprise when decisions are largely in the hands of professional managers rather than of shareholders (i.e. owners), together with the theoretical apparatus that is built up upon them.

---

[1] In earlier editions the name of Berle was inexplicably left out: Adolf A. Berle (with Gardiner C. Means), *The Modern Corporation and Private Property* (1932). This work had undoubtedly a considerable influence on J. K. Galbraith and is, more generally, acknowledged as of seminal significance.

# 13

# A New Certainty?

*From the New Economics to the New Classical Macroeconomics*

It is usually misleading, sometimes dangerously so, to apply the labels of political history, representing as they do successive encrustations of interpretation, to the broad history of ideas, not least so in that of economics. It has, however, become customary after the 'revolution' of the classics, and the 'marginal revolution' of the latter part of the nineteenth century, to continue to distinguish by similar names what appear, either to contemporaries or more often in retrospect, to be major new directions in which the discipline moves. Thus, it has been customary for some decades now to speak of the Keynesian revolution and of the anti-Keynesian counter-revolution and this pattern has been followed in the last few chapters. But while in political history revolutions and counter-revolutions are usually followed by periods of relative stability with first one, then the other, tendency having achieved a certain mastery, this is not entirely true in the history of economic thought of the last half century. Indeed, as has been stressed in successive editions of this history, few economic ideas, at least in their more generalized forms, disappear altogether; they continue to form the small change of daily political discourse, even if they have been discredited and abandoned by the professionals.

What is true is that the Keynesian revolution was successful enough to be followed by a period during which its authority was established and, indeed, largely unchallenged not only by scholars but also to a remarkable degree in the real world of economic action. This does not seem to have been quite the case after the massive counter-revolution, particularly in its monetary appearance, at least in the realm of scholarship. Where it did achieve a high degree of unquestioned authority – not universal and not as far as one can now tell of secular duration – was in its influence on certain politicians in some countries and, therefore, on the economic policy of those countries.

But before attempting to assess the longevity of the counter-revolution, a further description and analysis of its most recent manifestations is in order. Indeed, the gap between the accepted convictions of a large majority of the profession and the beliefs of politicians was vividly brought out when in March 1981 364 important British economists, many of them of much renown, published a letter claiming that the policies of the British Government of the day were misguided and that there was no basis in economic theory for their validity (*The Times*, 29 March 1981). For a while, their views seemed to conflict with actual economic experience. In March 1988, however, the group claimed that once again what was happening in the real world supported their opinion. They did not remain unanswered. In the introduction to a larger survey of economists' opinion in 1990 the original statement was described as 'infamous' (Ricketts and Shoesmith (eds), *British Economic Opinion* (Institute of Economic Affairs, 1990)), a word incidentally that seems to have become popular among the 'new right': Professor Minford, for example, described the Delors Report on European economic and monetary union in this way when commenting on a lecture by the Governor of the Bank of England, a co-author of that report! (*The Future of Monetary Arrangements in Europe* (Institute of Economic Affairs, 1989).) The word may have been intended to denote the opposite of 'famous'. However, according to the *Oxford Dictionary* – and common usage – it means 'notoriously vile or evil, abominable'.

One particular development of the last twenty years or so which is of so very general a scope and which has sometimes been claimed to be of so fundamental a significance for the whole basis of economic science that it requires somewhat fuller treatment is what has come to be known as the 'New Classical Economics' or sometimes the 'New Classical Macroeconomics'. One important element in it is that of 'Rational Expectations' and it seems convenient to begin with this. Without enquiring too closely into possible earlier traces of this school, we may follow the general practice of acknowledging as its founders Robert Lucas of the University of Chicago and Thomas Sargent of the University of Minnesota with Robert Barro, also of the University of Chicago (and now Harvard), as the third member of the original group; though an early statement is to be found in J. F. Muth's 'Rational Expectations and the Theory of Price' in *Econometrica* (July 1961).

The literature on the subject has grown rapidly and is now very large;

the following very modest selection should, however, suffice: R. E. Lucas and T. J. Sargent, *After Keynesian Macroeconomics* (1978) in 'After the Phillips Curve: Persistence of High Inflation and Unemployment', Federal Reserve Bank of Boston; edited by the same authors, *Rational Expectations and Econometric Practice* (1981); Sargent's article 'Rational Expectations' in the New Palgrave *Dictionary of Economics* (1987); C. L. E. Attfield, Demery and Duck, *Rational Expectations in Macroeconomics: An Introduction to Theory and Evidence* (1985); Willes, 'Rational Expectations as a Counterrevolution' in *The Public Interest*, Special Issue: 'Economics in Crisis' (1980); R. J. Barro, *Macroeconomics* (1984); Hoover, *The New Classical Macroeconomics: A Sceptical Enquiry* (1988), which is particularly useful not only because it covers the whole field and not only rational expectations, but also because its approach is 'sceptical'; Lejonhofvud, 'What Would Keynes Have Thought of Rational Expectations' with comments by L. Pasinetti and P. A. Samuelson in G. D. Worswick and J. S. Trevithik (eds), *Keynes and the Modern World* (1983) (papers presented at a conference celebrating the centenary of Keynes's birth). For those interested in the more recondite methodological aspects, Sheila C. Dow, *Macroeconomic Thought: A Methodological Approach* (1985) may be mentioned; and finally A. Klamer, *The New Classical Macroeconomics: Conversations with the New Classical Economists and Their Opponents* (1984), gives in many ways a more revealing insight than that afforded by the various authors' more formal writings.[1]

In some ways, Rational Expectations, at least in its ultimate practical relevance, is, according to taste, the foundation or the coping stone of the New Classical Macroeconomics. For this reason it is as well to set out briefly what it amounts to. The theory has its roots in the concept of rational behaviour and in the fairly substantial history and literature concerning it. The frontiers of this subject are very much wider than those of economic analysis and it would be going too far afield to examine all its aspects and implications. As far as economics is concerned, it stems in one sense from the notion of choice – e.g. in the doctrines of the Austrian school, particularly of Wieser – as the essence of the behaviour of economic man, or the 'economic agent', as it is fashionable nowadays to call him. (This new word to describe the

---

1 A highly interesting review article of this book makes some valuable substantive comments and criticisms of the NCE: Howitt, 'Conversations with Economists', *Journal of Monetary Economics* (1986).

individual in his economic activity could itself be the subject of a philosophical/psychological analysis of the new theoretical tendencies – 'agents' of whom or what?)

Indeed in the formulation of some Austrian economists, Mises and Hayek for example, choice becomes the essence of all human action as such. The term rational behaviour can be used to describe either what individual behaviour actually is – and is likely to be (i.e. forecasting) – or what it ought to be if each individual is to act in order to serve his own self-interest, this being regarded at least by implication, variously as either his principal motive (contrary somewhat to Adam Smith), or the one most easily used in the analysis of economic behaviour, or even as the one that 'ought' (in some sense) to prevail over others.

Rational Expectation is the proposition that forecasts affect outcomes and outcomes affect expectations, thus producing a 'mapping' from expectations to expectations. 'Economic agents' will eventually notice when they have made mistakes and will try to revise their methods of forecasting until they have achieved equilibrium, i.e. a situation in which they have in fact formed rational expectations. Putting it in a more conventional way, we must assume that all 'economic agents' act on the best information available to them as well as on the principles of economic theory (at least the fundamental ones); that, consequently, their forecasts will be 'unbiased' and they will rationally expect the consequences of whatever intervention the authorities attempt. As a result, and making the further assumption of flexible prices and wages, it will be impossible for government (or, more generally, 'the authority') to intervene in the economic process in a way that will not immediately be frustrated by the actions of the 'economic agents'.

This theory has been largely developed in relation to the efficacy of monetary policy; and much of the literature is devoted to demonstrating the futility of attempting to influence the major economic categories by monetary policy since rational expectations will (again, one supposes 'sooner or later') frustrate the action of the monetary authority. In fact the theory goes further, at least as formulated by Barro, in that a similar non-effective label is applied to fiscal policy. In an article called 'Are Government Bonds Net Wealth?' in the *Journal of Political Economy* (November 1974) Professor Barro argues (as Ricardo had briefly done but then dismissed this view) that there was no difference between financing government expenditure by taxation or by borrowing. If this is so (because households do not regard government bonds as part of their wealth), then governments cannot stimulate growth by deficit financing. More precisly, economic agents will regard government borrowing as merely postponing taxation, and will, therefore, increase their savings to meet expected future taxation, thus compensating for the dissaving which government borrowing represents.

Needless to say, this analysis is by no means unchallenged. It is not appropriate here to go into the details of this debate, but it is interesting to highlight this further implication of the rational expectations school for a non-interventionist economic policy. While not all the anti-Keynesian writers share all the views of the monetarist or rational expectations school, there is a certain family relationship between them all, namely the general rejection of macroeconomic management either of the Keynesian variety or of any of those belonging to what Professor Samuelson has called the 'neo-classical synthesis'.

Before examining further the consequences for economic management (obviously 180 degrees different from those of neo- or post-Keynesian economics), we must try to link the rational expectations concept into the broader stream of the neo-classical macroeconomics. This is the most up-to-date form which the market-clearing theory takes with its origin (somewhat equivocal, as we have seen) in Adam Smith, later simplied to the point of tautology in Say and Bastiat, put in more sophisticated, and mathematical, form by Walras and represented today by Arrow and Debreu. Reference has already been made to it and to the stringent conditions which need to be fulfilled if its propositions are to be a correct, relevant, representation of reality. On theoretical terms a linkage of the new formulation of the inevitable tendency of markets towards an equilibrium position with the rational expectations proposition (that intervention by authority, particularly in monetary policy, is useless since it will inevitably – sooner or later? – be frustrated by economic agents acting on rational expectations) produces a foundation for a complete non-interventionist body of theory.

While it would be wrong to accuse the authors of these theoretical constructions (notably someone like Kenneth Arrow) of ignoring the enormous gap between the conditions postulated in theory from those of the real economic world (e.g. in regard to price formation in labour markets), it is easy to see that they lend themselves readily to facile political slogans and, now and again, to consequential political experimentation. As already noted, some of the interventionist excesses that some of Keynes's followers – again particularly political users (and abusers) of his theories – the result of a kind of hubris born of some of the theories' early successes, produced a climate of disillusionment, in which even extreme – thus equally excessive – claims for non-interventionism could flourish, at least for a time.

There are, of course, some curious and not easily analysed alliances and differences, not only in the realm of theory (which is not surprising), but also in that of practical action. It is impossible here to go into all the varieties of combinations between believers in the rational expectations theory, the pure doctrine of macroeconomic equilibrium brought about by a new type of 'invisible hand' (brilliantly analysed by James Tobin in 'The Invisible Hand in Modern Macroeconomics' already referred to) and the hard core of monetarists who are generally staunch believers in an extreme form of *laissez-faire* but do not always see eye to eye with others (though as already stated there is a family relationship between them). This whole area of economic theory and theory of economic policy resembles sometimes a square dance in which positions and partners are subject to frequent change.

From a longer-term point of view concerning the present and future of economics, there is, however, a very clear-cut distinction between, on the one hand, a variety of mainstream economists whose analyses still retain much of Keynesian theory, and build on the more recent and refined versions of it, and, on the other, those who have in various ways carried forward the anti-Keynesian counter-revolution.[1]

It is interesting to observe that while Jevons thought that Ricardo had started economics on the wrong track, no neo- or post- or other form of Keynesian has yet suggested that Walras had done just that. On the contrary, many of them have shown great admiration for Walras; and some might even join with Schumpeter in regarding Walras's system as 'the Magna Carta of economic theory' since, as he believed, the setting out of the conditions of general equilibrium is the central problem of economics. Of course it would be wrong to dismiss out of hand the work from Walras to Arrow, which has established this 'general theory'; but the claim that it constitutes the be-all and end-all of economics as a science is difficult to sustain. In the first place, if this

1 For a short but comprehensive assessment of the rational expectations school by the foremost exponent of post- (or, as he would say, 'reconstructed') Keynesianism, see Samuelson in a discussion on 'What Keynes would have thought of rational expectations' initiated by Axel Lejonhufvud in G. D. Worswick and J. S. Trevithick (eds), *Keynes and the Modern World*, (1983), a volume recording the proceedings of the Keynes Centenary Conference, King's College, Cambridge, 1983, already referred to.

were to be accepted, it would mean eliminating – as not really being economics – by far the most voluminous part of to-day's work, that concerned with an enormous range of practical policy issues in particular sectors of the economy or of finance. These are not easily linked with the austere propositions of general equilibrium, but implicitly, and often explicitly, they include some kind of interventionist action; or they postulate market imperfections, more often than not historically conditioned, without any value judgment other than their effect on particular economic processes. If the claim that the new classical macroeconomics is indeed the acme of a scientific development making economics the equivalent of, say, Newtonian physics, the question would ineluctably arise as to how and where equivalent practical application (such as various branches of modern technology) are to be found. This is the point at which the nature and purpose of economics becomes once again the question it has been at earlier critical moments in the subject's history.

# Economics Yesterday, Today, and Tomorrow

> Aber die Grenzen der Nationalökonomie
> als Wissenschaft sind zu enge gezogen
> ... denn sie schlieszen die Politik aus,
> Was sie nicht sollten.
>   Ludwig Börne, *Von dem Gelde* (1809)

This lament by the nineteenth-century essayist and journalist (not an economist, but a social and literary critic), significantly made in an essay on money, was, of course, only a half truth when it was made. From its origin in the classical period to the present day, the separation of 'analytics' from policy (therefore, inevitably, from politics) has been a fluctuating phenomenon – periods of more intensive 'politicization' of the body of theory alternating with a more distinct and self-conscious separation (or at least attempts at such) between the two. In a sense, Börne posed the problem incorrectly. Can economics encompass politics? Has it at any time done so? That politics encompasses economics, there can be no doubt. From time to time, in democratic societies, problems other than economic ones (even in the widest sense) have been at the centre of political debate, but economic ones have never been far away; and more often than not – certainly in the last hundred years or so – they have usually been the crucial issues.

On the other hand, whether economics, i.e. the science as it has developed, can include politics in a meaningful sense and within the categories and method that it has created in order to become a science, is a much more debatable question despite the fact that the promotion of a vital political objective – material well-being – has implicitly and explicitly been the ultimate objective to which the science was to contribute by developing a greater understanding of economic processes. Leaving aside for a moment the question whether a 'systematic'

568

integration of politics into the corpus of economic analysis is feasible, there is no doubt that at various periods in its history, notably in our own day (in the thirty or forty years from the mid thirties to the mid seventies), most practitoners of the science believed that they had evolved a number of tools of macroeconomic management (out of the raw material of their analytical categories) which could be used by politicians to achieve a number of highly desirable goals: growth and full employment without inflation and – more uncertainly since beyond the authority of a single national government – expanding international trade and financial flows with a high degree of stability. The development of this belief, its apotheosis and its decline have been traced in Chapters 11 and 12.

As we have seen, there have been assaults on the general body of economic theory in the sixties and seventies from many quarters which, in part, reflect a frustration over the political relevance of economics similar to that expressed by Börne at the beginning of last century.

The pattern of economic management based primarily on an analysis of the role of the budget with its consequent emphasis on fiscal policy has been attacked, from the inside, as it were, by the monetarists. In another sense there has been an attack from within. Joan Robinson has continued the erosion of the neo-classical system, which she began in her celebrated *The Economics of Imperfect Competiton*. In the preface to the second edition of this book[1] she claims that 'perfect competition, supply and demand, consumers' sovereignty and marginal products still reign supreme in orthodox teaching'; and she reminds the reader that in her book she succeeded 'in proving within the framework of the orthodox theory that it is not true that wages are normally equal to the value of the marginal product of labour'. In a later work, *Economic Heresies, Some Old-Fashioned Questions in Economic Theory* (1971) she carries the attack further against the whole theoretical scheme of current work in economics.[2]

1 1969.
2 Joan Robinson speaks of a second crisis in economics (the first being the pre-Keynesian one over employment) in connection with the 'form of investment' (p. xiv) and generally believes that economics has shown itself incapable of dealing with the problems of the age, thus carrying much further some earlier doubts, expressed notably in *Economic Philosophy* (1962). Professor Gunnar Myrdal (in a speech at the American Economic Association meeting at New Orleans on December 28, 1971), on 'Crises and Cycles in the Development of Economics', shares Mrs Robinson's view that 'economic

In addition to attacks which come from the profession itself, and which cover a wide spectrum, the attacks from the outside, stemming from what are widely thought to be the inadequacies of economic analysis, and policies based upon it, to deal with the pressing problems of the real work have continued and grown in scope and intensity. They have covered the crucial questions of inflation, employment and growth, in their relation to each other, as well as the proper definition and wider evaluation of growth and its contents in their bearing on human welfare, all these involving directly the role of government in the management of the economy, thus the old problem of the agenda of the state.

In the light of the necessarily brief account given in Chapter 12 of some of the major areas of doubt, one is finally left with an impression of uncertainty – uncertainty both on the analytical and, even more obviously, the policy front. We have already met a situation in Economics some sixty years ago to which the word uncertainty could be applied. Uncertainty was then removed essentially by the appearance of the new Keynesian theory and its subsequent development to a point where considerable self-assurance became the hallmark of the New Economics. This seemed justified because there followed a period of considerable practical achievement, when it seemed possible to hope that the inter-war ghosts of hyper-inflation and massive unemployment were laid forever.

Uncertainty did, however, set in again. When an earlier edition of this history could say that 'in sum ... the state of affairs in economic theory is fairly reassuring', it seemed at the same time necessary even then to draw attention to 'some dangers inherent in the "New Economics"', since 'thinking in terms of the aggregates of the economic

---

science is up to a serious crisis ... very much more revolutionary in regard to our research approaches than ever was the Keynesian revolution three decades ago'. Professor Samuelson has not yet echoed the words of criticism he used twenty-five years ago when he spoke of the economics of the thirties, but, as has already been pointed out, the successive editions of his *Economics* have contained unmistakable signs of a growing broadening of concern with socio-economic and politico-economic matters though more recently there has been added as if in recognition of certain political tendencies increased emphasis on the market mechanism. It is also significant that the presidential addresses in 1971 both to the Royal Economic Society and to Section F of the British Association for the Advancement of Science should have reflected highly sceptical views on the state of the science. E. H. Phelps Brown, 'The Underdevelopment of Economics' and G. D. N. Worswick, 'Is Progress in Economic Science Possible', both in *Economic Journal*, March 1972. On the question of 'crisis' see further below.

system tends to foster a mechanical view'; and a warning was issued against believing that wise judgment in respect of policy can automatically be ensured by economic theory however refined.

Unfortunately, but perhaps inevitably, a degree of mechanistic thinking did tend to pervade economics at least as applied to policy. In the case of some schools of economics imbued with a deep-seated regard for the virtues of non-intervention by the state, such as the monetarists', a similar tendency to an absolute faith in the 'automatic pilot' of the money supply that can be 'locked in position' and ensure that the vessel will be kept on the desired course is however, and paradoxically, also to be observed. Such faith leads, as has already been said, to a dangerous 'hubris' on the part of the interventionists, confident that both statistics and analysis can be perfected to a point where the necessary changes of policy can be read off as if on a dial and then appropriate adjustments be applied to the controls with sufficient delicacy so as to produce the desired results. When a British Chancellor of the Exchequer, later Prime Minister, complained that he was expected to guide the economy on ancient statistics rather like running a train on an out-of-date timetable, he was only demonstrating how far politicians had come to share the touching faith of some economists and administrators that greater perfection of the mechanics of their craft would provide the answers to their problems.[1]

In the last ten years this position has been both more generalized and propounded with special vigour. It has gone beyond monetarism as such and taken the form of a revival of extreme non-interventionist doctrine (in its most extreme form involving even a rejection of monetarism itself and the advocacy of a 'privatization' of money). There is no doubt that the extremism of some interventionist writers and politicians has called forth an even more extreme reaction since it contrasted sharply with the poor practical results most strongly evident in the description of the economy for which the word 'stagflation' is now generally accepted and which has certainly not been absent in countries in which interventionism had been actively pursued. The ensuing contest became very acute indeed in the political arena where it has been the characteristic feature of public economic debate of the last decade. For reasons which would require a very elaborate study

---

1 For a searching analysis of 'fine tuning' see Bator, 'Fine Tuning' in *The New Palgrave Dictionary of Economics* (1987), vol. 2.

to unravel, its most vehement manifestations were in the English-speaking countries, particularly the United States and Britain, both traditionally regarded (particularly by themselves) as not given to extreme doctrinaire predilections but generally pragmatic in political conduct. In both countries, slogans such as 'rolling back the frontiers of the state' became common and produced consequences in fiscal policy, the 'supply-side' effect of lower taxation being extolled,[1] and removal of support for ailing industries, privatization of state-owned and controlled industries within a general principle of non-intervention and absolute reliance on the market mechanism becoming canons of economic policy.[2]

Unfortunately, the economy is not a laboratory in which results of experiments can be measured and analysed. All that can be said is that after some ten years of experience with a proclaimed non-interventionist policy (which in many countries transcended the customary political divisions between left and right), the results in terms of the usual criteria – growth, employment, absence of inflation or of international payments imbalance – are not reassuring. Indeed, the performance of those countries in which the doctrinal battle and its practical expression in policy action was much less virulent, e.g. Germany and Japan (and after 1983 also France), seems on the whole to have been better. Nor has excessive reliance on monetary policy been the striking success that has sometimes been claimed it would be.[3] Even in the fight against inflation monetary restrictionism has taken a long time to make its mark and it is not yet established that it will completely succeed, let alone what price in unemployment would be exacted if it were to succeed.[4] Thus neither reliance on market forces

1 See the short, but devastating analysis of 'supply-side' theory in Walter S. Salant, 'A Critical Look at Supply-side Theory' in *International Monetary Problems and Supply-side Economics: Essays in Honour of Lorie Tarshis* (1986).
2 Needless to say, that heady draught was, in practice, taken with a good deal of water. As the Conservative historian, Lord Blake, has pointed out: 'They (politicians) know how much of the art of politics lies in concealing behind a facade of rigid adherence to immutable principles those deviations or reversals, events and responsibility so often force on governments.' Robert Blake, *Disraeli* (1966) p. 764.
3 For a succinct and very fair summing-up of monetarism *versus* Keynesianism, including a judgement on the practical effects of undiluted monetarism see Modigliani, *The Debate over Stabilization Policy*, the Rafaele Mattioli Lectures (1986).
4 In a lecture twenty years ago, I remarked: 'It is, I suppose, possible to imagine that the adoption of a more restrictive monetary policy could so change expectations about future prospects for inflation and for the markets for goods, that inflationary wage settlements

to the exclusion of all policies that carry even the slightest interventionist taint, nor monetarism (which is, of course, interventionist, but has nevertheless some 'philosophical' relationship with *laissez-faire*) can be said to have succeeded in coping with stagflation – the phenomenon which in the end nullified so much of the considerable success over some twenty years of post-Keynesianism, the corpus of theory not confined to the problems of depression: i.e. that associated with (taken at random) Samuelson, Solow, Okun, Hicks, Meade, Tobin and many others.

Some economists have been directly involved as participants – be it as advisers to politicians or as commentators in this contest of philosophies of economic policy, without necessarily involving the vast bulk of analytical work. Nevertheless, as we have seen in the last three chapters, the claims of the real world have penetrated even the most theoretical activities of the professional and produced (at the very least) another wave of philosophic doubt.

To some extent, the uncertainty which has thus reappeared among both professionals and the general public, is clearly a reflection of a more general social and cultural *malaise* that shows itself in so many different ways at the present time, for example in an increased and more widely spread irreverence for anything 'established' and in a greater 'alienation' of youth than has been witnessed in any of the most industrialized countries of the world for well over a hundred years. What the deeper causes of this state of affairs may be cannot be examined here. It may be, as Professor Macpherson has maintained, that we are in the presence of the results of an evolution that started in the middle of the last century and has only now reached maturity. The process may be one by which the bases of the 'possessive market society' which 'puts every man on his own' and which 'is accurately reflected in the assumptions of possessive individualism' have been eroded to the point 'where the structure of market society no longer provides the necessary conditions for deducing a valid theory of political obligation from those assumptions' (those of possessive individualism).[1] It is certainly not easy in the face of the great structural changes of the economy with their effect on the balance between

---

would subside spontaneously as it were without much increase in unemployment having to occur. All I can say is that those who believe that will believe anything; so long as it has a happy ending.' (E. Roll, *Economic Policy and the U.K. Financial System* (Reading University, 1970).)

1 C. B. Macpherson, *The Political Theory of Possessive Individualism* (1962), pp. 271, 275.

individual effort and the broad direction both of the private and the national economy,[1] to recognize the view of society and the individual that is still largely implicit in the basic theorems of economics. In a world of increasingly complicated technology and automated production processes and of sophisticated financial, organizational and management techniques of the large corporation, often operating across many national boundaries, it is not easy for the individual, in whatever capacity he may be participating in the process, to detect readily a relevance to his own fate of any but the most elementary microeconomic principles or their connection with the macroeconomic analysis of aggregates, or the manipulation of these, by means of public policy. This, quite apart from the failures – or at best half-successes – of that policy to reconcile divergent objectives, is explanation enough for popular scepticism. Indeed, the dominant position which macroeconomics and management based on it, had achieved is not only an important pointer to the great changes in the socio-economic structure but also causes a further aggravation of the dilemma of maintaining the idea of the supremeacy of the individual – the twin in intellectual history of classical political economy – and managing large complex economies in an era of rapidly expanding populations and within a democratic political framework in an era of unprecedented technological change.

No wonder that in the relatively rare moments when he has the time and above all if he has the inclination to examine these transcendental questions, the economist should be perplexed. Many economists naturally avoid such a confrontation and take refuge in more and more refined theoretical work. Indeed, some would tend – as the dominant schools of the twenties also did – to deprecate preoccupation with these questions which pertain to social or political philosophy and which they regard as inferior to the more 'precise' tasks of positive economics. They do, of course, recognize that beyond the realm of positive economics, there lies that of politics; and in relation to it the traditional attitude requires of the economist not so much an abdication of political concern, but a separation of it from his analytical work, a recognition of the boundary between what he says as an economist pure and simple and what he may say as an economist, who has also applied some political, that is to say normative, judgments to

---

1 See: Andrew Shonfield, *Modern Capitalism, the Changing Balance of Public and Private Power* (1965) for an interesting discussion of the significance of these changes.

574

the problem under discussion. This separation, as it were, of the corpus of theory from social judgment is well brought out in a classic statement by Frank Knight on the system of free enterprise: 'that free enterprise is not a perfectly ideal system of social organization is a proposition not to be gainsaid' but 'its weaknesses and failures ... lie outside the field of the mechanics of exchange under the theoretical conditions of perfect competition'; and 'the values of life are not, in the main, reducible to satisfactions obtained from the consumption of exchangeable goods and services' ... for ... 'desires [are] the product of social influence' and 'productive capacities ... are derived from an uncertain mixture of conscientious effort, inheritance, pure luck and outright force and fraud'.[1] Broadly speaking, the vast majority of economists of the last fifty years or more would subscribe to some statement of this kind.

Lionel Robbins in a lecture explicitly devoted to this question, while taking generally the same line – 'economists *as economists* ... have nothing to say on the true ends of life: and that their propositions concerning what *is* or what *can be* involve in themselves no propositions concerning what *ought to be*'.[2] But he also takes the view that since 'a substantial number ... of our political judgments are made in very ignorance of consequences ... economic analysis, by pointing to the results of action rather than to action considered intrinsically' ... can make a contribution to rational action.[3]

How far such a process of creating something of a split personality in the economist is practicable must be a moot point; how far it is a prescription that is based on the right view – implicitly at least – of the process by which the whole body of economics, from Smith to Keynes at least, has developed is doubtful. It certainly requires that one be satisfied that in its most modern versions, economics has been more or less emancipated from its philosophical antecedents, has become, genuinely, a positive science, free from implicit assumptions of a normative character, but mature enough to be able to introduce 'desiderata' of a social character, thus creating a relationship between economic theory and policy virtually akin to that of, say, physics and chemistry on the one hand, and engineering on the other.

1 Frank H. Knight, 'Some Fallacies in the Interpretation of Social Cost' in *Quarterly Journal* (1924), reprinted in Kenneth J. Arrow and Tibor Scitovsky, *Readings in Welfare Economics* (1969), pp. 226–7.
2 Lord Robbins, *Politics and Economics, Papers in Political Economy* (1963), p. 7.
3 ibid., p. 22.

Even the most skilful of the representatives of the 'Neo-classical Synthesis', i.e. those who are active in the application of their theoretical propositions to specific issues of policy, would not be quite at ease with such a view. Curiously it is those who represent a diametrically opposite conception of the analytical approach, the economists of the neo-classical macroeconomics school, who would espouse a different and more complacent view of the state of economics. For them the prospect of general equilibrium, with markets clearing however distant the horizon and, given the tenets of the rational expectations school, that intervention is useless, i.e. worse than morally offensive to believers in *laissez-faire*, is enough to constitute not only a positive economics, but one which automatically also provides norms for action, i.e. inaction.

This view is usually seen in its crassest form where the labour market is concerned. As a notorious leader in the London *Times*, 'What every greengrocer knows', put it some years ago, it is quite simple: you have to put the price down if there is a likelihood of your goods (or services) remaining unsold. Even businessmen who might be basically attracted to the benefits of the action of completely free market forces may well hesitate to accept the analogy of the green-grocer's cauliflower still on display in the late afternoon with, say, several thousand workers in a Scottish steel mill whose employment was the result of corporate investment decisions, perhaps stimulated by takeovers or buyouts or by earlier 'job-creating' action by the state and who, as a result of changing policies, find themselves faced with imminent loss of jobs. Some, but not by any means the larger part, of professional economists have nevertheless taken refuge in the doctrine of the supremacy of the market. For some this has acquired almost the same philosophical potency as the class struggle and its predestined historic course in the Marxian system, or as 'fine-tuning' threatened to become among what Samuelson has called 'unreconstructed' Keynesians.

The search for the 'automatic pilot' seems to be an irrepressible urge. It may take different forms, but its essence remains the same: a single, simple principle of explanation that already contains within it the correct prescription for a policy which, if allowed to 'take over', will exempt society and its institutions from otherwise extremely difficult choices. It is an understandable desire on the part of politicians faced with a bewildering and kaleidoscopic array of problems and always – in the democratic countries – mindful of the ever-present electoral cycle.

It is more disturbing if it appears – which is fortunately not too often – among academic writers and their journalistic hangers-on. Then it acquires some of the attributes of religion and leads (as Marxism does) to identifying differing views with vice or virtue. It should be emphasized, however, that this form of irritationalism, so brilliantly castigated by Lecky, does not appear in the work of the many eminent post-Keynesians, some of whom have been mentioned in these pages.[1]

Is there, then, a crisis in Economics? This word has been applied at some earlier points in the subject's history. It has recently been given special emphasis by a collection of articles published in 1980 by the journal *The Public Interest*, as a fifteenth anniversary issue, under the unequivocal title of 'The Crisis in Economics' (edited by Irving Kristol and Daniel Bell).[2] A re-reading, after ten years, of this collection which brought together many eminent economists, from pure monetarist to neo- or post-Keynesians, from rational expectations proponents to one solitary Marxist, does not give one the feeling that the disarray and uncertainty demonstrated then has been at last dispelled. Indeed, if anything, the survey presented in this and the preceding two chapters, shows that on many basic issues concerning the nature, purpose and method of economic analysis there are still considerable differences of opinion.

This is so, notwithstanding the fact that the actual volume of controversial and polemical work within this area has somewhat subsided. What has taken place is a twofold development. On the one hand, the political debate over economic policy has undoubtedly become more vociferous and sharp in a decade which has seen the rise (and fall?) of *Reaganomics* and *Thatcherism*, the two most definite forms of the counter-revolution against what was (often wrongly) conceived of as an all-embracing Keynesian, i.e. unsound money, 'dirigiste', inflationary movement. On the other hand, in analytical work, the new classical macroeconomists and the representatives of the great post-Keynesian synthesis have gone on working more or less in separate compartments. It has to be said that there is so far little evidence that the

---

1 For a balanced and illuminating account of the different approaches to Macroeconomics see Bator, 'The State of Macroeconomics' in Steinherr and D. Weiserbs, *Employment and Growth* (1987).

2 The collection is discussed in detail in a review article: E. Roll, 'Economics in Crisis', *Encounter* (August 1981). See also an article written three years earlier: E. Roll, 'Has Economics a Future?', *Encounter* (1978) which reached somewhat more pessimistic conclusions.

former have been able to bring their theories (which employ more, and more advanced, mathematical techniques and thus widen the gap between themselves and the non-professional) down to earth, that is to apply them to practical problems, in contrast with the most elementary conclusions of neo-classical economics, such as the opportunity-cost principle well established for at least a century.

The 'synthetists', however, who have been, and are, patiently continuing not only to develop the post-Keynesian doctrines but also to apply them where possible to practical problems both of the private economy and of statecraft, have many advances to their credit.[1]

Some critics of modern theory – who recognize, however, its considerable contributions not only to the better understanding of the economic process but also to the fashioning of better policy instruments, and at times to their application – have cherished the hope that as Burke, two centuries ago, saw the age of chivalry succeeded by 'that of sophisters, economists and calculators', so we may now see that 'the age of calculators is gone, that of humanists is succeeding'[2] – this being clearly to imply an ability to infuse the theorems of economics, the calculations of the GNP and its constituents with moral values, or, put more neutrally, with humanly (politically?) acceptable objectives.

Whether one shares this hope or not, the fact that such hope can exist is an unmistakable sign of the continued vigour of the discipline. But even if this hope were to be realized, even if the development of a new 'normative' economics – making full use of the analytical advances – were possible, the ultimate dilemma of the relation between politics and economics, that is between those who wield power, albeit temporarily, and those who advise either directly or through the influence of their theoretical work, would still remain to be resolved. Plato, in speaking of philosopher-kings, took one alternative view, Kant was more pessimistic: 'That kings should philosophize or that

---

1 One example may be mentioned which, while at the furthest distance from theoretical work, is nevertheless closely related to it. Since 1970 the Brookings Institution has prepared an annual analysis, using to a large extent economists for the purpose, of the presidential budget from the point of view of its priorities and the means of achieving them. The eighth of these, Henry J. Aaron and others, *Setting National Priorities* (1990), is a most impressive document in which explicit policy objectives and alternative methods of achieving methods of achieving them are compared with proposed government policy, the whole being clearly inspired by up-to-date economic theory and based on considerable statistical work.

2 Shigeto Tsuru, *In Place of GNP* op. cit.

philosophers should become kings is not to be expected; nor is it to be desired: for the possession of power ineluctably corrupts the free judgement of reason.'[1]

1 Kant, Immanuel, *Zum Ewigen Frieden*, p. 48.

# Index